Financial Reporting and Analysis

CFA® PROGRAM CURRICULUM • VOLUME 2

LEVEL II
2011

CFA INSTITUTE

Learning Solutions

New York Boston San Francisco
London Toronto Sydney Tokyo Singapore Madrid
Mexico City Munich Paris Cape Town Hong Kong Montreal

Cover photograph courtesy of Hector Emanuel.

1 2 3 4 5 6 7 8 9 10 V313 15 14 13 12 11 10

099900000270552066

AG/JW

Please visit our website at *www.pearsoned.com*

PEARSON

ISBN 10: 0-558-52188-6
ISBN 13: 978-0-558-52188-2

CONTENTS

HOW TO USE THE CFA PROGRAM CURRICULUM

Congratulations on passing Level I of the Chartered Financial Analyst (CFA®) Program. This exciting and rewarding program of study reflects your desire to become a serious investment professional. You are participating in a program noted for its high ethical standards and the breadth of knowledge, skills, and abilities it develops. Your commitment to the CFA Program should be educationally and professionally rewarding.

The credential you seek is respected around the world as a mark of accomplishment and dedication. Each level of the program represents a distinct achievement in professional development. Successful completion of the program is rewarded with membership in a prestigious global community of investment professionals. CFA charterholders are dedicated to life-long learning and maintaining currency with the ever-changing dynamics of a challenging profession.

The CFA examination measures your degree of mastery of the assigned CFA Program curriculum. Therefore, the key to your success on the examination is reading and studying the CFA Program curriculum. The remaining sections provide background on the Candidate Body of Knowledge (CBOK™), the organization of the curriculum and tips for developing an effective study program.

Curriculum Development

The CFA Program curriculum is grounded in the practice of the investment profession. Utilizing the Global Body of Investment Knowledge (GBIK) collaborative website, CFA Institute performs a continuous practice analysis with investment professionals around the world to determine the knowledge, skills, and abilities that are relevant to the profession. Regional panels and targeted surveys are conducted annually to verify and reinforce the continuous feedback. The practice analysis process ultimately defines the Candidate Body of Knowledge (CBOK). The CBOK consists of four components:

- A broad topic outline that lists the major knowledge areas
- Topic area weights that indicate the relative exam weightings of the top-level topic areas
- Learning Outcome Statements (LOS) that advise candidates as to what they should be able to do with this knowledge (LOS are provided in candidate study sessions and at the beginning of each reading)
- The curriculum of material that candidates receive upon exam registration and are expected to master

A committee made up of practicing charterholders, in conjunction with CFA Institute staff, designs the CFA Program curriculum to deliver the CBOK to candidates. The examinations, also written by practicing charterholders, are designed to allow you to demonstrate your mastery of the CBOK as set forth in the CFA Program curriculum. As you structure your personal study program, you should emphasize mastery of the CBOK and the practical application of that knowledge. For more information on the practice analysis, CBOK, and development of the CFA Program curriculum, please visit www.cfainstitute.org/toolkit.

Organization of the Curriculum

The Level II CFA Program curriculum is organized into 10 topic areas. Each topic area begins with a brief statement of the material and the depth of knowledge expected.

Each topic area is then divided into one or more study sessions. These study sessions—18 sessions in the Level II curriculum—should form the basic structure of your reading and preparation.

Each study session includes a statement of its structure and objective, and is further divided into specific reading assignments. The outline on the inside front cover of each volume illustrates the organization of these 18 study sessions.

The reading assignments are the basis for all examination questions, and are selected or developed specifically to teach the CBOK. These readings are drawn from CFA Program-commissioned content, textbook chapters, professional journal articles, research analyst reports, and cases. Readings include problems and solutions as well as appendices to help you learn.

Reading-specific Learning Outcome Statements (LOS) are listed at the beginning of each reading. These LOS indicate what you should be able to accomplish after studying the reading. We encourage you to review how to properly use LOS, and the descriptions of commonly used LOS "command words," at www.cfainstitute.org/toolkit. The command words signal the depth of learning you are expected to achieve from the reading. You should use the LOS to guide and focus your study, as each examination question is based on an assigned reading and one or more LOS. However, the readings provide context for the LOS and enable you to apply a principle or concept in a variety of scenarios. The candidate is responsible for the entirety of all of the required material in a study session, the assigned readings as well as the end-of-reading questions and problems.

Features of the Curriculum

OPTIONAL SEGMENT BEGINS

- **Required vs. Optional Segments** - You should read all of the pages for an assigned reading. In some cases, however, we have reprinted an entire chapter or article and marked those parts of the reading that are not required as "optional." The CFA examination is based only on the required segments, and the optional segments are included only when they might help you to better understand the required segments (by seeing the required material in its full context). When an optional segment begins, you will see an icon and a solid vertical bar in the outside margin that will continue until the optional segment ends, accompanied by another icon. *Unless the material is specifically marked as optional, you should assume it is required.* Keep in mind that the optional material is provided strictly for your convenience and will not be tested. You should rely on the required segments and the reading-specific LOS in preparing for the examination.

OPTIONAL SEGMENT ENDS

- **Problems/Solutions** - *All questions and problems in the readings as well as their solutions (which are provided directly following the problems) are part of the curriculum and required material for the exam.* When appropriate, we have included problems within and after the readings to demonstrate practical application and reinforce your understanding of the concepts presented. The questions and problems are designed to help you learn these concepts and may serve as a basis for exam questions. Many of the questions are adapted from past CFA examinations.

- **Margins** - The wide margins in each volume provide space for your note-taking.
- **Two-Color Format** - To enrich the visual appeal and clarity of the exhibits, tables, and text, the curriculum is printed in a two-color format.
- **Six-Volume Structure** - For portability of the curriculum, the material is spread over six volumes.
- **Glossary and Index** - For your convenience, we have printed a glossary and index in each volume. Throughout the curriculum, a **bolded blue** word in a reading denotes a term defined in the glossary.
- **Source Material** - The authorship, publisher, and copyright owners are given for each reading for your reference. We recommend that you use this CFA Institute curriculum rather than the original source materials because the curriculum may include only selected pages from outside readings, updated sections within the readings, and has problems and solutions tailored to the CFA Program.
- **LOS Self-Check** - We have inserted checkboxes next to each LOS that you can use to track your progress in mastering the concepts in each reading.

Designing Your Personal Study Program

Create a Schedule - An orderly, systematic approach to examination preparation is critical. You should dedicate a consistent block of time every week to reading and studying. Complete all reading assignments and the associated problems and solutions in each study session. Review the LOS both before and after you study each reading to ensure that you have mastered the applicable content and can demonstrate the knowledge, skill, or ability described by the LOS and the assigned reading. Use the new LOS self-check to track your progress and highlight areas of weakness for later review.

You will receive periodic e-mail communications that contain important study tips and preparation strategies. Be sure to read these carefully.

CFA Institute estimates that you will need to devote a minimum of 10–15 hours per week for 18 weeks to study the assigned readings. Allow a minimum of one week for each study session, and plan to complete them all at least 30–45 days prior to the examination. This schedule will allow you to spend the final four to six weeks before the examination reviewing the assigned material and taking online sample and mock examinations.

At CFA Institute, we believe that candidates need to commit to a *minimum* of 270–300 hours reading and reviewing the curriculum and end-of-reading questions and problems. Many candidates have also incorporated the online sample examinations into their preparations during the final weeks before the exam. This recommendation, however, may substantially underestimate the hours needed for appropriate examination preparation depending on your individual circumstances, relevant experience, and academic background. You will undoubtedly adjust your study time to conform to your own strengths and weaknesses, and your educational and professional background.

You will probably spend more time on some study sessions than on others, but on average you should plan on devoting 15 hours per study session. You should allow ample time for both in-depth study of all topic areas and additional concentration on those topic areas for which you feel least prepared.

Candidate Preparation Toolkit - We have created the online toolkit to provide a single comprehensive location with resources and guidance for candidate preparation. In addition to in-depth information on study program planning, the CFA Program curriculum, and the online sample and mock examinations, the toolkit also contains curriculum errata, printable study session outlines, sample examination questions, and more. Errata that we have identified in the curriculum are corrected and listed periodically in the errata listing in the toolkit. We encourage you to use the toolkit as your central preparation resource during your tenure as a candidate. Visit the toolkit at www.cfainstitute.org/toolkit.

Online Sample Examinations - CFA Institute online sample examinations are intended to assess your exam preparation as you progress toward the end of your study. After each question, you will receive immediate feedback noting the correct response and indicating the relevant assigned reading, so you'll be able to identify areas of weakness for further study. The 120-minute sample examinations reflect the question formats, topics, and level of difficulty of the actual CFA examinations. Aggregate data indicate that the CFA examination pass rate was higher among candidates who took one or more online sample examinations than among candidates who did not take the online sample examinations. For more information on the online sample examinations, please visit www.cfainstitute.org/toolkit.

Online Mock Examinations - In response to candidate requests, CFA Institute has developed mock examinations that mimic the actual CFA examinations not only in question format and level of difficulty, but also in length. The three-hour online mock exams are intended to be taken after you complete your study of the full curriculum, so you can test your understanding of the CBOK and your readiness for the exam. To further differentiate, feedback is provided at the end of the exam, rather than after each question as with the sample exams. CFA Institute recommends that you take these mock exams at the final stage of your preparation toward the actual CFA examination. For more information on the online mock examinations, please visit www.cfainstitute.org/toolkit.

Tools to Measure Your Comprehension of the Curriculum

With the addition of the online mock exams, CFA Institute now provides three distinct ways you can practice for the actual CFA exam. The full descriptions are above, but below is a brief summary of each:

End-of-Reading Questions and Problems - These are found at the end of each reading in the printed curriculum, and should be used to test your understanding of the concepts.

Online Sample Exams - Available in Fall 2010, online sample exams are designed to assess your exam preparation, and can help you target areas of weakness for further study.

Online Mock Exams - In contrast to the sample exams, mock exams will be available in Spring 2011. Mock exams are designed to replicate the exam day experience, and should be taken near the end of your study period to prepare for exam day.

Preparatory Providers - After you enroll in the CFA Program, you may receive numerous solicitations for preparatory courses and review materials. When considering a prep course, make sure the provider is in compliance with the CFA Institute Prep Provider Guidelines Program. Just remember, there are no shortcuts to success on the CFA examinations; reading and studying the CFA curriculum is the key to success on the examination. The CFA examinations reference only the CFA Institute assigned curriculum—no preparatory course or review course materials are consulted or referenced. For more information on the Prep Provider Guidelines Program, visit www.cfainstitute.org/cfaprog/resources/prepcourse.html.

SUMMARY

Every question on the CFA examination is based on specific pages in the required readings and on one or more LOS. Frequently, an examination question is also tied to a specific example highlighted within a reading or to a specific end-of-reading question and/or problem and its solution. To make effective use of the curriculum, please remember these key points:

1. All pages printed in the Custom Curriculum are required reading for the examination except for occasional sections marked as optional. You may read optional pages as background, but you will not be tested on them.
2. All questions, problems, and their solutions - printed at the end of readings - are part of the curriculum and required study material for the examination.
3. You should make appropriate use of the CFA Candidate Toolkit and the online sample/mock examinations.
4. You should schedule and commit sufficient study time to cover the 18 study sessions, review the materials, and take sample/mock examinations.
5. **Note:** Some of the concepts in the study sessions may be superseded by updated rulings and/or pronouncements issued after a reading was published. Candidates are expected to be familiar with the overall analytical framework contained in the assigned readings. Candidates are not responsible for changes that occur after the material was written.

Feedback

At CFA Institute, we are committed to delivering a comprehensive and rigorous curriculum for the development of competent, ethically grounded investment professionals. We rely on candidate and member feedback as we work to incorporate content, design, and packaging improvements. You can be assured that we will continue to listen to your suggestions. Please send any comments or feedback to curriculum@cfainstitute.org. Ongoing improvements in the curriculum will help you prepare for success on the upcoming examinations, and for a lifetime of learning as a serious investment professional.

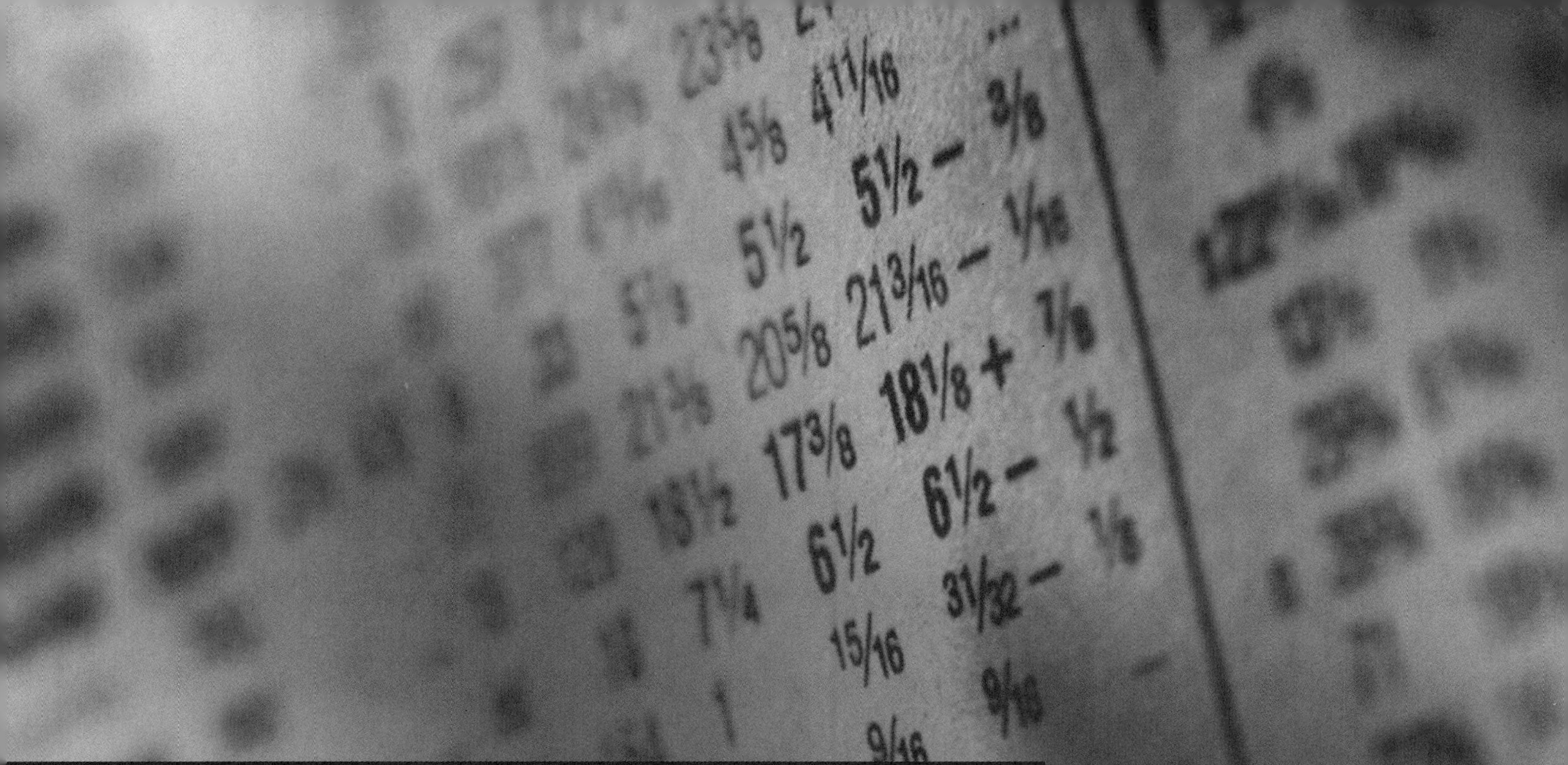

FINANCIAL REPORTING AND ANALYSIS

STUDY SESSIONS

Study Session 5	Inventories and Long-lived Assets
Study Session 6	Intercorporate Investments, Post-Employment and Share-Based Compensation, and Multinational Operations
Study Session 7	Earnings Quality Issues and Financial Ratio Analysis

TOPIC LEVEL LEARNING OUTCOME

The candidate should be able to 1) analyze and use financial statements and accompanying disclosures in the investment valuation process; 2) analyze a company's liquidity, profitability, financial stability, solvency, and asset utilization; and 3) analyze the effects of alternative accounting methods and assumptions on financial statements. The candidate should also be able to analyze differences between international and U.S. accounting standards and incorporate the findings into financial and valuation analyses.

Note:
In 2009, the Financial Accounting Standards Board (FASB) released the FASB Accounting Standards Codification™. The Codification is the single source of authoritative nongovernmental U.S. generally accepted accounting principles (U.S. GAAP) effective for periods ending after 15 September 2009. The Codification supersedes all previous U.S. GAAP standards. We have attempted to update the readings to reference or cross-reference the Codification as appropriate. Candidates are responsible for the content of international and U.S. accounting standards, not the reference numbers.

FINANCIAL RATIO LIST

Candidates should be aware that certain ratios may be defined differently. Such differences are part of the nature of practical financial analysis. For examination purposes, when a ratio is defined and calculated differently, candidates should use the definition provided in this list of ratios.

1. Current ratio = Current assets ÷ Current liabilities
2. Quick ratio = (Cash + Short-term marketable investments + Receivables) ÷ Current liabilities
3. Cash ratio = (Cash + Short-term marketable investments) ÷ Current liabilities
4. Defensive interval ratio = (Cash + Short-term marketable investments + Receivables) ÷ Daily cash expenditures
5. Receivables turnover ratio = Total revenue ÷ Average receivables
6. Days of sales outstanding (DSO) = Number of days in period ÷ Receivables turnover ratio
7. Inventory turnover ratio = Cost of goods sold ÷ Average inventory
8. Days of inventory on hand (DOH) = Number of days in period ÷ Inventory turnover ratio
9. Payables turnover ratio = Purchases ÷ Average trade payables
10. Number of days of payables = Number of days in period ÷ Payables turnover ratio
11. Cash conversion cycle (net operating cycle) = DOH + DSO − Number of days of payables
12. Working capital turnover ratio = Total revenue ÷ Average working capital
13. Fixed asset turnover ratio = Total revenue ÷ Average net fixed assets
14. Total asset turnover ratio = Total revenue ÷ Average total assets
15. Gross profit margin = Gross profit ÷ Total revenue
16. Operating profit margin = Operating profit ÷ Total revenue
17. Pretax margin = Earnings before tax but after interest ÷ Total revenue
18. Net profit margin = Net income ÷ Total revenue
19. Operating return on assets = Operating income ÷ Average total assets
20. Return on assets = Net income ÷ Average total assets
21. Return on equity = Net income ÷ Average shareholders' equity
22. Return on total capital = Earnings before interest and taxes ÷ (Interest bearing debt + Shareholders' equity)
23. Return on common equity = (Net income − Preferred dividends) ÷ Average common shareholders' equity
24. Tax burden = Net income ÷ Earnings before taxes
25. Interest burden = Earnings before taxes ÷ Earnings before interest and taxes
26. EBIT margin = Earnings before interest and taxes ÷ Total revenue
27. Financial leverage ratio (equity multiplier) = Average total assets ÷ Average shareholders' equity

28. Total debt = The total of interest-bearing short-term and long-term debt, excluding liabilities such as accrued expenses and accounts payable
29. Debt-to-assets ratio = Total debt ÷ Total assets
30. Debt-to-equity ratio = Total debt ÷ Total shareholders' equity
31. Debt-to-capital ratio = Total debt ÷ (Total debt + Total shareholders' equity)
32. Interest coverage ratio = Earnings before interest and taxes ÷ Interest payments
33. Fixed charge coverage ratio = (Earnings before interest and taxes + Lease payments) ÷ (Interest payments + Lease payments)
34. Dividend payout ratio = Common share dividends ÷ Net income attributable to common shares
35. Retention rate = (Net income attributable to common shares − Common share dividends) ÷ Net income attributable to common shares = 1 − Payout ratio
36. Sustainable growth rate = Retention rate × Return on equity
37. Earnings per share = (Net income − Preferred dividends) ÷ Weighted average number of ordinary shares outstanding
38. Book value per share = Common stockholders' equity ÷ Total number of common shares outstanding
39. Free cash flow to equity (FCFE) = Cash flow from operating activities − Investment in fixed capital + Net borrowing
40. Free cash flow to the firm (FCFF) = Cash flow from operating activities + Interest expense × (1 − Tax rate) − Investment in fixed capital *(Interest expense should be added back only if it was subtracted in determining cash flow from operating activities. This may not be the case for companies electing an alternative treatment under IFRS.)*

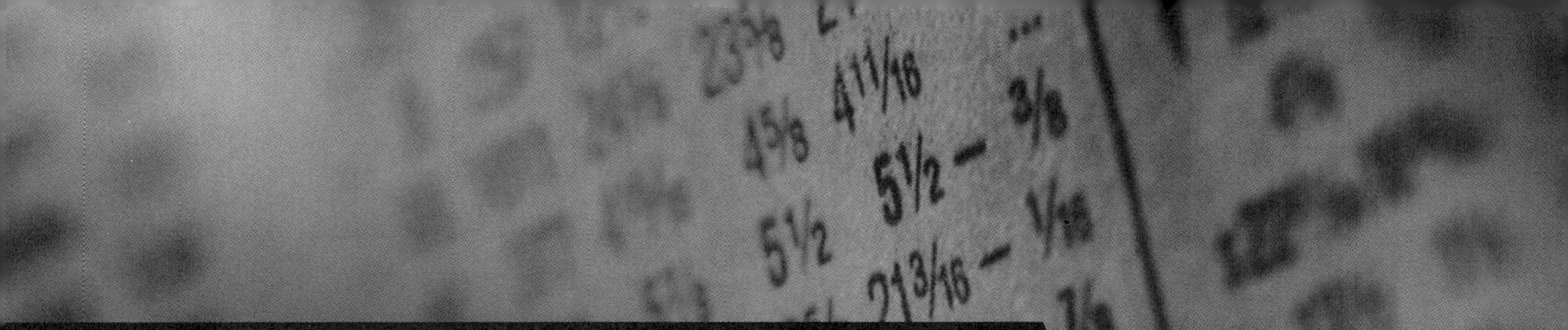

STUDY SESSION 5
FINANCIAL REPORTING AND ANALYSIS:
Inventories and Long-lived Assets

The readings in this study session focus on the implications that different accounting methods can have on financial statements and ratios. Comparing the performance of companies is challenging due to a variety of allowable accounting choices. Analysts must identify and understand the accounting differences and make adjustments to reported financial statements as needed to achieve comparability.

If inventory price levels change over time, the choice of inventory valuation method affects a company's financial statements and financial ratios. Analysts must know the various effects of the alternative inventory valuation methods, and be able to compare financial statements prepared using one method to those prepared using another method.

Analysts also must understand the effects on financial statements and financial ratios of 1) capitalizing versus expensing costs, 2) the choice of depreciation method, 3) asset impairment and revaluation, 4) leasing versus purchasing an asset, and 5) recording a lease as a finance lease versus an operating lease.

Note:
New rulings and/or pronouncements issued after the publication of the readings in financial reporting and analysis may cause some of the information in these readings to become dated. Candidates are expected to be familiar with the overall analytical framework contained in the study session readings, as well as the implications of alternative accounting methods for financial analysis and valuation, as provided in the assigned readings. Candidates are not responsible for changes that occur after the material was written.

READING ASSIGNMENTS

Reading 21 Inventories: Implications for Financial Statements and Ratios by Michael A. Broihahn, CFA

Reading 22 Long-lived Assets: Implications for Financial Statements and Ratios by Elaine Henry, CFA and Elizabeth A. Gordon

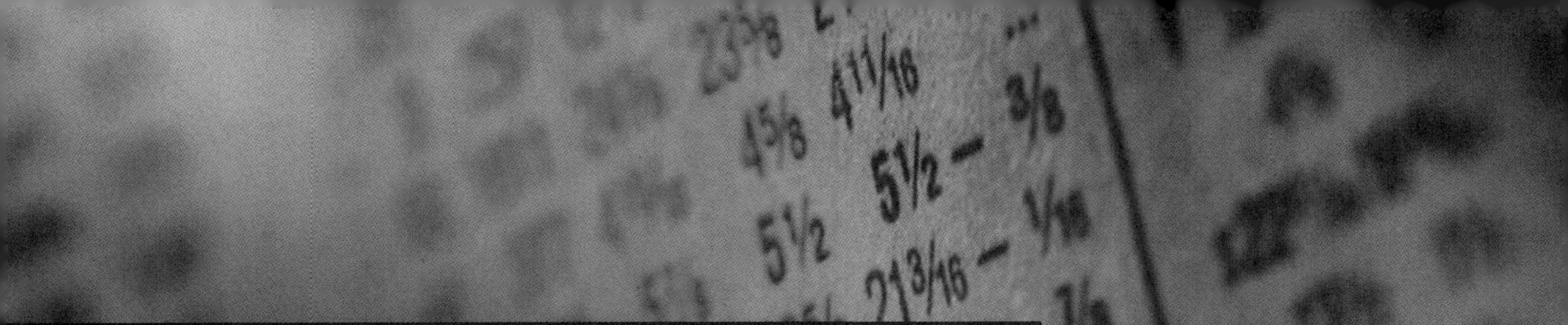

INVENTORIES: IMPLICATIONS FOR FINANCIAL STATEMENTS AND RATIOS

by Michael A. Broihahn, CFA

READING 21

LEARNING OUTCOMES

The candidate should be able to:	Mastery
a. explain and calculate the effect of inflation and deflation of inventory costs on the financial statements and ratios of companies that use different inventory valuation methods (cost formulas or cost flow assumptions);	☐
b. discuss LIFO reserve and LIFO liquidation and their effects on financial statements and ratios;	☐
c. demonstrate how to adjust a company's reported financial statements from LIFO to FIFO for purposes of comparison;	☐
d. discuss the implications of valuing inventory at net realisable value for financial statements and ratios;	☐
e. analyze and compare the financial statements and ratios of companies, including those that use different inventory valuation methods;	☐
f. discuss issues that analysts should consider when examining a company's inventory disclosures and other sources of information.	☐

Note:
New rulings and/or pronouncements issued after the publication of the readings in financial reporting and analysis may cause some of the information in these readings to become dated. Candidates are expected to be familiar with the overall analytical framework contained in the study session readings, as well as the implications of alternative accounting methods for financial analysis and valuation, as provided in the assigned readings. Candidates are not responsible for changes that occur after the material was written.

INTRODUCTION 1

Inventories and cost of sales (cost of goods sold) are significant items in the financial statements of many companies. Comparing the performance of these companies is challenging because of the allowable choices for valuing inventories: Differences in the choice of inventory valuation method can result in significantly different amounts being assigned to inventory and cost of sales. Financial statement analysis would be much easier if all companies used the same inventory valuation method or if inventory price levels remained constant over time. If there was no inflation or deflation with respect to inventory costs and thus unit costs were unchanged, the choice of inventory valuation method would be irrelevant. However, inventory price levels typically do change over time.

International Financial Reporting Standards (IFRS) permit the assignment of inventory costs (costs of goods available for sale) to inventories and cost of sales by three cost formulas: specific identification, first-in, first-out (FIFO), and weighted average cost.[1] U.S. generally accepted accounting principles (U.S. GAAP) allow the same three inventory valuation methods, referred to as cost flow assumptions in U.S. GAAP, but also include a fourth method called last-in, first-out (LIFO).[2] The choice of inventory valuation method affects the allocation of the cost of goods available for sale to ending inventory and cost of sales.

To evaluate a company's performance over time and relative to industry peers, analysts must clearly understand the various inventory valuation methods that companies use and the related impact on financial statements and financial ratios. This reading is organised as follows: Section 2 explains the effects of changing price levels on the financial statements of companies that use different inventory valuation methods. Section 3 discusses the LIFO method, LIFO reserve, and the effects of LIFO liquidations, and demonstrates the adjustments required to compare a company that uses LIFO with one that uses FIFO. Section 4 discusses the financial statement effects of a change in inventory valuation method. Section 5 demonstrates the financial statement effects of a decline in inventory value. Section 6 discusses issues analysts should consider when evaluating companies that carry inventory. A summary and practice problems in the CFA Institute item set format complete the reading.

2 INVENTORY AND CHANGING PRICE LEVELS

Each of the allowable inventory valuation methods involves a different assumption about cost flows. The choice of cost formula (IFRS terminology) or cost flow assumption (U.S. GAAP terminology) determines how the cost of goods available for sale during a period is allocated between inventory and cost of sales. Specific identification assumes that inventory items are not ordinarily interchangeable and that the cost flows match the actual physical flows of the inventory items. Cost of sales and inventory reflect the actual costs of the specific items sold and unsold (remaining in inventory).

[1] International Accounting Standard (IAS) 2 [Inventories].

[2] Financial Accounting Standards Board *Accounting Standards Codification* (FASB ASC) Topic 330 [Inventory].

First-in, first-out (FIFO) assumes that the inventory items purchased or manufactured first are sold first. The items remaining in inventory are assumed to be those most recently purchased or manufactured. In periods of rising inventory prices (inflation), the costs assigned to the units in ending inventory are higher than the costs assigned to the units sold. Conversely, in periods of declining inventory prices (deflation), the costs assigned to the units in ending inventory using FIFO are lower than the costs assigned to the units sold. In periods of changing prices, ending inventory values determined using FIFO more closely reflect current costs than do the cost of sales.

Weighted average cost assumes that the inventory items sold and those remaining in inventory are the same average age and cost. In other words, a mixture of older and newer inventory items is assumed to be sold and remaining in inventory. Weighted average cost assigns the average cost of the goods available for sale (beginning inventory plus purchases, conversion, and other costs) during the accounting period to the units that are sold as well as to the units in ending inventory. Weighted average cost per unit is calculated as total cost of goods available for sale divided by total units available for sale.

Companies typically record changes to inventory using either a periodic inventory system or a perpetual inventory system. Under a **periodic inventory system**, inventory values and costs of sales are determined at the end of the accounting period. Under a **perpetual inventory system**, inventory values and cost of sales are continuously updated to reflect purchases and sales. Under either system, the allocation of goods available for sale to cost of sales and ending inventory is the same if the inventory valuation method used is either specific identification or FIFO. This is not generally true for the weighted average cost method. Under a periodic inventory system, the amount of cost of goods available for sale allocated to cost of sales and ending inventory may be quite different using the FIFO method compared to the weighted average cost method. Under a perpetual inventory system, inventory values and cost of sales are continuously updated to reflect purchases and sales. As a result, the amount of cost of goods available for sale allocated to cost of sales and ending inventory is similar under the FIFO and weighted average cost methods. Because of lack of disclosure and the dominance of perpetual inventory systems, analysts typically do not make adjustments when comparing a company using the weighted average cost method with a company using the FIFO method.

Last-in, first-out (LIFO), which is allowed under U.S. GAAP but not allowed under IFRS, assumes that the inventory items purchased or manufactured most recently are sold first. The items remaining in inventory are assumed to be the oldest items purchased or manufactured. In periods of rising prices, the costs assigned to the units in ending inventory are lower than the costs assigned to the units sold. Similarly, in periods of declining prices, the costs assigned to the units in ending inventory are higher than the costs assigned to the units sold. In periods of changing prices and using LIFO, cost of sales more closely reflects current costs than do ending inventory values.

Using the LIFO method, the periodic and perpetual inventory systems will generally result in different allocations to cost of sales and ending inventory. Under either a perpetual or periodic inventory system, the use of the LIFO method will generally result in significantly different allocations to cost of sales and ending inventory compared to other inventory valuation methods. When inventory costs are increasing and inventory unit levels are stable or increasing, using the LIFO method will result in higher cost of sales and lower inventory carrying amounts than using the FIFO method. The higher cost of sales under LIFO will result in lower gross profit, operating income, income before taxes, and net income. Income tax expense will be lower under LIFO, causing the company's net operating cash flow to be higher. On the balance sheet, the lower inventory carrying amount will result in lower reported current assets, working capital, and total assets. Analysts must carefully assess the financial statement implications of the choice of inventory valuation method when comparing companies that use the LIFO method with companies that use the FIFO method.

The choice of inventory valuation method would be largely irrelevant if inventory unit costs remained relatively constant over time. The allocation of cost of goods available for sale to items sold and inventory items would be very similar regardless of the choice of inventory valuation method. However, inventory unit costs typically change over time and the choice of inventory valuation method does in fact result in potentially different allocations of cost of goods available for sale to inventory sold in the period and inventory on hand at the end of the period. The financial results of two essentially similar companies can look very different if the companies choose different inventory valuation methods. Cost of sales (cost of goods sold) on the income statement and inventory on the balance sheet will differ depending upon the inventory valuation method chosen.

An inventory valuation method that allocates more of the cost of goods available for sale to cost of sales and a corresponding lower amount to inventory will result in lower gross profit, net income, current assets, and total assets than an inventory method that allocates more of the cost of goods available for sale to inventory and a correspondingly lower amount to cost of sales. Therefore, the choice of inventory valuation method can have a direct impact on a company's financial statements and many of the financial ratios that are derived from them.

EXAMPLE 1

Impact of Inflation Using LIFO Compared to FIFO

Company L and Company F are identical in all respects except that Company L uses the LIFO method and Company F uses the FIFO method. Each company has been in business for five years and maintains a base inventory of 2,000 units each year. Each year, except the first year, the number of units purchased equaled the number of units sold. Over the five-year period, unit sales increased 10 percent each year and the unit purchase and selling prices increased at the beginning of each year to reflect inflation of 4 percent per year. In the first year, 20,000 units were sold at a price of \$15.00 per unit, and the unit purchase price was \$8.00.

1. What was the end of year inventory, sales, cost of sales, and gross profit for each company for each of the five years?
2. Compare the inventory turnover ratios (based on ending inventory carrying amounts) and gross profit margins over the five-year period and between companies.

Solution to 1:

Company L Using LIFO	Year 1	Year 2	Year 3	Year 4	Year 5
Ending inventory[a]	$ 16,000	$ 16,000	$ 16,000	$ 16,000	$ 16,000
Sales[b]	$300,000	$343,200	$392,621	$449,158	$513,837
Cost of sales[c]	160,000	183,040	209,398	239,551	274,046
Gross profit	$140,000	$160,160	$183,223	$209,607	$239,791

[a] Inventory is unchanged at $16,000 each year (2,000 units × $8). 2,000 of the units acquired in the first year are assumed to remain in inventory.

[b] Sales Year X = (20,000 × $15)$(1.10)^{X-1}(1.04)^{X-1}$. The quantity sold increases by 10 percent each year and the selling price increases by 4 percent each year.

[c] Cost of sales Year X = (20,000 × $8)$(1.10)^{X-1}(1.04)^{X-1}$. In Year 1, 20,000 units are sold with a cost of $8. In subsequent years, the number of units purchased equals the number of units sold, and the units sold are assumed to be those purchased in the year. The quantity purchased increases by 10 percent each year, and the purchase price increases by 4 percent each year.

Note that if the company sold more units than it purchased in a year, inventory would decrease. This is referred to as LIFO liquidation. The cost of sales of the units sold in excess of those purchased would reflect the inventory carrying amount. In this example, each unit sold in excess of those purchased would have a cost of sales of $8 and a higher gross profit.

Company F Using FIFO	Year 1	Year 2	Year 3	Year 4	Year 5
Ending inventory[a]	$ 16,000	$ 16,640	$ 17,306	$ 17,998	$ 18,718
Sales[b]	$300,000	$343,200	$392,621	$449,158	$513,837
Cost of sales[c]	160,000	182,400	208,732	238,859	273,326
Gross profit	$140,000	$160,800	$183,889	$210,299	$240,511

[a] Ending inventory Year X = 2,000 units × Cost in Year X = 2,000 units [$8 × $(1.04)^{X-1}$]. 2,000 units of the units acquired in Year X are assumed to remain in inventory.

[b] Sales Year X = (20,000 × $15)$(1.10)^{X-1}(1.04)^{X-1}$

[c] Cost of sales Year 1 = $160,000 (= 20,000 units × $8). There was no beginning inventory.

Cost of sales Year X (where X ≠ 1) = Beginning inventory plus purchases less ending inventory

= (Inventory at Year X–1) + [(20,000 × $8)$(1.10)^{X-1}(1.04)^{X-1}$] – (Inventory at Year X)

= 2,000($8)$(1.04)^{X-2}$ + [(20,000 × $8)$(1.10)^{X-1}(1.04)^{X-1}$] – [2,000($8)$(1.04)^{X-1}$]

For example, Cost of sales Year 2 = 2,000($8) + [(20,000 × $8)(1.10)(1.04)] – [2,000($8)(1.04)] = $16,000 + 183,040 – 16,640 = $182,400

Solution to 2:

	Company L					Company F				
Year	**1**	**2**	**3**	**4**	**5**	**1**	**2**	**3**	**4**	**5**
Inventory turnover	10.0	11.4	13.1	15.0	17.1	10.0	11.0	12.1	13.3	14.6
Gross profit margin (%)	46.7	46.7	46.7	46.7	46.7	46.7	46.9	46.8	46.8	46.8

Inventory turnover ratio = Cost of sales ÷ Ending inventory. The inventory turnover ratio increased each year for both companies because the units sold increased, whereas the units in ending inventory remained unchanged. The increase in the inventory turnover ratio is higher for Company L because Company L's cost of sales is increasing for inflation, but the inventory carrying amount is unaffected by inflation. It might appear that a company using the LIFO method manages its inventory more effectively, but this is deceptive. Both companies have identical quantities and prices of purchases and sales and only differ in the inventory valuation method used.

Gross profit margin = Gross profit ÷ Sales. The gross profit margin is stable under LIFO because both sales and cost of sales increase at the same rate of inflation. The gross profit margin is slightly higher under the FIFO method after the first year because a proportion of the cost of sales reflects an older purchase price.

3 THE LIFO METHOD

In the United States, the LIFO method is widely used (approximately 36 percent of U.S. companies use the LIFO method). The potential income tax savings are a benefit of using the LIFO method when inventory costs are increasing. The higher cash flows due to lower income taxes may make the company more valuable because the value of a company is based on the present value of its future cash flows. Under the "LIFO conformity rule," the U.S. tax code requires that companies using the LIFO method for tax purposes must also use the LIFO method for financial reporting. Under the LIFO method, ending inventory is assumed to consist of those units that have been held the longest. This generally results in ending inventories with carrying amounts lower than current replacement costs because inventory costs typically increase over time. Cost of sales will more closely reflect current replacement costs.

If the purchase prices (purchase costs) or production costs of inventory are increasing, the income statement consequences of using the LIFO method compared to other methods will include higher cost of sales, and lower gross profit, operating profit, income tax expense, and net income. The balance sheet consequences include lower ending inventory, working capital, total assets, retained earnings, and shareholders' equity. The lower income tax paid will result in higher net cash flow from operating activities. Some of the financial ratio effects are a lower current ratio, higher debt-to-equity ratios, and lower profitability ratios.

If the purchase prices or production costs of inventory are decreasing, it is unlikely that a company will use the LIFO method for tax purposes (and therefore for financial reporting purposes due to the LIFO conformity rule) because this will result in lower cost of sales, and higher taxable income and income taxes. However, if the company had elected to use the LIFO method and cannot justify changing the inventory valuation method for tax and financial reporting purposes when inventory costs begin to decrease, the income statement, balance sheet, and ratio effects will be opposite to the effects during a period of increasing costs.

The U.S. Securities Exchange Commission (SEC) has proposed the full adoption of IFRS by all U.S. reporting companies beginning in 2014. An important consequence of this proposal would be the complete elimination of the LIFO inventory method for financial reporting and, due to the LIFO conformity rule, tax reporting by U.S. companies. As a consequence of the restatement of financial statements to the FIFO or weighted average cost method, significant immediate income tax liabilities may arise in the year of transition from the LIFO method to either the FIFO or weighted average cost method.

3.1 LIFO Reserve

For companies using the LIFO method, U.S. GAAP requires disclosure, in the notes to the financial statements or on the balance sheet, of the amount of the LIFO reserve. The **LIFO reserve** is the difference between the reported LIFO inventory carrying amount and the inventory amount that would have been reported if the FIFO method had been used (in other words, the FIFO inventory value less the LIFO inventory value). The disclosure provides the information that analysts need to adjust a company's cost of sales (cost of goods sold) and ending inventory balance based on the LIFO method, to the FIFO method.

To compare companies using LIFO with companies not using LIFO, inventory is adjusted by adding the disclosed LIFO reserve to the inventory balance that is reported on the balance sheet. The reported inventory balance, using LIFO, plus the LIFO reserve equals the inventory that would have been reported under FIFO. Cost of sales is adjusted by subtracting the increase in the LIFO reserve during the period from the cost of sales amount that is reported on the income statement. If the LIFO reserve has declined during the period,[3] the decrease in the reserve is added to the cost of sales amount that is reported on the income statement. The LIFO reserve disclosure can be used to adjust the financial statements of a U.S. company using the LIFO method to make them comparable with a similar company using the FIFO method.

[3] This typically results from a reduction in inventory units and is referred to as LIFO liquidation. LIFO liquidation is discussed in Section 3.2.

EXAMPLE 2

Inventory Conversion from LIFO to FIFO

Caterpillar Inc. (NYSE: CAT), based in Peoria, Illinois, USA, is the largest maker of construction and mining equipment, diesel and natural gas engines, and industrial gas turbines in the world. Excerpts from CAT's consolidated financial statements are shown in Exhibits 1 and 2; notes pertaining to CAT's inventories are presented in Exhibit 3. Assume tax rates of 20 percent for 2008 and 30 percent for earlier years. The assumed tax rates are based on the provision for taxes as a percentage of consolidated profits before taxes rather than the U.S. corporate statutory tax rate of 35 percent.

1. What inventory values would CAT report for 2008, 2007, and 2006 if it had used the FIFO method instead of the LIFO method?
2. What amount would CAT's cost of goods sold for 2008 and 2007 be if it had used the FIFO method instead of the LIFO method?
3. What net income (profit) would CAT report for 2008 and 2007 if it had used the FIFO method instead of the LIFO method?
4. By what amount would CAT's 2008 and 2007 net cash flow from operating activities decline if CAT had used the FIFO method instead of the LIFO method?
5. What is the cumulative amount of income tax savings that CAT has generated through 2008 by using the LIFO method instead of the FIFO method?
6. What amount would be added to CAT's retained earnings (profit employed in the business) at 31 December 2008 if CAT had used the FIFO method instead of the LIFO method?
7. What would be the change in CAT's cash balance if CAT had used the FIFO method instead of the LIFO method?
8. Calculate and compare the following for 2008 under the LIFO method and the FIFO method: inventory turnover ratio, days of inventory on hand, gross profit margin, net profit margin, return on assets, current ratio, and total liabilities-to-equity ratio.

EXHIBIT 1 Caterpillar Inc. Consolidated Results of Operation (US$ Millions)

For the Years Ended 31 December	2008	2007	2006
Sales and revenues:			
Sales of Machinery and Engines	48,044	41,962	38,869
Revenue of Financial Products	3,280	2,996	2,648
Total sales and revenues	51,324	44,958	41,517

(*Exhibit continued on next page . . .*)

EXHIBIT 1 (continued)

For the Years Ended 31 December	2008	2007	2006
Operating costs:			
Cost of goods sold	38,415	32,626	29,549
⋮	⋮	⋮	⋮
Interest expense of Financial Products	1,153	1,132	1,023
⋮	⋮	⋮	⋮
Total operating costs	46,876	40,037	36,596
Operating profit	4,448	4,921	4,921
Interest expense excluding Financial Products	274	288	274
Other income (expense)	299	320	214
Consolidated profit before taxes	4,473	4,953	4,861
Provision for income taxes	953	1,485	1,405
Profit of consolidated companies	3,520	3,468	3,456
Equity in profit of unconsolidated affiliated companies	37	73	81
Profit	3,557	3,541	3,537

EXHIBIT 2 Caterpillar Inc. Consolidated Financial Position (US$ Millions)

31 December	2008	2007	2006
Assets			
Current assets:			
Cash and short-term investments	2,736	1,122	530
⋮	⋮	⋮	⋮
Inventories	8,781	7,204	6,351
Total current assets	31,633	25,477	23,663
⋮	⋮	⋮	⋮
Total assets	67,782	56,132	51,449

(Exhibit continued on next page . . .)

EXHIBIT 2 (continued)

31 December	2008	2007	2006
Liabilities			
Total current liabilities	26,069	22,245	19,822
⋮	⋮	⋮	⋮
Total liabilities	61,171	47,249	44,590
Redeemable noncontrolling interest (Note 25)[a]	524		
Stockholders' equity			
Common stock of $1.00 par value:			
Authorized shares: 900,000,000			
Issued shares (2008, 2007 and 2006—814,894,624) at paid-in amount	3,057	2,744	2,465
Treasury stock (2008—213,367,983 shares; 2007—190,908,490 shares and 2006—169,086,448 shares) at cost	(11,217)	(9,451)	(7,352)
Profit employed in the business	19,826	17,398	14,593
Comprehensive income (loss)	(5,579)	(1,808)	(2,847)
Total stockholders' equity	6,087	8,883	6,859
Total liabilities and stockholders' equity	67,782	56,132	51,449

[a]U.S. GAAP permitted the reporting of non-controlling interest as a liability or a mezzanine account between liabilities and equity.

EXHIBIT 3 Caterpillar Inc. Selected Notes to Consolidated Financial Statements

Note 1. Operations and Summary of Significant Accounting Policies

D. Inventories

Inventories are stated at the lower of cost or market. Cost is principally determined using the last-in, first-out (LIFO) method. The value of inventories on the LIFO basis represented about 70% of total inventories at December 31, 2008 and about 75% of total inventories at December 31, 2007 and 2006.

If the FIFO (first-in, first-out) method had been in use, inventories would have been $3,183 million, $2,617 million and $2,403 million higher than reported at December 31, 2008, 2007 and 2006, respectively.

(Exhibit continued on next page . . .)

EXHIBIT 3 (continued)

Note 9. Inventories

31 December (Millions of Dollars)	2008	2007	2006
Raw Materials	3,356	2,990	2,698
Work-in-process	1,107	863	591
Finished goods	4,022	3,066	2,785
Supplies	296	285	277
Total inventories	8,781	7,204	6,351

We had long-term material purchase obligations of approximately $363 million at December 31, 2008.

Solution to 1:

31 December (Millions of Dollars)	2008	2007	2006
Total inventories (LIFO method)	8,781	7,204	6,351
From Note 1. D (LIFO reserve)	3,183	2,617	2,403
Total inventories (FIFO method)	11,964	9,821	8,754

Solution to 2:

31 December (Millions of Dollars)	2008	2007
Cost of goods sold (LIFO method)	38,415	32,626
Less: Increase in LIFO reserve*	−566	−214
Cost of goods sold (FIFO method)	37,849	32,412

*From Note 1.D, the increase in LIFO reserve for 2008 is 566 (3,183 − 2,617) and for 2007 is 214 (2,617 − 2,403).

Solution to 3:

31 December (Millions of Dollars)	2008	2007
Net income (LIFO method)	3,557	3,541
Reduction in cost of goods sold (increase in operating profit)	566	214
Taxes on increased operating profit *	−113	−64
Net income (FIFO method)	4,010	3,691

*The taxes on the increased operating profit are assumed to be 113 (566 × 20%) for 2008 and 64 (214 × 30%) for 2007.

Solution to 4: The effect on a company's net cash flow from operating activities is limited to the impact of the change on income taxes paid; changes in allocating inventory costs to ending inventory and cost of goods sold do not change any cash flows except income taxes. Consequently, the effect of using FIFO on CAT's net operating cash flow from operating activities would be a decline of $113 million in 2008 and a decline of $64 million in 2007. These are the approximate incremental increases in income taxes that CAT would have incurred if the FIFO method had been used instead of the LIFO method (see solution to 3 above).

Solution to 5: Assuming tax rates of 20 percent for 2008 and 30 percent for earlier years, the cumulative amount of income tax savings that CAT has generated by using the LIFO method instead of FIFO is approximately $898 million (566 × 20% + 2,617 × 30%). Note 1.D indicates a LIFO reserve of $2,617 million at the end of 2007 and an increase in the LIFO reserve of $566 million in 2008. Therefore, under the FIFO method, cumulative gross profits would have been $2,617 million higher as of the end of 2007 and an additional $566 million higher as of the end of 2008. The estimated tax savings would be higher (lower) if income tax rates were assumed to be higher (lower).

Solution to 6: The amount that would be added to CAT's retained earnings is $2,285 million (3,183 − 898) or (566 × 80% + 2,617 × 70%). This represents the cumulative increase in operating profit due to the decrease in cost of goods sold (LIFO reserve of $3,183 million) less the assumed taxes on that profit ($898 million, see solution to 5 above).

Solution to 7: Under the FIFO method, an additional $898 million is assumed to have been paid in taxes and cash would be reduced accordingly. If CAT switched to FIFO, it would have an additional tax liability of $898 million as a consequence of the restatement of financial statements to the FIFO method. This illustrates the significant immediate income tax liabilities that may arise in the year of transition from the LIFO method to the FIFO method.

Solution to 8: CAT's ratios for 2008 under the LIFO and FIFO methods are as follows:

	LIFO	FIFO
Inventory turnover	4.81	3.47
Days of inventory on hand	76.1 days	105.5 days
Gross profit margin	20.04%	21.22%
Net profit margin	6.93%	7.81%
Return on assets	5.74%	6.26%
Current ratio	1.21	1.30
Total liabilities-to-equity ratio	10.05	7.31

Inventory turnover ratio = Cost of goods sold ÷ Average inventory

LIFO = 4.81 = 38,415 ÷ [(8,781 + 7,204) ÷ 2]
FIFO = 3.47 = 37,849 ÷ [(11,964 + 9,821) ÷ 2]

The ratio is higher under LIFO because, given rising inventory costs, cost of goods sold will be higher and inventory carrying amounts will be lower under LIFO. If an analyst made no adjustment for the difference in inventory methods, it might appear that a company using the LIFO method manages its inventory more effectively.

Days of inventory on hand = Number of days in period ÷ Inventory turnover ratio

LIFO = 76.1 days = (366 days* ÷ 4.81)
FIFO = 105.5 days = (366 days ÷ 3.47)

*2008 was a leap year.

Without adjustment, a company using the LIFO method might appear to manage its inventory more effectively. This is primarily the result of the lower inventory carrying amounts under LIFO.

Gross profit margin = Gross profit ÷ Total revenue

LIFO = 20.04 percent = [(48,044 − 38,415) ÷ 48,044]
FIFO = 21.22 percent = [(48,044 − 37,849) ÷ 48,044]

Revenue of financial products is excluded from the calculation of gross profit. Gross profit is sales of machinery and engines less cost of goods sold. The gross profit margin is lower under LIFO because the cost of goods sold is higher given rising inventory costs.

Net profit margin = Net income ÷ Total revenue

LIFO = 6.93 percent = (3,557 ÷ 51,324)
FIFO = 7.81 percent = (4,010 ÷ 51,324)

The net profit margin is lower under LIFO because the cost of goods sold is higher. The absolute percentage difference is less than that of the gross profit margin because of income taxes on the increased income reported under FIFO and because net income is divided by total revenue including sales of machinery and engines and revenue of financial products. The company appears to be less profitable under LIFO.

Return on assets = Net income ÷ Average total assets

LIFO = 5.74 percent = 3,557 ÷ [(67,782 + 56,132) ÷ 2]
FIFO = 6.26 percent = 4,010 ÷ [(67,782 + 3,183 − 898) + (56,132 + 2,617 − 785) ÷ 2]

The total assets under FIFO are the LIFO total assets increased by the LIFO reserve and decreased by the cash paid for the additional income taxes. The return on assets is lower under LIFO because the lower net income due to the higher cost of goods sold has a greater impact on the ratio than the lower total assets, which are the result of lower inventory carrying amounts. The company appears to be less profitable under LIFO.

Current ratio = Current assets ÷ Current liabilities

LIFO = 1.21 = (31,633 ÷ 26,069)
FIFO = 1.30 = [(31,633 + 3,183 − 898) ÷ 26,069]

The current ratio is lower under LIFO primarily because of lower inventory carrying amount. The company appears to be less liquid under LIFO.

Total liabilities-to-equity ratio = Total liabilities ÷ Total shareholders' equity

LIFO = 10.05 = (61,171 ÷ 6,087)
FIFO = 7.31 = [61,171 ÷ (6,087 + 2,285)]

The ratio is higher under LIFO because the addition to retained earnings under FIFO reduces the ratio. The company appears to be more highly leveraged under LIFO.

In summary, the company appears to be less profitable, less liquid, and more highly leveraged under LIFO. Yet, because a company's value is based on the present value of future cash flows, LIFO will increase the company's value because the cash flows are higher in earlier years due to lower taxes. LIFO is primarily used for the tax benefits it provides.

3.2 LIFO Liquidations

In periods of rising inventory unit costs, the carrying amount of inventory under FIFO will always exceed the carrying amount of inventory under LIFO. The LIFO reserve may increase over time as the result of the increasing difference between the older costs used to value inventory under LIFO and the more recent costs used to value inventory under FIFO. Also, when the number of inventory units manufactured or purchased exceeds the number of units sold, the LIFO reserve may increase as the result of the addition of new LIFO layers (the quantity of inventory units is increasing and each increase in quantity creates a new LIFO layer).

When the number of units sold exceeds the number of units purchased or manufactured, the number of units in ending inventory is lower than the number of units in beginning inventory, and a company using LIFO will experience a LIFO liquidation (some of the older units held in inventory are assumed to have been sold). If inventory unit costs have been rising from period to period and LIFO liquidation occurs, this will produce an inventory-related increase in gross profits. The increase in gross profits occurs because of the lower inventory carrying amounts of the liquidated units. The lower inventory carrying amounts are used for cost of sales and the sales are at the current prices. The gross profit on these units is higher than the gross profit that would be recognised using more current costs. These inventory profits caused by a LIFO liquidation, however, are one-time events and are not sustainable.

LIFO liquidations can occur for a variety of reasons. The reduction in inventory levels may be outside of management's control; for example, labour strikes at a supplier may force a company to reduce inventory levels to meet customer demands. In periods of economic recession or when customer demand is declining, a company may choose to reduce existing inventory levels rather than invest in new inventory. Analysts should be aware that management can potentially manipulate and inflate their company's reported gross profits and net income at critical times by intentionally reducing inventory quantities and liquidating older layers of LIFO inventory (selling some units of beginning inventory). During economic downturns, LIFO liquidation may result in higher gross profit than would otherwise be realised. If LIFO layers of inventory are temporarily depleted and not replaced by fiscal year-end, LIFO liquidation will occur, resulting in unsustainable higher gross profits. Therefore, it is imperative to review the LIFO reserve footnote disclosures to determine if LIFO liquidation has occurred. A decline in the LIFO reserve from the prior period may be indicative of LIFO liquidation.

EXAMPLE 3

LIFO Liquidation: Financial Statement Impact and Disclosure

The following excerpts are from the 2007 10-K of Sturm Ruger & Co., Inc. (NYSE:RGR):

> Item 7—Management's Discussion and Analysis of Financial Condition and Results of Operations
>
> Reduction in inventory generated positive cash flow for the Company, partially offset by the tax impact of the consequent LIFO liquidation, which generated negative cash flow as it created taxable income, resulting in higher tax payments.

Balance Sheets *(In thousands, except per share data)* **December 31**	**2007**	**2006**
Assets		
Current Assets		
⋮	⋮	⋮
Gross inventories:	64,330	87,477
Less LIFO reserve	(46,890)	(57,555)
Less excess and obsolescence reserve	(4,143)	(5,516)
Net inventories	13,297	24,406
⋮	⋮	⋮
Total Current Assets	73,512	81,785
⋮	⋮	⋮
Total Assets	$101,882	$117,066

Statements of Income *(In thousands, except per share data)* **Year ended December 31**	**2007**	**2006**
⋮	⋮	⋮
Total net sales	156,485	167,620
Cost of products sold	117,186	139,610
Gross profit	39,299	28,010
Expenses:		
⋮	⋮	⋮
Total expenses	30,184	27,088
Operating income	9,115	922
⋮	⋮	⋮
Total other income, net	7,544	921
Income before income taxes	16,659	1,843
Income taxes	6,330	739
Net income	$10,329	$1,104
Basic and Diluted Earnings Per Share	$ 0.46	$ 0.04
Cash Dividends Per Share	$ 0.00	$ 0.00

Notes to Financial Statements
1. Significant Accounting Policies

⋮

Inventories

Inventories are stated at the lower of cost, principally determined by the last-in, first-out (LIFO) method, or market. If inventories had been valued using the first-in, first-out method, inventory values would have been higher by approximately $46.9 million and $57.6 million at December 31, 2007 and 2006, respectively. During 2007 and 2006, inventory quantities were reduced. This reduction resulted in a liquidation of LIFO inventory quantities carried at lower costs prevailing in prior years as compared with the current cost of purchases, the effect of which decreased costs of products sold by approximately $12.1 million and $7.1 million in 2007 and 2006, respectively. There was no LIFO liquidation in 2005.

1. What is the decrease in the LIFO reserve on the balance sheet? How much less was cost of products sold in 2007, due to LIFO liquidation, according to the note disclosure?
2. How did the decreased cost of products sold compare to operating income in 2007?
3. How did the LIFO liquidation affect cash flows?

Solution to 1: The LIFO reserve decreased by $10,665 thousand (57,555 − 46,890) in 2007. The LIFO liquidation decreased costs of products sold by approximately $12.1 million in 2007. The decrease in the LIFO reserve is indicative of a LIFO liquidation but is not sufficient to determine the exact amount of the LIFO liquidation.

Solution to 2: The decreased cost of products sold of approximately $12.1 million exceeds the operating income of approximately $9 million.

Solution to 3: The LIFO liquidation (reduction in inventory) generated positive cash flow. The positive cash flow effect of the LIFO liquidation was reduced by its tax impact. The LIFO liquidation resulted in higher taxable income and higher tax payments.

EXAMPLE 4

LIFO Liquidation Illustration

Reliable Fans, Inc. (RF), a hypothetical company, sells high-quality fans and has been in business since 2006. Exhibit 4 provides relevant data and financial statement information about RF's inventory purchases and sales of fan inventory for the years 2006 through 2009. RF uses the LIFO method and a periodic inventory system. What amount of RF's 2009 gross profit is due to LIFO liquidation?

EXHIBIT 4 RF Financial Statement Information under LIFO

	2006	2007	2008	2009
Fans units purchased	12,000	12,000	12,000	12,000
Purchase cost per fan	$100	$105	$110	$115
Fans units sold	10,000	12,000	12,000	13,000
Sales price per fan	$200	$205	$210	$215
LIFO Method				
Beginning inventory	$0	$200,000	$200,000	$200,000
Purchases	1,200,000	1,260,000	1,320,000	1,380,000
Goods available for sale	1,200,000	1,460,000	1,520,000	1,580,000
Ending inventory*	(200,000)	(200,000)	(200,000)	(100,000)
Cost of goods sold	$1,000,000	1,260,000	$1,320,000	$1,480,000
Income Statement				
Sales	$2,000,000	$2,460,000	$2,520,000	$2,795,000
Cost of goods sold	1,000,000	1,260,000	1,320,000	1,480,000
Gross profit	$1,000,000	$1,200,000	$1,200,000	$1,315,000
Balance Sheet				
Inventory	$200,000	$200,000	$200,000	$100,000

*Ending inventory 2006, 2007, and 2008 = (2,000 × $100).
Ending inventory 2009 = (1,000 × $100).

Solution: RF's reported gross profit for 2009 is $1,315,000. RF's 2009 gross profit due to LIFO liquidation is $15,000. If RF had purchased 13,000 fans in 2009 rather than 12,000 fans, the cost of goods sold under the LIFO method would have been $1,495,000 (13,000 fans sold at $115.00 purchase cost per fan), and the reported gross profit would have been $1,300,000 ($2,795,000 less $1,495,000). The gross profit due to LIFO liquidation is $15,000 ($1,315,000 reported gross profit less the $1,300,000 gross profit that would have been reported without the LIFO liquidation). The gross profit due to LIFO liquidation may also be determined by multiplying the number of units liquidated times the difference between the replacement cost of the units liquidated and their historical purchase cost. For RF, 1,000 units times $15 ($115 replacement cost per fan less the $100 historical cost per fan) equals the $15,000 gross profit due to LIFO liquidation.

INVENTORY METHOD CHANGES

4

Companies on rare occasion change inventory valuation methods. Under IFRS, a change in method is acceptable only if the change "results in the financial statements providing reliable and more relevant information about the effects of transactions, other events, or conditions on the business entity's financial position, financial performance, or cash flows."[4] If the change is justifiable, then it is applied retrospectively.

This means that the change is applied to comparative information for prior periods as far back as is practicable. The cumulative amount of the adjustments relating to periods prior to those presented in the current financial statements is made to the opening balance of each affected component of equity (i.e., retained earnings or comprehensive income) of the earliest period presented. For example, if a company changes its inventory method in 2009 and it presents three years of comparative financial statements (2007, 2008, and 2009) in its annual report, it would retrospectively reflect this change as far back as possible. The change would be reflected in the three years of financial statements presented; the financial statements for 2007 and 2008 would be restated as if the new method had been used in these periods, and the cumulative effect of the change on periods prior to 2007 would be reflected in the 2007 opening balance of each affected component of equity. An exemption to the restatement applies when it is impracticable to determine either the period-specific effects or the cumulative effect of the change.

Under U.S. GAAP, the conditions to make a change in accounting policy and the accounting for a change in inventory policy are similar to IFRS.[5] U.S. GAAP, however, requires companies to thoroughly explain why the newly adopted inventory accounting method is superior and preferable to the old method. If a company decides to change from LIFO to another inventory method, U.S. GAAP requires a retrospective restatement as described above. However, if a company decides to change to the LIFO method, it must do so on a prospective basis and retrospective adjustments are not made to the financial statements. The carrying amount of inventory under the old method becomes the initial LIFO layer in the year of LIFO adoption.

Analysts should carefully evaluate changes in inventory valuation methods. Although the stated reason for the inventory change may be to better match inventory costs with sales revenue (or some other plausible business explanation), the real underlying (and unstated) purpose may be to reduce income tax expense (if changing to LIFO from FIFO or average cost), or to increase reported profits (if changing from LIFO to FIFO or average cost). As always, the choice of inventory valuation method can have a significant impact on financial statements and the financial ratios that are derived from them. As a consequence, analysts must carefully consider the impact of the change in inventory valuation methods and the differences in inventory valuation methods when comparing a company's performance with that of its industry or its competitors.

---

[4] IAS 8 [Accounting Policies, Changes in Accounting Estimates and Errors].

[5] FASB ASC Topic 250 [Accounting Changes and Error Corrections].

5 INVENTORY ADJUSTMENTS

Significant financial risk can result from the holding of inventory. The cost of inventory may not be recoverable due to spoilage, obsolescence, or declines in selling prices. IFRS state that inventories shall be measured (and carried on the balance sheet) at the lower of cost and net realisable value.[6] **Net realisable value** is the estimated selling price in the ordinary course of business less the estimated costs necessary to make the sale and estimated costs to get the inventory in condition for sale. The assessment of net realisable value is typically done item by item or by groups of similar or related items. In the event that the value of inventory declines below the carrying amount on the balance sheet, the inventory carrying amount must be written down to its net realisable value[7] and the loss (reduction in value) recognised as an expense on the income statement. This expense may be included as part of cost of sales or reported separately.

In each subsequent period, a new assessment of net realisable value is made. Reversal (limited to the amount of the original write-down) is required for a subsequent increase in value of inventory previously written down. The reversal of any write-down of inventories is recognised as a reduction in cost of sales (reduction in the amount of inventories recognised as an expense).

U.S. GAAP specify the lower of cost or market to value inventories.[8] This is broadly consistent with IFRS with one major difference: U.S. GAAP prohibit the reversal of write-downs. Market is defined as current replacement cost subject to upper and lower limits. Market cannot exceed net realisable value (selling price less reasonably estimated costs of completion and disposal). The lower limit of market is net realisable value less a normal profit margin. Any write-down reduces the value of the inventory, and the loss in value (expense) is generally reflected in the income statement in cost of goods sold.

An inventory write-down reduces both profit and the carrying amount of inventory on the balance sheet and thus has a negative effect on profitability, liquidity, and solvency ratios. However, activity ratios (for example, inventory turnover and total asset turnover) will be positively affected by a write-down because the asset base (denominator) is reduced. The negative impact on some key ratios, due to the decrease in profit, may result in the reluctance by some companies to record inventory write-downs unless there is strong evidence that the decline in the value of inventory is permanent. This is especially true under U.S. GAAP where reversal of a write-down is prohibited.

Analysts should consider the possibility of an inventory write-down because the impact on a company's financial ratios may be substantial. The potential for inventory write-downs can be high for companies in industries where technological obsolescence of inventories is a significant risk. Analysts should carefully evaluate prospective inventory impairments (as well as other potential asset impairments) and their potential effects on the financial ratios when debt covenants include financial ratio requirements. The breaching of debt covenants can have a significant impact on a company.

---

[6] IAS 2 paragraphs 28–33 [Inventories—Net realisable value].

[7] Frequently, rather than writing inventory down directly, an inventory valuation allowance account is used. The allowance account is netted with the inventory accounts to arrive at the carrying amount that appears on the balance sheet.

[8] FASB ASC Section 330-10-35 [Inventory—Overall—Subsequent Measurement].

Companies that use specific identification, weighted average cost, or FIFO methods are more likely to incur inventory write-downs than companies that use the LIFO method. Under the LIFO method, the *oldest* costs are reflected in the inventory carrying amount on the balance sheet. Given increasing inventory costs, the inventory carrying amounts under the LIFO method are already conservatively presented at the oldest and lowest costs. Thus, it is far less likely that inventory write-downs will occur under LIFO—and if a write-down does occur, it is likely to be of a lesser magnitude.

EXAMPLE 5

Effect of Inventory Write-downs on Financial Ratios

The Volvo Group (OMX Nordic Exchange: VOLV B), based in Göteborg, Sweden, is a leading supplier of commercial transport products such as construction equipment, trucks, busses, and drive systems for marine and industrial applications as well as aircraft engine components.[9] Excerpts from Volvo's consolidated financial statements are shown in Exhibits 5 and 6. Notes pertaining to Volvo's inventories are presented in Exhibit 7.

1. What inventory values would Volvo have reported for 2008, 2007, and 2006 if it had no allowance for inventory obsolescence?
2. Assuming that any changes to the allowance for inventory obsolescence are reflected in the cost of sales, what amount would Volvo's cost of sales be for 2008 and 2007 if it had not recorded inventory write-downs in 2008 and 2007?
3. What amount would Volvo's profit (net income) be for 2008 and 2007 if it had not recorded inventory write-downs in 2008 and 2007? Assume tax rates of 28.5 percent for 2008 and 30 percent for 2007.
4. What would Volvo's 2008 profit (net income) have been if it had reversed all past inventory write-downs in 2008? This question is independent of 1, 2, and 3. Assume a tax rate of 28.5 percent for 2008.
5. Compare the following for 2008 based on the numbers as reported and those assuming no allowance for inventory obsolescence as in questions 1, 2, and 3: inventory turnover ratio, days of inventory on hand, gross profit margin, and net profit margin.
6. CAT (Example 2) has no disclosures indicative of either inventory write-downs or a cumulative allowance for inventory obsolescence in its 2008 financial statements. Provide a conceptual explanation as to why Volvo incurred inventory write-downs for 2008 but CAT did not.

[9] As of this writing, the Volvo line of automobiles is not under the control and management of the Volvo Group.

EXHIBIT 5 Volvo Group Consolidated Income Statements (Swedish Krona in Millions, except per Share Data)

For the years ended 31 December	2008	2007	2006
Net sales	303,667	285,405	258,835
Cost of sales	(237,578)	(219,600)	(199,054)
Gross income	66,089	65,805	59,781
⋮	⋮	⋮	⋮
Operating income	15,851	22,231	20,399
Interest income and similar credits	1,171	952	666
Income expenses and similar charges	(1,935)	(1,122)	(585)
Other financial income and expenses	(1,077)	(504)	(181)
Income after financial items	14,010	21,557	20,299
Income taxes	(3,994)	(6,529)	(3,981)
Income for the period	10,016	15,028	16,318
Attributable to:			
Equity holders of the parent company	9,942	14,932	16,268
Minority interests	74	96	50
Profit	10,016	15,028	16,318

EXHIBIT 6 Volvo Group Consolidated Balance Sheets (Swedish Krona in Millions)

31 December	2008	2007	2006
Assets			
Total non-current assets	196,381	162,487	124,039
Current assets:			
Inventories	55,045	43,645	34,211
⋮	⋮	⋮	⋮
Cash and cash equivalents	17,712	14,544	10,757
Total current assets	176,038	159,160	134,388
Total assets	372,419	321,647	258,427

(*Exhibit continued on next page . . .*)

EXHIBIT 6 (continued)

31 December	2008	2007	2006
Shareholders' equity and liabilities			
Shareholders' equity:			
Share capital	2,554	2,554	2,554
Reserves	5,078	2,146	1,664
Retained earnings	66,436	62,570	66,418
Income for the period	9,942	14,932	16,268
Equity attributable to equity holders of the parent company	84,010	82,202	86,904
Minority interests	630	579	284
Total shareholders' equity	84,640	82,781	87,188
Total non-current provisions	29,031	26,202	19,864
Total non-current liabilities	92,608	71,729	45,457
Total current provisions	11,750	10,656	9,799
Total current liabilities	154,390	130,279	96,119
Total shareholders' equity and liabilities	372,419	321,647	258,427

EXHIBIT 7 Volvo Group Selected Notes to Consolidated Financial Statements

Note 1. Accounting Principles
Inventories
Inventories are reported at the lower of cost, in accordance with the first-in, first-out method (FIFO), or net realisable value. The acquisition value is based on the standard cost method, including costs for all direct manufacturing expenses and the apportionable share of the capacity and other related manufacturing costs. The standard costs are tested regularly and adjustments are made based on current conditions. Costs for research and development, selling, administration and financial expenses are not included. Net realisable value is calculated as the selling price less costs attributable to the sale.

(*Exhibit continued on next page . . .*)

EXHIBIT 7 (continued)

Note 2. Key sources of estimation uncertainty
Inventory obsolescence
Inventories are reported at the lower of cost, in accordance with the first-in, first-out method (FIFO), or net realisable value. The estimated net realisable value includes management consideration of out-dated articles, over-stocking, physical damages, inventory-lead-time, handling and other selling costs. If the estimated net realisable value is lower than cost, a valuation allowance is established for inventory obsolescence. The total inventory value, net of inventory obsolescence allowance, is per 31 December 2008, SEK (in millions) 55,045.

Note 18. Inventories

31 December (Millions of Krona)	2008	2007	2006
Finished products	39,137	28,077	20,396
Production materials, etc.	15,908	15,568	13,815
Total	**55,045**	**43,645**	**34,211**

Increase (decrease) in allowance for inventory obsolescence

31 December (Millions of Krona)	2008	2007	2006
Balance sheet, 31 December, preceding year	2,837	2,015	2,401
Increase in allowance for inventory obsolescence charged to income	1,229	757	186
Scrapping	(325)	(239)	(169)
Translation differences	305	2	(130)
Reclassifications, etc.	(524)	302	(273)
Balance sheet, 31 December	3,522	2,837	2,015

Solution to 1:

31 December (Swedish Krona in Millions)	2008	2007	2006
Total inventories, net	55,045	43,645	34,211
From Note 18. (Allowance for obsolescence)	3,522	2,837	2,015
Total inventories (without allowance)	58,567	46,482	36,226

Solution to 2:

31 December (Swedish Krona in Millions)	2008	2007
Cost of sales	237,578	219,600
Less: Increase in allowance for obsolescence*	−685	−822
Cost of sales (without allowance)	236,893	218,778

*From Note 18, the increase in allowance for obsolescence for 2008 is 685 (3,522 – 2,837) and for 2007 is 822 (2,837 – 2,015).

Solution to 3:

31 December (Swedish Krona in Millions)	2008	2007
Profit (Net income)	10,016	15,028
Reduction in cost of sales (increase in operating profit)	685	822
Taxes on increased operating profit*	−195	−247
Profit (without allowance)	10,506	15,603

*Taxes on the increased operating profit are assumed to be 195 (685 × 28.5%) for 2008 and 247 (822 × 30%) for 2007.

Solution to 4:

31 December (Swedish Krona in Millions)	2008
Profit (Net income)	10,016
Reduction in cost of sales (increase in operating profit)	3,522
Taxes on increased operating profit*	−1,004
Profit (after recovery of previous write-downs)	12,534

*Taxes on the increased operating profit are assumed to be 1,004 (3,522 × 28.5%) for 2008.

Solution to 5: The Volvo Group's financial ratios for 2008 with the allowance for inventory obsolescence and without the allowance for inventory obsolescence are as follows:

	With Allowance (As Reported)	Without Allowance (Adjusted)
Inventory turnover ratio	4.81	4.51
Days of inventory on hand	76.1	81.2
Gross profit margin	21.76%	21.99%
Net profit margin	3.30%	3.46%

Inventory turnover ratio = Cost of sales ÷ Average inventory

With allowance (as reported) = 4.81 = 237,578 ÷ [(55,045 + 43,645) ÷ 2]
Without allowance (adjusted) = 4.51 = 236,893 ÷ [(58,567 + 46,482) ÷ 2]

Inventory turnover is higher based on the numbers as reported because cost of sales will be higher (assuming inventory write-downs are reported as part of cost of sales), and inventory carrying amounts will be lower with an allowance for inventory obsolescence. The company appears to manage its inventory more efficiently when it has inventory write-downs.

Days of inventory on hand = Number of days in period ÷ Inventory turnover ratio

With allowance (as reported) = 76.1 days = (366 days* ÷ 4.81)
Without allowance (adjusted) = 81.2 days = (366 days ÷ 4.51)

*2008 was a leap year.

Days of inventory on hand are lower based on the numbers as reported because the inventory turnover is higher. A company with inventory write-downs might appear to manage its inventory more effectively. This is primarily the result of the lower inventory carrying amounts.

Gross profit margin = Gross income ÷ Net sales

With allowance (as reported) = 21.76 percent = [66,089 ÷ 303,667]
Without allowance (adjusted) = 21.99 percent = [(66,089 + 685) ÷ 303,667]

The gross profit margin is lower with inventory write-downs because the cost of sales is higher. This assumes that inventory write-downs are reported as part of cost of sales.

Net profit margin = Profit ÷ Net sales

With allowance (as reported) = 3.30 percent = (10,016 ÷ 303,667)
Without allowance (adjusted) = 3.46 percent = (10,506 ÷ 303,667]

The net profit margin is lower with inventory write-downs because the cost of sales is higher (assuming the inventory write-downs are reported as part of cost of sales). The absolute percentage difference is less than that of the gross profit margin because of income taxes on the increased income without write-downs.

The profitability ratios (gross profit margin and net profit margin) for Volvo Group would have been slightly better (higher) for 2008 if the company had not recorded inventory write-downs. The activity ratio (inventory turnover ratio) would appear less attractive without the write-downs. The inventory turnover ratio is slightly better (higher) with inventory write-downs because inventory write-downs increase cost of sales (numerator) and decrease the average inventory (denominator), making inventory management appear more efficient with write-downs.

Solution to 6: CAT uses the LIFO method whereas Volvo uses the FIFO method. Given increasing inventory costs, companies that use the FIFO inventory method are far more likely to incur inventory write-downs than those companies that use the LIFO method. This is because under the LIFO method, the inventory carrying amounts reflect the *oldest* costs and therefore the *lowest* costs given increasing inventory costs. Because inventory carrying amounts under the LIFO method are already conservatively presented, it is less likely that inventory write-downs will occur.

IAS 2 [Inventories] does not apply to the inventories of producers of agricultural and forest products and minerals and mineral products, nor to commodity broker–traders. These inventories may be measured at net realisable value (fair value less costs to sell and complete) according to well-established industry practices. If an active market exists for these products, the quoted market price in that market is the appropriate basis for determining the fair value of that asset. If an active market does not exist, a company may use market determined prices or values (such as the most recent market transaction price) when available for determining fair value. Changes in the value of inventory (increase or decrease) are recognised in profit or loss in the period of the change. U.S. GAAP is similar to IFRS in its treatment of inventories of agricultural and forest products and mineral ores. Mark-to-market inventory accounting is allowed for bullion.

6 FINANCIAL STATEMENT ANALYSIS ISSUES

IFRS and U.S. GAAP require companies to disclose, either on the balance sheet or in the notes to the financial statements, the carrying amounts of inventories in classifications suitable to the company. For manufacturing companies, these classifications might include production supplies, raw materials, work in progress, and finished goods. For a retailer, these classifications might include significant categories of merchandise or the grouping of inventories with similar attributes. These disclosures may provide signals about a company's future sales and profits.

For example, a significant increase (attributable to increases in unit volume rather than increases in unit cost) in raw materials and/or work-in-progress inventories may signal that the company expects an increase in demand for its products. This suggests an anticipated increase in sales and profit. However, a substantial increase in finished goods inventories while raw materials and work-in-progress inventories are declining may signal a decrease in demand for the company's products and hence lower future sales and profit. This may also signal a potential future write-down of finished goods inventory. Irrespective of the signal, an analyst should thoroughly investigate the underlying reasons for any significant changes in a company's raw materials, work-in-progress, and finished goods inventories.

Analysts also should compare the growth rate of a company's sales to the growth rate of its finished goods inventories, because this could also provide a signal about future sales and profits. For example, if the growth of inventories is greater than the growth of sales, this could indicate a decline in demand and a decrease in future earnings. The company may have to lower (mark down) the selling price of its products to reduce its inventory balances, or it may have to write down the value of its inventory because of obsolescence, both of which would negatively affect profits. Besides the potential for mark-downs or write-downs, having too much inventory on hand or the wrong type of inventory can have a negative financial effect on a company because it increases inventory-related expenses such as insurance, storage costs, and taxes. In addition, it means that the company has less cash and working capital available to use for other purposes.

Inventory write-downs may have a substantial impact on a company's activity, profitability, liquidity, and solvency ratios. It is critical for the analyst to be aware of industry trends toward product obsolescence and to analyze the financial ratios for their sensitivity to potential inventory impairment. Companies can minimise the impact of inventory write-downs by better matching their inventory composition and growth with prospective customer demand. To obtain additional information about a company's inventory and its future sales, a variety of sources of information are available. Analysts should consider the Management Discussion and Analysis (MD&A) or similar sections of the company's financial reports, industry-related news and publications, and industry economic data.

When conducting comparisons, differences in the choice of inventory valuation method can significantly affect the comparability of financial ratios between companies. A restatement from the LIFO method to the FIFO method is critical to make a valid comparison with companies using a method other than the LIFO method such as those companies reporting under IFRS.

EXAMPLE 6

Comparative Illustration

1. Using CAT's LIFO numbers as reported and FIFO adjusted numbers (Example 2) and Volvo's numbers as reported (Example 5), compare the following for 2008: inventory turnover ratio, days of inventory on hand, gross profit margin, net profit margin, return on assets, current ratio, total liabilities-to-equity ratio, and return on equity. For the current ratio, include current provisions as part of current liabilities. For the total liabilities-to-equity ratio, include provisions in total liabilities.
2. How much do inventories represent as a component of total assets for CAT using LIFO numbers as reported and FIFO adjusted numbers, and for Volvo using reported numbers in 2007 and 2008? Discuss any changes that would concern an analyst.
3. Using the reported numbers, compare the 2007 and 2008 growth rates of CAT and Volvo for sales, finished goods inventory, and inventories other than finished goods.

Solution to 1: The comparisons between Caterpillar and Volvo for 2008 are as follows:

	CAT(LIFO)	CAT(FIFO)	Volvo
Inventory turnover ratio	4.81	3.47	4.81
Days of inventory on hand	76.1 days	105.5 days	76.1 days
Gross profit margin	20.04%	21.22%	21.76%
Net profit margin	6.93%	7.81%	3.30%
Return on assets[a]	5.74%	6.26%	2.89%
Current ratio[b]	1.21	1.30	1.06
Total liabilities-to-equity ratio[c]	10.05	7.31	3.40
Return on equity[d]	47.5%	42.0%	12.0%

Note: Calculations for ratios previously calculated (see Examples 2 and 5) are not shown again.

[a]Return on assets = Net income ÷ Average total assets
Volvo = 2.89 percent = 10,016 ÷ [(372,419 + 321,647) ÷ 2]

[b]Current ratio = Current assets ÷ Current liabilities
Volvo = 1.06 = [176,038 ÷ (11,750 + 154,390)]
The question indicates to include current provisions in current liabilities.

[c]Total liabilities-to-equity ratio = Total liabilities ÷ Total shareholders' equity
Volvo = 3.40 = [(29,031 + 92,608 + 11,750 + 154,390) ÷ 84,640]
The question indicates to include provisions in total liabilities.

[d]Return on equity = Net income ÷ Average shareholders' equity
CAT (LIFO) = 47.5 percent = 3,557 ÷ [(6,087 + 8,883) ÷ 2]
CAT (FIFO) = 42.0 percent = 4,010 ÷ {[(6,087 + 3,183 − 898) + (8,883 + 2,617 − 785)] ÷ 2}
Volvo = 12.0 percent = 10,016 ÷ [(84,640 + 82,781) ÷ 2]

Comparing CAT (FIFO) and Volvo, it appears that Volvo manages its inventory more effectively. It has higher inventory turnover and less days of inventory on hand. CAT appears to have superior profitability based on net profit margins. CAT did report some losses as other comprehensive income in the balance sheet (see Exhibit 2) as indicated by the absolute increase in the negative accumulated other comprehensive income. The absolute increase in the negative accumulated other comprehensive income results in a reduction of shareholders' equity, which makes CAT's return on equity higher. The higher leverage of CAT also increases the return on equity. The sources of CAT's higher return on equity (reporting losses through other comprehensive income and higher leverage) should be of concern to an analyst. An analyst should investigate further, rather than reaching a conclusion based on ratios alone (in other words, try to identify the underlying causes of changes or differences in ratios).

Solution to 2: The 2008 and 2007 inventory to total assets ratios for CAT using LIFO and adjusted to FIFO and for Volvo as reported, are as follows:

	CAT (LIFO)	CAT (FIFO)	Volvo
2008	12.95%	17.08%	14.78%
2007	12.83%	16.94%	13.57%

Inventory to total assets

CAT (LIFO) 2008 = 12.95 percent = 8,781 ÷ 67,782

CAT (LIFO) 2007 = 12.83 percent = 7,204 ÷ 56,132

CAT (FIFO) 2008 = 17.08 percent = 11,964 ÷ (67,782 + 3,183 − 898)

CAT (FIFO) 2007 = 16.94 percent = 9,821 ÷ (56,132 + 2,617 − 785)

Volvo 2008 = 14.78 percent = 55,045 ÷ 372,419

Volvo 2007 =13.57 percent = 43,645 ÷ 321,647

Based on the numbers as reported, CAT appears to have a lower percentage of assets tied up in inventory than Volvo. However, when CAT's inventory is adjusted to FIFO, it has a higher percentage of its assets tied up in inventory than Volvo.

The increase in Volvo's inventory as a percentage of total assets is cause for some concern. Higher inventory typically results in higher maintenance costs (for example, storage and financing costs). In addition, Volvo may be building up slow moving or obsolete inventories that may result in future inventory write-downs for 2009. In Volvo's Note 18, the breakdown by inventory classification shows a small increase in the inventory of production materials. It appears that Volvo is planning on reducing production until it reduces its finished goods inventory. Looking at CAT's Note 9, all classifications of inventory seem to be increasing, and because these are valued using the LIFO method, there is some cause for concern. The company must be increasing inventory quantities and adding LIFO layers.

Solution to 3: CAT's and Volvo's 2008 and 2007 growth rates for sales (for CAT use Sales of machinery and engines and for Volvo use Net sales), finished goods, and inventories other than finished goods are as follows:

2008	**CAT (%)**	**Volvo (%)**
Sales	14.5	6.4
Finished goods	31.2	39.4
Inventories other than finished goods	15.0	2.2
2007		
Sales	8.0	10.3
Finished goods	10.1	37.7
Inventories other than finished goods	16.0	12.7

Growth rate = (Value for year − Value for previous year)/
Value for previous year

2008 CAT
Sales = 14.5 percent = (48,044 − 41,962) ÷ 41,962
Finished goods = 31.2 percent = (4,022 − 3,066) ÷ 3,066
Inventories other than finished goods = 15.0 percent = [(3,356 + 1,107 + 296) − (2,990 + 863 + 285)] ÷ (2,990 + 863 + 285)

2008 Volvo
Sales = 6.4 percent = (303,667 − 285,405) ÷ 285,405
Finished products = 39.4 percent = (39,137 − 28,077) ÷ 28,077
Inventories other than finished products = 2.2 percent = (15,908 − 15,568) ÷ 15,568

2007 CAT
Sales = 8.0 percent = (41,962 − 38,869) ÷ 38,869
Finished goods = 10.1 percent = (3,066 − 2,785) ÷ 2,785
Inventories other than finished goods = 16.0 percent = [(2,990 + 863 + 285) − (2,698 + 591 + 277)] ÷ (2,698 + 591 + 277)

2007 Volvo
Sales = 10.3 percent = (285,405 − 258,835) ÷ 258,835
Finished products = 37.7 percent = (28,077 − 20,396) ÷ 20,396
Inventories other than finished products = 12.7 percent = (15,568 − 13,815) ÷ 13,815

For both companies, the growth rates in finished goods inventory exceeds the growth rate in sales; this could be indicative of accumulating excess inventory. Volvo's growth rate in finished goods compared to its growth rate in sales is significantly higher, but the lower growth rates in finished goods inventory for CAT is potentially a result of using the LIFO method versus the FIFO method. It appears Volvo is aware that an issue exists and is planning on cutting back production given the relatively small increase in inventories other than finished products. Regardless, an analyst should do further investigation before reaching any conclusion about a company's future prospects for sales and profit.

EXAMPLE 7

Management Discussion and Analysis

The following excerpts commenting on inventory management are from the Volvo Group Annual Report, 2008:

> **From the CEO Comment**: In a declining economy, it is extremely important to act quickly to reduce the Group's cost level and ensure we do not build inventories, since large inventories generally lead to pressure on prices. . . . During the second half of the year, we implemented sharp production cutbacks to lower inventories of new trucks and construction equipment as part of efforts to maintain our product prices, which represent one of the most important factors in securing favorable profitability in the future. We have been successful in these efforts. During the fourth quarter, inventories of new trucks declined 13% and of new construction equipment by 19%. During the beginning of 2009, we have continued to work diligently and focused to reduce inventories to the new, lower levels of demand that prevail in most of our markets, and for most of our products.
>
> **From the Board of Directors' Report 2008**: Inventory reduction contributed to positive operating cash flow of SEK 1.8 billion in Industrial Operations. . . . The value of inventories increased during 2008 by SEK 11.4 billion. Adjusted for currency changes, the increase amounted to SEK 5.8 billion. The increase is mainly related to the truck operations and to construction equipment and is an effect of the rapidly weakening demand during the second half of the year. . . . In order to reduce the capital tied-up in inventory, a number of shutdown days in production were carried out during the end of year. Measures aimed at selling primarily trucks and construction equipment in inventory were prioritized. These measures have continued during the beginning of 2009. . . . Overcapacity within the industry can occur if there is a lack of demand, potentially leading to increased price pressure.
>
> **From Business Areas 2008 (Ambitions 2009)**: Execute on cost reduction and adjust production to ensure inventory levels in line with demand.

Assume inventory write-downs are reported as part of cost of sales. Based on the excerpts above, discuss the anticipated direction of the following for 2009 compared to 2008:

1. Inventory carrying amounts
2. Inventory turnover ratio
3. Sales
4. Gross profit margin
5. Return on assets
6. Current ratio

Solution to 1: Inventory carrying amounts are expected to decrease as the company cuts back on inventory levels and pressures are exerted on costs and prices.

Solution to 2: Inventory turnover ratio is expected to increase. Any potential change in cost of sales will be more than offset by the decline in inventory carrying amounts. For example, if cost of sales and inventory carrying amounts were 238 billion and 55 billion Swedish krona, before inventory write-downs totaling 1 billion Swedish krona, the inventory turnover ratio will change from 4.33 (238 ÷ 55) to 4.39 (237 ÷ 54).

Solution to 3: Unit sales and sales revenues are expected to decline due to decrease in demand and pressure on prices.

Solution to 4: Gross profit margin is difficult to predict. Sales revenues are expected to decline, but cost of sales as a percentage of sales revenue may decline if cost controls are effective, stay the same if cost controls are offset by increased inventory write-downs, or increase if inventory write-downs more than offset cost controls. In this case, an analyst might use 2008's gross profit margin of 21.8 percent as a reasonable prediction. It is less than the 2006 and 2007 gross profit margin of 23.1 percent and may already reflect cost controls, price pressures, and inventory write-downs.

Solution to 5: Return on assets is expected to decline. The positive effects of cost controls and reduction in assets is likely to be offset by decreased net income due to the declining sales revenues.

Solution to 6: The direction of change in the current ratio is difficult to predict. Current assets are expected to be reduced, but current liabilities are also expected to be reduced as costs are controlled and purchases are reduced resulting in lower accounts payable.

Analysts should seek out as much information as feasible when analyzing the performance of companies.

SUMMARY

Inventories and cost of sales (cost of goods sold) are significant items in the financial statements of many companies. Comparing the performance of these companies is challenging due to the allowable choices for valuing inventories; differences in the choice of inventory valuation method can result in significantly different amounts being assigned to inventory and the cost of sales. To evaluate a company's performance over time and relative to industry peers, analysts must clearly understand the various inventory valuation methods that companies use and the related impact on financial statements and financial ratios.

Key concepts in this reading are as follows:

- The allowable inventory valuation methods implicitly involve different assumptions about cost flows. The choice of inventory valuation method determines how the cost of goods available for sale during the period is allocated between inventory and cost of sales.
- Under IFRS, the cost of inventories is typically assigned by using either the first-in, first-out (FIFO) or weighted average cost formula. The specific identification method is required for inventories of items that are not ordinarily interchangeable and for goods or services produced and segregated for specific projects.
- Under U.S. GAAP, in addition to specific identification, FIFO and weighted average cost, last-in first-out (LIFO) is an accepted inventory valuation method. The LIFO method is widely used in the United States for both tax and financial reporting purposes because of potential income tax savings.
- The choice of inventory method affects the financial statements and any financial ratios that are based on them. As a consequence, the analyst must carefully consider inventory valuation method differences when evaluating a company's performance over time or in comparison to industry data or industry competitors.
- Under U.S. GAAP, companies that use the LIFO method must disclose in their financial notes the amount of the LIFO reserve or the amount that would have been reported in inventory if the FIFO method had been used. This information can be used to adjust reported LIFO inventory and cost of goods sold balances to the FIFO method for comparison purposes.
- LIFO liquidation occurs when the number of units in ending inventory declines from the number of units that were present at the beginning of the year. If inventory unit costs have generally risen from year to year, this will produce an inventory-related increase in gross profits.
- Consistency of inventory costing is required under both IFRS and U.S. GAAP. If a company changes an accounting policy, the change must be justifiable and applied retrospectively to the financial statements. An exception to the retrospective restatement is when a company reporting under U.S. GAAP changes to the LIFO method.
- Inventories are measured at the lower of cost and net realisable value under IFRS and the lower of cost and market under U.S. GAAP. Any write-down of inventory to net realisable value or market reduces the carrying amount of inventory on the balance sheet and profit on the income statement.
- Reversals of inventory write-downs may occur under IFRS but are not allowed under U.S. GAAP.

- Changes in the carrying amounts within inventory classifications (such as raw materials, work-in-process, and finished goods) may provide signals about a company's future sales and profits. Relevant information with respect to inventory management and future sales may be found in the Management Discussion and Analysis or similar items within the annual or quarterly reports, industry news and publications, and industry economic data.
- Inventory management may have a substantial impact on a company's activity, profitability, liquidity, and solvency ratios. It is critical for the analyst to be aware of industry trends and management's intentions.

PRACTICE PROBLEMS FOR READING 21

The following information relates to Questions 1–6[1]

John Martinson, CFA, is an equity analyst with a large pension fund. His supervisor, Linda Packard, asks him to write a report on Karp Inc. Karp prepares its financial statements in accordance with U.S. GAAP. Packard is particularly interested in the effects of the company's use of the LIFO method to account for its inventory. For this purpose, Martinson collects the financial data presented in Exhibits 1 and 2.

EXHIBIT 1 Balance Sheet Information (US$ Millions)

As of 31 December	2009	2008
Cash and cash equivalents	172	157
Accounts receivable	626	458
Inventories	620	539
Other current assets	125	65
Total current assets	1,543	1,219
Property and equipment, net	3,035	2,972
Total assets	4,578	4,191
Total current liabilities	1,495	1,395
Long-term debt	644	604
Total liabilities	2,139	1,999
Common stock and paid in capital	1,652	1,652
Retained earnings	787	540
Total shareholders' equity	2,439	2,192
Total liabilities and shareholders' equity	4,578	4,191

EXHIBIT 2 Income Statement Information (US$ Millions)

For the Year Ended 31 December	2009	2008
Sales	4,346	4,161
Cost of goods sold	2,211	2,147
Depreciation and amortisation expense	139	119
Selling, general, and administrative expense	1,656	1,637
Interest expense	31	18
Income tax expense	62	48
Net income	247	192

[1] Developed by Rodrigo Ribeiro, CFA (Montevideo, Uruguay).

Martinson finds the following information in the notes to the financial statements:

- The LIFO reserves as of 31 December 2009 and 2008 are $155 million and $117 million respectively, and
- The effective income tax rate applicable to Karp for 2009 and earlier periods is 20 percent.

1. If Karp had used FIFO instead of LIFO, the amount of inventory reported as of 31 December 2009 would have been *closest* to:

A. $465 million.

B. $658 million.

C. $775 million.

2. If Karp had used FIFO instead of LIFO, the amount of cost of goods sold reported by Karp for the year ended 31 December 2009 would have been *closest* to:

A. $2,056 million.

B. $2,173 million.

C. $2,249 million.

3. If Karp had used FIFO instead of LIFO, its reported net income for the year ended 31 December 2009 would have been higher by an amount *closest* to:

A. $30 million.

B. $38 million.

C. $155 million.

4. If Karp had used FIFO instead of LIFO, Karp's retained earnings as of 31 December 2009 would have been higher by an amount *closest* to:

A. $117 million.

B. $124 million.

C. $155 million.

5. If Karp had used FIFO instead of LIFO, which of the following ratios computed as of 31 December 2009 would *most likely* have been lower?

A. Cash ratio.

B. Current ratio.

C. Gross profit margin.

6. If Karp had used FIFO instead of LIFO, its debt to equity ratio computed as of 31 December 2009 would have:

A. increased.

B. decreased.

C. remained unchanged.

The following information relates to Questions 7–12[2]

Robert Groff, an equity analyst, is preparing a report on Crux Corp. As part of his report, Groff makes a comparative financial analysis between Crux and its two main competitors, Rolby Corp. and Mikko Inc. Crux and Mikko report under U.S. GAAP and Rolby reports under IFRS.

Groff gathers information on Crux, Rolby, and Mikko. The relevant financial information he compiles is in Exhibit 1. Some information on the industry is in Exhibit 2.

EXHIBIT 1 Selected Financial Information (US$ Millions)

	Crux	Rolby	Mikko
Inventory valuation method	LIFO	FIFO	LIFO
From the Balance Sheets			
As of 31 December 2009			
Inventory, gross	480	620	510
Valuation allowance	20	25	14
Inventory, net	460	595	496
Total debt	1,122	850	732
Total shareholders' equity	2,543	2,403	2,091
As of 31 December 2008			
Inventory, gross	465	602	401
Valuation allowance	23	15	12
Inventory, net	442	587	389
From the Income Statements			
Year Ended 31 December 2009			
Revenues	4,609	5,442	3,503
Cost of goods sold[a]	3,120	3,782	2,550
Net income	229	327	205
[a] Charges included in cost of goods sold for inventory write-downs*	13	15	15

* This does not match the change in the inventory valuation allowance because the valuation allowance is reduced to reflect the valuation allowance attached to items sold and increased for additional necessary write-downs.

	Crux	Rolby	Mikko
LIFO Reserve			
As of 31 December 2009	55	0	77
As of 31 December 2008	72	0	50
As of 31 December 2007	96	0	43
Tax Rate			
Effective tax rate	30%	30%	30%

[2] Developed by Rodrigo Ribeiro, CFA (Montevideo, Uruguay).

EXHIBIT 2 **Industry Information**

	2009	2008	2007
Raw materials price index	112	105	100
Finished goods price index	114	106	100

To compare the financial performance of the three companies, Groff decides to convert LIFO figures into FIFO figures, and adjust figures to assume no valuation allowance is recognized by any company.

After reading Groff's draft report, his supervisor, Rachel Borghi, asks him the following questions:

Question 1: Which company's gross profit margin would best reflect current costs of the industry?

Question 2: Would Rolby's valuation method show a higher gross profit margin than Crux's under an inflationary, a deflationary, or a stable price scenario?

Question 3: Which group of ratios usually appears more favorable with an inventory write-down?

7. Crux's inventory turnover ratio computed as of 31 December 2009, after the adjustments suggested by Groff, is *closest* to:

A. 5.67.

B. 5.83.

C. 6.13.

8. Rolby's net profit margin for the year ended 31 December 2009, after the adjustments suggested by Groff, is *closest* to:

A. 6.01%.

B. 6.20%.

C. 6.28%.

9. Compared with its unadjusted debt-to-equity ratio, Mikko's debt-to-equity ratio as of 31 December 2009, after the adjustments suggested by Groff, is:

A. lower.

B. higher.

C. the same.

10. The *best* answer to Borghi's Question 1 is:

A. Crux's.

B. Rolby's.

C. Mikko's.

11. The *best* answer to Borghi's Question 2 is:

A. Stable.

B. Inflationary.

C. Deflationary.

12. The *best* answer to Borghi's Question 3 is:

A. Activity ratios.

B. Solvency ratios.

C. Profitability ratios.

The following information relates to Questions 13–20[3]

ZP Corporation is a (hypothetical) multinational corporation headquartered in Japan that trades on numerous stock exchanges. ZP prepares its consolidated financial statements in accordance with U.S. GAAP. Excerpts from ZP's 2009 annual report are shown in Exhibits 1–3.

EXHIBIT 1 Consolidated Balance Sheets (¥ Millions)

31 December	2008	2009
Current assets		
Cash and cash equivalents	¥ 542,849	¥ 814,760
⋮	⋮	⋮
Inventories	608,572	486,465
⋮	⋮	⋮
Total current assets	4,028,742	3,766,309
⋮	⋮	⋮
Total assets	**¥ 10,819,440**	**¥ 9,687,346**
⋮	⋮	⋮
Total current liabilities	¥ 3,980,247	¥ 3,529,765
⋮	⋮	⋮
Total long-term liabilities	2,663,795	2,624,002
Minority interest in consolidated subsidiaries	218,889	179,843
Total shareholders' equity	3,956,509	3,353,736
Total liabilities and shareholders' equity	**¥ 10,819,440**	**¥ 9,687,346**

EXHIBIT 2 Consolidated Statements of Income (¥ Millions)

For the Years Ended 31 December	2007	2008	2009
Net revenues			
Sales of products	¥ 7,556,699	¥ 8,273,503	¥ 6,391,240
Financing operations	425,998	489,577	451,950
	7,982,697	8,763,080	6,843,190

(*Exhibit continued on next page . . .*)

[3] Developed by Karen O'Connor Rubsam, CFA (Fountain Hills AZ, U.S.A.).

EXHIBIT 2 (continued)

For the Years Ended 31 December	2007	2008	2009
Cost and expenses			
Cost of products sold	6,118,742	6,817,446	5,822,805
Cost of financing operations	290,713	356,005	329,128
Selling, general and administrative	827,005	832,837	844,927
⋮	⋮	⋮	⋮
Operating income (loss)	746,237	756,792	−153,670
⋮	⋮	⋮	⋮
Net income	¥ 548,011	¥ 572,626	¥ −145,646

EXHIBIT 3 Selected Disclosures in the 2009 Annual Report

Management's Discussion and Analysis of Financial Condition and Results of Operations

Cost reduction efforts were offset by increased prices of raw materials, other production materials and parts. . . . Inventories decreased during fiscal 2009 by ¥122.1 billion, or 20.1%, to ¥486.5 billion. This reflects the impacts of decreased sales volumes and fluctuations in foreign currency translation rates.

Management & Corporate Information

Risk Factors

Industry and Business Risks

The worldwide market for our products is highly competitive. ZP faces intense competition from other manufacturers in the respective markets in which it operates. Competition has intensified due to the worldwide deterioration in economic conditions. In addition, competition is likely to further intensify because of continuing globalization, possibly resulting in industry reorganization. Factors affecting competition include product quality and features, the amount of time required for innovation and development, pricing, reliability, safety, economy in use, customer service and financing terms. Increased competition may lead to lower unit sales and excess production capacity and excess inventory. This may result in a further downward price pressure.

ZP's ability to adequately respond to the recent rapid changes in the industry and to maintain its competitiveness will be fundamental to its future success in maintaining and expanding its market share in existing and new markets.

Notes to Consolidated Financial Statements

2. Summary of significant accounting policies:

Inventories. Inventories are valued at cost, not in excess of market. Cost is determined on the "average-cost" basis, except for the cost of finished products carried by certain subsidiary companies which is determined "last-in, first-out" ("LIFO") basis. Inventories valued on the LIFO basis totaled

(Exhibit continued on next page . . .)

EXHIBIT 3 (continued)

¥94,578 million and ¥50,037 million at December 31, 2008 and 2009, respectively. Had the "first-in, first-out" basis been used for those companies using the LIFO basis, inventories would have been ¥10,120 million and ¥19,660 million higher than reported at December 31, 2008 and 2009, respectively.

9. Inventories:
Inventories consist of the following:

31 December (¥ Millions)	2008	2009
Finished goods	¥ 403,856	¥ 291,977
Raw materials	99,869	85,966
Work in process	79,979	83,890
Supplies and other	24,868	24,632
	¥ 608,572	**¥ 486,465**

13. The MD&A indicated that the prices of raw material, other production materials, and parts increased. Based on the inventory valuation methods described in Note 2, which inventory classification would *least accurately* reflect current prices?

A. Raw materials.

B. Finished goods.

C. Work in process.

14. The 2008 inventory value as reported on the 2009 consolidated balance sheet if the company had used the FIFO inventory valuation method instead of the LIFO inventory valuation method for a portion of its inventory would be *closest* to:

A. ¥104,698 million.

B. ¥506,125 million.

C. ¥618,692 million.

15. What is the *least likely* reason why ZP may need to change its accounting policies regarding inventory at some point after 2009?

A. The U.S. SEC is likely to require companies to use the same inventory valuation method for all inventories.

B. The U.S. SEC is likely to prohibit the use of one of the methods ZP currently uses for inventory valuation.

C. One of the inventory valuation methods used for U.S. tax purposes may be repealed as an acceptable method.

16. If ZP had prepared its financial statement in accordance with IFRS, the inventory turnover ratio (using average inventory) for 2009 would be:

A. lower.

B. higher.

C. the same.

17. Inventory levels decreased from 2008 to 2009 for all of the following reasons *except*:

A. LIFO liquidation.

B. decreased sales volume.

C. fluctuations in foreign currency translation rates.

18. Which observation is *most likely* a result of looking only at the information reported in Note 9?

A. Increased competition has led to lower unit sales.

B. There have been significant price increases in supplies.

C. Management expects a further downturn in sales during 2010.

19. Note 2 indicates that, "Inventories valued on the LIFO basis totaled ¥94,578 million and ¥50,037 million at December 31, 2008 and 2009, respectively." Based on this, the LIFO reserve should *most likely*:

A. increase.

B. decrease.

C. remain the same.

20. The Industry and Business Risk excerpt states that, "Increased competition may lead to lower unit sales and excess production capacity and excess inventory. This may result in a further downward price pressure." The downward price pressure could lead to inventory that is valued above current market prices or net realisable value. Any write-downs of inventory are *least likely* to have a significant effect on the inventory valued using:

A. weighted average cost.

B. first-in, first-out (FIFO).

C. last-in, first-out (LIFO).

SOLUTIONS FOR READING 21

1. C is correct. Karp's inventory under FIFO equals Karp's inventory under LIFO plus the LIFO reserve. Therefore, as of 31 December 2009, Karp's inventory under FIFO equals:

   $$\begin{aligned}\text{Inventory (FIFO method)} &= \text{Inventory (LIFO method)} + \text{LIFO reserve}\\ &= \$620 \text{ million} + 155 \text{ million}\\ &= \$775 \text{ million}\end{aligned}$$

2. B is correct. Karp's cost of goods sold (COGS) under FIFO equals Karp's cost of goods sold under LIFO minus the increase in the LIFO reserve. Therefore, for the year ended 31 December 2009, Karp's cost of goods sold under FIFO equals:

   $$\begin{aligned}\text{COGS (FIFO method)} &= \text{COGS (LIFO method)} - \text{Increase in LIFO reserve}\\ &= \$2{,}211 \text{ million} - (155 \text{ million} - 117 \text{ million})\\ &= \$2{,}173 \text{ million}\end{aligned}$$

3. A is correct. Karp's net income (NI) under FIFO equals Karp's net income under LIFO plus the after-tax increase in the LIFO reserve. For the year ended 31 December 2009, Karp's net income under FIFO equals:

   $$\begin{aligned}\text{NI (FIFO method)} &= \text{NI (LIFO method)} + \text{Increase in LIFO reserve} \times (1 - \text{tax rate})\\ &= \$247 \text{ million} + 38 \text{ million} \times (1 - 20\%)\\ &= \$277.4 \text{ million}\end{aligned}$$

   Therefore, the increase in net income is:

   $$\begin{aligned}\text{Increase in NI} &= \text{NI (FIFO method)} - \text{NI (LIFO method)}\\ &= \$277 \text{ million} - 247 \text{ million}\\ &= \$30.4 \text{ million}\end{aligned}$$

4. B is correct. Karp's retained earnings (RE) under FIFO equals Karp's retained earnings under LIFO plus the after-tax LIFO reserve. Therefore, for the year ended 31 December 2009, Karp's retained earnings under FIFO equals:

   $$\begin{aligned}\text{RE (FIFO method)} &= \text{RE (LIFO method)} + \text{LIFO reserve} \times (1 - \text{tax rate})\\ &= \$787 \text{ million} + 155 \text{ million} \times (1 - 20\%)\\ &= \$911 \text{ million}\end{aligned}$$

   Therefore, the increase in retained earnings is:

   $$\begin{aligned}\text{Increase in RE} &= \text{RE (FIFO method)} - \text{RE (LIFO method)}\\ &= \$911 \text{ million} - 787 \text{ million}\\ &= \$124 \text{ million}\end{aligned}$$

5. A is correct. The cash ratio (cash and cash equivalents ÷ current liabilities) would be lower because cash would have been less under FIFO. Karp's income before taxes would have been higher under FIFO, and consequently taxes paid by Karp would have also been higher and cash would have been lower. There is no impact on current liabilities. Both Karp's current ratio and gross profit margin would have been higher if

FIFO had been used. The current ratio would have been higher because inventory under FIFO increases by a larger amount than the cash decreases for taxes paid. Because the cost of goods sold under FIFO is lower than under LIFO, the gross profit margin would have been higher.

6. B is correct. If Karp had used FIFO instead of LIFO, the debt-to-equity ratio would have decreased. No change in debt would have occurred, but shareholders' equity would have increased as a result of higher retained earnings.

7. B is correct. Crux's adjusted inventory turnover ratio must be computed using cost of goods sold (COGS) under FIFO and excluding charges for increases in valuation allowances.

COGS (adjusted) = COGS (LIFO method) − Charges included in cost of goods sold for inventory write-downs − Change in LIFO reserve
= \$3,120 million − 13 million − (55 million − 72 million)
= \$3,124 million

Note: Minus the change in LIFO reserve is equivalent to plus the decrease in LIFO reserve. The adjusted inventory turnover ratio is computed using average inventory under FIFO.

Ending Inventory (FIFO) = Ending Inventory (LIFO) + LIFO reserve
Ending Inventory 2009 (FIFO) = \$480 + 55 = \$535
Ending Inventory 2008 (FIFO) = \$465 + 72 = \$537
Average inventory = (\$535 + 537)/2 = \$536

Therefore, adjusted inventory turnover ratio equals:

Inventory turnover ratio = COGS/Average inventory = \$3,124/\$536
= 5.83

8. B is correct. Rolby's adjusted net profit margin must be computed using net income (NI) under FIFO and excluding charges for increases in valuation allowances.

NI (adjusted) = NI (FIFO method) + Charges, included in cost of goods sold for inventory write-downs, after-tax
= \$327 million + 15 million × (1 − 30%)
= \$337.5 million

Therefore, adjusted net profit margin equals:

Net profit margin = NI/Revenues = \$337.5/\$5,442 = 6.20%

9. A is correct. Mikko's adjusted debt-to-equity ratio is lower because the debt (numerator) is unchanged and the adjusted shareholders' equity (denominator) is higher. The adjusted shareholders' equity corresponds to shareholders' equity under FIFO, excluding charges for increases in valuation allowances. Therefore, adjusted shareholders' equity is higher than reported (unadjusted) shareholders' equity.

10. C is correct. Mikko's and Crux's gross margin ratios would better reflect the current gross margin of the industry than Rolby because both use LIFO. LIFO recognizes as cost of goods sold the cost of the most recently purchased units; therefore, it better reflects replacement cost. However, Mikko's gross margin ratio best reflects the current gross margin of the industry because Crux's LIFO reserve is decreasing. This could reflect a LIFO liquidation by Crux, which would distort gross profit margin.

11. B is correct. The FIFO method shows a higher gross profit margin than the LIFO method in an inflationary scenario, because FIFO allocates to cost of goods sold the cost of the oldest units available for sale. In an inflationary environment, these units are the ones with the lowest cost.

12. A is correct. An inventory write-down increases cost of sales and reduces profit and reduces the carrying value of inventory and assets. This has a negative effect on profitability and solvency ratios. However, activity ratios appear positively affected by a write-down because the asset base, whether total assets or inventory (denominator), is reduced. The numerator, sales, in total asset turnover is unchanged, and the numerator, cost of sales, in inventory turnover is increased. Thus, turnover ratios are higher and appear more favorable as the result of the write-down.

13. B is correct. Finished goods least accurately reflect current prices because some of the finished goods are valued under the "last-in, first-out" ("LIFO") basis. The costs of the newest units available for sale are allocated to cost of goods sold, leaving the oldest units (at lower costs) in inventory. ZP values raw materials and work in process using the weighted average cost method. While not fully reflecting current prices, some inflationary effect will be included in the inventory values.

14. C is correct. FIFO inventory = Reported inventory + LIFO reserve = ¥608,572 + 10,120 = ¥618,692. The LIFO reserve is disclosed in Note 2 of the notes to consolidated financial statements.

15. A is correct. The SEC does not require companies to use the same inventory valuation method for all inventories, so this is the *least likely* reason to change accounting policies regarding inventory. The SEC is currently evaluating whether all U.S. companies should be required to adopt IFRS. If the SEC requires companies to adopt IFRS, the LIFO method of inventory valuation would no longer be allowed.

16. A is correct. The inventory turnover ratio would be lower. The average inventory would be higher under FIFO, and cost of products sold would be lower by the increase in LIFO reserve. LIFO is not permitted under IFRS.

Inventory turnover ratio = Cost of products sold ÷ Average inventory

2009 inventory turnover ratio as reported
= 10.63 = ¥5,822,805/[(608,572 + 486,465)/2].

2009 inventory turnover ratio adjusted to FIFO as necessary
= 10.34 = [¥5,822,805 − (19,660 – 10,120)]/[(608,572 + 10,120 + 486,465 + 19,660)/2].

17. A is correct. No LIFO liquidation occurred during 2009; the LIFO reserve increased from ¥10,120 million in 2008 to ¥19,660 million in 2009. Management stated in the MD&A that the decrease in inventories reflected the impacts of decreased sales volumes and fluctuations in foreign currency translation rates.

18. C is correct. Finished goods and raw materials inventories are lower in 2009 when compared to 2008. Reduced levels of inventory typically indicate an anticipated business contraction.

19. B is correct. The decrease in LIFO inventory in 2009 would typically indicate that more inventory units were sold than produced or purchased. Accordingly, one would expect a liquidation of some of the older LIFO layers and the LIFO reserve to decrease. In actuality, the LIFO reserve *increased* from ¥10,120 million in 2008 to ¥19,660 million in 2009. This is not to be expected and is likely caused by the increase in prices of raw materials, other production materials, and parts of foreign currencies as noted in the MD&A. An analyst should seek to confirm this explanation.

20. C is correct. Inventories valued using LIFO are less likely to incur inventory write-downs than inventories valued using weighted average cost or FIFO. Under LIFO, the *oldest* costs are reflected in the inventory carrying value on the balance sheet. Given increasing inventory costs, the inventory carrying values under the LIFO method are already conservatively presented at the oldest and lowest costs. Thus, it is far less likely that inventory write-downs will occur under LIFO; and if a write-down does occur, it is likely to be of a lesser magnitude.

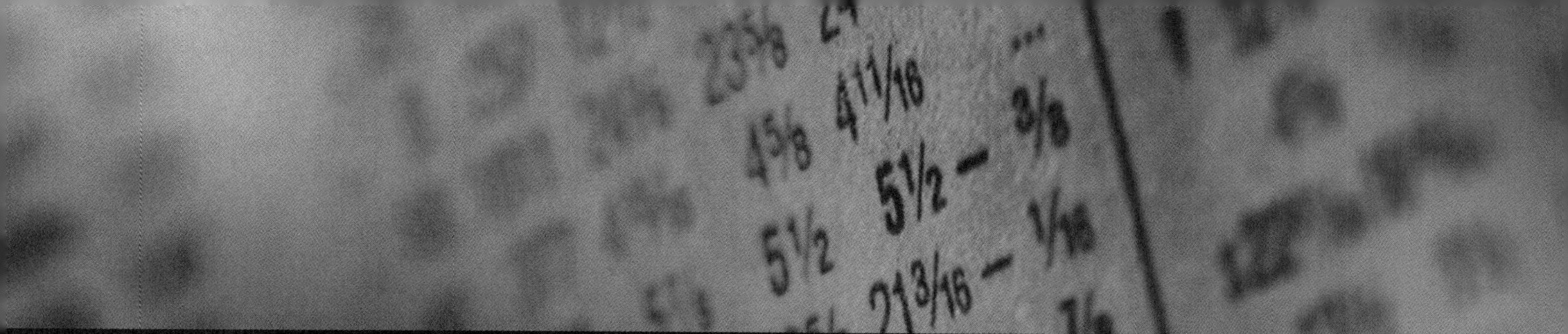

LONG-LIVED ASSETS: IMPLICATIONS FOR FINANCIAL STATEMENTS AND RATIOS

by Elaine Henry, CFA and Elizabeth A. Gordon

READING

22

LEARNING OUTCOMES

The candidate should be able to:	Mastery
a. discuss the implications for financial statements and ratios of capitalising versus expensing costs in the period in which they are incurred;	☐
b. discuss the implications for financial statements and ratios of the different depreciation methods for property, plant, and equipment;	☐
c. discuss the implications for financial statements and ratios of impairment and revaluation of property, plant, and equipment, and intangible assets;	☐
d. analyze and interpret the financial statement disclosures regarding long-lived assets;	☐
e. discuss the implications for financial statements and ratios of leasing assets instead of purchasing assets;	☐
f. discuss the implications for financial statements and ratios of finance leases and operating leases from the perspective of both the lessor and the lessee.	☐

INTRODUCTION 1

Long-lived assets include tangible assets such as property, plant, and equipment; identifiable intangible assets such as patents and trademarks; and goodwill. In this reading, we focus on the implications for financial statements and ratios of accounting choices involved in the financial reporting of tangible and identifiable intangible long-lived assets. Further, this reading considers both assets that a company owns and assets that a company leases.

Although companies must follow accounting standards, companies make numerous choices and decisions within what is allowed by those standards. In

Note:
New rulings and/or pronouncements issued after the publication of the readings in financial reporting and analysis may cause some of the information in these readings to become dated. Candidates are expected to be familiar with the overall analytical framework contained in the study session readings, as well as the implications of alternative accounting methods for financial analysis and valuation, as provided in the assigned readings. Candidates are not responsible for changes that occur after the material was written.

general, accounting choices related to long-lived assets affect the timing of expense recognition, which in turn affects the company's profitability for the current period and trends in profitability. Choices resulting in lower profits for the current period, such as expensing rather than capitalising expenditures, generally result in higher profits in a subsequent period and thus a more favorable trend. The choices may impact cash flows through taxes.

This reading is organised as follows: Section 2 describes and illustrates the implications for financial statements and ratios of capitalising versus expensing expenditures related to long-lived assets. Section 3 describes and illustrates the implications for financial statements and ratios of using different depreciation methods, depreciation periods, and residual value assumptions in allocating the cost of long-lived assets over time. Section 4 describes and illustrates the implications for financial statements and ratios of periodically estimating the recoverable value of long-lived assets, which can give rise to impairments and/or revaluations.

Section 5 describes the analysis and interpretation of financial statement disclosures about long-lived assets. In Section 6, we turn to leased assets and examine the issues involved in lease accounting, along with the financial statement effects of different kinds of leases. A summary and practice problems in the CFA Institute item set format complete the reading.

2 CAPITALISING VERSUS EXPENSING

This section discusses the implications for financial statements and ratios of capitalising versus expensing costs in the period in which they are incurred. In general, when a company acquires a long-lived tangible or intangible asset, the company records the asset in an amount equal to the acquisition cost plus the cost, if any, to get the asset ready for its intended use. When a company acquires a long-lived asset in a business combination, the accounting treatment differs.

To be recognised as a long-lived asset, tangible or intangible, future economic benefits must flow to the entity from the use of the asset. International Financial Reporting Standards (IFRS) specify that "The cost of an item of property, plant and equipment shall be recognised as an asset if, and only if: a) it is probable that future economic benefits associated with the item will flow to the entity; and b) the cost of the item can be measured reliably."[1] U.S. generally accepted accounting principles (U.S. GAAP), as contained in the Financial Accounting Standards Board (FASB) Accounting Standards Codification™ (ASC),[2] are similar.[3] Examples of property, plant, and equipment (PPE) include land, buildings, machinery, furniture, fixtures, and vehicles. Major spare parts that are expected to be used during more than one period or spare parts that

[1] IAS 16 [Property, Plant and Equipment], paragraph 7.

[2] The Codification is the single source of authoritative nongovernmental U.S. GAAP and supersedes previous U.S. GAAP standards. The Codification is effective for periods ending after 15 September 2009.

[3] FASB ASC Topic 360 [Property, Plant, and Equipment].

can be used only in connection with an item of PPE are treated as part of the PPE asset. (Minor spare parts and spare parts that are not specific to an item of PPE are usually expensed as consumed.) Examples of expenditures to get an asset ready for its intended use include purchase price, delivery, and installation.

Intangible assets lack physical substance. IFRS require that intangible assets be identifiable, under the control of the entity, and generators of future economic benefits.[4] Requirements under U.S. GAAP are similar.[5] Examples of identifiable intangible long-lived assets include patents, licenses, trademarks, brands, copyrights, and mailing lists. When assets are acquired as part of a business combination, a company records for each identifiable tangible and intangible asset acquired and each liability assumed an amount equal to the estimated fair value of the asset or the liability. If the purchase price exceeds the sum of the amounts allocated to identifiable assets and liabilities, the excess is recorded as goodwill.

Before turning to specific instances, we will consider the general financial statement impact of capitalising versus expensing and two analytical issues related to the decision—namely the effect on an individual company's trend analysis and on comparability across companies.

In the period of the expenditure, an expenditure that is capitalised increases the amount of assets on the balance sheet and appears as an investing cash outflow on the statement of cash flows. In subsequent periods, a company allocates the capitalised amount over the asset's useful life as depreciation or amortisation expense (except assets that are not depreciated, i.e., land, or amortised, e.g., intangible assets with indefinite lives). This expense reduces net income on the income statement and reduces the value of the asset on the balance sheet. Depreciation and amortisation are non-cash expenses and therefore, apart from their effect on taxable income and taxes payable, have no impact on the cash flow statement. In the section of the statement of cash flows that reconciles net income to operating cash flow, depreciation and amortisation expenses are added back to net income.

Alternatively, an expenditure that is expensed reduces net income by the after-tax amount of the expenditure in the period it is made. No asset is recorded on the balance sheet and thus no depreciation or amortisation occurs in subsequent periods. The lower amount of net income is reflected in lower retained earnings on the balance sheet. An expenditure that is expensed appears as an operating cash outflow in the period it is made. There is no effect on the financial statements of subsequent periods.

Example 1 illustrates the impact on the financial statements of capitalising versus expensing an expenditure.

EXAMPLE 1

Financial Statement Impact of Capitalising versus Expensing

Assume two identical (hypothetical) companies, CAP Inc. (CAP) and NOW Inc. (NOW), start with €1,000 cash and €1,000 common stock. Each year the companies recognise total revenues of €1,500 cash and make cash expenditures, excluding an equipment purchase, of €500. At the beginning of operations, each company pays €900 to purchase

[4] IAS 38 [Intangible Assets].

[5] FASB ASC Topic 350 [Intangibles—Goodwill and Other].

equipment. CAP estimates the equipment will have a useful life of three years and an estimated salvage value of €0 at the end of the three years. NOW estimates a much shorter useful life and expenses the equipment immediately. The companies have no other assets and make no other asset purchases during the three-year period. Assume the companies pay no dividends, earn zero interest on cash balances, have a tax rate of 30 percent, and use the same accounting method for financial and tax purposes.

The left side of Exhibit 1 shows CAP's financial statements, i.e., with the expenditure capitalised and depreciated at €300 per year based on the straight-line method of depreciation (€900 cost minus €0 salvage value equals €900, divided by a three-year life equals €300 per year). The right side of the exhibit shows NOW's financial statements, with the entire €900 expenditure treated as an expense in the first year. All amounts are in euro.

EXHIBIT 1 Capitalising versus Expensing

CAP Inc.
Capitalise €900 as Asset and Depreciate

For Year	1	2	3
Revenue	1,500	1,500	1,500
Cash expenses	500	500	500
Depreciation	300	300	300
Income before tax	700	700	700
Tax at 30%	210	210	210
Net income	490	490	490
Cash from operations	790	790	790
Cash used in investing	(900)	0	0
Total change in cash	(110)	790	790

As of	Time 0	End of Year 1	End of Year 2	End of Year 3
Cash	1,000	890	1,680	2,470
PP & E (net)	—	600	300	—
Total assets	1,000	1,490	1,980	2,470
Retained earnings	0	490	980	1,470
Common stock	1,000	1,000	1,000	1,000
Total shareholders' equity	1,000	1,490	1,980	2,470

NOW Inc.
Expense €900 Immediately

For Year	1	2	3
Revenue	1,500	1,500	1,500
Cash expenses	1,400	500	500
Depreciation	0	0	0
Income before tax	100	1,000	1,000
Tax at 30%	30	300	300
Net income	70	700	700
Cash from operations	70	700	700
Cash used in investing	0	0	0
Total change in cash	70	700	700

Time	Time 0	End of Year 1	End of Year 2	End of Year 3
Cash	1,000	1,070	1,770	2,470
PP & E (net)	—	—	—	—
Total assets	1,000	1,070	1,770	2,470
Retained earnings	0	70	770	1,470
Common stock	1,000	1,000	1,000	1,000
Total shareholders' equity	1,000	1,070	1,770	2,470

1. Which company reports higher net income over the three years? Total cash flow? Cash from operations?
2. Based on ROE and net profit margin, how does the profitability of the two companies compare?
3. Why does NOW report change in cash of €70 in Year 1, while CAP reports total change in cash of (€110)?

Solution to 1: Neither company reports higher total net income or cash flow over the three years. The sum of net income over the three years is identical (€1,470 total) whether the €900 is capitalised or expensed. Also, the sum of the change in cash (€1,470 total) is identical under either scenario. CAP reports higher cash from operations by an amount of €900 because, under the capitalisation scenario, the €900 purchase is treated as an investing cash flow.

Note: Because the companies use the same accounting method for both financial and taxable income, absent the assumption of zero interest on cash balances, expensing the €900 would have resulted in higher income and cash flow for NOW because the lower taxes paid in the first year (€30 versus €210) would have allowed NOW to earn interest income on the tax savings.

Solution to 2: In general, Ending shareholders' equity = Beginning shareholders' equity + Net income + Other comprehensive income − Dividends + Net capital contributions from shareholders. Because the companies in this example do not have other comprehensive income, did not pay dividends, and reported no capital contributions from shareholders, Ending retained earnings = Beginning retained earnings + Net income, and Ending shareholders' equity = Beginning shareholders' equity + Net income.

ROE is calculated as net income ÷ average shareholders' equity, and net profit margin is calculated as net income ÷ total revenue. For example, CAP had Year 1 ROE of 39 percent (€490/[(€1,000 + €1,490)/2]), and Year 1 net profit margin of 33 percent (€490 ÷ €1,500).

CAP Inc. Capitalise €900 as Asset and Depreciate				NOW Inc. Expense €900 Immediately			
For year	**1**	**2**	**3**	**For year**	**1**	**2**	**3**
ROE	39%	28%	22%	ROE	7%	49%	33%
Net profit margin	33	33	33	Net profit margin	5	47	47

As shown, capitalising results in higher profitability ratios (ROE and net profit margin) in the first year, and lower profitability ratios in subsequent years. For example, CAP's Year 1 ROE of 39 percent was higher than NOW's Year 1 ROE of 7 percent, but in Years 2 and 3, NOW reports superior profitability.

Note also that NOW's superior growth in net income between Year 1 and Year 2 is not attributable to superior performance compared to CAP but rather to the accounting decision to recognise the expense sooner than CAP. In general, all else equal, accounting decisions that result in recognising expenses sooner will give the appearance of greater subsequent growth. Comparison of the growth of the two companies' net incomes without an awareness of the difference in accounting methods would be misleading. As a corollary, NOW's income and profitability exhibit greater volatility across the three years, not because of more volatile performance but rather because of the different accounting decision.

Solution to 3: NOW reports an increase in cash of €70 in Year 1, whereas CAP reports a decrease in cash of €110 because NOW's taxes were €180 lower than CAP's taxes (€30 versus €210).

Note that this problem assumes the accounting method used by each company for its tax purposes is identical to the accounting method used by the company for its financial reporting. In many countries, companies are allowed to use different depreciation methods for financial reporting and taxes, which may give rise to deferred taxes.

As shown, discretion regarding whether to expense or capitalise expenditures can impede comparability across companies. Example 1 assumes the companies purchase a single asset in one year. Because the sum of net income over the three-year period is identical whether the asset is capitalised or expensed, it illustrates that although capitalising results in higher profitability compared to expensing in the first year, it results in lower profitability ratios in the subsequent years. Conversely, expensing results in lower profitability in the first year but higher profitability in later years, indicating a favorable trend.

Similarly, shareholders' equity for a company that capitalises the expenditure will be higher in the early years because the initially higher profits result in initially higher retained earnings. Example 1 assumes the companies purchase a single asset in one year and report identical amounts of total net income over the three-year period, so shareholders' equity (and retained earnings) for the firm that expenses will be identical to shareholders' equity (and retained earnings) for the capitalising firm at the end of the three-year period.

Although Example 1 shows companies purchasing an asset only in the first year, if a company continues to purchase similar or increasing amounts of assets each year, the profitability-enhancing effect of capitalising continues if the amount of the expenditures in a period continues to be more than the depreciation expense. Example 2 illustrates this point.

EXAMPLE 2

Impact of Capitalising versus Expensing for Ongoing Purchases

A company buys a £300 computer in Year 1 and capitalises the expenditure. The computer has a useful life of three years and an expected salvage value of £0, so the annual depreciation expense using the straight-line method is £100 per year. Compared to expensing the entire £300 immediately, the company's pre-tax profit in Year 1 is £200 greater.

1. Assume that the company continues to buy an identical computer each year at the same price. If the company uses the same accounting treatment for each of the computers, when does the profit-enhancing effect of capitalising versus expensing end?
2. If the company buys another identical computer in Year 4 using the same accounting treatment as the prior years, what is the effect on Year 4 profits of capitalising versus expensing these expenditures?

Solution to 1: The profit-enhancing effect of capitalising versus expensing would end in Year 3. In Year 3, the depreciation expense on each of the three computers bought in Years 1, 2, and 3 would total £300 (£100 + £100 + £100). Therefore, the total depreciation expense for Year 3 will be exactly equal to the capital expenditure in Year 3. The expense in Year 3 would be £300, regardless of whether the company capitalised or expensed the annual computer purchases.

Solution to 2: There is no impact on Year 4 profits. As in the previous year, the depreciation expense on each of the three computers bought in Years 2, 3, and 4 would total £300 (£100 + £100 + £100). Therefore, the total depreciation expense for Year 4 will be exactly equal to the capital expenditure in Year 4. Pre-tax profits would be reduced by £300, regardless of whether the company capitalised or expensed the annual computer purchases.

Compared to expensing an expenditure, capitalising the expenditure typically results in greater amounts reported as cash from operations. Capitalised expenditures are typically treated as an investment cash outflow whereas expenses reduce operating cash flows. Because cash flow from operating activities is an important consideration in some valuation models, companies may try to maximise reported cash flow from operations by capitalising expenditures that should be expensed. Valuation models that use free cash flow will consider not only operating cash flows but also investing cash flows. Analysts should be alert to evidence of companies manipulating reported cash flow from operations by capitalising expenditures that should be expensed.

In summary, holding all else constant, capitalising an expenditure enhances current profitability and increases reported cash flow from operations. The profitability-enhancing effect of capitalising continues so long as capital expenditures exceed the depreciation expense. Profitability-enhancing motivations for decisions to capitalise should be considered when analyzing performance. For example, a company may choose to capitalise more expenditures (within the allowable bounds of accounting standards) to achieve earnings targets for a given period. Expensing a cost in the period reduces current period profits but enhances future profitability and thus enhances the profit trend. Profit trend-enhancing motivations should also be considered when analyzing performance. If the company is in a reporting environment which requires identical accounting methods for financial reporting and taxes (unlike the United States, which permits companies to use depreciation methods for reporting purposes that differ from the depreciation method required by tax purposes), then expensing will have a more favorable cash flow impact because paying lower taxes in an earlier period creates an opportunity to earn interest income on the cash saved.

In contrast with the relatively simple examples above, it is generally neither possible nor desirable to identify individual instances involving discretion about whether to capitalise or expense expenditures. An analyst can, however, typically identify significant items of expenditure treated differently across companies. The items of expenditure giving rise to the most relevant differences across companies will vary by industry. This cross-industry variation is apparent in the following discussion of the capitalisation of expenditures.

2.1 Capitalisation of Interest Costs

Companies generally must capitalise interest costs associated with acquiring or constructing an asset that requires a long period of time to get ready for its intended use.[6] For example, constructing a building to sell or for a company's own use typically requires a substantial amount of time; any interest cost incurred, prior to completion, to finance construction is capitalised as part of the cost of the asset. The company determines the interest rate to use based on its existing borrowings or, if applicable, on a borrowing specifically incurred for constructing the asset. If a company takes out a loan specifically to construct a building, the interest cost on that loan during the time of construction would be capitalised as part of the building's cost.

As a consequence of this accounting treatment, a company's interest costs for a period can appear either on the balance sheet (to the extent they are capitalised) or on the income statement (to the extent they are expensed).

If the interest expenditure is incurred in connection with constructing an asset for the company's own use, the capitalised interest appears on the balance sheet as a part of the relevant long-lived asset. The capitalised interest is expensed over time as the property is depreciated—and is thus part of depreciation expense rather than interest expense. If the interest expenditure is incurred in connection with constructing an asset to sell, for example by a real estate construction company, the capitalised interest appears on the company's balance sheet as part of inventory. The capitalised interest is then expensed as part of the cost of sales when the asset is sold.

The treatment of capitalised interest poses certain issues that analysts should consider. First, capitalised interest appears as part of investing cash outflows, whereas expensed interest reduces operating cash flow. Although the treatment is consistent with accounting standards, an analyst may want to examine the impact on reported cash flows. Second, interest coverage ratios are solvency indicators measuring the extent to which a company's earnings (or cash flow) in a period covered its interest costs. To provide a true picture of a company's interest coverage, the entire amount of interest expenditure, both the capitalised portion and the expensed portion, should be used in calculating interest coverage ratios. Additionally, if a company is depreciating interest that it capitalised in a previous period, income should be adjusted to eliminate the effect of that depreciation. Example 3 illustrates the calculation.

---

[6] IAS 23 [Borrowing Costs] and FASB ASC Subtopic 835-20 [Interest—Capitalization of Interest] specify respectively IFRS and U.S. GAAP for capitalisation of interest costs. Although the standards are not completely converged, the standards are in general agreement.

EXAMPLE 3

Effect of Capitalised Interest Costs on Coverage Ratios and Cash Flow

MTR Gaming Group, Inc. (NASDAQGS: MNTG) disclosed the following information in one of the footnotes to its financial statements: "Interest is allocated and capitalized to construction in progress by applying our cost of borrowing rate to qualifying assets. Interest capitalized in 2007 and 2006 was $2.2 million and $6.0 million, respectively. There was no interest capitalized during 2008." (Form 10-K filed 13 March 2009).

EXHIBIT 2 MTR Gaming Group Selected Data, as Reported (Dollars in Thousands)

	2008	2007	2006
EBIT (from income statement)	432,686	389,268	268,800
Interest expense (from income statement)	40,764	34,774	17,047
Interest capitalised (from footnote)	0	2,200	6,000
Net cash provided by operating activities	14,693	14,980	42,206
Net cash from (used in) investing activities	41,620	(144,824)	(162,415)

1. Calculate and interpret MTR's interest coverage ratio with and without capitalised interest. Assume that capitalised interest increases depreciation expense by $475 thousand in 2008 and 2007, and by $365 thousand in 2006.
2. Calculate MTR's percentage change in operating cash flow from 2006 to 2007 and from 2007 to 2008. Assuming that financial reporting does not affect reporting for income taxes, what were the effects of capitalised interest on operating and investing cash flows?

Solution to 1: MTR did not capitalise any interest during 2008, so the interest coverage ratio for this year is affected only by depreciation expense related to previously capitalised interest. The interest coverage ratio, measured as earnings before interest and taxes (EBIT) divided by interest expense, was as follows for 2008:

10.61 ($432,686 ÷ $40,764) for 2008 without adjusting for capitalised interest; and
10.63 [($432,686 + $475) ÷ $40,764] including an adjustment to EBIT for depreciation of previously capitalised interest.

For the years 2007 and 2006, interest coverage ratios with and without capitalised interest were as follows:

For 2007

11.19 ($389,268 ÷ $34,774) without adjusting for capitalised interest; and

10.54 [($389,268 + $475) ÷ ($34,774 + $2,200)] including an adjustment to EBIT for depreciation of previously capitalised interest and an adjustment to interest expense for the amount of interest capitalised in 2007.

For 2006

15.77 ($268,800 ÷ $17,047) without adjusting for capitalised interest; and

11.68 [($268,800 + $365) ÷ ($17,047 + $6,000)] including an adjustment to EBIT for depreciation of previously capitalised interest and an adjustment to interest expense for the amount of interest capitalised in 2006.

Because MTR capitalises interest in previous years, EBIT is adjusted by adding in depreciation expense due to capitalised interest costs.

The above calculations indicate that MTR's interest coverage deteriorated over the three-year period from 2006 to 2008, even with no adjustments for capitalised interest. In both 2006 and 2007, the coverage ratio is lower when adjusted for capitalised interest. For 2006, the interest coverage ratio of 11.68 that includes capitalised interest is substantially lower than the ratio without capitalised interest.

Solution to 2: If the interest had been expensed rather than capitalised, operating cash flows would have been substantially lower in 2006, slightly lower in 2007, but unchanged in 2008. If the interest had been expensed rather than capitalised, the trend—at least in the last two years—would have been more favorable; operating cash flows would have increased rather than decreased over the 2007 to 2008 period. On an unadjusted basis, for 2008 compared with 2007, MTR's operating cash flow declined by 1.9 percent [($14,693 ÷ $14,980) − 1]. If the $2,200 of interest had been expensed rather than capitalised in 2007, the change in operating cash flow would have been positive, 15.0 percent {[$14,693 ÷ ($14,980 − $2,200)] − 1}.

If interest had been expensed rather than capitalised, the amount of cash outflow for investing activities would have been lower in 2006 and 2007 but unaffected in 2008. The percentage decline in cash outflows for investing activities from 2006 to 2007 would have been slightly smaller excluding capitalised interest from investing activities, 8.8 percent {[($144,824 − $2,200) ÷ ($162,415 − $6,000)] − 1}.

Generally, including capitalised interest in the calculation of interest coverage ratios provides a better assessment of a company's solvency. In assigning credit ratings, rating agencies include capitalised interest in coverage ratios. For example, Standard & Poor's calculates the EBIT interest coverage ratio as EBIT divided by gross interest (defined as interest prior to deductions for capitalised interest or interest income).

Maintaining a minimum interest coverage ratio is a financial covenant often included in lending agreements, e.g., bank loans and bond indentures. The definition of the coverage ratio can be found in the company's credit agreement. The definition is relevant because treatment of capitalised interest in calculating coverage ratios would affect an assessment of how close a company's actual ratios are to the levels specified by its financial covenants and thus the probability of breaching those covenants.

2.2 Capitalisation of Internal Development Costs

Costs to internally develop intangible assets are generally expensed when incurred, although there are exceptions, some of which are described in this section.

IFRS require that expenditures on *research* (or during the research phase of an internal project) be expensed rather than capitalised as an intangible asset. Research is defined as "original and planned investigation undertaken with the prospect of gaining new scientific or technical knowledge and understanding."[7] An example of an internal project is the search for alternative materials or systems to use in a production process. The research phase of an internal project refers to the period during which a company cannot demonstrate that an intangible asset will be created. IFRS allow companies to recognise an internal asset arising from *development* (or the development phase of an internal project) if certain criteria are met, including a demonstration of the technical feasibility of completing the intangible asset and the intent to use or sell the asset. Development is defined in IAS 38 as "the application of research findings or other knowledge to a plan or design for the production of new or substantially improved materials, devices, products, processes, systems, or services before the start of commercial production or use."

Generally, U.S. GAAP require that research and development costs be expensed, although there are certain exceptions.[8] For example, certain costs related to software development must be capitalised. Costs incurred to develop a software product for sale are expensed until the product's feasibility is established, and capitalised after the product's feasibility has been established. In addition, companies capitalise costs related directly to developing software for internal use, such as the costs of employees who help build and test the software. Even though standards require companies to capitalise software development costs after a product's feasibility is established, judgment in determining feasibility means that companies' capitalisation practices differ. For example, if only a short period elapses between the time a company establishes feasibility and the time that a company markets its products, it may conclude that the amount of development costs to be capitalised are immaterial and should be expensed. Exhibit 3 illustrates this concept.

[7] IAS 38 [Intangible Assets].

[8] FASB ASC Topic 730 [Research and Development]; FASB ASC Subtopic 350-40 [Intangibles—Internal-Use Software]; FASB ASC Subtopic 985-20 [Software—Costs of Software to be Sold, Leased, or Marketed].

EXHIBIT 3 Disclosure on Software Development Costs

Excerpt from Notes to Consolidated Financial Statements—Note 1 of Apple Inc. (NASDAQGS: AAPL):

> Research and development costs are expensed as incurred. Development costs of computer software to be sold, leased, or otherwise marketed are subject to capitalization beginning when a product's technological feasibility has been established and ending when a product is available for general release to customers. In most instances, the Company's products are released soon after technological feasibility has been established. Therefore, costs incurred subsequent to achievement of technological feasibility are usually not significant, and generally most software development costs have been expensed.
>
> In 2009 and 2008, the Company capitalized $71 million and $11 million, respectively, of costs associated with the development of Mac OS X Version 10.6 Snow Leopard ("Mac OS X Snow Leopard"), which was released during the fourth quarter of 2009. During 2007, the Company capitalized $75 million of costs associated with the development of Mac OS X Version 10.5 Leopard ("Mac OS X Leopard") and iPhone software. The capitalized costs are being amortized to cost of sales on a straight-line basis over a three year estimated useful life of the underlying technology.

Source: Apple's Form 10-K for the year ended 26 September 2009.

As with other types of expenditures, expensing rather than capitalising development costs results in lower net income in the current period. The cumulative effect will also reduce net income so long as the amount of the current period development costs is higher than the expense that would have resulted from amortising prior periods' capitalised development costs—the typical situation when a company's development costs are increasing. On the statement of cash flows, expensing rather than capitalising development costs results in an operating cash outflow rather than an investing cash outflow.

In comparing the financial performance of a company that expenses most or all software development costs, such as Apple, with another company that capitalises software development costs, adjustments can be made to make the two comparable. For the company that capitalises software development costs, an analyst can adjust a) the income statement to include software development costs as an expense and to exclude amortisation of prior years' software development costs; b) the balance sheet to exclude capitalised software (decrease assets and equity); and c) the statement of cash flows to decrease operating cash flows and decrease cash used in investing by the amount of the current period development costs. Any ratios that include income, long-lived assets, or cash flow from operations—such as return on equity—will also be affected.

EXAMPLE 4

Software Development Costs

You are working on a project involving the analysis of JHH Software, a (hypothetical) software development company that established technical feasibility for its first product in 2007. Part of your analysis involves computing certain market-based ratios, which you will use to compare JHH to another company that expenses all of its software development expenditures. Relevant data and excerpts from the company's annual report are included in Exhibit 4.

EXHIBIT 4 JHH Software (Dollars in Thousands, except Per-Share Amounts)

CONSOLIDATED STATEMENT OF EARNINGS–abbreviated

For year ended 31 December	2009	2008	2007
Total revenue	$91,424	$91,134	$96,293
Total operating expenses	78,107	78,908	85,624
Operating income	13,317	12,226	10,669
Provision for income taxes	3,825	4,232	3,172
Net income	$ 9,492	$ 7,994	$ 7,497
Earnings per share (EPS)	$1.40	$0.82	$0.68

STATEMENT OF CASH FLOWS–abbreviated

For year ended 31 December	2009	2008	2007
Net cash provided by operating activities	$15,007	$14,874	$15,266
Net cash used in investing activities*	(11,549)	(4,423)	(5,346)
Net cash used in financing activities	(8,003)	(7,936)	(7,157)
Net change in cash and cash equivalents	($ 4,545)	$ 2,515	$ 2,763
**Includes software development expenses of*	*($ 6,000)*	*($ 4,000)*	*($ 2,000)*
and includes capital expenditures of	*($ 2,000)*	*($ 1,600)*	*($ 1,200)*

Additional information:

For year ended 31 December	2009	2008	2007
Market value of outstanding debt	0	0	0
Amortisation of capitalised software development expenses	($ 2,000)	($ 667)	0
Depreciation expense	($ 2,200)	($ 1,440)	($ 1,320)
Market price per share of common stock	$42	$26	$17
Shares of common stock outstanding (thousands)	6,780	9,765	10,999

Footnote disclosure of accounting policy for software development:

Expenses that are related to the conceptual formulation and design of software products are expensed to research and development as incurred. The company capitalises expenses that are incurred to produce the finished product after technological feasibility has been established.

1. Compute the following ratios for JHH based on the reported financial statements for fiscal year ended 31 December 2009, with no adjustments. Next, determine the approximate impact on these ratios if the company had expensed rather than capitalised its investments in software. (Assume the financial reporting does not affect reporting for income taxes. There would be no change in the effective tax rate.)
   - A. P/E: Price/Earnings per share.
   - B. P/CFO: Price/Operating cash flow per share.
   - C. EV/EBITDA: Enterprise value/EBITDA, where enterprise value is defined as the total market value of all sources of a company's financing, including equity and debt, and EBITDA is earnings before interest, taxes, depreciation, and amortisation.
2. Interpret the changes in the ratios.

Solution to 1: (Dollars are in thousands, except per-share amounts.) JHH's 2009 ratios are presented in the following table:

Ratios	As Reported	As Adjusted
A. P/E ratio	30.0	42.9
B. P/CFO	19.0	31.6
C. EV/EBITDA	16.3	24.7

A. Based on the information as reported, the P/E ratio was 30.0 ($42 ÷ $1.40). Based on EPS adjusted to expense software development costs, the P/E ratio was 42.9 ($42 ÷ $0.98).

- Price: Assuming that the market value of the company's equity is based on its fundamentals, the price per share is $42, regardless of a difference in accounting.
- EPS: As reported, EPS was $1.40. Adjusted EPS was $0.98. Expensing software development costs would have reduced JHH's 2009 operating income by $6,000, but the company would have reported no amortisation of prior years' software costs, which would have increased operating income by $2,000. The net change of $4,000 would have reduced operating income from the reported $13,317 to $9,317. The effective tax rate for 2009 ($3,825 ÷ $13,317) is 28.72 percent, and using this effective tax rate would give an adjusted net income of $6,641 [$9,317 × (1 − 0.2872)], compared to $9,492 before the adjustment. The EPS would therefore be reduced from the reported $1.40 to $0.98 (adjusted net income of $6,641 ÷ 6,780 shares).

B. Based on information as reported, the P/CFO was 19.0 ($42 ÷ $2.21). Based on CFO adjusted to expense software development costs, the P/CFO was 31.6 ($42 ÷ $1.33).

- Price: Assuming that the market value of the company's equity is based on its fundamentals, the price per share is $42, regardless of a difference in accounting.
- CFO per share, as reported, was $2.21 (total operating cash flows $15,007 ÷ 6,780 shares).

- CFO per share, as adjusted, was $1.33. The company's $6,000 expenditure on software development costs was reported as a cash outflow from investing activities, so expensing those costs would reduce cash from operating activities by $6,000, from the reported $15,007 to $9,007. Dividing adjusted total operating cash flow of $9,007 by 6,780 shares results in cash flow per share of $1.33.

C. Based on information as reported, the EV/EBITDA was 16.3 ($284,760 ÷ $17,517). Based on EBITDA adjusted to expense software development costs, the EV/EBITDA was 24.7 ($284,760 ÷ $11,517).

- Enterprise Value: Enterprise value is the sum of the market value of the company's equity and debt. JHH has no debt, and therefore the enterprise value is equal to the market value of its equity. The market value of its equity is $284,760 ($42 per share × 6,780 shares).
- EBITDA, as reported, was $17,517 (earnings before interest and taxes of $13,317 plus $2,200 depreciation plus $2,000 amortisation).
- EBITDA, adjusted for expensing software development costs by the inclusion of $6,000 development expense and the exclusion of $2,000 amortisation of prior expense, would be $11,517 (earnings before interest and taxes of $9,317 plus $2,200 depreciation plus $0 amortisation).

Solution to 2: Expensing software development costs would decrease historical profits, operating cash flow, and EBITDA, and would thus increase all market multiples. So JHH's stock would appear more expensive if it expensed rather than capitalised the software development costs.

If the unadjusted market-based ratios were used in the comparison of JHH to its competitor that expenses all software development expenditures, then JHH might appear to be under-priced when the difference is solely related to accounting factors. JHH's adjusted market-based ratios provide a better basis for comparison.

For the company in Example 4, current period software development expenditures exceed the amortisation of prior periods' capitalised software development expenditures. As a result, expensing rather than capitalising software development costs would have the effect of lowering income. If, however, software development expenditures slowed such that current expenditures were lower than the amortisation of prior periods' capitalised software development expenditures, then expensing software development costs would have the effect of increasing income relative to capitalising it.

This section illustrated how decisions about capitalising versus expensing impact financial statements and ratios. Earlier expensing lowers current profits but enhances trends, whereas capitalising now and expensing later enhances current profits. The next section illustrates how decisions about depreciation methods can impact financial statements and ratios.

3 DEPRECIATION

Capitalised costs of long-lived tangible assets (other than land, which is not depreciated) and long-lived intangible assets with finite useful lives are allocated to subsequent periods via depreciation and amortisation expense, respectively. From this point forward, the term *depreciation* should be read as though it refers to depreciation or amortisation as appropriate. This section first examines the financial statement impact of choices about depreciation methods and judgments about useful lives and residual values. We then illustrate one use of financial disclosures to analyze long-lived assets.

3.1 Depreciation Methods

This section compares the financial statement impact of various depreciation methods. The method chosen should reflect the pattern in which the asset's future economic benefits are consumed. Accelerated depreciation methods, such as the double-declining balance method, result in higher depreciation expense (lower income) in earlier years and lower depreciation expense (higher income) in later years. Straight-line methods result in an even depreciation expense over the life of an asset. Production-based methods such as the units-of-production method can potentially result in variable depreciation expense.

EXAMPLE 5

Financial Statement Impact of Alternative Depreciation Methods

You are analyzing three (hypothetical) companies: EVEN-LI Co., SOONER Inc., and AZUSED Co. Each of the companies buys an identical piece of box-manufacturing equipment at a cost of $2,300, and each estimates the equipment's salvage value of $100. However, each company uses a different method of depreciation, as disclosed in the footnotes to their financial statements (including relevant assumptions).

Depreciation Method and Relevant Assumptions

- EVEN-LI uses the straight-line method and estimates the useful life of the equipment at four years.
- SOONER uses the double-declining balance method for the first year, switching to straight-line for the remaining years and estimates the useful life of the equipment at four years.
- AZUSED uses units-of-production method, assuming total productive capacity of 800 boxes. (Assume the following production: 200 boxes in Year 1; 300 boxes in Year 2; 200 boxes in Year 3; and 100 boxes in Year 4.)

Exhibit 5 presents the year-by-year book value, depreciation expense, and accumulated depreciation for each company.

EXHIBIT 5 **Comparative Year-by-Year Book Value, Depreciation Expense, and Accumulated Depreciation**

	Beginning Net Book Value ($)	Depreciation Expense ($)	Accumulated Year-End Depreciation ($)	Ending Net Book Value ($)
EVEN-LI Co.				
Year 1	2,300	550	550	1,750
Year 2	1,750	550	1,100	1,200
Year 3	1,200	550	1,650	650
Year 4	650	550	2,200	100
SOONER Inc.				
Year 1	2,300	1,150	1,150	1,150
Year 2	1,150	350	1,500	800
Year 3	800	350	1,850	450
Year 4	450	350	2,200	100
AZUSED Co.				
Year 1	2,300	550	550	1,750
Year 2	1,750	825	1,375	925
Year 3	925	550	1,925	375
Year 4	375	275	2,200	100

Assume the following for each company: Revenues in each year were $3,000; expenses, other than depreciation and tax, were $1,000; and the tax rate is 32 percent.

1. Calculate each company's net profit margin (net income divided by sales) for each of the four years.
2. Assess the impact of the depreciation method on the comparative net profit margins.

Solution to 1: Calculations in Exhibit 6 are as follows:

- Income before tax = Revenues of $3,000 − Expenses (other than depreciation) of $1,000 − Depreciation expense for each company
- Net income = Income before tax × (1 minus tax rate)
- Net profit margin = Net income ÷ Sales

EXHIBIT 6 Net Profit Margin

EVEN-LI Co.	Income before Tax ($)	Net Income ($)	Net Profit Margin (%)
Year 1	1,450	986	32.9
Year 2	1,450	986	32.9
Year 3	1,450	986	32.9
Year 4	1,450	986	32.9
SOONER Inc.			
Year 1	850	578	19.3
Year 2	1,650	1,122	37.4
Year 3	1,650	1,122	37.4
Year 4	1,650	1,122	37.4
AZUSED Co.			
Year 1	1,450	986	32.9
Year 2	1,175	799	26.6
Year 3	1,450	986	32.9
Year 4	1,725	1,173	39.1

Solution to 2: Because revenues and expenses other than depreciation are assumed equal in each year, EVEN-LI, which uses straight-line depreciation, reports the same income before tax, net income, and net profit margin for each of the four years. SOONER, which uses an accelerated depreciation method in the first year, reports lower income before tax, net income, and net profit margin in the initial year because its depreciation expense is higher in that year. This company shows a positive trend in income and net profit margin, at least at the beginning of the asset's life. AZUSED, which employs a usage-based depreciation method, reports income before tax, net income, and a net profit margin that varies with the variations in usage of the asset.

Note that the cumulative net income ($3,944) is the same over the four-year period for all three companies. However, if a company's value is based on the present value of future cash flows, the company with higher cash flows in earlier years due to lower taxes may have a higher value.

3.2 Estimates Required for Depreciation Calculations

Estimates required for depreciation calculations include the useful life of the equipment (or its total lifetime productive capacity) and its expected residual value at the end of that useful life. A longer useful life and higher expected residual value decrease the amount of annual depreciation relative to a shorter useful life and lower expected residual value.

A company makes estimates used in the calculation of depreciation expense when depreciable assets are acquired, or it may adopt estimates for major asset groups. The estimates are periodically reviewed. When a company determines that a change in an estimate is needed, the change is made going forward (prospectively). That is, the new estimate is applied to the current carrying amount going forward. Below is an example of how to incorporate a change in estimates to calculate depreciation expense and its effect on income.

EXAMPLE 6

Changing Estimates Used in the Depreciation Expense Calculation

Peacock Company, a (hypothetical) manufacturer of ornamental hardware, acquired a piece of machinery for $1,100,000 on 2 January Year 1. Originally, Peacock estimated the equipment would have a useful life of five years and $100,000 residual value. In December, Year 3, Peacock determines that the useful life should be extended from five years to eight years. The residual value does not change. It uses the straight-line depreciation method.

1. What amount of depreciation expense is reported in Year 1 and Year 2?
2. What amount of depreciation expense is reported in Year 3?
3. What is the effect on income before taxes of the change in the useful life in Year 3?

Solution to 1: In Year 1 and Year 2, Peacock's depreciation expense is $200,000 [(acquisition cost − residual value) ÷ estimated years of useful life = ($1,100,000 − $100,000) ÷ 5].

Solution to 2: The depreciation expense in Year 3 is $100,000. To estimate the amount of depreciation expense in Year 3, Peacock first determines the carrying amount of the machine (which is the amount of the machine remaining to be depreciated) and the machine's remaining useful life at the beginning of Year 3. The carrying amount of the machine is $700,000, determined as its acquisition cost of $1,100,000 less accumulated depreciation of $400,000 ($200,000 depreciation expense per year times two years). The remaining useful life of the machine is six years, determined as the new useful life of eight years less the two years the machine has already been used. The new depreciation expense of $100,000 is calculated as the carrying amount of $700,000 less the residual value of $100,000 divided by six years [($700,000 − $100,000)/6].

Solution to 3: Income before taxes increases by $100,000 ($200,000 original depreciation expenses less $100,000 new depreciation expense) due to extending the machine's useful life.

In Exhibit 7, Franklin Towers Enterprises, Inc., a Chinese company listed on the OTCBB, discloses its increase in the useful lives used to estimate the depreciation of production equipment and its rationale for this change.

EXHIBIT 7 Disclosure of Changes in Estimates Used to Calculate Depreciation Expense

Franklin Towers Enterprises, Inc. (OTCBB: FRTW), disclosure of change in estimates used to calculate depreciation expense from its fiscal 2008 10-K filing.

NOTE 5—Property and Equipment

During the first quarter of 2008, management reviewed the useful lives and residual value of the Company's machinery and equipment and compared to industry standards. Management has determined the production equipment acquired in 2007, which were originally estimated to have 5–7 years useful lives should be increased to 10-years useful lives and with a residual value of 5% of their original cost. Accordingly, effective January 1, 2008, the Company has changed the depreciation lives for the production equipment and auxiliary equipment to 10 years.

Additional estimates are required to allocate depreciation expense between the cost of sales (cost of goods sold) and selling, general, and administrative expenses (SG&A). Footnotes to the financial statements often disclose some information regarding which income statement line item includes depreciation, although the exact amount of detail disclosed by individual companies varies. Including a higher proportion of depreciation expense in cost of sales lowers the gross margin and lowers the operating expenses, but does not affect the operating margin. When comparing two companies, apportionment of depreciation to cost of sales versus SG&A can contribute to explaining differences in gross margins and operating expenses.

The processes of depreciation and amortisation serve to allocate the cost of long-lived assets over the useful life of the asset, periodically reflecting a portion of the historical cost as depreciation or amortisation expense and correspondingly reducing the carrying amount of the asset. The next section focuses on two types of accounting processes that can change the carrying amount of an asset differently than the periodic allocation of the asset's cost: impairment and revaluation.

4 IMPAIRMENT AND REVALUATION OF LONG-LIVED ASSETS

Impairment charges reflect an unanticipated decline in the value of an asset. Both IFRS and U.S. GAAP require companies to write down the carrying amount of impaired assets.[9] Impairment reversals—namely, writing the value of an asset back up if the value of the asset increases—is permitted under IFRS. Under U.S.

[9] IAS 36 [Impairment of Assets] defines an impairment loss as "the amount by which the carrying amount of an asset or a cash-generating unit exceeds its recoverable amount." FASB ASC Glossary defines impairment as "the condition that exists when the carrying amount of a long-lived asset (asset group) exceeds its fair value."

GAAP, however, reversing an impairment charge on an asset held for use is prohibited.

Another accounting process that can change the value of an asset differently than the periodic allocation of the asset's cost is the use of the revaluation model for valuing long-lived assets. Note the revaluation model is not allowed under U.S. GAAP, and the discussion therefore pertains exclusively to IFRS.

4.1 Impairment of Long-lived Tangible Assets Held for Use

For long-lived tangible assets held for use, impairment losses are recognised when the asset's carrying amount is not recoverable and its carrying amount exceeds its fair value. Both of these concepts are based on the asset's carrying amount relative to its expected future cash flows. However, IFRS and U.S. GAAP differ somewhat in both the guidelines for determining that impairment has occurred and in the measurement of any impairment loss. Under IAS 36, an impairment loss is measured as the excess of carrying amount over the recoverable amount of the asset. The recoverable amount is defined as "the higher of its fair value less costs to sell and its value in use." Value in use is a discounted measure of expected future cash flows. Under U.S. GAAP, a two-step test is used to determine whether an asset is impaired. First, recoverability is assessed: An asset's carrying amount is considered not recoverable when the asset's carrying amount exceeds the undiscounted expected future cash flows. Second, if the asset's carrying amount is considered not recoverable, the impairment loss is measured as the difference between the asset's fair value and carrying amount.

The impairment loss will reduce the carrying amount of the asset on the balance sheet and will reduce net income on the income statement. The impairment loss is a non-cash item and will not affect cash flow from operations. As with any accounting estimate, management's estimate of an impairment loss may be affected by a motivation to manage earnings.

EXAMPLE 7

Implications of Impairment Charges in Financial Statement Analysis

Assume that OmeTech (a hypothetical company) owns one asset with a carrying amount of $2,000. The asset is manufacturing equipment that produces two products: the Ome-Gizmo and the Tech-Gizmo. An adverse event occurs that requires evaluation of the asset for impairment; one of OmeTech's competitors wins a lawsuit confirming its right to a patent on the technology underlying the Tech-Gizmo, leaving OmeTech with a single product. Because the equipment is highly specialised and can now only be used to manufacture a single product for which there is finite demand, OmeTech believes that this adverse event reduces the recoverable value of its manufacturing equipment to an amount below its carrying cost. Based on new estimates that the future cash flows from the equipment will total $300 per year for the next five years, and an assumed discount rate of 10 percent, the company estimates the fair value of the equipment is now $1,137 (calculated as the present value of a $300 per year cash flow for five years). The company thus determines it has an impairment loss of $863.

1. Where will the impairment loss appear in the company's financial statements?
2. How should the impairment loss be viewed in the context of evaluating past earnings and cash flow?
3. How should the impairment loss be viewed in the context of projecting future earnings and cash flow?
4. Compare and contrast the determination and reporting of any impairment loss under IFRS and U.S. GAAP.

Solution to 1: On the balance sheet, the impairment loss will reduce the carrying amount of the relevant long-lived asset, with detail on the impairment loss itself in the footnotes to the financial statements and the MD&A. On the income statement (and thus ultimately in the retained earnings account on the balance sheet), the impairment loss will reduce income. In the operating section of the statement of cash flows, the reconciliation of net income to cash flows from operating activities will add back the impairment charge because it represents a non-cash item.

Solution to 2: Because the historical depreciation charge was insufficient to represent the full decline in the equipment's value, historical earnings may have been overstated. In evaluating past earnings, it should be understood that recognition and measurement of impairment charges are highly judgmental and thus can offer the potential for a company to manage its earnings. The direction of earnings management, to the extent that it exists, depends on what is motivating the management team. For example, a new management team might be motivated to show improvements in future performance, so recognising a substantial impairment charge in the current period will contribute to presenting a favorable trend. Alternatively, a management team that is close to missing a targeted earnings benchmark might be motivated to underestimate the impairment loss. In the context of evaluating past cash flow, an impairment charge does not affect cash flow. However, if the impairment loss relates to an asset that was relatively recently acquired, comparing the impairment loss to the amount invested to acquire the asset may offer some insight into management's ability to make successful acquisitions.

Solution to 3: In projecting future earnings, impairment losses would typically be considered non-recurring and thus would not be included in future projections. In projecting future cash flows, the impairment loss can provide some guidance. In this hypothetical example with only a single machine, the disclosures would provide a fairly transparent picture of management's expectations about its future cash flows. If an analyst or other user of the financial statements made identical assumptions of a five-year remaining life of the equipment and a 10 percent discount rate, the user could derive the expected future annual cash flows by calculating what annuity a present value of $1,137 would yield over five years at an interest rate of 10 percent, namely $300 per annum. The information from the impairment loss could be used as an input to an analyst's own future cash flow projections, based on his own expectations about the company's sales and profit margins, given information and assumptions about future demand for the product and competitive pressures.

Solution to 4: In this example, an impairment loss of $863 will be reported under both IFRS and U.S. GAAP. Under IFRS, the asset is considered impaired if its carrying amount is greater than its recoverable amount. The company thus determines it has an impairment loss of $863 ($2,000 carrying amount less the $1,137 present value of future cash flows). Under U.S. GAAP, the first step in determining impairment is assessing recoverability by comparing the carrying amount to future undiscounted cash flows. Because the carrying amount of $2,000 is greater than the $1,500 future undiscounted cash flows (five years at $300 per year), the recoverability test is not satisfied. The second step under U.S. GAAP then compares the carrying amount to fair value to determine the impairment loss of $863.

In practice, neither companies' businesses nor their disclosures are as simplistic as the above example. Nonetheless, impairment disclosures can provide similarly useful information. Exhibit 8 provides a footnote from the financial statements of Abitibi-Consolidated. The footnote provides information about three properties assessed for potential impairment. Based on the information, we can estimate that the company forecasts undiscounted future cash flows on the three properties of around C$1,014 million (32 percent more than the book value of the three properties: C$250 million + C$174 million + C$344 million). An assumption that the average remaining life of these assets is approximately the same as the estimated remaining life of the company's overall PPE asset base of 9.4 years, would indicate projected annual future cash flows from these three properties of C$108 million (C$1,014 million ÷ 9.4 years). While this cash flow projection is clearly a broad estimate, it could provide a useful basis of comparison for an analyst's own projections based on his own assumptions about the future cash flows of the company.

EXHIBIT 8 Disclosure of Impairment of Long-lived Assets

Excerpt from Financial Statement Footnotes of Abitibi-Consolidated Inc. (NYSE: ABY; TSX:A):

IMPAIRMENT OF LONG-LIVED ASSETS

During the fourth quarter of 2006, the Company conducted the initial step of the impairment tests on the Bridgewater, United Kingdom, paper mill and on the "Wood products" segment as a result of operating losses. The Company also conducted the initial step on the indefinitely idled Lufkin, Texas, paper mill. Estimates of future cash flows used to test the recoverability of a long-lived asset are mainly derived in the same manner as the projections of cash flows used in the initial step of the goodwill impairment test. In

(Exhibit continued on next page . . .)

EXHIBIT 8 (continued)

addition, the impairment test for the Lufkin paper mill was performed in light of a scenario of the mill's restart producing lightweight coated paper under a partnership structure.

The Company concluded that the recognition of an impairment charge for the business units analyzed was not required, as the estimated undiscounted cash flows exceeded the book values by at least 32%. Certain paper mills and sawmills are particularly sensitive to the key assumptions. Given the inherent imprecision and corresponding importance of the key assumptions used in the impairment test, it is reasonably possible that changes in future conditions may lead management to use different key assumptions, which could require a material change in the book value of these assets. The total book value of these assets was $250 million, $174 million and $344 million for the "Newsprint", "Commercial printing papers" and "Wood products" segments, respectively, as at December 31, 2006.

Source: Form 40-F for the year ended 31 December 2006, page 5, filed 15 March 2007.

Continuously testing the value of all these assets would obviously be impractical, so accounting standards set guidelines for when the tests must be done. For all long-lived assets, IFRS require that companies assess annually whether there are any indications that an asset might be impaired and then undertake an impairment test if such indications are present.[10] In contrast, U.S. GAAP require that companies only undertake an impairment test for an asset group within property, plant, and equipment if "events or changes in circumstances indicate that its carrying amount may not be recoverable."[11] IFRS and U.S. GAAP require that goodwill and identifiable intangible assets that are not amortised be tested for impairment annually, or more frequently when there are indications that impairment might have occurred. Examples of indicators that give rise to the need to test for impairment include a significant adverse change in an asset's physical condition, a significant adverse change in legal or economic factors, or a significant decrease in the market price among others.[12]

4.2 Revaluation of Long-lived Assets

The revaluation model of accounting for long-lived assets is an alternative to the historical cost model and is available under IFRS, but not under U.S. GAAP. Only the historical cost model is available under U.S. GAAP. Companies using IFRS have a choice of using the cost model or the revaluation model, although the majority uses the cost model.

Under the historical cost model, long-lived assets are reported at historical cost less accumulated depreciation or accumulated amortisation, adjusted for any impairment. Under the revaluation model, long-lived assets are reported at their fair value. IAS 16 states that the assets are to be reported at their fair value

[10] IAS 36, paragraph 9.

[11] FASB ASC 360-10-35-21.

[12] IAS 36, paragraph 12, FASB ASC 350-20-35-30, and FASB ASC 360-10-35-21.

less any subsequent accumulated depreciation and subsequent impairment losses, but requires revaluations be made frequently enough that the carrying amount does not differ materially from fair value. Required frequency of revaluation depends on the significance of periodic changes. Fair value of tangible long-lived assets is usually determined by professional appraisal using market-based evidence, but can be based on a discounted cash flow or replacement cost analysis in the absence of market-based evidence, e.g., if the asset is very specialized and seldom sold.[13]

IFRS allow a company to use the revaluation model for some classes of assets and the cost model for other classes, but the company must apply the same model to all assets within a particular class of assets. IFRS define a class of assets as a "grouping of assets of a similar nature and use in an entity's operations."[14] Examples of separate classes include land, buildings, furniture and fixtures, office equipment, machinery, ships, aircraft, and motor vehicles. If an asset is revalued, the company must revalue all items within the class simultaneously to avoid selective revaluation.

Whether an asset revaluation affects earnings depends on whether the revaluation initially increases or decreases an asset's carrying amount. If an asset revaluation initially decreases the carrying amount, the decrease is recognised in profit or loss (similar to an asset impairment). Later, if the asset's carrying amount increases due to an increase in fair value, the increase is recognised in profit or loss to the extent that it reverses a revaluation decrease of the same asset previously recognised in profit or loss. In contrast, if an asset revaluation initially increases the carrying amount, the increase in the asset's carrying amount bypasses the income statement, is reported as other comprehensive income, and appears in equity under the heading of revaluation surplus. Any subsequent decrease in the asset's value first decreases the revaluation surplus, then goes to income. When an asset is retired or disposed of, any related amount of revaluation surplus included in equity is transferred directly to retained earnings.

Asset revaluations offer several considerations for financial statement analyses. First, an increase in the carrying amount of depreciable long-lived assets increases total assets and shareholders' equity, so asset revaluations that increase the carrying amount of an asset can be used to reduce reported leverage. Defining leverage as average total assets divided by average shareholders' equity, increasing both the numerator (assets) and denominator (equity) by the same amount, leads to a decline in the ratio. (Mathematically, when a ratio is greater than one, as in this case, an increase in both the numerator and the denominator by the same amount leads to a decline in the ratio.) Therefore, the leverage motivation for the revaluation should be considered in analysis. For example, a company may revalue assets up if it is seeking new capital or approaching leverage limitations set by financial covenants.

Second, assets revaluations that decrease the carrying amount of the assets reduce net income. In the year of the revaluation, profitability measures such as return on assets and return on equity decline. However, because total assets and shareholders' equity are also lower, the company may appear more profitable in future years. Additionally, reversals of downward revaluations also go through income, thus increasing earnings. Managers can then opportunistically time the reversals to manage earnings and increase income. Third, asset revaluations that increase the carrying amount of an asset initially increase depreciation expense,

[13] For intangible long-lived assets, discounted cash flows and cost approach are typically used because market values are generally not obtainable.

[14] IAS 36, paragraph 37.

total assets, and shareholders' equity. Therefore, profitability measures, such as return on assets and return on equity, would decline. Although upward asset revaluations also generally decrease income (through higher depreciation expense), the increase in the value of the long-lived asset is presumably based on increases in the operating capacity of the asset, which will likely be evidenced in increased future revenues.

Finally, an analyst should consider who did the appraisal—i.e., an independent external appraiser or management—and how often revaluations are made. Appraisals of the fair value of long-lived assets involve considerable judgment and discretion. Presumably, appraisals of assets from independent external sources are more reliable. How often assets are revalued can provide an indicator of whether their reported value continues to be representative of their fair values.

EXAMPLE 8

Asset Revaluation

You are analyzing RevUp PLC, a (hypothetical) company which is planning to raise new debt in the coming year. Part of your analysis involves understanding the company's solvency to help determine its capacity to handle additional debt. You observe that in Year 2 RevUp made an asset revaluation that increased the reported value of its assets by €150 million and increased depreciation expense by €25 million. Other relevant data and excerpts from the company's annual report are included in Exhibit 9.

EXHIBIT 9 RevUp PLC
Excerpts from Financial Statements

Line Items (€ in Millions)	Year 1	Year 2
At 31 December:		
Property, plant, and equipment, net	700	750
Total assets	3,000	3,650
Total liabilities	1,400	1,900
Revaluation surplus (part of shareholders' equity)	—	150
Total shareholders' equity	1,600	1,750
For the year ended 31 December:		
Depreciation expense	100	125
Income before taxes	1,000	975
Tax expense	400	400
Net income	600	575

1. Compute the company's financial leverage (defined as average total assets ÷ average shareholders' equity) based on reported Year 2 financial statements, with no adjustments, and with adjustment for the impact of the asset revaluation on leverage. (Assume the asset revaluation is not taxable, and any increases in depreciation expense related to the revaluation are not tax deductible, so there would be no change in taxes.)

2. Interpret the change in leverage.

Solution to 1: RevUp's Year 2 ratios are as follows:

	With Asset Revaluation (As Reported)	Without Asset Revaluation (As Adjusted)
Leverage	1.99	2.03

Based on information as reported, leverage with the €150 million asset revaluation was 1.99 (average total assets ÷ average shareholders' equity).

- Average total assets: €3,325. [(beginning assets of €3,000 + ending assets of €3,650) ÷ 2]
- Average shareholders' equity: €1,675. [(beginning shareholders' equity of €1,600 + ending shareholders' equity of €1,750) ÷ 2]

Based on information as reported without the €150 million asset revaluation, leverage was 2.03.

- Average total assets: €3,250. [(beginning assets of €3,000 + ending assets of €3,500) ÷ 2].
  Ending assets = €3,650 − the €150 increase in the value of the asset surplus.
- Average shareholders' equity: €1,600. [(beginning shareholders' equity of €1,600 + ending shareholders' equity of €1,600) ÷ 2]
  Ending shareholders' equity = (€1,750 − €150).

Solution to 2: Increasing the value of the assets through revaluation decreases leverage. Therefore, RevUp appears to have more capacity for any new debt issues.

FINANCIAL STATEMENT DISCLOSURES: ANALYSIS AND DISCLOSURE

5

In this section, we discuss analysis and interpretation of disclosures of long-lived assets. Disclosure of long-lived assets can be used to assess a company's usage of its assets, the average age of assets, and the average remaining useful life of assets. A company must disclose the depreciation method(s), the gross carrying amount, and the accumulated depreciation at the balance sheets dates for each class of property, plant, and equipment (ASC 360-10-50 and IAS 16). Under IFRS, the measurement bases, the useful lives (or equivalently the depreciation rate) used, and a reconciliation of the carrying amount at the beginning and end of the period also must be disclosed (IAS 16).[15]

As noted in Section 4.2, IFRS permit companies to measure PPE either under a cost model, i.e., historical cost (initially recognised acquisition cost) minus accumulated depreciation, or under a revaluation model, i.e., fair value.[16] Under the revaluation model, the relationship between carrying amount, accumulated depreciation, and depreciation expense will differ when the carrying amount differs significantly from the depreciated historical cost. Under U.S. GAAP, only the cost model is permitted. The following discussion applies primarily to PPE reported under the cost model.

Disclosures about long-lived assets appear throughout the financial statements: in the balance sheet, the income statement, the statement of cash flows, and the notes. The balance sheet reports PPE at historical cost net of accumulated depreciation and net of any impairment charges. For the income statement, depreciation expense may or may not appear as a separate line item. Under IFRS, whether the income statement discloses depreciation expense separately depends on whether the company is using a "nature of expense" method or a "function of expense" method. Under the nature of expense method, a company aggregates expenses "according to their nature (for example, depreciation, purchases of materials, transport costs, employee benefits and advertising costs), and does not reallocate them among functions within the entity."[17] Under the function of expense method, a company classifies expenses according to the function, for example as part of cost of sales or of SG&A (selling, general, and administrative expenses). At a minimum, a company using the function of expense method must disclose cost of sales, but the other line items vary.

The statement of cash flows reflects acquisitions and disposals of fixed assets in the investing section. In addition, when prepared using the indirect method, the statement of cash flows typically shows depreciation expense (or depreciation plus amortisation) as a line item in the adjustments of net income to cash flow from operations. The notes to the financial statements describe the company's accounting method(s), the range of estimated useful lives, historical cost by main category of fixed asset, accumulated depreciation, and annual depreciation expense.

The fixed asset turnover ratio (total revenue divided by average net fixed assets) reflects the relationship between total revenues and investment in PPE. The higher this ratio, the higher the amount of sales a company is able to generate with a given amount of investment in fixed assets.

Asset age and remaining useful life are important indicators of a company's need to reinvest in productive capacity. The older the assets and the shorter the remaining life, the more a company may need to reinvest to maintain productive capacity. The amount of depreciation expense and the amount of net PPE can be used to estimate the average remaining useful life of a company's asset base. Specifically, the average remaining useful life of a company's assets can be estimated as net PPE divided by depreciation expense. In this section, we discuss this

---

[15] Most U.S. companies disclose asset useful lives by asset class as part of the description of the depreciation method used.

[16] Research indicates that revaluations of property, plant, and equipment permitted under IFRS but prohibited under U.S. GAAP are an important cause of the lack of comparability of financial statements prepared under the two sets of standards. For example, see J. L. Haverty, "Are IFRS and U.S. GAAP converging? Some Evidence from People's Republic of China Companies Listed on the New York Stock Exchange," *Journal of International Accounting, Auditing and Taxes*, Volume 15, Issue 1 (2006): 48–71.

[17] IAS 1, paragraph 102.

analysis as well as the estimation of the average age of a company's depreciable assets. To estimate the average age of the asset base, divide accumulated depreciation by depreciation expense.

These estimates simply reflect the following relationships for assets accounted for on a historical cost basis: total historical cost minus accumulated depreciation equals net PPE; and, under straight-line depreciation, total historical cost less salvage value divided by estimated useful life equals annual depreciation expense. Equivalently, total historical cost less salvage value divided by annual depreciation expense equals estimated useful life. Assuming straight-line depreciation and no salvage value (for simplicity), we have the following:

Estimated total useful life	=	Time elapsed since purchase (age)	+	Estimated remaining life
Historical cost ÷ annual depreciation expense	=	Estimated total useful life		
Historical cost	=	Accumulated depreciation	+	Net PPE

Equivalently,

Estimated total useful life	=	Estimated age of equipment	+	Estimated remaining life
Historical cost ÷ annual depreciation expense	=	Accumulated depreciation ÷ annual depreciation expense	+	Net PPE ÷ annual depreciation expense

The application of these estimates can be illustrated by a hypothetical example of a company with a single depreciable asset. Assume the asset initially cost \$100, had an estimated useful life of ten years, and an estimated salvage value of \$0. Each year, the company records a depreciation expense of \$10, so accumulated depreciation will equal \$10 times the number of years since the asset was acquired (when the asset is seven years old, accumulated depreciation will be \$70). Equivalently, the age of the asset will equal accumulated depreciation divided by the annual depreciation expense.

In practice, such estimates are difficult to make with great precision. Companies use depreciation methods other than the straight-line method and have numerous assets with varying useful lives and salvage values, including some assets that are fully depreciated, so this approach produces an estimate only. Moreover, fixed asset disclosures are often quite general. Consequently, these estimates may be primarily useful to identify areas for further investigation.

One further measure compares a company's current reinvestment in productive capacity. Comparing annual capital expenditures to annual depreciation expense provides an indication of whether productive capacity is being maintained. It is a very general indicator of the rate at which a company is replacing its PPE relative to the rate at which PPE is being depreciated.

EXAMPLE 9

Using Fixed Asset Disclosure to Compare Companies' Fixed Asset Turnover and Average Age of Depreciable Assets

You are analyzing the property, plant, and equipment of three international paper and paper products companies:

- AbitibiBowater Inc. (NYSE: ABY) is a Canadian company that manufactures newsprint, commercial printing papers, and other wood products.
- International Paper Company (NYSE: IP) is a U.S. paper and packaging company.
- UPM-Kymmene Corporation (UPM) is a Finnish company that manufactures fine and specialty papers, newsprint, magazine papers, and other related products. The company's common stock is listed on the Helsinki and New York stock exchanges.

Exhibit 10 presents selected information from the companies' financial statements.

EXHIBIT 10

	ABY	IP	UPM
Currency, Millions of:	**Canadian $**	**U.S. $**	**Euro €**
Historical cost total PPE, end of year	9,013	29,815	16,382
Accumulated depreciation, end of year	4,553	15,613	10,694
Net PPE, end of year	4,460	14,202	5,688
Land included in PPE	161	Not separated	347
Average net PPE	5,067	12,172	5,934
Net sales	6,771	24,829	9,461
Annual depreciation expense (annual impairment)	726	1,347	745 (182)
Capital expenditure	186	1,002	558
Accounting standards	Canadian GAAP	U.S. GAAP	IFRS
PPE measurement	Historical cost	Historical cost	Historical cost
Depreciation method	Straight-line	Units-of-production for pulp and paper mills;* straight-line for other	Straight-line
Useful life of assets, in years, except as noted	20–40 (buildings); 5–20 (machinery and equipment); 40 (power plants)	Straight-line depreciation rates are 2.5% to 8.5% (buildings), and 5% to 33% (machinery and equipment)	25–40 (buildings); 15–20 (heavy equip.); 5–15 (light equip.)

*Pulp and paper mills' historical cost as disclosed in a footnote totals $21,819 million. Depreciation expense and accumulated depreciation are not separately reported for mills.

Sources:
For ABY, Form 10-K for the year ended 31 December 2008, filed 31 March 2009.
For IP, Form 10-K for the year ended 31 December 2008, filed 20 February 2009.
For UPM, annual report for the year ended 31 December 2008.

1. Based on the above data for each company, estimate the total useful life, age, and remaining useful life of PPE.
2. Interpret the estimates. What items might affect comparisons across these companies?
3. How does each company's 2008 depreciation expense compare to its capital expenditures for the year?
4. Calculate and compare fixed asset turnover for each company.

Solution to 1: The following table presents the estimated total useful life, estimated age, and estimated remaining useful life of PPE for each of the companies.

Estimates	ABY	IP	UPM
Estimated total useful life (years)	12.4	22.1	22.0
Estimated age (years)	6.3	11.6	14.4
Estimated remaining life (years)	6.1	10.5	7.6

The computations are explained using UPM's data. The estimated total useful life of PPE is total historical cost of PPE of €16,382 divided by annual depreciation expense of €745, giving 22.0 years. Estimated age and estimated remaining life are obtained by dividing accumulated depreciation of €10,694 and net PPE of €5,688 by the annual depreciation expense of €745, giving 14.4 years and 7.6 years, respectively.

Ideally, the estimates of asset lives illustrated in this example should exclude land, which is not depreciable, when the information is available; however, IP does not separately disclose land. We will use UPM, for which land appeared to be disclosed separately in the above table, to illustrate the estimates with adjusting for land. As an illustration of the calculations to exclude land, excluding UPM's land would give an estimated total useful life for the non-land PPE of 21.5 years [(total cost €16,382 minus land cost of €347) divided by annual depreciation expense of €745 million].

Solution to 2: The estimated total useful life suggests that IP and UPM depreciate PPE over a much longer period than ABY: 22.1 and 22.0 years for IP and UPM, respectively, versus 12.4 years for ABY. This result can be compared, to an extent, to the useful life of assets noted by the companies, and the composition of fixed assets. For instance, ABY and UPM depreciate their buildings over similar periods and their equipment over the same period (5 to 20 years). That the estimated useful life of PPE overall differs so much between the companies suggests that equipment reflects a higher proportion of ABY's assets. An inspection of the companies' footnoted information (not shown above) on asset composition confirms that equipment accounts for a larger portion of ABY gross fixed assets (86 percent) compared to UPM (76 percent).

The estimated age of the equipment suggests that ABY has the newest PPE with an estimated age of 6.3 years. Additionally, the estimates suggest that around 50 percent of ABY's assets' useful lives have passed (6.3 years ÷ 12.4 years, or equivalently, C$4,553 million ÷ C$9,013 million). In comparison, around 67 percent of the useful lives of the PPE of UPM have passed. Items that can affect comparisons across the companies include business differences, such as differences in composition of the companies' operations and differences in acquisition and divestiture activity. In addition, the companies all report under different accounting standards, and IP discloses that it uses the units-of-production method for the largest component of its PPE. Differences in disclosures, e.g., in the categories of assets disclosed, also can affect comparisons.

Solution to 3: Capital expenditure as a percentage of depreciation is 26 percent for ABY, 74 percent for IP, and 75 percent for UPM. Based on this measure, IP and UPM are replacing their PPE at rates closer to the rate PPE is being depreciated. ABY's measure suggests the company is replacing its PPE at a slower rate than the PPE is being depreciated, consistent with the company's apparently newer asset base.

Solution to 4: Fixed asset turnover for each company is presented below, calculated as total revenues divided by average net PPE. Net sales is used as an approximation for total revenues, because differences like sales returns are not consistently disclosed by companies. We can see that IP's fixed asset turnover is highest, implying it is able to generate more sales from each unit of investment in fixed assets.

	ABY	IP	UPM
Fixed asset turnover	1.3	2.0	1.6
Currency, millions of:	*Canadian $*	*U.S. $*	*Euro €*
Net sales	6,771	24,829	9,461
Average net PPE	5,067	12,172	5,934

6 LEASING

A lease is a contract between the owner of an asset—the **lessor**—and another party seeking use of the assets—the **lessee**. Through the lease, the lessor grants the right to use the asset to the lessee. The right to use the asset can be a long period, such as 20 years, or a much shorter period such as a month. In exchange for the right to use the asset, the lessee makes periodic lease payments to the lessor. A lease, then, is a form of financing to the lessee provided by the lessor that enables the lessee to purchase the *use* of the leased asset.

6.1 The Lease versus Buy Decision

There are several advantages to leasing an asset compared to purchasing it. Leases can provide less costly financing, usually require little, if any, down payment, and are often at fixed interest rates. The negotiated lease contract may contain less restrictive provisions than other forms of borrowing. A lease can also reduce the risks of obsolescence, residual value, and disposition to the lessee because the lessee does not own the asset. The lessor may be better positioned to manage servicing the asset and to take advantage of tax benefits of ownership. As a result, leasing the asset may be less costly than owning the asset for the lessee.

Leases also have perceived financial and tax reporting advantages. While providing a form of financing, certain types of leases are not reported as debt on the balance sheet. The items leased under these types of leases also do not appear as assets on the balance sheet. Therefore, no interest expense or depreciation expense is included in the income statement. Additionally, in some countries such as the United States, financial reporting standards may differ from reporting under tax regulations; thus, in some cases, a company may own an asset for tax purposes (and thus obtain deductions for depreciation expense for tax purposes) while not reflecting the ownership in its financial statements. A lease that is structured to provide a company with the tax benefits of ownership while not requiring the asset to be reflected on the company's financial statements is known as a **synthetic lease**.

6.2 Finance versus Operating Leases

Recall the differences in economic substance and accounting for the two main types of leases—finance and operating. The economic substance of a finance (or capital)[18] lease is different from an operating lease, as are the implications of each for the financial statements of the lessee and lessor. In substance, a **finance lease** is equivalent to the purchase of some asset (lease to own) by the buyer (lessee) that is directly financed by the seller (lessor). An **operating lease** is an agreement allowing the lessee to use the asset for a period of time, essentially a rental.

Under IFRS, if substantially *all* the risks and rewards incidental to ownership are transferred to the lessee, the lease is classified as a finance lease and the lessee reports a leased asset and a lease obligation on the balance sheet.[19] Otherwise, the lease is reported as an operating lease. While a similar principle of the transfer of benefits and risks guides U.S. GAAP, U.S. accounting standards are more prescriptive in their criteria for classifying finance and operating leases. Under U.S. GAAP, a lease that meets any one of four specific requirements is classified as a finance lease.[20]

The following example illustrates and compares the accounting and financial statement effects of buying an asset using debt, leasing an asset under an operating lease, and leasing an asset under a finance lease.

[18] Finance lease is IFRS terminology and capital lease is U.S. GAAP terminology. IAS 17 [Leases] and FASB ASC Topic 840 [Leases].

[19] International accounting for leases is prescribed under IAS 17 [Leases].

[20] The four criteria are: 1) ownership of the leased asset transfers to lessee at end of lease, 2) the lease contains an option for the lessee to purchase the leased asset cheaply (bargain purchase option), 3) the lease term is 75 percent or more of the useful life of the leased asset, and 4) the present value of lease payments is 90 percent or more of the fair value of the leased asset (ASC 840-10-25-1).

EXAMPLE 10

Comparison of Accounting and Financial Statement Effects of the Buy versus Lease Decision

Bi-ly Company is considering the following alternatives in obtaining the use of a new piece of equipment at the beginning of Year 1:

Alternative 1: Buy the equipment and finance the purchase with new debt.

Alternative 2: Lease the equipment under an operating lease (the equipment is not reported as an asset, and the lease payments each period are treated as an operating expense on the income statement).

Alternative 3: Lease the equipment under a finance lease (the equipment is reported as an asset, and an obligation is recorded equal to the present value of future lease payments).

The fair value of the equipment, having a five-year useful life and no salvage value, is $1,000. If Bi-ly leases the equipment, annual lease payments would be $264 due at the end of each year. Bi-ly's discount rate is 10 percent. The company uses straight-line depreciation. (For illustration, assume the company can record the lease as either operating or financing.)

1. For each alternative under consideration, determine the effect on assets and liabilities at the beginning of Year 1.
2. For each alternative, determine the effect on the income statement in Year 1.
3. For each alternative, calculate Bi-ly's return on assets and debt-to-asset ratio at the end of Year 1. For simplicity, assume that—excluding any effects of Bi-ly's choice among the three alternatives for obtaining the assets—total assets at the beginning and end of the year are $4,500, total liabilities at the beginning and end of the year are $3,000, and net income for the year is $800.

Solution to 1: At the beginning of Year 1, Bi-ly would show the following assets and debt:

Alternative	1	2	3
Buy/Lease	Buy	Lease	Lease
Finance/Accounting	Issue new debt	Operating	Finance*
Long-lived asset	$1,000		$1,000
Debt/lease obligation	$1,000		$1,000

*Under a finance lease, the present value of five future lease payments of $264 discounted at 10 percent is reported on the balance sheet as a lease obligation and an asset of $1,000 (rounded).

Solution to 2: For Year 1, Bi-ly would show the following expenses related to the equipment:

Alternative	1	2	3
Rent expense		$264	
Depreciation expense	$200		$200
Interest expense	100		100
Total expenses	$300	$264	$300

For Alternatives 1 and 3, depreciation expense is the acquisition cost of $1,000 divided by the five-year useful life. Salvage value is 0.

For Alternatives 1 and 3, interest expense is the beginning balance of debt, $1,000, times the discount rate of 10 percent. Each year the interest expense will decline.

For Alternative 2, rent expense is the lease payment of $264.

Solution to 3: To calculate the return on assets:

Alternative	1	2	3
Net income, excluding new asset	$800	$800	$800
Add additional expenses (solution to 2 above)	300	264	300
Net income, adjusted	$500	$536	$500
Total assets, beginning, excluding new asset	$4,500	$4,500	$4,500
Add additional asset (solution to 1 above)	1,000		1,000
Total assets, beginning, adjusted	$5,500	$4,500	$5,500
Total assets, end, excluding new asset	$4,500	$4,500	$4,500
Add additional asset*	800		800
Total assets, end, adjusted	$5,300	$4,500	$5,300
Average total assets	$5,400	$4,500	$5,400
Return on assets, adjusted	9.3%	11.9%	9.3%

* The book value of the new asset at the end of the year is its beginning balance of $1,000 less $200 accumulated depreciation.

In this example, the highest return on assets is found when the equipment is leased under an operating lease, which is expected because net income is highest and the asset base is lowest. Buying an asset and seeking to finance it with new debt and leasing it under a finance lease result in the same return on assets.

To calculate the debt-to-asset ratio at the end of the year:

Alternative	1	2	3
Total assets, end, excluding new asset	$4,500	$4,500	$4,500
Add additional asset	800		800
Total assets, end, adjusted	$5,300	$4,500	$5,300
Total liabilities, end, excluding new asset	$3,000	$3,000	$3,000
Add additional debt*	837		837
Total liabilities, end, adjusted	$3,837	$3,000	$3,837
Debt-to-asset ratio	0.724	0.667	0.724

* Additional debt at the end of the first year is the present value of the four remaining debt/lease payments of $264 discounted at 10 percent (and rounded).

In this example, the lowest debt-to-asset ratio is found when the equipment is financed through an operating lease. Buying an asset and seeking to finance it with new debt and leasing it under a finance lease result in the same return on assets.

6.2.1 Accounting and Reporting by the Lessee

A finance lease is economically similar to borrowing money and buying an asset; therefore, a company that enters into a finance lease as the lessee reports an asset (leased asset) and related debt (lease payable) on the balance sheet. The initial value of both the leased asset and the lease payable is the lower of the fair value of the leased asset or the present value of future lease payments. On the income statement, the company reports interest expense on the debt; and if the asset acquired is depreciable, the company reports depreciation expense. (The lessor, as we illustrate in Section 6.2.2, reports the sale of an asset and the lease as a receivable.)

Because an operating lease is economically similar to renting an asset, the lessee records a lease expense on its income statement during the period it uses the asset. No asset or liability is recorded on its balance sheet. The main accounting differences between a finance lease and an operating lease are that under a finance lease, reported debt and assets are higher and expenses are generally higher in the early years. Because of the higher reported assets, debt and expenses—and therefore the lower ROA, all else equal—lessees often prefer operating leases to finance leases. As we illustrate in the next section, lessors' preferences generally differ. Lessors would prefer a finance lease because, under an operating lease, lessors continue to show the asset and its associated financing on their balance sheets.

On the lessee's statement of cash flows, for an operating lease, the full lease payment is shown as an operating cash outflow. For a finance lease, only the portion of the lease payment relating to interest expense potentially reduces operating cash flows;[21] the portion of the lease payment that reduces the lease liability appears as a cash outflow in the financing section.

A company reporting a lease as an operating lease will typically show higher profits in early years, higher return measures in early years, and a stronger solvency position than an identical company reporting an identical lease as a finance lease. However, the company reporting the lease as a finance lease will show higher operating cash flows because a portion of the lease payment will be reflected as a financing cash outflow rather than an operating cash outflow.

Example 11 illustrates the effect on a lessee's income, debt, and cash flows when reporting a lease as a finance lease versus an operating lease.

EXAMPLE 11

Financial Statement Impact of a Finance versus Operating Lease for the Lessee

Assume two similar (hypothetical) companies, CAPBS Inc. and OPIS Inc., enter into similar lease agreements for a piece of machinery on 1 January Year 1. The leases require four annual payments of €28,679 starting on 1 January Year 1. The useful life of the machine is four years and its salvage value is zero. CAPBS accounts for the lease as a finance lease and uses straight-line depreciation, while OPIS has determined the lease is an operating lease. For simplicity, this example assumes that the accounting rules governing these hypothetical companies do not mandate either type of lease. The present value of lease payments and fair value of the equipment is €100,000. (A reminder relevant for present value calculations: Lease payments are made at the beginning of each period.)

At the beginning of Year 1, before entering into the lease agreements, both companies reported liabilities of €100,000 and equity of €200,000. Each year the companies receive total revenues of €50,000, and all revenues are cash. Assume the companies have a tax rate of 30 percent, and use the same accounting for financial and tax purposes. Both companies' discount rate is 10 percent. In order to focus only on the differences in the type of lease, assume neither company incurs expenses other than those associated with the lease, and neither invests excess cash.

1. Which company reports higher expenses/net income in Year 1? Over the four years?
2. Which company reports higher total cash flow over the four years? Cash flow from operations?
3. Based on return on equity (ROE), how do the two companies' profitability measures compare?
4. Based on the ratio of debt-to-equity, how do the two companies' solvency positions compare?

[21] Interest expense may be classified as a financing cash flow or an operating cash flow under IFRS (IAS 7, paragraph 33) but is classified as an operating cash flow under U.S. GAAP (FASB ASC, paragraph 230-10-45-17).

Solution to 1: In Year 1 and Year 2, CAPBS reports higher expenses because the depreciation expense and interest expense of its finance lease exceeds the lease expense of OPIS's operating lease. Therefore, OPIS reports higher net income in Year 1 and Year 2. The companies' total expense over the entire four-year period, however, is equal, as is the companies' total net income.

Each year, OPIS reports lease expense of €28,679 associated with its operating lease. For CAPBS, its finance lease is treated as being economically similar to borrowing money and purchasing an asset. So, on its income statement, CAPBS reports depreciation expense on the leased asset acquired and interest expense on the lease liability.

The table below shows by year CAPBS's depreciation expense and book values on the leased asset.

Year	Acquisition Cost (a)	Depreciation Expense (b)	Accumulated Depreciation (c)	Carrying Amount (Year End) (d)
1	€100,000	€ 25,000	€ 25,000	€75,000
2	100,000	25,000	50,000	50,000
3	100,000	25,000	75,000	25,000
4	100,000	25,000	100,000	0
		€100,000		

- Column (a) is acquisition cost of €100,000 of the leased equipment.
- Column (b) is depreciation expense of €25,000 per year, calculated using the straight line convention, as the acquisition costs less salvage value divided by useful life [(€100,000 − €0)/4 years].
- Column (c) is the accumulated depreciation on the leased asset, calculated as the prior year's accumulated depreciation plus the current year's depreciation expense.
- Column (d) is the carrying amount at year end of the leased equipment, which is the difference between the acquisition cost and accumulated depreciation.

The table below shows CAPBS's lease payment, interest expense, and carrying amount for its lease liability by year.[22]

Year	Lease Liability, 1 January (a)	Annual Lease Payment, 1 January (b)	Interest (at 10%; Accrued in Previous Year) (c)	Reduction of Lease Liability, 1 January (d)	Lease Liability on 31 December after Lease Payment on 1 January Same Year (e)
1	€100,000	€ 28,679	€ 0	€ 28,679	€71,321
2	71,321	28,679	7,132	21,547	49,774
3	49,774	28,679	4,977	23,702	26,072
4	26,072	28,679	2,607	26,072	0
		€114,717	€14,717	€100,000	

[22] The computations included throughout the example were made using an Excel worksheet; small discrepancies in the calculations are due to rounding.

- Column (a) is the lease liability at the beginning of the year.

  Year 1: €100,000

  Years thereafter: lease liability at end of previous year
- Column (b) is the annual lease payment made at the beginning of the year. Part of the lease payment pays any interest accrued in the previous year, and the remainder of the lease payment reduces the lease liability. For example, in Year 2, the €28,679 paid on 1 January reduces the interest payable of €7,132 that accrued in Year 1 (0.10 × 71,321) and then reduces the lease liability by €21,547.
- Column (c) is the interest portion of the 1 January lease payment made on that date. This amount of interest was accrued as interest payable during the *prior* year and is reported as the interest expense of the *prior* year.
- Column (d) is the reduction of the lease liability, which is the difference between the annual lease payment and the interest portion.
- Column (e) is the lease liability on 31 December of a given year just before the lease payment is made on the first day of the next year. It is equal to the lease liability on 1 January of the same year (column a) less the reduction of the lease liability (column d).

The table below summarizes and compares the income statement effects of the lease for CAPBS and OPIS. Notice that over the four-year lease, both companies report the same total amount of expense but CAPBS shows higher expenses earlier in the life of the lease.

	CAPBS			OPIS	
Year	**Depreciation Expense**	**Interest Expense**	**Total**	**Lease Expense**	**Difference**
1	€ 25,000	€ 7,132	€ 32,132	€ 28,679	€3,453
2	25,000	4,977	29,977	28,679	1,298
3	25,000	2,607	27,607	28,679	(1,072)
4	25,000	—	25,000	28,679	(3,679)
Total	€100,000	€14,717	€114,717	€114,717	€ (0)

The complete income statements for CAPBS and OPIS are presented below. Notice under the assumption that the same accounting is used for financial and tax purposes, CAPBS's taxes are lower in Year 1 and Year 2. The lower taxes in the earlier years reflect the higher expenses in those years.

Income Statements	CAPBS 1	CAPBS 2	CAPBS 3	CAPBS 4	CAPBS Total	OPIS 1	OPIS 2	OPIS 3	OPIS 4	OPIS Total
Sales	€50,000	€50,000	€50,000	€50,000	€200,000	€50,000	€50,000	€50,000	€50,000	€200,000
Depreciation expense	25,000	25,000	25,000	25,000	€100,000					
Interest expense	7,132	4,977	2,607		14,717					
Lease expense	—	—	—	—	—	28,679	28,679	28,679	28,679	114,717
Income before taxes	17,868	20,023	22,393	25,000	85,283	21,321	21,321	21,321	21,321	85,283
Tax expense	5,360	6,007	6,718	7,500	25,585	6,396	6,396	6,396	6,396	25,585
Net income	€12,508	€14,016	€15,675	€17,500	€ 59,698	€14,925	€14,925	€14,925	€14,925	€ 59,698

Solution to 2: On the statement of cash flows, observe that over the four years, both CAPBS and OPIS report the same total change in cash of €59,698. Operating cash flows reported by CAPBS are higher because a portion of the lease payment each year is categorised as a financing cash flow rather than an operating cash flow. In the first two years, CAPBS's change in cash is higher due to its lower taxes in those years.

Statements of Cash Flows	CAPBS 1	CAPBS 2	CAPBS 3	CAPBS 4	CAPBS Total	OPIS 1	OPIS 2	OPIS 3	OPIS 4	OPIS Total
Sales	€50,000	€50,000	€50,000	€50,000	€200,000	€50,000	€50,000	€50,000	€50,000	€200,000
Interest paid	—	7,132	4,977	2,607	€14,717					
Taxes paid	5,360	6,007	6,718	7,500	25,585	6,396	6,396	6,396	6,396	€25,585
Lease expense	—	—	—	—	—	28,679	28,679	28,679	28,679	114,717
Operating cash flows	44,640	36,861	38,305	39,893	159,698	14,925	14,925	14,925	14,925	59,698
Payment to reduce lease liability	(28,679)	(21,547)	(23,702)	(26,072)	(100,000)					
Financing cash flows	(28,679)	(21,547)	(23,702)	(26,072)	(100,000)	—	—	—	—	—
Total change in cash	€15,960	€15,314	€14,603	€13,821	€ 59,698	€14,925	€14,925	€14,925	€14,925	€ 59,698

Solution to 3: Based on ROE, CAPBS looks less profitable than OPIS in the earlier years. Computing ROE requires forecasting shareholders' equity. In general, ending Shareholders' equity = Beginning shareholders' equity + Net income + Other comprehensive income − Dividends + Net capital contributions by shareholders. Because the companies in this example do not have other comprehensive income, did not pay dividends, and experienced no capital contributions from shareholders, Ending shareholders' equity = Beginning shareholders' equity + Net income. The forecasts are presented below.

CAPBS	0	1	2	3	4
Retained earnings	€0	€12,508	€26,523	€42,198	€59,698
Common stock	200,000	200,000	200,000	200,000	200,000
Total shareholders' equity	€200,000	€212,508	€226,523	€242,198	€259,698

OPIS	0	1	2	3	4
Retained earnings	€0	€14,925	€29,849	€44,774	€59,698
Common stock	200,000	200,000	200,000	200,000	200,000
Total shareholders' equity	€200,000	€214,925	€229,849	€244,774	€259,698

ROE is calculated as net income divided by average shareholders' equity. For example, CAPBS Inc. had Year 1 ROE of 6.1 percent: €12,508/ [(€200,000 + €212,508) ÷ 2].

	CAPBS				OPIS			
	1	2	3	4	1	2	3	4
ROE	6.1%	6.4%	6.7%	7.0%	7.2%	6.7%	6.3%	5.9%

Solution to 4: Based on the ratio of debt-to-equity, the solvency position of CAPBS appears weaker than that of OPIS.

For the debt-to-equity ratio, take the total shareholders' equity from Part 3 above. Initially, both companies had reported liabilities of €100,000. For OPIS, the amount of total liabilities remains constant at €100,000. For CAPBS, add the lease liability at the end of the year and the amount of accrued interest payable at the end of each year from Part 1 above. So at the end of Year 1, CAPBS's total liabilities are €178,453 (€100,000 + €71,321 lease liability + €7,132 accrued interest payable at the end of the year), and its debt-to-equity ratio is 0.84 (€178,453 ÷ €212,508). At the end of Year 2, CAPBS total liabilities equal €154,751 (€100,000 + €49,774 lease liability + €4,977 accrued interest payable at the end of the year). The remaining years are computed in the same manner. The table below presents the ratios for each year.

	CAPBS				OPIS			
	1	2	3	4	1	2	3	4
Total debt	178,453	154,751	128,679	100,000	100,000	100,000	100,000	100,000
Shareholders' equity	212,508	226,523	242,198	259,698	214,925	229,849	244,774	259,698
Debt-to-equity ratio	0.84	0.68	0.53	0.39	0.47	0.44	0.41	0.39

In summary, a company reporting a lease as an operating lease will typically show higher profits in early years, higher return measures in early years, and a stronger solvency position than an identical company reporting an identical lease as a finance lease.[23] However, the company reporting the lease as a finance lease will show higher operating cash flows because a portion of the lease payment will be reflected as a financing cash outflow rather than an operating cash outflow.

The precisely defined accounting standards in the United States that determine when a company should report a capital (finance) versus an operating lease enable a company to structure a lease so as to avoid meeting any of the four capital lease criteria and thereby record an operating lease. Similar to debt disclosures, lease disclosures show payments under both capital and operating leases for the next five years and afterwards. Future payments under U.S. GAAP are disclosed year by year for the first five years and then aggregated for all subsequent years. Under IFRS, future payments are disclosed for the first year, in aggregate for Years 2–5, and then in aggregate for all subsequent years. These disclosures can help to estimate the extent of a company's off-balance sheet lease financing through operating leases. Example 12 illustrates the disclosures and how these disclosures can be used to determine the effect on the financial statements if all operating leases were capitalised.

EXAMPLE 12

Financial Statement Impact of Treating Operating Leases as Finance Leases for the Lessee

CEC Entertainment, Inc. (NYSE: CEC) has significant commitments under capital (finance) and operating leases. Presented below is selected financial statement information and note disclosure to the financial statements for the company.

[23] Example 11 assumes the company uses the straight-line depreciation method, which is common under IFRS and U.S. GAAP. If the company estimated depreciation expense based on the "economic" depreciation of the leased asset, there would be no difference in reported income under a finance lease and operating lease.

Commitments and Contingencies Footnote from CEC's Financial Statements:
8. Commitments and contingencies:
The company leases certain restaurants and related property and equipment under operating and capital leases. All leases require the company to pay property taxes, insurance, and maintenance of the leased assets. The leases generally have initial terms of 10 to 20 years with various renewal options.

Scheduled annual maturities of the obligations for capital and operating leases as of 28 December 2008 are as follows (US$ thousands):

Years	Capital	Operating
2009	$1,683	$66,849
2010	1,683	66,396
2011	1,683	66,558
2012	1,600	65,478
2013	1,586	63,872
Thereafter	9,970	474,754
Minimum future lease payments	$18,205	$803,907
Less amounts representing interest	(5,997)	
Present value of future minimum lease payments	$12,208	
Less current portion	(806)	
Long-term finance lease obligation	$11,402	

Selected Financial Statement Information for CEC:

	28 December 2008	30 December 2007
Total liabilities	$608,854	$519,900
Shareholders' equity	128,586	217,993

1. A. Calculate the implicit interest rate used to discount the "scheduled annual maturities" under capital leases to obtain the "present value of future minimum lease payments" of $12,208 disclosed in the Commitments and Contingencies footnote. To simplify the calculation, assume that future minimum lease payments on the company's capital leases for the "thereafter" lump sum are as follows: $1,586 on 31 December of each year from 2014 to 2019, and $454 in 2020. Assume annual lease payments are made at the end of each year.

B. Why is the implicit interest rate estimate in Part A important in assessing a company's leases?

2. If the operating lease agreements had been treated as capital leases, what additional amount would be reported as a lease obligation on the balance sheet at 28 December 2008? To simplify the calculation, assume that future minimum lease payments on the company's operating leases for the "thereafter" lump sum are as follows: $63,872 on 31 December each year from 2014 to 2020, and $27,650 in 2021. Based on the implicit interest rate obtained in Part 1A, use 7.245 percent to discount future cash flows on the operating leases.
3. What would be the effect on the debt-to-equity ratio of treating all operating leases as finance leases (i.e., the ratio of total liabilities to equity) at 28 December 2008?

Solution to 1A: The implicit interest rate on finance leases is 7.245 percent. The implicit interest rate used to discount the finance lease payments is the internal rate of return on the stream of cash flows; i.e., the interest rate that will make the present value of the lease payments equal to $12,208. You can use an Excel spreadsheet or a financial calculator for the computations. Set the cash flow at time zero equal to $12,208 (note on Excel and on most financial calculators, you will input this amount as a negative number), input each of the annual payments on the finance leases, and solve for the internal rate of return.

To demonstrate how the internal rate of return corresponds to the individual present values, refer to the following schedule of the undiscounted minimum lease payments based on information from footnote 8 and the assumptions given. Exhibit 11 presents the present value computations.

EXHIBIT 11 Present Value Computations Implicit Interest Rate (Internal Rate of Return) based on Capital Leases (7.245%)

Fiscal Year	Years to Discount	Minimum Capital Lease Payment	Times Present Value Factor	Equals Present Value
2009	1	1,683	$1/(1+\text{interest rate})^1$	1,569
2010	2	1,683	$1/(1+\text{interest rate})^2$	1,463
2011	3	1,683	$1/(1+\text{interest rate})^3$	1,364
2012	4	1,600	$1/(1+\text{interest rate})^4$	1,210
2013	5	1,586	$1/(1+\text{interest rate})^5$	1,118
2014	6	1,586	$1/(1+\text{interest rate})^6$	1,042
2015	7	1,586	$1/(1+\text{interest rate})^7$	972
2016	8	1,586	$1/(1+\text{interest rate})^8$	906
2017	9	1,586	$1/(1+\text{interest rate})^9$	845
2018	10	1,586	$1/(1+\text{interest rate})^{10}$	788
2019	11	1,586	$1/(1+\text{interest rate})^{11}$	735
2020	12	454	$1/(1+\text{interest rate})^{12}$	196
Undiscounted sum of minimum future lease payments		$18,205		
Present value of future minimum lease payments				$12,208

The interest rate of 7.245 percent approximately equates the future minimum lease payments with the present value of future minimum lease payments of $12,208 that CEC reports.

Solution to 1B: The implicit interest rate is important because it will be used to estimate the present value of the lease obligations reported as a liability, the value of the leased assets on the balance sheet, the interest expense, and the lease amortisation on the income statement. For instance, by selecting a higher rate a company could, if desired, opportunistically reduce the present value of its finance leases and thus its reported debt. The reasonableness of the implicit interest rate can be gauged by comparing it to the interest rates of the company's other debt instruments outstanding, which are disclosed in financial statement footnotes, and by considering recent market conditions. Note, however, that the interest rate implicit in capitalisation of the finance lease obligations reflects the interest rate at the time the lease occurred and thus may differ from current rates.

Solution to 2: If the operating leases had been treated as finance leases, the additional amount that would be reported as a lease obligation on the balance sheet at 28 December 2008, using a discount rate of 7.245 percent determined in Part 1 above, is $520,256. Exhibit 12 presents the present value computations. An alternative short cut approach is to divide the discounted finance lease cash flows of $12,208 by the undiscounted finance lease cash flows of $18,205 and then apply the resulting percentage of 67.06 percent to the undiscounted operating lease cash flows of $803,907. The shortcut approach estimates the present value of the operating lease payments as $539,100, which is close to the estimate obtained using the longer method. It is likely to be most accurate when the timing and relative quantities of the two sets of cash flows are similar.

Exhibit 12 Present Value Computations (Implicit Interest Rate: 7.245%)

Fiscal Year	Years to Discount	Operating Lease Payments	Times Present Value Factor	Equals Present Value
2009	1	66,849	$1/(1+0.07245)^1$	$62,333
2010	2	66,396	$1/(1+0.07245)^2$	57,728
2011	3	66,558	$1/(1+0.07245)^3$	53,960
2012	4	65,478	$1/(1+0.07245)^4$	49,498
2013	5	63,872	$1/(1+0.07245)^5$	45,022
2014	6	63,872	$1/(1+0.07245)^6$	41,981
2015	7	63,872	$1/(1+0.07245)^7$	39,145
2016	8	63,872	$1/(1+0.07245)^8$	36,500
2017	9	63,872	$1/(1+0.07245)^9$	34,034
2018	10	63,872	$1/(1+0.07245)^{10}$	31,735
2019	11	63,872	$1/(1+0.07245)^{11}$	29,591
2020	12	63,872	$1/(1+0.07245)^{12}$	27,592
2021	13	27,650	$1/(1+0.07245)^{13}$	11,138
Undiscounted sum of future operating lease payment		$803,907		
Present value of future operating lease payments				$520,256

Solution to 3: The debt-to-equity ratio almost doubles, increasing to 8.78x from 4.73x when capitalising the operating leases. The adjusted debt-to-equity ratio is computed as follows:

	Unadjusted for Operating Leases	Adjustment to Capitalise Operating Leases	Adjusted to Capitalise Operating Leases
Total liabilities	$608,854	$520,256	$1,129,110
Common shareholders' equity	128,586		128,586
Debt-to-equity ratio	4.73x		8.78x

6.2.2 Accounting and Reporting by the Lessor

Lessors that report under U.S. GAAP determine whether a lease is a finance (also called "capital lease") or operating lease using the same four criteria as a lessee, plus additional revenue recognition criteria. If a lessor enters into an operating lease, the lessor records any lease revenue when earned. The lessor also continues to report the leased asset on the balance sheet and the asset's associated depreciation expense on the income statement.

Under a finance lease, the lessor reports a lease receivable based on the present value of future lease payments, and the lessor also reduces its assets by the carrying amount of the asset leased. Under U.S. GAAP, the carrying amount of the asset leased relative to the present value of lease payments distinguishes a direct financing lease from a sales-type lease. The income statement will show interest revenue on the lease.

EXAMPLE 13

Financial Statement Impact of a Direct Financing Lease versus Operating Lease for the Lessor

Assume two similar (hypothetical) companies, DIRFIN Inc. and LOPER Inc., own a similar piece of machinery and make similar agreements to lease the machinery on 1 January Year 1. In the lease contract, each company requires four annual payments of €28,679 starting on 1 January Year 1. The useful life of the machine is four years and its salvage value is zero. DIRFIN Inc. accounts for the lease as a direct financing lease whereas LOPER has determined the lease is an operating lease. (For simplicity, this example assumes that the accounting rules governing these hypothetical companies do not mandate either type of lease.) The present value of lease payments and fair value of the equipment is €100,000.

At the beginning of Year 1, before entering into the lease agreement, both companies reported liabilities of €100,000 and equity of

€200,000. Assets on hand include the asset about to be leased. Each year the companies receive total revenues of €50,000 cash, apart from any revenue earned on the lease. Assume the companies have a tax rate of 30 percent, and use the same accounting for financial and tax purposes. Both companies' discount rate is 10 percent. In order to focus only on the differences in the type of lease, assume that neither company incurs revenues or expenses other than those associated with the lease and that neither invests excess cash.

1. Which company reports higher expenses/net income in Year 1? Over the four years?
2. Which company reports higher total cash flow over the four years? Cash flow from operations?
3. Based on ROE, how do the two companies' profitability measures compare?

Solution to 1: LOPER reports higher expenses in Year 1 because, under an operating lease, the lessor retains ownership of the asset and continues to report associated depreciation expense. DIRFIN, treating the lease as a finance lease, does not reflect ownership of the asset or the associated depreciation expense. DIRFIN has higher net income in Year 1 because the interest revenue component of the lease payment in that year exceeds the lease revenue net of depreciation reported by LOPER.

On its income statement, LOPER reports depreciation expense for the asset it has leased and lease revenue based on the lease payment received. The table below shows LOPER's depreciation and book values on leased equipment by year.[24]

Year	Cost (a)	Depreciation Expense (b)	Accumulated Depreciation (c)	Book Value (Year End) (d)
1	€100,000	€ 25,000	€ 25,000	€75,000
2	100,000	25,000	50,000	50,000
3	100,000	25,000	75,000	25,000
4	100,000	25,000	100,000	0
		€100,000		

- Column (a) is the cost of €100,000 of the leased equipment.
- Column (b) is depreciation expense of €25,000 per year, calculated using the straight-line method as the cost less the salvage value divided by the useful life [(€100,000 − €0) ÷ 4 years].
- Column (c) is the accumulated depreciation on the leased asset calculated as the prior year's accumulated depreciation plus the current year's depreciation expense.

[24] The computations included throughout the example were made using an Excel worksheet; small apparent discrepancies in the calculations are due to the rounding.

- Column (d) is the ending book value of the leased equipment, which is the difference between the cost and accumulated depreciation.

DIRFIN, however, records the lease as a direct financing lease. It removes the leased asset from its assets and records a lease receivable. On its income statement, DIRFIN reports interest revenues earned from financing the lease. The table below shows DIRFIN's interest revenues and carrying amounts on the lease receivable.

Year	Lease Receivable, 1 January (a)	Annual Lease Payment Received, 1 January (b)	Interest (at 10%; Accrued in Previous Year) (c)	Reduction of Lease Receivable, 1 January (d)	Lease Receivable on 31 December after Lease Payment on 1 January of Same Year (e)
1	€100,000	€ 28,679	€ 0	€ 28,679	€71,321
2	71,321	28,679	7,132	21,547	49,774
3	49,774	28,679	4,977	23,702	26,072
4	26,072	28,679	2,607	26,072	0
		€114,717	€14,717	€100,000	

- Column (a) is the lease receivable at the beginning of the year.
- Column (b) is annual lease payment received at the beginning of the year, which is allocated to interest and reduction of the lease receivable.
- Column (c) is interest accrued in the previous year calculated as the lease receivable outstanding for the year times the interest rate.
- Column (d) is the reduction of the lease receivable, which is the difference between the annual lease payments received and interest. Because the lease payment is due on 1 January, this amount of interest is a receivable at the end of the *prior* year and is reported as interest revenue in the *prior* year.
- Column (e) is the lease receivable after the lease payment is received and at the end of the year. It is the lease receivable at 1 January (Column a) less the reduction of the lease receivable (Column d).

The table below summarises and compares the income statement effects of the lease for DIRFIN and LOPER. Notice that over the four-year lease, both companies report the same total amount of revenue, but DIRFIN's revenues in the earlier years of the lease are higher than the net of lease revenues less depreciation reported by LOPER in those years.

	DIRFIN	LOPER			
Year	Lease Revenue	Lease Revenue	Depreciation Expense	Total	Difference
1	€ 7,132	€ 28,679	€ 25,000	€ 3,679	€ 3,453
2	4,977	28,679	25,000	3,679	1,298
3	2,607	28,679	25,000	3,679	(1,072)
4	—	28,679	25,000	3,679	(−3,679)
Total	€14,717	€114,717	€100,000	€14,717	€ 0

The complete income statements for DIRFIN and LOPER are presented below. Notice that, under the assumption that the same accounting is used for financial and tax purposes, DIRFIN's taxes are higher than those of LOPER in Years 1 and 2.

Income Statements	DIRFIN					LOPER				
	1	2	3	4	Total	1	2	3	4	Total
Sales	€50,000	€50,000	€50,000	€50,000	€200,000	€50,000	€50,000	€50,000	€50,000	€200,000
Depreciation expense						(25,000)	(25,000)	(25,000)	(25,000)	(100,000)
Interest revenue	7,132	4,977	2,607		14,717					
Lease revenue	—	—	—	—	—	28,679	28,679	28,679	28,679	114,717
Income before taxes	€57,132	€54,977	€52,607	€50,000	€214,717	€53,679	€53,679	€53,679	€53,679	€214,717
Tax expense	17,140	16,493	15,782	15,000	64,415	16,104	16,104	16,104	16,104	64,415
Net income	€39,992	€38,484	€36,825	€35,000	€150,302	€37,575	€37,575	€37,575	€37,575	€150,302

Solution to 2: Looking at the statement of cash flows, observe that operating cash flows reported by DIRFIN are lower, but investing cash flows are higher than LOPER. Over the four years, both DIRFIN and LOPER report the same total change in cash.

Statements of Cash Flows	DIRFIN					LOPER				
	1	2	3	4	Total	1	2	3	4	Total
Net income	€39,992	€38,484	€36,825	€35,000	€150,302	€37,575	€37,575	€37,575	€37,575	€150,302
Increase (decrease) in interest receivable	7,132	(2,155)	(2,370)	(2,607)	0					
Add back depreciation expense	—	—	—	—	—	25,000	25,000	25,000	25,000	100,000
Operating cash flows	€32,860	€40,639	€39,195	€37,607	€150,302	€62,575	€62,575	€62,575	€62,575	€250,302
Payments received on finance leases	28,679	21,547	23,702	26,072	100,000					
Investing cash flows	28,679	21,547	23,702	26,072	100,000	—	—	—	—	—
Change in cash	€61,540	€62,186	€62,897	€63,679	€250,302	€62,575	€62,575	€62,575	€62,575	€250,302

Solution to 3: Based on ROE, DIRFIN appears more profitable than LOPER in the early years of the lease.

Computing ROE requires forecasting shareholders' equity. In general, Ending shareholders' equity = Beginning shareholders' equity + Net income + Other comprehensive income − Dividends + Net capital contributions by shareholders. Because the companies in this example do not have other comprehensive income, do not pay dividends, and have no capital contributions, Ending shareholders' equity = Beginning shareholders' equity + Net income. The forecasts are presented below.

DIRFIN	0	1	2	3	4
Retained earnings	€ 0	€ 39,992	€ 78,477	€115,302	€150,302
Common stock	200,000	200,000	200,000	200,000	200,000
Total shareholders' equity	€200,000	€239,992	€278,477	€315,302	€350,302

LOPER	0	1	2	3	4
Retained earnings	€ 0	€ 37,575	€ 75,151	€112,726	€150,302
Common stock	200,000	200,000	200,000	200,000	200,000
Total shareholders' equity	€200,000	€237,575	€275,151	€312,726	€350,302

ROE is calculated as net income divided by average shareholders' equity. For example, DIRFIN Inc. had Year 1 ROE of 18.2 percent: €39,992/[(€200,000 + €239,992)/2].

	DIRFIN				LOPER			
	1	2	3	4	1	2	3	4
ROE	18.2%	14.8%	12.4%	10.5%	17.2%	14.7%	12.8%	11.3%

From the comparisons above, DIRFIN looks more profitable in the early years of the lease, but less profitable in the later years.

U.S. GAAP make a further distinction in defining two types of non-operating leases: 1) **direct financing leases**, and 2) **sales-type leases** from the lessor's perspective.[25] A direct financing lease results when the present value of lease payments (and thus the amount recorded as a lease receivable) equals the carrying amount of the leased asset. Because there is no "profit" on the asset itself, the lessor is essentially providing financing to the lessee, and the revenues earned by the lessor are financing in nature (i.e., interest revenue). If, however, the present value of lease payments (and thus the amount recorded as a lease receivable) exceeds the carrying value of the leased asset, the lease is treated as a sale.

[25] IFRS does not make the distinction between a sales-type lease and a direct financing lease. However, a similar treatment to "sales-type" is allowed for finance leases originated by "manufacturer or dealer lessors," within the general provisions for finance leases.

When a company enters into a sales-type lease, a lease agreement in which the present value of lease payment is greater than the value of the leased asset to the lessor, it will show a profit on the transaction in the year of inception and interest revenue over the life of the lease.

EXAMPLE 14

Financial Statement Impact of a Sales-type Lease for the Lessor

Assume a (hypothetical) company, Selnow Inc., owns a piece of machinery and enters into an agreement to lease the machinery on 1 January Year 1. In the lease contract, the company requires four annual payments of €28,679 starting on 1 January Year 1. The present value of the lease payments (using a 10 percent discount rate) is €100,000, and the fair value of the equipment is €90,000. The useful life of the machinery is four years and its salvage value is zero.

1. Is the lease a direct financing or sales-type lease?
2. What is Selnow's income related to the lease in Year 1? In Year 2? Ignore taxes.

Solution to 1: This is a sales-type lease: The present value of lease payments is more than the lessor's carrying amount of the leased asset. The difference between the present value of the lease payments and the carrying amount of the leased asset is the lessor's profit from selling the machinery. The lessor will record a profit of €10,000 on the sale of the leased equipment in Year 1 (€100,000 present value of lease payments receivable less €90,000 value of leased equipment).

Solution to 2: In Year 1, Selnow shows income of €17,132 related to the lease. One part of this is the €10,000 gain on the sale of the lease equipment (sales revenues of €100,000 less costs of goods sold of €90,000). Selnow also shows interest revenue of €7,132 on its financing of the lease (lease receivable of €71,321 after the initial lease payment is received times the 10 percent discount rate). In Year 2, Selnow reports only the interest revenue of €4,977 (lease receivable of €49,774 after the 1 January lease payment is received times the 10 percent discount rate). The table below shows lease payments received, interest revenue, and reduction of the lease receivable for Selnow's sales-type lease. Note that this table is the same as DIRFIN's table in the previous example with the direct financing lease. They are the same because the present value of the lease payments in both cases is the same. It is the fair value of the equipment that differs between the two examples.

Year	Lease Receivable, 1 January (a)	Annual Lease Payment Received, 1 January (b)	Interest (at 10%; Accrued in Previous Year) (c)	Reduction of Lease Receivable, 1 January (d)	Lease Receivable on 31 December after Lease Payment on 1 January of Same Year (e)
1	€100,000	€ 28,679	€ 0	€ 28,679	€71,321
2	71,321	28,679	7,132	21,547	49,774
3	49,774	28,679	4,977	23,702	26,072
4	26,072	28,679	2,607	26,072	0
		€114,717	€14,717	€100,000	

SUMMARY

This reading describes how companies' decisions about accounting for tangible and intangible long-lived assets affect their financial statements. Compared to expensing an expenditure in the current period, capitalising an expenditure results in higher profits and higher operating cash flows in the year of the expenditure. For capitalised amounts that are to be depreciated (or amortised), estimating a longer useful life and a higher salvage value results in higher profits in the earlier years of the asset's life.

After an asset is acquired, if its value declines such that its recoverable value is lower than its carrying amount, a company must record an impairment charge against income to reflect that change. Under IFRS, companies can subsequently revalue the asset if its value increases, but under U.S. GAAP, revaluation is not permitted. Another key difference between IFRS and U.S. GAAP reporting for long-lived assets is that IFRS (but *not* U.S. GAAP) offer companies two distinct alternatives for reporting long-lived assets: the historical cost model or the revaluation model.

As an alternative to acquiring an asset, a company may choose to lease an asset. Leases are generally characterised as either operating leases, which is similar to renting the asset, or capital leases, which is similar to purchasing the asset. As a lessee, a capital lease increases both the company's reported assets and liabilities, generally increasing leverage. An operating lease does not change the company's balance sheet.

Key points include the following:

- Expenditures related to long-lived assets are included as part of the value of assets on the balance sheet, i.e., capitalised, if they are expected to provide future benefits, typically beyond one year.
- Although capitalising expenditures, rather than expensing, results in higher reported profit in the initial year, it results in lower profits in subsequent years; however, if a company continues to purchase similar or increasing amounts of assets each year, the profitability-enhancing effect of capitalising continues.
- Capitalising an expenditure rather than expensing it results in greater amounts reported as cash from operations.
- Including capitalised interest in the calculation of interest coverage ratios provides a better assessment of a company's solvency.
- If companies apply different approaches to capitalising software development costs, adjustments can be made to make the two comparable.
- Significant estimates required for depreciation calculations include the useful life of the equipment (or its total lifetime productive capacity) and its expected residual value at the end of that useful life. A longer useful life and higher expected residual value decrease the amount of annual depreciation relative to a shorter useful life and lower expected residual value.
- Intangible assets with finite useful lives are amortised over their useful lives.
- Intangible assets with indefinite useful lives are not amortised, but are tested for impairment whenever changes in events or circumstances indicate that the carrying amount of an asset may not be recoverable (and at least annually in the case of identifiable intangible assets with indefinite useful lives and goodwill).

- In contrast with depreciation and amortisation charges, which serve to allocate the cost of a long-lived asset over its useful life, impairment charges reflect a decline in the fair value of an asset to an amount lower than its carrying amount.
- Impairment disclosures can provide useful information about a company's expected cash flows.
- Under IFRS, companies can use the historical cost model or the revaluation model to report long-lived assets.
- Under U.S. GAAP, the value of long-lived assets must be reported at depreciated historical cost. This value may be decreased by impairment charges, but cannot be increased. IFRS, however, permit impairment losses to be reversed.
- Estimates of average age and remaining useful life of a company's assets reflect the relationship between assets accounted for on a historical cost basis and depreciation amounts.
- The average remaining useful life of a company's assets can be estimated as net PPE divided by depreciation expense, although the accounting useful life may not necessarily correspond to the economic useful life.
- To estimate the average age of the asset base, divide accumulated depreciation by depreciation expense.
- Accounting standards generally define two types of leases: operating leases and finance (or capital) leases. U.S. GAAP specify four criteria to determine when a lease is classified as a capital lease. IFRS are less prescriptive in determining the classification of a lease as a finance lease.
- When a lessee reports a lease as an operating lease rather than a finance lease, it usually appears more profitable in early years of the lease and less so later, and it appears more solvent over the whole period.
- When a company has a substantial amount of operating leases, adjusting reported financials to include the impact of capitalising these leases better reflects the company's solvency position.
- When a lessor reports a lease as a finance lease rather than an operating lease, it usually appears more profitable in early years of the lease.
- In direct financing leases under U.S. GAAP, a lessor earns only interest revenue. In a sales-type lease under U.S. GAAP, a lessor earns both interest revenue and a profit (or loss) on the sale of the leased asset.

PRACTICE PROBLEMS FOR READING 22

The following information relates to Questions 1–6[1]

Melanie Hart, CFA, is a transportation analyst. Hart has been asked to write a research report on Altai Mountain Rail Company (AMRC). Like other companies in the railroad industry, AMRC's operations are capital intensive, with significant investments in such long-lived tangible assets as property, plant, and equipment. In November of 2008, AMRC's board of directors hired a new team to manage the company. In reviewing the company's 2009 annual report, Hart is concerned about some of the accounting choices that the new management has made. These choices differ from those of the previous management and from common industry practice. Hart has highlighted the following statements from the company's annual report:

Statement 1: "In 2009, AMRC spent significant amounts on track replacement and similar improvements. AMRC expensed rather than capitalised a significant proportion of these expenditures."

Statement 2: "AMRC uses the straight-line method of depreciation for both financial and tax reporting purposes to account for plant and equipment."

Statement 3: "In 2009, AMRC recognized an impairment loss of €50 million on a fleet of locomotives. The impairment loss was reported as 'other income' in the income statement and reduced the carrying amount of the assets on the balance sheet."

Statement 4: "AMRC acquires the use of many of its assets, including a large portion of its fleet of rail cars, under long-term lease contracts. In 2009, AMRC acquired the use of equipment with a fair value of €200 million under 20-year lease contracts. These leases were classified as operating leases. Prior to 2009, most of these lease contracts were classified as finance leases."

Exhibits 1 and 2 contain AMRC's 2009 consolidated income statement and balance sheet. AMRC prepares its financial statements in accordance with International Financial Reporting Standards.

EXHIBIT 1 Consolidated Statement of Income

For the Years Ended 31 December	2009		2008	
	€ Millions	% Revenues	€ Millions	% Revenues
Operating revenues	2,600	100.0	2,300	100.0
Operating expenses				
Depreciation	(200)	(7.7)	(190)	(8.3)
Lease payments	(210)	(8.1)	(195)	(8.5)
Other operating expense	(1,590)	(61.1)	(1,515)	(65.9)
Total operating expenses	(2,000)	(76.9)	(1,900)	(82.6)

(Exhibit continued on next page . . .)

[1] Developed by Christopher Anderson, CFA (Lawrence KS, U.S.A.).

EXHIBIT 1 (continued)

For the Years Ended 31 December	2009		2008	
	€ Millions	% Revenues	€ Millions	% Revenues
Operating income	600	23.1	400	17.4
Other income	(50)	(1.9)	—	0.0
Interest expense	(73)	(2.8)	(69)	(3.0)
Income before taxes	477	18.4	331	14.4
Income taxes	(189)	(7.3)	(125)	(5.4)
Net income	288	11.1	206	9.0

EXHIBIT 2 Consolidated Balance Sheet

As of 31 December	2009		2008	
Assets	€ Millions	% Assets	€ Millions	% Assets
Current assets	500	9.4	450	8.5
Property & equipment:				
Land	700	13.1	700	13.2
Plant & equipment	6,000	112.1	5,800	109.4
Total property & equipment	6,700	125.2	6,500	122.6
Accumulated depreciation	(1,850)	(34.6)	(1,650)	(31.1)
Net property & equipment	4,850	90.6	4,850	91.5
Total assets	5,350	100.0	5,300	100.0
Liabilities and Shareholders' Equity				
Current liabilities	480	9.0	430	8.1
Long-term debt	1,030	19.3	1,080	20.4
Other long-term provisions and liabilities	1,240	23.1	1,440	27.2
Total liabilities	2,750	51.4	2,950	55.7
Shareholders' equity				
Common stock and paid-in-surplus	760	14.2	760	14.3
Retained earnings	1,888	35.3	1,600	30.2
Other comprehensive losses	(48)	(0.9)	(10)	(0.2)
Total shareholders' equity	2,600	48.6	2,350	44.3
Total liabilities & shareholders' equity	5,350	100.0	5,300	100.0

1. With respect to Statement 1, which of the following is the *most likely* effect of management's decision to expense rather than capitalise these expenditures?
   - A. 2009 net profit margin is higher than if the expenditures had been capitalised.
   - B. 2009 total asset turnover is lower than if the expenditures had been capitalised.
   - C. Future profit growth will be higher than if the expenditures had been capitalised.
2. With respect to Statement 2, what would be the *most likely* effect in 2010 if AMRC were to switch to an accelerated depreciation method for both financial and tax reporting?
   - A. Net profit margin would decrease.
   - B. Total asset turnover would increase.
   - C. Cash flow from operating activities would increase.
3. With respect to Statement 3, what is the *most likely* effect of the impairment loss?
   - A. Net income in years prior to 2009 was likely understated.
   - B. Net profit margins in years after 2009 will likely exceed the 2009 net profit margin.
   - C. Cash flow from operating activities in 2009 was likely lower due to the impairment loss.
4. Based on Exhibits 1 and 2, the *best estimate* of the average remaining useful life of the company's plant and equipment at the end of 2009 is:
   - A. 20.75 years.
   - B. 24.25 years.
   - C. 30.00 years.
5. With respect to Statement 4, if AMRC had used its old classification method for its leases instead of its new classification method, its 2009 total asset turnover ratio would *most likely* be:
   - A. lower.
   - B. higher.
   - C. the same.
6. With respect to Statement 4 and Exhibit 1, if AMRC had used its old classification method for its leases instead of its new classification method, the *most likely* effect on its 2009 ratios would be a:
   - A. higher net profit margin.
   - B. higher fixed asset turnover.
   - C. higher total liabilities-to-total assets ratio.

The following information relates to Questions 7–13[2]

Brian Jordan is interviewing for a junior equity analyst position at Orion Investment Advisors. As part of the interview process, Mary Benn, Orion's Director of Research, provides Jordan with information about two hypothetical

[2] Developed by Philip Fanara Jr., CFA (Hyattsville MD, U.S.A.).

companies, Alpha and Beta, and asks him to comment on the information on their financial statements and ratios. Both companies prepare their financial statements in accordance with International Financial Reporting Standards (IFRS) and are identical in all respects except for their accounting choices.

Jordan is told that at the beginning of the current fiscal year, both companies purchased a major new computer system and began building new manufacturing plants for their own use. Alpha capitalised and Beta expensed the cost of the computer system; Alpha capitalised and Beta expensed the interest costs associated with the construction of the manufacturing plants. In mid-year, both companies leased new office headquarters. Alpha classified the lease as an operating lease, and Beta classified it as a finance lease.

Benn asks Jordan, "What was the impact of these decisions on each company's current fiscal year financial statements and ratios?"

Jordan responds, "Alpha's decision to capitalise the cost of its new computer system instead of expensing it results in lower net income, lower total assets, and higher cash flow from operating activities in the current fiscal year. Alpha's decision to capitalise its interest costs instead of expensing them results in a lower fixed asset turnover ratio and a higher interest coverage ratio. Alpha's decision to classify its lease as an operating lease instead of a finance lease results in higher net income, higher cash flow from operating activities, and stronger solvency and activity ratios compared to Beta."

Jordan is told that Alpha uses the straight-line depreciation method and Beta uses an accelerated depreciation method; both companies estimate the same useful lives for long-lived assets. Many companies in their industry use the units-of-production method.

Benn asks Jordan, "What are the financial statement implications of each depreciation method, and how do you determine a company's need to reinvest in its productive capacity?"

Jordan replies, "All other things being equal, the straight-line depreciation method results in the least variability of net profit margin over time, while an accelerated depreciation method results in a declining trend in net profit margin over time. The units-of-production can result in a net profit margin trend that is quite variable. I use a three-step approach to estimate a company's need to reinvest in its productive capacity. First, I estimate the average age of the assets by dividing net property, plant, and equipment by annual depreciation expense. Second, I estimate the average remaining useful life of the assets by dividing accumulated depreciation by depreciation expense. Third, I add the estimates of the average remaining useful life and the average age of the assets in order to determine the total useful life."

Jordan is told that at the end of the current fiscal year, Alpha revalued a manufacturing plant; this increased its reported carrying amount by 15 percent. There was no previous downward revaluation of the plant. Beta recorded an impairment loss on a manufacturing plant; this reduced its carrying by 10 percent.

Benn asks Jordan "What was the impact of these decisions on each company's current fiscal year financial ratios?"

Jordan responds, "Beta's impairment loss increases its debt to total assets and fixed asset turnover ratios, and lowers its cash flow from operating activities. Alpha's revaluation increases its debt to capital and return on assets ratios, and reduces its return on equity."

At the end of the interview, Benn thanks Jordan for his time and states that a hiring decision will be made shortly.

7. Jordan's response about the financial statement impact of Alpha's decision to capitalise the cost of its new computer system is most likely *correct* with respect to:

A. lower net income.

B. lower total assets.

C. higher cash flow from operating activities.

8. Jordan's response about the ratio impact of Alpha's decision to capitalise interest costs is most likely *correct* with respect to the:

A. interest coverage ratio.

B. fixed asset turnover ratio.

C. interest coverage and fixed asset turnover ratios.

9. Jordan's response about the impact of Alpha's decision to classify its lease as an operating lease instead of finance lease is most likely *incorrect* with respect to:

A. net income.

B. solvency and activity ratios.

C. cash flow from operating activities.

10. Jordan's response about the impact of the different depreciation methods on net profit margin is most likely *incorrect* with respect to:

A. accelerated depreciation.

B. straight-line depreciation.

C. units-of-production depreciation.

11. Jordan's response about his approach to estimating a company's need to reinvest in its productive capacity is most likely *correct* regarding:

A. estimating the average age of the asset base.

B. estimating the total useful life of the asset base.

C. estimating the average remaining useful life of the asset base.

12. Jordan's response about the effect of Beta's impairment loss is most likely *incorrect* with respect to the impact on its:

A. debt to total assets.

B. fixed asset turnover.

C. cash flow from operating activities.

13. Jordan's response about the effect of Alpha's revaluation is most likely *correct* with respect to the impact on its:

A. return on equity.

B. return on assets.

C. debt to capital ratio.

SOLUTIONS FOR READING 22

1. C is correct. Expensing rather than capitalising an investment in long-term assets will result in higher expenses and lower net income and net profit margin in the current year. Future years' incomes will not include depreciation expense related to these expenditures. Consequently, year-to-year growth in profitability will be higher. If the expenses had been capitalised, the carrying amount of the assets would have been higher and the 2009 total asset turnover would have been lower.

2. C is correct. In 2010, switching to an accelerated depreciation method would increase depreciation expense and decrease income before taxes, taxes payable, and net income. Cash flow from operating activities would increase because of the resulting tax savings.

3. B is correct. 2009 net income and net profit margin are lower because of the impairment loss. Consequently, net profit margins in subsequent years are likely to be higher. An impairment loss suggests that insufficient depreciation expense was recognized in prior years, and net income was overstated in prior years. The impairment loss is a non-cash item and will not affect operating cash flows.

4. A is correct. The estimated average remaining useful life is 20.75 years.

$$\begin{aligned}\text{Estimate of remaining useful life} &= \text{Net plant and equipment}\\ &\quad \div \text{Annual depreciation expense}\\ \text{Net plant and equipment} &= \text{Gross P\&E} - \text{Accumulated depreciation}\\ &= €6000 - €1850 = €4150\\ \text{Estimate of remaining useful life} &= \text{Net P\&E} \div \text{Depreciation expense}\\ &= €4150 \div €200 = 20.75\end{aligned}$$

5. A is correct. When leases are classified as finance leases, the lessee initially reports an asset and liability at a carrying amount equal to the lower of the fair value of the leased asset or the present value of the future lease payments. Under an operating lease, the lessee does not report an asset or liability. Therefore, total asset turnover (total revenue ÷ average total assets) would be lower if the leases were classified as finance leases.

6. C is correct. Total liabilities-to-assets would be higher. When leases are classified as finance leases, the lessee initially reports an asset and liability at a carrying amount equal to the lower of the fair value of the leased asset or the present value of the future lease payments. Both the numerator and denominator would increase by an equal amount, but the proportional increase in the numerator is higher and the ratio would be higher. The following exhibit shows what would happen to 2009 total liabilities, assets, and total liabilities-to-assets if €200 million, the fair value of the leased equipment, is added to AMRC's total liabilities and assets. This simple example ignores the impact of accounting for the 2009 lease payment.

	2009 Actual Under Operating Lease	2009 Hypothetical Under Finance Lease
Total liabilities	€2,750	€2,950
Total assets	€5,350	€5,550
Total liabilities-to-assets	51.4%	53.2%

The depreciation and interest expense under a finance lease tends to be higher than the operating lease payment in the early years of the lease. The finance lease would result in lower net income and net profit margin. Long-lived (fixed) assets are higher under a finance lease and fixed asset turnover is lower.

7. C is correct. The decision to capitalise the costs of the new computer system results in higher cash flow from operating activities; the expenditure is reported as an outflow of investing activities. The company allocates the capitalised amount over the asset's useful life as depreciation or amortisation expense rather than expensing it in the year of expenditure. Net income and total assets are higher in the current fiscal year.

8. B is correct. Alpha's fixed asset turnover will be lower because the capitalised interest will appear on the balance sheet as part of the asset being constructed. Therefore, fixed assets will be higher and the fixed asset turnover ratio (total revenue/average net fixed assets) will be lower than if it had expensed these costs. Capitalised interest appears on the balance sheet as part of the asset being constructed instead of being reported as interest expense in the period incurred. However, the interest coverage ratio should be based on interest payments, not interest expense (earnings before interest and taxes/interest payments), and should be unchanged. To provide a true picture of a company's interest coverage, the entire amount of interest expenditure, both the capitalised portion and the expensed portion, should be used in calculating interest coverage ratios.

9. C is correct. The cash flow from operating activities will be lower, not higher, because the full lease payment is treated as an operating cash outflow. With a finance lease, only the portion of the lease payment relating to interest expense potentially reduces operating cash outflows. A company reporting a lease as an operating lease will typically show higher profits in early years, because the lease expense is less than the sum of the interest and depreciation expense. The company reporting the lease as an operating lease will typically report stronger solvency and activity ratios.

10. A is correct. Accelerated depreciation will result in an improving, not declining, net profit margin over time, because the amount of depreciation expense declines each year. Under straight-line depreciation, the amount of depreciation expense will remain the same each year. Under the units-of-production method, the amount of depreciation expense reported each year varies with the number of units produced.

11. B is correct. The estimated average total useful life of a company's assets is calculated by adding the estimates of the average remaining useful life and the average age of the assets. The average age of the assets is estimated by dividing accumulated depreciation by depreciation expense. The average remaining useful life of the asset base is estimated by dividing net property, plant, and equipment by annual depreciation expense.

12. C is correct. The impairment loss is a non-cash charge and will not affect cash flow from operating activities. The debt to total assets and fixed asset turnover ratios will increase, because the impairment loss will reduce the carrying amount of fixed assets and therefore total assets.

13. A is correct. In an asset revaluation, the carrying amount of the assets increases. The increase in the asset's carrying amount bypasses the income statement and is reported as other comprehensive income and appears in equity under the heading of revaluation surplus. Therefore, shareholders' equity will increase, but net income will not be affected, so return on equity will decline. Return on assets and debt to capital ratios will also decrease.

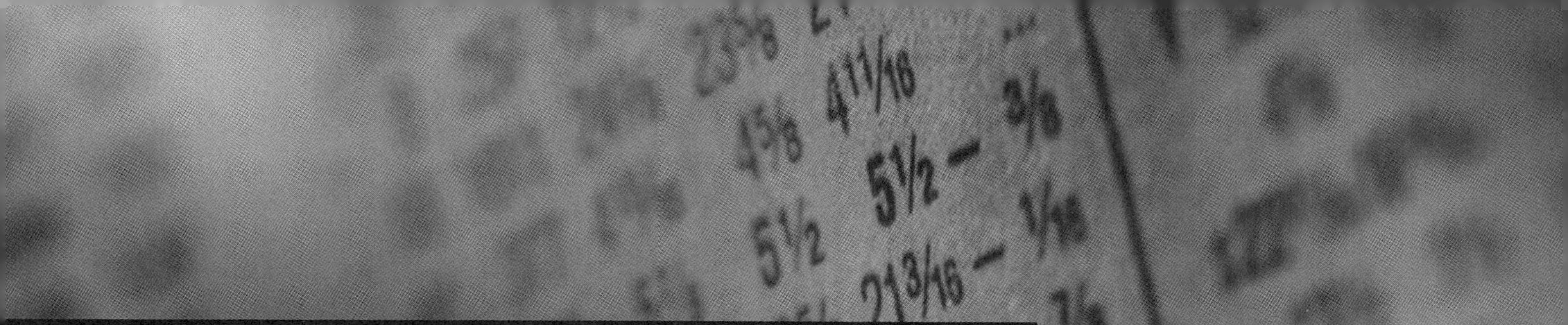

STUDY SESSION 6

FINANCIAL REPORTING AND ANALYSIS:

Intercorporate Investments, Post-Employment and Share-Based Compensation, and Multinational Operations

Intercorporate investments receive different accounting treatments depending on the percentage ownership, amount of control, and other variables concerning the relation between the company making the investment and the investee.

An analysis of intercorporate investments is necessary to separate operating performance from investing performance and to understand the potential accounting distortions that arise as a result of accounting rules and/or earnings management ploys that may occur. The analyst also must understand the comparative financial statement effects that occur from the consolidation or proportionate consolidation of intercorporate investments.

Mergers and acquisitions can also be an important component of management strategy. The accounting standards that govern business combinations are the result of a joint project between the IASB and the FASB. Both IFRS and U.S. GAAP have eliminated the use of the uniting of interest (pooling of interest) method. The acquisition method, which replaces the purchase method, is now the only accepted method. The structure and scope of business combinations create comparability challenges because the financial statements of the acquiring company may be radically changed. The analyst should understand the comparative financial statement effects that occur from business combinations, and the consolidation or proportionate consolidation of intercorporate investments.

In 2009, the FASB eliminated the use of Qualifying Special Purpose Entities (QSPEs), changed the requirements for derecognizing financial assets, and increased the disclosure requirements for companies that are involved with Special Purpose Entities (SPEs) or Variable Interest Entities (VIEs). The new standards have increased the transparency and comparability of financial statements and further converged U.S. GAAP with IFRS.

Note:
New rulings and/or pronouncements issued after the publication of the readings in financial reporting and analysis may cause some of the information in these readings to become dated. Candidates are expected to be familiar with the overall analytical framework contained in the study session readings, as well as the implications of alternative accounting methods for financial analysis and valuation, as provided in the assigned readings. Candidates are not responsible for changes that occur after the material was written.

Recent changes in accounting for pensions and other post-employment benefits require more obligations to be reported on the balance sheet. IFRS and U.S. GAAP have both changed in a similar, but not identical fashion. Employee stock options were previously excluded from the income statement, but were disclosed in the footnotes. IFRS and U.S. GAAP now require employee stock options to be expensed.

Multinational companies often have subsidiaries in different countries that maintain their books and records in a local currency. Floating exchange rates present an additional challenge. Transactions and translations in a parent company's financial statements must be analyzed to evaluate a company's performance and financial position.

READING ASSIGNMENTS

Reading 23 Intercorporate Investments
International Financial Statement Analysis, by Thomas R. Robinson, CFA, Jan Hendrik van Greuning, CFA, Elaine Henry, CFA, and Michael A. Broihahn, CFA

Reading 24 Employee Compensation: Post-Employment and Share-Based
International Financial Statement Analysis, by Thomas R. Robinson, CFA, Jan Hendrik van Greuning, CFA, Elaine Henry, CFA, and Michael A. Broihahn, CFA

Reading 25 Multinational Operations
International Financial Statement Analysis, by Thomas R. Robinson, CFA, Jan Hendrik van Greuning, CFA, Elaine Henry, CFA, and Michael A. Broihahn, CFA

INTERCORPORATE INVESTMENTS

by Susan Perry Williams

READING 23

LEARNING OUTCOMES

The candidate should be able to:	Mastery
a. describe the classification, measurement, and disclosure under the International Financial Reporting Standards (IFRS) for 1) investments in financial assets, 2) investments in associates, 3) joint ventures, 4) business combinations, and 5) special purpose and variable interest entities (SPEs, VIEs);	□
b. distinguish between IFRS and U.S. GAAP in the classification, measurement, and disclosure of investments in financial assets, investments in associates, joint ventures, business combinations, and special purpose and variable interest entities;	□
c. analyze the effects on financial ratios of the different methods used to account for intercorporate investments.	□

INTRODUCTION 1

Intercorporate investments can have a significant impact on the investing entity's financial performance and position. Companies invest in the debt and equity securities of other companies to diversify their asset base, enter new markets, obtain competitive advantages, and achieve additional profitability. Debt securities include commercial paper, corporate and government bonds and notes, redeemable preferred stock, and asset-backed securities. Equity securities include common stock and nonredeemable preferred stock. The percentage of equity ownership a company acquires in an investee depends on the resources available, the ability to acquire the shares, and the desired level of influence or control.

Note:
New rulings and/or pronouncements issued after the publication of the readings in financial reporting and analysis may cause some of the information in these readings to become dated. Candidates are expected to be familiar with the overall analytical framework contained in the study session readings, as well as the implications of alternative accounting methods for financial analysis and valuation, as provided in the assigned readings. Candidates are not responsible for changes that occur after the material was written.

The accounting standards that apply to the classification, measurement, and disclosure of intercorporate investments are increasingly reflective of a joint project undertaken by the International Accounting Standards Board (IASB) and the U.S. Financial Accounting Standards Board (FASB). The objective of this project is to remove differences between the sets of standards and to converge on a set of high-quality standards. The IASB and the FASB have issued a series of pronouncements that focus on the measurement, classification, and disclosure of intercorporate investments. These pronouncements have reduced differences between the two accounting standards and have improved the relevance, transparency, and comparability of information provided in financial statements.

As examples of the movement towards convergence, in December of 2007, the FASB issued two new standards: SFAS 141(R), *Business Combinations*,[1] and SFAS 160, *Noncontrolling Interests in Consolidated Financial Statements*.[2] These statements introduced significant changes in the accounting for and reporting of business acquisitions and noncontrolling interests in a subsidiary. Both apply to business combinations occurring on or after 15 December 2008, with early adoption prohibited. In January 2008, the IASB revised IFRS 3, *Business Combinations* and amended IAS 27, *Consolidated and Separate Financial Statements*. These new requirements became effective on 1 July 2009, although entities were permitted to adopt them earlier. This reading includes accounting standards issued by IASB and FASB through 31 December 2008.

Although convergence between IFRS and U.S. GAAP is occurring and accounting is the same or similar for many transactions, differences still remain. In the case of differences, there is generally enough transparency in the disclosures to allow financial statement users to adjust for the differences. Understanding the appropriate accounting treatment for different intercorporate investments and the similarities and differences that exist between IFRS and U.S. GAAP will enable analysts to make better comparisons between companies and improve investment decision making. The terminology used in this reading is IFRS oriented. U.S. GAAP may not use identical terminology but in most cases, the terminology is similar.

This reading is organized as follows: Section 2 explains the basic categorization of corporate investments. Section 3 describes reporting for investments in financial assets; in this reading, financial assets are limited to debt and equity securities of other entities. Section 4 describes reporting for investments in associates where significant influence can exist, and Section 5 describes reporting for joint ventures, a common, important type of investment where control is shared. Section 6 describes reporting for business combinations, the parent/subsidiary relationship, and consolidated financial statements. Section 7 describes reporting for variable

[1] FASB ASC Topic 805 [Business Combinations].

[2] FASB ASC Topic 810 [Consolidation].

interest and special purpose entities. A summary and practice problems in the CFA Institute item set format complete the reading.

BASIC CORPORATE INVESTMENT CATEGORIES

2

In general, investments in marketable debt and equity securities can be categorized as 1) investments in financial assets in which the investor has no significant influence or control over the operations of the investee, 2) investments in associates in which the investor can exert significant influence (but not control) over the investee, and 3) business combinations, including investments in subsidiaries, in which the investor has control over the investee. The distinction between investments in financial assets, investments in associates, and business combinations is based on the degree of influence or control rather than purely on the percent holding. However, lack of influence is generally presumed when the investor holds less than a 20 percent equity interest, significant influence is generally presumed between 20 percent and 50 percent, and control is presumed when the percentage of ownership exceeds 50 percent. A fourth category, investments in joint ventures, indicates shared control by two or more entities.

The following excerpt is from the 2007 Annual Report of Volvo Group, a Swedish manufacturer of commercial vehicles, and illustrates the categorization in practice:

> Consolidated financial statements comprise the Parent Company, subsidiaries, joint ventures, and associated companies. Subsidiaries are defined as companies in which Volvo holds more than 50% of the voting rights or in which Volvo otherwise has a controlling interest. Joint ventures are companies over which Volvo has joint control together with one or more external parties. Associated companies are companies in which Volvo has a significant influence, which is normally when Volvo's holding equals at least 20% but less than 50% of the voting rights.

A summary of the accounting treatments and relevant standards for various types of corporate investment is presented in Exhibit 1 (the headings in Exhibit 1 use the terminology of IFRS; U.S. GAAP categorizes intercorporate investments similarly but not identically). The reader should be alert to the fact that value measurement and/or the treatment of changes in value can vary depending on the portfolio classification and whether IFRS or U.S. GAAP is used. The alternative treatments are discussed in greater depth later in this reading.

EXHIBIT 1 Summary of Accounting Treatments for Investments

	In Financial Assets	In Associates	Business Combinations	In Joint Ventures
Influence	Not significant	Significant	Controlling	Shared Control
Typical percentage interest	Usually <20%	Usually 20%–50%	Usually > 50%	Varies

(Exhibit continued on next page . . .)

EXHIBIT 1 (continued)

	In Financial Assets	In Associates	Business Combinations	In Joint Ventures
Accounting Treatment	Classified into one of four categories based on management intent and type of security. *Debt only*: ► Held-to-maturity (amortized cost, changes in value ignored unless deemed as impaired) *Debt and Equity*: ► Held for trading (fair value, changes in value recognized in profit or loss) ► Available-for-sale (fair value, changes in value recognized in equity) ► Designated at fair value (fair value, changes in value recognized in profit or loss)	Equity method	Consolidation	IFRS: Equity method or proportionate consolidation U.S. GAAP: Equity method (except for unincorporated ventures in specialized industries)
Applicable IFRS	IAS 39	IAS 28	IAS 27 IFRS 3	IAS 31
Applicable U.S. GAAP	SFAS 115[3] SFAS 157 SFAS 159	SFAS 142[4] SFAS 159 APB 18	ARB 51[5] SFAS 141R SFAS 142 SFAS 160	SFAS 94[6]

3 INVESTMENTS IN FINANCIAL ASSETS

Investments in financial assets are considered passive; the investor cannot exert significant influence or control over the operations of the investee. IFRS and U.S. GAAP are similar regarding the accounting for investments in financial assets. IFRS has three basic categories of investments in financial assets: 1) held-to-maturity, 2) fair value through profit or loss, and 3) available-for-sale.

[3] Superseded by FASB ASC Topic 320 [Investments–Debt and Equity Securities].
[4] Superseded by FASB ASC Topic 323 [Investments–Equity Method and Joint Ventures].
[5] Superseded by FASB ASC Topics 805 [Business Combinations] and 810 [Consolidations].
[6] Superseded by FASB ASC Topic 323 [Investments–Equity Method and Joint Ventures].

Under IFRS, fair value through profit or loss includes held for trading financial assets and those designated as fair value through profit or loss, whereas U.S. GAAP has two separate categories: held for trading, and investments designated at fair value. These categories determine the reporting for the investments.

Generally, investments in financial assets are initially recognized at fair value. Dividend and interest income from investments in financial assets, regardless of categorization, are reported in the income statement. The reporting of subsequent changes in fair value and the treatment of transaction costs, however, depends on the classification of the financial asset investment.

3.1 Held-to-Maturity

Held-to-maturity investments are investments in financial assets with fixed or determinable payments and fixed maturities (debt securities) that the investor has the positive intent and ability to hold to maturity. Held-to-maturity investments are exceptions from the general requirement (under both IFRS and U.S. GAAP) that investments in financial assets are subsequently recognized at fair value. Therefore, strict criteria apply before this designation can be used. Under both IFRS and U.S. GAAP, the investor must have a positive intent and ability to hold the security to maturity.

Reclassifications and sales prior to maturity may call into question the company's intent and ability. Under IFRS, an entity is not permitted to classify any financial assets as held-to-maturity if it has, during the current or two preceding financial reporting years, sold or reclassified more than an insignificant amount of held-to-maturity investments before maturity unless the sale or reclassification meets certain criteria. Similarly, under U.S. GAAP, a sale (and by inference a reclassification) is taken as an indication that intent was not truly present and use of the held-to-maturity category will be precluded.

IFRS require that held-to-maturity securities be initially recognized at fair value plus transaction costs, whereas U.S. GAAP require held-to-maturity securities be initially recognized at cost including transaction costs. In most cases, however, initial fair value is equal to cost excluding transaction costs, so the treatment is identical. At each reporting date (subsequent to initial recognition), IFRS and U.S. GAAP require that held-to-maturity securities are reported at amortized cost using the effective interest rate method,[7] unless objective evidence of impairment exists. Any difference—discount or premium—between maturity (par) value and fair value, typically including transaction costs, existing at the time of purchase is amortized over the life of the security. A discount (par value exceeds fair value) occurs when the stated interest rate is less than the effective rate, and a premium (fair value exceeds par value) occurs when the stated interest rate is greater than the effective rate. Amortization impacts the carrying value of the security. Any interest payments received are adjusted for amortization and are reported as interest income. If the security is sold before maturity (with the potential consequences described above), any realized gains or losses arising from the sale are recognized in profit or loss of the period.

---

[7] The effective interest method is a method of calculating the carrying value of a debt security and allocating the interest income to the period in which it is earned. It is based on the effective interest rate calculated at the time of purchase. Under U.S. GAAP, the calculation of the effective interest rate is generally based on *contractual* cash flows over the asset's *contractual* life. Under IFRS, the effective rate is based on the *estimated* cash flows over the *expected* life of the asset. Contractual cash flows over the full contractual term of the security are only used if the expected cash flows over the expected life of the security cannot be reliably estimated.

3.2 Held for Trading[8]

Held for trading investments are debt or equity securities acquired with the intent to sell them in the near term. Held for trading securities are reported at fair value. Transaction costs are not included in fair value at initial or subsequent recognition points. At each reporting date, the held for trading investments are remeasured and recognized at fair value with any unrealized gains and losses arising from changes in fair value reported in profit or loss. Also included in profit or loss are interest received on debt securities and dividends received on equity securities.

3.3 Available-for-Sale

Available-for-sale investments are debt and equity securities not classified as held-to-maturity or held for trading, and not designated at fair value through profit or loss. Under both IFRS and U.S. GAAP, investments classified as available-for-sale are initially measured at fair value, plus transaction costs. At each subsequent reporting date, the investments are remeasured and recognized at fair value, excluding transaction costs, with any unrealized gains or losses arising from changes in fair value reported in equity as other comprehensive income. The amount reported in other comprehensive income is net of taxes. When they are sold, the cumulative gain or loss previously recognized in other comprehensive income is reclassified (i.e., reversed out of comprehensive income) and reported as a reclassification adjustment on the income statement. Interest (calculated using the effective method) from debt securities and dividends from equity securities are included in profit or loss.

IFRS and U.S. GAAP differ on the treatment of foreign exchange gains and losses on available-for-sale debt securities.[9] Under IFRS, for the purpose of recognizing foreign exchange gains and losses, a debt security is treated as if it were carried at amortized cost in the foreign currency. Exchange rate differences arising from changes in amortized cost are recognized in profit or loss, and other changes in the carrying amount are recognized in other comprehensive income. In other words, the total change in fair value of an available-for-sale debt security is divided into two components, with any portion attributable to foreign exchange gains and losses recognized on the income statement (in profit or loss) and the remaining portion recognized in other comprehensive income. Under U.S. GAAP, the total change in fair value of available-for-sale debt securities (including foreign exchange rate gains or losses) is included in other comprehensive income. For equity securities, under IFRS and U.S. GAAP, the gain or loss that is recognized in other comprehensive income arising from changes in fair value includes any related foreign exchange component. There is no separate recognition of foreign exchange gains or losses.

---

[8] Under IFRS, securities classified as fair value through profit or loss include securities classified as held for trading.

[9] Under IAS 21 a debt security is defined as a monetary item, because the holder (investor) has the right to receive a fixed or determinable number of units of currency in the form of contractual interest payments. An equity instrument is not considered a monetary item.

3.4 Designated at Fair Value[10]

Both IFRS and U.S. GAAP allow entities to initially designate investments at fair value that might otherwise be classified as available-for-sale or held-to-maturity. The accounting treatment for investments designated at fair value is similar to that of held for trading investments. At each subsequent reporting date, the investments are remeasured at fair value with any unrealized gains and losses arising from changes in fair value as well as any interest and dividends received included in profit or loss.

The accounting treatment for investments in financial assets under IFRS is illustrated in Exhibit 2. This excerpt from the 2007 Annual Report of Deutsche Bank, a global investment bank, describes how its investments are classified, measured, and reported on its financial statements.

EXHIBIT 2 Deutsche Bank 2007 Annual Report

NOTES TO THE CONSOLIDATED FINANCIAL STATEMENTS

FINANCIAL ASSETS AND LIABILITIES AT FAIR VALUE THROUGH PROFIT OR LOSS

The Group classifies certain financial assets and financial liabilities as either held for trading or designated at fair value through profit or loss. They are carried at fair value and are presented as financial assets at fair value through profit or loss and financial liabilities at fair value through profit or loss, respectively. Related realized and unrealized gains and losses are included in net gains (losses) on financial assets/liabilities at fair value through profit or loss.

TRADING ASSETS AND LIABILITIES—financial instruments are classified as held for trading if they have been originated, acquired or incurred principally for the purpose of selling or repurchasing them in the near term, or they form part of a portfolio of identified financial instruments that are managed together and for which there is evidence of a recent actual pattern of short-term profit-taking.

FINANCIAL ASSETS CLASSIFIED AS AVAILABLE FOR SALE

Financial assets that are not classified at fair value through profit or loss or as loans are classified as AFS. A financial asset classified as AFS is initially recognized at its fair value plus transaction costs that are directly attributable to the acquisition of the financial asset. The amortization of premiums and accretion of discount are recorded in net interest income. Financial assets classified as AFS are carried at fair value with the changes in fair value reported in equity, in net gains (losses) not recognized in the income statement, unless the asset is subject to a fair value hedge, in which case changes in fair value resulting from the risk being hedged are recorded in other income. For monetary financial assets classified as AFS (for example, debt instruments), changes in carrying amounts relating to changes in foreign exchange rate are recognized in the income statement and other changes in carrying amount are recognized in equity as indicated above. For financial assets classified as AFS that are not monetary items (for example, equity instruments), the gain or loss that is recognized in equity includes any related foreign exchange component.

(Exhibit continued on next page . . .)

[10] IFRS uses the term "fair value through profit or loss," whereas U.S. GAAP uses the term "designated at fair value."

EXHIBIT 2 (continued)

DETERMINATION OF FAIR VALUE

Fair value is defined as the price at which an asset or liability could be exchanged in a current transaction between knowledgeable, willing parties, other than in a forced or liquidation sale. Where available, fair value is based on observable market prices or parameters or derived from such prices or parameters. Where observable prices or inputs are not available, valuation techniques appropriate for the particular instrument are applied. These valuation techniques involve some level of management estimation and judgment, the degree of which will depend on the price transparency for the instrument or market and the instrument's complexity. The valuation process to determine fair value also includes making appropriate adjustments to the valuation model outputs to consider factors such as close out costs, liquidity and credit risk (both counterparty credit risk in relation to financial assets and the Bank's own credit risk in relation to financial liabilities).

3.5 Reclassification of Investments

Both IFRS and U.S. GAAP permit entities to reclassify their intercorporate investments; however, there are certain restrictions and criteria that must be met. Reclassification may result in changes in how the asset value is measured and how unrealized gains or losses are recognized.

IFRS generally prohibits the reclassification of securities into or out of the designated at fair value category,[11] and reclassification out of the held for trading category is severely restricted. Held-to-maturity (debt) securities can be reclassified as available-for-sale if a change in intention or a change in ability to hold the security until maturity occurs. At the time of reclassification to available-for-sale, the security is remeasured at fair value with the difference between its carrying amount (amortized cost) and fair value recognized in other comprehensive income. Recall that the reclassification has implications for the use of the held-to-maturity category for existing debt securities and new purchases. A mandatory reclassification and a prohibition from future use may result from the reclassification.

Debt securities initially designated as available-for-sale may be reclassified to held-to-maturity if a change in intention or ability has occurred. The fair value carrying amount of the security at the time of reclassification becomes its new (amortized) cost. Any previous gain or loss that had been recognized in other comprehensive income is amortized to profit or loss over the remaining life of the security using the effective interest method. Any difference between the new amortized cost of the security and its maturity value is amortized over the remaining life of the security using the effective method.

Any financial asset classified as available-for-sale may be reclassified at cost, in the rare instances where there is no reliable measure of fair value and no evidence of impairment. However, if a reliable fair value measure becomes available, the financial asset must be reclassified to the available-for-sale category with changes in value recognized in other comprehensive income.

[11] In rare circumstances IFRS permits reclassification of a financial asset if it is no longer held for the purpose of selling it in the near term. The financial asset is reclassified at its fair value with any gain or loss recognized in profit or loss, and the fair value on the date of its reclassification becomes its new cost or amortized cost.

U.S. GAAP allows reclassifications (transfers) of securities between all categories using the fair value of the security at the date of transfer. However, recall that the reclassification of securities from the held-to-maturity category has implications for the use of this category for other securities. The treatment of unrealized holding gains and losses on the transfer date, however, depends on the initial classification of the security. For a security initially classified as held for trading that is being reclassified as available-for-sale, any unrealized gains and losses (arising from the difference between its carrying value and current fair value) are recognized in income. For a security transferred into the held for trading category, the unrealized gains or losses are recognized immediately. In the case of transfer from available-for-sale, the cumulative amount of gains and losses previously recognized in other comprehensive income is recognized in income on the date of transfer. For a debt security transferred into the available-for-sale category from held-to-maturity, the unrealized holding gain or loss at the date of the transfer (i.e., the difference between the fair value and amortized cost) is reported in other comprehensive income. For a debt security transferred into the held-to-maturity category from available-for-sale, the cumulative amount of gains or losses previously reported in other comprehensive income will be amortized over the remaining life of the security as an adjustment of yield (interest income) in the same manner as a premium or discount.

3.6 Impairments

A financial asset (in this case debt or equity securities) becomes impaired whenever its carrying amount is expected to permanently exceed its recoverable amount. There are key differences in the approaches that IFRS and U.S. GAAP take to determine if a financial asset is impaired and how the impairment loss is measured and reported.

Under IFRS, at the end of each reporting period, financial assets not carried at fair value through profit or loss (individually or as a group) need to be assessed, whether there is any objective evidence that the assets are impaired. Since investments classified as fair value through profit or loss and held for trading are reported at fair value, any impairment loss will have already been recognized in profit or loss as the events were occurring or will be recognized in profit or loss immediately.

A debt security is impaired if one or more events (loss events) occur after initial recognition that has impact on its estimated future cash flows that can be reliably estimated. Although it may not be possible to identify a single specific event that caused the impairment, the combined effect of several events may cause the impairment. Losses expected as a result of future events no matter how likely are not recognized. Examples of loss events causing impairment are:

- Significant financial difficulty of the issuer;
- Default or delinquency in interest or principal payments;
- The borrower experiences financial difficulty and receives a concession from the lender as a result; and
- It becomes probable that the borrower will enter bankruptcy or other financial reorganization.

The disappearance of an active market because an entity's financial instruments are no longer publicly traded is not evidence of impairment. A downgrade of an entity's credit rating or a decline in fair value of a security below its cost or amortized cost is also not by itself evidence of impairment. However, it may be evidence of impairment when considered with other available information.

For equity securities, objective evidence of a loss event includes:

- Significant changes in the technological, market, economic, and/or legal environments that have an adverse affect on the investee and indicate that the initial cost of the equity investment may not be recovered.
- A significant or prolonged decline in the fair value of an equity investment below its cost.

For held-to-maturity (debt) investments that have become impaired, the amount of the loss is measured as the difference between the security's carrying value and the present value of its estimated future cash flows discounted at the security's original effective interest rate (the effective interest rate computed at initial recognition). The carrying amount of the security is then reduced either directly or through the use of an allowance account, and the amount of the loss is recognized in profit or loss. If in a subsequent period the amount of the impairment loss decreases and the decrease can be objectively related to an event occurring after the impairment was recognized (for example, an improvement in the debtor's credit rating), the previously recognized impairment loss can be reversed either directly (by increasing the carrying value of the security) or by adjusting the allowance account. The amount of this reversal is then recognized in profit or loss.

For available-for-sale securities that have become impaired, the cumulative loss that had been recognized in other comprehensive income is reclassified from equity to profit or loss as a reclassification adjustment. The amount of the cumulative loss to be reclassified is the difference between acquisition cost (net of any principal repayment and amortization) and current fair value, less any impairment loss that has previously been recognized in profit or loss. Impairment losses on available-for-sale equity securities cannot be reversed. However, impairment losses on available-for-sale debt securities can be reversed if a subsequent increase in fair value can be objectively related to an event occurring after the impairment loss was recognized in profit and loss. In this case, the impairment loss is reversed with the amount of the reversal recognized in profit or loss.

Exhibit 3 contains an excerpt from Deutsche Bank's 2007 annual report that describes how impairment losses for its financial assets are determined, measured, and recognized on its financial statements.

EXHIBIT 3 Excerpt from Deutsche Bank 2007 Annual Report

IMPAIRMENT OF FINANCIAL ASSETS

At each balance sheet date, the Group assesses whether there is objective evidence that a financial asset or a group of financial assets is impaired. A financial asset or group of financial assets is impaired and impairment losses are incurred if there is:

- objective evidence of impairment as a result of a loss event that occurred after the initial recognition of the asset and up to the balance sheet date ("a loss event");
- the loss event had an impact on the estimated future cash flows of the financial asset or the group of financial assets; and
- a reliable estimate of the amount can be made.

(Exhibit continued on next page . . .)

EXHIBIT 3 (continued)

IMPAIRMENT OF FINANCIAL ASSETS CLASSIFIED AS AVAILABLE FOR SALE

For financial assets classified as AFS, management assesses at each balance sheet date whether there is objective evidence that an asset or group of assets is impaired. In the case of equity investments classified as AFS, objective evidence would include a significant or prolonged decline in the fair value of the investment below cost. In the case of debt securities classified as AFS, impairment is assessed based on the same criteria as for loans.

Where there is evidence of impairment, the cumulative unrealized loss previously recognized in equity, in net gains (losses) not recognized in the income statement, is removed from equity and recognized in the income statement for the period, reported in net gains (losses) on financial assets available for sale. This amount is determined as the difference between the acquisition cost (net of any principal repayments and amortization) and current fair value of the asset less any impairment loss on that investment previously recognized in the income statement. Reversals of impairment losses on equity investments classified as AFS are not reversed through the income statement; increases in their fair value after impairment are recognized in equity.

Reversals of impairment of debt securities are recognized in the income statement if the recovery is objectively related to a specific event occurring after the impairment loss was recognized in the income statement.

Under U.S. GAAP, the determination of impairment and the calculation of the impairment loss are different than under IFRS. For securities classified as available-for-sale or held-to-maturity, the investor is required to determine at each balance sheet date, whether the decline in value is other than temporary. For debt securities classified as held-to-maturity, this means that the investor will be unable to collect all amounts due according to the contractual terms existing at acquisition. If the decline in fair value is deemed to be other than temporary, the cost basis of the security is written down to its fair value, which then becomes the new cost basis of the security. The amount of the write-down is treated as a realized loss and reported on the income statement.

For available-for-sale securities (both debt and equity) if the decline in fair value is other than temporary, the cost basis of the security is written down to its fair value, which becomes the new cost basis, and the amount of the write-down is treated as a realized loss. However, the new cost basis cannot be increased for subsequent increases in fair value. Instead, subsequent increases in fair value (and decreases if other than temporary) are treated as unrealized gains or losses and included in other comprehensive income.

EXAMPLE 1

Accounting for Investments in Debt Securities

In this example, two fictitious companies are used. On 1 January 2008, Baxter Inc. invested £300,000 in Cartel Co. debt securities (with a 6 percent stated rate on par value, payable each 31 December). The par value of the securities was £275,000. On 31 December 2008, the fair value of Baxter's investment in Cartel is £350,000.

Assume that the market interest rate in effect when the bonds were issued was 4.5 percent.[12] If the investment is designated as held-to-maturity, the investment is reported at amortized cost using the effective interest method. A portion of the amortization table is as follows:

End of Year	Interest Payment (£)	Interest Income (£)	Amortization (£)	Carrying Value (£)
0				300,000
1*	16,500	13,500	3,000	297,000
2	16,500	13,365	3,135	293,865
3	16,500	13,224	3,276	290,589

* 6% × par value of £275,000 = £16,500 and 4.5% × carrying value of £300,000 = £13,500

1. How would this investment be reported on the balance sheet, income statement, and statement of shareholders' equity at 31 December 2008, under either IFRS or U.S. GAAP (accounting is essentially the same in this case), if Baxter designated the investment as 1) held-to-maturity, 2) held for trading, 3) available-for-sale, or 4) designated at fair value?
2. How would the gain be recognized if the debt securities were sold on 1 January 2009 for £352,000?
3. How would this investment appear on the balance sheet at 31 December 2009?
4. How would the classification and reporting differ if Baxter had invested in Cartel's equity securities instead of its debt securities?

Solution to 1:

	Income Statement	Balance Sheet	Statement of Shareholders' Equity
Held-to-maturity	Interest income £13,500 (£16,500 − £3,000 or £300,000 × 4.5%)	Reported at amortized cost of £297,000	No effect
Held for trading security	Interest income £13,500 and £53,000 unrealized gain is recognized through profit	Reported at fair value £350,000	No effect
Available-for-sale	Interest income of £13,500	Reported at fair value £350,000	£53,000 unrealized gain (net of tax) is reported as other comprehensive income
Designated at fair value	Interest income £13,500 and £53,000 unrealized gain is recognized through profit	Reported at fair value £350,000	No effect

[12] The effective interest rate method applies the market rate in effect when the bonds were issued to the current amortized cost (book value) of the bonds to obtain interest income for the period. Assume that the debt securities' contractual cash flows are equal to estimated cash flows and that its contractual life is equal to its expected life.

Solution to 2: If the debt securities were sold on 1 January 2009 for £352,000, the amount of the realized gain would be as follows:

Held-to-maturity: gain on income statement of £55,000 (£352,000 − £297,000)

Fair value through profit or loss (held for trading): gain on income statement of £2,000 (£352,000 − £350,000)

Available-for-sale: gain on income statement of £55,000 = (£352,000 − £350,000) + £53,000 (removed from other comprehensive income)

Solution to 3: If the investment was classified as held-to-maturity, the reported amount at amortized cost at the end of Year 2 on the balance sheet would be £293,865. If the investment was classified as either held for trading securities, available-for-sale, or designated at fair value, it would be measured at its fair value at the end of Year 2.

Solution to 4: If the investment had been in Cartel Co. equity securities rather than debt securities, the analysis would change in the following ways:

- There would not be a held-to-maturity option.
- Dividend income (if any) would replace interest income.

The convergence between IFRS and U.S. GAAP in the classification and reporting standards for investments in financial assets has made it easier for analysts to evaluate investment returns. Analysts typically evaluate performance separately for operating and investing activities. Analysis of operating performance should exclude items related to investing activities such as interest income, dividends, and realized and unrealized gains and losses. For comparative purposes, analysts should exclude nonoperating assets in the determination of return on net operating assets. IFRS (IAS 7) and U.S. GAAP (SFAS 115)[13] require disclosure of fair value of each class of investment in financial assets. Using market values and adjusting pro forma financial statements for consistency improves assessments of performance ratios across companies.

INVESTMENTS IN ASSOCIATES 4

Under both IFRS and U.S. GAAP, when an entity (investor) holds 20 to 50 percent of the voting rights of an associate (investee), either directly or indirectly (i.e., through subsidiaries), it is presumed (unless circumstances demonstrate otherwise) that the entity has (or can exercise) significant influence, but not control, over the investee's business activities.[14] Conversely, if the investor holds,

[13] FASB ASC Section 320-10-50 [Investments–Debt and Equity Securities–Overall–Disclosure].

[14] The determination of significant influence under IFRS also includes currently exercisable or convertible warrants, call options, or convertible securities that the investor owns, which give it additional voting power or reduce another party's voting power over the financial and operating policies of the investee. Under U.S. GAAP, the determination of an investor's voting stock interest is based only on the voting shares outstanding at the time of the purchase. The existence and effect of securities with potential voting rights are not considered.

directly or indirectly, less than 20 percent of the voting power of the associate (investee), it is presumed that the investor does not have (or cannot exercise) significant influence, unless such influence can be demonstrated. IAS 28 (IFRS) and SFAS 142 and APB 18 (U.S. GAAP)[15] apply to most investments in which an investor has significant influence; they also provide guidance on accounting for investments in associates using the equity method. These standards note that significant influence may be evidenced by

- representation on the board of directors;
- participation in the policy-making process;
- material transactions between the investor and the investee;
- interchange of managerial personnel; or
- technological dependency.

Being able to exert significant influence means that the financial and operating performance of the investee is partly attributable to the management decisions and operational skills of the investor. The equity method of accounting for the investment reflects the economic reality of this relationship and provides a more objective basis for reporting investment income.

Under the equity method of accounting, the investment is initially recognized at cost and is increased (decreased) to recognize the investor's share of the investee's profit (loss) and decreased by any distributions (dividends) received from the investee after the acquisition date. As a result the change in the investment account reflects the investor's proportionate share of the change in the investee's net assets. The investor also reports its share of the investee's profit or loss on its income statement.

4.1 Equity Method of Accounting: Basic Principles

Under the equity method of accounting, the equity investment is initially recorded on the investor's balance sheet at cost. In subsequent periods, the carrying amount of the investment is adjusted to recognize the investor's proportionate share of the investee's earnings or losses, and these earnings or losses are reported in income. Dividends or other distributions received from the investee are treated as a return of capital and reduce the carrying amount of the investment and are not reported in the investor's profit or loss. The equity method is often referred to as "one-line consolidation" since the investor's proportionate ownership interest in the assets and liabilities of the investee is disclosed as a single line item (net assets) on its balance sheet, and the investor's share of the revenues and expenses of the investee is disclosed as a single line item on its income statement (contrast these disclosures with the disclosures on consolidated statements in Section 6). Equity method investments are classified as noncurrent assets on the balance sheet. The investor's share of the profit or loss of equity method investments, and the carrying amount of those investments, must be separately disclosed on the income statement and balance sheet.

[15] SFAS 142.

EXAMPLE 2

Equity Method: Balance in Investment Account

Branch (a fictitious company) purchases a 20 percent interest in Williams (a fictitious company) for €200,000 on 1 January 2008. Williams reports income and dividends as follows:

	Income	Dividends
2008	€200,000	€ 50,000
2009	300,000	100,000
2010	400,000	200,000
	€900,000	€350,000

Calculate the investment in Williams that appears on Branch's balance sheet as of the end of 2010.

Solution:
Investment in Williams at 31 December 2010:

Initial cost	€200,000	
Equity income 2008	€40,000	= (20% of €200,000 Income)
Dividends received 2008	(€10,000)	= (20% of €50,000 Dividends)
Equity income 2009	€60,000	= (20% of €300,000 Income)
Dividends received 2009	(€20,000)	= (20% of €100,000 Dividends)
Equity income 2010	€80,000	= (20% of €400,000 Income)
Dividends received 2010	(€40,000)	= (20% of €200,000 Dividends)
Balance	€310,000	= [€200,000 + 20% × (€900,000 − €350,000)]

This simple example implicitly assumes that the purchase price equals the purchased equity in the book value of Williams' net assets. Sections 4.2 and 4.3 will cover the more common case in which the purchase price does not equal the proportional share of the book value of the investee's net assets.

Using the equity method, the investor includes its share of the investee's profit and losses on the income statement. The equity investment is carried at cost, plus its share of post-acquisition income less dividends received. The recorded investment value can decline as a result of investee losses or a permanent decline in the investee's market value (see Section 4.5 for treatment of impairments). If the investment value is reduced to zero, the investor usually discontinues the equity method and does not record further losses. If the investee subsequently reports profits, the equity method is resumed after the investor's share of the profits equals the share of losses not recognized during the suspension of the equity method. Exhibit 4 contains an excerpt from Deutsche Bank's 2007 annual report in which it describes the accounting treatment for its investments in associates.

EXHIBIT 4 Excerpt from Deutsche Bank 2007 Annual Report

ASSOCIATES AND JOINTLY CONTROLLED ENTITIES

An associate is an entity in which the Group has significant influence, but not a controlling interest, over the operating and financial management policy decisions of the entity. Significant influence is generally presumed when the Group holds between 20% and 50% of the voting rights. The existence and effect of potential voting rights that are currently exercisable or convertible are considered in assessing whether the Group has significant influence. Among the other factors that are considered in determining whether the Group has significant influence are representation on the board of directors (supervisory board in the case of German stock corporations) and material intercompany transactions. The existence of these factors could require the application of the equity method of accounting for a particular investment even though the Group's investment is for less than 20% of the voting stock.

A jointly controlled entity exists when the Group has a contractual arrangement with one or more parties to undertake activities through entities which are subject to joint control.

[14] EQUITY METHOD INVESTMENTS

Investments in associates and jointly controlled entities are accounted for using the equity method of accounting unless they are held for sale. As of December 31, 2007, there were two significant associates which were accounted for as held for sale. For information on assets held for sale please refer to Note [22].

As of December 31, 2007, the following investees were significant, representing 75% of the carrying value of equity method investments.

Investment[1]	Ownership Percentage
AKA Ausfuhrkredit-Gesellschaft mit beschränkter Haftung, Frankfurt	26.89
Beijing Gouhua Real Estate Co., Ltd., Beijing	30.00
Compañia Logistica de Hidrocarburos CLH, S.A., Madrid[2]	5.00
DB Global Masters (Fundamental Value Trading II) Fund Ltd, George Town	27.88
DB Phoebus Lux S.à.r.l., Luxembourg[3]	74.90
Deutsche Interhotel Holding GmbH & Co. KG, Berlin	45.51
Discovery Russian Realty Paveletskaya Project Ltd., George Town	33.33
DMG & Partners Securities Pte. Ltd., Singapore	49.00
Fincasa Hipotecaria, S.A. de C.V. Sociedad Financiera de Objeto Limitado, Mexico City	49.00
Fondo Immobiliare Chiuso Piramide Globale, Milan	42.45
Force 2005-1 Limited Partnership, St. Helier	40.00
Gemeng International Energy Group Company Limited, Taiyuan[2]	19.00
Hanoi Building Commercial Joint Stock Bank, Hanoi[2]	10.00
K&N Kenanga Holdings Bhd, Kuala Lumpur[2]	16.55
Ligusterfonds, Amsterdam	25.85
Makkolli Trading Ltd, Hamilton	45.00
MFG Flughafen-Grundstücksverwaltungsgesellschaft mbH & Co. BETA KG, Gruenwald	25.03
Mountaineer Natural Gas Trust, Wilmington	50.00
Paternoster Limited, Douglas	30.99

(Exhibit continued on next page . . .)

EXHIBIT 4 (continued)

Investment[1]	Ownership Percentage
PX Holdings Limited, Stockton on Tees	43.00
Redwood Russia PLP1 Limited, St. Helier	40.10
Rongde Asset Management Company Limited, Beijing	40.70
RREEF America REIT III, Inc., Chicago[2]	9.67
RREEF Global Opportunities Fund II LLC, Wilmington[2]	9.90
STC Capital YK, Tokyo	50.00
SWIP Multi Manager Global Real Estate Fund, London	24.70
SWIP Property Trust, London	37.38
SWIP UK Income Fund, London	35.99
SWIP UK Smaller Cos, London	34.24
VCG Venture Capital Gesellschaft mbH & Co. Fonds III KG, Munich	36.98

[1] All significant equity method investments are investments in associates.
[2] The Group has significant influence over the investee through board seats or other measures.
[3] The Group does not have a controlling financial interest in the investee.

Summarized aggregated financial information of these significant equity method investees were as follows:

In € m	Dec 31, 2007	Dec 31, 2006
Total assets	22,107	20,062
Total liabilities	13,272	12,113
Revenues	2,368	2,344
Net income/loss	528	1,195

The following are the components of the net income (loss) from all equity method investments:

In € m	2007	2006
Net income (loss) from equity method investments:		
Pro rata share of investees' net income (loss)	358	207
Net gains (losses) on disposal of equity method investments[1]	9	217
Impairments	(14)	(5)
Total net income (loss) from equity method investments	**353**	**419**

[1] Net gains (losses) on disposal of equity method investments in 2006 included a gain of €131 million from the sale of the Group's remaining holding in EUROHYPO AG.

There was no unrecognized share of losses of an investee, neither for the period, or cumulatively.

Equity method investments for which there are published price quotations had a carrying value of €160 million and a fair value of €168 million as of December 31, 2007 and a carrying value of €219 million and a fair value of €228 million as of December 31, 2006.

It is interesting to note the explanations for the treatment as associates when the ownership percentage is less than 20 percent or is greater than 50 percent. The equity method reflects the strength of the relationship between the investor and its associates. In the instances where the percentage ownership is less than 20 percent, Deutsche Bank uses the equity method because it has significant influence over these associates' operating and financial policies either through its representation on their boards of directors and/or material intercompany transactions. The equity method provides a more objective basis for reporting investment income than the accounting treatment for investments in financial assets, since the investor can potentially influence the timing of dividend distributions.

4.2 Investment Costs That Exceed the Book Value of the Investee

The cost (purchase price) to acquire shares of an investee is often greater than the book value of those shares. This is because many of the investee's assets and liabilities reflect historical cost rather than fair values. IFRS allow an entity to measure its property, plant, and equipment using either historical cost or fair value (less accumulated depreciation).[16] U.S. GAAP, however, require the use of historical cost (less accumulated depreciation) to measure property, plant, and equipment.[17]

When the cost of the investment exceeds the investor's proportionate share of the investee's (associate's) net identifiable assets (e.g., inventory, property, plant and equipment), the difference is first allocated to specific assets (or categories of assets). These differences are then amortized to the investor's proportionate share of the investee's profit or loss over the economic lives of the assets whose fair values exceeded book values. It should be noted that the allocation is not recorded formally; what appears initially in the investment account on the balance sheet of the investor is the cost. Over time, as the differences are amortized, the balance in the investment account will come closer to representing the ownership percentage of the book value of the net assets of the associate.

IFRS and U.S GAAP both treat the difference between the cost of the acquisition and investor's share of the fair value of the net identifiable assets as goodwill. Therefore, any remaining difference between the acquisition cost and the fair value of net identifiable assets that cannot be allocated to specific assets is treated as goodwill and is not amortized. Instead it is reviewed for impairment on a regular basis, and written down for any identified impairment. Goodwill, however, is included in the carrying amount of the investment, since investment is reported as a single line item on the investor's balance sheet.[18]

[16] After initial recognition, an entity can choose to use either a cost model or a revaluation model to measure its property, plant, and equipment. Under the revaluation model, property, plant, and equipment whose fair value can be measured reliably can be carried at a revalued amount. This revalued amount is its fair value at the date of the revaluation less any subsequent accumulated depreciation.

[17] Successful companies should be able to generate, through the productive use of assets, economic value in excess of the resale value of the assets themselves. Therefore, investors may be willing to pay a premium in anticipation of future benefits. These benefits could be as a result of general market conditions, the investor's ability to exert significant influence on the investee, or other synergies.

[18] If the investor's share of the fair value of the associate's net assets (identifiable assets, liabilities, and contingent liabilities) is greater than the cost of the investment, the difference is excluded from the carrying amount of the investment and instead included as income in the determination of the investor's share of the associate's profit or loss in the period in which the investment is acquired.

EXAMPLE 3

Equity Method Investment in Excess of Book Value

Assume that the hypothetical Blake Co. acquires 30 percent of the outstanding shares of the hypothetical Brown Co. At the acquisition date, book values and fair values of Brown's recorded assets and liabilities are as follows:

	Book Value	Fair Value
Current assets	€ 10,000	€ 10,000
Plant and equipment	190,000	220,000
Land	120,000	140,000
	€320,000	€370,000
Liabilities	100,000	100,000
Net assets	€220,000	€270,000

Blake Co. believes the value of Brown Co. is higher than the fair value of its identifiable net assets. They offer €100,000 for a 30 percent interest in Brown Co. Part of the excess purchase price is attributable to the €50,000 difference between book value and fair value of the identifiable assets and so the remaining amount is attributable to goodwill. Calculate goodwill.

Solution:

Purchase price	€100,000
30 percent of book value of Brown (30% × €220,000)	66,000
Excess purchase price	€ 34,000
Attributable to net assets	
Plant and equipment (30% × €30,000)	€ 9,000
Land (30% × €20,000)	6,000
Goodwill (residual)	19,000
	€ 34,000

As illustrated above, goodwill is the residual excess not allocated to identifiable assets or liabilities.

4.3 Amortization of Excess Purchase Price

The excess purchase price allocated to the assets and liabilities is accounted for in a manner that is consistent with the accounting treatment for the specific asset or liability to which it is assigned. Amounts allocated to assets and liabilities that are expensed (such as inventory) or periodically depreciated or amortized (plant, property, and intangible assets) must be treated in a similar manner. These allocated amounts are not reflected on the financial statements of the investee (associate), and the investee's income statement will not reflect the necessary periodic adjustments. Therefore, the investor must directly record these adjustment effects by reducing the carrying amount of the investment on its balance sheet and by reducing its share of the investee's profit recognized on its income statement. Amounts allocated to assets or liabilities that are not systematically amortized (e.g., land) will continue to be reported at their fair value as of the date the investment was acquired. As stated above, goodwill is included in the carrying amount of the investment instead of being separately recognized. It is not amortized since it is considered to have an indefinite life.

Using the example above and assuming a 10-year useful life for plant, property, and equipment and using straight-line depreciation, the annual amortization is as follows:

Account	Excess Price (€)	Useful Life	Amortization/Year (€)
Plant and equipment	9,000	10 years	900
Land	6,000	Indefinite	0
Goodwill	19,000	Indefinite	0

Annual amortization would reduce the investor's share of the investee's reported income (equity income) and the balance in the investment account by €900 for each year over the 10-year period.

EXAMPLE 4

Equity Method Investments with Goodwill

On 1 January 2009 Parker Company acquired 30 percent of Prince Inc. common shares for the cash price of €500,000 (both companies are fictitious). It is determined that Parker has the ability to exert significant influence on Prince's financial and operating decisions. The following information concerning Prince's assets and liabilities on 1 January 2009 is provided:

Prince, Inc.

	Book Value	Fair Value	Difference
Current assets	€ 100,000	€ 100,000	€ 0
Plant and equipment	1,900,000	2,200,000	300,000
	€2,000,000	€2,300,000	€300,000
Liabilities	800,000	800,000	0
Net assets	€1,200,000	€1,500,000	€300,000

The plant and equipment are depreciated on a straight-line basis and have 10 years of remaining life. Prince reports net income for 2009 of €100,000 and pays dividends of €50,000. Calculate the following:

1. Goodwill included in the purchase price.
2. Investment in associate (Prince) at the end of 2009.

Solution to 1:

Purchase price	€500,000
Acquired equity in book value of Prince's net assets (30% × €1,200,000)	360,000
Excess purchase price	€140,000
Attributable to plant and equipment (30% × €300,000)	90,000
Goodwill (residual)	50,000
	€140,000

Solution to 2: Investment in associate

Purchase price	€500,000
Parker's share of Prince's net income (30% × €100,000)	30,000
Dividends received (30% of €50,000)	(15,000)
Amortization of excess purchase price attributable to plant and equipment (€90,000 ÷ 10 years)	(9,000)
31 December 09 balance in investment in Prince	€506,000

An alternate way to look at the balance in the investment account is that it reflects the basic valuation principle of the equity method. At any point in time, the investment account balance equals the investor's (Parker) proportionate share of the net equity (net assets at book value) of the investee (Prince) plus the unamortized balance of the original excess purchase price. Applying this principle to this example:

2009 Beginning net assets =	€1,200,000
Plus: Net income	100,000
Less: Dividends	(50,000)
2009 Ending net assets	€1,250,000
Parker's proportionate share of Prince's recorded net assets (30% × €1,250,000)	€375,000
Unamortized excess purchase price (€140,000 − 9,000)	131,000
Investment in Prince	€506,000

Note that the unamortized excess purchase price is a cost incurred by Parker, not Prince. Therefore, the total amount is included in the investment account balance.

4.4 Fair Value Option

Both IFRS (39) and U.S. GAAP (SFAS 159)[19] give the investor the option to account for their equity method investment at fair value. Under U.S. GAAP this option is available to all entities; however, under IFRS, its use is restricted to venture capital organizations, mutual funds, unit trusts, and similar entities, including investment-linked insurance funds.

[19] FASB ASC Section 825-10-25 [Financial Instruments–Overall–Recognition].

Both standards require that the election to use the fair value option occur at the time of initial recognition and is irrevocable. Subsequent to initial recognition, the investment is reported at fair value with unrealized gains and losses arising from changes in fair value as well as any interest and dividends received included in the investor's profit or loss (income). Under the fair value method, the investment account on the investor's balance sheet does not reflect the investor's proportionate share of the investee's profit or loss, dividends, or other distributions. In addition, the excess of cost over the fair value of the investee's identifiable net assets is not amortized, nor is goodwill created.

4.5 Impairment

Both IFRS and U.S. GAAP require periodic reviews of equity method investments for impairment. If the fair value of the investment is below its carrying value and this decline is deemed to be other than temporary, an impairment loss must be recognized.

Under IFRS (39), there must be objective evidence of impairment as a result of one or more (loss) events that occurred after the initial recognition of the investment, and that loss event has an impact on the investment's future cash flows, which can be reliably estimated. Because goodwill is included in the carrying amount of the investment and is not separately recognized, it is not separately tested for impairment. Instead, the entire carrying amount of the investment is tested for impairment by comparing its recoverable amount with its carrying amount.[20] The impairment loss is recognized on the income statement, and the carrying amount of the investment on the balance sheet is either reduced directly or through the use of an allowance account.

U.S. GAAP takes a different approach. If the fair value of the investment declines below its carrying value *and* the decline is determined to be permanent, U.S. GAAP (APB Opinion 18)[21] requires an impairment loss to be recognized on the income statement and the carrying value of the investment on the balance sheet is reduced to its fair value.

Both IFRS and U.S. GAAP prohibit the reversal of impairment losses even if the fair value later increases.

Section 6.4.5 of this reading discusses impairment tests for the goodwill attributed to a controlling investment (consolidated subsidiary). Note the distinction between the disaggregated goodwill impairment test for consolidated statements and the total fair value of impairment test for equity method investments.

4.6 Transactions with Associates

An investor company can influence the terms and timing of transactions with its associates so profits from such transactions cannot be realized until confirmed through use or sale to third parties. Accordingly, the investor company's share of any unrealized profit must be deferred by reducing the amount recorded under the equity method. In the subsequent period(s) when this deferred profit is considered confirmed, it is added back to the equity income. At that time, the equity income is again based on the recorded values in the associate's accounts.

---

[20] Recoverable amount is the higher of "value in use" or net selling price. Value in use is equal to the present value of estimated future cash flows expected to arise from the continuing use of an asset and from its disposal at the end of its useful life. Net selling price is equal to fair value less cost to sell.

[21] FASB ASC Section 323-10-35 [Investments–Equity Method and Joint Ventures–Overall–Subsequent Measurement].

Transactions between the two affiliates may be **upstream** (associate to investor) or **downstream** (investor to associate). In an upstream sale, the profit on the intercompany transaction is recorded on the associate's income (profit or loss) statement. The investor's share of the unrealized profit is thus included in equity income on the investor's income statement. In a downstream sale, the profit is recorded on the investor's income statement. Both IFRS (IAS 28) and U.S. GAAP (Interpretation 1 of APB 18)[22] require that the unearned profits be eliminated to the extent of the investor's interest in the associate. The result is an adjustment to equity income on the investor's income statement.

EXAMPLE 5

Equity Method with Sale of Inventory: Upstream Sale

On 1 January 2009, Wicker Company acquired a 25 percent interest in Foxworth Company (both companies are fictitious) for €1,000,000 and used the equity method to account for its investment. The book value of Foxworth's net assets on that date was €3,800,000. An analysis of fair values revealed that all assets and liabilities were equal to book values except for a building. The building was undervalued by €40,000 and has a 20-year remaining life. The company used straight-line depreciation for the building. Foxworth paid €3,200 in dividends in 2009. During 2009, Foxworth reported net income of €20,000. During the year, Foxworth sold inventory to Wicker. At the end of the year, there was €8,000 profit from the upstream sale in Wicker's inventory because the goods had not been sold to an outside party.

1. Calculate the equity income to be reported as a line item on Wicker's 2009 income statement.
2. Calculate the balance in the investment in Foxworth to be reported on the 31 December 2009 balance sheet.

Purchase price	€1,000,000
Acquired equity in book value of Foxworth's net assets (25% × €3,800,000)	950,000
Excess purchase price	€ 50,000
Attributable to:	
Building (25% × €40,000)	€ 10,000
Goodwill (residual)	40,000
	€ 50,000

Solution to 1: Equity Income

Wicker's share of Foxworth's reported income (25% × €20,000)	€5,000
Amortization of excess purchase price attributable to building, (€10,000 ÷ 20)	(500)
Unrealized profit (25% × €8,000)	(2,000)
Equity income 2009	€2,500

[22] FASB ASC Topic 323 [Investments–Equity Method and Joint Ventures].

Solution to 2: Investment in Foxworth:

Purchase price	€1,000,000
Equity income 2009	2,500
Dividends received (25% × €3,200)	(800)
Investment in Foxworth, 31 Dec 2009	€1,001,700
Composition of investment account:	
Wicker's proportionate share of Foxworth's net equity (net assets at book value) [25% × (€3,800,000 + (20,000 − 8,000) − 3,200)]	€952,200
Unamortized excess purchase price (€50,000 − 500)	49,500
	€1,001,700

EXAMPLE 6

Equity Method with Sale of Inventory: Downstream Sale

Jones Company owns 25 percent of Jason Company (both fictitious companies) and appropriately applies the equity method of accounting. Amortization of excess purchase price, related to undervalued assets at the time of the investment, is €8,000 per year. During 2009 Jones sold €96,000 of inventory to Jason for €160,000. Jason resold €120,000 of this inventory during 2009. The remainder was sold in 2010. Jason reports income from its operations of €800,000 in 2009 and €820,000 in 2010.

1. Calculate the equity income to be reported as a line item on Jones's 2009 income statement.
2. Calculate the equity income to be reported as a line item on Jones's 2010 income statement.

Solution to 1: Equity Income 2009

Jones's share of Jason's reported income (25% × €800,000)	€200,000
Amortization of excess purchase price	(8,000)
Unrealized profit (25% × €16,000)	(4,000)
Equity income 2009	€188,000

Jones's profit on the sale to Jason = €160,000 − 96,000 = €64,000

Jason sells 75% (€120,000/160,000) of the goods purchased from Jones; 25% is unsold.

Total unrealized profit = €64,000 × 25% = €16,000

Jones's share of the unrealized profit = €16,000 × 25% = €4,000

Alternative approach:

Jones's profit margin on sale to Jason: 40 percent (€64,000/€160,000)

Jason's inventory of Jones's goods at 31 Dec 2009: €40,000

Jones's profit margin on this was 40% × 40,000 = €16,000

Jones's share of profit on unsold goods = €16,000 × 25% = €4,000

Solution to 2: Equity Income 2010

Jones's share of Jason's reported income (25% × €820,000)	€205,000
Amortization of excess purchase price	(8,000)
Realized profit (25% × €16,000)	4,000
Equity income 2010	€201,000

Jason sells the remaining 25 percent of the goods purchased from Jones.

4.7 Disclosure

The notes to the financial statements are an integral part of the information necessary for investors. Both IFRS and U.S. GAAP require disclosure about the assets, liabilities, and results of equity method investments. For example, in their 2007 annual report, Deutsche Bank reports that:

> Investments in associates and jointly controlled entities are accounted for under the equity method of accounting. The Group's share of the results of associates and jointly controlled entities is adjusted to conform with the accounting policies of the Group. Unrealized gains on transactions are eliminated to the extent of the Group's interest in the investee.
>
> Under the equity method of accounting, the Group's investments in associates and jointly controlled entities are initially recorded at cost, and subsequently increased (or decreased) to reflect both the Group's pro-rata share of the post acquisition net income (or loss) of the associate or jointly controlled entity and other movements included directly in the equity of the associate or jointly controlled entity. Goodwill arising on the acquisition of an associate or a jointly controlled entity is included in the carrying value of the investment (net of any accumulated impairment loss). Equity method losses in excess of the Group's carrying value of the investment in the entity are charged against other assets held by the Group related to the investee. If those assets are written down to zero, a determination is made whether to report additional losses based on the Group's obligation to fund such losses.

For practical reasons, associated companies' results are sometimes included in the investor's accounts with a certain time lag, normally not more than one quarter. Dividends from associated companies are not included in investor income because it would be a double counting. Applying the equity method recognizes the investor's full share of the associate's income. Dividends received involve exchanging a portion of equity interest for cash. In the consolidated balance sheet, the book value of shareholdings in associated companies is increased by the investor's share of the company's net income and reduced by amortization of surplus values and the amount of dividends received.

4.8 Issues for Analysts

Equity method accounting presents several challenges for analysis. First, analysts should question whether the equity method is appropriate. For example, an investor holding 19 percent of an associate may in fact exert significant influence but may attempt to avoid using the equity method to avoid reporting associate losses. On the other hand, an investor holding 25 percent of an associate may be unable to exert significant influence and may be unable to access cash flows, and yet prefers the equity method to capture associate income.

Second, the investment account represents the investor's percentage ownership in the net assets of the investee company through "one-line consolidation." There can be significant assets and liabilities of the investee that are not reflected on the investor's balance sheet, which will significantly affect debt ratios. Net margin ratios could be overstated because income for the associate is included in investor net income but is not specifically included in sales. An investor may actually control the investee with less than 50 percent ownership but prefer the financial results using the equity method. Careful analysis can reveal financial performance driven by accounting structure.

Finally, the analyst must consider the quality of the equity method earnings. The equity method assumes that a percentage of each dollar earned by the investee company is earned by the investor (i.e., a fraction of the dollar equal to the fraction of the company owned), even if cash is not received. Analysts should, therefore, consider potential restrictions on dividend cash flows (the statement of cash flows).

5 JOINT VENTURES

Joint ventures—ventures undertaken and controlled by two or more parties—can be a convenient way to enter foreign markets, conduct specialized activities, and engage in risky projects. They can be organized in a variety of different forms and structures. Some joint ventures are primarily contractual relationships, whereas others have common ownership of assets. They can be partnerships, corporations, or other legal forms (unincorporated associations, for example).

Joint ventures are defined differently under IFRS and U.S. GAAP. This can result in the same arrangement being classified differently under the two standards. In turn, this can affect reported financial results, ratios, and covenants.

IFRS identify the following common characteristics of joint ventures: 1) contractual arrangement exists between two or more venturers and 2) the contractual arrangement establishes joint control. IFRS distinguish between three types of joint ventures with each type having specific accounting requirements, although proportionate consolidation is the generally preferred accounting treatment. Proportionate consolidation requires the venturer's share of the assets, liabilities, income, and expenses of the joint venture to be *combined on a line-by-line* basis with similar items on the venturer's financial statements. The three types of joint venture identified under IFRS are:

- **Jointly controlled operations**: Each venturer uses its own assets and other resources for a specific project, rather than establishing a separate entity from the venturers. For example, two or more venturers combine their operations, resources, and expertise to manufacture, market, and distribute jointly a particular product. Each venturer recognizes in its financial statements the assets that it controls, the liabilities and expenses that it incurs, and its share of the revenue generated by the joint venture.

- **Jointly controlled assets**: The venturers jointly control and/or jointly own assets. These assets are used to obtain benefits for the venturers. For example, oil production companies may jointly control and operate an oil pipeline. Each venturer recognizes in its own accounting records and financial statements its share of the jointly controlled assets (classified by the nature of the assets), any liabilities it has incurred on behalf of those assets as well as its share of jointly incurred liabilities, any profit earned from the use of its share of the jointly controlled assets, together with its share of any expense incurred by the joint venture. In addition, it would recognize any expense (for example, interest expense related to financing the venturer's interest in the assets) it has incurred directly in respect of its interest in the joint venture.
- **Jointly controlled entities**: The predominant arrangement involves the establishment of a separate entity (corporation, partnership) in which each venturer has an interest. The project or venture is then conducted through this incorporated or unincorporated separate entity. The entity operates in the same way as other entities, except that a contractual arrangement between the venturers establishes joint control over the economic activity of the entity. To account for this arrangement, IAS 31 recommends using proportionate consolidation but permits the equity method.[23]

Proportionate consolidation requires the venturer's share of the assets, liabilities, income, and expenses of the joint venture to be *combined on a line-by-line* basis with similar items on the venturer's financial statements.[24] In contrast, as explained in Section 4, the equity method results in a single line item (equity in income of the joint venture) on the income statement and a single line item (investment in joint venture) on the balance sheet.

Because the single line item on the income statement under the equity method reflects the net effect of the sales and expenses of the joint venture, the total income recognized is identical under the two methods. In addition, because the single line item on the balance sheet item (investment in joint venture) under the equity method reflects the investors' share of the net assets of the joint venture, the total net assets of the investor is identical under both methods. There can be significant differences, however, in ratio analysis between the two methods because of the differential effects on values for total assets, liabilities, sales, expenses, etc.

---

[23] In September 2007, the IASB, as part of its convergence project with the FASB, issued a proposal to revise IAS 31 in two respects. The first change would be to eliminate the use of proportionate consolidation to account for jointly controlled entities. The second would be to change from treating the form of the arrangement as the most significant factor in determining the accounting. Instead, a dual approach would be used to account for joint arrangements that involve both jointly controlled assets and jointly controlled entities. Under this approach, the parties would account first for the assets and liabilities of the joint arrangement and use a residual approach to equity accounting for the joint venture portion of the joint arrangement.

[24] Under proportionate consolidation, the venturer has a choice between two presentation formats. First, the venture partner may include its share of the assets, liabilities, revenues, and expenses of the jointly controlled entity with similar items under its sole control. Alternatively, it can separately recognize its share of the joint venture's assets, liabilities, revenues, and expenses, although still placing them within the proper grouping. In either case, the same category totals will be presented.

Under U.S. GAAP the term joint venture refers only to a jointly controlled separate entity in which business activities are conducted. A corporate joint venture is a corporation that is owned and operated by two or more venturers as a separate and specific business for the mutual benefit of the venturers.[25] APB 18 requires the use of the equity method to account for joint ventures. Proportionate consolidation is generally not permitted except for unincorporated entities operating in certain industries.

EXAMPLE 7

Joint Venture (Jointly Controlled Entity)

Assume that hypothetical Companies A and B enter into a joint venture, each with a 50 percent interest. The second column presents the financial statement for the joint venture in its first year. Columns 3 and 4 reflect the financial results for Company A under the two methods of accounting for its interest in the joint venture.

		Company A Venturer	
	Joint Venture	Equity Method*	Proportionate Consolidation
Income Statement			
Sales	€400,000	€1,000,000	€1,200,000
Equity in joint venture income		60,000	
Cost of sales	200,000	500,000	600,000
Other expenses	80,000	240,000	280,000
Net income	€120,000	€ 320,000	€ 320,000
Balance Sheet			
Cash	€ 40,000	€ 400,000	€ 420,000
Inventory		500,000	500,000
Investment in joint venture		450,000	
Other assets	1,160,000	1,500,000	2,080,000
	€1,200,000	€2,850,000	€3,000,000
Accounts payable		€ 200,000	€ 200,000
Long-term debt	€ 300,000	1,650,000	1,800,000
Capital stock		600,000	600,000
Retained earnings		400,000	400,000
Venturers' equity (Companies A and B)	900,000		
	€1,200,000	€2,850,000	€3,000,000

* The data (other than the subtotals) shown under the equity method are the same as if there had been no joint venture except for "Equity in joint venture income," "Investment in joint venture," and "Retained earnings."

[25] FASB ASC Topic 323 [Investments–Equity Method and Joint Ventures].

First, examine the income statement. Notice that net income is €320,000 using either the equity method or proportionate consolidation. But sales, cost of sales, and expenses are different because under the equity method the net effect of sales, cost of sales, and expenses is reflected in the €60,000 equity in joint venture income.

On the balance sheet, the line item "investment in joint venture" observed under the equity method is replaced by the proportionate share of each balance sheet account in the proportionate consolidation method. The single line item is replaced with a line-by-line consolidation. In other words, because the venturer has a 50 percent interest in the joint venture, 50 percent of joint venture assets and liabilities are included in the proportionate balance sheet.

The analyst will observe differences in performance ratios based on the accounting method used for joint ventures.

	Equity Method	Proportionate Consolidation
Net profit margin	32.0%	26.7%
Return on assets	11.2%	10.7%
Debt/Equity	1.65	1.80

The proportional consolidation method is the preferred method for joint ventures under IFRS because it more effectively conveys the economic scope of an entity's operations when those operations include interests in one or more jointly controlled entities.

BUSINESS COMBINATIONS

6

Business combinations (controlling interest investments) involve the combination of two or more entities into a larger economic entity. Business combinations are typically motivated by expectations of added value through synergies, including elimination of duplicate costs, tax advantages, coordination of the production process, and efficiency gains in the management of assets.

Under IFRS, there is no distinction among business combinations based on the resulting structure of the larger economic entity. For all business combinations, one of the parties to the business combination is identified as the acquirer. Under U.S. GAAP, an acquirer is identified, but business combinations are categorized as merger, acquisition, or consolidation based on the structure after the combination. Each of these types of business combinations has distinctive characteristics that are described in Exhibit 5. Exhibit 5 also describes the features of variable interest and special purpose entities. Variable interest and special purpose entities are additional instances where control is exerted by another entity.

EXHIBIT 5 **Types of Business Combinations**

Merger

The distinctive feature of a merger is that only one of the entities remains in existence. One hundred percent of the target is absorbed into the acquiring company. Company A may issue common stock,

(Exhibit continued on next page . . .)

EXHIBIT 5 (continued)

preferred stock, bonds, or pay cash to acquire the net assets. The net assets of Company B are transferred to Company A. Company B ceases to exist and Company A is the only entity that remains.

Company A + Company B = Company A

Acquisition

The distinctive feature of an acquisition is the legal continuity of the entities. Each entity continues operations but is connected through a parent–subsidiary relationship. Each entity is an individual that maintains separate financial records, but the parent (the acquirer) provides consolidated financial statements in each reporting period. Unlike a merger or consolidation, the acquiring company does not need to acquire 100 percent of the target. In fact, in some cases, it may acquire less than 50 percent and still exert control (see Section 6.4.2). If the acquiring company acquires less than 100 percent, noncontrolling (minority) shareholders' interests are reported on the consolidated financial statements.

Company A + Company B = (Company A + Company B)

Consolidation

The distinctive feature of a consolidation is that a new legal entity is formed and none of the predecessor entities remain in existence. A new entity is created to take over the net assets of Company A and Company B. Company A and Company B cease to exist and Company C is the only entity that remains.

Company A + Company B = Company C

Special Purpose Entities

The distinctive feature of a special purpose (variable interest) entity is that control is not usually based on voting control, because equity investors do not have a sufficient amount at risk for the entity to finance its activities without additional subordinated financial support. Furthermore, the equity investors may lack a controlling financial interest. The sponsoring company usually creates a special purpose entity (SPE) for a narrowly defined purpose. IFRS require consolidation if the substance of the relationship indicates control by the sponsor. Variable interests will be discussed more thoroughly in Section 7.

In the past, business combinations could be accounted for either as a purchase transaction or as a uniting (or pooling) of interests. The accounting standards that currently govern business combinations are reflective of the joint project between IASB and FASB to converge on a single set of high-quality accounting standards. As part of the first phase of the project, in 2001 the FASB issued SFAS 141, *Business Combinations* and SFAS 142, *Goodwill and other Intangible Assets.*[26] In 2004, the IASB issued IFRS 3, *Business Combinations.* These standards prohibited the use of the pooling of interests (uniting of interest) method, required the use of the acquisition (purchase) method, and prohibited the amortization of goodwill.

In the second phase of the joint project, the FASB and IASB further reduced differences between IFRS and U.S. GAAP and ensured that the standards would be

[26] SFAS 141 and 142 are superseded by FASB ASC Topics 805 [Business Combinations] and 350 [Intangibles–Goodwill and Other].

applied consistently. In December 2007, the FASB issued two new standards, SFAS 141(R), *Business Combinations*, and SFAS 160, *Noncontrolling Interests in Consolidated Financial Statements*.[27] Both statements applied prospectively to business combinations occurring on or after 15 December 2008, with early adoption prohibited. In January 2008, the IASB issued a revised IFRS 3, *Business Combinations* and an amended IAS 27, *Consolidated and Separate Financial Statements*. These "new" standards became effective on 1 July 2009, although entities were permitted to adopt them earlier. These standards are expected to improve the relevance, representational faithfulness, transparency, and comparability of information provided in financial statements about business combinations and their effects on the reporting entity.

IFRS 3(R) and SFAS 141(R)[28] now require that all business combinations be accounted for as acquisitions, whereby one entity (the parent) takes management control of another entity (subsidiary), or the parent takes control of the subsidiary's assets and liabilities. The acquisition method developed by the IASB and the FASB replaces the purchase method, and substantially reduces any differences between IFRS and U.S. GAAP for business combinations. By requiring acquirers to account for business combinations in a similar manner, it should make it easier for analysts to evaluate how the operations of acquirer and the target business will combine and the effect of this combination on the combined entity's subsequent financial performance and position.

6.1 Pooling of Interests

Prior to June 2001, under U.S. GAAP, combining companies that met twelve strict criteria could use the **pooling of interests accounting method** for the business combination. Companies not meeting these criteria used the purchase method. In a pooling of interests, the combined companies were portrayed as if they had always operated as a single economic entity. Consequently, assets and liabilities were recorded at book values, and the pre-combination retained earnings were included in the balance sheet of the combined companies. This treatment was consistent with the view that there was a continuity of ownership and no new basis of accounting existed. Similar rules applied under IFRS, which used the term **uniting of interests** in reference to the same concept. IFRS permitted use of the uniting of interests method until March 2004. Currently, neither IFRS nor U.S. GAAP allows use of the pooling/uniting of interests method.

In contrast, a combination accounted for as a purchase is viewed as a purchase of net assets, and those net assets are recorded at fair values. An increase in the value of depreciable assets resulted in additional depreciation expense. As a result, for the same level of revenue, the purchase method resulted in lower reported income than the pooling of interests method. For this reason, managers had a tendency to favor the pooling of interests method.

Although the pooling of interests method is no longer allowed, companies may continue to use pooling of interests accounting for business combinations that occurred prior to its disallowance as a method. We discuss the method here because pooling of interests accounting was commonly used and will have an impact on financial statements for the foreseeable future. Because of the ongoing effect, an understanding of pooling of interests will facilitate the analyst's assessment of the performance and financial position of the company.

6.2 Acquisition Method

IFRS and U.S. GAAP currently require the acquisition method of accounting for business combinations, although both have a few specific exemptions.

[27] SFAS 141(R) and 160 are superseded by FASB ASC Topic 805 [Business Combinations].

[28] FASB ASC Topic 805 [Business Combinations].

Fair value of the net assets acquired at the acquisition date is the appropriate measurement for acquisitions. The fair value is usually equal to the consideration given by the acquiring firm. Direct costs of the business combination, such as professional and legal fees, valuation experts, and consultants, are expensed as incurred.

The acquisition method (which replaces the purchase method) addresses three major accounting issues that often arise in business combinations and the preparation of consolidated (combined) financial statements:

- The recognition and measurement of the assets and liabilities of the combined entities;
- The initial recognition and subsequent accounting for goodwill; and
- The recognition and measurement of the noncontrolling interest.

6.2.1 Recognition and Measurement of Identifiable Assets and Liabilities

IFRS and U.S. GAAP require that the acquirer measure the identifiable assets and liabilities of the acquiree (acquired entity) at fair value as of the date of the acquisition. The acquirer must also recognize any assets and liabilities that the acquiree had not previously recognized as assets and liabilities in its financial statements. For example, identifiable intangible assets (brand name, patent) that the acquiree developed internally would be recognized by the acquirer.

6.2.2 Recognition and Measurement of Contingent Liabilities[29]

On the acquisition date, the acquirer must recognize any contingent liability assumed in the acquisition if 1) it is a present obligation that arises from past events, and 2) it can be measured reliably. Costs that the acquirer expects (but is not obliged) to incur, however, are not recognized as liabilities as of the acquisition date. Instead, the acquirer recognizes these costs in future periods as they are incurred. For example, expected restructuring costs arising from exiting an acquiree's business will be recognized in the period in which they are incurred.

There is a small difference between IFRS and U.S. GAAP in their inclusion of contingent liabilities. IFRS include contingent liabilities if their fair values can be reliably measured. U.S. GAAP includes only those contingent liabilities that are probable and can be reasonably estimated.

6.2.3 Recognition and Measurement of Indemnification Assets

On the acquisition date, the acquirer must recognize an indemnification asset if the seller (acquiree) contractually indemnifies the acquirer for the outcome of a contingency or an uncertainty related to all or part of a specific asset or liability. The seller may also indemnify the acquirer against losses above a specified amount on a liability arising from a particular contingency. For example, the seller guarantees that an acquired contingent liability will not exceed a specified amount. In this situation, the acquirer recognizes an indemnification asset at the same time it recognizes the indemnified liability, with both measured on the same basis. If the indemnification relates to an asset or a liability that is recog-

---

[29] A contingent liability must be recognized even if it is not probable that an outflow of resources or economic benefits will be used to settle the obligation.

nized at the acquisition date and measured at its acquisition date fair value, the acquirer will also recognize the indemnification asset at the acquisition date at its acquisition date fair value.

6.2.4 Recognition and Measurement of Financial Assets and Liabilities

At the acquisition date, the acquirer can reclassify the financial assets and liabilities of the acquiree on the basis of the contractual terms, economic conditions, and the acquirer's operating or accounting policies and other pertinent conditions, as they exist at the acquisition date. For example, the acquirer may chose to reclassify particular financial assets of the acquiree as fair value through profit or loss instead of available-for-sale or held-to-maturity.

6.2.5 Recognition and Measurement of Goodwill

Goodwill represents the value that the acquirer sees in the acquiree beyond the fair value of the acquiree's tangible and identifiable intangible assets.[30] Under current IFRS (IAS 36), goodwill is recognized as the fair value of the acquisition (purchase price) less the acquirer's share of the fair value of all identifiable tangible and intangible assets, liabilities, and contingent liabilities acquired. This is sometimes referred to as "partial goodwill." U.S. GAAP (SFAS 142)[31] considers the entity as a whole. Goodwill is recognized as the fair value of the acquisition less the fair value of identifiable net assets. IFRS also permits this 100 percent goodwill under the "full goodwill" option on a transaction-by-transaction basis. Because goodwill is considered to have an indefinite life, it is not amortized. Instead, it is tested for impairment annually or more frequently if events or circumstances indicate that goodwill might be impaired.

6.2.6 Recognition and Measurement when Acquisition Price Is Less than Fair Value

Occasionally, a company faces adverse circumstances such that its market value drops below the fair value of its net assets. In an acquisition where the purchase price is less than the fair value of the target's net assets, the acquisition is considered to be a **bargain acquisition**. Any contingent consideration must be measured and recognized at fair value at the time of the business combination. Any subsequent changes in value of the contingent consideration are recognized in profit or loss. IFRS requires the difference between the fair value of the acquired net assets and the purchase price to be recognized immediately as a gain in profit or loss. Under U.S. GAAP, for business combinations prior to 15 December 2008, the difference was allocated as a pro rata reduction in the fair value of the acquired assets other than cash and cash equivalents, trade receivables, inventory, financial assets carried on the balance sheet at fair value, assets to be disposed of by sale, and deferred tax assets. If an amount remained after the eligible assets were reduced to zero, the excess was recognized as an extraordinary gain. For business combinations on or after 15 December 2008, the treatment of a bargain purchase is the same as that under IFRS.

---

[30] Goodwill is only recognized under the acquisition or purchase methods. Under the uniting (pooling) of interest method, goodwill was not created since the combined companies are treated as if they had always operated as a single entity.

[31] FASB ASC Topic 805 [Business Combinations].

EXAMPLE 8

Acquisition Method Post-Combination Balance Sheet

Franklin Company, headquartered in France, acquired 100 percent of the outstanding shares of Jefferson, Inc. by issuing 1,000,000 shares of its €1 par common stock (€15 market value). Immediately before the transaction, the two companies compiled the following information:

	Franklin Book Value (000)	Jefferson Book Value (000)	Jefferson Fair Value (000)
Cash and receivables	€10,000	€ 300	€ 300
Inventory	12,000	1,700	3,000
PP&E (net)	27,000	2,500	4,500
	€49,000	€4,500	€7,800
Current payables	8,000	600	600
Long-term debt	16,000	2,000	1,800
	24,000	2,600	2,400
Net assets	€25,000	€1,900	€5,400
Shareholders' equity:			
Capital stock (€1 par)	€ 5,000	€400	
Additional paid in capital	6,000	700	
Retained earnings	€14,000	€800	

Show the balances in the post-combination balance sheet using the acquisition method.

Solution: Acquisition Method
Under the acquisition method the purchase price allocation would be as follows:

Fair value of the stock issued	
(1,000,000 shares at market value of €15)	€15,000,000
Book value of Jefferson's net assets	1,900,000
Excess purchase price	€13,100,000
Fair value of the stock issued	€15,000,000
Fair value allocated to identifiable net assets	5,400,000
Goodwill	€ 9,600,000

Allocation of excess purchase price (based upon the differences between fair values and book values):

Inventory	€ 1,300,000
PPE (net)	2,000,000
Long-term debt	200,000
Goodwill	9,600,000
	€13,100,000

Both IFRS and U.S. GAAP record the fair value of the acquisition at the market value of the stock issued, or €15,000,000. In this case, the fair value exceeds the book value of Jefferson's net assets by €13,100,000. Inventory, PPE (net), and long-term debt are adjusted to fair values. The excess of fair value over the fair value of identifiable net assets results in goodwill recognition of €9,600,000.

The post-combination balance sheet of the combined entity would appear as follows:[32]

Franklin Consolidated Balance Sheet (Acquisition Method) (000)

Cash and receivables	€10,300
Inventory	15,000
PP&E (net)	31,500
Goodwill	9,600
Total assets	€66,400
Current payables	€ 8,600
Long-term debt	17,800
Total liabilities	€26,400
Capital stock (€1 par)	€ 6,000
Additional paid in capital	20,000
Retained earnings	14,000
Total stockholders' equity	€40,000
Total liabilities and stockholders' equity	€66,400

Assets and liabilities are combined using book values of Franklin plus fair values for the assets and liabilities acquired from Jefferson. For example, the book value of Franklin's inventory (€12,000,000) is added to the fair value of inventory acquired from Jefferson (€3,000,000) for a combined inventory of €15,000,000. Long-term debt has a book value of €16,000,000 on Franklin's pre-acquisition statements, and Jefferson's fair value of debt is €1,800,000. The combined long-term debt is recorded as €17,800,000.

[32] Under the uniting (pooling) of interests method (which required an exchange of common shares), the shares issued by Franklin would be measured at their par value. In addition, the assets and liabilities of both companies would be combined at their book values resulting in no goodwill being recognized. The retained earnings of Jefferson would also be combined with that of Franklin on the consolidated balance sheet.

Franklin's post-merger financial statement reflects in stockholders' equity the stock issued by Franklin to acquire Jefferson. Franklin issues stock with a par value of €1,000,000; however, the stock is measured at fair value under both IFRS and U.S. GAAP. Therefore, the consideration exchanged is 1,000,000 shares at market value of €15, or €15,000,000. Prior to the transaction, Franklin had 5,000,000 shares of €1 par stock outstanding (€5,000,000). The combined entity reflects the Franklin capital stock outstanding of €6,000,000 (€5,000,000 plus the additional 1,000,000 shares of €1 par stock issued to effect the transaction). Franklin's additional paid in capital of €6,000,000 is increased by the €14,000,000 additional paid in capital from the issuance of the 1,000,000 shares (€15,000,000 less par value of €1,000,000) for a total of €20,000,000. At the acquisition date, only the acquirer's retained earnings are carried to the combined entity. Earnings of the target are included on the consolidated income statement and retained earnings only in post-acquisition periods.

6.3 Impact of the Acquisition Method on Financial Statements, Post-Acquisition

In the periods subsequent to the business combination, the financial statements continue to be affected by the acquisition method. Net income reflects the performance of the combined entity. Under the acquisition method, amortization/depreciation is based on historical cost of Franklin's assets and the fair value of Jefferson's assets. Using Example 8, in the year the inventory is sold, the cost of goods sold would be €15,000,000, and depreciation on PP&E would be €2,000,000 higher over the life of the asset (€31.5 million versus €29.5 million).[33]

6.4 Consolidated Financial Statements

Consolidated financial statements combine the results of operations for distinct legal entities, the parent and its subsidiaries, as if they were one economic unit. IFRS and U.S. GAAP both require consolidation, but each is based on a different control model. The control model is important when considering variable interest and special purpose entities. These entities will be discussed in more detail in Section 7 but some of the implications are mentioned below.

Under the principles-based framework of IFRS, consolidation is required when one company (the parent) has the ability to govern (control) the financial and operating policies of another company (the subsidiary). Control is presumed to exist when the parent owns either directly or indirectly (i.e., through its subsidiaries), more than half of the voting shares of another entity (voting interest model). In situations where the parent owns half or less of the voting share, consolidation is based on an overall assessment of all of the relevant factors, including the allocation of risks and benefits between the parties.

[33] Under the pooling method, cost of goods sold and depreciation expense would be lower, since both would be based on the book value of the Jefferson's assets. Therefore, analysts must be aware of companies that used the uniting (pooling) of interests prior to the method being disallowed. This is because in the periods after pooling was disallowed, the assets of an entity that had used uniting of interests (pooling) may be understated and income overstated relative to companies that used the acquisition method. These differences will affect the comparability of return on investment ratios.

U.S. GAAP uses a two-component consolidation model that includes both a variable interest component and a voting interest (control) component. Under the variable interest component, FIN 46(R)[34] requires the primary beneficiary of a variable interest entity (VIE) to consolidate the VIE regardless of its voting interests (if any) in the VIE or its decision-making authority. The primary beneficiary is defined as the party that will absorb the majority of the VIE's expected losses, receive the majority of the VIE's expected residual returns, or both.

6.4.1 The Consolidation Process

Consolidation combines the assets, liabilities, revenues, and expenses of subsidiaries with the parent company. Transactions between the parent and subsidiary (intercompany transactions) are eliminated to avoid double counting and premature income recognition. Consolidated statements are presumed to be more meaningful in terms of representational faithfulness. It is important for the analyst to consider the differences in IFRS and U.S. GAAP, valuation bases, and other factors that could impair the validity of comparative analyses.

6.4.2 Business Combination with Less than 100 Percent Acquisition

In a merger or consolidation, the acquirer purchases 100 percent of the equity of the target company. In an acquisition, however, the acquirer does not have to purchase 100 percent of the equity of the target in order to achieve control. The acquiring company may purchase less than 100 percent of the target because it may be constrained by resources or it may be unable to acquire all the outstanding shares. As a result, both the acquirer and the target remain separate legal entities. Both IFRS and U.S. GAAP presume a company has control if it owns more than 50 percent of the voting shares of an entity. In this case, the acquiring company is viewed as the parent, and the target company is viewed as the subsidiary. Both the parent and the subsidiary prepare their own financial records, but the parent also prepares consolidated financial statements at each reporting period. The consolidated financial statements are the primary source of information for investors and analysts.

6.4.3 Noncontrolling (Minority) Interests: Balance Sheet

A noncontrolling (minority) interest is the portion of the subsidiary's equity (residual interest) that is held by third parties (i.e., not owned by the parent). Noncontrolling interests are created when the parent acquires less than a 100 percent controlling interest in a subsidiary.

IFRS and U.S. GAAP (SFAS 160)[35] have converged on how noncontrolling interests are classified. Both now require noncontrolling interests in consolidated subsidiaries to be presented on the consolidated balance sheet as a separate component of stockholders' equity. Previously, companies using IFRS reported noncontrolling interests as equity, whereas those applying U.S. GAAP reported noncontrolling interests either as liabilities or between (mezzanine section) liabilities and equity.

IFRS and U.S. GAAP still differ, however, on the measurement of noncontrolling interests. Under IFRS, the parent can measure the noncontrolling interest at either its fair value (full goodwill method) or at the noncontrolling interest's proportionate share of the acquiree's identifiable net assets (partial goodwill method). Under U.S. GAAP, the parent must use the full goodwill method and measure the noncontrolling interest at fair value.

Example 9 illustrates the current differences in reporting requirements.

---

[34] FASB ASC Topic 810 [Consolidation].

[35] FASB ASC Topic 810 [Consolidation].

EXAMPLE 9

Goodwill

On 1 January 2009, the hypothetical Parent Co. acquired 90 percent of the outstanding shares of the hypothetical Subsidiary Co. in exchange for shares of Parent Co.'s no par common stock with a fair value of €180,000. The fair market value of the subsidiary's shares on the date of the exchange was €200,000. Below is selected financial information from the two companies immediately prior to the exchange of shares (before the parent recorded the acquisition):

	Parent	Subsidiary	
	Book Value	Book Value	Fair Value
Cash and receivables	€ 40,000	€ 15,000	€ 15,000
Inventory	125,000	80,000	80,000
PP&E (net)	235,000	95,000	155,000
	€400,000	€190,000	€250,000
Payables	55,000	20,000	20,000
Long-term debt	120,000	70,000	70,000
	175,000	90,000	90,000
Net assets	€225,000	€100,000	€160,000
Shareholders' equity:			
Capital stock (no par)	€87,000	€34,000	
Retained earnings	€138,000	€66,000	

1. Calculate the value of PP&E on the consolidated balance sheet under both IFRS and U.S. GAAP.
2. Calculate the value of goodwill and the value of the noncontrolling interest at the acquisition date under the full goodwill method.
3. Calculate the value of goodwill and the value of the noncontrolling interest at the acquisition date under the partial goodwill method.

Solution to 1: Relative to fair value, the PP&E of the subsidiary is understated by €60,000. Under the acquisition method (IFRS and U.S. GAAP), as long as the parent has control over the subsidiary (i.e., regardless of whether the parent had purchased 51 percent or 100 percent of the subsidiary's stock), it would include 100 percent of the subsidiary's assets and liabilities at fair value on the consolidated balance sheet. Therefore, PP&E on the consolidated balance sheet would be valued at €390,000.

Solution to 2: Under the full goodwill method (mandatory under U.S. GAAP and optional under IFRS), goodwill on the consolidated balance sheet would be the difference between the total fair value of the subsidiary and the fair value of the subsidiary's identifiable net assets.

Fair value of the subsidiary	€200,000
Fair value of subsidiary's identifiable net assets	160,000
Goodwill	€ 40,000

The value of the noncontrolling interest is equal to the noncontrolling interest's proportionate share of the subsidiary's fair value. The noncontrolling interest's proportionate share of the subsidiary is 10 percent, and the fair value of the subsidiary is €200,000 on the acquisition date. Under the full goodwill method, the value of the noncontrolling interest would be €20,000 (10% × €200,000).

Solution to 3: Under the partial goodwill method (IFRS only), goodwill on the parent's consolidated balance sheet would be €36,000, the difference between the purchase price and the parent's proportionate share of the subsidiary's identifiable assets.

Acquisition price	€180,000
90% of fair value	144,000
Goodwill	€ 36,000

The value of the noncontrolling interest is equal to the noncontrolling interest's proportionate share of the fair value of the subsidiary's identifiable net assets. The noncontrolling interest's proportionate share is 10 percent, and the fair value of the subsidiary's identifiable net assets on the acquisition date is €160,000. Under the partial goodwill method, the value of the noncontrolling interest would be €16,000 (10% × €160,000).

Regardless of which method is used, goodwill is not amortized under either IFRS or U.S. GAAP but it is tested for impairment at least annually.

For comparative purposes, below is the balance sheet at the acquisition date under the full goodwill and partial goodwill methods.

Comparative Consolidated Balance Sheet at Acquisition Date: Acquisition Method

	Full Goodwill	Partial Goodwill
Cash and receivables	€ 55,000	€ 55,000
Inventory	205,000	205,000
PP&E (net)	390,000	390,000
Goodwill	40,000	36,000
Total assets	€690,000	€686,000

(continued on next page. . .)

	Full Goodwill	Partial Goodwill
Payables	€ 75,000	€ 75,000
Long-term debt	190,000	190,000
Total liabilities	€265,000	€265,000
Shareholders' equity:		
Noncontrolling interests	€ 20,000	€ 16,000
Capital stock (no par)	€267,000	€267,000
Retained earnings	138,000	138,000
Total equity	€425,000	€421,000
Total liabilities and shareholders' equity	€690,000	€686,000

6.4.4 Noncontrolling (Minority) Interests: Income Statement

On the income statement, noncontrolling (minority) interests are presented as a line item reflecting the allocation of profit or loss for the period. Intercompany transactions, if any, are eliminated in full.

Using assumed data consistent with the facts in Example 9, the amounts included for the subsidiary in the consolidated income statements under IFRS and U.S. GAAP are presented below:

	Full Goodwill	Partial Goodwill
Sales	€250,000	€250,000
Cost of goods sold	137,500	137,500
Interest expense	10,000	10,000
Depreciation expense	39,000	39,000
Income from continuing operations	€ 63,500	€ 63,500
Noncontrolling interest (10%)	(6,350)	(6,350)
Consolidated net income to shareholders	€ 57,150	€ 57,150

Income to the parent's shareholders is €57,150 using either method. This is because the fair value of the PP&E is allocated to noncontrolling shareholders as well as to the controlling shareholders under the full goodwill and the partial goodwill methods. Therefore, the noncontrolling interests will share in the adjustment for excess depreciation due to the €60,000 increase in PP&E. Since depreciation expense is the same under both methods, it results in identical net income to all shareholders, whichever method is used to recognize goodwill and to measure the noncontrolling interest.

Although net income to shareholders is the same, the impact on ratios would be different, because total assets and stockholders' equity would differ.

Impact on Ratios		
	Full Goodwill (%)	**Partial Goodwill (%)**
Return on assets	8.28	8.33
Return on equity	13.44	13.57

Over time, the value of the subsidiary will change as a result of net income and changes in equity. As a result, the value of the noncontrolling interest on the parent's consolidated balance sheet will also change.

6.4.5 Goodwill Impairment

Although goodwill is not amortized, it must be tested for impairment at least annually or more frequently if events or changes in circumstances indicate that it might be impaired. If it is probable that some or all of the goodwill will not be recovered through the profitable operations of the combined entity, it should be partially or fully written off by charging it to an expense. Once written down, goodwill cannot be later restored.

IFRS and U.S. GAAP differ on the definition of the levels at which goodwill is assigned and tested for impairment.

Under IFRS, at the time of acquisition, the total amount of goodwill recognized is allocated to each of the acquirer's cash-generating units that will benefit from the expected synergies resulting from the combination with the target. A cash-generating unit represents the lowest level within the combined entity at which goodwill is monitored for impairment purposes.[36] Goodwill impairment testing is then conducted under a one-step approach. The recoverable amount of a cash-generating unit is calculated and compared with the carrying value of the cash-generating unit.[37] An impairment loss is recognized if the recoverable amount of the cash-generating unit is less than its carrying value. The impairment loss (the difference between these two amounts) is first applied to the goodwill that has been allocated to the cash-generating unit. Once this has been reduced to zero, the remaining amount of the loss is then allocated to all of the other assets in the unit on a pro rata basis.

Under U.S. GAAP, at the time of acquisition, the total amount of goodwill recognized is allocated to each of the acquirer's reporting units. A reporting unit is an operating segment or component of an operating segment that is one level below the operating segment as a whole. Goodwill impairment testing is then conducted under a two-step approach: identification of impairment and then measurement of the loss. First, the carrying amount of the reporting unit (including goodwill) is compared to its fair value. If the carrying value of the reporting unit exceeds its fair value, an impairment loss has occurred. The second step is then performed to measure the amount of the impairment loss. The amount of the impairment loss is the difference between the implied fair value

36 A cash-generating unit is the smallest identifiable group of assets that generates cash inflows that are largely independent of the cash inflows from other assets or groups of assets.

37 The recoverable amount of a cash-generating unit is the higher of net selling price (i.e., fair value less costs to sell) and its value in use. Value in use is the present value of the future cash flows expected to be derived from the cash-generating unit. The carrying value of a cash-generating unit is equal to the carrying value of the unit's assets and liabilities including the goodwill that has been allocated to that unit.

of the reporting unit's goodwill and its carrying amount. The implied fair value of goodwill is determined in the same manner as in a business combination (it is the difference between the fair value of the reporting unit and the fair value of the reporting unit's assets and liabilities). The impairment loss is applied to the goodwill that has been allocated to the reporting unit. After the goodwill of the reporting unit has been eliminated, no other adjustments are made to the carrying values of any of the reporting unit's other assets or liabilities.

Under both IFRS and U.S. GAAP, the impairment loss is recorded as a separate line item in the consolidated income statement.

EXAMPLE 10

Goodwill Impairment: IFRS

The cash-generating unit of a French company has a carrying value of €1,400,000, which includes €300,000 of allocated goodwill. The recoverable amount of the cash-generating unit is determined to be €1,300,000, and the estimated fair value of its identifiable net assets is €1,200,000. Calculate the impairment loss.

Solution:

Recoverable amount of unit	€1,300,000
Carrying amount of unit	1,400,000
Impairment loss	€ 100,000

The impairment loss of €100,000 is reported on the income statement, and the goodwill allocated to the cash-generating unit would be reduced by €100,000 to €200,000.

If the recoverable amount of the cash-generating unit had been €800,000 instead of €1,300,000, the impairment loss recognized would be €600,000. This would first be absorbed by the goodwill allocated to the unit (€300,000). Once this has been reduced to the zero, the remaining amount of the impairment loss (€300,000) would then be allocated on a pro rata basis to the other assets within the unit.

EXAMPLE 11

Goodwill Impairment: U.S. GAAP

A reporting unit of a U.S. corporation (e.g., a division) has a fair value of $1,300,000 and a carrying value of $1,400,000 that includes recorded goodwill of $300,000. The estimated fair value of the identifiable net assets of the reporting unit is $1,200,000. Calculate the impairment loss.

Solution:

Step 1 – Determination of an Impairment Loss

Since the fair value of the reporting unit is less than its carrying book value, an impairment loss must be recognized.

Fair market value of unit: $1,300,000 < $1,400,000

Step 2 – Measurement of the Impairment Loss

Fair market value of unit	$1,300,000
Less: net assets	1,200,000
Implied goodwill	$ 100,000

Current carrying value of goodwill	$ 300,000
Less: implied goodwill	100,000
Impairment loss	$ 200,000

The impairment loss of $200,000 is reported on the income statement, and the goodwill allocated to the reporting unit would be reduced by $200,000 to $100,000.

If the fair market value of the reporting unit and its net assets were $800,000 (instead of $1,300,000), the implied goodwill would be a negative $400,000. In this case, the maximum amount of the impairment loss recognized would be $300,000, the carrying amount of goodwill.

6.5 Financial Statement Presentation Subsequent to the Business Combination

The presentation of consolidated financial statements is similar under IFRS and U.S. GAAP. For example, selected financial statements for GlaxoSmithKline are shown in Exhibits 6 and 7. GlaxoSmithKline is a leading pharmaceutical company headquartered in the United Kingdom.

The consolidated balance sheet in Exhibit 6 combines the operations of GlaxoSmithKline and its subsidiaries. The analyst can observe that in 2007 GlaxoSmithKline had investments in financial assets (other investments of £517,000,000 and liquid investments of £1,153,000,000), and investments in associates and joint ventures of £329,000,000. In 2007 GlaxoSmithKline acquired a 100 percent interest in three companies. The increase in goodwill on the balance sheet reflects the fact that GlaxoSmithKline paid an amount in excess of the fair value of the identifiable net assets in these acquisitions. The analyst can also note that GlaxoSmithKline is the parent company in a less than 100 percent acquisition. The minority interest of £307,000,000 in the equity section is the portion of the combined entity that accrues to noncontrolling shareholders. Because the company used the partial goodwill method under IFRS, the noncontrolling interest was reflected at the acquisition date based on the noncontrolling interest's share of the fair value of the net assets acquired.

EXHIBIT 6 GlaxoSmithKline Consolidated Balance Sheet at 31 December 2007

	Notes	2007 £m	2006 £m
Non-current assets			
Property, plant and equipment	17	**7,821**	6,930
Goodwill	18	**1,370**	758
Other intangible assets	19	**4,456**	3,293
Investments in associates and joint ventures	20	**329**	295
Other investments	21	**517**	441
Deferred tax assets	14	**2,196**	2,123
Derivative financial instruments	41	**1**	113
Other non-current assets	22	**687**	608
Total non-current assets		**17,377**	14,561
Current assets			
Inventories	23	**3,062**	2,437
Current tax recoverable	14	**58**	186
Trade and other receivables	24	**5,495**	5,237
Derivative financial instruments	41	**475**	80
Liquid investments	32	**1,153**	1,035
Cash and cash equivalents	25	**3,379**	2,005
Assets held for sale	26	**4**	12
Total current assets		**13,626**	10,992
Total assets		**31,003**	25,553
Current liabilities			
Short-term borrowings	32	**(3,504)**	(718)
Trade and other payables	27	**(4,861)**	(4,831)
Derivative financial instruments	41	**(262)**	(40)
Current tax payable	14	**(826)**	(621)
Short-term provisions	29	**(892)**	(1,055)
Total current liabilities		**(10,345)**	(7,265)
Non-current liabilities			
Long-term borrowings	32	**(7,067)**	(4,772)
Deferred tax liabilities	14	**(887)**	(595)
Pensions and other post-employment benefits	28	**(1,383)**	(2,339)
Other provisions	29	**(1,035)**	(528)
Derivative financial instruments	41	**(8)**	(60)
Other non-current liabilities	30	**(368)**	(346)
Total non-current liabilities		**(10,748)**	(8,640)
Total liabilities		**(21,093)**	(15,905)
Net assets		**9,910**	9,648
Equity			
Share capital	33	**1,503**	1,498
Share premium account	33	**1,266**	858
Retained earnings	34	**6,475**	6,965
Other reserves	34	**359**	65
Shareholders' equity		**9,603**	9,386
Minority interests	34	**307**	262
Total equity		**9,910**	9,648

The consolidated income statement for GlaxoSmithKline is presented in Exhibit 7. IFRS and U.S. GAAP have similar formats for consolidated income statements. Each line item (e.g., turnover [sales], cost of sales, etc.) includes 100 percent of the parent and the subsidiary transactions after eliminating any upstream (subsidiary sells to parent) or downstream (parent sells to subsidiary) intercompany transactions. The portion of income accruing to noncontrolling shareholders is presented as a separate line item on the consolidated income statement. Note that net income would be the same under IFRS and U.S. GAAP.[38] The analyst will need to make adjustments for any analysis comparing specific line items that might differ between IFRS and U.S. GAAP.

EXHIBIT 7 **GlaxoSmithKline Consolidated Income Statement for the Year Ended 31 December 2007**

		2007			2006	2005
	Notes	Business performance £m	Restructuring cost £m	Total £m	£m	£m
Turnover	6	22,716	—	**22,716**	23,225	21,660
Cost of sales		(5,206)	(111)	**(5,317)**	(5,010)	(4,764)
Gross profit		17,510	(111)	**17,399**	18,215	16,896
Selling, general and administration		(6,817)	(137)	**(6,954)**	(7,257)	(7,250)
Research and development		(3,237)	(90)	**(3,327)**	(3,457)	(3,136)
Other operating income	8	475	—	**475**	307	364
Operating profit	9,10	7,931	(338)	**7,593**	7,808	6,874
Finance income	11	262	—	**262**	287	257
Finance costs	12	(453)	—	**(453)**	(352)	(451)
Share of after tax profits of associates and joint ventures	13	50	—	**50**	56	52
Profit before taxation		7,790	(338)	**7,452**	7,799	6,732
Taxation	14	(2,219)	77	**(2,142)**	(2,301)	(1,916)
Profit after taxation for the year		5,571	(261)	**5,310**	5,498	4,816
Profit attributable to minority interests		96	—	**96**	109	127
Profit attributable to shareholders		5,475	(261)	**5,214**	5,389	4,689
		5,571	(261)	**5,310**	5,498	4,816
Basic earnings per share (pence)	15			**94.4p**	95.5p	82.6p
Diluted earnings per share (pence)	15			**93.7p**	94.5p	82.0p

[38] It is possible, however, for differences to arise through the application of different accounting rules (e.g., valuation of fixed assets).

6.6 Additional Issues in Business Combinations That Impair Comparability

Accounting for business combinations is a complex topic. In addition to the basics covered so far in this reading, we briefly mention some of the more common issues that impair comparability between IFRS and U.S. GAAP.

6.6.1 Contingent Assets and Liabilities

Under IFRS, the cost of an acquisition is allocated to the fair value of assets, liabilities, and contingent liabilities. Contingent liabilities are recorded separately as part of the cost allocation process, provided that their fair values can be measured reliably. Subsequently, the contingent liability is measured at the higher of the amount initially recognized or the best estimate of the amount required to settle. Contingent assets are not recognized under IFRS.

Under U.S. GAAP, contractual contingent assets and liabilities are recognized and recorded at their fair values at the time of acquisition. Noncontractual contingent assets and liabilities must also be recognized and recorded only if it is "more likely than not" they meet the definition of an asset or a liability at the acquisition date. Subsequently, a contingent liability is measured at the higher of the amount initially recognized or the best estimate of the amount of the loss. A contingent asset, however, is measured at the lower of the acquisition date fair value or the best estimate of the future settlement amount.

6.6.2 Contingent Consideration

Contingent consideration may be negotiated as part of the acquisition price. For example, the parent may agree to pay additional money to the subsidiary's shareholders if certain sales or profit levels are attained by the combined entity. Under both IFRS and U.S. GAAP, contingent consideration is initially measured at fair value. IFRS and U.S. GAAP classify contingent consideration as either a financial liability or equity. In addition, U.S. GAAP allows contingent consideration to also be classified as an asset. In subsequent periods, changes in the fair value of liabilities (and assets, in the case of U.S. GAAP) are recognized in the consolidated income statement. Both IFRS and U.S. GAAP do not remeasure equity classified contingent consideration; instead, settlement is accounted for within equity.

6.6.3 In-Process R&D

IFRS and U.S. GAAP recognize in-process research and development (R&D) acquired in a business combination as a separate intangible asset and measure it at fair value (if it can be measured reliably). In subsequent periods, R&D is subject to amortization upon completion or impairment.

6.6.4 Restructuring Costs

IFRS and U.S. GAAP do not recognize restructuring costs that are associated with the business combination as part of the cost of the acquisition. Instead, they are recognized as an expense in the periods the restructuring costs are incurred.

VARIABLE INTEREST AND SPECIAL PURPOSE ENTITIES

7

Special purpose entities (SPEs) are enterprises that are created to accommodate specific needs of the sponsoring entity.[39] The sponsoring entity (on whose behalf the SPE is created) frequently transfers assets to the SPE, obtains the right to use assets held by the SPE, or performs services for the SPE, while other parties (capital providers) provide funding to the SPE. SPEs can be a legitimate financing mechanism for a company to segregate certain activities and thereby reduce risk. SPEs may take the form of a corporation, trust, partnership, or unincorporated entity. They are often created with legal arrangements that impose strict and sometimes permanent limits on the decision-making powers of their governing board or management.

Beneficial interest in an SPE may take the form of a debt instrument, an equity instrument, a participation right, or a residual interest in a lease. Some beneficial interests may simply provide the holder with a fixed or stated rate of return, while beneficial interests give the holder the rights or the access to future economic benefits of the SPE's activities. In most cases, the creator/sponsor of the entity retains a significant beneficial interest in the SPE even though it may own little or none of the SPE's voting equity.

In the past, sponsors were able to avoid consolidating SPEs on their financial statements because they did not have "control" (i.e., own a majority of the voting interest) of the SPE. SPEs were structured so that the sponsoring company had financial control over their assets or operating activities, while third parties held the majority of the voting interest in the SPE.

These outside equity participants often funded their investments in the SPE with debt that was either directly or indirectly guaranteed by the sponsoring companies. The sponsoring companies, in turn, were able to avoid the disclosure of many of these guarantees as well as their economic significance. In addition, many sponsoring companies created SPEs to facilitate the transfer of assets and liabilities from their own balance sheets. As a result, they were able to recognize large amounts of revenue and gains, because these transactions were accounted for as sales. By avoiding consolidation, sponsoring companies did not have to report the assets and the liabilities of the SPE; financial performance as measured by unconsolidated financial statements was potentially misleading. The benefit to the sponsoring company was improved asset turnover, lower operating and financial leverage metrics, and higher profitability.

Enron, for example, used SPEs to obtain off-balance sheet financing and artificially improve its financial performance. Its subsequent collapse was partly attributable to its guarantee of the debt of the SPEs it had created.

To address the accounting issues arising from the misuse and abuse of SPEs, the IASB and the FASB have augmented their existing consolidation models to take into account financial arrangements where parties other than the holders of the majority of the voting interests exercise financial control over another entity. In addition, they have revised their standards concerning the measurement, reporting, and disclosure of all guarantees.

Currently, IAS 27 requires the consolidation of entities when the substance of the relationship indicates that the entity is controlled by the reporting entity.

[39] The term "special purpose entity" is used by IFRS and "variable interest entity" is used by U.S. GAAP.

However, the standard does not provide explicit guidance about the circumstances under which an SPE should be consolidated. SIC 12 does provide indicators of control:

- The SPE activities are conducted for the benefit of the sponsoring entity.
- The sponsoring entity has decision-making powers to obtain benefits.
- The sponsoring entity is able to absorb the risks and rewards of the SPE.
- The sponsoring entity has a residual interest in the SPE.

Under the revised IAS 39, a financial guarantee contract is defined as a contract that requires the issuer to make specified payments to reimburse the holder for a loss it incurs because a specified debtor fails to make payment when due. IFRS 3 requires financial guarantees to be initially recognized at fair value and in subsequent periods to be reported at the higher of the best estimate to settle the guarantee or the amount initially recognized.

In developing new accounting standards to address the consolidation issue, the FASB used the more general term variable interest entity (VIE) to more broadly define an entity that is financially controlled by one or more parties that do not hold a majority voting interest. Therefore, under U.S. GAAP, a VIE includes other entities besides SPEs. SFAS 140 and Interpretation FIN 46R provide guidance for U.S. GAAP,[40] which classifies special purpose entities as variable interest entities if:

1. total equity at risk is insufficient to finance activities without financial support from other parties, or
2. equity investors lack any one of the following:
   a. the ability to make decisions;
   b. the obligation to absorb losses; or
   c. the right to receive return.

Common examples of variable interests are entities created to lease real estate or other property, entities created for the securitization of financial assets, or entities created for R&D activity.

Under FIN 46R, the primary beneficiary of a VIE must consolidate it as its subsidiary regardless of how much of an equity investment it has in the VIE. The primary beneficiary (which is often the sponsor) is the entity that is expected to absorb the majority of the VIE's expected losses, receive the majority of the VIE's residual returns, or both. If one entity will absorb a majority of the VIE's expected losses and another unrelated entity will receive a majority of the VIE's expected residual returns, the entity absorbing a majority of the losses must consolidate the VIE. If there are noncontrolling interests in the VIE, these would also be shown in the consolidated balance sheet and consolidated income statement of the primary beneficiary.

7.1 Qualifying Special Purpose Entities

Prior to the revision of SFAS 140 and FIN 46 (effective 15 December 2008), it was possible under U.S. GAAP to structure a special purpose entity in a way that did not meet the variable interest criteria and consolidation requirements. To be a **qualifying special purpose entity** (QSPE) an entity had to 1) be independent and

[40] SFAS 140 and FIN 46R are superseded by FASB ASC Topic 810 [Consolidation].

legally separate from the sponsoring company, 2) have complete control over its assets, and 3) hold only financial assets. In addition, the sponsoring company had to be *bankruptcy remote*, which means that its financial risk was limited to either its investment or to an explicit recourse obligation in the SPE.

Therefore, a sponsor company did not have to consolidate a QSPE since it was not its primary beneficiary (i.e., it had no control over the entity's assets, nor was it expected to absorb the majority of its expected losses). This enabled the sponsoring company to derecognize the transferred assets (remove them from their balance sheet) and report the transaction as a sale.

The subprime crisis in 2007 and the resulting credit crisis in 2008 revealed that many of the sponsoring companies (transferors) had more continuing involvement with the transferred assets than they should have had in order to derecognize the assets and record the original transaction as a sale. Many banks and other financial institutions were forced to place the assets that were previously transferred to QSPEs back on their balance sheets and recognize substantial losses due to a decline in value of these assets. As a result, many financial statements users voiced concerns about their inability to understand the nature of the transferor's relationship with the QSPE, its maximum risk exposure, and the extent of its risk exposure.

The elimination of QSPEs by the FASB is intended to increase the transparency and comparability of companies involved with VIEs and further convergence, since QSPEs did not exist under IFRS. Revisions in SFAS 140 and FIN 46R have provided financial statement users with a better understanding of a company relationship with a VIE in terms of the extent of its involvement, its maximum risk exposure, and the current status of its exposure. The revised accounting standards have increased the consolidation of entities that formerly met the QSPE criteria and reduced the types of transferred financial assets that would have previously been eligible for derecognition and classified as a sale. In addition, sponsoring companies are now required to disclose the risks that they continue to be exposed to from their continuing involvement in transferred assets.

In an effort to more closely align with IFRS, the revised FIN 46R replaced a quantitative-based risks and reward calculation with a principles-based approach. This makes it easier to determine which enterprise will receive the majority of the expected residual returns from the VIE and which is expected to absorb the majority of expected losses.

7.2 Illustration of an SPE for a Leased Asset

Consider the situation in which a sponsoring company creates a special purpose entity with minimal and independent third party equity. The SPE borrows from the debt market and acquires or constructs an asset. The asset may be acquired from the sponsoring company or from an outside source. The sponsoring company then leases the asset, and the cash flow from lease payments is used to repay the debt and provide a return to equity holders. Because the asset is pledged as collateral, risk is reduced and a lower interest rate may be offered by the financing organization. In addition, because equity investors are not exposed to all the business risks of the sponsoring company but only those of the restricted SPE, they may be more willing to invest in this relatively safe investment. The sponsor retains the risk of default and receives the benefits of ownership of the leased asset through a residual value guarantee. Under these conditions, the sponsor is the primary beneficiary and consolidates the SPE.

In 1996, Dreamworks Animation SKG entered into an agreement with financial institutions to construct their Glendale animation campus in Glendale, California. The 326,000 square foot facility houses a majority of Dreamworks

EXHIBIT 8 Illustration of SPE for a Leased Asset

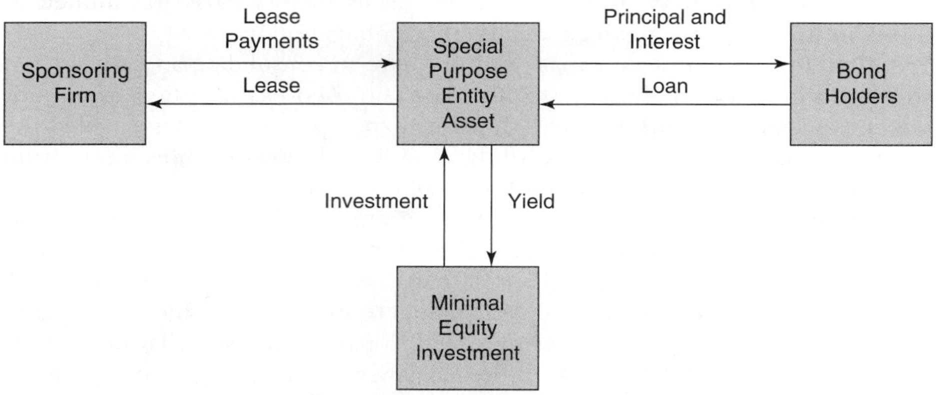

employees. In 2002, Dreamworks created a special purpose entity that acquired the property from the financial institution for $73.0 million. The special purpose entity leases the facility back to Dreamworks. It has been determined that Dreamworks Animation SKG is the primary beneficiary of the SPE. Dreamworks Animation SKG discloses the following information about its use of special purpose entities in its 2007 annual report:

> Our Glendale animation campus is approximately 326,000 square feet and houses a majority of our employees. The lease of the Glendale animation campus, which had originally been with a financial institution that had acquired and financed the Glendale animation campus for $76.5 million, was renegotiated in March 2002 through the creation of a special-purpose entity that acquired the property from the financial institution for $73.0 million. The lease term with the special-purpose entity was originally for a five-year term and was subsequently extended through October 2009.
>
> In connection with the adoption of FASB Interpretation No. 46 "Consolidation of Variable Interest Entities," the special-purpose entity associated with this financing was consolidated by us as of December 31, 2003 and, as such, the balance of the obligation is presented on the consolidated balance sheets as $70.1 million of bank borrowings and other debt and a $2.9 million non-controlling minority interest.
>
> In addition, in accordance with FIN 46R, the Company consolidates the special-purpose entity that acquired its Glendale animation campus in March 2002 (see Note 8). Accordingly, $63.9 million of property, plant and equipment, net of $9.1 million of accumulated depreciation, which represents the lower of the cost or fair value of the Glendale animation campus, and $70.1 million of debt and a $2.9 million minority interest, respectively, are included in the accompanying consolidated balance sheets as of December 31, 2007 and 2006.
>
> The entire amount of the obligation, $73.0 million, is due and payable in October 2009, bears interest primarily at 30-day commercial paper rates and is fully collateralized by the underlying real property. In connection with the adoption of FIN46R, the special purpose entity associated with this financing was consolidated by the Company as of December 31, 2003 and, as such, the balance of the obligation is presented on the consolidated balance sheets as $70.1 million of bank borrowings and other debt and a $2.9 million minority interest.

Source: Dreamworks Animation SKG, Inc. Form 10K, 2007.

7.3 Securitization of Assets

Special purpose entities are often established for the securitization of receivables. The SPE issues debt to acquire all or a portion of the sponsoring company receivables. Repayment of the debt and interest are made with the cash flow generated by the receivables.

For example, Fiat S.p.A. sells its trade receivables to an SPE to improve its cash flows in a cost-effective manner. Fiat, one of the largest industrial companies in Italy, is engaged principally in the manufacture and sale of automobiles, agricultural and construction equipment, trucks, and commercial vehicles. Regarding the sale of receivables, in its 2007 Annual report Fiat states:

> The Group sells a significant part of its financial, trade and tax receivables through either securitisation programs or factoring transactions. A securitisation transaction entails the sale of a portfolio of receivables to a securitisation vehicle. This special purpose entity finances the purchase of the receivables by issuing asset-backed securities (i.e. securities whose repayment and interest flow depend upon the cash flow generated by the portfolio). Asset-backed securities are divided into classes according to their degree of seniority and rating: the most senior classes are placed with investors on the market; the junior class, whose repayment is subordinated to the senior classes, is normally subscribed for by the seller. The residual interest in the receivables retained by the seller is therefore limited to the junior securities it has subscribed for. In accordance with SIC 12—Consolidation—Special Purpose Entities (SPE), all securitisation vehicles are included in the scope of consolidation, because the subscription of the junior asset-backed securities by the seller entails its control in substance over the SPE. Furthermore, factoring transactions may be with or without recourse to the seller; certain factoring agreements without recourse include deferred purchase price clauses (i.e. the payment of a minority portion of the purchase price is conditional upon the full collection of the receivables), require a first loss guarantee of the seller up to a limited amount or imply a continuing significant exposure to the receivables cash flow. These kinds of transactions do not meet IAS 39 requirements for assets derecognition, since the risks and rewards have not been substantially transferred. Consequently, all receivables sold through both securitisation and factoring transactions which do not meet IAS 39 derecognition requirements are recognised as such in the Group financial statements even though they have been legally sold; a corresponding financial liability is recorded in the consolidated balance sheet as "Asset-backed financing." Gains and losses relating to the sale of such assets are not recognised until the assets are removed from the Group balance sheet.

Securitizations raise several issues for the analyst. First, the analyst should assess the relationship to ensure that SPEs are consolidated when appropriate. Second, securitization can have a significant impact on operating cash flows and financial leverage and may need to be adjusted for analysis. Finally, securitization may affect the volatility of operating cash flows.

7.4 Consolidated versus Nonconsolidated Securitization Transactions

A common type of QSPE is a securitization transaction. To illustrate the differences between a consolidated and nonconsolidated securitization transaction consider the following:

Securitized Transaction: Qualified Special Purpose Entity	Securitized Transaction: Special Purpose Entity

▶ Originator of receivables sells financial assets to an SPE.
▶ The originator does not own or hold or expect to receive beneficial interest.
▶ SFAS 140 (before 2008 revision) allowed seller to derecognize the sold assets if transferred assets
  ▶ have been isolated from the transferor and are beyond the reach of bankruptcy, and
  ▶ are financial assets.
	▶ Originator of receivables sells financial assets to an SPE.
	▶ Seller is primary beneficiary; absorbs risks and rewards.
	▶ Seller maintains some level of control.
	▶ Seller is required to consolidate.
	▶ Seller's balance sheet would still show receivables as an asset.
	▶ Debt of SPE would appear on seller's balance sheet.

IFRS do not recognize a qualifying special purpose entity. As Deutsche Telekom AG notes in its 2006 20-F filing with the SEC:

> We have entered into agreements to sell, on a continual basis, certain eligible trade receivables to Special Purpose Entities (SPEs). Under IFRS, these SPEs are consolidated and included in our consolidated financial statements, whereas under U.S. GAAP, these SPEs are considered Qualifying Special Purpose Entities (QSPEs) and are therefore not consolidated. As a result, the transferred receivables are removed from the balance sheet, with a gain or loss recognized on the sale for U.S. GAAP. The measurement of the gain or loss depends on the carrying bases of the transferred receivables, allocated between the receivables sold and the interests and obligations retained, based on their relative fair values as of the date of transfer. Under these agreements, we retain without remuneration the servicing obligation relating to the sold receivables, which are recognized for U.S. GAAP, but not for IFRS.

EXAMPLE 12

Receivables Securitization

Odena, an Italian auto manufacturer, wants to raise €55M in capital by borrowing against its financial receivables. To accomplish this objective, Odena can choose between two alternatives:

Alternative 1: Borrow directly against the receivables; or

Alternative 2: Create a special purpose entity, invest €5M in the SPE, have the SPE borrow €55M, and then use the funds to purchase €60M of receivables from Odena.

Using the financial statement information provided below, describe the effect of each Alternative on Odena, assuming that Odena will not have to consolidate the SPE.

Odena
Balance Sheet

Cash	€ 30,000,000
Accounts receivable	60,000,000
Other assets	40,000,000
Total assets	€130,000,000
Current liabilities	€ 27,000,000
Noncurrent liabilities	20,000,000
Total liabilities	€ 47,000,000
Shareholder equity	€ 83,000,000
Total liabilities and equity	€130,000,000
Current ratio	3.33
Long-term debt to equity	0.24
Equity to total assets	0.64
Accounts receivable turnover	2.50X

Alternative 1: Odena's cash will increase by €55M (to €85M) and its debt will increase by €55M (to €75M). Its sales and net income will not change.

Odena: Alternative 1
Balance Sheet

Cash	€ 85,000,000
Accounts receivable	60,000,000
Other assets	40,000,000
Total assets	€185,000,000
Current liabilities	€ 27,000,000
Noncurrent liabilities	75,000,000
Total liabilities	€102,000,000
Shareholder equity	€ 83,000,000
Total liabilities and equity	€185,000,000
Current ratio	5.37
Long-term debt to equity	0.90
Equity to total assets	0.44

From a ratio perspective, Odena's equity to total assets ratios would be lower, but its debt to equity and current ratios would be higher. However, profitability ratios such as return on assets and return on total capital would be lower.

Alternative 2: Odena's accounts receivable will decrease by €60M and its cash will increase by €55 (it invests €5M in cash in the SPE). However, if Odena is able to sell the receivables to the SPE for more than their carrying value (for example, €65), it would also report a gain on the sale in its profit and loss. Equally important, the SPE may be able to borrow the funds at a lower rate than Odena, since they are bankruptcy remote from Odena (i.e., out of reach of Odena's creditors), and the lenders to the SPE are the claimants on its assets (i.e., the purchased receivables).

Odena: Alternative 2
Unconsolidated Balance Sheet

Cash	€ 85,000,000
Accounts receivable	0
Investment in SPE	5,000,000
Other assets	40,000,000
Total assets	€130,000,000
Current liabilities	€ 27,000,000
Noncurrent liabilities	20,000,000
Total liabilities	€ 47,000,000
Shareholder equity	€ 83,000,000
Total liabilities and equity	€130,000,000
Current ratio	3.15
Long-term debt to equity	0.24
Equity to total assets	0.64

From a ratio perspective, Odena's debt to equity and equity to total assets ratios would be unaffected by the sale; however, its accounts receivable turnover ratio would improve. In addition, if the receivables are transferred (sold) at a gain, Odena's profitability ratios (net profit margin, return on total capital, return on equity, and return on assets) would be higher.

SPE
Balance Sheet

Accounts receivable	€60,000,000
Total assets	€60,000,000
Long-term debt	€55,000,000
Equity	5,000,000
Total liabilities and equity	€60,000,000

If Odena consolidates the SPE, its financial balance sheet would look like the following:

Odena: Alternative 2
Consolidated Balance Sheet

Cash	€ 85,000,000	
Accounts receivable	60,000,000	
Other assets	40,000,000	
Total assets	€185,000,000	
Current liabilities	€ 27,000,000	
Noncurrent liabilities	75,000,000	
Total liabilities	€102,000,000	
Shareholder equity	€ 83,000,000	
Total liabilities and equity	€185,000,000	
Current ratio		5.37
Long-term debt to equity		0.90
Equity to total assets		0.45

Therefore, the consolidated balance sheet of Odena would look exactly the same as if it borrowed directly against the receivables. In addition, as result of the consolidation, the transfer (sale) of the receivables to the SPE would be reversed along with any gain Odena recognized on the sale.

Capital One, in its 2007 10-K filing, provides a reconciliation that illustrates the effect of the securitization on some common performance inputs. The first column reflects the information as reported and does not include consolidation of qualified special purpose entities. The third column reflects the "as if" consolidated. This provides the analyst with an example of how off-balance sheet accounting can affect financial analysis ratios.

EXHIBIT 9 Capital One Reconciliation

The Company's consolidated financial statements prepared in accordance with accounting principles generally accepted in the United States ("GAAP") are referred to as its "reported" financial statements. Loans included in securitization transactions which qualify as sales under GAAP have been removed from the Company's "reported" balance sheet. However, servicing fees, finance charges, and other fees, net of charge-offs, and interest paid to investors of securitizations are recognized as servicing and securitizations income on the "reported" income statement.

The Company's "managed" consolidated financial statements reflect adjustments made related to effects of securitization transactions qualifying as sales under GAAP. The Company generates earnings from

(Exhibit continued on next page . . .)

EXHIBIT 9 (continued)

its "managed" loan portfolio which includes both the on-balance sheet loans and off-balance sheet loans. The Company's "managed" income statement takes the components of the servicing and securitizations income generated from the securitized portfolio and distributes the revenue and expense to appropriate income statement line items from which it originated. For this reason, the Company believes the "managed" consolidated financial statements and related managed metrics to be useful to stakeholders.

As of and for the year ended December 31, 2007:

(Dollars in millions)	Total Reported	Securitization Adjustments[1]	Total Managed[2]
Income Statement Measures[3]			
Net interest income	$ 6,530	$4,490	$11,020
Non-interest income	8,054	(2,288)	5,766
Total revenue	$14,584	$2,202	$16,786
Provision for loan losses	2,637	2,201	4,838
Net charge-offs	1,961	2,201	4,162
Balance Sheet Measures			
Loans held for investment	$101,805	$49,557	$151,362
Total assets	150,590	48,707	199,297
Average loans held for investment	93,837	51,185	145,022
Average earning assets	124,426	49,076	173,502
Average total assets	148,983	50,410	199,393
Delinquencies	3,721	2,143	5,864

[1] Income statement adjustments for the year ended December 31, 2007 reclassify the net of finance charges of $6,334.8 million, past due fees of $1,004.1 million, other interest income of $(167.3) million and interest expense of $2,681.7 million; and net charge-offs of $2,201.5 million to non-interest income from net interest income and provision for loan losses, respectively.

[2] The managed loan portfolio does not include auto loans which have been sold in whole loan sale transactions where the Company has retained servicing rights.

[3] Based on continuing operations.

The impact is apparent in this example. Noninterest income is higher and total assets are lower when the qualified special purpose entity is not consolidated. Therefore, noninterest return on assets is significantly higher without consolidation (5.34 percent versus 2.89 percent).

There is also significant debt that is not reported on the balance sheet when the special purpose entity is not required to be consolidated. This disclosure by Capital One illustrates the effect of off-balance sheet special purpose entities and the usefulness of this type of financial information for performance analysis.

SUMMARY

Intercompany investments play a significant role in business activities and create significant challenges for the analyst in assessing company performance. Investments in other corporations can take five basic forms: investments in financial assets, investments in associates, joint ventures, business combinations, and investments in special purpose and variable interest entities. Key concepts are as follows:

- Investments in financial assets are those in which the investor has no significant influence. They can be designated as held-to-maturity investments, held for trading securities, or available-for-sale securities. IFRS and U.S. GAAP treat investments in financial assets in a similar manner.
  - Held-to-maturity investments are carried at cost.
  - Held for trading securities are carried at fair value; unrealized gains and losses are reported on the profit or loss (income) statement.
  - Available-for-sale securities are carried at fair value; unrealized gains and losses are reported in other comprehensive income in the equity section of the balance sheet.
  - Gains or losses on investments designated as fair value are reported on the profit and loss (income) statement.
  - Both IFRS and U.S. GAAP allow investments that would be classified as either held-to-maturity or available-for-sale to be carried at fair value, with unrealized losses reported in profit or loss (income statement).
- Investments in associates are those in which the investor has significant influence, but not control, over the investee's business activities. Because the investor can exert significant influence over financial and operating policy decisions, IFRS and U.S. GAAP require the equity method of accounting because it provides a more objective basis for reporting investment income.
  - The equity method requires the investor to recognize income as earned rather than when dividends are received.
  - The equity investment is carried at cost, plus its share of post-acquisition income (after adjustments) less dividends received.
  - The equity investment is reported as a single line item on the balance sheet and on the income statement.
- Joint ventures are entities owned and operated by a small group of investors with shared common control. IFRS and U.S. GAAP apply different standards to joint ventures. IFRS favor proportionate consolidation, which requires the venturer's share of the assets, liabilities, income, and expenses of the joint venture to be combined on a line-by-line basis with similar items in the venturer's financial statements. However, IFRS does allow the use of the equity method to account for jointly controlled entities. U.S. GAAP requires the equity method accounting for joint ventures.
- Business combinations can be structured as mergers, acquisitions, or consolidations under U.S. GAAP. IFRS makes no such distinction amongst business combinations.

- An acquisition allows for the legal continuity for each of the combining companies. Both companies continue as separate entities through a parent–subsidiary relationship.
  - If the acquiring company acquires less than 100 percent, noncontrolling (minority) shareholders' interests are reported on the consolidated financial statements.
  - Consolidated financial statements are prepared in each reporting period.
- Current IFRS and U.S. GAAP accounting standards require the use of the acquisition method to account for business combinations. Fair value is the appropriate measurement for identifiable assets and liabilities acquired in the business combination. If the acquisition is less than 100 percent, IFRS allow the noncontrolling interest to be measured at either its fair value (full goodwill) or at the noncontrolling interest's proportionate share of the acquiree's identifiable net assets (partial goodwill). U.S. GAAP requires the noncontrolling interest to be measured at fair value (full goodwill).
- Goodwill is the difference between the acquisition value and the fair value of the target's identifiable net tangible and intangible assets. Because it is considered to have an indefinite life, it is not amortized. Instead, it is evaluated at least annually for impairment. Impairment losses are reported on the income statement. IFRS use a one-step approach to determine and measure the impairment loss, whereas U.S. GAAP use a two-step approach.
- Special purpose (SPEs) and variable interest entities (VIEs) are required to be consolidated by the entity which is expected to absorb the majority of the expected losses or receive the majority of expected residual benefits.
- U.S. GAAP has eliminated the use of qualified special purpose entities resulting in a convergence with IFRS over the accounting treatment of SPEs.

PRACTICE PROBLEMS FOR READING 23

The following information relates to Questions 1–6

Cinnamon, Inc. is a diversified manufacturing company headquartered in the United Kingdom. It complies with IFRS. In 2009, Cinnamon held a 19 percent passive equity ownership interest in Cambridge Processing that was classified as available-for-sale. During the year, the value of this investment rose by £2 million. In December 2009, Cinnamon announced that it would be increasing its ownership interest to 50 percent effective 1 January 2010 through a cash purchase. Cinnamon and Cambridge have no intercompany transactions.

Peter Lubbock, an analyst following both Cinnamon and Cambridge, is curious how the increased stake will affect Cinnamon's consolidated financial statements. He asks Cinnamon's CFO how the company will account for the investment, and is told that the decision has not yet been made. Lubbock decides to use his existing forecasts for both companies' financial statements to compare the outcomes of alternative accounting treatments.

Lubbock assembles abbreviated financial statement data for Cinnamon (Exhibit 1) and Cambridge (Exhibit 2) for this purpose.

EXHIBIT 1 Selected Financial Statement Information for Cinnamon, Inc. (£ Millions)

Year ending 31 December	2009	2010*
Revenue	1,400	1,575
Operating income	126	142
Net income	62	69
31 December	**2009**	**2010***
Total assets	1,170	1,317
Shareholders' equity	616	685

*Estimates made prior to announcement of increased stake in Cambridge.

EXHIBIT 2 Selected Financial Statement Information for Cambridge Processing (£ Millions)

Year ending 31 December	2009	2010*
Revenue	1,000	1,100
Operating income	80	88
Net income	40	44
Dividends paid	20	22
31 December	**2009**	**2010**
Total assets	800	836
Shareholders' equity	440	462

* Estimates made prior to announcement of increased stake by Cinnamon.

1. In 2009, Cinnamon's earnings before taxes includes a contribution (in £ millions) from its investment in Cambridge Processing that is *closest* to:
   - **A.** £3.8.
   - **B.** £5.8.
   - **C.** £7.6.
2. In 2010, if Cinnamon is deemed to have control over Cambridge, it will *most likely* account for its investment in Cambridge using:
   - **A.** the equity method.
   - **B.** the acquisition method.
   - **C.** proportionate consolidation.
3. At 31 December 2010, Cinnamon's shareholders' equity on its balance sheet would *most likely* be:
   - **A.** highest if Cinnamon is deemed to have control of Cambridge.
   - **B.** independent of the accounting method used for the investment in Cambridge.
   - **C.** highest if Cinnamon is deemed to have significant influence over Cambridge.
4. In 2010, Cinnamon's net profit margin would be *highest* if:
   - **A.** it is deemed to have control of Cambridge.
   - **B.** it had not increased its stake in Cambridge.
   - **C.** it is deemed to have significant influence over Cambridge.
5. At 31 December 2010, assuming control and recognition of goodwill, Cinnamon's reported debt to equity ratio will *most likely* be highest if it accounts for its investment in Cambridge using the:
   - **A.** equity method.
   - **B.** full goodwill method.
   - **C.** partial goodwill method.

6. Compared to Cinnamon's operating margin in 2009, if it is deemed to have control of Cambridge, its operating margin in 2010 will *most likely* be:

A. lower.

B. higher.

C. the same.

The following information relates to Questions 7–12

Zimt, AG is a consumer products manufacturer headquartered in Austria. It complies with IFRS. In 2009, Zimt held a 10 percent passive stake in Oxbow Limited that was classified as held for trading securities. During the year, the value of this stake declined by €3 million. In December 2009, Zimt announced that it would be increasing its ownership to 50 percent effective 1 January 2010.

Franz Gelblum, an analyst following both Zimt and Oxbow, is curious how the increased stake will affect Zimt's consolidated financial statements. Because Gelblum is uncertain how the company will account for the increased stake, he uses his existing forecasts for both companies' financial statements to compare various alternative outcomes.

Gelblum gathers abbreviated financial statement data for Zimt (Exhibit 1) and Oxbow (Exhibit 2) for this purpose.

EXHIBIT 1 Selected Financial Statement Estimates for Zimt AG (€ Millions)

Year ending 31 December	2009	2010*
Revenue	1,500	1,700
Operating income	135	153
Net income	66	75
31 December	**2009**	**2010**
Total assets	1,254	1,421
Shareholders' equity	660	735

* Estimates made prior to announcement of increased stake in Oxbow.

EXHIBIT 2 Selected Financial Statement Estimates for Oxbow Limited (€ Millions)

Year ending 31 December	2009	2010*
Revenue	1,200	1,350
Operating income	120	135
Net income	60	68
Dividends paid	20	22
31 December	**2009**	**2010**
Total assets	1,200	1,283
Shareholders' equity	660	706

* Estimates made prior to announcement of increased stake by Zimt.

7. In 2009, Zimt's earnings before taxes includes a contribution (in € millions) from its investment in Oxbow Limited *closest* to:
   - A. (€0.6) million.
   - B. (€1.0) million.
   - C. €2.0 million.
8. At 31 December 2010, Zimt's total assets balance would *most likely* be:
   - A. highest if Zimt is deemed to have control of Oxbow.
   - B. highest if Zimt is deemed to have significant influence over Oxbow.
   - C. unaffected by the accounting method used for the investment in Oxbow.
9. Based on Gelblum's estimates, if Zimt is deemed to have significant influence over Oxbow, its 2010 net income (in € millions) would be *closest* to:
   - A. €75.
   - B. €109.
   - C. €143.
10. Based on Gelblum's estimates, if Zimt is deemed to have joint control of Oxbow, and Zimt uses the proportionate consolidation method, its 31 December 2010 total liabilities (in € millions) will *most likely* be *closest* to:
    - A. €686.
    - B. €975.
    - C. €1,263.
11. Based on Gelblum's estimates, if Zimt is deemed to have control over Oxbow, its 2010 consolidated sales (in € millions) will be *closest* to:
    - A. €1,700.
    - B. €2,375.
    - C. €3,050.

12. Based on Gelblum's estimates, Zimt's net income in 2010 will *most likely* be:

- **A.** highest if Zimt is deemed to have control of Oxbow.
- **B.** highest if Zimt is deemed to have significant influence over Oxbow.
- **C.** independent of the accounting method used for the investment in Oxbow.

The following information relates to Questions 13–18

Burton Howard, CFA, is an equity analyst with Maplewood Securities. Howard is preparing a research report on Confabulated Materials, SA, a publicly traded company based in France that complies with IFRS. As part of his analysis, Howard has assembled data gathered from the financial statement footnotes of Confabulated's 2009 Annual Report and from discussions with company management. Howard is concerned about the effect of this information on Confabulated's future earnings.

Information about Confabulated's investment portfolio for the years ended 31 December 2008 and 2009 is presented in Exhibit 1. As part of his research, Howard is considering the possible effect on reported income of Confabulated's accounting classification for fixed income investments.

EXHIBIT 1 **Confabulated's Investment Portfolio (€ Thousands)**

Characteristic	Bugle AG	Cathay Corp	Dumas SA
Classification	Available-for-sale	Held-to-maturity	Held-to-maturity
Cost*	€25,000	€40,000	€50,000
Market value, 31 December 2008	29,000	38,000	54,000
Market value, 31 December 2009	28,000	37,000	55,000

* All securities were acquired at par value.

In addition, Confabulated's annual report discusses a transaction under which receivables were securitized through a special purpose entity (SPE) for Confabulated's benefit.

13. The balance sheet carrying value of Confabulated's investment portfolio (in € thousands) at 31 December 2009 is *closest* to:

- **A.** 112,000.
- **B.** 115,000.
- **C.** 118,000.

14. The balance sheet carrying value of Confabulated's investment portfolio at 31 December 2009 would have been higher if which of the securities had been reclassified as a held for trading security?

A. Bugle.

B. Cathay.

C. Dumas.

15. Compared to Confabulated's reported interest income in 2009, if Dumas had been classified as available-for-sale, the interest income would have been:

A. lower.

B. the same.

C. higher.

16. Compared to Confabulated's reported earnings before taxes in 2009, if Bugle had been classified as a held for trading security, the earnings before taxes (in € thousands) would have been:

A. the same.

B. €1,000 lower.

C. €3,000 higher.

17. Confabulated's reported interest income would be higher if the cost was the same but the par value (in € thousands) of:

A. Bugle was €28,000.

B. Cathay was €37,000.

C. Dumas was €55,000.

18. Confabulated's special purpose entity is *most likely* to be:

A. held off-balance sheet.

B. consolidated on Confabulated's financial statements.

C. consolidated on Confabulated's financial statements only if it is a "qualifying SPE."

The following information relates to Questions 19–24

BetterCare Hospitals, Inc. operates a chain of hospitals throughout the United States. The company has been expanding by acquiring local hospitals. Its largest acquisition, that of Statewide Medical, was made in 2001 under the pooling of interests method. BetterCare complies with U.S. GAAP.

BetterCare is currently forming a 50/50 joint venture with Supreme Healthcare under which the companies will share control of several hospitals. BetterCare plans to use the equity method to account for the joint venture. Supreme Healthcare complies with IFRS and will use the proportionate consolidation method to account for the joint venture.

Erik Ohalin is an equity analyst who covers both companies. He has estimated the joint venture's financial information for 2010 in order to prepare his estimates of each company's earnings and financial performance. This information is presented in Exhibit 1.

EXHIBIT 1 **Selected Financial Statement Forecasts for Joint Venture ($ Millions)**

Year ending 31 December	2010
Revenue	1,430
Operating income	128
Net income	62
31 December	**2010**
Total assets	1,500
Shareholders' equity	740

Supreme Healthcare recently announced it had formed a special purpose entity through which it plans to sell up to $100 million of its accounts receivable. Supreme Healthcare has no voting interest in the SPE, but it is expected to absorb any losses that it may incur. Ohalin wants to estimate the impact this will have on Supreme Healthcare's consolidated financial statements.

19. Compared to accounting principles currently in use, the pooling method BetterCare used for its Statewide Medical acquisition has *most likely* caused its reported:

A. revenue to be higher.

B. total equity to be lower.

C. total assets to be higher.

20. Based on Ohalin's estimates, the amount of joint venture revenue (in $ millions) included on BetterCare's consolidated 2010 financial statements should be *closest* to:

A. $0.

B. $715.

C. $1,430.

21. Based on Ohalin's estimates, the amount of joint venture net income included on the consolidated financial statements of each venturer will *most likely* be:

A. higher for BetterCare.

B. higher for Supreme Healthcare.

C. the same for both BetterCare and Supreme Healthcare.

22. Based on Ohalin's estimates, the amount of the joint venture's 31 December 2010 total assets (in $ millions) that will be included on Supreme Healthcare's consolidated financial statements will be *closest* to:

A. $0.

B. $750.

C. $1,500.

23. Based on Ohalin's estimates, the amount of joint venture shareholders' equity at 31 December 2010 included on the consolidated financial statements of each venturer will *most likely* be:

A. higher for BetterCare.

B. higher for Supreme Healthcare.

C. the same for both BetterCare and Supreme Healthcare.

24. If Supreme Healthcare sells its receivables to the SPE, its consolidated financial results will *most likely* show:

A. a higher revenue for 2010.

B. a higher cash balance at 31 December 2010.

C. the same accounts receivable balance at 31 December 2010.

The following information relates to Questions 25–30

Percy Byron, CFA, is an equity analyst with a U.K.-based investment firm. One firm Byron follows is NinMount PLC, a U.K.-based company. On 31 December 2008, NinMount paid £320 million to purchase a 50 percent stake in Boswell Company. The excess of the purchase price over the fair value of Boswell's net assets was attributable to previously unrecorded licenses. These licenses were estimated to have an economic life of six years. The fair value of Boswell's assets and liabilities other than licenses was equal to their recorded book values. NinMount and Boswell both use the pound sterling as their reporting currency and prepare their financial statements in accordance with IFRS.

Byron is concerned whether the investment should affect his "buy" rating on NinMount common stock. He knows NinMount could choose one of several accounting methods to report the results of its investment, but NinMount has not announced which method it will use. Byron forecasts that both companies' 2009 financial results (excluding any merger accounting adjustments) will be identical to those of 2008.

NinMount's and Boswell's condensed income statements for the year ended 31 December 2008, and condensed balance sheets at 31 December 2008, are presented in Exhibits 1 and 2, respectively.

EXHIBIT 1 NinMount PLC and Boswell Company Income Statements for the Year Ended 31 December 2008 (£ millions)

	NinMount	Boswell
Net sales	950	510
Cost of goods sold	(495)	(305)
Selling expenses	(50)	(15)
Administrative expenses	(136)	(49)
Depreciation & amortization expense	(102)	(92)
Interest expense	(42)	(32)
Income before taxes	125	17
Income tax expense	(50)	(7)
Net income	75	10

EXHIBIT 2 **NinMount PLC and Boswell Company Balance Sheets at 31 December 2008 (£ millions)**

	NinMount	Boswell
Cash	50	20
Receivables—net	70	45
Inventory	130	75
Total current assets	250	140
Property, plant, & equipment—net	1,570	930
Investment in Boswell	320	—
Total assets	2,140	1,070
Current liabilities	110	90
Long-term debt	600	400
Total liabilities	710	490
Common stock	850	535
Retained earnings	580	45
Total equity	1,430	580
Total liabilities and equity	2,140	1,070

Note: Balance sheets reflect the purchase price paid by NinMount, but do not yet consider the impact of the accounting method choice.

25. NinMount's current ratio on 31 December 2008 *most likely* will be highest if the results of the acquisition are reported using:

A. the equity method.
B. consolidation with full goodwill.
C. consolidation with partial goodwill.

26. NinMount's long-term debt to equity ratio on 31 December 2008 *most likely* will be lowest if the results of the acquisition are reported using:

A. the equity method.
B. consolidation with full goodwill.
C. consolidation with partial goodwill.

27. Based on Byron's forecast, if NinMount deems it has acquired control of Boswell, NinMount's consolidated 2009 depreciation and amortization expense (in £ millions) will be *closest* to:

A. 102.
B. 148.
C. 204.

28. Based on Byron's forecast, NinMount's net profit margin for 2009 *most likely* will be highest if the results of the acquisition are reported using:

A. the equity method.
B. consolidation with full goodwill.
C. consolidation with partial goodwill.

29. Based on Byron's forecast, NinMount's 2009 return on beginning equity *most likely* will be the same under:

A. either of the consolidations, but different under the equity method.

B. the equity method, consolidation with full goodwill, and consolidation with partial goodwill.

C. none of the equity method, consolidation with full goodwill, or consolidation with partial goodwill.

30. Based on Byron's forecast, NinMount's 2009 total asset turnover ratio on beginning assets under the equity method is *most likely*:

A. lower than if the results are reported using consolidation.

B. the same as if the results are reported using consolidation.

C. higher than if the results are reported using consolidation.

SOLUTIONS FOR READING 23

1. A is correct. Dividends from equity securities that are classified as available-for-sale are included in income when earned. Cinnamon would record its 19 percent share of the dividends paid by Cambridge; this is £3.8 million (£20 × 0.19). Though the value of Cinnamon's stake in Cambridge Processing rose by £2 million during the year, under IFRS any unrealized gains or losses for available-for-sale securities are reported in the equity section of the balance sheet as part of other comprehensive income until the securities are sold.
2. B is correct. If Cinnamon is deemed to have control over Cambridge, it would use the acquisition method to account for Cambridge and prepare consolidated financial statements. Proportionate consolidation is used for joint ventures; the equity method is used for some joint ventures and when there is significant influence but not control.
3. A is correct. If Cinnamon is deemed to have control over Cambridge, consolidated financial statements would be prepared and Cinnamon's shareholders' equity would increase and include the amount of the noncontrolling interest. If Cinnamon is deemed to have significant influence, the equity method would be used and there would be no change in the shareholders' equity of Cinnamon.
4. C is correct. If Cinnamon is deemed to have significant influence, it would report half of Cambridge's net income as a line item on its income statement, but no additional revenue is shown. Its profit margin is thus higher than if it consolidated Cambridge's results, which would impact revenue and income, or if it only reported 19 percent of Cambridge's dividends (no change in ownership).
5. C is correct. The full and partial goodwill method will have the same amount of debt; however, shareholders' equity will be higher under full goodwill (and the debt to equity ratio will be lower). Therefore, the debt to equity will be higher under partial goodwill. If control is assumed, Cinnamon cannot use the equity method.
6. A is correct. Cambridge has a lower operating margin (88/1,100 = 8.0%) than Cinnamon (142/1,575 = 9.0%). If Cambridge's results are consolidated with Cinnamon's, the consolidated operating margin will reflect that of the combined company, or 230/2,675 = 8.6%.
7. B is correct. Oxbow was classified as a held for trading security. Held for trading securities are reported at fair value, with unrealized gains and losses included in income. The income statement also includes dividends from equity securities that are classified as held for trading. The €3 million decline in the value of Zimt's stake would reduce income by that amount. Zimt would record its share of the dividends paid (0.1 × €20 million = €2 million). The net effect of Zimt's stake in Oxbow Limited would be to reduce Zimt's income before taxes by €1 million for 2009.
8. A is correct. When a company is deemed to have control of another entity, it records all of the other entity's assets on its own consolidated balance sheet.

9. B is correct. If Zimt is deemed to have significant influence, it would use the equity method to record its ownership. Under the equity method, Zimt's share of Oxbow's net income would be recorded as a single line item. Net income of Zimt = 75 + 0.5(68) = 109.

10. B is correct. Under the proportionate consolidation method, Zimt's balance sheet would show its own total liabilities of €1,421 − 735 = €686 plus half of Oxbow's liabilities of €1,283 − 706 = €577. €686 + (0.5 × 577) = €974.5.

11. C is correct. Under the assumption of control, Zimt would record its own sales plus 100 percent of Oxbow's. €1,700 + 1,350 = €3,050.

12. C is correct. Net income is not affected by the accounting method used to account for active investments in other companies. "One-line consolidation" and consolidation result in the same impact on net income; it is the disclosure that differs.

13. C is correct. Held for trading and available-for-sale securities are carried at market value, whereas held-to-maturity securities are carried at historical cost. €28,000 + 40,000 + 50,000 = €118,000.

14. C is correct. If Dumas had been classified as a held for trading security, its carrying value would have been the €55,000 fair value rather than the €50,000 historical cost.

15. B is correct. The coupon payment is recorded as interest income whether securities are held-to-maturity or available-for-sale. No adjustment is required for amortization since the bonds were bought at par.

16. B is correct. Unrealized gains and losses are included in income when securities are classified as held for trading securities. During 2009 there was an unrealized loss of €1,000.

17. C is correct. The difference between historical cost and par value must be amortized when securities are classified as held-to-maturity. If the par value is more than the initial cost, the amortization increases interest income.

18. B is correct. Under IFRS, SPEs must be consolidated if they are conducted for the benefit of the sponsoring entity. Further, under IFRS, SPEs cannot be classified as qualifying. Under U.S. GAAP, qualifying SPEs do not have to be consolidated.

19. B is correct. Statewide Medical was accounted for under the pooling of interest method, which causes all of Statewide's assets and liabilities to be reported at historical book value. The excess of assets over liabilities generally is lower using the historical book value method than using the fair value method (this latter method must be used under currently required acquisition accounting). It would have no effect on revenue.

20. A is correct. Under the equity method, BetterCare would record its interest in the joint venture's net profit as a single line item, but would show no line-by-line contribution to revenues or expenses.

21. C is correct. Net income will be the same under the equity method and proportional consolidation. However, sales, cost of sales, and expenses are different because under the equity method the net effect of sales, cost of sales, and expenses is reflected in a single line.

22. B is correct. Under the proportionate consolidation method, Supreme Healthcare's consolidated financial statements will include its 50 percent share of the joint venture's total assets.

23. C is correct. The choice of equity method or proportionate consolidation does not affect reported shareholders' equity.

24. C is correct. Although Supreme Healthcare has no voting interest in the SPE, it is expected to absorb any losses that the SPE incurs. Therefore, Supreme Healthcare "in substance" controls the SPE and would consolidate it. On the consolidated balance sheet, the accounts receivable balance will be the same since the sale to the SPE will be reversed upon consolidation.

25. A is correct. The current ratio using the equity method of accounting is Current assets/Current liabilities = £250/£110 = 2.27. Using consolidation (either full or partial goodwill), the current ratio = £390/£200 = 1.95. Therefore, the current ratio is highest using the equity method.

26. A is correct. Using the equity method, long-term debt to equity = £600/£1,430 = 0.42. Using the consolidation method, long-term debt to equity = long-term debt/equity = £1,000/£1,750 = 0.57. Equity includes the £320 noncontrolling interest under either consolidation. It does not matter if the full or partial goodwill method is used since there is no goodwill.

27. C is correct. The projected depreciation and amortization expense will include NinMount's reported depreciation and amortization (£102), Boswell's reported depreciation and amortization (£92), and amortization of Boswell's licenses (£10 million). The licenses have a fair value of £60 million. £320 purchase price indicates a fair value of £640 for the net assets of Boswell. The net book (fair) value of the recorded assets is £580. The previously unrecorded licenses have a fair value of £60 million. The licenses have a remaining life of six years; the amortization adjustment for 2008 will be £10 million. Therefore, Projected depreciation and amortization = £102 + £92 + £10 = £204 million.

28. A is correct. Net income is the same using any of the methods but under the equity method, net sales are only £950; Boswell's sales are not included in the net sales figure. Therefore, net profit margin is highest using the equity method.

29. A is correct. Net income is the same using any of the choices. Beginning equity under the equity method is £1,430. Under either of the consolidations, beginning equity is £1,750 since it includes the £320 noncontrolling interest. Return on beginning equity is highest under the equity method.

30. A is correct. Using the equity method, Total asset turnover = Net sales/Beginning total assets = £950/£2,140 = 0.444. Total asset turnover on beginning assets using consolidation = £1,460/£2,950 = 0.495. Under consolidation, Assets = £2,140 − 320 + 1,070 + 60 = £2,950. Therefore, total asset turnover is lowest using the equity method.

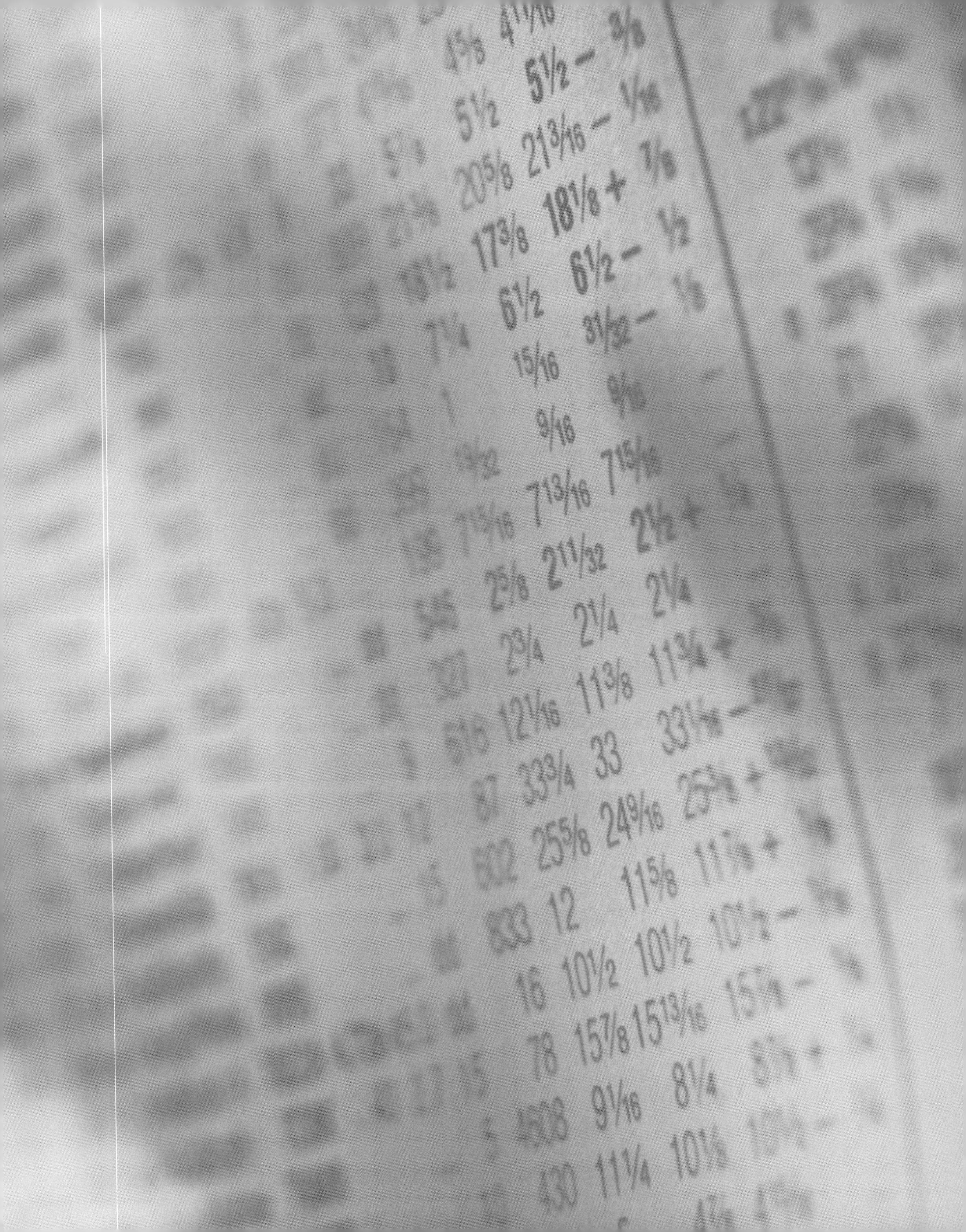

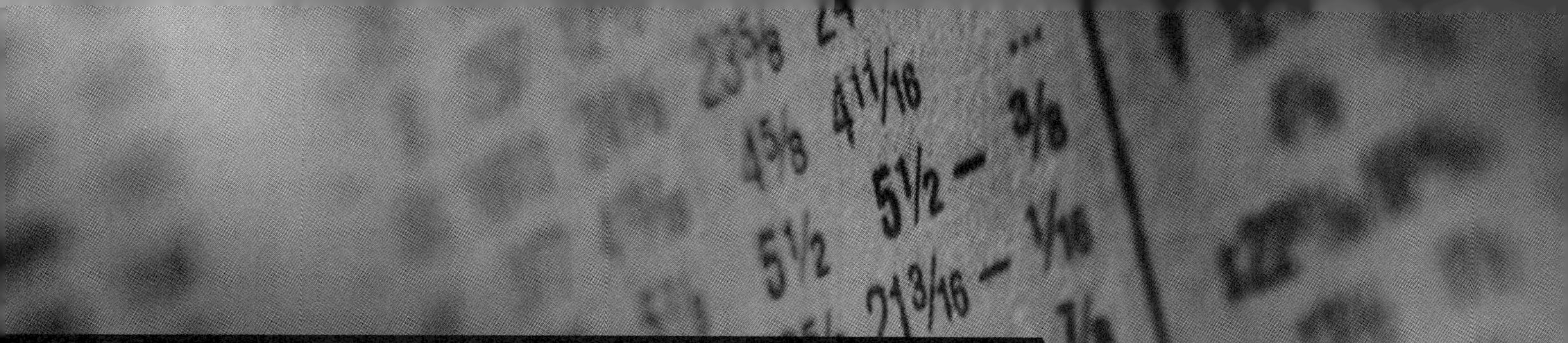

EMPLOYEE COMPENSATION: POST-EMPLOYMENT AND SHARE-BASED

by Elaine Henry, CFA and Elizabeth A. Gordon

READING 24

LEARNING OUTCOMES

The candidate should be able to:	Mastery
a. discuss the types of post-employment benefit plans and the implications for financial reports;	☐
b. explain the measures of a defined benefit pension plan's liability (i.e., defined benefit obligation and projected benefit obligation);	☐
c. describe the components of a company's defined benefit pension expense;	☐
d. explain the impact of a defined benefit plan's assumptions on the defined benefit obligation and periodic expense;	☐
e. explain the impact on financial statements of International Financial Reporting Standards (IFRS) and U.S. Generally Accepted Accounting Principles (U.S. GAAP) for pension and other post-employment benefits that permit items to be reported in the footnotes rather than in the financial statements;	☐
f. evaluate pension plan footnote disclosures including cash flow related information;	☐
g. evaluate the underlying economic liability (or asset) of a company's pension and other post-employment benefits;	☐
h. calculate the underlying economic pension expense (income) and other post-employment expense (income) based on disclosures;	☐
i. discuss the issues involved in accounting for share-based compensation;	☐
j. explain the impact on financial statements of accounting for stock grants and stock options, and the importance of companies' assumptions in valuing these grants and options.	☐

Note:
New rulings and/or pronouncements issued after the publication of the readings in financial reporting and analysis may cause some of the information in these readings to become dated. Candidates are expected to be familiar with the overall analytical framework contained in the study session readings, as well as the implications of alternative accounting methods for financial analysis and valuation, as provided in the assigned readings. Candidates are not responsible for changes that occur after the material was written.

1 INTRODUCTION

This reading covers two complex aspects of employee compensation: post-employment (retirement) benefits and share-based compensation. Retirement benefits include pensions and other post-employment benefits such as health insurance. Examples of share-based compensation are stock options and stock grants.

A common issue underlying both aspects of employee compensation is the difficulty in measuring the value of the compensation. One factor contributing to the difficulty is that employees earn the benefits in the periods that they provide service but typically receive the benefits in future periods, so measurement requires a significant number of assumptions.

This reading provides an overview of the methods companies use to estimate and measure the benefits they provide to their employees and how this information is reported in their financial statements. For the most part, there has been significant convergence between IFRS and U.S. GAAP in the accounting treatment for pensions, other post-employment benefits, and share-based compensation. Although this reading focuses primarily on IFRS, instances where U.S. GAAP significantly differ are discussed.

The reading is organized as follows: Section 2 addresses pensions and other post-employment benefits, and Section 3 covers share-based compensation, with a focus primarily on the accounting for and analysis of stock options. A summary and practice problems conclude the reading.

2 PENSIONS AND OTHER POST-EMPLOYMENT BENEFITS

This section discusses the accounting and reporting of pensions and other post-employment benefits by the companies that provide these benefits (accounting and reporting by pension and other retirement funds are not covered in this reading). Under IFRS, IAS 19 provides the principal source of guidance in accounting for pensions and other post-employment benefits. Under U.S. GAAP, the guidance is spread across six standards (SFAS 87, 88, 106, 112, 132, 158).[1]

The discussion begins with an overview of the types of benefits and measurement issues involved, including the accounting treatment for defined contribution plans. It then continues with financial statement reporting of pension plans and other post-employment benefits including an overview of critical assumptions used to value these benefits. The section concludes with a discussion of evaluating defined benefit pension plan and other post-employment benefit disclosures.

[1] These standards are superseded by FASB ASC Topics 712 [Compensation–Nonretirement Postemployment Benefits]; 715 [Compensation–Retirement Benefits]; 960 [Plan Accounting–Defined Benefit Pension Plans]; 962 [Plan Accounting–Defined Contribution Pension Plans]; and 965 [Plan Accounting–Health and Welfare Benefit Plans].

2.1 Types of Post-Employment Benefit Plans and Implications for Financial Reports

Companies (sponsors) may offer various types of benefits to their employees following retirement, including pension plans, health care plans, medical insurance, and life insurance. Some of these benefits involve payments in the current period but many are promises of future benefits. The objective of accounting for employee benefits is to measure the cost associated with providing these benefits and to recognise these costs in the sponsoring company's financial statements during the employees' periods of service. Complexity arises because the sponsoring company must make a series of assumptions to estimate the value of future benefits. The assumptions required to estimate and recognise these future benefits can have a significant impact on the company's presentation of operating performance and financial position. In addition, differences in assumptions can reduce comparability across companies.

Pension plans may be either defined contribution plans or defined benefit plans. The accounting treatment for the former is relatively simple. Typically, under a **defined contribution** (DC) plan, individual accounts are established for participating employees.[2] The employees and the employer may each contribute to the plan. After the employer makes its agreed-upon contribution into the plan (typically, a fund or an insurance company) on behalf of an employee (generally in the same period in which the employee provides the service), the employer has no obligation to make further payments beyond this amount. These plans are known as "defined contribution" because the amount of the employer's contribution into the pension plan is specified (defined) at the outset. The future value of the plan's assets depends on the performance of the investments within the plan. Any gains or losses related to the investments accrue to the employee. In other words, in DC pension plans, the employee bears the risk that plan assets will be sufficient to meet future needs. From a financial statement perspective, the employer's contributions into the plan, if any, are recorded as an expense on the income statement. Since the employer's obligation is limited to its contribution, no significant pension-related liability accrues on the balance sheet.[3]

In contrast with defined contribution plans, in **defined benefit** (DB) pension plans, the amount of pension benefit to be provided is defined, usually by reference to age, years of service, compensation, etc. For example, a DB pension plan may provide for the retiree to be paid, annually until death, 1 percent of the final year's salary times the number of years of service. The pension payments to be paid in the future represent a liability or obligation of the company. This requires the employer to make various actuarial assumptions (employee turnover, average retirement age, life expectancy after retirement) and computations in order to measure this future obligation. Under IFRS and U.S. GAAP, all plans other than those explicitly structured as defined contribution plans are classified as defined benefit plans. DB plans include both formal plans and those informal arrangements that create a constructive obligation by the employer to its employees.[4]

---

[2] The establishment of individual accounts for each employee is not required under IFRS but is a requirement under U.S. GAAP. For practical purposes, individual accounts are generally established.

[3] An accrual (current liability) is recognised at the end of the reporting period for any unpaid contributions.

[4] For example, a company has a constructive obligation if the benefits it promises are not linked solely to the amount of its contributions or if it indirectly or directly guarantees a specified return.

Most defined benefit pension plans are funded through a separate legal entity, typically a pension trust; and the assets of the trust are used to make the payments to retirees. The sponsoring company, however, is not only responsible for making current contributions to the plan; they also must ensure that there are sufficient assets in the plan to pay the ultimate benefits promised to plan participants. Current contributions to the plan may only partially satisfy the total obligation. As a result, the actual cost (expense) incurred is not based solely on current contributions. Instead, the employer must estimate the total cost of the benefits promised and then allocate them to the periods in which the employees render services. This further increases the complexity because the timing of contributions into the plan and the timing of payments from the plan can differ significantly from when the services are rendered and the benefits earned.

Most countries have regulatory requirements specifying minimal funding levels for DB pension plans, but those requirements vary by country.[5] If the amount of assets in the DB pension trust exceeds the present value of the estimated liability, the DB pension plan is said to be overfunded; conversely, if the amount of assets in the pension trust is less than the estimated liability, the plan is said to be underfunded. Because the company has promised a defined amount of benefit to the employees, it is obligated to make those pension payments regardless of whether the pension plan assets generate sufficient returns to provide that benefit when it is due. In other words, the company bears the investment risk.

Similar to DB pension plans, **other post-employment benefits** (OPB) are promises by the company to pay benefits in the future, such as life insurance premiums and all or part of health care insurance for its retirees. Under IFRS, OPB often fit the definition of defined benefit plans with similar accounting treatment as defined benefit pension plans. However, the complexity may be even greater because of the need to estimate future increases in costs, such as health care, over a long time horizon. Unlike DB pension plans, however, companies may not be required to fund an OPB in advance to the same degree as DB pension plans. This is partly because OPB may represent a much smaller financial liability and partly because they are often easier to eliminate should the costs become onerous.

Exhibit 1 summarizes these three types of post-employment benefits.

EXHIBIT 1 Types of Post-Employment Benefits

Type of Benefit	Amount of Post-Employment Benefit to Employee	Obligation of Sponsoring Company	Sponsoring Company's Pre-funding of Its Future Obligation
Defined contribution pension plan	Amount of future benefit is *not* defined. ► Actual future benefit will depend on the investment performance of plan assets. ► Investment risk is borne by the employee.	Obligation is limited to the amount contributed to the plan. The amount of the company's contribution is defined and made on a periodic basis. There is no additional future obligation.	Not applicable.

(Exhibit continues on next page . . .)

[5] For instance, the U.S. Pension Protection Act of 2006 established funding requirements for U.S. DB plans. It went into effect in 2008.

EXHIBIT 1 (continued)

Type of Benefit	Amount of Post-Employment Benefit to Employee	Obligation of Sponsoring Company	Sponsoring Company's Pre-funding of its Future Obligation
Defined benefit pension plan	Amount of future benefit is defined. ► Benefit is based on plan formula (often a function of length of service and final year's compensation). ► Investment risk is borne by company.	The amount of the future obligation, based on the plan formula, must be estimated in the current period.	Companies typically pre-fund the plans by contributing funds to a pension trust. Regulatory requirements to pre-fund vary by country.
Other post-employment benefits (e.g., retirees' health care)	Amount of future benefit depends on plan specifications and type of benefit.	The eventual benefits are specified. The amount of the future obligation must be estimated in the current period.	Companies typically do not pre-fund other post-employment benefit obligations.

Information about a company's pension plans often appears throughout the company's footnote disclosures and not just in a single footnote. Exhibit 2 provides excerpts of pension plan disclosures from Volvo Group's 2007 annual report. The Volvo Group is a Swedish company which manufactures cars, trucks, busses, construction equipment, and aircraft equipment components. The company is listed on the OMX Nordic Exchange in Stockholm.

The first excerpt in the exhibit is taken from Note 1 of Notes to the Consolidated Financial Statements and succinctly summarizes the company's accounting for pensions and other post-employment benefits. The note explains that "actuarial calculations should be made for all defined benefit plans in order to determine the present value of obligations for benefits vested by its current and former employees." It then goes on to explain factors that cause changes in this obligation, and how the pension related amount disclosed on its balance sheet amount was determined. The second excerpt is taken from Note 2, "key sources of estimation uncertainty," and describes the assumptions used to determine the company's pension obligation and period costs. This disclosure illustrates the complexity of defined benefit accounting and the significant impact of various assumptions that are used to determine the present value of the future obligation as well as the net periodic cost.

The third excerpt is taken from Note 24, which shows the funded status (underfunded) of the Volvo Group's defined benefit plans and discusses the assumptions used in the calculations. The pension liability shown on the Volvo Group's balance sheet for 2007 is SEK 10,216, which is the present value of the defined benefit obligation, reduced by the fair value of the plan's assets, and adjusted for unrecognised actuarial gains and past service costs.

EXHIBIT 2 Excerpts from the Pension Plan Disclosures of the Volvo Group

Excerpt 1

Pensions and similar obligations (Postemployment benefits)

Volvo applies IAS 19, Employee Benefits, for pensions and similar obligations. In accordance with IAS 19, actuarial calculations should be made for all defined-benefit plans in order to determine the present value of obligations for benefits vested by its current and former employees. The actuarial calculations are prepared annually and are based upon actuarial assumptions that are determined close to the balance sheet date each year. Changes in the present value of obligations due to revised actuarial assumptions are treated as actuarial gains or losses which are amortized over the employees' average remaining service period to the extent these exceed the corridor value for each plan. Deviations between expected return on plan assets and actual return are treated as actuarial gains or losses. Provisions for post-employment benefits in Volvo's balance sheet correspond to the present value of obligations at year-end, less fair value of plan assets, unrecognized actuarial gains or losses and unrecognized unvested past service costs. See Note 24.

Excerpt 2

Pensions and other post-employment benefits

Provisions and costs for post-employment benefits, i.e. mainly pensions and health-care benefits, are dependent on assumptions used by actuaries in calculating such amounts. The appropriate assumptions and actuarial calculations are made separately for each population in the respective countries of Volvo's operations. The assumptions include discount rates, health care cost trends rates, inflation salary growth, long-term return on plan assets, retirement rates, mortality rates and other factors. Discount rate assumptions are based on long-term high quality corporate bond and government bond yield available at year-end. Health care cost trend assumptions are developed based on historical cost data, the near-term outlook, and an assessment of likely long-term trends. Inflation assumptions are based on an evaluation of external market indicators. The salary growth assumptions reflect the long-term actual experience, the near-term outlook and assumed inflation. Retirement and mortality rates are based primarily on officially available mortality statistics. The actuarial assumptions are reviewed on an annual basis and modifications are made to them when it is deemed appropriate to do so. Actual results that differ from management's assumptions are accumulated and amortized over future periods and, therefore, generally affect the recognized expense and recorded provisions in such future periods. See Note 24 for more information regarding costs and assumptions for post-employment benefits. At December 31, 2007 net provisions for post-employment benefits amounted to 7,643 (6,651).

Excerpt 3

Volvo's pension foundation in Sweden was formed in 1996 to secure obligations relating to retirement pensions for salaried employees in Sweden in accordance with the ITP plan (a Swedish individual pension plan). Plan assets amounting to 2,456 was contributed to the foundation at its formation, corresponding to the value of the pension obligations at that time. Since its formation, net contributions of 1,472, whereof 52 during 2007, have been made to the foundation. The plan assets in Volvo's Swedish pension foundation are invested in Swedish and

(Exhibit continues on next page . . .)

EXHIBIT 2 (continued)

foreign stocks and mutual funds, and in interest-bearing securities, in accordance with a distribution that is determined by the foundation's Board of Directors. At December 31, 2007, the fair value of the foundation's plan assets amounted to 6,648 (6,394), of which 43% (45) was invested in shares or mutual funds. At the same date, retirement pension obligations attributable to the ITP plan amounted to 7,847 (6,560). In the valuation of Volvo's pension liability for the Swedish companies, the life-expectancy assumptions was changed during 2007. Men are now assumed to live about two years longer than previously. The increase for women is about one year. The changed life-expectancy assumptions increased the pension obligation by about 14%. However, this increase has not affected the carrying amount of the Volvo Group's liabilities immediately since Volvo applies the corridor approach to actuarial gains and losses. Swedish companies can secure new pension obligations through balance sheet provisions or pension fund contributions. Furthermore, a credit insurance must be taken out for the value of the obligations. In addition to benefits relating to retirement pensions, the ITP plan also includes, for example, a collective family pension, which Volvo finances through insurance with the Alecta insurance company. According to an interpretation from the Swedish Financial Accounting Standards Council's interpretations committee, this is a multi-employer defined benefit plan. For fiscal year 2007, Volvo did not have access to information from Alecta that would have enabled this plan to be reported as a defined benefit plan. Accordingly, the plan has been reported as a defined contribution plan. Alecta's funding ratio is 152,0% (143.1%). Alecta's current funding ratio exceeds the target of 140%. Accordingly, Alecta's Board of Directors has decided to reduce premiums for defined benefit plans and family pensions by 40% during 2008.

Volvo's subsidiaries in the United States mainly secure their pension obligations through transfer of funds to pension plans. At the end of 2007, the total value of pension obligations secured by pension plans of this type amounted to 10,928 (11,830). At the same point in time, the total value of the plan assets in these plans amounted to 12,195 (12,226), of which 58% (60) was invested in shares or mutual funds. The regulations for securing pension obligations stipulate certain minimum levels concerning the ratio between the value of the plan assets and the value of the obligations. During 2007, Volvo contributed 0 (2,858) to the pension plans.

During 2007 Volvo has made extra contributions to the pension plans in Great Britain in the amount of 135 (646).

In 2008, Volvo estimate [sic] to transfer an amount of not more than SEK 1 billion to pension plans.

Source: The Volvo Group, 2007 Annual Report.

The following sections provide additional detail on how DB pension plan liabilities and periodic costs are measured, the financial statement impact of reporting pension and other post-employment benefits, and how footnote disclosures can be used to gain insights about the underlying economics of a company's defined benefit plans.

2.2 Measuring a Defined Benefit Pension Plan's Liabilities

Under IFRS, the **projected unit credit method** is used to estimate the **defined benefit obligation**, the liability of a defined benefit pension. Under the projected unit credit method, each period of service (e.g., year of employment) gives rise to an additional unit of benefit (credit) that the employee is entitled to at retirement. In other words, for each period in which employees provide services, they earn a portion of the post-employment benefits that the company has promised to pay. The employer measures each unit of service as it is earned, to determine the amount of benefits that it is obligated to pay in future reporting periods.

The objective of the projected unit credit method is to allocate the entire expected retirement costs (benefits) for an employee over the employee's service periods. The defined benefit obligation represents the actuarial present value of all the units of benefit (credit) that the employee is entitled to (i.e., has earned) as a result of prior and current periods of service. This obligation is based upon actuarial assumptions about demographic variables such as employee turnover and life expectancy and upon estimates of financial variables such as future inflation and the expected long-term return on the plan's assets. If the pension benefit formula is based on employees' future compensation levels, then the unit of benefit earned each period will reflect this estimate.

Under both IFRS and U.S. GAAP, the assumed rate of increase in compensation, the expected annual increase in compensation over the employee service period, can have a significant impact on the defined benefit obligation. Another key assumption is the discount rate, the interest rate used to calculate the present value of the future benefits. It represents the rate at which the defined benefit obligation could be effectively settled. This rate is based on current rates of return on high quality corporate bonds with durations consistent with the durations of the benefit.[6]

Under both defined benefit and defined contribution plans, the benefits that employees earn may be conditional on remaining with the company for a specified period of time. "Vesting" refers to a provision in pensions plans whereby an employee gains rights to future benefits only after meeting certain criteria such as providing a pre-specified number of years of service. If the employee leaves the company before meeting the criteria, they may be entitled to none or a portion of the benefits they have earned up until that point. However, once the employee has met the vesting requirements, they are entitled to receive the benefits they have earned in prior periods (i.e., since the employee has become vested, benefits are not forfeited if the employee leaves the company).

Employee service prior to the vesting date creates an obligation because at each successive reporting date, the amount of future service that an employee will have to provide before becoming entitled to the benefit is reduced. In measuring the defined benefit obligation, the company considers the probability that some employees may not satisfy the vesting requirements (i.e., may leave before the vesting period) and uses this probability to calculate the current service costs and the present value of the obligation.

U.S. GAAP use three measures to estimate the liabilities of a defined benefit pension plan; each measure is increasingly more inclusive. The **vested benefit**

[6] Under U.S. GAAP, entities can use the rate of return on quality fixed income instruments (similar to IFRS); however, the U.S. Securities and Exchange Commission has stated that the term "high quality" means that a bond has received one of the two highest ratings given by a recognised ratings agency.

obligation is the "actuarial present value of vested benefits" (SFAS 87, 106).[7] The **accumulated benefit obligation** is "the actuarial present value of benefits (whether vested or non-vested) attributed by the pension benefit formula to employee service rendered before a specified date and based on employee service and compensation (if applicable) prior to that date" (SFAS 87, 96).[8] Both the vested benefit obligation and the accumulated benefit obligation are based on the amounts promised as a result of an employee's service up to a specific date.

The third measure of a defined benefit pension plan's liabilities is the **projected benefit obligation**. This measure includes not only the benefit obligation attributable to an employee's service up to a specific date, but also an estimate of benefit obligations based on future compensation levels where applicable. It is defined as "the actuarial present value as of a date of all benefits attributed by the pension benefit formula to employee service rendered prior to that date." The projected benefit obligation is calculated in a similar manner to the defined benefit obligation under IFRS. It is measured using assumptions as to future compensation levels if the pension benefit formula is based on those future compensation levels (pay-related, final-pay, final-average-pay, or career-average-pay plans). If the pension benefit formula is not linked to future compensation levels, the accumulated benefit obligation and projected benefit obligation will be equal. For analysis, the projected benefit obligation is typically the most relevant measure because it assumes that the company will continue to operate in the future (the so-called "going-concern assumption") and recognises that benefits will increase with future compensation increases.

In the remainder of this reading, unless otherwise specified, the term defined benefit (DB) pension obligation will refer to the obligation inclusive of any effects of estimated future compensation levels; i.e., the "defined benefit obligation" under IFRS and "projected benefit obligation" under U.S. GAAP.

2.3 Measuring a Defined Benefit Pension Plan's Periodic Costs

Broadly, the periodic cost of a company's defined benefit pension plan can be thought of as the increase in its pension obligation, offset by earnings on pension plan assets. As will be discussed, current accounting rules do not require companies to reflect this entire amount as an expense of the period; however, it is a useful starting point for understanding periodic pension expense.

Items that can increase a company's DB pension obligation in a particular period include the following: 1) employees' service during the period, which increases the amount of pension benefit the employee will be paid in retirement (current service costs); 2) interest expense accrued on the beginning pension obligation; 3) changes to the terms of a pension plan that increase the benefit obligation applicable to employees' service during previous periods (past service costs); and 4) actuarial gains and losses. Actuarial gains and losses can occur when changes are made to the assumptions on which a company's estimated pension obligation has been based (e.g., employee turnover, mortality rates, retirement ages, compensation increases, etc.).

Items that can decrease a company's DB pension obligation in a particular period are curtailments and settlements. Increases in a company's pension obligations are offset by earnings on the pension plan assets. Accounting standards allow companies to use the expected return instead of the actual return on plan assets because the (potentially) sizeable fluctuations in actual return from period

[7] FASB ASC Topic 715 [Compensation–Retirement Benefits].

[8] FASB ASC Topic 715 [Compensation–Retirement Benefits].

to period could distort the company's operating results. In addition, because pension plan assets are intended as long-term investments, if the expected returns are accurately estimated, differences between the actual return and the expected return should offset over the long term. A curtailment occurs when a company either significantly reduces the number of employees that are covered by a plan, or amends the plan so that future service by current employees no longer qualifies for benefits.[9] A settlement occurs when a company eliminates all future obligations for all or part of the future promised benefits.[10]

IFRS and U.S. GAAP use somewhat different terminology for items that are substantively the same. For example, the increase in the present value of a company's estimated pension obligation that results from employees' service during a period is known as the "current service cost" in IFRS and as the "service cost component of net periodic pension cost" in U.S. GAAP. An increase in the present value of a company's estimated pension obligation that results from changes to the terms of a pension plan applicable to employees' service during previous periods is known as "past service cost" in IFRS and "prior service cost" in U.S. GAAP. In the remainder of this reading, we will use the IFRS terms "current service cost" and "past service cost."

2.4 Financial Statement Reporting of Pension and Other Post-Employment Benefits

The next few sections describe how pensions and other post-employment benefits are reflected on the financial statements of the sponsoring company.

2.4.1 Balance Sheet

Companies make contributions to defined contribution plans as the expense arises. Any accrual recognised at the end of the reporting period for any unpaid contributions is simple to calculate and generally insignificant. The discussion in this section therefore relates to defined benefit plans and other post-employment benefits where a liability does accrue and thus must be measured and reported. As noted, companies typically contribute to a trust fund that holds assets specifically dedicated to satisfying their liabilities for DB plans.

IFRS (IAS 19, paragraph 54) require companies to report a defined benefit liability on their balance sheet equal to the net total of the following amounts: the present value of the defined benefit obligation at the balance sheet date, plus any actuarial gains (less any actuarial losses) not recognised, minus any past service costs not yet recognised, minus the fair value at the balance sheet date of plan assets (if any) out of which the obligations are to be settled directly. Some actuarial gains or losses or past service costs might not yet be recognised because IFRS (and U.S. GAAP) allow companies to "smooth" the effects of these two items over time rather than immediately reflecting the total amount of the effect as income or expense. The next section on expenses explains the smoothing mechanism.

If the fair value of plan assets exceeds the obligations reported, the company would report a pension asset.[11] An asset may arise if a defined benefit plan has

---

[9] Curtailments generally result from such events as restructurings, plant closings, and the discontinuance of an operation.

[10] A settlement would occur if a company makes a lump sum payment to (or on behalf) of plan participants in exchange for their rights to receive specified post-employment benefits.

[11] A pension asset would result if fair value of plan assets > defined benefit obligation + unrecognised actuarial gains (minus actuarial losses) − unrecognised past service cost.

been overfunded or in certain cases where actuarial gains are recognised. IFRS restrict the amount of the asset that can be reported on the balance sheet to the lower of:

- the amount determined under IAS 19, paragraph 54, or
- the total of any cumulative unrecognised net actuarial losses and past service costs and the present value of any economic benefits available in the form of refunds from the plan or reductions in future contributions to the plan.

The amount of the asset that is not reported on the balance sheet is disclosed in the footnotes to the company's financial statements.

U.S. GAAP SFAS 158[12] was adopted in 2006 with phase-in provisions for measurement, recognition, and disclosure. It represents the first phase in a comprehensive review of the accounting for post-employment benefits. Changes arising from the adoption of this standard by U.S. based companies are also relevant for anticipating future changes for companies using IFRS.

SFAS 158 requires companies to report on their balance sheet the funded status of their defined benefit plans, which is equal to the difference between the defined benefit obligation and the fair value of the plans assets. If the plan is underfunded (defined benefit obligation is greater than the fair value of plan assets), a pension liability would be reported; and if the plan is overfunded (defined benefit obligation is less than the fair value of plan assets), a pension asset would be reported. U.S. GAAP do not restrict the amount of the pension asset that can be reported on the balance sheet.

Prior to SFAS 158, U.S. accounting standards allowed companies to recognise the funded position of its benefit plans, net of adjustments for various unamortized costs (similar to the adjustments still allowed under IFRS). These unamortized costs were included in equity (accumulated other comprehensive income). SFAS 158 not only requires more complete recognition of liabilities related to post-employment benefits, it also requires companies to disclose the financial statement effects of implementing the new requirements. For companies with underfunded plans, the adoption of SFAS 158 has resulted in increasing liabilities (to reflect the full underfunded position of the pension plan) and reducing equity by the amount of unamortized costs, net of tax; and an increase of deferred tax assets, reflecting the future tax deductions.

Example 1 illustrates the effect of a defined benefit pension plan on reported pension plan assets and disclosure under IFRS and U.S. GAAP. Example 2 illustrates the effect of a defined benefit pension plan on reported pension plan liabilities and equity under IFRS and U.S. GAAP.

EXAMPLE 1

Determination of the Amount of Pension Asset to Be Reported on the Balance Sheet

The following information pertains to a hypothetical company's pension plan as of 31 December 2009:

- The present value of a company's defined benefit obligation is £5,485 and the fair value of the pension plan assets is £5,798.

[12] FASB ASC Topic 715 [Compensation–Retirement Benefits].

- The company has an unrecognised transition liability of £50, unrecognised actuarial losses of £59, and unrecognised past service costs of £70.
- The present value of available future refunds and reductions in future contributions (funded status) is £313.

Calculate the amount of the pension asset that the company would report on its 2009 balance sheet under IFRS. Is any additional disclosure required? How would the reporting differ under U.S. GAAP?

Solution:
The company's pension plan is overfunded by £492, calculated as follows:

Present value of defined benefit obligation	£5,485
Unrecognised transition liability	(50)
Unrecognised actuarial losses	(59)
Unrecognised past service costs	(70)
Fair value of plan assets	(5,798)
Overfunded amount	(£492)

The total of the unrecognised net actuarial losses, past service costs and the present value of future refunds (or reductions in future contributions to the plan) is:

Unrecognised actuarial losses	£ 59
Unrecognised past service costs	70
Present value of future refunds	313
Total	£442

Because £442 is lower than £492, the company would report a pension asset on its balance sheet of £442. The amount of the asset not reported on the balance sheet £50 (£492 − 442) is disclosed in the footnotes. Under U.S. GAAP, the company would report a pension asset of £313 on its balance sheet, which is the difference between the defined benefit obligation and the plan's assets (£5,485 − £5,798). The amount under U.S. GAAP, £313, differs from the total of the reported and disclosed pension assets, £492, under IFRS due to the different treatment of unrecognised (unamortized costs).

EXAMPLE 2

Effect of Company's Defined Benefit Pension Plan on Its Liabilities and Equity

The following information pertains to a hypothetical company's pension plan as of 31 December 2009:

- The present value of the company's defined benefit obligation is 6,723, and the fair value of the pension plan's assets is 4,880.
- The company has unrecognised actuarial losses of 255 and unrecognised past service costs of 170.

Calculate the amount that the company would report as a liability and in equity on its 2009 balance sheet under IFRS and U.S. GAAP.

Solution:

Under IFRS, the company would report pension liabilities of:

Present value of defined benefit obligation	6,723
Less: Unrecognised actuarial losses	(255)
Less: Unrecognised past service costs	(170)
Less: Fair value of plan assets	(4,880)
Pension liabilities	1,418

However, if the company had chosen to recognise actuarial gains and losses immediately, it would not subtract the amount of unrecognised actuarial losses to determine the pension liabilities. Instead, it would report the actuarial losses in the statement of recognised income and expense.[13]

Under U.S. GAAP, the company would report pension liabilities of:

Fair value of plan assets	(4,880)
Present value of defined benefit obligation	6,723
Pension liabilities	1,843

Under U.S. GAAP (SFAS 158), the company would report the full underfunded status of its pension plan; i.e., the difference between the fair value of plan assets and the present value of the defined benefit obligation. In accumulated comprehensive income (equity), it would report:

Unrecognised actuarial losses	(255)
Unrecognised past service costs	(170)
Total	(425)

This amount would be adjusted each period, as the unrecognised actuarial losses and past service costs are amortized to pension expense over the remaining service life of its employees.

The IASB and the FASB have identified accounting for pensions and post-employment benefits as a major project for collaborative efforts. Subsequent anticipated changes in accounting standards will address those aspects of current accounting standards that smooth the income effects of fluctuations in the values of pension assets and liabilities (discussed in the following section). The changes arising under SFAS 158 by U.S. based companies are relevant for anticipating future changes for companies using IFRS, and it is important for analysts to understand the financial statement effects of this standard.

In Example 3, one disclosure refers to an Additional Minimum Liability (AML), a concept that will no longer be relevant for U.S. GAAP after completion of the phasing-in of SFAS 158. Smoothing adjustments under the prior U.S. accounting standards resulted in the funded position reflected on a company's balance sheet differing from the actual funded position of the plan; when the

[13] This is similar to the statement of comprehensive income under U.S. GAAP.

difference between the reported and actual funded positions became too great, the old standards required an adjustment to make the reported position closer to the actual funded position. The adjustments were reflected as an AML. Example 3 is taken prior to the complete phasing-in of SFAS 158; the company separately disclosed the AML effect at that time.

EXAMPLE 3

Impact of New Pension Accounting and Analysis of Trends in Key Financial Ratios

Companies are required to disclose the impact of the new accounting standard for pensions, SFAS 158. These disclosures can be particularly important in trend analysis. Exhibit 3 presents pension disclosures and supplemental information for Caterpillar (CAT).

EXHIBIT 3 Caterpillar Inc. Pension Disclosures and Selected Supplemental Information

Pension disclosure: Excerpt from Note 1 (L) in the company's Form 10-K filed 22 February 2008. Page A-13.

> **SFAS 158**—In September 2006, the FASB issued Statement of Financial Accounting Standards No. 158 (SFAS 158), "Employers' Accounting for Defined Benefit Pension and Other Postretirement Plans—an amendment of FASB Statements No. 87, 88, 106 and 132R." SFAS 158 requires recognition of the overfunded or underfunded status of pension and other postretirement benefit plans on the balance sheet. . . . The following summarizes the effect of the required changes in the AML, as well as the impact of the initial adoption of SFAS 158, as of December 31, 2006.

Initial adoption of SFAS 158 (*Millions of dollars*)	**31 Dec. 2006 Prior to AML and SFAS 158 Adjustments**	**AML Adjustment per SFAS 87**	**SFAS 158 Adjustment**	**31 Dec. 2006 Post AML and SFAS 158 Adjustments**
Prepaid expenses and other current assets	$2,467	$—	$(1,829)	$638
Investments in unconsolidated affiliated companies	568	—	(6)	562
Deferred income taxes	552	(97)	1,494	1,949
Intangible assets	639	(60)	(192)	387
Accrued wages, salaries and employee benefits	1,440	—	(502)	938
Liability for post-employment benefits	3,625	(386)	2,640	5,879
Accumulated other comprehensive income	(405)	229	(2,671)	(2,847)

Pension disclosure: Excerpt from Management's Discussion and Analysis in the company's Form 10-K filed 22 February 2008. Page A-63.

> The adoption of the balance sheet recognition provisions reduced December 31, 2006 assets by approximately $500 million, increased liabilities by approximately $2.20 billion and reduced stockholders' equity by approximately $2.70 billion. Also, we reclassified approximately $500 million from current liabilities to long-term liabilities based on the classification guidelines provided in SFAS 158. We did not incur any violation of debt covenant agreements as a result of the reduction in stockholders' equity. We do not expect the adoption of the year-end measurement date will have a material impact on our financial statements.

Selected Supplemental Information for Caterpillar Inc. (from financial statements in the company's Form 10-K's filed 23 February 2007 and 24 February 2005)

(Millions of dollars)	2006	2005	2004	2003	2002
Net income	$3,537	$2,854	$2,035	$1,099	$798
Ending shareholders' equity	6,859	8,432	7,467	6,078	5,472
Long term debt, including current maturities	22,141	20,176	19,368	17,527	15,686
Pension & post-employment related liabilities	5,879	3,161	3,126	3,172	3,333

Using the information from Exhibit 3:

1. Calculate Caterpillar's return on equity (ROE) and debt-to-capital ratios with and without pension-related liabilities, for 2006:
   a. using the financial information as reported, which includes the adjustments for AML and SFAS 158, and
   b. based on the financial information as it would have been without AML and SFAS 158 adjustments.
2. Describe the effect of SFAS 158 on Caterpillar's 2006 ROE.
3. Describe the effect of SFAS 158 on Caterpillar's 2006 debt-to-capital ratio.
4. Explain the implications for an analysis of the trends for Caterpillar, based on its ROE and debt-to-capital ratio from 2003 to 2006.

Solution to 1: For CAT, the calculation of ROE and debt-to-capital ratios using the financial information reported, and the financial information with the impact of AML and SFAS 158 removed is as follows:

($ Millions)	2006 as Reported	2006 w/out AML and SFAS 158
Net income	$3,537	$3,537
Ending shareholders' equity (E)	6,859	9,301[a]
Long-term debt, including current maturities	22,141	22,141
Pension & post-employment related liabilities	5,879	3,625
ROE*	46.26%	39.89%
LTD/(LTD + E) where LTD includes pension-related liabilities	80.33%	73.48%
LTD/(LTD + E) where LTD excludes pension-related liabilities	76.35%	70.42%

* Beginning shareholders' equity = $8,432
[a] 6,859 + 2,671 − 229 = 9,301

Solution to 2: SFAS 158 does not affect reported income but does reduce reported shareholders' equity, thus increasing ROE.

Solution to 3: SFAS 158 reduces reported shareholders' equity, thus increasing its debt-to-capital ratio. CAT's 2006 debt-to-total capital ratio increases from 70.42 percent to 76.35 percent; and if pension liabilities are treated as debt, the ratio increases from 73.48 percent to 80.33 percent.

Solution to 4: In examining the trends in its profitability (for example, as measured by ROE) and leverage (for example, as measured by debt-to-capital), an analyst should recognise that the accounting change—rather than an actual economic change—creates the appearance of an improvement in the company's profitability ratios and shows a deterioration rather than improvement in the company's leverage ratios. While CAT shows a positive trend in profitability as measured by ROE, the 2006 ratios based on the reported numbers overstate the improvement from prior years. Similarly, CAT shows increasing leverage in 2006 based on the reported financials; however, the apparent trend toward higher leverage is actually the result of the change in accounting for pensions.

For CAT, the ratios for 2003 to 2006 are:

	2006 as Reported	2006 w/out SFAS 158	2005	2004	2003
ROE	46.26%	39.89%	35.90%	30.05%	19.03%
LTD/(LTD + E) where LTD includes pension-related liabilities	80.33	73.48	73.46	75.08	77.30
LTD/(LTD + E) where LTD excludes pension-related liabilities	76.35	70.42	70.53	72.17	74.25

In Example 3, the solution shows the debt-to-capital ratio both with and without pension-related liabilities included as debt. The argument for including pension-related liabilities in the calculation is that these liabilities reflecting underfunded defined benefit pension and other post-employment plans are indeed debt-like in nature. One difference in pension-related liabilities and debt is that pension-related liabilities are often tax deductible; therefore, a further refinement in analyses similar to the one shown above is to reflect the pension-related liabilities after taxes. Note, however, that companies do include tax considerations in reporting under SFAS 158. Exhibit 3 shows that Caterpillar reflects a $1,494 increase in deferred income tax asset. Rating agencies such as Moody's Investors Service adjust to record the underfunded pension obligations as debt on a gross basis.

2.4.2 Pension Expense

Pension expense for defined contribution pension plans is straightforward; it is simply an amount equal to the company's annual contribution to the plans adjusted for changes in year-end accruals. The discussion in this section relates to pension expense for defined benefit plans, which has several components.

For DB plans, actuarial assumptions and estimates of financial variables play a central role in determining periodic costs (as well as the defined benefit obligation); differences in these assumptions may result in a lack of comparability in financial reporting. As a consequence, it is imperative that financial statement users review the key assumptions and methods that companies use. Exhibit 4 provides an example of the type of footnote disclosures that companies are required to make about the assumptions and estimates used in determining the defined benefit obligation and periodic costs. Notice that the Volvo Group uses different actuarial assumptions and estimates for each country where it sponsors a defined benefit plan. Under U.S. GAAP, companies are required to make similar disclosures.

EXHIBIT 4 Example of Footnote Disclosures

The following tables disclose information about defined benefit plans in the Volvo Group. Volvo report the difference between the obligations and the plan assets adjusted for actuarial gains and losses in the balance sheet. The information refers to assumptions applied for actuarial calculations, periodical costs and the value of obligations and plan assets at year-end. The tables also include reconciliation of obligations and plan assets during the year and the difference between fair values and carrying amounts reported on the balance sheet date.

Assumptions Applied for Actuarial Calculations, %	December 31 2006	December 31 2007
Sweden		
Discount rate	4.00	4.50
Expected return on plan assets[1]	6.00	6.00
Expected salary increases	3.20	3.20
Inflation	1.50	2.00
United States		
Discount rate	5.50	5.75–6.25
Expected return on plan assets[1]	7.65	7.65
Expected salary increases	3.50	3.50
Inflation	2.50	2.50
France		
Discount rate	4.25	5.25
Expected salary increases	3.00	3.00
Inflation	2.00	2.00
Great Britain		
Discount rate	5.00	5.75
Expected return on plan assets[1]	5.00–5.80	5.30–6.10
Expected salary increases	4.00–4.60	4.20–4.90
Inflation	3.00	3.40

[1] Applicable for the following accounting period. These assumptions reflect the expected long-term return rate on plan assets, based upon historical yield rates for different categories of investments and weighted in accordance with the foundation's investment policy. The expected return has been calculated net of administrative expenses and applicable taxes.

Source: The Volvo Group, 2007 Annual Report. Notes to the Consolidated Financial Statements, Note 24.

The periodic cost (economic expense) of a company's DB pension plan can be thought of as the increase in its pension obligations, offset by earnings on the pension plan's assets. As will be discussed, IFRS and U.S. GAAP do not require companies to reflect this entire amount as an expense. Items that can increase a company's pension liability in a particular period include the following: current service costs; interest expense accrued on the pension obligation; past service costs; actuarial losses; and losses on curtailments or settlements.[14]

Increases in a company's pension obligation are offset by earnings on the pension plan's assets, including interest income, dividend income, gains or losses on sales of securities, and unrealized gains and losses (i.e., changes in the value of the assets held by the plan). Note that the amount of assets in the plan increases when the company makes contributions and decreases when the plan pays out benefits to current retirees; however, such changes are essentially deposits into and withdrawals from the plan, not earnings on the plan's assets.

Under IFRS and U.S. GAAP, current service costs and interest expense on the pension obligation increase a company's pension liability in a particular period and are fully and immediately reflected as components of a company's defined benefit pension expense. In contrast, both IFRS and U.S. GAAP include various provisions (sometimes referred to as smoothing mechanisms because they result in a smoother pattern of income) providing for some of the effects of past service costs and of actuarial gains and losses to be reflected in a company's DB pension expense over time.

Past service costs arise when a defined benefit plan is introduced or the benefits under an existing plan are changed. These changes are in return for past employee service, but recognition under IFRS is spread over the period until the "new" benefits become vested. Therefore, past service costs are recognised over the vesting period despite the fact that the cost refers to employee service in previous periods. Past service costs are measured as the change in the defined benefit obligation resulting from the plan amendment. Amendments that increase benefits payable also increase pension expense, and those that reduce benefits payable (negative past service costs) reduce pension expense.

Under IFRS, past service costs are recognised immediately in the period when the change occurs, to the extent that the benefits are vested, or amortized on a straight-line basis over the average period until the benefits become vested and reported as an expense on the income statement. Unamortized past service costs are disclosed in the footnotes and used to calculate the funded status of the plan and the resulting pension liability or asset that is reported on the balance sheet.

Under U.S. GAAP, past (prior) service costs are reported in other comprehensive income in the period in which the change occurs. In subsequent periods, these costs are amortized over the average service lives of the affected employees and reported as a component of pension expense. Unamortized past service costs are reported in accumulated other comprehensive income (shareholders' equity) and are not included in the determination of the funded status of the plan.

Actuarial assumptions represent the "best estimates" of the variables that will determine the ultimate cost of providing post-employment benefits. They include demographic assumptions such as mortality rates and rates of employee turnover, and financial assumptions such as the discount rate, the rate of future salary increases, and the expected return on plan assets. Actuarial gains and losses result from two sources: changes in the actuarial assumptions used in determining the benefit obligation, and differences between the expected and actual returns on pension plan assets. In theory, the differences between expected and actual returns are due to short-term fluctuations in market

[14] Actuarial gains and curtailment gains would decrease a company's pension liability.

returns; over the long term, expected and actual returns should approach the same amount. Therefore, in the long term, actuarial gains and losses arising from differences between the expected and actual returns on plan assets should offset one another.

Under IFRS and U.S. GAAP, companies may recognise actuarial gains and losses immediately, in the period of occurrence, or defer recognition using one of the methods described below. Companies must disclose the method used. Under IFRS, actuarial gains and losses that are recognised immediately can either be reported on the income statement or as other comprehensive income. Actuarial gains and losses treated as other comprehensive income are not reported on the income statement, which can reduce the volatility of pension expense but can increase the volatility of shareholders' equity. Under U.S. GAAP, actuarial gains and losses that are recognised immediately are included as a component of pension expense. Under IFRS and U.S. GAAP, if the recognition of actuarial gains and losses is deferred, then companies use either the corridor method or the faster recognition method to determine the minimum amount to be reported on the income statement.

Under the corridor method, the net cumulative unrecognised actuarial gains and losses at the beginning of the reporting period are compared with the defined benefit obligation and the fair value of plan assets at the beginning of the period. If the cumulative amount of unrecognised actuarial gains and losses becomes too large (i.e., exceeds 10 percent of the greater of the defined benefit obligation or the fair value of plan assets), then the excess is amortized over the expected average remaining working lives of the employees participating in the plan and is included as a component of pension expense. The term "corridor" refers to the 10 percent range, and it is only amounts in excess of the corridor that must be amortized. Actuarial gains or losses can also be amortized more quickly than under the corridor method using the faster recognition method, provided that the company applies the method of amortization to both gains and losses consistently in all periods presented.

Under IFRS, similar to the treatment of unamortized past service costs, unamortized actuarial gains and losses are disclosed in the footnotes rather than being shown on the balance sheet unless the company chooses to recognise the actuarial gains and losses immediately in other comprehensive income. Under U.S. GAAP, if either the corridor or faster recognition method is used, any actuarial gains and losses not recognised in earnings must be reported in other comprehensive income in the period they occur, and the unamortized portion of actuarial gains and losses are reported in accumulated other comprehensive income (shareholders' equity) on the balance sheet until it is subsequently amortized, i.e., recognised in earnings.

IFRS do not require companies to present the various components of pension expense as a net amount (i.e., within a single line item) on the income statement. Instead, companies may disclose portions of net pension expense within different line items on the income statement. For example, companies can record the interest cost and the expected return on plan assets as a part of financing costs on the income statement. U.S. GAAP, however, require all components of net periodic pension expense to be aggregated and presented as a net amount within the same line item on the income statement. Both sets of standards require total pension expense to be disclosed in the footnotes to the financial statements.

An income statement prepared under IFRS will include current service costs, interest cost, the expected return on plan assets, past service costs, the effect of any settlement or curtailment, and perhaps actuarial gains and losses (if the company does not choose to recognise them in a statement of recognised income and expense). Under U.S. GAAP, the net periodic pension expense reported on the income statement will include current service costs, interest cost, the expected return on plan assets (or the actual return), the amortization of past service costs, actuarial gains and losses to the extent recognised, the amortization of any net transition asset or obligation existing at the date of the initial application of SFAS 158, and the effect of settlement or curtailment gains or losses.[15] In summary, the components of a company's defined benefit pension expense are listed in Exhibit 5.

EXHIBIT 5 Components of a Company's Defined Benefit Pension Expense

Component	Effect on Defined Benefit Pension Expense	Direction of Effect on Defined Benefit Pension Expense
Service costs: Estimated increase in the pension obligation resulting from employees' service during the period.	Immediately and fully recognised.	Increases the expense.
Interest expense on the opening pension obligation.	Immediately and fully recognised.	Increases the expense.
Past service costs: Increase in the pension obligation resulting from changes to the terms of a pension plan applicable to employees' service during previous periods.	IFRS: Vested employees' portion expensed immediately; unvested employees' portion expensed over average period until vesting. U.S. GAAP: Portion not immediately recognised as an expense is shown in other comprehensive income and subsequently amortized over service life of employees.	Typically increases the expense.
Actuarial gains and losses, including changes in a company's pension obligation arising from changes in actuarial assumptions as well as differences between the actual and expected returns on plan assets.	IFRS: 1) Recognised immediately either in the income statement or as other comprehensive income (equity); or 2) deferred and amortized using the corridor or faster recognition method. If the cumulative unrecognised amount of actuarial gains and losses exceeds specified levels,* a portion of the excess is recognised as an expense. U.S. GAAP: Recognised immediately as an expense or deferred and amortized using the corridor or faster recognition method.* All amounts not immediately recognised as an expense are included in other comprehensive income.	May increase or decrease the expense.

(Exhibit continues on next page . . .)

[15] The unamortized portion of the transition asset or liability is included in accumulated other comprehensive income.

EXHIBIT 5 (continued)

Component	Effect on Defined Benefit Pension Expense	Direction of Effect on Defined Benefit Pension Expense
Return on plan assets.	*Expected return* on plan assets is immediately and fully recognised as a reduction of pension expense. Any differences between expected and actual return is considered part of actuarial gains and losses and treated as described above.	Decreases the expense.**

* If the cumulative amount of unrecognised actuarial gains and losses exceeds 10 percent of the greater of the value of the plan assets or of the present value of the DB obligation (under U.S. GAAP, the projected benefit obligation), the difference must be amortized over the service lives of the employees.

** If the actual return on plan assets is lower than the expected return on plan assets such that the cumulative difference becomes large enough to require amortization, the amortization of the difference increases pension expense.

2.4.3 Effect of Assumptions and Actuarial Gains and Losses on Pension and Other Post-Employment Benefits Expense

As noted, periodic pension expense for a defined contribution pension plan is approximately equal to the company's contribution to the plan in the period. The discussion in this section relates to the effect of assumptions on expenses for DB pension plans and for other post-employment benefits.

For DB pension plans, the company's pension obligation is an estimate based on many assumptions. The amount of future pension payments requires assumptions about employee turnover, length of service, and rate of increase in compensation levels. The length of time the pension payments will be made requires assumptions about employees' life expectancy post-employment. Finally, the present value of these future payments requires assumptions about the appropriate discount rate and the rate at which interest will subsequently accrue on the pension liability. Changes in any of the assumptions will increase or decrease the pension obligation. An increase in pension obligation resulting from changes in actuarial assumptions would be considered an actuarial loss, and a decrease would be considered an actuarial gain. The estimate of the company's pension liability affects several components of annual pension expense, apart from actuarial gains and losses. First, the service cost component of annual pension expense is essentially the amount by which the pension liability increases as a result of the employees' service during the year. Second, the interest cost component of annual pension expense is based on the amount of the liability. Third, the past service cost component of annual pension expense is the amount by which the pension liability increases because of changes to the plan.

Estimates related to plan assets also affect annual pension expense. Because a company's pension expense includes the expected return on pension assets rather than the actual return, the assumptions about the "expected return" on plan assets can have a significant impact. Also, the expected return on plan assets requires estimating in which future period the benefits will be paid. As noted above, a divergence of actual returns on pension assets from expected returns results in an actuarial gain or loss.

Understanding the effect of assumptions on the estimated pension obligation and on periodic expenses is important both for interpreting a company's financial statements and for evaluating whether a company's assumptions appear relatively conservative or aggressive.

The following example, using a single employee, illustrates the calculation of the defined benefit obligation and current service costs, using the projected unit credit method, for an individual employee under four different scenarios. The fourth scenario illustrates the impact on a company's pension obligation of changes in certain key estimates.

EXAMPLE 4

Calculation of Defined Benefit Pension Obligation for an Individual Employee

The following information applies to each of the four scenarios. Assume that a (hypothetical) company establishes a defined benefit pension plan. The employee has a current salary of €50,000 and is expected to work for five more years before retiring. The assumed discount rate is 6 percent and the assumed annual compensation increase is 4.75 percent. For simplicity, assume that there are no changes in actuarial assumptions, all compensation increases are awarded on the first day of the service year, and no additional adjustments are made to reflect the probability that the employee may leave the company at an earlier date.

Current salary	€50,000.00
Years until retirement	5
Annual compensation increases	4.75%
Discount rate	6.00%
Final year's estimated salary[a]	€60,198.56

[a] Final years estimated salary = Current year's salary × [(1 + Annual compensation increase)$^{\text{Years until retirement}}$]

At the end of Year 1, final year's estimated salary = €50,000 × [(1 + 0.0475)^4] = €60,198.56, assuming that the employee's salary increases by 4.75 percent each year.

With no change in assumption about the rate of increase in compensation or date of retirement, the estimate of the final year salary will remain unchanged.

At the end of Year 2, assuming the employee's salary actually increased by 4.75 percent, final year's estimated salary = €52,375 × [(1 + 0.0475)^3] = €60,198.56.

Scenario 1: Benefit is paid as a lump sum amount upon retirement

The plan will pay a lump sum pension benefit equal to 1.5 percent of the employee's final salary for each year of service beyond the date of establishment. The lump sum payment to be paid upon retirement = (Final salary × Benefit formula) × Years of service = (€60,198.56 × 0.015) × 5 = €4,514.89.

Annual unit credit (benefit) per service year = Value at retirement divided by Years of service = €4,514.89/5 = €902.98.

If the discount rate (the interest rate at which the defined benefit obligation could be effectively settled) was assumed to be 0%, the amount of annual unit credit per service year would be the amount of the company's annual obligation, and the closing obligation each year would simply be the annual unit credit multiplied by the number of past and current years of service. However, because the discount rate assumption would not equal 0%, the future obligation resulting from current and prior service is discounted to measure the value of the obligation at any point in time.

The following table shows how the obligation builds up for this employee.

Year	1	2	3	4	5
Estimated annual salary	€50,000.00	€52,375.00	€54,862.81	€57,468.80	€60,198.56
Benefits attributed to:					
Prior years[a]	€0.00	€902.98	€1,805.96	€2,708.94	€3,611.92
Current year[b]	902.98	902.98	902.98	902.98	902.97
Total benefits earned	€902.98	€1,805.96	€2,708.94	€3,611.92	€4,514.89
Opening obligation[c]	0.00	€715.24	€1,516.31	€2,410.94	€3,407.47
Interest cost at 6%[d]	0.00	42.91	90.98	144.66	204.45
Current service costs[e]	715.24	758.16	803.65	851.87	902.97
Closing obligation[f]	€715.24	€1,516.31	€2,410.94	€3,407.47	€4,514.89

[a] The benefit attributed to prior years = Annual unit credit × Years of prior service
For Year 2, €902.98 × 1 = €902.98
For Year 3, €902.98 × 2 = €1,805.96

[b] The benefit attributed to current year = Annual unit credit based on benefit formula = Final year's estimated salary × Benefit formula = Value at retirement date/Years of service = (€60,198.56 × 1.5%) = €4,514.89/5 = €902.98

[c] The opening obligation is the closing obligation at the end of the previous year, but can also be viewed as the present value of benefits earned in prior years:
Benefits earned in prior years/[(1 + Discount rate)$^{\text{Years until retirement}}$]
Opening obligation Year 1 = 0
Opening obligation Year 2 = €902.98/[(1 + 0.06)^4] = €715.24
Opening obligation Year 3 = €1,805.96/[(1 + 0.06)^3] = €1,516.32

[d] The interest cost is the increase in the present value of the defined benefit obligation due to the passage of time: Interest Cost = Opening obligation × Discount rate
For Year 2 = €715.24 × 0.06 = €42.91
For Year 3 = €1,516.32 × 0.06 = €90.98

[e] Current service costs are the present value of annual units credits earned in the current period: Annual unit credit/[(1 + Discount rate)$^{\text{Years until retirement}}$]
For Year 1 = €902.98/[(1 + 0.06)^4] = €715.24
For Year 2 = €902.98/[(1 + 0.06)^3] = €758.16
Note: Given no change in actuarial assumptions and estimates of financial growth, the current service costs in any year (except the first) are the previous year's current service costs increased by the discount rate; the current service costs increase with the passage of time.

[f] The closing obligation is the opening obligation plus the interest cost and the current service costs, but can also be viewed as the present value of benefits earned in prior and current years. There is a slight difference due to rounding.
Total benefits earned/[(1 + Discount rate)$^{\text{Years until retirement}}$]
Closing obligation Year 1 = €902.98/[(1 + 0.06)^4] = €715.24
Closing obligation Year 2 = €1,805.96/[(1 + 0.06)^3] = €1,516.32
At Year 3 = €2,708.94/[(1 + 0.06)^2] = €2,410.95

Scenario 2: Prior years of service, and benefit paid as a lump sum upon retirement
The plan will pay a lump sum pension benefit equal to 1.5 percent of the employee's final salary for each year of service beyond the date of establishment. In addition, at the time the pension plan is established, the employee is given credit for 10 years of prior service with immediate vesting. The lump sum

payment to be paid upon retirement = (Final salary × Benefit formula) × Years of service = (€60,198.56 × 0.015) × 15 = €13,544.68.

Annual unit credit = Value at retirement date/Years of service = €13,544.68/15 = €902.98.

The following table shows how the obligation builds up for this employee.

Year	1	2	3	4	5
Benefits attributed to:					
Prior years[a]	€9,029.78	€9,932.76	€10,835.74	€11,738.72	€12,641.70
Current years	902.98	902.98	902.98	902.98	902.98
Total benefits earned	€9,932.76	€10,835.74	€11,738.72	€12,641.70	€13,544.68
Opening obligation[b]	6,747.58	€7,867.67	€9,097.89	€10,447.41	€11,926.13
Interest at 6%	404.85	472.06	545.87	626.85	715.57
Current service costs	715.24	758.16	803.65	851.87	902.98
Closing obligation	€7,867.67	€9,097.89	€10,447.41	€11,926.13	€13,544.68

[a] Benefits attributed to prior years of service = Annual unit credit × Years of prior service: At beginning of Year 1 = (€60,198.56 × 0.015) × 10 = €9,029.78.

[b] Opening obligation is the present value of the benefits attributed to prior years = Benefits attributed to prior years/(1 + Discount rate)$^{\text{Number of years to retirement}}$

At beginning of year 1 = €9,029.78/$(1.06)^5$ = €6,747.58. This is treated as past service costs in Year 1 since there was no previous recognition and there is immediate vesting.

Scenario 3: Employee to receive benefit payments for 20 years (no prior years of service)

Years of receiving pension 20

Estimated annual payment for each of the 20 years = (Estimated final salary × Benefit formula) × Years of service = (€60,198.56 × 0.015) × 5 = €4,514.89.

Value at the end of Year 5 (retirement date) of the estimated future payments = PV of €4,514.89 for 20 years at 6% = €51,785.46.[16]

Annual unit credit = Value at retirement date/Years of service = €51,785.46/5 = €10,357.09.

Year	1	2	3	4	5
Benefit attributed to:					
Prior years	€0.00	€10,357.09	€20,714.18	€31,071.27	€41,428.36
Current year	10,357.09	10,357.09	10,357.09	10,357.09	10,357.10
Total benefits earned	€10,357.09	€20,714.18	€31,071.27	€41,428.36	€51,785.46
Opening obligation	€0.00	€8,203.79	€17,392.03	€27,653.32	€39,083.36
Interest at 6%		492.23	1,043.52	1,659.20	2,345.00
Current service costs	8,203.79	8,696.01	9,217.77	9,770.84	10,357.10
Closing obligation	€8,203.79	€17,392.03	€27,653.32	€39,083.36	€51,785.46

[16] This is a simplification of the valuation process for illustrative purposes. For instance, the actuarial valuation would use mortality rates, not just assumed life expectancy. Additionally, annualizing the present value of an ordinary annuity probably understates the liability because the actual benefit payments are usually made monthly or bi-weekly rather than annually.

Scenario 4: Employee to receive benefit payments for 20 years and is given credit for 10 years of prior service with immediate vesting

Estimated annual payment for each of the 20 years = (Estimated final salary × Benefit formula) × Years of service = (€60,198.56 × 0.015) × (10 + 5) = €13,544.68.

Value at the end of Year 5 (retirement date) of the estimated future payments = PV of €13,544.68 for 20 years at 6% = €155,356.41.

Annual unit credit = Value at retirement date/Years of service = €155,356.41/15 = €10,357.09.

Year	1	2	3	4	5
Benefit attributed to:					
Prior years	€103,570.94	€113,928.03	€124,285.12	€134,642.21	€144,999.30
Current year	10,357.09	10,357.09	10,357.09	10,357.09	10,357.11
Total benefits earned	€113,928.03	€124,285.12	€134,642.21	€144,999.30	€155,356.41
Opening obligation[a]	€77,394.23	€90,241.67	€104,352.18	€119,831.08	€136,791.79
Interest at 6%	4,643.65	5,414.50	6,261.13	7,189.87	8,207.51
Current service costs	8,203.79	8,696.01	9,217.77	9,770.84	10,357.11
Closing obligation	€90,241.67	€104,352.18	€119,831.08	€136,791.79	€155,356.41

[a] This is treated as past service costs in Year 1 since there was no previous recognition and there is immediate vesting.

Based on Scenario 4 (10 years of prior service and the employee receives benefits for 20 years after retirement):

1. What is the effect on the Year 1 closing pension obligation of a 1 percent increase in the assumed discount rate—from 6 percent to 7 percent?
2. What is the effect on the Year 1 closing pension obligation of a 1 percent increase in the assumed annual compensation increase—from 4.75 percent to 5.75 percent? Treat this as being independent of Question 1.

Solution to 1: The estimated final salary and the estimated annual payments after retirement are unchanged at €60,198.56 and €13,544.68, respectively. However, the value at the retirement date is changed. Value at the end of Year 5 (retirement date) of the estimated future payments = PV of €13,544.68 for 20 years at 7% = €143,492.53. Annual unit credit = Value at retirement date/Years of service = €143,492.53/15 = €9,566.17.

Year	1
Benefit attributed to:	
Prior years	€ 95,661.69
Current year	9,566.17
Total benefits earned	€105,227.86
Opening obligation	€ 68,205.46
Interest at 7%	4,774.38
Current service costs	7,297.99
Closing obligation	€ 80,277.83

A 1 percent increase in the assumed discount rate (from 6 percent to 7 percent) would *decrease* the Year 1 closing pension obligation by €90,241.67 − €80,277.83 = €9,963.84.

Solution to 2: The estimated final salary is [€50,000 × (1 + 0.0575)^4] = €62,530.44. Estimated annual payment for each of the 20 years = (Estimated final salary × Benefit formula) × Years of service = (€62,530.44 × 0.015) × (10 + 5) = €14,069.35. Value at the end of Year 5 (retirement date) of the estimated future payments = PV of €14,069.35 for 20 years at 6% = €161,374.33. Annual unit credit = Value at retirement date/Years of service = €161,374.33/15 = €10,758.29.

Year	**1**
Benefit attributed to:	
Prior years	€107,582.89
Current year	10,758.29
Total benefits earned	€118,341.18
Opening obligation	€ 80,392.19
Interest at 6%	4,823.53
Current service costs	8,521.57
Closing obligation	€ 93,737.29

A 1 percent increase in the assumed annual compensation increase (from 4.75 percent to 5.75 percent) would *increase* the pension obligation by €93,737.29 − €90,241.67 = €3,495.62.

Example 4 illustrates that increases in the assumed discount rate will *decrease* a company's pension obligation. In the case above, there is a slight increase in the interest component of the pension obligation and pension expense. However, the interest component of the pension obligation and pension expense (calculated as the discount rate times the obligation at the beginning of the year) may decrease because the decrease in the opening obligation may more than offset the effect of the increase in the discount rate; an exception occurs when the pension obligation is of a short duration; i.e., time to retirement is short.

Example 4 also illustrates that increases in the assumed rate of annual compensation increase will *increase* a company's pension obligation—when the pension formula is based on final year's salary. In addition, a higher assumed rate of annual compensation increase will increase the service components and the interest component of a company's periodic pension expense due to an increased annual unit credit and the resulting increased obligation. An increase in life expectancy will also increase the pension obligation unless the promised pension payments are independent of life expectancy; e.g., paid as a lump sum or over a fixed period.

Finally, because the expected return on plan assets reduces pension expense, a higher expected return will decrease pension expense. Exhibit 6

EXHIBIT 6 Impact of Key DB Pension Assumptions on Balance Sheet and Periodic Expense

Assumption	Impact of Assumption on Balance Sheet	Impact of Assumption on Periodic Expense
Higher discount rate	Lower obligation	The interest cost will typically be lower due to lower obligation
Higher rate of compensation increase	Higher obligation	Higher service costs
Higher expected return on plan assets		Lower pension expense

summarizes the impact of some key estimates on the balance sheet and the periodic benefit-related expense.

Accounting for other post-employment benefits also requires assumptions and estimates. For example, assumed trends in health care costs are an important component of estimating costs of post-employment health care plans. A higher assumed medical expense inflation rate will result in a higher post-employment medical obligation. Companies also estimate various patterns of health care cost trend rates—for example, higher in the near term, but becoming lower after some point in time. For post-employment health plans, an increase in the assumed inflationary trends in health care costs or an increase in life expectancy will increase the obligation and associated periodic expense of these plans.

The next section evaluates disclosures of pension and other post-employment benefits, including disclosures about key assumptions.

2.5 Evaluating Disclosures of Pension and Other Post-Employment Benefits

Several aspects of the accounting for pensions and other post-employment benefits described above can affect comparative financial analysis using ratios based on financial statements. First, differences in key assumptions can affect comparisons across companies. Second, differences between IFRS and U.S. GAAP in how the funded status of the pension plan is determined, in the amount of resulting pension liability or pension asset that is reported, and in footnote disclosures can affect company comparisons. Third, the smoothing mechanisms within the accounting standards can obscure the underlying economic expense. Fourth, under U.S. GAAP, all of the components of pension expense are reported within a single line item that is treated as an operating expense on the income statement, even though some of the components are of a financial nature (specifically, interest expense and the expected return on assets). However, under IFRS the components of pension expense can be included in various line items. Finally, cash flow information may not be comparable because some portion of the amount of contributions might be better treated as a financing activity rather than an investing activity.

Information related to pensions can be obtained from various portions of the footnote disclosure and appropriate analytical adjustments can be made. In the following sections, we examine pension plan footnote disclosures to address analytical issues.

2.5.1 Assumptions

Companies disclose their assumptions about discount rates, expected compensation increases, medical expense inflation, and expected return on plan assets (see Volvo's assumptions in Exhibit 4). Comparing these assumptions over time and across companies provides a basis to assess any conservative or aggressive biases. Some companies also disclose the effects of a change in their assumptions.

Exhibit 7 presents the assumed discount rates (Panel A) and assumed annual compensation increases (Panel B) to estimate pension obligations for four companies operating in the automotive and equipment manufacturing sector. The Volvo Group (a Swedish-based company) and Fiat S.p.A. (an Italian-based company) use IFRS. General Motors and Ford Motor Company are U.S.-based companies that use U.S. GAAP. All of these companies have both U.S. and non-U.S. defined benefit pension plans; this facilitates comparison.

EXHIBIT 7

	2007	2006	2005
Panel A. Assumed Discount Rates Used to Estimate Pension Obligations (%)			
Fiat S.p.A. (Italy)	4.70	3.98	3.53
The Volvo Group (Sweden)	4.50	4.00	4.00
General Motors (non-U.S. plans)	5.72	4.76	4.72
Ford Motor Company (non-U.S. plans)	5.58	4.91	4.58
Fiat S.p.A. (U.S. plans)	5.80	5.80	5.50
The Volvo Group (U.S. plans)	5.75–6.25	5.50	5.75
General Motors (U.S. plans)	6.35	5.90	5.70
Ford Motor Company (U.S. plans)	6.25	5.86	5.61
Panel B. Assumed Annual Compensation Increases Used to Estimate Pension Obligations (%)			
Fiat S.p.A. (Italy)	4.60	3.65	2.58
The Volvo Group (Sweden)	3.20	3.20	3.20
General Motors (non-U.S. plans)	3.60	3.00	3.10
Ford Motor Company (non-U.S. plans)	3.21	3.30	3.44
Fiat S.p.A. (U.S. plans)	n.a.	n.a.	n.a.
The Volvo Group (U.S. plans)	3.50	3.50	3.50
General Motors (U.S. plans)	5.25	5.00	4.90
Ford Motor Company (U.S. plans)	3.80	3.80	4.00

The assumed discount rates used to estimate pension obligations are based on the market interest rates of high quality corporate fixed income investments with a maturity profile similar to the timing of a company's future pension payments. The trend in discount rates across the companies (in both their U.S. plans and non-U.S. plans) is similar: increasing discount rates from 2005 to 2007. General Motors has the highest assumed discount rates for both its non-U.S. and U.S. DB plans. Recall that a higher discount rate assumption results in a lower estimated pension obligation. Therefore, the use of a higher discount rate compared to its peers may indicate a less-conservative bias.

Explanations for differences in the level of the assumed discount rates, apart from bias, are differences in the regions involved and differences in the timing of obligations. In this example, difference in regions might explain the difference in rates used for the non-U.S. plans but would not explain the difference in the rates shown for the four companies for their U.S. plans. However, the range of discount rates used is less for the U.S. plans than for the non-U.S. plans. The timing of obligations under the companies' DB pension plans likely varies, so the relevant market interest rates selected as the discount rate will vary accordingly. Because the timing of the obligations is not disclosed, differences in the timing of pension obligations cannot be ruled out as an explanation for differences in discount rates.

Another important consideration is whether the assumptions are internally consistent. For example, do a company's assumed discount rates and assumed compensation increases reflect a consistent view of inflation? For Volvo, both the assumed discount rates and the assumed annual compensation increases (for both its non-U.S. and U.S. plans) are lower than those of the other companies, so the assumptions appear internally consistent. The assumptions are consistent with plans located in lower inflation regions. However, unlike the increasing trend in its discount rate, Volvo's assumed annual rate of compensation increase is unchanged over the period, possibly reflecting the terms of the company's agreement with its labor union. Recall that a lower rate of compensation increase results in a lower estimated pension obligation.

In Ford's U.S. and non-U.S. pension plans, the assumed discount rate is increasing and the assumed rate of compensation increase is decreasing. Each of these will reduce the pension obligation. Therefore, holding all else equal, Ford's pension liability is decreasing due to the higher assumed discount rate and the reduced assumed rate of compensation increase. For Fiat's U.S. plan, no annual rate of compensation increase assumption is disclosed. An explanation for the omission can be found in the company's descriptive disclosure that "benefits for salaried employees in the United States were frozen for pay and service as of December 31, 2000." The assumptions about the annual rate of compensation increases provide potentially interesting information about a company independent of pension considerations.

Exhibit 8 presents a comparison of the four companies' assumptions about the expected return on U.S. pension assets. Recall that a higher expected return on plan assets lowers the periodic pension expense. (Of course, a higher expected return on plan assets presumably reflects more risky investments, so it would be inadvisable for a company to simply invest in riskier investments to reduce periodic pension expense.) Analysts should compare the company's assumptions in the context of its chosen asset allocation.

Although the disclosure for Fiat and Volvo does not separately disclose plan assets for the U.S. plans, comparison of the overall asset allocations yields some insights. General Motors shows the highest expected return and Volvo shows the lowest expected returns assumption. A higher expected return is consistent with

EXHIBIT 8 Assumed Expected Return on U.S. Pension Expense (%)

	2007	2006	2005
Fiat S.p.A. (U.S. plans)	8.00	8.25	8.25
The Volvo Group (U.S. plans)	7.65	7.65	7.65
General Motors (U.S. plans)	8.50	9.00	9.00
Ford Motor Company (U.S. plans)	8.25	8.50	8.50

EXHIBIT 9 Allocation of Plan Assets (Equity/Debt/Other; in Percent)

	2007	2006	2005
Fiat S.p.A. (all plan assets)	58/39/3	56/39/5	54/42/4
The Volvo Group (all plan assets)	49/41/10	51/40/9	n.a.
General Motors (U.S. plans)	26/52/22	38/43/19	47/32/21
Ford Motor Company (U.S. plans)	51/46/3	72/27/1	73/27/0

a greater portion of plan assets being allocated to riskier investments such as equities. This does not seem to be the case. Recall that a higher expected return on plan assets lowers a company's pension expense.

Companies with post-employment health care plans, a type of defined benefit plan, also disclose assumptions about increases in health care costs. The assumptions are typically that the inflation rate in health care costs will taper off to some lower, constant rate at some year in the future. That future inflation rate is known as the ultimate health care trend rate. Holding all else equal, the following assumptions would each result in a higher benefit obligation and a higher periodic expense:

- a higher assumed near term increase in health care costs;
- a higher assumed ultimate health care trend rate; and
- a later year in which the ultimate health care trend rate is assumed to be reached.

Conversely, holding all else equal, the following assumptions would each result in a lower benefit obligation and a lower periodic expense:

- a lower assumed near term increase in health care costs;
- a lower assumed ultimate health care trend rate; and
- an earlier year in which the ultimate health care trend rate is assumed to be reached.

Example 5 examines two companies' assumptions about trends in U.S. health care costs.

EXAMPLE 5

Comparison of Assumptions about Trends in U.S. Health Care Costs

In addition to disclosing assumptions about health care costs, companies also disclose information on the sensitivity of the measurements of both the obligation and periodic expense to a change in those assumptions. Exhibit 10 presents information obtained from the footnotes to the financial statements for CNH Global N.V. (a Dutch manufacturer of construction and mining equipment) and Caterpillar Inc. (a U.S. manufacturer of construction and mining equipment, engines, and turbines).

Panel A in the exhibit shows the companies' assumptions about health care costs and the amounts each reported for post-employment health care benefit plans. For example, CNH assumes that the initial year's (2008) increase in health care costs will be 9 percent, and this rate of increase will decline to 5 percent over the next 5 years; i.e., 8 percent increase in the second year, 7 percent increase in the third year, 6 percent increase in the fourth year, and 5 percent increase in the fifth year and each year thereafter. Caterpillar assumes a lower initial year increase and a more gradual and longer decline to the ultimate health care trend rate.

Panel B in the exhibit shows the effect of a 1 percent increase or decrease in the assumed health care cost trend rates. A one-percentage point increase in the assumed health care cost trend rates would increase Caterpillar's 2007 service and interest cost component of the other post-employment benefit costs by $32 million and the related obligation by $395 million. A one-percentage point increase in the assumed health care cost trend rates would increase CNH Global's 2007 service and interest cost component of the other post-employment benefit costs by $9 million and the related obligation by $106 million.

EXHIBIT 10 Post-Employment Health Care Plan Disclosures

Panel A. Assumptions and Reported Amounts for U.S. Post-Employment Health Care Benefit Plans

	Assumptions about Health Care Costs			Amounts Reported for Other Post-Employment Benefits ($ Millions)	
	Initial Health Care Trend Rate	Ultimate Health Care Trend Rate	Year Ultimate Trend Rate Attained	Accumulated Benefit Obligation Year End 2007	Periodic Expense for Benefits for 2007
CNH Global N.V.	9.0% (I)	5%	2012	$1,221	$121
Caterpillar Inc.	7.9 (I)	5	2016	5,455	311

Panel B. Effect of 1 Percent Increase (Decrease) in Assumed Health Care Cost Trend Rates on 2007 Total Accumulated Post-Employment Benefit Obligations and Periodic Expense

	1% Increase	1% Decrease
CNH Global N.V.	+$106 million (Obligation) +$9 million (Expense)	−$90 million (Obligation) −$7 million (Expense)
Caterpillar Inc.	+$395 million (Obligation) +$32 million (Expense)	−$346 million (Obligation) −$28 million (Expense)

Sources: Caterpillar information is from the company's Form 10-K filed 22 February 2008, Note 14 (pages A-25 and A-28) and Management's Discussion and Analysis (page A-65). CNH Global information is from the company's 2007 Form 20-F, Note 12 (pages F-38, F-40, and F-42).

Based on the information in Exhibit 10, answer the following questions:

1. Which company's assumptions about health care costs appear less conservative?
2. What would be the effect of adjusting the post-employment benefit obligation and the periodic post-employment benefit expense of the less conservative company for a 1 percent increase in health care cost trend rates? Does this make the two companies more comparable?

Solution to 1: Caterpillar's assumptions about health care costs appear less conservative than CNH's. Caterpillar's initial assumed health care cost increase of 7.9 percent is significantly lower than CNH's assumed 9.0 percent. This lower assumed initial rate is partially offset by a more gradual and longer decline to the ultimate health care trend rate. CNH's assumption is that the ultimate health care cost trend rate will be reached four years earlier than Caterpillar's assumption.

A year-by-year extrapolation of the companies' assumed health care cost trend rates is shown below. Year-to-year change in assumed growth in health care costs are estimated by extrapolating from the assumptions as follows: (initial health care trend rate − ultimate health care trend rate) ÷ years until the ultimate trend rate is reached.

	2008	2009	2010	2011	2012	2013	2014	2015	2016
CNH	9.00%	8.00%	7.00%	6.00%	5.00%	5.00%	5.00%	5.00%	5.00%
Caterpillar	7.90	7.5375	7.175	6.8125	6.45	6.0875	5.725	5.3625	5.00

Solution to 2: The sensitivity disclosures indicate that a 1 percent increase in the assumed health care cost trend rate would increase Caterpillar's post-employment benefit obligation by $395 million and the periodic cost by $32 million. This would make the underlying assumptions more consistent and analysis based on the adjusted numbers better, since the numbers are more comparable.

A 1 percent increase is reasonable, in this case, given the difference in the initial trends of 1.1 percent and a more gradual decline in the less conservative company's trend rates. If the initial difference was not close to 1 percent, an analysis based on linear sensitivity could be used to estimate the impact. Note that the sensitivity to an increase more or less than 1 percent cannot be assumed to be exactly linear; this is an approximation. If the difference in the initial trend rate was 2 percent, the adjustment would use the impact of a 1 percent change multiplied by 2 as an approximation of the adjustment required for comparability.

This section has explored the use of pension and other post-employment benefits disclosures to assess a company's assumptions and explore how the assumptions can affect comparisons across companies. The following sections turn to the use of disclosures in understanding the underlying economics of a company's pension and other post-employment benefits.

2.5.2 Underlying Economic Liability (or Asset)

A company's balance sheet reports the net funded position (or simply *funded position* or *funded status*) of a company's pension and other post-employment benefits. From an economic perspective, the net funded position is the difference between the defined benefit obligations and the fair value of any assets out of which the obligations are to be settled directly. Footnotes to the financial statements disclose the components of the net funded position. Under current IFRS, the present value of the defined benefit obligation may be adjusted for a number of deferred items. In addition, there is a limitation on the amount of a pension asset that can be reported. Thus, the amount reported under IFRS is not necessarily equivalent to the economic perspective of the net funded position. Analysts look at the footnotes to find the gross benefit obligation and the fair value of the assets allocated to pay the obligation in order to arrive at the economic net funded position.

Under U.S. GAAP (SFAS 158), companies now report the entire net pension obligation (funded status) on the balance sheet without any adjustments; this is equivalent to the economic net funded position. An overfunded plan results in an asset (with no limitations on the amount that can be shown), and an underfunded plan results in a liability.

Under both standards, the amount appearing in the balance sheet is a net amount. Some analysts use information from the footnotes to adjust a company's assets and liabilities for the gross amount of the benefit plan assets and the gross amount of the benefit plan liabilities. A related adjustment is to include the actual return on plan assets as income and the interest on the plan liability as an expense (U.S. GAAP only, since it is already included in interest expense under IFRS). Such adjustments effectively consolidate the benefit plans with the sponsoring company. An argument for making such adjustments is that they reflect the underlying economic liabilities and assets of a company; however, it should be recognised that actual consolidation is precluded by laws protecting a pension or other benefit plan as a separate legal entity.

At a minimum, an analyst will compare the gross benefit obligation (i.e., the benefit obligation without deducting related plan assets) to the sponsoring company's total assets, shareholders' equity, and earnings. If the gross benefit obligation is large relative to these items, a small change in the pension liability can have a significant financial impact on the sponsoring company.

2.5.3 Underlying Economic Expense (or Income)

As illustrated in Exhibit 11, the two main reasons for changes in the economic net funded status of a DB pension plan are the economic periodic costs (as opposed to reported periodic costs) of the pension plan, and contributions into the plan by the sponsoring company. Benefits paid to retirees decrease the pension obligations and the plan assets by an identical amount and thus have no impact on the net funded status. The economic periodic costs of a company's DB pension plan comprise net increases in pension obligations (excluding the impact of benefits paid) offset by earnings on pension plan assets. So the economic periodic costs of a company's DB pension plan can be calculated in either of the following ways: by summing each item (other than benefits paid) that increases or decreases the pension obligation and deducting actual returns on pension plan assets; or equivalently, by taking the contributions made by the sponsoring company and adjusting for the change in the plan's net funded status over the period. Because the computations yield equivalent results, analysts can use the approach they consider most intuitive to determine the economic pension expense.

Example 6 illustrates the estimation of economic pension expense for Coach, Inc. (NYSE: COH), which prepares its financial statements in accordance with U.S. GAAP. The estimation of pension expense is shown first for U.S. GAAP because the reported and economic net funded positions are equivalent; this allows the use of the format of Exhibit 11 to estimate the economic pension expense.

EXHIBIT 11 **Summary of Underlying Economic Liability (or Asset) and Economic Expense of the Period**

Beginning of Period Economic Liability or Asset →	Economic Expense of the Period	Benefits Paid Out of and Contributions into the Pension Plan →	End of Period Economic Liability or Asset
Beginning pension obligations	▶ Service costs increase the obligation and the economic expense of the period ▶ Interest costs increase the obligation and the economic expense of the period ▶ Actuarial gains/losses affecting pension obligation may increase or decrease the obligation and the economic expense of the period	Benefits paid to retirees decrease the pension obligation	Ending pension obligation
Beginning plan assets	Actual returns on plan assets (typically) increase the plan assets and thus decrease the economic expense of the period	Benefits paid to retirees decrease the plan assets Contributions by sponsoring company increase the plan assets	Ending plan assets
Beginning net funded position ▶ If negative, economic liability ▶ If positive, economic asset	Increases in the economic costs of the period minus decreases in the economic costs of the period equals net economic expense of the period	Contributions by sponsoring company increase the plan assets	Ending net funded position ▶ If negative, economic liability ▶ If positive, economic asset

EXAMPLE 6

Summary of Underlying Economic Liability (or Asset)

The following information is from Note 11 of the 2008 Annual Report of Coach, Inc. (in $ thousands).

- Beginning pension obligation was $7,818, and beginning plan assets were $4,968.
- Service costs of $777, interest costs of $384, and foreign exchange impact of $281 increased Coach's pension obligation.

- Actuarial gains of $792 and benefits paid to retired employees of $398 decreased Coach's pension obligation.
- Actual returns on the plan assets totaled $166.
- Coach contributed $931 to the plan.
- Reported net periodic benefit cost was $1,110, which includes service costs of $777, interest costs of $384, amortization of net actuarial loss of $263, and expected return on plan assets of $314. ($777 + $384 + $263 − $314 = $1,110)

This information is presented using the Exhibit 11 format below:

Beginning of Period Economic Liability or Asset →	Economic Expense of the Period	Benefits Paid Out of and Contributions into the Pension Plan →	End of Period Economic Liability or Asset
Beginning pension obligation: $7,818	Service costs: $777 Interest costs: $384 Actuarial gain: −$792 Foreign exchange impact: $281	Benefits paid to retirees: −$398	Ending pension obligation: $8,070
Beginning plan assets: $4,968	Actual returns on plan assets: $166	Benefits paid to retirees: −$398 Contributions by the company: $931	Ending plan assets: $5,667
Beginning net funded position: −$2,850	Total net economic expense of the period is calculated by summing the above: $777 + $384 − $792 + $281 − $166 = $484 Or alternatively, calculated as company contributions adjusted for the change in the net funded position: $931 − $447 = $484*	Contributions by the company: $931	Ending net funded position: −$2,403

* The change in the net funded position of $447 is calculated as −$2,403 − $2,850. While still underfunded, the funding position improved by $447. If there had been no economic expense, the contributions would have increased the funded position by $931. The economic expense is $484.

Based on this information, the economic expense of the period equals $484 compared with the reported periodic pension cost of $1,110. This is primarily due to the smoothing mechanisms permitted under accounting standards. Specifically, the expected returns on plan assets of $314 differed from actual returns of $166, and an amortization expense for previous actuarial losses of $263 differed from the period's actuarial gain of $792. The final difference is the foreign exchange impact of $281.

As discussed earlier, the pension expense shown on a company's income statement does not reflect the economic expense of the period primarily because, under certain conditions, accounting standards permit several components of pension expense to be smoothed into income over time. (Recall that the components of the cost that may be smoothed into income over time include past service costs and actuarial gains and losses. Also, recall that actuarial gains and losses result from two sources: changes in the actuarial assumptions used in determining the benefit obligation, and differences between the expected and actual returns on pension plan assets.) To better reflect the company's operating performance, analysts can adjust for these items to obtain the underlying economic expense (or income) and financial ratios based on it. Using either of the alternative calculations to estimate the economic pension expense of the period effectively includes actual returns on plan assets, all actuarial gains and losses arising in the period on the pension obligation, and all service costs arising in the period (whether they relate to current service or past service), and effectively excludes any amortization of past service costs, amortization of net actuarial gains and losses, and expected returns on plan assets.

Below is an example illustrating the estimation of economic pension expense for Novartis Group [NYSE (ADR): NVS], which prepares its financial statements in accordance with IFRS.

EXAMPLE 7

Adjusting Pension and Other Post-Employment Benefits Expense to Underlying Economic Expense

Use the following post-employment benefit information reported by Novartis Group (Novartis Group Annual Report, 2007) to answer the following. All amounts are in millions.

1. Estimate the economic benefit expense of the period and compare to the reported net periodic benefit cost.
2. Adjust reported net income to reflect the underlying economic benefit expense. Novartis' net income from continuing operations in fiscal 2007 is $6,540 and the effective tax rate is 12.6 percent.

Information Based on Note 26: Post-Employment Benefits

Change in Benefit Obligation	
Benefit obligation at beginning of year	$16,767
Benefit obligations related to discontinued operations	−197
Service cost	424
Interest cost	615
Actuarial (gain) loss	−586
Plan amendments	−94
Currency translation effects	1,056
Benefit payments	−996
Contributions of associates	116
Benefit obligation at end of year	$17,105

Change in Plan Assets	
Fair value of plan assets at beginning of year	$17,515
Plan assets related to discontinued operations	−199
Expected return on plan assets	804
Actuarial gains	4
Currency translation effects	1,088
Novartis group contributions	59
Contributions of associates	116
Plan amendments	−36
Benefits paid	−996
Fair value of plan assets at end of year	$18,355
Funded Status	$1,250*
Components of net periodic benefit costs:	
Service costs	$424
Interest cost	615
Expected return on plan assets	−804
Recognised past service costs	−20
Curtailment and settlement gains	−29
Net periodic benefit cost	$186

* Net asset in the balance sheet is $1,201 as a result of adjustment for unrecognised past service cost and limitation on recognition of fund surplus. Recall that IFRS restrict the amount of the asset that can be reported on the balance sheet.

Solution to 1:

Calculation of Economic Benefit Expense

Below is the economic benefit expense calculated as the sum of each item (other than benefits paid and contributions of associates) that increases or decreases the benefit obligation and deducting actual returns on plan assets. Two alternative methods of estimating the actual returns on plan assets are shown. The first alternative sums each item that increases or decreases the fair value of the plan assets (other than benefits paid and contributions). The second takes the change in fair value of the plan assets and adjusts the amount for the contributions and benefits paid. The adjustments are required because, if the contributions had not been made, the assets would have been lower. Similarly, if the benefits had not been paid, the assets would have been higher.

Sum of individual items impacting the benefit obligation		
Benefit obligations related to discontinued operations	−$197	
Service cost	424	
Interest cost	615	
Actuarial (gain) loss	−586	
Plan amendments	−94	
Currency translation effects	1,056	$1,218

Less: Actual return on plan assets		
Method 1, Estimating Returns		
Plan assets related to discontinued operations	−199	
Expected return on plan assets	804	
Actuarial gains	4	
Currency translation effects	1,088	
Plan amendments	−36	
Method 2, Estimating Returns		
Change in fair value of plan assets	$840	
Novartis group contributions	−59	
Contributions of associates	−116	
Benefits paid	996	1,661
Economic benefit expense		−$443

Alternate Calculation of Economic Benefit Expense
Calculated as the change in the net benefit obligation, excluding contributions.

Employer's contribution		$59
Change in the benefit obligation		
Net funded position at beginning of period (overfunded)	$748	
$16,767 benefit obligation minus $17,515 plan assets		
Less: Net funded position at end of period (overfunded)	−1,250	
Increase in net funded position		−502
Economic benefit expense		−$443

The economic benefit expense is –$443; this is essentially $443 of economic benefit income. This is a result of returns on plan assets that exceeded the increase in benefit obligations.

The reported net period benefit cost is $186. There is a difference between the reported and economic benefit expense of $629. The difference is largely due to actuarial gains on the benefit obligation and currency translation effect; these are not included in the reported periodic benefit expense.

Solution to 2: Adjusting to economic benefit expense decreases benefit expense from the reported amount of $186 to −$443 (credit); this is a $629 before-tax reduction in expenses. The after-tax reduction in expenses is [$629 × (1 − 0.126)] = $550.

Net income from continuing operations for Novartis would increase from $6,540 to $7,090, or by 8.41 percent, if adjusted for economic benefit expense. In companies where the benefit expense is a greater percentage of income, the effects are expected to be greater.

Reported net income from continuing operations	$6,540
Adjusted for after-tax decrease in pension expense	550
Adjusted net income from operations	$7,090

Another issue with the reported periodic pension or benefit expense is that conceptually the components of pension expense could be classified as operating, investing, or financing costs. However, the expense is generally treated as a single item and deducted as an operating expense. It can be argued that only the current service cost component of the pension expense is an operating expense, whereas the interest component and asset returns are both non-operating. The interest cost component of pension expense is conceptually similar to the interest cost on any of the company's other liabilities. The pension liability is essentially equivalent to a borrowing from employees, and the interest costs of that borrowing can be considered financing costs. Similarly, the return on pension plan assets is conceptually similar to returns on any of the company's other financial assets.

To better reflect a company's operating performance, an adjustment can be made to operating income by adding back the full pension expense and then subtracting the service costs or the total of service costs and settlements and curtailments. Note that this approach excludes from operating income the amortization of past service costs and the amortization of net actuarial gains and losses. This adjustment also eliminates the interest cost component and the return on plan assets component from the company's operating income. The interest cost component would be added to the company's interest expense, and the return on plan assets would be treated as non-operating income. Recall that the *expected* return on plan assets is included as a component of pension expense. The difference between the actual and expected return is shown as a component of other comprehensive income. This difference can be taken to the current year so that current year earnings reflect the *actual return* on plan assets. This adjustment changes net income, and potentially introduces earnings volatility. The reclassification of interest expense would not change net income. Example 8 illustrates adjustments to operating and non-operating incomes.

EXAMPLE 8

Adjusting Pension and Other Post-Employment Benefits Expense to Underlying Economic Expense and Reclassifying Components between Operating and Non-operating Incomes

SABMiller plc is a U.K.-based company that brews and distributes beer and other beverages. The following information was taken from the 2008 Annual Report. All amounts are in millions of U.S. dollars.

Excerpt from Consolidated Income Statement for the year ended 31 March 2008

SABMiller plc

Revenue	$21,410
Net operating expenses	−17,962
Operating income	3,448
Interest payable and similar charges	−721
Interest receivable and similar income	265
Share of post-tax results of associates	272
Profit before taxation	$ 3,264

Excerpt from Note 30: Pensions and post-retirement benefits

(Components of the amount recognised in net operating expenses for pension and other post-retirement benefits.)

Current service costs	$44
Interest costs	121
Expected return on plan assets	(81)
Settlements and curtailments	(11)
Total	$73
Actual return (loss) on plan assets	$(9)

Use the fiscal 2008 pension-related information below to estimate operating income and income before taxes for the period adjusted to include the economic pension and other post-retirement benefits expense.

Solution: The total reported expense for pension and post-retirement benefits is $73. If the actual return (loss) on plan assets is used instead of expected return on plan assets, the total expense is $163 [(44 + 121 + 9 − 11) or (73 + 81 + 9)]; $163 is an estimate of the economic expense for pension and other post-retirement benefits. The profit before taxation adjusted for the economic expense is $3,174.

However, in addition to the adjustment for economic expense, there is concern about the classification of all components of benefits expense as operating expense. Operating income adjusted to include only the current service costs and settlements and curtailments of the economic pension expense is $3,488; the $73 total pension and other post-employment benefits expense is excluded from operating income, and then the $44 current service costs component and the −$11 of settlements and curtailments are included as operating expenses. The $121 of interest costs are reclassified as interest payable and similar charges. The *actual* return on plan assets is added as investment income (loss). All adjustments are summarized below:

	Reported	Adjustments	Adjusted
Revenue	$21,410		$21,410
Net operating expenses	−17,962	(73 − 33)	−17,922
Operating income	3,448		3,488
Interest charges	−721	−121	−842
Interest income	265		265
Share of post-tax results of associates	272		272
Investment income (loss)		− 9	−9
Profit before taxation	$ 3,264		$ 3,174

The adjustments result in a higher operating income but a lower profit before taxation. Net finance costs have increased from $456 to $577.

2.5.4 Cash Flow Information

For a sponsoring company, the cash flow impact of pension and other post-employment benefits is the amount of contributions that the company makes to fund the plan; or for unfunded plans, the amount of benefits paid. The amount of contributions a company makes to fund a pension or other post-employment benefit plan is partially determined by regulations of the countries in which the company operates. Companies may choose to make contributions in excess of those required by regulation. In the United States, for example, the amount of contributions to DB pension plans is governed by ERISA (the Employee Retirement and Income Security Act) and depends on the funded status of the plan.

The previous section described the economic pension expense of a period. If a sponsoring company's periodic contributions to a plan exceed the economic pension expense of the period, the excess can be viewed from an economic perspective as a reduction of the pension obligation. The contribution covers not only the pension obligation arising in the current period, but also the pension obligations of another period. Such a contribution would be similar in concept to making a principal payment on a loan in excess of the scheduled principal payment. Conversely, a periodic contribution that is less than the economic pension expense of the period can be viewed as a source of financing.

In Example 7, Novartis had a negative economic benefit expense of $443 million and company contributions to the plan of $59 million for the year ended 31 March 2008. The excess of $502 million can be viewed as a reduction of the benefit obligation. The company covered not only the benefit obligation arising in the year ended 31 March 2008, but also part of the benefit obligation from other period(s). Similarly, in Example 6, Coach had an economic pension expense of $484 and contributions of $931. The excess of $447 can be viewed as a reduction of the pension obligation. Where the amounts of benefit obligations are material, an analyst may choose to adjust the cash flows that a company presents in its statement of cash flows. In this instance, the adjustment would reclassify the excess as an outflow related to financing activities rather than to operating activities. Example 9 describes such an adjustment.

EXAMPLE 9

Adjusting Cash Flow

Vassilika Doukas is analyzing the statement of cash flows of a hypothetical company, GeoRace plc, as part of a valuation. Doukas suggests to her colleague, Dimitri Krontiras, that the difference between the company's contributions to the pension plan and the economic pension costs incurred during a period is similar to a form of borrowing or a repayment of borrowing depending on the direction of the difference; this affects the company's reported cash from operating activities and cash from financing activities. Based on information from the company's annual report (currency in £ millions), she estimates that the company's economic pension expense was £437; however, the company disclosed a contribution of £504. GeoRace reported cash inflow from operating activities of £6,161 and cash outflow from financing activities of £1,741. The company's effective tax rate was 28.7 percent.

Use the information provided to answer the following questions:

1. How did the company's 2007 contribution to the pension plan compare to the economic expense for the year?
2. How would cash from operating activities and financing activities be adjusted to illustrate Doukas's interpretation of the difference between the company's contribution and the economic pension cost?

Solution to 1: The company's contribution to the pension plan in 2007 was £504. The contribution was £67 more than the economic pension expense of £437. The £67 difference equals £47.8 on an after-tax basis, using the effective tax rate of 28.7 percent.

Economic pension expense	£437	
Company's contribution	504	
Amount by which the sponsoring company's contribution exceeds economic pension expense (pre-tax)	£67	
Tax rate	28.7%	
After-tax amount by which the sponsoring company's contribution exceeds economic pension expense	£48	£67 × (1−0.2870)

Solution to 2: The company's contribution to the pension plan in 2007 was £67 (£48 after tax) greater than the 2007 economic pension expense. Interpreting the excess contribution as similar to a repayment of borrowing (financing use of funds) rather than as an operating cash flow increases the company's cash outflow from financing activities from £1,741 to £1,789 and increases the cash inflow from operations by £48.

SHARE-BASED COMPENSATION 3

In this section, we provide an overview of executive compensation focusing on share-based compensation. We first briefly discuss common components of executive compensation packages, their objectives, and advantages and disadvantages of share-based compensation. The discussion of share-based compensation then moves to accounting and reporting of stock grants before concentrating on stock options. The explanation of accounting and reporting stock options includes discussion of fair value accounting, the choice of valuation models, assumptions used, common disclosures, and important dates in measuring and reporting compensation expense.

Employee compensation packages are structured to fulfill varied objectives including satisfying employees' needs for liquidity, retaining employees, and motivating employees. Common components of employee compensation packages are salary, bonuses, and share-based compensation.[17] The salary component

[17] An extensive overview of different employee compensation mechanisms can be found in Lynch and Perry (2003).

provides for the liquidity needs of an employee. Bonuses, generally in the form of cash, motivate and reward employees for short- or long-term performance or goal achievement linking pay to performance. Share-based compensation is intended to align employees' interests with those of the shareholders. Both IFRS (IFRS 2) and U.S. GAAP (SFAS 123R)[18] require a company to disclose in their annual report (or proxy statement) key elements of management compensation. This enables analysts to understand the nature and extent of the share-based payment arrangements that existed during the reporting period. Below are examples of the description of the component and objectives of executive compensation programs for companies that report under IFRS and under U.S. GAAP. Exhibit 12 shows the disclosure for the executive compensation program of SABMiller plc (London Stock Exchange: SAB); SABMiller plc reports under IFRS.

In the United States, similar disclosures are required in a company's proxy statement that is filed with the SEC. Exhibit 13 shows the disclosure of American Eagle Outfitters, Inc.'s (NYSE: AEO) executive compensation program including a description of the key elements and objectives.

Share-based compensation, in addition to theoretically aligning the interests of employees (management), has the advantage of requiring no cash outlays.[19] However, a compensation expense is recorded and it reduces earnings as further discussed below. Although share-based compensation is generally viewed as motivating employees and aligning managers' interests with those of the share-

EXHIBIT 12 Excerpts from Remuneration Report of SABMiller plc

The committee's policy is to ensure that executive directors and members of the executive committee are rewarded for their contribution to the group's operating and financial performance at levels which take account of industry, market and country benchmarks, and that their remuneration is appropriate to their scale of responsibility and performance, and will attract, motivate and retain individuals of the necessary calibre. The committee takes account of the need to be competitive in the different parts of the world in which the company operates. The committee has implemented its policy of agreeing a remuneration package for each executive director comprising an annual base salary, an annual cash bonus, long-term incentives through participation in share option and share award plans, pension contributions, other security and health benefits, and benefits in kind. The base salaries, pensions and other benefits provided are intended to establish a level of fixed pay which is competitive with appropriate comparators. The variable pay elements provided by short-term and long-term incentives form a significant proportion of executive directors' pay and are intended to provide the opportunity for executives to earn superior total pay for superior company and individual performance. The table and charts below show the ratios of performance-related compensation to base salary and benefits of the executive directors, and the relative value of the different elements, including the target bonus and fair value of the long-term share-based compensation awarded in the year under review.

Source: SABMiller plc, Annual Report 2008.

[18] FASB ASC Topic 718 [Compensation–Stock Compensation].

[19] While issuing employee stock options requires no initial cash outlay, the company implicitly foregoes issuing new shares of stock (and receiving cash) when the options are exercised.

EXHIBIT 13 Excerpts from Executive Compensation Disclosures of American Eagle Outfitters, Inc.

Compensation Program Elements
Our executive compensation program is designed to place a large amount of pay at risk based on company performance for all executives. Our philosophy serves to cultivate a pay-for-performance environment. Our executive compensation plan design has five key elements:

- Base Salary
- Annual Incentive Bonus
- Long-term Incentive Cash Plan ("LTICP")
- Restricted Stock ("RS")
- Non-Qualified Stock Options ("NSO")

Three of the elements (Annual Incentive Bonus, Long-term Incentive Cash Plan, and Restricted Stock) are entirely "at risk" based on company performance and are subject to forfeiture if the Company does not achieve threshold performance goals. Company performance below threshold levels results in forfeiture of all elements of direct compensation other than base salary and Non-Qualified Stock Options. At threshold performance, the CEO's total annual compensation declines by an average 45% relative to target performance.

We strategically allocate compensation between short-term and long-term components and between cash and equity in order to maximize executive performance and retention. While we endeavor to design compensation packages consistently for our executives, long-term compensation and equity awards comprise an increasingly larger proportion of total compensation as position level increases. The portion of total pay attributable to long-term incentive cash/equity compensation increases at successively higher levels of management, which ensures that executive compensation closely aligns with changes in shareholder value and achievement of performance objectives and that executives are held accountable for results relative to position level.

Source: American Eagle Outfitters, Inc. Proxy Statement (Form Def 14A) filed 9 May 2008.

holders, there are several disadvantages of share-based compensation. One disadvantage is that the recipient of the share-based compensation may have limited influence over the company's market value (consider the scenario of overall market decline), so share-based compensation does not necessarily provide the desired incentives. Another disadvantage is that the increased ownership may lead managers to be risk averse. That is, fearing a large market value decline (and loss in individual wealth), managers may seek less risky (and less profitable) projects. An opposite effect, excessive risk-taking, can also occur with the awarding of options. Because options have skewed pay-out that rewards excessive risk-taking, managers may seek more risky projects. Finally, when share-based compensation is granted to employees, existing shareholders' ownership is diluted.

For financial reporting, a company reports compensation expense during the period in which employees earn their salary. Accounting for cash payments and cash bonuses is relatively straightforward. When the employee has earned the salary or bonus, an expense is recorded. Typically, compensation expense for managers is reported in sales, general, and administrative expenses on the income statement.

Share-based compensation is more varied and can include stock, stock options, or stock appreciation rights and phantom shares. By granting shares or share options in addition to other compensation, companies are paying additional compensation for services rendered by employees. Companies use the fair value of the shares granted to measure the value of these services, because of the difficulty of measuring directly the fair value of the employees' services received.

This results in the reporting of compensation expense for share-based compensation at fair value under IFRS (IFRS 2) and U.S. GAAP (SFAS 123R). However, the specifics of the accounting depend on the type of share-based compensation given to the employee. Under both IFRS and U.S. GAAP, the usual disclosures required for share-based compensation include: 1) the nature and extent of share-based compensation arrangements during the period, 2) how the fair value of a share-based grant was determined, and 3) the effect of share-based compensation on the company's income for the period and on its financial position.

Two common forms of share-based compensation are discussed below: stock grants and stock options.

3.1 Stock Grants

A company can grant stock to employees outright, with restrictions, or contingent upon performance. For an outright stock grant, compensation expense is reported based on the fair value of the stock on the grant date—generally the market value at grant date. Compensation expense is allocated over the period benefited by the employee's service, referred to as the service period.

Another type of stock award is a restricted stock grant that is given subject to the shares being returned to the company if certain conditions are not met. Common restrictions include the requirement that employees remain with the company for a specified period or that certain performance goals are met. Compensation expense for restricted stock grants is equal to the fair value (usually market value) of the shares issued at the grant date. This compensation expense is allocated over the employee service period.

Shares granted contingent on meeting performance goals are called performance shares. The amount of the grant is usually determined by performance measures other than the change in stock price, such as accounting earnings or return on assets. Basing the grant on accounting performance addresses employees' concerns that stock price is beyond their control. However, it can provide incentives to manipulate accounting numbers. Compensation expense is equal to the fair value (usually market value) of the shares issued at the grant date. This compensation expense is allocated over the employee service period.

3.2 Stock Options

Like stock grants, compensation expense related to option grants is reported at fair value under IFRS 2 and SFAS 123(R).[20] Both accounting standards require

[20] Prior to the adoption of SFAS 123(R) in January 2006, U.S. companies were allowed to use the intrinsic value of the stock options granted to measure compensation expense. The intrinsic value is the difference between the market price on the day the options are granted and the exercise price of the option. In most cases, the exercise price of the stock options granted was equal to the market value of the stock on the grant date, so the intrinsic value of the options was zero and so was the compensation expense.

fair value to be estimated using an appropriate valuation model. Using the fair value of stock options granted rather than the intrinsic value generally results in increased compensation expense.

Whereas the fair value of stock grants is usually based on the market value at the date of the grant, the fair value of option grants must be estimated. Because features of employee stock options generally differ from traded options, companies must choose a valuation model rather than rely on a market value. One critical element in estimating fair value is the choice of valuation or option pricing model. Several models are commonly used, such as the Black–Scholes option pricing model or a binomial model. Accounting standards do not prescribe a certain model. Generally, though, the valuation method should be 1) consistent with the fair value measurement, 2) based on established principles of financial economic theory, and 3) reflect all substantive characteristics of the award.

Once a valuation model is selected, a company must determine the inputs to the option pricing model, often including such items as exercise price, stock price volatility, estimated life of each award, estimated number of options that will be forfeited, and the risk-free rate of interest.[21] Some inputs are known at the time of the grant, such as the exercise price. Other critical inputs are highly subjective—such as stock price volatility or the estimated life of stock options—and can greatly change the estimated fair value and thus compensation expense. Higher volatility, longer estimated life, and higher risk-free interest rate increase the estimated fair value, while a higher assumed dividend yield decreases the estimated fair value.

Using different assumptions coupled with different valuation models can significantly impact the fair value of employee stock options. Exhibit 14 shows an excerpt from GlaxoSmithKline, plc explaining the assumptions used in valuing its granted stock options; the company also discloses the model used.

In accounting for stock options, there are several important dates including the grant date, vesting date, exercise date, and expiration date. The **grant date** is the day that options are granted to employees. The **service period** is usually the period between the grant date and the vesting date.

The **vesting date** is the date that employees can first exercise stock options. The vesting can be immediate or over a future period. If the share-based payments vest immediately (i.e., no further period of service is required), then expense is recognised on the grant date. If the share-based awards do not vest until a specified service period is completed, compensation expense is recognised and allocated over the service period. If the share-based awards are conditional upon the achievement of a performance condition or a market condition (i.e., a target share price), then compensation expense is recognised over the estimated service period. The **exercise date** is the date when employees actually exercise the options and convert them to stock. If the options go unexercised, they may expire at some predetermined future date, commonly 5 or 10 years from the grant date.

The grant date is also usually the date that compensation expense is measured if both the number of shares and option price are known. If facts affecting the value of options granted depend on events after the grant date, then compensation expense is measured at the exercise date. In Example 10, Coca-Cola, Inc. (NYSE: KO) reported, in the 2007 Form 10-K, $313 million of compensation expense from option grants. It also disclosed that $441 million, related to stock options already granted, would be recognised as compensation expense over the next 1.8 years.

---

[21] The estimated life of an option award incorporates such assumptions as employee turnover, and is usually shorter than the expiration period.

EXHIBIT 14 Assumptions Used in Stock Options Pricing Models: Excerpts from Financial Statements of GlaxoSmithKline, plc

Note 42—Employee share schemes

Option pricing

For the purposes of valuing options to arrive at the stock-based compensation charge, the Black–Scholes option pricing model has been used. The assumptions used in the model for 2005, 2006 and 2007 are as follows:

	2007	2006	2005
Risk-free interest rate	4.7%–5.3%	4.2%–5.0%	4.0%–4.8%
Dividend yield	4.0%	3.3%	3.0%
Volatility	17%–25%	18%–29%	21%–28%
Expected lives of options granted under:			
Share option schemes	5 years	5 years	5 years
Savings-related share option schemes	3 years	3 years	3 years
Weighted average share price for grants in the year:			
Ordinary shares	£14.41	£14.64	£13.15
ADSs	$57.59	$51.40	$47.42

Volatility was determined based on the three year share price history. The fair value of performance share plan grants take into account market conditions. Expected lives of options were determined based on weighted average historic exercises of options.

Source: GlaxoSmithKline Form 10-K filed 27 February 2008.

EXAMPLE 10

Disclosure of Stock Options Current Compensation Expense, Vesting, and Future Compensation Expense

Using information from Coca-Cola, Inc.'s Note 15 to financial statements, given below, determine the following:

1. Total compensation expense in future years as options vest.
2. Compensation expense in 2008 and 2009 for options already granted.

Excerpts from Note 15: Stock Compensation Plans in the Notes to Financial Statements of Coca-Cola, Inc.

Our total stock-based compensation expense was approximately $313 million, $324 million and $324 million in 2007, 2006 and 2005, respectively. These amounts were recorded in selling, general and administrative expenses in our consolidated statements of income. The total income tax benefit recognised in the income statement for share-based compensation arrangements was approximately $91 million, $93 million and $90 million in 2007, 2006 and 2005, respectively. As of December 31, 2007, we had approximately $441 million of total unrecognised compensation cost related to non-vested share-based compensation arrangements granted under our plans. This cost is expected to be recognised as stock-based compensation expense over a weighted-average period of 1.8 years as stock based compensation expense.

. . .

Stock options granted in December 2003 and thereafter generally become exercisable over a four-year annual vesting period and expire 10 years from the date of grant. Stock options granted from 1999 through July 2003 generally become exercisable over a four-year annual vesting period and expire 15 years from the date of grant. Prior to 1999, stock options generally became exercisable over a three-year vesting period and expired 10 years from the date of grant.

Source: Coca-Cola, Inc. Form 10-K filed 28 February 2008.

Solution to 1: Coca-Cola, Inc. discloses that unrecognised compensation expense relating to stock options already granted totals $441 million.

Solution to 2: The options already granted will vest over the next 1.8 years. Compensation expense related to stock options already granted will be $245 million ($441/1.8 years) in 2008 and $196 in 2009 ($441 total less $245 expensed in 2008). New options may also be granted in the future, raising the reported compensation expense.

3.3 Other Issues Related to Share-Based Compensation

In addition to decreasing income through compensation expense, stock options have the potential to dilute earnings per share. Both stock grants and stock options allow the employee to obtain direct ownership in the company. Other types of share-based compensation, such as stock appreciation rights (SARs) or phantom stock, compensate an employee based on changes in the value of shares without requiring the employee to hold the shares. With SARs, an employee's compensation is based on increases in a company's share price. Like other forms of share-based compensation, SARs serve to motivate employees and align their interest with shareholders. Two additional advantages of SARs are: 1) the potential for risk aversion is limited because employees have limited downside risk and unlimited upside potential similar to employee stock options, and 2) shareholder ownership is not diluted. A disadvantage is that SARs require a current-period cash outflow. Similar to other share-based compensation, SARs are valued at fair value, and compensation expense is allocated over the service period of the employee. While phantom share plans are similar to other types of share-based compensation, they differ somewhat because compensation is based on the performance of hypothetical stock rather than the company's actual stock. Unlike SARs, phantom shares can be used by private companies or business units within a company that are not publicly traded, or by highly illiquid companies.

SUMMARY

This reading discussed two different forms of employee compensation: post-employment benefits and share-based compensation. While different, the two share similarities in that they are forms of compensation outside of the standard salary arrangements. They also involve complex valuation, accounting, and reporting issues. While IFRS and U.S. GAAP are converging on accounting and reporting, it is important to note that differences in a country's social system, laws, and regulations can result in differences in a company's pension and share-based compensation plans that may be reflected in the company's earnings and financial reports.

Key points include the following:

- Defined contribution pension plans specify (define) only the amount of contribution to the plan; the eventual amount of the pension benefit to the employee will depend on the value of an employee's plan assets at the time of retirement.
- Defined benefit pension plans specify (define) the amount of the pension benefit, often determined by a plan formula, under which the eventual amount of the benefit to the employee is a function of length of service and final salary.
- Accounting for a defined benefit plan entails:
  1. Estimating the defined benefit obligation (the amount of future benefits) using actuarial assumptions and demographic variables;
  2. Estimating the present value of the defined benefit obligation and the related current service costs using the project unit credit method;
  3. Determining the actuarial gains and losses and the amount of these actuarial gains and losses to be recognised;
  4. Estimating any past service costs; and
  5. Determining the fair value of plan assets.
- Differences exist in countries' regulatory requirements for companies to fund defined benefit pension plan obligations.
- Defined benefit pension plan obligations are funded by the sponsoring company contributing assets to a pension trust, a separate legal entity.
- IFRS use one method to estimate a defined benefit plan's liabilities: the defined benefit obligation. U.S. GAAP, however, use three measures, with each increasingly more inclusive: the vested benefit obligation, the accumulated benefit obligation, and the projected benefit obligation.
- For analysis, the defined (projected) benefit obligation is typically the most appropriate measure because it recognises future salary increases.
- Balance sheet reporting is less analytically relevant for defined contribution plans because companies make contributions to defined contribution plans as the expense arises and thus no liabilities accrue for that type of plan.
- IFRS require companies to report on their balance sheet a pension liability or asset equal to the defined benefit obligation minus the fair value of plan assets, with certain adjustments for unrecognised actuarial gains or losses and any past service costs. However, IFRS restrict the amount of a pension asset that can be reported.

- U.S. GAAP require companies to report on their balance sheet a pension liability or asset equal to the projected benefit obligation minus the fair value of plan assets, with no additional adjustments. There is no limit on the amount of a pension asset that can be reported.
- Because the IASB and the FASB have identified pensions and other post-employment benefit accounting as a major area for collaborative efforts, SFAS 158 (adopted in 2006) is relevant for anticipating future changes for companies using IFRS.
- Pension expense includes the following components: current service costs, interest expense, past service costs, actuarial gains and losses, and expected return on plan assets (which reduces pension expense). IFRS do not require companies to present the various components of pension expense as a net amount (i.e., one line item) on the income statement. Instead, companies may disclose portions of net pension expense within different line items on the income statement. U.S. GAAP, however, require all components of net periodic pension expense to be aggregated and presented as a net amount (a single line item) on the income statement.
- Estimates of the future obligation under defined benefit pension plans and other post-employment benefits are sensitive to numerous assumptions, including discount rates, assumed annual compensation increases, expected return on plan assets, and assumed health care cost inflation.
- Employee compensation packages are structured to fulfill varied objectives including satisfying employees' needs for liquidity, retaining employees, and providing incentives to employees.
- Common components of employee compensation packages are salary, bonuses, and share-based compensation.
- Share-based compensation serves to align employees' interests with those of the shareholders. It includes stocks and stock options.
- Share-based compensation has the advantage of requiring no current-period cash outlays.
- Share-based compensation is reported at fair value under IFRS and U.S. GAAP.
- The valuation technique, or option pricing model, that a company uses is an important choice in determining fair value and is disclosed.
- Key assumptions and input into option pricing models include items such as exercise price, stock price volatility, estimated life of each award, estimated number of options that will be forfeited, and the risk-free rate of interest. Certain assumptions are highly subjective, such as stock price volatility or the expected life of stock options, and can greatly change the estimated fair value and thus compensation expense.

PRACTICE PROBLEMS FOR READING 24

The following information relates to Questions 1–6

Kensington plc is based in the United Kingdom and offers its employees a defined benefit pension plan. Kensington complies with IFRS. The company's effective tax rate for 2009 is 28 percent. Excerpts from a financial statement footnote on Kensington's retirement plans are presented in Exhibit 1.

EXHIBIT 1 Kensington plc Defined Benefit Pension Plan

(in Millions)	2009
Components of net periodic benefit cost	
Service cost	£ 96
Interest cost	1,557
Expected return plan assets	−1,874
Recognised past service cost	169
Recognised net actuarial loss	95
Net periodic pension cost	£ 43
Change in benefit obligation	
Benefit obligations at beginning of year	£28,416
Service cost	96
Interest cost	1,557
Actuarial (gains) losses	–306
Past service costs	132
Foreign exchange impact	–42
Benefits paid	–1,322
Benefit obligations at end of year	£28,531
Change in plan assets	
Fair value of plan assets at beginning of year	£23,432
Expected return plan assets	1,874
Actuarial loss	−572
Employer contributions	693
Benefits paid	−1,322
Fair value of plan assets at end of year	£24,105
Funded Status	−£4,426
Unrecognised past service cost	185
Unrecognised actuarial gain	−318
Net asset/(liability) in the balance sheet	−£4,559

Practice Problems and Solutions: 1–24 taken from *International Financial Statement Analysis*, by Thomas R. Robinson, CFA, Jan Hendrik van Greuning, CFA, Elaine Henry, CFA, and Michael A. Broihahn, CFA.

1. At year-end 2009, £28,531 million represents:
   A. the funded status of the plan.
   B. the defined benefit obligation.
   C. the fair value of the plan's assets.
2. The economic pension expense for Kensington's defined benefit plan is *closest* to:
   A. £135 million.
   B. £1,251 million.
   C. £2,509 million.
3. The difference between Kensington's estimated economic pension expense for the period and its reported net periodic pension cost is *closest* to:
   A. £92 million.
   B. £1,208 million.
   C. £1,302 million.
4. To adjust Kensington's reported net income to reflect the company's underlying economic pension expense, an analyst would decrease net income by an amount *closest* to:
   A. £26 million.
   B. £66 million.
   C. £92 million.
5. To reflect the funded status of Kensington's defined benefit pension plan, an analyst would adjust Kensington's 2009 balance sheet by decreasing liabilities by an amount *closest* to:
   A. £104 million.
   B. £133 million.
   C. £639 million.
6. An adjustment to Kensington's statement of cash flows to reclassify the company's excess contribution for 2009 would *most likely* entail reclassifying £558 million (excluding income tax effects) as an outflow related to:
   A. investing activities rather than operating activities.
   B. financing activities rather than operating activities.
   C. operating activities rather than financing activities.

The following information relates to Questions 7–12

Passaic Industries is based in France and offers its employees both a defined benefit pension plan and stock options. Passaic prepares its financial statements in accordance with IFRS. Several of the disclosures related to these plans are presented in Exhibits 1, 2, and 3.

EXHIBIT 1 **Components of Pension Cost (Income)**

(in Millions)	Year ended 31 December 2009	2008	2007
Components of cost (income)			
Service cost	€ 908	€ 910	€ 831
Interest cost	2,497	2,457	2,378
Expected return on plan assets	(3,455)	(3,515)	(3,378)
Recognised past service costs	188	185	180
Recognised net actuarial loss (gain)	912	1,266	440
Net periodic benefit cost	€1,050	€1,303	€ 451

EXHIBIT 2 **Funded Status of Plan**

(in Millions)	At 31 December 2009	2008
Change in benefit obligation		
Beginning balance	€45,183	€42,781
Service cost	908	910
Interest cost	2,497	2,457
Plan participants' contributions	9	12
Amendments	156	270
Actuarial (gain) loss	(925)	2,778
Settlement/curtailment/acquisitions/dispositions, net	85	(1,774)
Benefits paid	(2,331)	(2,251)
Ending balance	€45,582	€45,183
Change in plan assets		
Beginning balance at fair value	€43,484	€38,977
Expected return on plan assets	3,455	3,515
Actuarial gain	784	1,945
Company contribution	526	2,604
Plan participants' contributions	9	12
Settlement/curtailment/acquisitions/dispositions, net	216	(1,393)
Benefits paid	(2,286)	(2,208)
Exchange rate adjustment	15	32
Ending balance at fair value	€46,203	€43,484
Funded Status	€ 621	(€ 1,699)
Unrecognised past service cost	104	218
Unrecognised actuarial loss (gain)	237	(115)
Net asset (liability) in the balance sheet	€ 962	(€ 1,596)

EXHIBIT 3 Volatility Assumptions Used to Value Stock Option Grants

Grant Year	Weighted Average Expected Volatility (%)
2009 valuation assumptions	
2005–2009	21.50
2008 valuation assumptions	
2004–2008	23.00

7. If Passaic had reported under U.S. GAAP, with regard to its defined benefit pension plan, Passaic's year-end 2009 balance sheet *most likely* would report a:

A. €621 million asset.

B. €962 million asset.

C. €621 million liability.

8. The net periodic pension cost reported on the Passaic Industries income statement for the year ending 31 December 2009 is *closest* to:

A. €908 million.

B. €1,050 million.

C. €2,331 million.

9. The Passaic Industries statement of cash flows for the year ended 31 December 2009 shows the reconciliation of net income to cash flows from operating activities for the period. The associated net adjustment to net income related to the defined benefit plan is *closest* to:

A. €524 million.

B. €526 million.

C. €1,050 million.

10. The estimated increase in the pension obligation due to benefits earned by current employees in 2009 is *closest* to:

A. €908 million.

B. €1,050 million.

C. €2,331 million.

11. In 2009, the actual return on Passaic's plan assets is *closest* to:

A. −€1,760 million.

B. €3,445 million.

C. €4,239 million.

12. Compared to 2009 net income as reported, if Passaic Industries had used the same expected volatility assumption for its 2009 option grants that it had used in 2008, its 2009 net income would have been:

A. lower.

B. higher.

C. the same.

The following information relates to Questions 13–18

Stereo Warehouse is an Australian retailer that offers employees a defined benefit pension plan and stock options as part of its compensation package. Stereo Warehouse prepares its financial statements in accordance with the requirements of Australian equivalents to International Financial Reporting Standards (AIFRS).

Peter Friedland, CFA, is an equity analyst concerned with earnings quality. He is particularly interested in whether the discretionary assumptions the company is making regarding compensation plans are contributing to the recent earnings growth at Stereo Warehouse. He gathers information from the company's regulatory filings regarding the pension plan assumptions in Exhibit 1, the actual asset allocation for the pension plan in Exhibit 2, and the assumptions related to option valuation in Exhibit 3.

EXHIBIT 1 Assumptions Used for Stereo Warehouse Defined Benefit Plan

	2009	2008	2007
Expected long-term rate of return on plan assets	6.06%	6.14%	6.79%
Discount rate	4.85	4.94	5.38
Estimated future salary increases	4.00	4.44	4.25
Inflation	3.00	2.72	2.45

EXHIBIT 2 Allocation of Stereo Warehouse Defined Benefit Plan Assets

	2009	2008
Equity securities	90%	80%
Debt securities	10	20

EXHIBIT 3 Option Valuation Assumptions

	2009	2008	2007
Risk-free rate	4.6%	3.8%	2.4%
Expected life	5.0 yrs	4.5 yrs	5.0 yrs
Dividend yield	1.0%	0.0%	0.0%
Expected volatility	29%	31%	35%

13. Compared to the 2009 reported financial statements, if Stereo Warehouse had used the same expected long-term rate of return on plan assets assumption in 2009 as it used in 2007, its year-end 2009 pension obligation would *most likely* have been:
    - **A.** lower.
    - **B.** higher.
    - **C.** the same.
14. Compared to the reported 2009 financial statements, if Stereo Warehouse had used the same discount rate as it used in 2007, it would have *most likely* reported lower:
    - **A.** net income.
    - **B.** total liabilities.
    - **C.** cash flow from operating activities.
15. Compared to the assumptions Stereo Warehouse used to compute its net periodic pension cost in 2008, earnings in 2009 were *most favorably* impacted by the change in the:
    - **A.** discount rate.
    - **B.** estimated future salary increases.
    - **C.** expected long-term rate of return on plan assets.
16. Compared to the pension assumptions Stereo Warehouse used in 2008, which of the following pair of assumptions used in 2009 are *most likely* internally inconsistent?
    - **A.** Estimated future salary increases, inflation.
    - **B.** Discount rate, estimated future salary increases.
    - **C.** Expected long-term rate of return on plan assets, discount rate.
17. Compared to the reported 2009 financial statements, if Stereo Warehouse had used the 2007 expected volatility assumption to value its employee stock options, it would have *most likely* reported higher:
    - **A.** net income.
    - **B.** compensation expense.
    - **C.** deferred compensation liability.
18. Compared to the assumptions Stereo Warehouse used to value stock options in 2008, earnings in 2009 were most favorably impacted by the change in the:
    - **A.** expected life.
    - **B.** risk free rate.
    - **C.** dividend yield.

The following information relates to Questions 19–24

Andreas Kordt is an equity analyst examining the financial statements of Aero Euro. Aero Euro is based in Belgium and complies with IFRS. Kordt believes that the accounting guidelines for defined benefit plans do not reflect the underlying economic financial conditions, and he intends to adjust Aero Euro's financial statements accordingly. He also wants to compare the reported financial statements to those of a company that follows U.S. GAAP. As an initial step, he collected certain information relating to the plans, which is presented in Exhibits 1 and 2.

EXHIBIT 1 Pension Plan Assumptions for Aero Euro

	2009	2008	2007
Discount rate	4.51%	4.49%	4.55%
Expected rate of salary increases	2.62	2.70	2.91
Expected long-term rate of return on plan assets	5.70	5.70	5.13

EXHIBIT 2 Information Related to Aero Euro's Defined Benefit Plans

	Pension benefits (in € Millions)		
	2009	2008	2007
Benefit obligation at beginning of year	10,921	10,313	9,208
Service cost	368	359	275
Interest cost	489	461	447
Employees' contribution	40	36	32
Plan amendments	150	49	16
Settlements/curtailments	(28)	(11)	(1)
Benefits paid	(423)	(398)	(352)
Actuarial loss/(gain)	68	106	707
Currency translation adjustment	(3)	6	(19)
Benefit obligation at end of year	11,582	10,921	10,313
Fair value of plan assets at beginning of year	12,538	10,782	9,936
Actual return on plan assets	936	1,763	920
Employers' contributions	323	358	261
Employees' contributions	40	36	32
Settlements/curtailments	(6)	(6)	—
Benefits paid	(423)	(398)	(352)
Currency translation adjustment	(4)	3	(15)
Fair value of plan assets at end of year	13,404	12,538	10,782
Funded status	1,822	1,617	469
Unrecognised prior service cost	190	59	25
Unrecognised actuarial (gains)/losses	(857)	(710)	322
Net asset (liability) in the balance sheet	1,155	966	816

(Exhibit continues on next page . . .)

EXHIBIT 2 (continued)

	Pension benefits (in € Millions)		
	2009	**2008**	**2007**
Amounts recorded in the balance sheet:			
Pension asset	2,097	1,903	1,767
Provision for retirement benefits	(942)	(937)	(951)
Net amount recognised	1,155	966	816
Net periodic cost:			
Service cost	368	359	275
Interest cost	489	461	447
Expected return on plan assets	(714)	(616)	(532)
Settlement/curtailment	(18)	(8)	—
Recognised prior service cost	19	12	15
Recognised actuarial (gain) loss	(1)	16	(4)
Other	—	(1)	—
Net periodic cost	143	223	201

19. At year-end 2009, €11,582 million represents the total present value of benefits Aero Euro's employees:

A. would receive if they left the company.

B. are expected to earn during their career.

C. have earned in the current and prior periods.

20. Aero Euro's underlying economic pension expense for 2009 is *closest* to:

A. €118 million.

B. €143 million.

C. €323 million.

21. The 2009 net periodic pension cost recognised in Aero Euro's income statement is *closest* to:

A. €143 million.

B. €423 million.

C. €1,155 million.

22. Adjusting Aero Euro's 2009 balance sheet to reflect the underlying economic position of the company's defined benefit plan would result in a €667 increase in:

A. assets.

B. liabilities.

C. shareholders' equity.

23. Compared to the reported 2009 financial statements, if Aero Euro used the 2007 expected rate of salary increase assumption in 2009, it would have *most likely* reported higher:

A. net income.

B. benefit obligation.

C. recognised prior service costs.

24. Compared to the reported 2009 financial statements, if Aero Euro used the 2007 expected long-term rate of return on plan assets in 2009, it would have *most likely* reported higher:

A. net assets.

B. net income.

C. pension expense.

The following information relates to Questions 25–30

Dorothy Gale is a junior analyst with a large mutual fund. She is examining selected financial and footnote data for Eastern Distillers Corporation (EDC), which has a defined benefit pension plan and follows IFRS. Before comparing the company's ratios with industry statistics, Gale would like to examine the impact of the pension plan and related assumptions on EDC's financial statements and ratios. The defined benefit pension plan covers most full-time employees, whose average age is 35. Abbreviated financial information assembled from the financial statements and footnotes is presented below.

Eastern Distillers Corporation (EDC)
Selected Financial Information
(Expressed in Millions)

Year Ended 30 April	2008	2007	2006
Net sales	€2,134	€2,009	€1,906
Operating income	348	322	307
Income before income taxes	343	318	296
Taxes on income	125	116	111
Net income	218	202	185

30 April	2008	2007	2006
Total assets	€1,802	€1,735	€1,494
Total liabilities	754	818	677

Components of net periodic pension benefit (income) expense:

Year Ended 30 April	2008	2007	2006
Service cost	€12	€10	€ 9
Interest cost	21	19	18
Expected return on plan assets	(38)	(33)	(29)
Recognised prior service cost	1	1	1
Recognised net actuarial (gain) loss	(3)	(3)	(3)
Net periodic benefit (income) expense	€ (7)	€ (6)	€ (4)

Change in pension benefit obligation:

30 April	2008	2007
Obligation at beginning of year	€327	€284
Service cost	12	10
Interest cost	21	19
Plan amendments	1	5
Actuarial loss (gain)	(17)	23
Benefits paid	(15)	(14)
Obligation at end of year	€329	€327

Change in plan assets:

30 April	2008	2007
Fair value at beginning of year	€478	€407
Expected return on plan assets	38	33
Actuarial gains (losses)	14	51
Company contributions	1	1
Benefits paid	(15)	(14)
Fair value at end of year	€516	€478

Plan assets consist primarily of stocks and bonds.

Funded status:

30 April	2008	2007
Funded status	€187	€151
Unrecognised actuarial (gains) losses	(130)	(99)
Unrecognised prior service costs	10	11
Net asset (liability) in the balance sheet	€ 67	€ 63

Year Ended 30 April	2008	2007	2006
Discount rate	7.8%	6.5%	7.0%
Expected return on plan assets	10.0	10.0	10.0
Rate of compensation increase	4.5	4.0	4.0

25. All else equal, the change in the discount rate from 2007 to 2008 will cause:

A. increased future pension expense and a higher benefit obligation.

B. increased future pension expense and a lower benefit obligation.

C. decreased future pension expense and a lower benefit obligation.

26. All else equal, the change in the rate of compensation increase from 2007 to 2008 will cause:

A. increased future pension expense and a higher benefit obligation.

B. increased future pension expense and a lower benefit obligation.

C. decreased future pension expense and a lower benefit obligation.

27. Under IFRS, EDC's 2008 net pension asset (liability) is *closest* to:

A. €67 million asset.

B. €187 million asset.

C. €187 million liability.

28. Under U.S. GAAP, EDC's 2008 net pension asset (liability) is *closest* to:

A. €67 million asset.

B. €187 million asset.

C. €187 million liability.

29. Which most closely describes the reporting of pension expense (income) under U.S. GAAP compared to IFRS for EDC?

A. The net amount reported and the presentation may differ.

B. There is no difference in the net amount reported or in the presentation.

C. There would be no difference in the net amount reported, but would be a difference in the presentation.

30. If EDC's actual return on plan assets had been 15 percent for 2008, the impact on reported pension expense and plan assets for 2008 would be:

A. no change in pension expense, but an increase in plan assets.

B. a decrease in pension expense, but no change in plan assets.

C. a decrease in pension expense and an increase in plan assets.

The following information relates to Questions 31–36 and is based on "Intercorporate Investments" and this reading

Howard Burke, CFA, is an equity analyst with Southern Oak Securities. Burke is preparing a research report on SeaBriar Corporation, a U.S.-based, publicly traded company that complies with U.S. GAAP. As part of his analysis, Burke gathers information from the financial statement footnotes of SeaBriar's 2008 annual report, first quarter interim financial statements, and other public sources. Burke is concerned about the impact of this information on SeaBriar's future earnings.

Information about SeaBriar's fixed income investment portfolio for the year ended 31 December 2008, and for the quarter ended 31 March 2009, is presented in Exhibit 1. As part of his research, Burke is considering the possible effect on reported income if SeaBriar reclassifies its held-to-maturity securities to either held for trading or available-for-sale securities.

EXHIBIT 1 **SeaBriar's Investment Portfolio (US$ Millions)**

Characteristic	Alvin, Inc.	Baron, Inc.	Cora, Inc.	Dunbar, Inc.
Classification as of 31 December 2008 and 31 March 2009	Held for trading	Available-for-sale	Held-to-maturity	Held-to-maturity
Cost*	15	25	40	50
Market value, 31 December 2008	16	29	38	54
Market value, 31 March 2009	16	28	37	55

* All held-to-maturity securities were purchased at par value.

SeaBriar sponsors a defined benefit pension plan for its relatively young (average age of 37) employee workforce. Selected pension plan data from SeaBriar's 2008 annual report is shown in Exhibit 2.

EXHIBIT 2 **Selected Pension Plan Financial Data from SeaBriar's 2008 Annual Report (US$ Millions except Percentage Amounts)**

As of 31 December:	2008	2007
Fair value of plan assets	$888	$806
Actual return on plan assets	29	188
Employer contributions	158	172
Benefits paid	105	99
Projected benefit obligation	1,307	1,246
Pension expense:		
Service cost	$ 76	$ 72
Interest cost	90	88
Expected return on assets	(64)	(56)
Loss (gain) amortized	6	8
Pension expense	$108	$112
Pension assumptions:		
Expected return on plan assets	8.0%	8.0%
Rate of compensation growth	4.5	4.5
Discount rate	7.2	7.2

The industry average assumptions for 2008 were as follows:

► Expected return on plan assets	8.25%
► Rate of compensation growth	4.25
► Discount rate	7.50

31. The balance sheet value of SeaBriar's investment portfolio (in millions) at 31 March 2009 is *closest* to:

A. $127.

B. $130.

C. $134.

32. If SeaBriar had reclassified the held-to-maturity securities as of 1 January 2009, its reported income in the first quarter of 2009 would have been *highest* if it had classified:

A. both Cora and Dunbar as held for trading securities.

B. Cora as a held for trading security and Dunbar as an available-for-sale security.

C. Cora as an available-for-sale security and Dunbar as a held for trading security.

33. SeaBriar's 2008 underlying economic pension expense (in millions) is *closest* to:

A. $102.

B. $137.

C. $143.

34. If SeaBriar had used the industry average expected return on plan assets assumption in 2008 instead of its own, it would *most likely* result in:

A. a lower reported pension expense.

B. a higher reported pension expense.

C. a lower projected benefit obligation.

35. If SeaBriar had used the industry average rate of compensation growth assumption in 2008 instead of its own, it would *most likely* result in:

A. a lower net income.

B. a lower fair value of plan assets.

C. a lower projected benefit obligation.

36. If SeaBriar had used the industry average discount rate assumption in 2008 instead of its own, it would *most likely* result in:

A. a higher pension expense.

B. a higher fair value of plan assets.

C. a lower projected benefit obligation.

SOLUTIONS FOR READING 24

1. B is correct. The year-end benefit obligation represents the defined benefit obligation.
2. A is correct. The economic pension expense (in £ millions) is calculated as follows:

Change in benefit obligation	£ 115
Benefits paid	1,322
Adjusted change in liability	£1,437
Change in plan assets	£ 673
Employer contributions	−693
Benefits paid	1,322
Adjusted change in assets	£1,302
Economic pension expense	£135
Alternatively:	
Underfunding, beginning of 2009	−£4,984
Underfunding, end of 2009	−4,426
Reduction in underfunding	£ 558
Employer contribution	£693
Less: Reduction in underfunding	558
Economic pension expense	£135

3. A is correct. The economic pension expense is £135 million. Kensington's reported net periodic pension cost for the period is £43 million. The difference is £135 million − £43 million = £92 million.
4. B is correct. The company's economic pension expense is £135 million, but its reported net periodic pension cost is £43 million, a difference of £92 million. That amount must be adjusted for taxes: £92 million × (1 − 0.28) = £66.2 million. The economic pension expense is higher than the reported net periodic pension cost so net income would be adjusted down by about £66 million.
5. B is correct. The liability reported on Kensington's balance sheet is £4,559 million. However, the funded status of the plan is £4,426 million (underfunded), the difference between the defined benefit obligation and the fair value of plan assets (£28,531 million − £24,105 million). To adjust the balance sheet to reflect the funded status of the plan, the liability on the balance sheet would be decreased by £133 million, the difference between the reported liability and the funded status of the plan (£4,559 million − £4,426 million).
6. B is correct. Kensington's economic pension expense for the period was £135 million. The company's contributions to the plan for the year were £693 million. The £558 million difference between these numbers can be viewed as a reduction of the overall pension obligation. To adjust the statement of cash flows to reflect this view, an analyst would reclassify the £558 million (excluding income tax effects) as an outflow related to financing activities rather than operating activities.

7. A is correct. Under U.S. GAAP, the funded status of the DB plan is reported without adjustment. Passaic would report an asset of €621 million. Under IFRS, Passaic's balance sheet reflects the present value of the defined benefit obligation at the balance sheet date, plus any unrecognised actuarial gains (less any actuarial losses not recognised), minus any past service cost not yet recognised, minus the fair value at the balance sheet date of plan assets. The resulting amount is an asset of €962 million as shown at the bottom of Exhibit 2.
8. B is correct. The net periodic pension cost recorded in the income statement is €1,050 million, the net periodic benefit cost. Unlike U.S. GAAP, IFRS does not require the various components of pension cost to be reported as a net amount. As a result, companies are allowed to disclose the individual components within different line items on the income statement.
9. A is correct. The company's net periodic benefit cost (non-cash expense) of €1,050 million is added back, and the contributions (cash outflow) of €526 million are deducted from net income as part of the reconciliation between net income and cash flow from operating activities. The net effect is to add €524 million to the net income in the reconciliation to cash flow from operations.
10. A is correct. In 2009 the service cost was €908 million. Service costs represent the estimated increase in the pension obligation resulting from employees' service during the period.
11. C is correct. The actual return on plan assets is €4,239 million, which is the expected return on plan assets plus actuarial gains (€3,455 million + €784 million).
12. A is correct. In 2009 Passaic used a lower volatility assumption than it did in 2008. Lower expected volatility reduces the fair value of an option and thus the reported expense. Using the 2008 volatility estimate would have resulted in higher expense and thus lower net income.
13. C is correct. The assumed long-term rate of return on plan assets is not a component that is used in calculating the pension obligation, so there would be no change.
14. B is correct. A higher discount rate (5.38% instead of 4.85%) will reduce the present value of the pension obligation (liability). In most cases, a higher discount rate will decrease the interest cost component of the net periodic cost, because the decrease in the obligation will more than offset the increase in the discount rate (except if the pension obligation is of short duration). Therefore, net periodic pension cost would have been lower, and reported net income higher. Cash flow from operating activities should not be affected by the change.
15. B is correct. In 2009 the three relevant assumptions were lower than in 2008. Lower expected salary increases reduce the service cost component of the periodic pension cost. A lower discount rate will increase the defined benefit obligation and increase the interest cost component of the periodic pension cost (the increase in the obligation will, in most cases, more than offset the decrease in the discount rate). Reducing the expected return on plan assets typically increases the periodic pension cost.
16. A is correct. The company's inflation estimate rose from 2008 to 2009. However, it lowered its estimate of future salary increases. Normally, salary increases will be positively related to inflation.

17. B is correct. A higher volatility assumption increases the value of the stock option and thus the compensation expense, which in turn reduces net income. There is no associated liability for stock options.

18. C is correct. A higher dividend yield reduces the value of the call option and thus option expense. The lower expense results in higher earnings. Higher risk-free rates and expected lives result in higher call option values.

19. C is correct. The defined benefit obligation at year-end 2009 is €11,582 million and represents the actuarial present value of all benefits (future payments) that all employees have earned based on their service up until 31 December 2009, regardless of whether the benefits have vested.

20. A is correct. The economic pension expense (in € millions) is calculated as follows:

Change in benefit obligation	€ 661
Benefits paid	423
Adjusted change in liability	€1,084
Change in plan assets	€866
Employer contributions	−323
Benefits paid	423
Adjusted change in assets	€966
Economic pension expense	€118
Alternatively:	
Overfunding, beginning of 2009	€1,617
Overfunding, end of 2009	1,822
Increase in overfunding	€ 205
Employer contribution	€323
Less: increase in overfunding	205
Economic pension expense	€118

21. A is correct. The net periodic pension cost of €143 million is the amount recognised in the income statement. Unlike U.S. GAAP, IFRS does not require the various components of pension cost as a net amount. As a result, companies are allowed to disclose the individual components within different line items on the income statement.

22. C is correct. The net funded status of the plan is €1,822 million, but only €1,155 million is recognised on the balance sheet: an asset of €2,097 million, a liability of €942 million, and net assets (equity) of €1,155 million. The net result of balance sheet adjustments would be an increase (in € millions) of €1,822 − €1,155 = €667 to shareholders' equity. The actual funded status shows the underlying financial position, and that is a net asset (equity) of €1,822 million, or €667 million higher than is reported. The amounts reported in the balance sheet for pension asset and provision for retirement benefits would each change to reflect the net impact of €667 million.

23. B is correct. Using the higher 2007 expected rate of salary increases would have increased current service cost and the benefit obligation, reducing net income. It would not affect prior service costs and related recognition.

24. C is correct. Using the lower 2007 expected return on plan assets would increase pension expense, reduce net income, and have no effect on net assets.

25. C is correct. The discount rate assumption was increased from 6.5 percent to 7.8 percent. The increase in the discount rate will generally reduce both the pension expense and the projected benefit obligation.

26. A is correct. The rate of compensation increase was increased from 4.0 percent to 4.5 percent. This will increase the pension expense and the projected benefit obligation.

27. A is correct. After adjusting for unrecognised prior service costs and actuarial gains, the overfunded (by €187 million) pension plan has a reported net pension asset of €67 million under IFRS.

28. B is correct. Under U.S. GAAP, EDC has a funded status and reported net pension asset of €187 million.

29. A is correct. The net amount reported may vary depending on the treatment of prior service costs and actuarial gains and losses. Under GAAP, the net pension expense (income) is reported as a single amount, whereas under IFRS, the various components of net pension expense (income) do not have to be presented as a single net amount.

30. A is correct. EDC uses expected return on plan assets rather than actual return to arrive at current pension expense, so the actual return on plan assets does not affect reported pension expense. Plan assets, however, would increase if the actual return on plan assets had been 15 percent (in 2008, the actual return on plan assets was $(38 + 14)/478 = 10.9$ percent). Both U.S. GAAP and IFRS allow the use of expected return.

31. C is correct. The reported value at 31 March 2009 is $16 + 28 + 40 + 50 = $134 million. Held for trading and available-for-sale securities are reported at their market value and held-to-maturity securities are reported at their amortized cost. In this case the held for trading securities were purchased at par value, so amortized cost equals historical cost.

32. C is correct. Dunbar's unrecognised gain of $5 million ($55 million market value at 31 March 2009 − $50 million amortized cost) would be included in income, while Cora's unrecognised loss would be reported in other comprehensive income (equity). Income would be higher by $5 million.

33. B is correct. The underlying economic pension expense = \$137 million, calculated as the change in the pension obligation less the change in pension plan assets adjusted for cash contributions and benefit payments:

Change in benefit obligation	\$ 61
Benefits paid	105
Adjusted change in benefit obligation	\$166
Change in plan assets	\$82
Less employer contributions	−158
Benefits paid	105
Adjusted change in plan assets	\$29
Economic pension expense	\$137

34. A is correct. A higher expected return on assets would decrease SeaBriar's reported pension expense because the expected return on assets is subtracted when calculating the GAAP determined pension expense. The industry expected return of 8.25% is higher than SeaBriar's expected return on assets of 8.0%.

35. C is correct. A lower rate of compensation growth (4.25% industry vs. 4.5% SeaBriar for 2008) would decrease the projected benefit obligation and pension expense. As a result, net income would be higher. The rate of compensation growth has no impact on the plan assets.

36. C is correct. A higher discount rate (7.5% industry vs. 7.2% SeaBriar for 2006) would decrease the projected benefit obligation. In most cases, a higher discount rate will decrease the interest cost component of the net periodic cost, because the decrease in the obligation will more than offset the increase in the discount rate (except if the pension obligation is of short duration). Therefore, given the young work force, the pension expense would be lower. The discount rate has no impact on the plan assets.

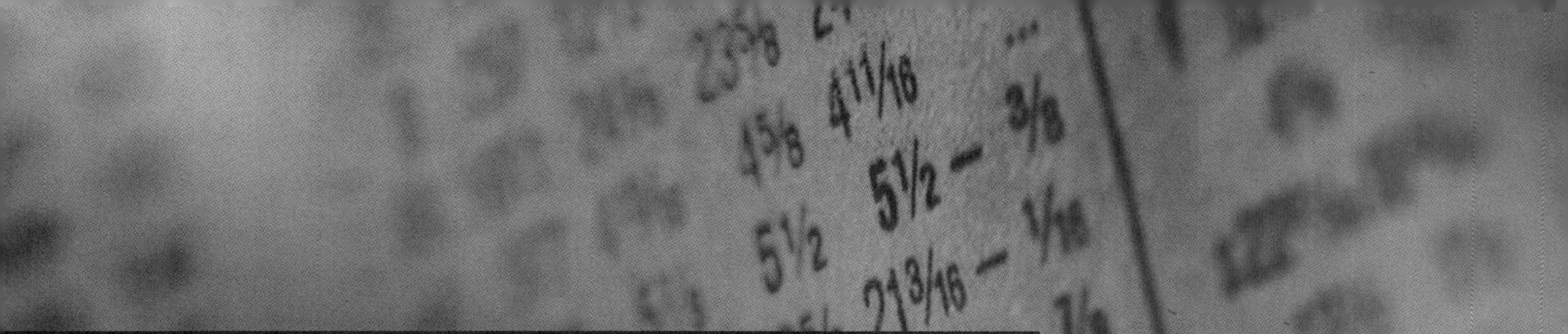

MULTINATIONAL OPERATIONS

by Timothy S. Doupnik

READING 25

LEARNING OUTCOMES

The candidate should be able to:	Mastery
a. distinguish among presentation currency, functional currency, and local currency;	☐
b. analyze the impact of changes in exchange rates on the translated sales of the subsidiary and parent company;	☐
c. compare and contrast the current rate method and the temporal method, analyze and evaluate the effects of each on the parent company's balance sheet and income statement, and determine which method is appropriate in various scenarios;	☐
d. calculate the translation effects, evaluate the translation of a subsidiary's balance sheet and income statement into the parent company's currency, and analyze the different effects of the current rate method and the temporal method on the subsidiary's financial ratios;	☐
e. analyze how using the temporal method versus the current rate method will affect the parent company's financial ratios;	☐
f. illustrate and analyze alternative accounting methods for subsidiaries operating in hyperinflationary economies.	☐

Note:
New rulings and/or pronouncements issued after the publication of the readings in financial reporting and analysis may cause some of the information in these readings to become dated. Candidates are expected to be familiar with the overall analytical framework contained in the study session readings, as well as the implications of alternative accounting methods for financial analysis and valuation, as provided in the assigned readings. Candidates are not responsible for changes that occur after the material was written.

INTRODUCTION 1

According to the World Trade Organization, merchandise exports worldwide exceeded US$10 trillion in 2005.[1] The top five exporting countries, in order, were Germany, the United States, China, Japan, and France. From 2000 to 2005, international trade grew by 62 percent.

[1] World Trade Organization, *International Trade Statistics 2006*, Table A6.

The U.S. Department of Commerce identified 239,100 U.S. companies as exporters in 2005. Only 3 percent of those companies were large (more than 500 employees). The vast majority of U.S. companies with export activity were small- or medium-sized entities.

The point made by these statistics is that many companies engage in transactions that cross national borders. The parties to these transactions must agree on the currency in which to settle the transaction. Generally this will be the currency of either the buyer or the seller. Exporters that receive payment in foreign currency and allow the purchaser time to pay must carry a foreign currency receivable on their books. Conversely, importers that agree to pay in foreign currency will have a foreign currency account payable. To be able to include them in the total amount of accounts receivable (payable) reported on the balance sheet, these foreign currency-denominated accounts receivable (payable) must be translated into the currency in which the exporter (importer) keeps its books and presents financial statements.

The prices at which foreign currencies can be purchased or sold are called foreign exchange rates. Because foreign exchange rates fluctuate over time, the value of foreign currency payables and receivables also fluctuates. The major accounting issue related to foreign currency transactions is how to reflect the changes in value for foreign currency payables and receivables in the financial statements.

Many companies have operations located in foreign countries. As examples, the Swiss food products company Nestlé SA reports that it has subsidiaries in more than 90 different countries, and U.S.-based Coca-Cola Company discloses that it has 144 foreign wholly owned subsidiaries located in 40 countries around the world. Foreign subsidiaries are generally required to keep accounting records in the currency of the country in which they are located. To prepare consolidated financial statements, the parent company must translate the foreign currency financial statements of its foreign subsidiaries into its own currency. Nestlé, for example, must translate the assets and liabilities its various foreign subsidiaries carry in foreign currency into Swiss francs to be able to consolidate those amounts with the Swiss franc assets and liabilities located in Switzerland.

A multinational company like Nestlé is likely to have two types of foreign currency activities that require special accounting treatment. Most multinationals 1) engage in transactions that are denominated in a foreign currency, and 2) invest in foreign subsidiaries that keep their books in a foreign currency. To prepare consolidated financial statements, a multinational company must translate the foreign currency amounts related to both types of international activities into the currency in which the company presents its financial statements.

This reading presents the accounting for foreign currency transactions and the translation of foreign currency financial statements. The conceptual issues related to these accounting topics are discussed and the specific rules embodied in International Financial Reporting Standards (IFRS) and U.S. GAAP are demonstrated through examples. Fortunately, differences between IFRS and U.S. GAAP with respect to foreign currency translation issues are minimal.

Analysts need to understand the impact that fluctuations in foreign exchange rates have on the financial statements of a multinational company and how foreign currency gains and losses, whether realized or not, are reflected in the company's financial statements.

FOREIGN CURRENCY TRANSACTIONS 2

When companies from different countries agree to conduct business with one another, they must decide which currency will be used. For example, if a Mexican electronic components manufacturer agrees to sell goods to a customer in Finland, the two parties must agree whether the Finnish company will pay for the goods in Mexican pesos, euros, or perhaps even a third currency such as the U.S. dollar. If the transaction is denominated in Mexican pesos, the Finnish company has a foreign currency transaction but the Mexican company does not. To account for the inventory being purchased and the account payable in Mexican pesos, the Finnish company must translate the Mexican peso amounts into euros using appropriate exchange rates. Although the Mexican company also has entered into an international transaction (an export sale), it does not have a foreign currency transaction and no translation is necessary. It simply records the sales revenue and account receivable in Mexican pesos, which is the currency in which it keeps its books and prepares financial statements.

The currency in which financial statement amounts are presented is known as the **presentation currency**. In most cases, the presentation currency of a company will be the currency of the country where the company is located. Finnish companies are required to keep accounting records and present financial results in euros, U.S. companies in U.S. dollars, Chinese companies in Chinese yuan, and so on.

Another important concept in accounting for foreign currency activities is the **functional currency**, which is the currency of the primary economic environment in which an entity operates. Normally, the functional currency is the currency in which an entity primarily generates and expends cash. In most cases, the functional currency of an entity will be the same as its presentation currency. And, because most companies primarily generate and expend cash in the currency of the country where they are located, the functional and presentation currencies are most often the same as the **local currency** where the company operates.

Because the local currency generally is an entity's functional currency, a multinational corporation with subsidiaries in a variety of different countries is likely to have a variety of different functional currencies. The Thai subsidiary of a Japanese parent company, for example, is likely to have the Thai baht as its functional currency whereas the Japanese parent's functional currency is the Japanese yen. But in some cases, the foreign subsidiary could have the parent's functional currency as its own. Intel Corporation, for example, has determined that all of its significant foreign subsidiaries have the U.S. dollar as their functional currency.

By definition, a foreign currency is any currency other than the functional currency of a company and **foreign currency transactions** are transactions that are denominated in a currency other than the company's functional currency. Foreign currency transactions occur when a company 1) makes an import purchase or an export sale that is denominated in a foreign currency, or 2) borrows or lends funds where the amount to be repaid or received is denominated in a foreign currency. In each of theses cases, the company has an asset or a liability that is denominated in a foreign currency.

2.1 Foreign Currency Transaction Exposure to Foreign Exchange Risk

Assume that FinnCo, a Finnish-based company, imports goods from Mexico in January under 90-day credit terms and the purchase is denominated in Mexican pesos. By deferring payment until April, FinnCo runs the risk that from the date the purchase is made until the date of payment, the value of the Mexican peso might increase relative to the euro. FinnCo would then need to spend more euros to settle its Mexican peso account payable. In this case, FinnCo is said to have an **exposure to foreign exchange risk**. Specifically, FinnCo has a foreign currency **transaction exposure**. Transaction exposure related to imports and exports can be summarized as follows:

> *Import purchase*. A transaction exposure arises when the importer is obligated to pay in foreign currency and is allowed to defer payment until sometime after the purchase date. The importer is exposed to the risk that from the purchase date until the payment date the foreign currency might increase in value, thereby increasing the amount of functional currency that must be spent to acquire enough foreign currency to settle the account payable.
>
> *Export sale*. A transaction exposure arises when the exporter agrees to be paid in foreign currency and allows payment to be made sometime after the purchase date. The exporter is exposed to the risk that from the purchase date until the payment date the foreign currency might decrease in value, thereby decreasing the amount of functional currency into which the foreign currency can be converted when it is received.

The major issue in accounting for foreign currency transactions is how to account for the foreign currency risk; that is, how to reflect in the financial statements the change in value of the foreign currency asset or liability. Both International Accounting Standard (IAS) 21, "The Effects of Changes in Foreign Exchange Rates," and FASB Statement (SFAS) 52, "Foreign Currency Translation," require the change in the value of the foreign currency asset or liability resulting from a foreign currency transaction to be treated as a gain or loss reported on the income statement.[2]

---

[2] The content of SFAS 52 is included in FASB ASC Topic 830 [Foreign Currency Matters].

2.1.1 Accounting for Foreign Currency Transactions with Settlement before Balance Sheet Date

Example 1 demonstrates the accounting that would be done by FinnCo assuming that it purchased goods on account from a Mexican supplier who required payment in Mexican pesos, and that it made payment before the balance sheet date. The basic principle is that all transactions are recorded at the spot rate on the date of the transaction. The foreign currency risk on *transactions*, therefore, only arises when the transaction date and the payment date are different.

EXAMPLE 1

Accounting for Foreign Currency Transactions with Settlement before the Balance Sheet Date

FinnCo purchases goods from its Mexican supplier on 1 November 2008; the purchase price is 100,000 Mexican pesos. Credit terms allow payment in 45 days, and FinnCo makes payment of 100,000 pesos on 15 December 2008. FinnCo's functional and presentation currency is the euro. Spot exchange rates between the euro (€) and Mexican peso (Ps.) are as follows:

1 November 2008	Ps. 1 = €0.0684
15 December 2008	Ps. 1 = €0.0703

FinnCo's fiscal year end is 31 December. How will FinnCo account for this foreign currency transaction and what effect will it have on the 2008 financial statements?

Solution: The euro value of the Mexican peso account payable on 1 November 2008 was €6,840 (Ps. 100,000 × €0.0684). FinnCo could have paid for its inventory on 1 November by converting 6,840 euros into 100,000 Mexican pesos. Instead, the company purchases 100,000 Mexican pesos on 15 December 2008, when the value of the peso has increased to €0.0703. Thus, FinnCo pays 7,030 euros to purchase 100,000 Mexican pesos. This results in a loss of 190 euros (€7,030 − €6,840).

Although the cash outflow to acquire the inventory is €7,030, the cost included in the inventory account is only €6,840. This represents the amount that FinnCo could have paid if it had not waited 45 days to settle its account. By deferring payment, and because the Mexican peso increased in value between the transaction date and settlement date, FinnCo has to pay an additional 190 euros. A foreign exchange loss of €190 will be reported in FinnCo's net income in 2008. This is a realized loss in that the company actually spent an additional 190 euros to purchase its inventory. The net effect on the financial statements can be seen as follows:

Balance Sheet						**Income Statement**		
Assets		**= Liabilities +**	**Stockholders' Equity**			**Revenues and Gains**	**Expenses and Losses**	
Cash	− 7,030		Retained earnings	−190	←		Foreign exchange loss	−190
Inventory	+ 6,840							
	−190							

2.1.2 Accounting for Foreign Currency Transactions with Intervening Balance Sheet Dates

Another important issue related to the accounting for foreign currency transactions is what should be done, if anything, if a balance sheet date falls between the initial transaction date and the settlement date. For foreign currency transactions that occur with settlement dates that fall in subsequent accounting periods, both IFRS and U.S. GAAP require adjustments to reflect intervening changes in currency exchange rates. Foreign currency transaction gains and losses are reported on the income statement, creating one of the very few situations in which accounting rules allow, indeed require, companies to include (recognize) an unrealized gain or loss in income before it has been realized.

Subsequent foreign currency transaction gains and losses are recognized from the balance sheet date through the date the transaction is settled. Adding together foreign currency transaction gains and losses for both accounting periods (transaction initiation to balance sheet date and balance sheet date to transaction settlement) produces an amount equal to the actual realized gain or loss on the foreign currency transaction.

EXAMPLE 2

Accounting for Foreign Currency Transaction with Intervening Balance Sheet Date

FinnCo sells goods to a customer in the United Kingdom for £10,000 on 15 November 2008, with payment to be received in British pounds on 15 January 2009. FinnCo's functional and presentation currency is the euro. Spot exchange rates between the euro (€) and British pound (£) are as follows:

15 November 2008	£1 = €1.460
31 December 2008	£1 = €1.480
15 January 2009	£1 = €1.475

FinnCo's fiscal year end is 31 December. How will FinnCo account for this foreign currency transaction and what effect will it have on the 2008 and 2009 financial statements?

Solution: The euro value of the British pound account receivable at each of the three relevant dates is determined as follows:

		Account Receivable (£10,000)	
Date	€ per £ Exchange Rate	Euro Value	Change in Euro Value
15 Nov 2008	€1.460	14,600	N/A
31 Dec 2008	€1.480	14,800	+ 200
15 Jan 2009	€1.475	14,750	− 50

A change in the euro value of the British pound receivable from 15 November to 31 December would be recognized as a foreign currency transaction gain or loss on FinnCo's 2008 income statement. In this case, the increase in the value of the British pound results in a transaction gain of €200 [£10,000 × (€1.48 − €1.46)]. Note that the gain recognized in 2008 income is unrealized and remember that this is one of few situations where companies include an unrealized gain in income.

Any change in the exchange rate between the euro and British pound that occurs from the balance sheet date (31 December 2008) to the transaction settlement date (15 January 2009) likewise will result in a foreign currency transaction gain or loss. In our example, the British pound weakened slightly against the euro during this period, resulting in an exchange rate of €1.475 per British pound on 15 January 2009. The £10,000 account receivable now has a value of €14,750, which is a decrease in value of €50 from 31 December 2008. FinnCo will recognize a foreign currency transaction loss on 15 January 2009 of €50 that will be included in the company's calculation of net income for the first quarter of 2009.

From the transaction date to the settlement date, the British pound has increased in value by €0.015 (€1.475 − €1.46), which generates a realized foreign currency transaction gain of €150. A gain of €200 was recognized in 2008 and a loss of €50 is recognized in 2009. Over the two month period, the net gain recognized in the financial statements is equal to the actual realized gain on the foreign currency transaction.

In Example 2, FinnCo's British pound account receivable resulted in a net foreign currency transaction gain because the British pound strengthened (increased) in value between the transaction date and the settlement date. In this case FinnCo has an asset exposure to foreign exchange risk. This asset exposure benefited the company because the foreign currency strengthened. If FinnCo instead had a British pound account payable, a liability exposure would have existed. The euro value of the British pound account payable would have increased as the British pound strengthened and FinnCo would have recognized a foreign currency transaction loss as a result.

Whether a change in exchange rate results in a foreign currency transaction gain or loss depends on 1) the nature of the exposure to foreign exchange risk (asset or liability) and 2) the direction of change in the value of the foreign currency (strengthens or weakens).

		Foreign Currency	
Transaction	**Type of Exposure**	**Strengthens**	**Weakens**
Export sale	Asset (account receivable)	Gain	Loss
Import purchase	Liability (account payable)	Loss	Gain

A foreign currency receivable arising from an export sale creates an asset exposure to foreign exchange risk. If the foreign currency strengthens, the receivable increases in value in terms of the company's functional currency and a foreign currency transaction gain arises. The company will be able to convert the foreign currency when received into more units of functional currency because the foreign currency has strengthened. Conversely, if the foreign currency weakens, the foreign currency receivable loses value in terms of the functional currency and a loss results.

A foreign currency payable resulting from an import purchase creates a liability exposure to foreign exchange risk. If the foreign currency strengthens, the payable increases in value in terms of the company's functional currency and a foreign currency transaction loss arises. The company will have to spend more units of functional currency to be able to settle the foreign currency liability because the foreign currency has strengthened. Conversely, if the foreign currency weakens, the foreign currency payable loses value in terms of the functional currency and a gain exists.

2.2 Analytical Issues

Both IFRS (IAS 21) and U.S. GAAP (FASB 52) require foreign currency transaction gains and losses to be reported in net income (even if they have not yet been realized), but neither standard indicates where on the income statement these gains and losses should be placed. The two most common treatments are 1) as a component of other operating income/expense or 2) as a component of nonoperating income/expense, in some cases as a part of net financing cost. The calculation of operating profit margin is affected by where foreign currency transaction gains or losses are placed on the income statement.

EXAMPLE 3

Placement of Foreign Currency Transaction Gains/Losses on the Income Statement—Effect on Operating Profit

Assume that FinnCo had the following income statement information in both 2008 and 2009, excluding a foreign currency transaction gain of €200 in 2008 and a transaction loss of €50 in 2009.

	2008	2009
Revenues	€20,000	€20,000
Cost of goods sold	12,000	12,000
Other operating expenses, net	5,000	5,000
Nonoperating expenses, net	1,200	1,200

FinnCo is deciding between two alternatives for the treatment of foreign currency transaction gains and losses. Alternative 1 calls for the reporting of foreign currency transaction gains/losses as part of "other operating expenses, net." Under Alternative 2, the company would report this information as part of "nonoperating expenses, net."

FinnCo's fiscal year end is 31 December. What impact will the decision of Alternatives 1 and 2 have on the company's gross profit margin, operating profit margin, and net profit margin for 2008? For 2009?

Solution: Remember that a gain would serve to reduce expenses whereas a loss would have the effect of increasing expenses.

2008—Transaction Gain of €200

	Alternative 1		Alternative 2	
Revenues	€20,000		€20,000	
Cost of goods sold	12,000		12,000	
Gross profit	8,000		8,000	
Other operating expenses, net	4,800	incl. gain	5,000	
Operating profit	3,200		3,000	
Nonoperating expenses, net	1,200		1,000	incl. gain
Net profit	€ 2,000		€ 2,000	

Profit margins in 2008 under the two alternatives would be calculated as follows:

	Alternative 1	Alternative 2
Gross profit margin	€8,000/€20,000 = 40.0%	€8,000/€20,000 = 40.0%
Operating profit margin	3,200/20,000 = 16.0%	3,000/20,000 = 15.0%
Net profit margin	2,000/20,000 = 10.0%	2,000/20,000 = 10.0%

2009—Transaction Loss of €50

	Alternative 1		Alternative 2	
Revenues	€20,000		€20,000	
Cost of goods sold	12,000		12,000	
Gross profit	8,000		8,000	
Other operating expenses, net	5,050	incl. loss	5,000	
Operating profit	2,950		3,000	
Nonoperating expenses, net	1,200		1,250	incl. loss
Net profit	€ 1,750		€ 1,750	

Profit margins in 2009 under the two alternatives would be calculated as follows:

	Alternative 1	Alternative 2
Gross profit margin	€8,000/€20,000 = 40.0%	€8,000/€20,000 = 40.0%
Operating profit margin	2,950/20,000 = 14.75%	3,000/20,000 = 15.0%
Net profit margin	1,750/20,000 = 8.75%	1,750/20,000 = 8.75%

Gross profit and net profit are unaffected, but operating profit differs under the two alternatives. In 2008, the operating profit margin is larger under Alternative 1, which includes the transaction gain as part of "other operating expenses, net." In 2009, Alternative 1 results in a smaller operating profit margin than Alternative 2. Alternative 2 has the same operating profit margin in both periods. Because exchange rates do not fluctuate by the same amount or in the same direction from one accounting period to the next, Alternative 1 will cause greater volatility in operating profit and operating profit margin over time.

Because accounting standards do not provide guidance on the placement of foreign currency transaction gains and losses on the income statement, companies are free to choose among the alternatives. Two companies in the same industry could choose different alternatives, which would distort the direct comparison of operating profit and operating profit margins between those companies.

A second issue that should be of interest to analysts relates to the fact that unrealized foreign currency transaction gains and losses are included in net income when the balance sheet date falls between the transaction and settlement dates. The implicit assumption underlying this accounting requirement is that the unrealized gain or loss as of the balance sheet date is reflective of the ultimate net gain or loss to the company. In reality, though, the ultimate net gain or loss may vary dramatically because of the possibility for changes in trend and volatility of currency prices.

This effect was seen in the previous hypothetical Example 2 with FinnCo. Using actual currency exchange rate data shows that the real-world effect can also be quite dramatic. Assume that a French company purchased goods from a Canadian supplier on 1 December 2006, with payment of 100,000 Canadian dollars (C$) to be made on 15 May 2007. Actual exchange rates between the Canadian dollar and euro during the period 1 December 2006 and 15 May 2007, the euro value of the Canadian dollar account payable, and foreign currency transaction gain or loss are shown below:

		Account Payable (C$100,000)	
	€ per C$	**€ Value**	**Change in € Value (Gain/Loss)**
01 Dec 06	0.6656	66,560	N/A
31 Dec 06	0.6504	65,040	1,520 gain
31 Mar 07	0.6490	64,900	140 gain
15 May 07	0.6658	66,580	1,680 loss

As the Canadian dollar weakened against the euro in late 2006 and early 2007, the French company would have recorded a foreign currency transaction gain of €1,520 in the fourth quarter of 2006 and an additional transaction gain of €140 in the first quarter of 2007. The Canadian dollar reversed course and strengthened against the euro in the second quarter of 2007, resulting in a transaction loss of €1,680. At the time payment is made on 15 May 2007, the French company realizes a net foreign currency transaction loss of €20 (€66,580 − €66,560). In this case, the transaction gains reported in net income in 2006 and the first quarter of 2007 did not accurately reflect the loss that ultimately was realized.

2.3 Disclosures Related to Foreign Currency Transaction Gains and Losses

Because accounting rules allow companies to choose where they present foreign currency transaction gains and losses on the income statement it is useful for companies to disclose both the amount of transaction gain or loss that is included in income and the presentation alternative they have selected. IAS 21 requires disclosure of "the amount of exchange differences recognized in profit or loss" and SFAS 52 requires disclosure of "the aggregate transaction gain or loss included in determining net income for the period," but neither standard specifically requires disclosure of the line item in which these gains and losses are located.

Exhibit 1 provides disclosures from BASF AG's 2006 Annual Report that the German company made related to foreign currency transaction gains and losses. Exhibit 2 presents similar disclosures found in the Netherlands-based Heineken NV's 2006 Annual Report. Both companies use IFRS to prepare their consolidated financial statements.

BASF's income statement in Exhibit 1 does not include a separate line item for foreign currency gains and losses. From Note 5 in Exhibit 1, an analyst can determine that BASF has chosen to include "Gains from foreign currency transactions" in Other operating income. Of the total amount of €934.1 million reported as Other operating income in 2006, €119.7 million is attributable to foreign currency transaction gains. It is not possible to determine from BASF's financial statements whether these gains were realized in 2006 or not. And any unrealized gain reported in 2006 income might or might not be realized in 2007.

Note 6 in Exhibit 1 indicates that "Losses from foreign currency transactions" in 2006 were €48.4 million, making up 2.5 percent of Other operating expenses. Combining foreign currency transaction gains and losses results in a net gain of €71.3 million, which comprised 1.06 percent of BASF's Income from operations.

EXHIBIT 1 **Excerpts from BASF AG's 2006 Annual Report Related to Foreign Currency Transactions**

Consolidated Statements of Income Million €	**Explanation in Notes**	**2006**	**2005**
Sales	(4)	52,609.7	42,744.9
Cost of sales		37,697.5	29,566.8
Gross profit on sales		**14,912.2**	**13,178.1**
Selling expenses		4,995.5	4,329.9
General and administrative expenses		893.2	780.1
Research and development expenses		1,276.6	1,063.7

(Exhibit continued on next page . . .)

EXHIBIT 1 (continued)

Consolidated Statements of Income Million €	Explanation in Notes	2006	2005
Other operating income	(5)	934.1	600.2
Other operating expenses	(6)	1,931.1	1,775.1
Income from operations		**6,749.9**	**5,829.5**
Income from companies accounted for using the equity method		35.0	5.6
Other income from participations		36.7	342.4
Interest result		(371.9)	(170.0)
Other financial result		77.0	(81.9)
Financial result	(7)	**(223.2)**	**96.1**
Income before taxes and minority interests		**6,526.7**	**5,925.6**
Income taxes	(8)	3,060.6	2,758.1
Income before minority interests		**3,466.1**	**3,167.5**
Minority interests	(9)	250.9	160.8
Net income		**3,215.2**	**3,006.7**

Notes

1. Summary of Accounting Policies

Foreign currency transactions: The cost of assets acquired in foreign currencies and revenues from sales in foreign currencies are recorded at the exchange rate at the date of the transaction. Foreign currency receivables and liabilities are valued at the exchange rates on the balance sheet date.

5. Other Operating Income

Million €	**2006**	**2005**
Reversal and adjustment of provisions	275.2	118.4
Revenue from miscellaneous revenue-generating activities	62.3	85.3
Gains from foreign currency transactions	119.7	43.3
Gains from the translation of financial statements in foreign currencies	10.8	57.3
Gains from disposal of property, plant and equipment and divestitures	127.8	107.4
Gains on the reversal of allowance for doubtful receivables	89.0	92.1
Other	249.3	96.4
	934.1	600.2

Gains from foreign currency transactions represent gains arising from foreign currency positions and foreign currency derivatives as well as from the valuation of receivables and liabilities denominated in foreign currencies at the spot rate at the balance sheet date.

6. Other Operating Expenses

Million €	**2006**	**2005**
Integration and restructuring measures	399.4	446.5
Environmental protection and safety measures, costs of demolition and planning costs related to the preparation of capital expenditure projects not subject to mandatory capitalization	180.5	158.3
Amortization of intangible assets and depreciation of property, plant and equipment	430.3	204.6
Costs from miscellaneous revenue-generating activities	85.1	84.7
Losses from foreign currency transactions	48.4	189.5
Losses from the translation of financial statements in foreign currencies	51.6	23
Losses from the disposal of property, plant and equipment	21.8	15.5

(Exhibit continued on next page . . .)

EXHIBIT 1 (continued)

Notes

Million €	**2006**	**2005**
Oil and gas exploration expenses	167.3	172.9
Expenses from additions to allowances for doubtful receivables	90.4	102.9
Other	456.3	377.2
	1,931.1	1,775.1

Losses from foreign currency transactions include losses from foreign currency positions and derivatives and the valuation of receivables and liabilities in foreign currencies at the closing rate on the balance sheet date.

In Exhibit 2 below, Heineken's Note 2, Basis of Preparation, part (c) explicitly states that the euro is the company's functional currency. Note 3(b)*(i)* indicates that monetary assets and liabilities denominated in foreign currencies at the balance sheet are translated to the functional currency and foreign currency differences arising on the translation (i.e., translation gains and losses) are recognized on the income statement. Note 3(o) discloses that foreign currency gains are included in Other finance income and foreign currency losses are included in Other finance expense. These two amounts are combined into a part of the line item reported on the income statement as Other net finance income. Note 11, Other net finance income, shows that a net translation loss of €16 million existed in 2006 and a net gain of €19 million arose in 2005. The net foreign currency transaction gain in 2005 amounted to 1.63 percent of Heineken's profit before income tax that year, while the net translation loss in 2006 represented 0.94 percent of the company's profit before income tax in that year.

EXHIBIT 2 Excerpts from Heineken NV's 2006 Annual Report Related to Foreign Currency Transactions

Consolidated Income Statement for the Year Ended 31 December 2006 in Millions of EUR	**Note**	**2006**	**2005**
Revenue	5	**11,829**	**10,796**
Other income	7	**379**	**63**
Raw materials, consumables and services	8	7,376	6,657
Personnel expenses	9	2,241	2,180
Amortisation, depreciation and impairments	10	786	768
Total expenses		**10,403**	**9,605**
Results from operating activities		**1,805**	**1,254**
Interest income		52	60
Interest expenses		(185)	(199)
Other net finance income	11	11	25
Net finance expenses		**(122)**	**(114)**
Share of profit of associates		27	29
Profit before income tax		**1,710**	**1,169**
Income tax expense	12	(365)	(300)
Profit		**1,345**	**869**

(Exhibit continued on next page . . .)

EXHIBIT 2 (continued)

	2006	2005
Attributable to:		
Equity holders of the Company (net profit)	1,211	761
Minority interest	134	108
Profit	**1,345**	**869**

Notes

2. Basis of preparation

(c) Functional and presentation currency

These consolidated financial statements are presented in euros, which is the company's functional currency. All financial information presented in euros has been rounded to the nearest million.

3. Significant accounting policies

(b) Foreign currency

(i) Foreign currency transactions

Transactions in foreign currencies are translated to the respective functional currencies of Heineken entities at the exchange rates at the dates of the transactions. Monetary assets and liabilities denominated in foreign currencies at the balance sheet date are retranslated to the functional currency at the exchange rate at that date. . . . Foreign currency differences arising on retranslation are recognised in the income statement, except for differences arising on the retranslation of available-for-sale (equity) investments.[3]

(o) Interest income, interest expenses and other net finance expenses

Other finance income comprises dividend income, gains on the disposal of available-for-sale financial assets, changes in the fair value of financial assets at fair value through profit or loss, foreign currency gains, and gains on hedging instruments that are recognised in the income statement. Dividend income is recognised on the date that Heineken's right to receive payment is established, which in the case of quoted securities is the ex-dividend date.

Other finance expenses comprise unwinding of the discount on provisions, changes in the fair value of financial assets at fair value through profit or loss, foreign currency losses, impairment losses recognised on financial assets, and losses on hedging instruments that are recognised in the income statement.

11. Other net finance income

In millions of EUR	**2006**	**2005**
Impairment investments	—	(6)
Dividend income	13	13
Exchange rate differences	(16)	19
Other	14	(1)
	11	**25**

In applying U.S. GAAP's SFAS 52 to account for its foreign currency transactions, Yahoo! Inc. reported the following in its Quantitative and Qualitative Disclosures about Market Risk in its 2006 Annual Report:

> In the year ended December 31, 2006, we recorded net foreign currency transaction gains, realized and unrealized, of approximately $5 million, net losses of $8 million and net gains of $6 million in 2005 and 2004, respectively, which were recorded in other income, net on the consolidated statements of income.

[3] Note that this excerpt uses "retranslation" in the same way that "translation" is used throughout the rest of this reading.

Yahoo! explicitly acknowledges that both realized and unrealized foreign currency transaction gains and losses are reflected in income, specifically as a part of nonoperating activities. The net foreign currency transaction gain in 2006 of $5 million represented only 0.6 percent of the company's net income for the year.

Companies often neglect to disclose either the location or the amount of foreign currency transaction gains and losses, presumably because the amounts involved are immaterial. The disclosure made by Altria Group, Inc. in its 2006 Annual Report is indicative of this approach. Note 2, Summary of Significant Accounting Policies, contains a subheading "Foreign Currency Translation," in which the company states:

> Transaction gains and losses are recorded in the consolidated statements of earnings and were not significant for any of the periods presented.

There are several reasons why the amount of transaction gains and losses can be immaterial for a company:

1. The company engages in a limited number of foreign currency transactions that involve relatively small amounts of foreign currency.
2. The exchange rates between the company's functional currency and the foreign currencies in which it has transactions tend to be relatively stable.
3. Gains on some foreign currency transactions are naturally offset by losses on other transactions, such that the net gain or loss is immaterial. For example, if a U.S. company sells goods to a customer in Canada with payment in Canadian dollars to be received in 90 days and at the same time purchases goods from a supplier in Canada with payment to be made in Canadian dollars in 90 days, any loss that arises on the Canadian dollar receivable due to a weakening in the value of the Canadian dollar will be exactly offset by a gain of equal amount on the Canadian dollar payable.
4. The company engages in foreign currency hedging activities to offset the foreign exchange gains and losses that arise from foreign currency transactions. Hedging foreign exchange risk is a common practice for many companies engaged in foreign currency transactions.

The two most common types of hedging instruments used to minimize foreign exchange risk are foreign currency forward contracts and foreign currency options. Corning, Inc. describes its foreign exchange risk management approach in its 2006 Annual Report in Note 15, Hedging Activities. An excerpt from that note follows:

> We operate and conduct business in many foreign countries and as a result are exposed to movements in foreign currency exchange rates. Our exposure to exchange rate effects includes:
>
> - Exchange rate movements on financial instruments and transactions denominated in foreign currencies that impact earnings, and
> - Exchange rate movements upon translation of net assets in foreign subsidiaries for which the functional currency is not the U.S. dollar that impact our net equity.[4]
>
> Our most significant foreign currency exposures related to Japan, Korea, Taiwan, and western European countries. We selectively enter

[4] The translation of currency for foreign subsidiaries will be covered in the next section.

> into foreign exchange forward and option contracts with durations generally 15 months or less to hedge our exposure to exchange rate risk on foreign source income and purchases. The hedges are scheduled to mature coincident with the timing of the underlying foreign currency commitments and transactions. The objective of these contracts is to neutralize the impact of exchange rate movements on our operating results.
>
> We engage in foreign currency hedging activities to reduce the risk that changes in exchange rates will adversely affect the eventual net cash flows resulting from the sale of products to foreign customers and purchases from foreign suppliers. The hedge contracts reduce the exposure to fluctuations in exchange rate movements because the gains and loses associated with foreign currency balances and transactions are generally offset with gains and losses of the hedge contracts. Because the impact of movements in foreign exchange rates on the value of hedge contracts offsets the related impact on the underlying items being hedged, these financial instruments help alleviate the risk that might otherwise result from currency exchange rate fluctuations.

Corning goes on to indicate that "changes in the fair value of undesignated hedges are recorded in current period earnings in the other income, net component, *along with the foreign currency gains and losses arising from the underlying monetary assets or liabilities in the consolidated statement of operations*" (p. 171, emphasis added). Amounts, however, are not disclosed, presumably because they are immaterial.

3 TRANSLATION OF FOREIGN CURRENCY FINANCIAL STATEMENTS

Many companies have operations in foreign countries. Most operations located in foreign countries keep their accounting records and prepare financial statements in the local currency. For example, the U.S. subsidiary of German automaker BMW AG keeps its books in U.S. dollars. IFRS and U.S. GAAP require parent companies to prepare consolidated financial statements in which the assets, liabilities, revenues, and expenses of both domestic and foreign subsidiaries are added to those of the parent company. To prepare worldwide consolidated statements, parent companies must translate the foreign currency financial statements of their foreign subsidiaries into the parent company's presentation currency. BMW AG, for example, must translate the U.S. dollar financial statements of its U.S. subsidiary and the South African rand financial statements of its South African subsidiary into euros to consolidate these foreign operations.

The IASB (in IAS 21) and FASB (in SFAS 52) have established very similar rules for the translation of foreign currency financial statements. To fully understand the results from applying these rules, however, several conceptual issues must first be examined.

3.1 Translation Conceptual Issues

In translating foreign currency financial statements into the parent company's presentation currency, two questions must be addressed:

1. What is the appropriate exchange rate to be used in translating each financial statement item?

2. How should the translation adjustment that inherently arises from the translation process be reflected in the consolidated financial statements? In other words, how is the balance sheet brought back into balance?

These issues and the basic concepts underlying the translation of financial statements are demonstrated through the following example.

Spanco is a hypothetical Spanish-based company that uses the euro as its presentation currency. Spanco establishes a wholly owned subsidiary, Amerco, in the United States on 31 December 2008 by investing €10,000 when the exchange rate between the euro and the U.S. dollar is €1 = US$1. The equity investment of €10,000 is physically converted into US$10,000 to begin operations. In addition, Amerco borrows US$5,000 from local banks on 31 December 2008. Amerco purchases inventory that costs US$12,000 on 31 December 2008, and retains US$3,000 in cash. Amerco's balance sheet at 31 December 2008 appears as follows:

Amerco Balance Sheet at 31 December 2008 (in U.S. Dollars)

Cash	$3,000	Notes payable	$5,000
Inventory	12,000	Common stock	10,000
Total	$15,000	Total	$15,000

To prepare a consolidated balance sheet in euros at 31 December 2008, Spanco must translate all of the U.S. dollar balances on Amerco's balance sheet at the €1 = US$1 exchange rate. The translation worksheet at 31 December 2008 is as follows:

Translation Worksheet for Amerco
31 December 2008

	USD	Exchange Rate (€)	EUR
Cash	$ 3,000	1.00	€ 3,000
Inventory	12,000	1.00	12,000
Total	$15,000		€15,000
Notes payable	5,000	1.00	5,000
Common stock	10,000	1.00	10,000
Total	$15,000		€15,000

By translating each U.S. dollar balance at the same exchange rate (€1.00), Amerco's translated balance sheet in euros reflects an equal amount of total assets and total liabilities plus equity and remains in balance.

During the first quarter of 2009, Amerco engages in no transactions. However, during that period the U.S. dollar weakens against the euro such that the exchange rate at 31 March 2009 is €0.80 = US$1.

To prepare a consolidated balance sheet at the end of the first quarter 2009, Spanco now must choose between the current exchange rate of €0.80 and the historical exchange rate of €1.00 to translate Amerco's balance sheet amounts into euros. The original investment made by Spanco of €10,000 is a historical fact, so the company wants to translate Amerco's common stock in such a way that it continues to reflect this amount. This is achieved by translating common stock of US$10,000 into euros using the historical exchange rate of €1 = US$1.

Two different approaches for translating the foreign subsidiary's assets and liabilities are:

1. All assets and liabilities are translated at the **current exchange rate** (the spot exchange rate on the balance sheet date), or
2. Only **monetary assets and liabilities** are translated at the current exchange rate; **nonmonetary assets and liabilities** are translated at **historical exchange rates** (the exchange rates that existed when the assets and liabilities were acquired). Monetary items are cash and receivables (payables) that are to be received (paid) in a fixed number of currency units. Nonmonetary assets include inventory, fixed assets, and intangibles, and nonmonetary liabilities include deferred revenue.

These two different approaches are demonstrated and the results analyzed in turn.

3.1.1 All Assets and Liabilities Are Translated at the Current Exchange Rate

The translation worksheet at 31 March 2009 in which all assets and liabilities are translated at the current exchange rate (€0.80) is as follows:

Translation Worksheet for Amerco 31 March 2009

	U.S. Dollar	Exchange Rate (€)	Euro	Change in Euro Value Since 31 Dec 2008
Cash	$ 3,000	0.80 C	€ 2,400	−€ 600
Inventory	12,000	0.80 C	9,600	−2,400
Total	$15,000		€12,000	−€3,000
Notes payable	5,000	0.80 C	4,000	−1,000
Common stock	10,000	1.00 H	10,000	0
Subtotal	$15,000		14,000	−1,000
Translation adjustment			(2,000)	−2,000
Total			€12,000	−€3,000

Note: C = current exchange rate; H = historical exchange rate

By translating all assets at the lower current exchange rate, total assets are written down from 31 December 2008 to 31 March 2009 in terms of their euro value by €3,000. Liabilities are written down by €1,000. To keep the euro translated balance sheet in balance, a *negative* translation adjustment of €2,000 is created and included in stockholders' equity on the consolidated balance sheet.

Those foreign currency balance sheet accounts that are translated using the current exchange rate are revalued in terms of the parent's functional currency. This process is very similar to the revaluation of foreign currency receivables and payables related to foreign currency transactions. The net translation adjustment that results from translating individual assets and liabilities at the current exchange rate can be viewed as the *net* foreign currency translation gain or loss caused by a change in the exchange rate:

(€600)	loss on cash
(€2,400)	loss on inventory
€1,000	gain on notes payable
(€2,000)	net translation loss

The negative translation adjustment (net translation loss) does not result in a cash outflow of €2,000 for Spanco and thus is unrealized. The loss could be realized, however, if Spanco were to sell Amerco at its book value of US$10,000. The proceeds from the sale would be converted into euros at €0.80 per US$1, resulting in a cash inflow of €8,000. Because Spanco originally invested €10,000 in its U.S. operation, a *realized* loss of €2,000 would result.

The second conceptual issue related to the translation of foreign currency financial statements is whether the unrealized net translation loss should be included in the determination of consolidated net income currently or should be deferred in the stockholders' equity section of the consolidated balance sheet until the loss is realized through sale of the foreign subsidiary. There is some debate as to which of these two treatments is most appropriate. This issue is discussed in more detail after considering the second approach for translating assets and liabilities.

3.1.2 Only Monetary Assets and Monetary Liabilities Are Translated at the Current Exchange Rate

Now assume only monetary assets and monetary liabilities are translated at the current exchange rate. The translation worksheet at 31 March 2009 in which only monetary assets and liabilities are translated at the current exchange rate (€0.80) is as follows:

Translation Worksheet for Amerco 31 March 2009

	U.S. Dollar	Exchange Rate (€)	Euro	Change in Euro Value Since 31 Dec 2008
Cash	$ 3,000	0.80 C	€ 2,400	−€600
Inventory	12,000	1.00 H	12,000	0
Total	$15,000		€14,400	−€600
Notes payable	5,000	0.80 C	4,000	−1,000
Common stock	10,000	1.00 H	10,000	0
Subtotal	$15,000		14,000	−1,000
Translation adjustment			400	400
Total			€14,400	−€600

Note: C = current exchange rate; H = historical exchange rate

Using this approach, cash is written down by €600 but inventory continues to be carried at its euro historical cost of €12,000. Notes payable is written down by €1,000. To keep the balance sheet in balance, a positive translation adjustment of €400 must be included in stockholders' equity. The translation adjustment reflects the *net* translation gain or loss related to monetary items only:

(€600)	loss on cash
€1,000	gain on notes payable
€400	net translation gain

The positive translation adjustment (net translation gain) also is *unrealized*. However, the gain could be *realized* if:

1. The subsidiary uses its cash (US$3,000) to pay as much of its liabilities as possible, and
2. The parent sends enough euros to the subsidiary to pay its remaining liabilities (US$5,000 − US$3,000 = US$2,000). At 31 December 2008, at the €1.00 per US$1 exchange rate, Spanco would have sent €2,000 to Amerco to pay liabilities of US$2,000. At 31 March 2009, given the €0.80 per US$1 exchange rate, the parent needs to send only €1,600 to pay US$2,000 of liabilities. As a result, Spanco would enjoy a foreign exchange gain of €400.

The second conceptual issue again arises under this approach. Should the unrealized foreign exchange gain be recognized in current period net income or deferred on the balance sheet as a separate component of stockholders' equity? The answer to this question, as provided by IFRS and U.S. GAAP, is described in Section 3.2, Translation Methods.

3.1.3 Balance Sheet Exposure

Those assets and liabilities translated at the *current* exchange rate are revalued from balance sheet to balance sheet in terms of the parent company's presentation currency. These items are said to be *exposed* to translation adjustment. Balance sheet items translated at *historical* exchange rates do not change in parent currency value and therefore are not exposed to translation adjustment. Exposure to translation adjustment is referred to as balance sheet translation, or accounting exposure.

A foreign operation will have a **net asset balance sheet exposure** when assets translated at the current exchange rate are greater in amount than liabilities translated at the current exchange rate. A **net liability balance sheet exposure** exists when liabilities translated at the current exchange rate are greater than assets translated at the current exchange rate. Another way to think about the issue is to realize that there is a net asset balance sheet exposure when exposed assets are greater in amount than exposed liabilities and a net liability balance sheet exposure when exposed liabilities are greater in amount than exposed assets. The sign (positive or negative) of the current period's translation adjustment is a function of two factors: 1) the nature of the balance sheet exposure (asset or liability) and 2) the direction of change in the exchange rate (strengthens or weakens). The relationship between exchange rate fluctuations, balance sheet exposure, and the current period's translation adjustment can be summarized as follows:

	Foreign Currency (FC)	
Balance Sheet Exposure	**Strengthens**	**Weakens**
Net asset	Positive translation adjustment	Negative translation adjustment
Net liability	Negative translation adjustment	Positive translation adjustment

These relationships are the same as those summarized in Section 2.2 with respect to foreign currency transaction gains and losses. In reference to the example in Section 3.1.2, for instance, exposed assets ($3,000) were less than exposed liabilities ($5,000), implying that there was a net liability exposure. Further, the foreign currency (US$) weakened, resulting in a positive translation adjustment.

The combination of balance sheet exposure and direction of exchange rate change determines whether the current period's translation adjustment will be positive or negative. After the initial period of operations, a cumulative translation adjustment is required to keep the translated balance sheet in balance. The cumulative translation adjustment will be the sum of the translation adjustments that arise over successive accounting periods. For example, assume that Spanco translates all of Amerco's assets and liabilities using the current exchange rate (a net asset balance sheet exposure exists), which due to a weakening U.S. dollar in the first quarter of 2009 resulted in a negative translation adjustment at 31 March 2009 of €2,000 (as shown in Section 3.1.1). Assume further that in the second quarter of 2009, the U.S. dollar strengthens against the euro and there still is a net asset balance sheet exposure, which results in a *positive* translation adjustment of €500 for that quarter. Although the current period translation adjustment for the second quarter of 2009 is positive, the cumulative translation adjustment at 30 June 2009 still will be negative, but the amount now will be only €1,500.

3.2 Translation Methods

The two approaches to translating foreign currency financial statements described in the previous section are known as 1) the **current rate method** (all assets and liabilities are translated at the current exchange rate), and 2) the **monetary/nonmonetary method** (only monetary assets and liabilities are translated at the current exchange rate). A variation of the monetary/nonmonetary method requires not only monetary assets and liabilities but also nonmonetary assets and liabilities that are measured at their current value on the balance sheet date to be translated at the current exchange rate. This variation of the monetary/nonmonetary method sometimes is referred to as the **temporal method**. The basic idea underlying the temporal method is that assets and liabilities should be translated in such a way that the measurement basis (either current value or historical cost) in the foreign currency is preserved after translating to the parent's presentation currency. To achieve this objective, assets and liabilities carried on the foreign currency balance sheet at a current value should be translated at the current exchange rate, and assets and liabilities carried on the foreign currency balance sheet at historical costs should be translated at historical exchange rates. Although neither the IASB nor the FASB specifically refer to translation methods by name, the procedures required by IFRS and U.S. GAAP in translating foreign currency financial statements essentially require the use of either the current rate or the temporal method.

Which method is appropriate for an individual foreign entity depends on that entity's functional currency. As noted earlier, the functional currency is the currency of the primary economic environment in which an entity operates. A foreign entity's functional currency can be either the parent's presentation currency or another currency, typically the currency of the country in which the foreign entity is located. Exhibit 3 lists the factors that IAS 21 indicates should be considered in determining a foreign entity's functional currency. Although not identical, SFAS 52 provides similar indicators for determining a foreign entity's functional currency.

When the functional currency indicators listed in Exhibit 3 are mixed and the functional currency is not obvious, IAS 21 indicates that management should use its best judgment in determining the functional currency. However, in this case, indicators 1 and 2 should be given priority over indicators 3 through 9.

EXHIBIT 3 Factors Considered in Determining the Functional Currency

In accordance with IAS 21, The Effects of Changes in Foreign Exchange Rates, the following factors should be considered in determining an entity's functional currency:

1. The currency that influences sales prices for goods and services.
2. The currency of the country whose competitive forces and regulations mainly determine the sales price of its goods and services.
3. The currency that mainly influences labor, material, and other costs of providing goods and services.
4. The currency in which funds from financing activities are generated.
5. The currency in which receipts from operating activities are usually retained.

Additional factors to consider in determining whether the foreign entity's functional currency is the same as the parent's are:

6. Whether the activities of the foreign operation are an extension of the parent's or are carried out with a significant amount of autonomy.
7. Whether transactions with the parent are a large or a small proportion of the foreign entity's activities.
8. Whether cash flows generated by the foreign operation directly affect the cash flow of the parent and are available to be remitted to the parent.
9. Whether operating cash flows generated by the foreign operation are sufficient to service existing and normally expected debt or whether the foreign entity will need funds from the parent to service its debt.

The following three steps outline the functional currency approach required by both IFRS and U.S. GAAP in translating foreign currency financial statements into the parent's presentation currency:

1. Identify the functional currency of the foreign entity.
2. Translate foreign currency balances into the foreign entity's functional currency.
3. Use the current exchange rate to translate the foreign entity's functional currency balances into the parent's presentation currency, if they are different.

To illustrate how this approach is applied, consider a U.S. parent company with a Mexican subsidiary that keeps its accounting records in Mexican pesos. Assume that the vast majority of the subsidiary's transactions are carried out in Mexican pesos but it also has an account payable in Guatemalan quetzals. In applying the three steps, the U.S. parent company first determines that the Mexican peso is the functional currency of the Mexican subsidiary. Second, the Mexican subsidiary translates its foreign currency balances, i.e., the Guatemalan quetzal account payable, into Mexican pesos using the current exchange rate. In step 3, the Mexican peso financial statements (including the translated account payable) are translated into U.S. dollars using the current rate method.

Now assume that the primary operating currency of the Mexican subsidiary is the U.S. dollar, which thus is identified as the Mexican subsidiary's functional currency. In that case, in addition to the Guatemalan quetzal account payable, all of the subsidiary's accounts that are denominated in Mexican pesos also are considered to be foreign currency balances (because they are not denominated in the subsidiary's functional currency, which is the U.S. dollar). Along with the Guatemalan quetzal balance, each of the Mexican peso balances must be translated into U.S. dollars as if the subsidiary kept its books in U.S. dollars. Assets and liabilities carried at current value in Mexican pesos are translated into U.S. dollars using the current exchange rate, and assets and liabilities carried at historical cost in Mexican pesos are translated into U.S. dollars using historical exchange rates. After completing this step, the Mexican subsidiary's financial statements are stated in terms of U.S. dollars, which is both the subsidiary's functional currency and the parent's presentation currency. As a result, there is no need to apply step 3.

The procedures to be followed in applying the functional currency approach embodied in IFRS and U.S. GAAP are described in more detail in the following two sections.

3.2.1 Foreign Currency Is the Functional Currency

In most cases, a foreign entity will primarily operate in the currency of the country where it is located, which will be different from the currency in which the parent company presents its financial statements. For example, the Japanese subsidiary of a French parent company is likely to have the Japanese yen as its functional currency, whereas the French parent company must prepare consolidated financial statements in euros. When a foreign entity has a functional currency that is different from the parent's presentation currency, the foreign entity's foreign currency financial statements are translated into the parent's presentation currency using the following procedures:

1. All assets and liabilities are translated at the current exchange rate at the balance sheet date.
2. Stockholders' equity accounts are translated at historical exchange rates.
3. Revenues and expenses are translated at the exchange rate that existed when the transactions took place. For practical reasons, a rate that approximates the exchange rates at the dates of the transactions, such as an average exchange rate, may be used.

These procedures essentially describe the current rate method.

Under both IAS 21 and SFAS 52, when the current rate method is used, the cumulative translation adjustment needed to keep the translated balance sheet in balance is reported as a separate component of stockholders' equity.

The basic concept underlying the current rate method is that the entire investment in a foreign entity is exposed to translation gain or loss. Therefore, all assets and all liabilities must be revalued at each successive balance sheet date. But the net translation gain or loss that results from this procedure is unrealized and will be realized only when the entity is sold. In the meantime, the unrealized translation gain or loss that accumulates over time is deferred on the balance sheet as a separate component of stockholders' equity. When a specific foreign entity is sold, the cumulative translation adjustment related to that entity is reported as a realized gain or loss in net income.

The current rate method results in a net asset balance sheet exposure (except in the rare case in which an entity has negative stockholders' equity):

Items Translated at Current Exchange Rate
Total assets > Total liabilities → Net asset balance sheet exposure

When the foreign currency increases in value (strengthens), application of the current rate method results in an increase in the positive cumulative translation adjustment (or a decrease in the negative cumulative translation adjustment) reflected in stockholders' equity. When the foreign currency decreases in value (weakens), the current rate method results in a decrease in the positive cumulative translation adjustment (or increase in the negative cumulative translation adjustment) in stockholders' equity.

3.2.2 Parent's Presentation Currency Is the Functional Currency

In some cases, a foreign entity might have the parent's presentation currency as its functional currency. For example, a German-based manufacturer might have a 100 percent-owned distribution subsidiary in Switzerland that primarily uses the euro in its day-to-day operations. But as a Swiss company, the subsidiary is required to record its transactions and keep its books in Swiss francs. In that situation, the subsidiary's Swiss franc financial statements must be translated into euros as if the subsidiary's transactions had originally been recorded in euros. SFAS 52 refers to this process as *remeasurement*. IAS 21 does not refer to this process as remeasurement, but instead describes this situation as "reporting foreign currency transactions in the functional currency." To achieve the objective of translating to the parent's presentation currency as if the subsidiary's transactions had been recorded in that currency, the following procedures are used:

1. a. Monetary assets and liabilities are translated at the current exchange rate.
   b. Nonmonetary assets and liabilities measured at historical cost are translated at historical exchange rates.
   c. Nonmonetary assets and liabilities measured at current value are translated at the exchange rate at the date when the current value was determined.
2. Stockholders' equity accounts are translated at historical exchange rates.
3. a. Revenues and expenses, other than those expenses related to nonmonetary assets (as explained in 3.b. below), are translated at the exchange rate that existed when the transactions took place (for practical reasons, average rates may be used).
   b. Expenses related to nonmonetary assets, such as cost of goods sold (inventory), depreciation (fixed assets), and amortization (intangible assets), are translated at the exchange rates used to translate the related assets.

These procedures essentially describe the temporal method.

Under the temporal method, companies must keep record of the exchange rates that exist when nonmonetary assets (inventory, prepaid expenses, fixed assets, and intangible assets) are acquired, because these assets (normally measured at historical cost) are translated at historical exchange rates. Keeping track of the historical exchange rates for these assets is not necessary under the current rate method. Translating these assets (and their related expenses) at historical exchange rates complicates application of the temporal method.

The historical exchange rates used to translate inventory (and cost of goods sold) under the temporal method will differ depending on the cost flow assumption—first in, first out (FIFO), last in, first out (LIFO), or average cost—used to account for inventory. Ending inventory reported on the balance sheet is translated at the exchange rate that existed when the inventory assumed to still be on hand at the balance sheet date (using FIFO or LIFO) was acquired. If FIFO is used, ending inventory is assumed to be composed of the most recently acquired items and thus inventory will be translated at relatively recent exchange rates. If LIFO is used, ending inventory is assumed to consist of older items and thus inventory will be translated at older exchange rates. The weighted average exchange rate for the year is used when inventory is carried at weighted average cost. Similarly, cost of goods sold is translated using the exchange rates that existed when the inventory items assumed to have been sold during the year (using FIFO or LIFO) were acquired. If weighted average cost is used to account for inventory, cost of goods sold will be translated at the weighted average exchange rate for the year.

Under both IAS 21 and SFAS 52, when the temporal method is used, the translation adjustment needed to keep the translated balance sheet in balance is reported as a gain or loss in net income. SFAS 52 refers to these as *remeasurement* gains and losses.

The basic assumption supporting the recognition of a translation gain or loss in income when the temporal method is used is that if the foreign entity primarily uses the parent's currency in its day-to-day operations, then the foreign entity's monetary items that are denominated in a foreign currency generate translation gains and losses that will be realized in the near future and thus should be reflected in current net income.

The temporal method generates either a net asset or a net liability balance sheet exposure, depending on whether assets translated at the current exchange rate, i.e., monetary assets and nonmonetary assets measured on the balance sheet date at current value (exposed assets), are greater than or less than liabilities translated at the current exchange rate, i.e., monetary liabilities and nonmonetary liabilities measured on the balance sheet date at current value (exposed liabilities):

Items Translated at Current Exchange Rate
Exposed assets > Exposed liabilities → Net asset balance sheet exposure
Exposed assets < Exposed liabilities → Net liability balance sheet exposure

Most liabilities are monetary liabilities. Only cash and receivables are monetary assets, and nonmonetary assets generally are measured at their historical cost. As a result, liabilities translated at the current exchange rate (exposed liabilities) often exceed assets translated at the current exchange rate (exposed assets), which results in a net liability balance sheet exposure when the temporal method is applied.

3.2.3 Translation of Retained Earnings

Stockholders' equity accounts are translated at historical exchange rates under both the current rate and the temporal methods. This creates somewhat of a problem in translating retained earnings (R/E), which is the accumulation of previous years' income less dividends over the life of the company. At the end of the first year of operations, foreign currency (FC) retained earnings are translated into the parent's currency (PC) as follows:

Net income in FC		[Translated according to the method used to translate the income statement]	=	Net income in PC
− Dividends in FC	×	Exchange rate when dividends declared	=	− Dividends in PC
R/E in FC				R/E in PC

Retained earnings in parent currency at the end of the first year becomes the beginning retained earnings in parent currency for the second year, and the translated retained earnings in the second year (and subsequent years) is then calculated in the following manner:

Beginning R/E in FC		[From last year's translation]	→	Beginning R/E in PC
+ Net income in FC		[Translated according to the method used to translate the income statement]	=	+ Net income in PC
− Dividends in FC	×	Exchange rate when dividends declared	=	− Dividends in PC
Ending R/E in FC				Ending R/E in PC

The following table summarizes the translation rules as discussed in Sections 3.2.1 and 3.2.2.

EXHIBIT 4 **Rules for the Translation of a Foreign Subsidiary's Foreign Currency Financial Statements into the Parent's Presentation Currency under IFRS and U.S. GAAP**

	Foreign Subsidiary's Functional Currency	
	Foreign Currency	**Parent's Presentation Currency**
Translation method:	**Current Rate Method**	**Temporal Method**
Exchange rate at which financial statement items are translated from the foreign subsidiary's bookkeeping currency to the parent's presentation currency:		
Assets		
Monetary, e.g., cash; receivables	Current rate	Current rate
Nonmonetary		
► measured at current value, e.g., marketable securities; inventory measured at market under the lower of cost or market rule	Current rate	Current rate
► measured at historical costs, e.g., inventory measured at cost under the lower of cost or market rule; property, plant & equipment; intangible assets	Current rate	Historical rates
Liabilities		
Monetary, e.g., accounts payable; accrued expenses; long-term debt; deferred income taxes	Current rate	Current rate
Nonmonetary		
► measured at current value	Current rate	Current rate
► not measured at current value, e.g., deferred revenue	Current rate	Historical rates
Equity		
Other than retained earnings	Historical rates	Historical rates
Retained earnings	Beginning balance plus translated net income less dividends translated at historical rate	Beginning balance plus translated net income less dividends translated at historical rate
Revenues	Average rate	Average rate
Expenses		
Most expenses	Average rate	Average rate
Expenses related to assets translated at historical exchange rate, e.g., cost of goods sold; depreciation; amortization	Average rate	Historical rates
Treatment of the translation adjustment in the parent's consolidated financial statements	Accumulated as a separate component of equity	Included as gain or loss in net income

3.2.4 Highly Inflationary Economies

When a foreign entity is located in a highly inflationary economy, the entity's functional currency is irrelevant in determining how to translate its foreign currency financial statements into the parent's presentation currency. IAS 21 requires that the financial statements of the foreign entity first be restated for local inflation using the procedures outlined in IAS 29, "Financial Reporting in Hyperinflationary Economies." Then, the inflation-restated foreign currency financial statements are translated into the parent's presentation currency using the current exchange rate (i.e., using the current rate method).

U.S. GAAP requires a very different approach for translating the foreign currency financial statements of foreign entities located in highly inflationary economies. SFAS 52 does not allow restatement for inflation, but instead requires the temporal method to translate financial statements kept in a highly inflationary currency. However, despite the use of the temporal method, the resulting translation adjustment is included as a gain or loss in determining net income.

SFAS 52 defines a highly inflationary economy as one in which the cumulative three-year inflation rate exceeds 100 percent. This equates to an average of approximately 26 percent per year. IAS 21 does not provide a specific definition of high inflation, but IAS 29 does indicate that a cumulative inflation rate approaching or exceeding 100 percent over three years would be one indicator of hyperinflation. If a country in which a foreign entity is located ceases to be classified as highly inflationary, the functional currency of that foreign entity must be identified to determine the appropriate method for translating the entity's foreign currency financial statements.

The FASB initially proposed that companies restate for inflation and then translate the financial statements, but this approach met with stiff resistance from U.S. multinational corporations. By requiring the temporal method, SFAS 52 ensures that companies avoid a "disappearing plant problem" that exists when the current rate method is used in a country with high inflation. In a highly inflationary economy, as the local currency loses purchasing power within the country, it also tends to weaken in value in relation to other currencies. Translating the historical cost of assets such as land and buildings at progressively lower exchange rates causes these assets to slowly disappear from the parent company's consolidated financial statements. Example 4 demonstrates the effect of three different translation approaches when books are kept in the currency of a highly inflationary economy.

EXAMPLE 4

Foreign Currency Translation in a Highly Inflationary Economy

Turkey was one of the few remaining highly inflationary countries at the beginning of the 21st century. Annual inflation rates and selected exchange rates between the Turkish lira (TL) and U.S. dollar during the period 2000–2002 were as follows:

Date	Exchange Rates	Year	Inflation Rate (%)
01 Jan 2000	TL 542,700 = US$1		
31 Dec 2000	TL 670,800 = US$1	2000	38
31 Dec 2001	TL 1,474,525 = US$1	2001	69
31 Dec 2002	TL 1,669,000 = US$1	2002	45

Assume that a U.S.-based company established a subsidiary in Turkey on 1 January 2000. The U.S. parent sent the subsidiary US$1,000 on 1 January 2000 to purchase a piece of land at a cost of TL 542,700,000 (TL 542,700/US$ × US$1,000 = TL 542,700,000). Assuming no other assets or liabilities, what are the annual and cumulative translation gains or losses that would be reported under each of three possible translation approaches?

Solution:

Approach 1: Translate Using the Current Rate Method

The historical cost of the land is translated at the current exchange rate, which results in a new translated amount at each balance sheet date.

Date	Carrying Value	Current Exchange Rate	Translated Amount in US$	Annual Translation Gain (Loss)	Cumulative Translation Gain (Loss)
01 Jan 2000	TL 542,700,000	542,700	$1,000	N/A	N/A
31 Dec 2000	542,700,000	670,800	809	($191)	($191)
31 Dec 2001	542,700,000	1,474,525	368	(441)	(632)
31 Dec 2002	542,700,000	1,669,000	325	(43)	(675)

At the end of three years, land that was originally purchased with US$1,000 would be reflected on the parent's consolidated balance sheet at US$325 (and remember that land is not a depreciable asset). A cumulative translation loss of US$675 would be reported as a separate component of stockholders' equity on 31 December 2002. Because this method accounts for adjustments in exchange rates but does not account for likely changes in the local currency values of assets, it does a poor job accurately reflecting the economic reality of situations such as the one in our example. That is the major reason this approach is not acceptable under either IFRS or U.S. GAAP.

Approach 2: Translate Using the Temporal Method (SFAS 52)

The historical cost of land is translated using the historical exchange rate, which results in the same translated amount at each balance sheet date.

Date	Carrying Value	Historical Exchange Rate	Translated Amount in US$	Annual Translation Gain (Loss)	Cumulative Translation Gain (Loss)
01 Jan 2000	TL 542,700,000	542,700	$1,000	N/A	N/A
31 Dec 2000	542,700,000	542,700	1,000	N/A	N/A
31 Dec 2001	542,700,000	542,700	1,000	N/A	N/A
31 Dec 2002	542,700,000	542,700	1,000	N/A	N/A

Under this approach, land continues to be reported on the parent's consolidated balance sheet at its original cost of US$1,000 each year. There is no translation gain or loss related to balance sheet items translated at historical exchange rates. This approach is required by SFAS 52 and ensures that nonmonetary assets do not disappear from the translated balance sheet.

Approach 3: Restate for Inflation/Translate Using Current Exchange Rate (IAS 21)

The historical cost of the land is restated for inflation and then the inflation-adjusted historical cost is translated using the current exchange rate.

Date	Inflation Rate (%)	Restated Carrying Value	Current Exchange Rate	Translated Amount in US$	Annual Translation Gain (Loss)	Cumulative Translation Gain (Loss)
01 Jan 00		TL 542,700,000	542,700	$1,000	N/A	N/A
31 Dec 00	38	748,926,000	670,800	1,116	$116	$116
31 Dec 01	69	1,265,684,940	1,474,525	858	(258)	(142)
31 Dec 02	45	1,835,243,163	1,669,000	1,100	242	100

Under this approach, land is reported on the parent's 31 December 2002 consolidated balance sheet at US$1,100 with a cumulative, unrealized gain of US$100. Although the cumulative translation gain on 31 December 2002 is unrealized, it could have been realized if 1) the land had appreciated in TL value by the rate of local inflation, 2) the Turkish subsidiary sold the land for TL 1,835,243,163, and 3) the sale proceeds were converted into US$1,100 at the current exchange rate on 31 December 2002.

This approach is required by IAS 21. It is the approach that perhaps best represents economic reality in the sense that it reflects both the likely change in the local currency value of the land as well as the actual change in the exchange rate.

3.3 Illustration of Translation Methods (Excluding Hyperinflationary Economies)

To demonstrate the procedures required by IAS 21 and SFAS 52 in translating foreign currency financial statements, assume that Interco is a European-based company that has the euro as its presentation currency. On 1 January 2008, Interco establishes a wholly owned subsidiary in Canada, Canadaco. In addition to Interco making an equity investment in Canadaco, a long-term note payable to a Canadian bank was negotiated to purchase property and equipment. The subsidiary begins operations with the following balance sheet in Canadian dollars (C$):

Canadaco Balance Sheet
1 January 2008 (in Canadian Dollars)

Assets	
Cash	$1,500,000
Property and equipment	3,000,000
	$4,500,000
Liabilities and Equity	
Long-term note payable	$3,000,000
Capital stock	1,500,000
	$4,500,000

Canadaco purchases and sells inventory in 2008, generating net income of C$1,180,000, out of which C$350,000 in dividends are paid. The company's income statement and statement of retained earnings for 2008 and balance sheet at 31 December 2008 follow:

Canadaco Income Statement and Statement of Retained Earnings 2008 (in Canadian Dollars)

Sales	$12,000,000
Cost of sales	(9,000,000)
Selling expenses	(750,000)
Depreciation expense	(300,000)
Interest expense	(270,000)
Income tax	(500,000)
Net income	1,180,000
Less: Dividends, 1 Dec 08	(350,000)
Retained earnings, 31 Dec 2008	$ 830,000

Canadaco Balance Sheet 31 December 2008 (in Canadian Dollars)

Assets		**Liabilities and Equity**	
Cash	$ 980,000	Accounts payable	$ 450,000
Accounts receivable	900,000	Total current liabilities	450,000
Inventory	1,200,000	Long-term notes payable	3,000,000
Total current assets	3,080,000	Total liabilities	3,450,000
Property and equipment	3,000,000	Capital stock	1,500,000
Less: accumulated depreciation	(300,000)	Retained earnings	830,000
Total	$5,780,000	Total	$5,780,000

Inventory is measured at historical cost on a FIFO basis.

To translate Canadaco's Canadian dollar financial statements into euros for consolidation purposes, the following exchange rate information was gathered:

Date	€ per C$
1 January 2008	0.70
Average, 2008	0.75
Weighted average rate when inventory was acquired	0.74
1 December 2008 when dividends were declared	0.78
31 December 2008	0.80

During 2008, the Canadian dollar strengthened steadily against the euro from an exchange rate of €0.70 at the beginning of the year to €0.80 at year end.

The translation worksheet below shows Canadaco's translated financial statements under each of the two translation methods. Assume first that Canadaco's functional currency is the Canadian dollar and therefore the current rate method must be used. The Canadian dollar income statement and statement of retained earnings are translated first. Income statement items for 2008 are translated at the average exchange rate for 2008 (€0.75), and dividends are translated at the exchange rate that existed when they were declared (€0.78). The ending balance in retained earnings at 31 December 2008 of €612,000 is transferred to the C$ balance sheet. The remaining balance sheet accounts are then translated. Assets and liabilities are translated at the current exchange rate on the balance sheet date of 31 December 2008 (€0.80), and the capital stock account is translated at the historical exchange rate (€0.70) that existed on the date that Interco made the capital contribution. A positive translation adjustment of €202,000 is needed as a balancing amount, which is reported in the stockholders' equity section of the balance sheet.

If instead Interco determines that Canadaco's functional currency is the euro, the parent's presentation currency, the temporal method must be applied as shown in the far right columns of the table. The differences in procedure from the current rate method are that inventory, property, and equipment (and accumulated depreciation), as well as their related expenses (cost of goods sold and depreciation), are translated at the historical exchange rates that existed when the assets were acquired: €0.70 in the case of property and equipment, and €0.74 for inventory. The balance sheet is translated first, with €472,000 determined as the amount of retained earnings needed to keep the balance sheet in balance. This amount is transferred to the income statement and statement of retained earnings as the ending balance in retained earnings at 31 December 2008. Income statement items then are translated, with cost of goods sold and depreciation expense being translated at historical exchange rates. A negative translation adjustment of €245,000 is determined as the amount that is needed to arrive at the ending balance in retained earnings of €472,000, and is reported as a translation loss on the income statement.

The positive translation adjustment under the current rate method can be explained by the fact that Canadaco has a net asset balance sheet exposure (total assets exceed total liabilities) during 2008 and the Canadian dollar strengthened against the euro. The negative translation adjustment (translation loss) under the temporal method is due to the fact that Canadaco has exposed liabilities (accounts payable plus notes payable) that exceed exposed assets (cash plus receivables) during 2008 when the Canadian dollar strengthened against the euro.

Canadaco Income Statement and Statement of Retained Earnings 2008

		Current Rate		Temporal	
	C$	Exch. Rate	€	Exch. Rate	€
Sales	12,000,000	0.75 A	9,000,000	0.75 A	9,000,000
Cost of goods sold	(9,000,000)	0.75 A	(6,750,000)	0.74 H	(6,660,000)
Selling expenses	(750,000)	0.75 A	(562,500)	0.75 A	(562,500)
Depreciation expense	(300,000)	0.75 A	(225,000)	0.70 H	(210,000)
Interest expense	(270,000)	0.75 A	(202,500)	0.75 A	(202,500)
Income tax	(500,000)	0.75 A	(375,000)	0.75 A	(375,000)

(continued on next page . . .)

(continued)

		Current Rate		Temporal	
	C$	Exch. Rate	€	Exch. Rate	€
Income before trans. gain (loss)	1,180,000		885,000		990,000
Translation gain (loss)	N/A		N/A	to balance	(245,000)
Net income	1,180,000		885,000		745,000
Less: Dividends, 12/1/2008	(350,000)	0.78 H	(273,000)	0.78 H	(273,000)
Retained earnings, 12/31/2008	830,000		612,000	from B/S	472,000

Note: C = current exchange rate; A = average-for-the-year exchange rate; H = historical exchange rate

Canadaco Balance Sheet
31 December 2008

		Current Rate		Temporal	
	C$	Exch. Rate	€	Exch. Rate	€
Assets					
Cash	980,000	0.80 C	784,000	0.80 C	784,000
Accounts receivable	900,000	0.80 C	720,000	0.80 C	720,000
Inventory	1,200,000	0.80 C	960,000	0.74 H	888,000
Total current assets	3,080,000		2,464,000		2,392,000
Property and equipment	3,000,000	0.80 C	2,400,000	0.70 H	2,100,000
Less: accumulated depreciation	(300,000)	0.80 C	(240,000)	0.70 H	(210,000)
Total assets	5,780,000		4,624,000		4,282,000
Liabilities and Equity					
Accounts payable	450,000	0.80 C	360,000	0.80 C	360,000
Total current liabilities	450,000		360,000		360,000
Long-term notes payable	3,000,000	0.80 C	2,400,000	0.80 C	2,400,000
Total liabilities	3,450,000		2,760,000		2,760,000
Capital stock	1,500,000	0.70 H	1,050,000	0.70 H	1,050,000
Retained earnings	830,000	from I/S	612,000	to balance	472,000
Translation adjustment	N/A	to balance	202,000		N/A
Total	5,780,000		4,624,000		4,282,000

Note: C = current exchange rate; A = average-for-the-year exchange rate; H = historical exchange rate

3.4 Translation Analytical Issues

The two different translation methods used to translate Canadaco's C$ financial statements into euros result in very different amounts that will be included in Interco's consolidated financial statements. The chart below summarizes some of these differences:

	Translation Method		
Item	Current Rate (€)	Temporal (€)	Difference (%)
Net income	885,000	745,000	+18.8
Income before translation gain (loss)	885,000	990,000	−10.6
Total assets	4,624,000	4,282,000	+8.0
Total equity	1,864,000	1,522,000	+22.5

In this particular case, the current rate method results in a significantly larger net income than the temporal method. This occurs because under the current rate method the translation adjustment is not included in the calculation of income. If the translation loss were excluded from net income, the temporal method would result in a significantly larger amount of net income. The combination of smaller net income under the temporal method and a positive translation adjustment reported on the balance sheet under the current rate method results in a much larger amount of total equity under the current rate method. Total assets also are larger under the current rate method because all assets are translated at the current exchange rate, which is higher than the historical exchange rates at which inventory and fixed assets are translated under the temporal method.

To examine the impact that translation has on the underlying relationships that exist in Canadaco's C$ financial statements, several significant ratios are calculated from the original C$ financial statements and the translated (€) financial statements and presented in the table below.

	C$	Current Rate (€)	Temporal (€)
Current ratio			
Current assets	3,080,000	2,464,000	2,392,000
Current liabilities	450,000	360,000	360,000
	6.84	6.84	6.64
Debt-to-assets ratio			
Total debt	3,000,000	2,400,000	2,400,000
Total assets	5,780,000	4,624,000	4,282,000.00
	0.52	0.52	0.56
Debt-to-equity ratio			
Total debt	3,000,000	2,400,000	2,400,000
Total equity	2,330,000	1,864,000	1,522,000
	1.29	1.29	1.58

(continued on next page . . .)

	C$	Current Rate (€)	Temporal (€)
Interest coverage			
EBIT	1,950,000	1,462,500	1,567,500
Interest payments	270,000	202,500	202,500
	7.22	7.22	7.74
Gross profit margin			
Gross profit	3,000,000	2,250,000	2,340,000
Sales	12,000,000	9,000,000	9,000,000
	0.25	0.25	0.26
Operating profit margin			
Operating profit	1,950,000	1,462,500	1,567,500
Sales	12,000,000	9,000,000	9,000,000
	0.16	0.16	0.17
Net profit margin			
Net income	1,180,000	885,000	745,000
Sales	12,000,000	9,000,000	9,000,000
	0.10	0.10	0.08
Receivables turnover			
Sales	12,000,000	9,000,000	9,000,000
Accounts receivable	900,000	720,000	720,000
	13.33	12.50	12.50
Inventory turnover			
Cost of goods sold	9,000,000	6,750,000	6,660,000
Inventory	1,200,000	960,000	888,000
	7.50	7.03	7.50
Fixed asset turnover			
Sales	12,000,000	9,000,000	9,000,000
Property & equipment (net)	2,700,000	2,160,000	1,890,000
	4.44	4.17	4.76
Return on assets			
Net income	1,180,000	885,000	745,000
Total assets	5,780,000	4,624,000	4,282,000
	0.20	0.19	0.17
Return on equity			
Net income	1,180,000	885,000	745,000
Total equity	2,330,000	1,864,000	1,522,000
	0.51	0.47	0.49

Comparing the current rate method (€) and temporal method (€) columns in the above table shows that financial ratios calculated from Canadaco's translated financial statements (in €) differ significantly depending on which method of translation is used. Of the ratios presented, only receivables turnover is the same under both translation methods. This is the only ratio presented in which there is no difference in the type of exchange rate used to translate the items that comprise the numerator and the denominator. Sales are translated at the average exchange rate and receivables are translated at the current exchange rate under both methods. For each of the other ratios, at least one of the items included in either the numerator or the denominator is translated at a different type of rate (current, average, or historical rate) under the temporal method than under the current rate method. For example, the current ratio has a different value under the two translation methods because inventory is translated at the current exchange rate under the current rate method and at the historical exchange rate under the temporal method. In this case, because the €/C$ exchange rate at 31 December 2008 (€0.80) is higher than the historical exchange rate when the inventory was acquired (€0.74), the current ratio is larger under the current rate method of translation.

Comparing the ratios in the C$ and current rate method (€) columns of the above table shows that many of the underlying relationships that exist in Canadaco's C$ financial statements are preserved when the current rate method of translation is used (i.e., the ratio calculated from the C$ and € translated amounts is the same). The current ratio, the leverage ratios (debt-to-assets and debt-to-equity ratios), the interest coverage ratio, and the profit margins (gross profit margin, operating profit margin, and net profit margin) are the same in the C$ and current rate method (€) columns of the above table. This occurs because each of the ratios is calculated using information from either the balance sheet or the income statement, but not both. Those ratios that compare amounts from the balance sheet with amounts from the income statement (e.g., turnover and return ratios) are different. In this particular case, each of the turnover and return ratios is larger when calculated from the C$ amounts than when calculated using the current rate (€) amounts. The underlying C$ relationships are distorted when translated using the current rate method because the balance sheet amounts are translated using the current exchange rate while revenues and expenses are translated using the average exchange rate. (These distortions would not exist if revenues and expenses also were translated at the current exchange rate.)

Comparing the ratios in the C$ and temporal method (€) columns of the table shows that translation using the temporal method distorts all of the underlying relationships that exist in the C$ financial statements, except inventory turnover. Moreover, it is not possible to generalize the direction of the distortion across ratios. In Canadaco's case, using the temporal method results in a larger gross profit margin and operating profit margin but a smaller net profit margin as compared with the values of these ratios calculated from the original C$ amounts. Similarly, receivables turnover is smaller, inventory turnover is the same, and fixed asset turnover is larger when calculated from the translated amounts.

In translating Canadaco's C$ financial statements into euros, the temporal method results in a smaller amount of net income than the current rate method only because IFRS and U.S. GAAP require the resulting translation loss to be included in net income when the temporal method is used. The translation loss arises because the C$ strengthened against the euro and Canadaco has a larger amount of liabilities translated at the current exchange rate (monetary liabilities) than it has assets translated at the current exchange rate (monetary assets). If Canadaco had a net monetary asset exposure (i.e., if monetary assets exceeded monetary liabilities), a translation gain would arise and net income under the temporal method (including the translation gain) would be greater than under the current rate method. Example 5 demonstrates how different types of balance sheet exposure under the temporal method can affect translated net income.

EXAMPLE 5

Impacts of Different Balance Sheet Exposures under the Temporal Method

Canadaco begins operations on 1 January 2008, with cash of C$1,500,000 and property and equipment of C$3,000,000. In Case A, Canadaco finances the acquisition of property and equipment with a long-term note payable, and begins operations with net monetary liabilities of C$1,500,000 (C$3,000,000 long-term note payable less C$1,500,000 cash). In Case B, Canadaco finances the acquisition of property and equipment with capital stock, and begins operations with net monetary assets of C$1,500,000. To isolate the effect that balance sheet exposure has on net income under the temporal method, assume that Canadaco continues to have C$270,000 in interest expense in Case B, even though there is no debt financing. This assumption is inconsistent with reality, but it allows us to more clearly see the effect that balance sheet exposure has on net income. The only difference between Case A and Case B is the net monetary asset/liability position of the company, as shown below:

Canadaco Balance Sheet 1 January 2008

(in Canadian Dollars)	Case A	Case B
Assets		
Cash	$1,500,000	$1,500,000
Property and equipment	3,000,000	3,000,000
	$4,500,000	$4,500,000
Liabilities and Equity		
Long-term note payable	$3,000,000	$ 0
Capital stock	1,500,000	4,500,000
	$4,500,000	$4,500,000

Canadaco purchases and sells inventory in 2008, generating net income of C$1,180,000, out of which dividends of C$350,000 are paid. The company has total assets of C$5,780,000 at 31 December 2008. Canadaco's functional currency is determined to be the euro, the parent's presentation currency, and the company's Canadian dollar financial statements are translated into euros using the temporal method. Relevant exchange rates are:

Date	€ per C$
1 January 2008	0.70
Average, 2008	0.75
Weighted average rate when inventory was acquired	0.74
1 December 2008 when dividends were declared	0.78
31 December 2008	0.80

What impact does the nature of Canadaco's net monetary asset or liability position have on the euro translated amounts?

Solution: Translation of Canadaco's 31 December 2008 balance sheet under the temporal method in Case A and Case B is shown below:

Canadaco Balance Sheet
31 December 2008
Temporal Method

	Case A: Net Monetary Liabilities			Case B: Net Monetary Assets		
	C$	**Exch. Rate**	**€**	**C$**	**Exch. Rate**	**€**
Assets						
Cash	980,000	0.80 C	784,000	980,000	0.80 C	784,000
Accounts receivable	900,000	0.80 C	720,000	900,000	0.80 C	720,000
Inventory	1,200,000	0.74 H	888,000	1,200,000	0.74 H	888,000
Total current assets	3,080,000		2,392,000	3,080,000		2,392,000
Property and equipment	3,000,000	0.70 H	2,100,000	3,000,000	0.70 H	2,100,000
Less: accum. deprec.	(300,000)	0.70 H	(210,000)	(300,000)	0.70 H	(210,000)
Total assets	5,780,000		4,282,000	5,780,000		4,282,000
Liabilities and Equity						
Accounts payable	450,000	0.80 C	360,000	450,000	0.80 C	360,000
Total current liabilities	450,000		360,000	450,000		360,000
Long-term notes pay	3,000,000	0.80 C	2,400,000	0		0
Total liabilities	3,450,000		2,760,000	450,000		360,000
Capital stock	1,500,000	0.70 H	1,050,000	4,500,000	0.70 H	3,150,000
Retained earnings	830,000		472,000	830,000		772,000
Total	5,780,000		4,282,000	5,780,000		4,282,000

Note: C = current exchange rate; A = average-for-the-year exchange rate; H = historical exchange rate

To keep the balance sheet in balance, retained earnings must be €472,000 in Case A (net monetary liability exposure) and €772,000 in Case B (net monetary asset exposure). The difference in retained earnings of €300,000 is equal to the translation loss that results from holding a C$ note payable during a period in which the C$ strengthens against the euro. This difference is determined by multiplying the amount of long-term note payable in Case A by the change in exchange rate during the year [C$3,000,000 × (€0.80 − €0.70) = C$300,000]. Notes payable are exposed to foreign exchange risk under the temporal method, whereas capital stock is not. Canadaco could avoid the €300,000 translation loss related to long-term debt by financing the acquisition of property and equipment with equity rather than debt.

Translation of Canadaco's 2008 income statement and statement of retained earnings under the temporal method for Case A and Case B is shown below:

Canadaco Income Statement and Statement of Retained Earnings 2008
Temporal Method

	Case A: Net Monetary Liabilities			Case B: Net Monetary Assets		
	C$	Exch. Rate	€	C$	Exch. Rate	€
Sales	12,000,000	0.75 A	9,000,000	12,000,000	0.75 A	9,000,000
Cost of goods sold	(9,000,000)	0.74 H	(6,660,000)	(9,000,000)	0.74 H	(6,660,000)
Selling expenses	(750,000)	0.75 A	(562,500)	(750,000)	0.75 A	(562,500)
Depreciation expense	(300,000)	0.70 H	(210,000)	(300,000)	0.70 H	(210,000)
Interest expense	(270,000)	0.75 A	(202,500)	(270,000)	0.75 A	(202,500)
Income tax	(500,000)	0.75 A	(375,000)	(500,000)	0.75 A	(375,000)
Income before translation gain (loss)	1,180,000		990,000	1,180,000		990,000
Translation gain (loss)	N/A		(245,000)	N/A		55,000
Net income	1,180,000		745,000	1,180,000		1,045,000
Less: Dividends on 1 December 2008	(350,000)	0.78 H	(273,000)	(350,000)	0.78 H	(273,000)
Retained earnings on 31 December 2008	830,000		472,000	830,000		772,000

Note: C = current exchange rate; A = average-for-the-year exchange rate; H = historical exchange rate

Income before translation gain (loss) is the same in both cases. To obtain the amount of retained earnings needed to keep the balance sheet in balance, a translation loss of €245,000 must be subtracted from net income in Case A (net monetary liabilities), whereas a translation gain of €55,000 must be added to net income in Case B (net monetary assets). The difference in net income between the two cases is €300,000, which is equal to the translation loss related to the long-term note payable.

When the temporal method is used, companies have more ability to manage their exposure to translation gain (loss) than when the current rate method is used. If a company can manage the balance sheet of a foreign subsidiary such that monetary assets equal monetary liabilities, no balance sheet exposure exists. Elimination of balance sheet exposure under the current rate method occurs only when total assets equal total liabilities. This is difficult to achieve because it would require the foreign subsidiary to have no stockholders' equity.

For Canadaco, in 2008, applying the current rate method results in larger euro amounts of total assets and total equity being reported in the consolidated financial statements than would result from applying the temporal method. The direction of these differences between the two translation methods is determined by the direction of change in the exchange rate between the Canadian dollar and the euro. For example, total exposed assets are greater under the current rate method because all assets are translated at the current exchange rate. The current exchange rate at 31 December 2008 is greater than the exchange rates that existed when the nonmonetary assets were acquired, which is the translation rate for these assets under the temporal method. Therefore, the current rate method results in a larger amount of total assets because the Canadian dollar strengthened against the euro. The current rate method would result in a smaller amount of total assets than the temporal method if the Canadian dollar had weakened against the euro.

Applying the current rate method also results in a much larger amount of stockholders' equity than the temporal method. A positive translation adjustment arises under the current rate method, which is included in equity, whereas a translation loss reduces total equity (through retained earnings) under the temporal method.

Example 6 shows the effect that the direction of change in the exchange rate has on the translated amounts. Canadaco's Canadian dollar financial statements are translated into euros, first assuming no change in the exchange rate during 2008, and then assuming the Canadian dollar strengthens and weakens against the euro. Using the current rate method to translate the foreign currency financial statements into the parent's presentation currency, the foreign currency strengthening increases the revenues, income, assets, liabilities, and total equity reported on the parent company's consolidated financial statements. Likewise, smaller amounts of revenues, income, assets, liabilities, and total equity would be reported if the foreign currency weakens against the parent's presentation currency.

When the temporal method is used to translate the foreign currency financial statements, foreign currency strengthening still increases revenues, assets, and liabilities reported in the parent's consolidated financial statements. Net income and stockholders' equity, however, translate into smaller amounts (assuming that the foreign subsidiary has a net monetary liability position) because of the translation loss. The opposite results are obtained when the foreign currency weakens against the parent's presentation currency.

EXAMPLE 6

Effect of Direction of Change in the Exchange Rate on Translated Amounts

Canadaco's Canadian dollar (C$) financial statements are translated into euros (€) under three assumptions: 1) the Canadian dollar remains stable against the euro, 2) the Canadian dollar strengthens against the euro, and 3) the Canadian dollar weakens against the euro. Relevant exchange rates are as follows:

	€ per C$		
Date	**Stable**	**Strengthens**	**Weakens**
1 January 2008	0.70	0.70	0.70
Average, 2008	0.70	0.75	0.65
Weighted average rate when inventory was acquired	0.70	0.74	0.66
Rate when dividends were declared	0.70	0.78	0.62
31 December 2008	0.70	0.80	0.60

What amounts will be reported on the parent's consolidated financial statements under the three different exchange rate assumptions if Canadaco's Canadian dollar financial statements are translated using the:

1. current rate method?
2. temporal method?

Solution to 1:

Current Rate Method: Using the current rate method, Canadaco's Canadian dollar financial statements would be translated into euros as follows under the three different exchange rate assumptions:

Canadaco Income Statement and Statement of Retained Earnings 2008
Current Rate Method

		C$ Stable		C$ Strengthens		C$ Weakens	
	C$	Exch. Rate	€	Exch. Rate	€	Exch. Rate	€
Sales	12,000,000	0.70	8,400,000	0.75 A	9,000,000	0.65 A	7,800,000
Cost of goods sold	(9,000,000)	0.70	(6,300,000)	0.75 A	(6,750,000)	0.65 A	(5,850,000)
Selling expenses	(750,000)	0.70	(525,000)	0.75 A	(562,500)	0.65 A	(487,500)
Deprec. expense	(300,000)	0.70	(210,000)	0.75 A	(225,000)	0.65 A	(195,000)
Interest expense	(270,000)	0.70	(189,000)	0.75 A	(202,500)	0.65 A	(175,500)
Income tax	(500,000)	0.70	(350,000)	0.75 A	(375,000)	0.65 A	(325,000)
Net income	1,180,000		826,000		885,000		767,000
Less: Dividends	(350,000)	0.70	(245,000)	0.78 H	(273,000)	0.62 H	(217,000)
Retained earnings	830,000		581,000		612,000		550,000

Note: C = current exchange rate; A = average-for-the-year exchange rate; H = historical exchange rate

Compared to the translated amount of sales and net income under a stable Canadian dollar assumption, a stronger Canadian dollar results in a larger amount of sales and net income being reported in the consolidated income statement, and a weaker Canadian dollar results in a smaller amount of sales and net income being reported in consolidated net income.

Canadaco Balance Sheet
31 December 2008
Current Rate Method

		C$ Stable		C$ Strengthens		C$ Weakens	
	C$	Exch. Rate	€	Exch. Rate	€	Exch. Rate	€
Assets							
Cash	980,000	0.70	686,000	0.80 C	784,000	0.60 C	588,000
Accounts receivable	900,000	0.70	630,000	0.80 C	720,000	0.60 C	540,000
Inventory	1,200,000	0.70	840,000	0.80 C	960,000	0.60 C	720,000
Total current assets	3,080,000		2,156,000		2,464,000		1,848,000
Property and equipment	3,000,000	0.70	2,100,000	0.80 C	2,400,000	0.60 C	1,800,000
Less: accum. deprec.	(300,000)	0.70	(210,000)	0.80 C	(240,000)	0.60 C	(180,000)
Total assets	5,780,000		4,046,000		4,624,000		3,468,000

(Continued on next page . . .)

(continued)

		C$ Stable		C$ Strengthens		C$ Weakens	
	C$	**Exch. Rate**	**€**	**Exch. Rate**	**€**	**Exch. Rate**	**€**
Liabilities and Equity							
Accounts payable	450,000	0.70	315,000	0.80 C	360,000	0.60 C	270,000
Total current liabilities	450,000		315,000		360,000		270,000
Long-term notes pay	3,000,000	0.70	2,100,000	0.80 C	2,400,000	0.60 C	1,800,000
Total liabilities	3,450,000		2,415,000		2,760,000		2,070,000
Capital stock	1,500,000	0.70	1,050,000	0.70 H	1,050,000	0.70 H	1,050,000
Retained earnings	830,000		581,000		612,000		550,000
Translation adjustment	N/A		0		202,000		(202,000)
Total equity	2,330,000		1,631,000		1,864,000		1,398,000
Total	5,780,000		4,046,000		4,624,000		3,468,000

Note: C = current exchange rate; A = average-for-the-year exchange rate; H = historical exchange rate

The translation adjustment is zero when the Canadian dollar remains stable for the year; it is positive when the Canadian dollar strengthens and negative when the Canadian dollar weakens. Compared to the amounts that would appear in the euro consolidated balance sheet under a stable Canadian dollar assumption, a stronger Canadian dollar results in a larger amount of assets, liabilities, and equity being reported on the consolidated balance sheet, and a weaker Canadian dollar results in a smaller amount of assets, liabilities, and equity being reported on the consolidated balance sheet.

Solution to 2:

Temporal Method: Using the temporal method, Canadaco's financial statements would be translated into euros as follows under the three different exchange rate assumptions:

Canadaco Balance Sheet 31 December 2008

		Temporal Method					
		C$ Stable		C$ Strengthens		C$ Weakens	
	C$	**Exch. Rate**	**€**	**Exch. Rate**	**€**	**Exch. Rate**	**€**
Assets							
Cash	980,000	0.70	686,000	0.80 C	784,000	0.60 C	588,000
Accounts receivable	900,000	0.70	630,000	0.80 C	720,000	0.60 C	540,000
Inventory	1,200,000	0.70	840,000	0.74 H	888,000	0.66 H	792,000
Total current assets	3,080,000		2,156,000		2,392,000		1,920,000

(Continued on next page . . .)

(continued)

	C$	C$ Stable Exch. Rate	C$ Stable €	C$ Strengthens Exch. Rate	C$ Strengthens €	C$ Weakens Exch. Rate	C$ Weakens €
Property and equipment	3,000,000	0.70	2,100,000	0.70 H	2,100,000	0.70 H	2,100,000
Less: accum. deprec.	(300,000)	0.70	(210,000)	0.70 H	(210,000)	0.70 H	(210,000)
Total assets	5,780,000		4,046,000		4,282,000		3,810,000
Liabilities and Equity							
Accounts payable	450,000	0.70	315,000	0.80 C	360,000	0.60 C	270,000
Total current liabilities	450,000		315,000		360,000		270,000
Long-term notes pay	3,000,000	0.70	2,100,000	0.80 C	2,400,000	0.60 C	1,800,000
Total liabilities	3,450,000		2,415,000		2,760,000		2,070,000
Capital stock	1,500,000	0.70	1,050,000	0.70 H	1,050,000	0.70 H	1,050,000
Retained earnings	830,000		581,000		472,000		690,000
Total equity	2,330,000		1,631,000		1,522,000		1,740,000
Total	5,780,000		4,046,000		4,282,000		3,810,000

Note: C = current exchange rate; A = average-for-the-year exchange rate; H = historical exchange rate

Compared to the stable Canadian dollar scenario, a stronger Canadian dollar results in a larger amount of assets and liabilities, but a smaller amount of equity reported on the consolidated balance sheet. A weaker Canadian dollar results in a smaller amount of assets and liabilities, but a larger amount of equity reported on the consolidated balance sheet.

Canadaco Income Statement and Statement of Retained Earnings 2008 Temporal Method

	C$	C$ Stable Exch. Rate	C$ Stable €	C$ Strengthens Exch. Rate	C$ Strengthens €	C$ Weakens Exch. Rate	C$ Weakens €
Sales	12,000,000	0.70	8,400,000	0.75 A	9,000,000	0.65 A	7,800,000
Cost of sales	(9,000,000)	0.70	(6,300,000)	0.74 H	(6,660,000)	0.66 H	(5,940,000)
Selling expenses	(750,000)	0.70	(525,000)	0.75 A	(562,500)	0.65 A	(487,500)
Depreciation expense	(300,000)	0.70	(210,000)	0.70 H	(210,000)	0.70 H	(210,000)
Interest expense	(270,000)	0.70	(189,000)	0.75 A	(202,500)	0.65 A	(175,500)
Income tax	(500,000)	0.70	(350,000)	0.75 A	(375,000)	0.65 A	(325,000)
Income before translation gain (loss)	1,180,000		826,000		990,000		662,000

(Continued on next page . . .)

(continued)

		C$ Stable		C$ Strengthens		C$ Weakens	
	C$	Exch. Rate	€	Exch. Rate	€	Exch. Rate	€
Translation gain (loss)	N/A		0		(245,000)		245,000
Net income	1,180,000		826,000		745,000		907,000
Less: Dividends	(350,000)	0.70	(245,000)	0.78 H	(273,000)	0.62 H	(217,000)
Retained earnings	830,000		581,000		472,000		690,000

Note: C = current exchange rate; A = average-for-the-year exchange rate; H = historical exchange rate

No translation gain or loss exists when the Canadian dollar remains stable during the year. Because the subsidiary has a net monetary liability exposure to changes in the exchange rate, a stronger Canadian dollar results in a translation loss and a weaker Canadian dollar results in a translation gain. Compared to a stable Canadian dollar, a stronger Canadian dollar results in a larger amount of sales and a smaller amount of net income reported on the consolidated income statement. This difference in direction is due to the translation loss that is included in net income. (As was demonstrated in Example 5, a translation gain would have resulted if the subsidiary had a net monetary asset exposure.) A weaker Canadian dollar results in a smaller amount of sales, but a larger amount of net income than if the Canadian dollar had remained stable.

Exhibit 5 summarizes the relationships illustrated in Examples 5 and 6, focusing on the typical effect that a strengthening or weakening of the foreign currency has on financial statement amounts compared to what these amounts would be if the foreign currency were to remain stable.

3.5 Translation when a Foreign Subsidiary Operates in a Hyperinflationary Economy

As noted earlier, IAS 21 and SFAS 52 differ substantially in their approach to translating the foreign currency financial statements of foreign entities operating in the currency of a hyperinflationary economy. SFAS 52 simply requires the foreign currency financial statements of such an entity to be translated as if the parent's currency is the functional currency, i.e., the temporal method must be used with the resulting translation gain or loss reported in net income. IAS 21 requires the foreign currency financial statements first to be restated for inflation using the procedures of IAS 29, and then the inflation-adjusted financial statements are translated using the current exchange rate.

IAS 29 requires the following procedures in adjusting financial statements for inflation:

EXHIBIT 5 Effect of Currency Exchange Rate Movement on Financial Statements

	Temporal Method, Net Monetary Liability Exposure	Temporal Method, Net Monetary Asset Exposure	Current Rate Method
Foreign currency strengthens relative to parent's presentation currency	↑ Revenues ↑ Assets ↑ Liabilities ↓ Net income ↓ Shareholders' equity Translation loss	↑ Revenues ↑ Assets ↑ Liabilities ↑ Net income ↑ Shareholders' equity Translation gain	↑ Revenues ↑ Assets ↑ Liabilities ↑ Net income ↑ Shareholders' equity Positive translation adjustment
Foreign currency weakens relative to parent's presentation currency	↓ Revenues ↓ Assets ↓ Liabilities ↑ Net income ↑ Shareholders' equity Translation gain	↓ Revenues ↓ Assets ↓ Liabilities ↓ Net income ↓ Shareholders' equity Translation loss	↓ Revenues ↓ Assets ↓ Liabilities ↓ Net income ↓ Shareholders' equity Negative translation adjustment

Balance Sheet

- Monetary assets and monetary liabilities are not restated because they are already expressed in terms of the monetary unit current at the balance sheet date. Monetary items consist of cash, receivables, and payables.
- Nonmonetary assets and nonmonetary liabilities are restated for changes in the general purchasing power of the monetary unit. Most nonmonetary items are carried at historical cost. In these cases, the restated cost is determined by applying to the historical cost the change in the general price index from the date of acquisition to the balance sheet date. Some nonmonetary items are carried at revalued amounts, for example, property, plant, and equipment revalued according to the allowed alternative treatment in IAS 16, "Property, Plant and Equipment." These items are restated from the date of revaluation.
- All components of stockholders' equity are restated by applying the change in the general price level from the beginning of the period or, if later, from the date of contribution to the balance sheet date.

Income Statement

- All income statement items are restated by applying the change in the general price index from the dates when the items were originally recorded to the balance sheet date.
- The net gain or loss in purchasing power that arises from holding monetary assets and monetary liabilities during a period of inflation is included in net income.

The procedures for adjusting financial statements for inflation are similar in concept to the procedures followed when using the temporal method for translation. By restating nonmonetary assets and liabilities along with stockholders' equity in terms of the general price level at the balance sheet date, these items are carried at their historical amount of purchasing power. Only the monetary items, which are not restated for inflation, are exposed to inflation risk. The effect of that exposure is reflected through the purchasing power gain or loss on the net monetary asset or liability position.

Holding cash and receivables during a period of inflation results in a **purchasing power loss**, whereas holding payables during inflation results in a **purchasing power gain**. This can be demonstrated through the following examples.

Assume that the general price index (GPI) at 1 January 2008 is 100; that is, a representative basket of goods and services can be purchased on that date for $100. At the end of 2008, the same basket of goods and services costs $120; thus, the country has experienced an inflation rate of 20 percent ([$120 − $100]/$100). Cash of $100 can be used to acquire one basket of goods at 1 January 2008. One year later, however, when the GPI stands at 120, the same $100 in cash can now purchase only 83.3 percent of a basket of goods and services. At the end of 2008 it now takes $120 to purchase the same amount as $100 could purchase at the beginning of the year. The difference between the amount of cash needed to purchase one market basket at year end ($120) and the amount actually held ($100) results in a purchasing power loss of $20 from holding cash of $100 during the year.

Borrowing money during a period of inflation increases purchasing power. Assume that a company expects to receive $120 in cash at the end of 2008. If it waits until the cash is received, the company will be able to purchase exactly 1.0 baskets of goods and services when the GPI stands at 120. If instead, the company borrows $120 at 1 January 2008 when the GPI is 100, it can acquire 1.2 baskets of goods and services. This results in a purchasing power gain of $20. Of course, there is an interest cost associated with the borrowing that offsets a portion of this gain.

A net purchasing power gain will arise when a company holds a greater amount of monetary liabilities than monetary assets, and a net purchasing power loss will result when the opposite situation exists. As such, purchasing power gains and losses are analogous to the translation gains and losses that arise when the currency is weakening in value and the temporal method of translation is applied.

Although the procedures required by SFAS 52 and IAS 21 for translating the foreign currency financial statements in high inflation countries are fundamentally different, the results, in a rare occurrence, can be very similar. Indeed, if the exchange rate between two currencies changes by exactly the same percentage amount as the change in the general price index in the highly inflationary country, then the two methodologies produce the same results. This is demonstrated in Example 7.

EXAMPLE 7

Translation of Foreign Currency Financial Statements of a Foreign Entity Operating in a High Inflation Country

ABC Company formed a subsidiary in a foreign country on 1 January 2008, through a combination of debt and equity financing. The foreign subsidiary acquired land on 1 January 2008, which it rents to a local farmer. The foreign subsidiary's financial statements for its first year of operations, in foreign currency units (FC), are as follows:

Foreign Subsidiary Income Statement

(in FC)	2008
Rent revenue	1,000
Interest expense	(250)
Net income	750

Foreign Subsidiary Balance Sheets

(in FC)	1 Jan 08	31 Dec 08
Cash	1,000	1,750
Land	9,000	9,000
Total	10,000	10,750
Note payable (5 percent)	5,000	5,000
Capital stock	5,000	5,000
Retained earnings	0	750
Total	10,000	10,750

The foreign country experienced significant inflation in 2008, especially in the second half of the year. The general price index during 2008 was:

1 January 2008	100
Average, 2008	125
31 December 2008	200

The rate of inflation in 2008 was 100 percent, and the foreign country clearly meets the definition of a highly inflationary economy under both IFRS and U.S. GAAP.

As a result of the high rate of inflation in the foreign country, the FC weakened substantially during the year relative to other currencies. Relevant exchange rates between ABC's presentation currency (U.S. dollars) and the FC during 2008 were:

	$ per FCU
1 January 2008	1.00
Average, 2008	0.80
31 December 2008	0.50

What amounts will ABC Company include in its consolidated financial statements for the year ended 31 December 2008 related to this foreign subsidiary?

Solution: Assuming that ABC Company wishes to prepare its consolidated financial statements in accordance with IFRS, the foreign subsidiary's 2008 financial statements would be restated for local inflation and then translated into ABC's presentation currency using the current rate method as follows:

	FC	Restatement Factor	Inflation-Adjusted FC	Exch. Rate	$
Cash	1,750	200/200	1,750	0.50	875
Land	9,000	200/100	18,000	0.50	9,000
Total	10,750		19,750		9,875
Note payable	5,000	200/200	5,000	0.50	2,500
Capital stock	5,000	200/100	10,000	0.50	5,000
Retained earnings	750		4,750	0.50	2,375
Total	10,750		19,750		9,875
Revenues	1,000	200/125	1,600	0.50	800
Interest expense	(250)	200/125	(400)	0.50	(200)
Subtotal	750		1,200		600
Purchasing power gain/loss			3,550	0.50	1,775
Net income			4,750		2,375

All financial statement items are restated to the GPI at 31 December 2008. The net purchasing power gain of FC 3,550 can be explained as follows:

Gain from holding note payable	FC 5,000 × (200 − 100)/100 =	FC 5,000
Loss from holding beginning balance in cash	−1,000 × (200 − 100)/100 =	(1,000)
Loss from increase in cash during the year	−750 × (200 − 125)/125 =	(450)
Net purchasing power gain (loss)		FC 3,550

Note that all inflation-adjusted FC amounts are translated at the current exchange rate, and thus no translation adjustment is needed.

Now assume that ABC Company wishes to comply with U.S. GAAP in preparing its consolidated financial statements. In that case, the foreign subsidiary's FC financial statements are translated into U.S. dollars using the temporal method, with the resulting translation gain/loss reported in net income, as follows:

	FC	Exch. Rate	$
Cash	1,750	0.50 C	875
Land	9,000	1.00 H	9,000
Total	10,750		9,875
Note payable	5,000	0.50 C	2,500
Capital stock	5,000	1.00 H	5,000
Retained earnings	750		2,375
Total	10,750		9,875

(continued on next page . . .)

	FC	Exch. Rate	$
Revenues	1,000	0.80 A	800
Interest expense	(250)	0.80 A	(200)
Subtotal	750		600
Translation gain*			1,775
Net income			2,375

* The dividend is zero and the increase in retained earnings is $2,375 (from the balance sheet); so, net income is $2,375, and thus the translation gain is $1,775.

Note: C = current exchange rate; A = average-for-the-year exchange rate; H = historical exchange rate

Application of the temporal method as required by U.S. GAAP in this situation results in exactly the same U.S. dollar amounts as were obtained under the restate/translate approach required by IFRS. The equivalence of results under the two approaches exists because of the exact one-to-one inverse relationship between the change in the GPI in the foreign country and the change in the dollar value of the FC, as predicted by the theory of purchasing power parity. The GPI doubled and the FC lost half its purchasing power, which caused the FC to lose half its value in dollar terms. To the extent that this relationship does not hold, and it rarely if ever does, the two different methodologies will generate different translated amounts. For example, if the 31 December 2008 exchange rate had adjusted to only $0.60 per FC (rather than $0.50 per FC), then translated net income would have been $2,050 under U.S. GAAP and $2,850 under IFRS.

3.6 Companies Use Both Translation Methods at the Same Time

Under both IFRS and U.S. GAAP it is possible that a multinational corporation will need to use both the current rate and the temporal methods of translation at a single point in time. This will be true when some foreign subsidiaries have a foreign currency as their functional currency (and therefore are translated using the current rate method) and other foreign subsidiaries have the parent's currency as their functional currency (and therefore are translated using the temporal method). As a result, the consolidated financial statements of a multinational corporation can reflect at the same time both a net translation gain or loss that is included in the determination of net income (from foreign subsidiaries translated using the temporal method) and a separate cumulative translation adjustment that is reported on the balance sheet in stockholders' equity (from foreign subsidiaries translated using the current rate method).

Exxon Mobil Corporation is an example of a company that has a mixture of foreign currency and parent currency functional currency subsidiaries, as evidenced by the following excerpt from its 2006 Annual Report:

> **Exxon Mobil Corporation, Note 1. Summary of Significant Accounting Policies Foreign Currency Translation.** The Corporation selects the functional reporting currency for its international subsidiaries based on the currency of the primary economic environment in which each subsidiary operates. Downstream and Chemical operations primarily use the local currency. However, the U.S. dollar is used in highly inflationary

> countries (primarily in Latin America) and Singapore, which predominantly sells into the U.S. dollar export market. Upstream operations which are relatively self-contained and integrated within a particular country, such as Canada, the United Kingdom, Norway and continental Europe, use the local currency. Some Upstream operations, primarily in Asia, West Africa, Russia and the Middle East, use the U.S. dollar because they predominantly sell crude and natural gas production into U.S. dollar-denominated markets. For all operations, gains or losses from remeasuring foreign currency transactions into the functional currency are included in income.

Because of the judgment involved in determining the functional currency of foreign operations, two companies operating in the same industry might apply this judgment differently. For example, while Exxon Mobil has identified the local currency as the functional currency for many of its international subsidiaries, Chevron Corporation has designated the U.S. dollar as the functional currency for substantially all of its overseas operations as indicated in the company's 2006 Annual Report:

> **Chevron Corporation, Note 1. Summary of Significant Accounting Policies Currency Translation.** The U.S. dollar is the functional currency for substantially all of the company's consolidated operations and those of its equity affiliates. For those operations, all gains and losses from currency translations are currently included in income. The cumulative translation effects for those few entities, both consolidated and affiliated, using functional currencies other than the U.S. dollar are included in the currency translation adjustment in "Stockholders' Equity."

Evaluating net income reported by Exxon Mobil against net income reported by Chevron presents a comparability problem. This problem can be partially resolved by adding the translation adjustments reported in stockholders' equity to net income for both companies. The feasibility of this solution is dependent on the level of detail disclosed by multinational corporations with respect to the translation of foreign currency financial statements.

3.7 Disclosures Related to Translation Methods

Both IAS 21 and SFAS 52 require two types of disclosures related to foreign currency translation:

1. the amount of exchange differences recognized in net income, and
2. the amount of cumulative translation adjustment classified in a separate component of equity, along with a reconciliation of the amount of cumulative translation adjustment at the beginning and end of the period.

SFAS 52 also specifically requires disclosure of the amount of translation adjustment transferred from stockholders' equity and included in current net income as a result of the disposal of a foreign entity.

The amount of exchange differences recognized in net income consists of

- foreign currency *transaction* gains and losses, and
- *translation* gains and losses resulting from application of the temporal method.

Neither IAS 21 nor SFAS 52 requires disclosure of the two separate amounts that comprise the total exchange difference recognized in net income, and most companies do not provide disclosure at that level of detail. However, BASF AG (shown in Exhibit 1) is an exception. Note 5 in BASF's annual report separately discloses gains from foreign currency transactions and gains from translation of financial statements, both of which are included in the line item "Other Operating Income" on the income statement, as shown below:

5. Other Operating Income

Million €	**2006**	**2005**
Reversal and adjustment of provisions	275.2	118.4
Revenue from miscellaneous revenue-generating activities	62.3	85.3
Gains from foreign currency transactions	119.7	43.3
Gains from the translation of financial statements in foreign currencies	10.8	57.3
Gains from disposal of property, plant and equipment and divestitures	127.8	107.4
Gains on the reversal of allowance for doubtful receivables	89.0	92.1
Other	249.3	96.4
	934.1	600.2

The company provides a similar level of detail in Note 6 related to "Other Operating Expenses."

Disclosures related to foreign currency translation commonly are found in both the Management Discussion & Analysis (MD&A) and the Notes to Financial Statements sections of an annual report. Exhibit 6 provides foreign currency-related disclosures made by Swedish appliance manufacturer Electrolux AB in its 2006 annual report along with an analysis of those disclosures. As a company based in the European Union, Electrolux uses IFRS in preparing its consolidated financial statements.

EXHIBIT 6 Disclosures Related to Foreign Currency Translation: Electrolux AB 2006 Annual Report

Electrolux provides the following information related to exchange rate exposure in its discussion of Financial Risks and Commitment in the MD&A:

Exchange-rate exposure

Operations in a number of different countries throughout the world expose Electrolux to the effects of changes in exchange rates. These affect Group income through translation of income statements in foreign subsidiaries to SEK, i.e., translation exposure, as well as through exports of products and sales outside the country of manufacture, i.e., transaction exposure.

Translation exposure is related mainly to EUR and USD. Transaction exposure is greatest in EUR, USD, GBP and HUF. The Group's global presence and widespread production and sales enable exchange-rate effects to be balanced.

The last sentence suggests that natural hedges exist among Electrolux's different exchange rate exposures that results in a relatively small *net* gain or loss arising from fluctuations in exchange rates.

(Exhibit continued on next page . . .)

EXHIBIT 6 (continued)

Note 1, Accounting and Valuation Principles, discloses the principles used by the company to account for foreign currency translation:

Foreign currency translations

Foreign currency transactions are translated into the functional currency using the exchange rates prevailing at the dates of the transactions.

The consolidated financial statements are presented in SEK, which is the Parent Company's functional and presentation currency.

The balance sheets of foreign subsidiaries have been translated into SEK at year-end rates. The income statements have been translated at the average rates for the year. Translation differences thus arising have been taken directly to equity.

Prior to consolidation, the financial statements of subsidiaries in countries with highly inflationary economies and whose functional currency is other than the local currency have been remeasured into their functional currency and the exchange-rate differences arising from that remeasurement have been charged to income. When the functional currency is the local currency, the financial statements have been restated in accordance with IAS 29. When a foreign operation is partially disposed of or sold, exchange differences that were recorded in equity are recognized in the income statement as part of the gain or loss on sales.

Monetary assets and liabilities in foreign currency

Monetary assets and liabilities denominated in foreign currency are valued at year-end exchange rates and the exchange-rate differences are included in the income statement, except when deferred in equity for the effective part of a qualifying net investment hedge.

Exposure from net investments (balance sheet exposure)

The net of assets and liabilities in foreign subsidiaries constitute a net investment in foreign currency, which generates a translation difference in connection with consolidation. This exposure can have an impact on the Group's equity, and on the capital structure, and is hedged according to the Financial Policy. The Financial Policy stipulates the extent to which the net investments can be hedged and also sets the benchmark for risk measurement. The benchmark was changed at the end of 2006 and only investments with an equity capitalization exceeding 60% are hedged unless the exposure is considered too high by the Group. The result of this change is that only a limited number of currencies are hedged on a continuous basis. Group Treasury is allowed to deviate from the benchmark under a given risk mandate. Hedging of the Group's net investments is implemented within the Parent Company in Sweden.

Notes 4 and 9 indicate that the company includes exchange rate differences as components of both operating income and financial income and expense. Note 9, Financial Income and Financial Expenses, discloses that: *Exchange-rate differences on foreign currency loans and borrowings, net* amounted to SEK 46 million in 2006 (approximately 1.2 percent of pretax income). These are one type of transaction gain or loss.

Note 4, Net Sales and Operating Income, indicates that in 2006: *The Group's operating income includes net-exchange-rate differences in the amount of SEK 76 million.* This represented approximately 2 percent of pretax income. Although not explicitly stated, the amount of exchange rate difference included in operating income presumably includes both transaction gains and losses related to foreign currency accounts payable and accounts receivable as well as translation gains and losses related to those foreign subsidiaries whose financial statements are translated using the temporal method.

(Exhibit continued on next page . . .)

EXHIBIT 6 (continued)

Note 1 shown above indicates that translation differences arising from the translation of the foreign currency financial statements of local currency functional currency subsidiaries are taken directly to equity. The equity section of the consolidated balance sheet is as follows:

Equity Attributable to Equity Holders of the Parent Company (SEK in Millions)	Note	31 December 2006	31 December 2005
Share capital	20	1,545	1,545
Other paid-in capital		2,905	2,905
Other reserves	18	−11	1,653
Retained earnings		8,754	19,784
		13,193	**25,887**
Minority interests		1	1
Total equity		13,194	25,888

Note 18 reveals that translation differences are included in "Other reserves" as a "Currency translation reserve" as shown below:

Note 18, Other Reserves in Equity

	Other Reserves			
(SEK in Millions)	Available-for-Sale Instruments	Hedging Reserve	Currency Translation Reserve	Total Other Reserves
Opening balance, 1 January 2005			(489)	(489)
Effects of changes in accounting principles		7		7
Opening balance, 1 January 2005, after adoption of IAS 32 and IAS 39		7	(489)	(482)
Available-for-sale instruments				
Gain/loss taken to equity	24			24
Cash flow hedges				
Gain/loss taken to equity		16		16
Transferred to profit and loss on sale		(7)		(7)
Exchange differences on translation of foreign operations				–
Equity hedge			(615)	(615)
Translation difference			2,717	2,717
Net income recognized directly in equity	24	9	2,102	2,135
Closing balance, 31 December 2005	24	16	1,613	1,653

(Exhibit continued on next page . . .)

EXHIBIT 6 (continued)

(SEK in Millions)	Other Reserves: Available-for-Sale Instruments	Hedging Reserve	Currency Translation Reserve	Total Other Reserves
Available-for-sale instruments				
Gain/loss taken to equity	30			30
Cash flow hedges				
Gain/loss taken to equity		(34)		(34)
Transferred to profit and loss on sale				
Exchange differences on translation of foreign operations				
Equity hedge			421	421
Translation difference	—	—	(2,081)	(2,081)
Net income recognized directly in equity	30	(34)	(1,660)	(1,664)
Closing balance, 31 December 2006	54	(18)	(47)	(11)

The opening balance in the currency translation reserve on 1 January 2005 was a negative SEK 489 million. The translation adjustment in 2005 was a positive SEK 2,717 million. Assuming that most if not all of Electrolux's foreign subsidiaries have more assets than liabilities, the positive sign of the adjustment suggests that, on average, the functional currencies in which the company's foreign subsidiaries operate strengthened against the Swedish krona (SEK) in 2005. The opposite is true in 2006 as evidenced by the negative translation difference of SEK 2,081 million. The currency translation reserve also includes amounts related to equity hedges. Although there is no further description of these items, it is reasonable to assume that these reflect the gains and losses on financial instruments used to hedge the translation differences related to balance sheet exposure. The effect of the equity hedges is of the opposite sign from the translation difference in each year indicating that the hedges were effective in partially offsetting the translation difference. Nonetheless, the balance in the currency translation reserve fluctuates greatly from year-to-year; from SEK −489 million at 31 December 04 to SEK +1,613 million at 31 December 05 and SEK −47 million at 31 December 06.

Exhibit 7 provides an analysis of the foreign currency-related disclosures made in 2006 by Yahoo! Inc., a U.S.-based company that prepares financial statements in accordance with U.S. GAAP.

As noted in the previous section, because of the judgment involved in determining the functional currency of foreign operations, two companies operating in the same industry might use different predominant translation methods. As a result, income reported by these companies is not directly comparable. Exxon Mobil Corporation and Chevron Corporation, both operating in the petroleum industry, are an example of two companies for which this is the case. Whereas Chevron has identified the U.S. dollar as the functional currency for substantially all of its foreign subsidiaries, Exxon Mobil indicates that its downstream and chemical operations, as well as some of its upstream operations, primarily use the local currency as the functional currency. As a result Chevron primarily uses the temporal method with translation gains and losses included in income,

EXHIBIT 7 Disclosures Related to Foreign Currency Translation: Yahoo! Inc. 2006 Annual Report

Yahoo! Inc. is a U.S.-based provider of internet services. In the Management Discussion & Analysis section of the 2006 Annual Report, the company reports that 32 percent of revenues are generated from international operations, up from 30 percent in 2005 and 28 percent in 2004 (p. 44). As part of its Quantitative and Qualitative Disclosures about Market Risk, the company states that:

> The growth in our international operations has increased our exposure to foreign currency fluctuations. Revenues and related expenses generated from our international subsidiaries are generally denominated in the functional currencies of the local countries. Primary currencies include Euros, British Pounds, Japanese Yen, Korean Won and Australian Dollars. The statements of income of our international operations are translated into United States dollars at the average exchange rate in each applicable period. To the extent the United States dollar strengthens against foreign currencies, the translation of these foreign currency denominated transactions results in reduced revenues, operating expense and net income for our International segment. Similarly, our revenues, operating expenses and net income will increase for our International segment, if the United States dollar weakens against foreign currencies.

Note that Yahoo! describes its foreign currency risk from the perspective of how the U.S. dollar fluctuates against foreign currencies. If the U.S. dollar strengthens, then foreign currencies must weaken, which will result in reduced revenues, expenses, and income from foreign operations.

The stockholders' equity section of Yahoo!'s consolidated balance sheet includes the following line item, in which several types of unrealized gains and losses have been accumulated:

	31 December	
	2005	**2006**
Accumulated other comprehensive income (loss)	(35,965)	150,505

The consolidated statement of stockholders' equity provides detail on the components comprising Accumulated other comprehensive income (loss). The relevant portion of that statement appears below:

	Years Ended 31 December		
	2004	**2005**	**2006**
Accumulated other comprehensive income (loss)			
Balance, beginning of year	3,598	535,736	(35,965)
Net change in unrealized gains/losses on available-for-sale securities, net of tax	471,425	(491,532)	38,018
Foreign currency translation adjustments, net of tax	60,713	(80,169)	148,452
Balance, end of year	535,736	(35,965)	150,505

The foreign currency translation adjustments arise from applying the current rate method to translate the foreign currency functional currency financial statements of foreign subsidiaries. Assuming that Yahoo!'s foreign subsidiaries have positive net assets, the negative translation adjustment in 2005 is the result of a weakening in the foreign functional currencies in which Yahoo!'s foreign subsidiaries operate. Conversely, this can

(Exhibit continued on next page . . .)

EXHIBIT 7 (continued)

be viewed as a strengthening in the U.S. dollar. The positive translation adjustment in 2006 results from a strengthening in foreign currencies (weakening in the U.S. dollar). If these translation adjustments had been included in the calculation of income, net income would have been as follows:

	2005	2006	% Change
Net income	$1,896,230	$751,391	−60.4
Foreign currency translation adjustment	(80,169)	148,452	
	$1,816,061	$899,843	−50.5

The percentage decrease in reported net income from 2005 to 2006 of 60.4 percent would have been somewhat smaller if the translation adjustments had been treated as gains and losses in net income.

while Exxon Mobil uses the current rate method to a much greater extent, with the resulting translation adjustments excluded from income. To make the income of these two companies more comparable, an analyst can use the disclosures related to translation adjustments to include these as gains and losses in determining an adjusted amount of income. Example 8 demonstrates this process for Exxon Mobil and Chevron.

EXAMPLE 8

Comparing Net Income for Exxon Mobil Corporation and Chevron Corporation

Exxon Mobil Corporation uses the current rate method to translate the foreign currency financial statements of a substantial number of its foreign subsidiaries and includes the resulting translation adjustments in the "Accumulated other nonowner changes in equity" line item in the stockholders' equity section of the consolidated balance sheet. Detail on the items composing "Accumulated other nonowner changes in equity," including "Foreign exchange translation adjustment," is provided in the consolidated statement of shareholders' equity.

Chevron Corporation uses the temporal method to translate the foreign currency financial statements of substantially all of its foreign subsidiaries. However, for those few entities using functional currencies other than the U.S. dollar, the current rate method is used and the resulting translation adjustments are included in the "Accumulated other comprehensive loss" component of stockholders' equity. The consolidated statement of stockholders' equity provides detail on the changes in the component of stockholders' equity, including a "Currency translation adjustment."

Combining net income from the income statement and the change in the cumulative translation adjustment account from the statement of stockholders' equity, an adjusted net income in which translation adjustments are treated as gains and losses can be calculated for each company as shown in the table below (amounts in millions of U.S. dollars):

Exxon Mobil	2006	2005	2004
Reported net income	39,500	36,130	25,330
Translation adjustment	2,754	(2,619)	2,177
Adjusted net income	42,254	33,511	27,507

Chevron	2006	2005	2004
Reported net income	17,138	14,099	13,328
Translation adjustment	55	(5)	36
Adjusted net income	17,193	14,094	13,364

The sign (positive or negative) of the translation adjustment is the same for both companies in each of the years 2004–2006. But Exxon Mobil has significantly larger translation adjustments than Chevron because Exxon Mobil designates the local currency as functional currency for a substantially larger portion of its foreign operations.

A comparison of the relative amounts of net income generated by the two companies is different depending on whether reported net income or adjusted net income is used. Exxon Mobil's reported net income in 2004 is 1.90 times larger than Chevron's, whereas its adjusted net income is 2.06 times larger. This is shown in the table below, which also shows that the year-to-year percentage change in the ratio of net income between the two companies differs significantly depending on the income measure used. For example, based on reported net income, the ratio of net income decreased from 2005 to 2006 by 10 percent (from 2.56 down to 2.30); based on adjusted net income, the ratio increased from 2005 to 2006 by 3 percent (from 2.38 to 2.46).

	2006	2005	2004
Exxon Mobil reported net income/ Chevron reported net income	2.30	2.56	1.90
Year-to-year % change	−10%	+35%	
Exxon Mobil adjusted net income/ Chevron adjusted net income	2.46	2.38	2.06
Year-to-year % change	+3%	+16%	

Including translation adjustments as gains and losses in the measurement of an adjusted net income provides a more comparable basis for evaluating the profitability of two companies that are using different predominant translation methods. However, bringing the translation adjustments into the calculation of adjusted net income still might not provide truly comparable measures because of the different impact that the different translation methods have on reported net income. For example, both Exxon Mobil and Chevron reported a positive translation adjustment in 2006 because foreign currencies generally strengthened against the U.S. dollar that year. Assuming Chevron's U.S. dollar functional currency foreign subsidiaries mostly had net monetary liability positions, application of the temporal method in a year in which foreign currencies strengthened against the U.S. dollar resulted in a net translation loss that was included in net income. Because Exxon Mobil, on the other hand, has designated many of its foreign subsidiaries as foreign currency functional currency operations, a similar loss would not be recognized; instead a positive translation adjustment would result (knowing that Exxon has positive net assets). All else equal, Chevron's 2006 adjusted net income is likely to be less than Exxon Mobil's adjusted net income simply because Chevron has designated a larger portion of its foreign operations as having the U.S. dollar as the functional currency.

Some analysts believe that all nonowner changes in stockholders' equity, such as translation adjustments, should be included in the determination of net income. This is referred to as **clean-surplus accounting**, as opposed to **dirty-surplus accounting**, in which some income items are reported as part of stockholders' equity rather than as gains and losses on the income statement. One of the **dirty-surplus items** found in both IFRS and U.S. GAAP financial statements is the translation adjustment that arises when a foreign currency is determined to be the functional currency of a foreign subsidiary. Disclosures made in accordance with IFRS and U.S. GAAP provide analysts with the detail needed to be able to calculate net income on a clean-surplus basis. In fact, both sets of standards allow (but do not specifically require) companies to prepare a statement of comprehensive income in which unrealized gains and losses that have been deferred in stockholders' equity are included in a measure of comprehensive income. Chevron Corporation is one U.S. company that has elected to prepare a statement of comprehensive income. Exhibit 8 presents Chevron's consolidated statement of comprehensive income as shown in the company's 2006 annual report.

EXHIBIT 8 Excerpt from Chevron Corporation 2006 Annual Report Consolidated Statement of Comprehensive Income

	Year Ended 31 December		
Millions of Dollars	**2006**	**2005**	**2004**
Net income	$17,138	$14,099	$13,328
Currency translation adjustment			
Unrealized net change arising during period	55	(5)	36
Unrealized holding (loss) gain on securities			
Net (loss) gain arising during period	(88)	(32)	35
Reclassification to net income of net realized (gain)	–	–	(44)
Total	(88)	(32)	(9)
Net derivatives gain (loss) on hedge transactions			
Net gain (loss) arising during period			
Before income taxes	2	(242)	(8)
Income taxes	6	89	(1)
Reclassification to net income of net realized gain (loss)			
Before income taxes	95	34	–
Income taxes	(36)	(12)	–
Total	67	(131)	(9)
Minimum pension liability adjustment			
Before income taxes	(88)	89	719
Income taxes	50	(31)	(247)
Total	(38)	58	472
Other comprehensive (loss) gain, net of tax	(4)	(110)	490
Comprehensive income	$17,134	$13,989	$13,818

Chevron has four "dirty-surplus items" that are required under U.S. GAAP to be reported as "other comprehensive income" in stockholders' equity rather than as gains and losses in net income. In the statement of comprehensive income, these items are added to net income to determine comprehensive income. The first of these four items is the currency translation adjustment that arises when the current rate method is used to translate the foreign currency financial statements of those foreign operations that have been determined to have a foreign currency as their functional currency.

SUMMARY

The translation of foreign currency amounts is an important accounting issue for companies with multinational operations. Fluctuations in foreign exchange rates cause the functional currency values of foreign currency assets and liabilities resulting from foreign currency transactions as well as from foreign subsidiaries to change over time, giving rise to foreign exchange differences that must be reflected in the financial statements. Determining how to measure these foreign exchange differences and whether to include them in the calculation of net income are the major issues in accounting for multinational operations.

- The local currency is the national currency of the country where an entity is located. The functional currency is the currency of the primary economic environment in which an entity operates. Normally, the local currency is an entity's functional currency. For accounting purposes, any currency other than an entity's functional currency is a foreign currency for that entity. The currency in which financial statement amounts are presented is known as the presentation currency. In most cases, the presentation currency will be the same as the local currency.
- When an export sale (import purchase) on account is denominated in a foreign currency, the sales revenue (inventory) and foreign currency account receivable (account payable) are translated into the seller's (buyer's) functional currency using the exchange rate on the transaction date. Any change in the functional currency value of the foreign currency account receivable (account payable) that occurs from the transaction date to the settlement date is recognized as a foreign currency transaction gain or loss in net income.
- If a balance sheet date falls between the transaction date and the settlement date, the foreign currency account receivable (account payable) is translated at the exchange rate at the balance sheet date. The change in the functional currency value of the foreign currency account receivable (account payable) is recognized as a foreign currency transaction gain or loss in income. Analysts should understand that these gains and losses are unrealized at the time they are recognized, and might or might not be realized when the transactions are settled.
- A foreign currency transaction gain arises when an entity has a foreign currency receivable and the foreign currency strengthens or it has a foreign currency payable and the foreign currency weakens. A foreign currency transaction loss arises when an entity has a foreign currency receivable and the foreign currency weakens or it has a foreign currency payable and the foreign currency strengthens.
- Companies must disclose the net foreign currency gain or loss included in income. They may choose to report foreign currency transaction gains and losses as a component of operating income or as a component of non-operating income. If two companies choose to report foreign currency transaction gains and losses differently, making a direct comparison of operating profit and operating profit margin between the two companies is questionable.
- To prepare consolidated financial statements, foreign currency financial statements of foreign operations must be translated into the parent company's presentation currency. The major conceptual issues related to

this translation process are what is the appropriate exchange rate for translating each financial statement item and how should the resulting translation adjustment be reflected in the consolidated financial statements. Two different translation methods are used worldwide.

- Under the current rate method, assets and liabilities are translated at the current exchange rate, equity items are translated at historical exchange rates, and revenues and expenses are translated at the exchange rate that existed when the underlying transaction occurred. For practical reasons, an average exchange rate is often used to translate income items.
- Under the temporal method, monetary assets (and nonmonetary assets measured at current value) and monetary liabilities (and nonmonetary liabilities measured at current value) are translated at the current exchange rate. Nonmonetary assets and liabilities not measured at current value and equity items are translated at historical exchange rates. Revenues and expenses, other than those expenses related to nonmonetary assets, are translated at the exchange rate that existed when the underlying transaction occurred. Expenses related to nonmonetary assets are translated at the exchange rates used for the related assets.
- Under both IFRS and U.S. GAAP, the functional currency of a foreign operation determines the method to be used in translating its foreign currency financial statements into the parent's presentation currency and whether the resulting translation adjustment is recognized in income or as a separate component of equity.
- The foreign currency financial statements of a foreign operation that has a foreign currency as its functional currency are translated using the current rate method and the translation adjustment is accumulated as a separate component of equity. The cumulative translation adjustment related to a specific foreign entity is transferred to net income when that entity is sold or otherwise disposed of. The balance sheet risk exposure associated with the current rate method is equal to the foreign subsidiary's net asset position.
- The foreign currency financial statements of a foreign operation that has the parent's presentation currency as its functional currency are translated using the temporal method and the translation adjustment is included as a gain or loss in income. U.S. GAAP refers to this process as remeasurement. The balance sheet exposure associated with the temporal method is equal to the foreign subsidiary's net monetary asset/liability position (adjusted for nonmonetary items measured at current value).
- IFRS and U.S. GAAP differ with respect to the translation of foreign currency financial statements of foreign operations located in a highly inflationary country. Under IFRS, the foreign currency statements are first restated for local inflation and then translated using the current exchange rate. Under U.S. GAAP, the foreign currency financial statements are translated using the temporal method, without any restatement for inflation.
- Application of the different translation methods for a given foreign operation can result in very different amounts reported in the parent's consolidated financial statements.
- Companies must disclose the total amount of translation gain or loss reported in income and the amount of translation adjustment included in a separate component of stockholders' equity. Companies are not required

to separately disclose the component of translation gain or loss arising from foreign currency transactions and the component arising from application of the temporal method.

- Disclosures related to translation adjustments reported in equity can be used to include these as gains and losses in determining an adjusted amount of income following a clean-surplus approach to income measurement.

Foreign currency translation rules are well-established in both IFRS and U.S. GAAP. Fortunately, except for the treatment of foreign operations located in highly inflationary countries, there are no major differences between the two sets of standards in this area. The ability to understand the impact of foreign currency translation on the financial results of a company using IFRS should apply equally as well in the analysis of financial statements prepared in accordance with U.S. GAAP.

PRACTICE PROBLEMS FOR READING 25

The following information relates to Questions 1–6

Pedro Ruiz is an analyst for a credit rating agency. One of the companies he follows, Eurexim SA, is based in France and complies with International Financial Reporting Standards (IFRS). Ruiz has learned that Eurexim used €220 million of its own cash and borrowed an equal amount to open a subsidiary in Ukraine. The funds were converted into hryvnia (UAH) on 31 December 2007 at an exchange rate of €1.00 = UAH 6.70 and used to purchase UAH 1,500 million in fixed assets and UAH 300 of inventories.

Ruiz is concerned about the effect that the subsidiary's results might have on Eurexim's consolidated financial statements. He calls Eurexim's Chief Financial Officer, but learns little. Eurexim is not willing to share sales forecasts and has not even made a determination as to the subsidiary's functional currency.

Absent more useful information, Ruiz decides to explore various scenarios to determine the potential impact on Eurexim's consolidated financial statements. Ukraine is not currently in a hyperinflationary environment, but Ruiz is concerned that this situation could change. Ruiz also believes the euro will appreciate against the hryvnia for the foreseeable future.

1. If Ukraine's economy becomes highly inflationary, Eurexim will *most likely* translate inventory by:

A. restating for inflation and using the temporal method.

B. restating for inflation and using the current rate method.

C. using the temporal method with no restatement for inflation.

2. Given Ruiz's belief about the direction of exchange rates, Eurexim's gross profit margin would be *highest* if it accounts for the Ukraine subsidiary's inventory using:

A. FIFO and the temporal method.

B. weighted average cost and the temporal method.

C. FIFO and the current rate method.

3. If the euro is chosen as the Ukraine subsidiary's functional currency, Eurexim will translate its fixed assets using the:

A. average rate for the reporting period.

B. rate in effect when the assets were purchased.

C. rate in effect at the end of the reporting period.

4. If the euro is chosen as the Ukraine subsidiary's functional currency, Eurexim will translate its accounts receivable using the:

A. rate in effect at the transaction date.

B. average rate for the reporting period.

C. rate in effect at the end of the reporting period.

5. If the hryvnia is chosen as the Ukraine subsidiary's functional currency, Eurexim will translate its inventory using the:

A. average rate for the reporting period.

B. rate in effect at the end of the reporting period.

C. rate in effect at the time the inventory was purchased.

6. Based on the information available and Ruiz's expectations regarding exchange rates, if the hryvnia is chosen as the Ukraine subsidiary's functional currency, Eurexim will *most likely* report:

A. an addition to the cumulative translation adjustment.

B. a subtraction from the cumulative translation adjustment.

C. a translation gain or loss as a component of net income.

The following information relates to Questions 7–12

Consolidated Motors is a U.S.-based corporation that sells mechanical engines and components used by electric utilities. Its Canadian subsidiary, Consol-Can, operates solely in Canada. It was created on 31 December 2006 and Consolidated Motors determined at that time that it should use the U.S. dollar as its functional currency.

Chief Financial Officer Monica Templeton was asked to explain to the Board of Directors how exchange rates affect the financial statements of both Consol-Can and the consolidated financial statements of Consolidated Motors. For the presentation, Templeton collects Consol-Can's balance sheets for the years ended 2006 and 2007 (Exhibit 1), as well as relevant exchange rate information (Exhibit 2).

EXHIBIT 1 Consol-Can Condensed Balance Sheet Fiscal Years Ending 31 December (Canadian $, in Millions)

Account	2007	2006
Cash	135	167
Accounts receivable	98	–
Inventory	77	30
Fixed assets	100	100
Accumulated depreciation	(10)	–
Total assets	400	297
Accounts payable	77	–
Long-term debt	175	175
Common stock	100	100
Retained earnings	48	–
Total liabilities and shareholders' equity	400	275

EXHIBIT 2 Exchange Rate Information

	U.S. $/Canadian $
Rate on 31 December 2006	0.86
Average rate in 2007	0.92
Weighted average rate for inventory purchases	0.92
Rate on 31 December 2007	0.95

Templeton explains that Consol-Can uses the FIFO inventory accounting method, and that purchases of C$300 million and the sell-through of that inventory occurred evenly throughout 2007. Her presentation includes reporting the translated amounts in U.S. currency for each item, as well as associated translation-related gains and losses. The Board responds with several questions.

- Would there be a reason to change the functional currency to the Canadian dollar?
- Would there be any translation effects for Consolidated Motors if the functional currency for Consol-Can were changed to the Canadian dollar?
- Would a change in the functional currency have any impact on financial statement ratios for the parent company?
- What would be the balance sheet exposure to translation effects if the functional currency were changed?

7. After translating Consol-Can's inventory and long-term debt into the parent currency (US$), the amounts reported on Consolidated Motor's financial statements at 31 December 2007 would be *closest* to (in millions):

A. $71 for inventory and $161 for long-term debt.

B. $71 for inventory and $166 for long-term debt.

C. $73 for inventory and $166 for long-term debt.

8. After translating Consol-Can's 31 December 2007 balance sheet into the parent currency, the translated value of retained earnings will be *closest* to:

A. $41 million.

B. $44 million.

C. $46 million.

9. In response to the Board's first question, Templeton should reply that such a change would be *most* justified if:

A. the inflation rate in the United States became hyperinflationary.

B. management wanted to flow more of the gains through net income.

C. Consol-Can were making autonomous decisions about operations, investing, and financing.

10. In response to the Board's second question, Templeton should note that if the change is made, the consolidated financial statements for Consolidated Motors would begin to recognize:

A. realized gains and losses on monetary assets and liabilities.

B. realized gains and losses on nonmonetary assets and liabilities.

C. unrealized gains and losses on nonmonetary assets and liabilities.

11. In response to the Board's third question, Templeton should note that the change will *most likely* affect:

A. the cash ratio.

B. fixed asset turnover.

C. receivables turnover.

12. In response to the Board's fourth question, the balance sheet exposure (in C$ millions) would be *closest* to:

A. −19.

B. 148.

C. 400.

The following information relates to Questions 13–18

Romulus Corp. is a U.S.-based company that prepares its financial statements in accordance with U.S. GAAP. Romulus Corp. has two European subsidiaries: Julius and Augustus. Anthony Marks, CFA, is an analyst trying to forecast Romulus's 2008 results. Marks has prepared separate forecasts for both Julius and Augustus, as well as for Romulus's other operations (prior to consolidating the results.) He is now considering the impact of currency translation on the results of both the subsidiaries and the parent company's consolidated financials. His research has provided the following insights:

- The results for Julius will be translated into U.S. dollars using the current rate method.
- The results for Augustus will be translated into U.S. dollars using the temporal method.
- Both Julius and Augustus use the FIFO method to account for inventory.
- Julius had year-end 2007 inventory of €340 million. Marks believes Julius will report €2,300 in sales and €1,400 in cost of sales in 2008.

Marks also forecasts the 2008 year-end balance sheet for Julius (Exhibit 1). Data and forecasts related to euro/dollar exchange rates are presented in Exhibit 2.

EXHIBIT 1 Forecasted Balance Sheet Data for Julius 31 December 2008 (€ Millions)

Cash	50
Accounts receivable	100
Inventory	700
Fixed assets	1,450
Total assets	2,300
Liabilities	700
Common stock	1,500
Retained earnings	100
Total liabilities and shareholder equity	2,300

EXHIBIT 2 Exchange Rates ($/€)

31 December 2007	1.47
31 December 2008	1.61
2008 average	1.54
Rate when fixed assets were acquired	1.25
Rate when 2007 inventory was acquired	1.39
Rate when 2008 inventory was acquired	1.49

13. Based on the translation method being used for Julius, the subsidiary is *most likely*:

A. a sales outlet for Romulus's products.

B. a self-contained, independent operating entity.

C. using the U.S. dollar as its functional currency.

14. To account for its foreign operations, Romulus has *most likely* designated the euro as the functional currency for:

A. Julius only.

B. Augustus only.

C. both Julius and Augustus.

15. When Romulus consolidates the results of Julius, any unrealized exchange rate holding gains on monetary assets should be:

A. reported as part of operating income.

B. reported as a nonoperating item on the income statement.

C. reported directly to equity as part of the cumulative translation adjustment.

16. When Marks translates his forecasted balance sheet for Julius into U.S. dollars, total assets at 31 December 2008 (dollars in millions) will be *closest* to:

A. $1,429.

B. $2,392.

C. $3,703.

17. When Marks converts his forecasted income statement data into U.S. dollars, the 2008 gross profit margin for Julius will be *closest* to:

A. 39.1 percent.

B. 40.9 percent.

C. 44.6 percent.

18. Relative to the gross margins the subsidiaries report in local currency, Romulus's consolidated gross margin *most likely*:

A. will not be distorted by currency translations.

B. would be distorted if Augustus were using the same translation method as Julius.

C. will be distorted due to the translation and inventory accounting methods Augustus is using.

The following information relates to Questions 19–24

Redline Products, Inc. is a U.S.-based multinational with subsidiaries around the world. One such subsidiary, Acceletron, operates in Singapore, which has seen mild but not excessive rates of inflation. Acceletron was acquired in 2000 and has never paid a dividend. It records inventory using the FIFO method.

Chief Financial Officer Margot Villiers was asked by Redline's Board of Directors to explain how the functional currency selection and other accounting choices affect Redline's consolidated financial statements. She gathers Acceletron's financial statements denominated in Singapore dollars (SGD) in Exhibit 1 and the U.S. dollar/Singapore dollar exchange rates in Exhibit 2. She does not intend to identify the functional currency actually in use, but rather to use Acceletron as an example of how the choice of functional currency affects the consolidated statements.

EXHIBIT 1 Selected Financial Data for Acceletron 31 December 2007 (SGD Millions)

Cash	SGD	125
Accounts receivable		230
Inventory		500
Fixed assets		1,640
Accumulated depreciation		(205)
Total assets	SGD	2,290
Accounts payable		185
Long-term debt		200
Common stock		620
Retained earnings		1,285
Total liabilities and equity		2,290
Total revenues	SGD	4,800
Net income	SGD	450

EXHIBIT 2 Exchange Rates Applicable to Acceletron

Exchange Rate in Effect at Specific Times	USD per SGD
Rate when first 1,000 of fixed assets were acquired	0.568
Rate when remaining 640 of fixed assets were acquired	0.606
Rate when long-term debt was issued	0.588
31 December 2006	0.649
Weighted average rate when inventory was acquired	0.654
Average rate in 2007	0.662
31 December 2007	0.671

19. Compared to using the Singapore dollar as Acceletron's functional currency for 2007, if the U.S. dollar were the functional currency, it is *most likely* that Redline's consolidated:

A. inventories will be higher.

B. receivable turnover will be lower.

C. fixed asset turnover will be higher.

20. If the U.S. dollar were chosen as the functional currency for Acceletron in 2007, Redline could reduce its balance sheet exposure to exchange rates by:

A. selling SGD 30 of fixed assets for cash.

B. issuing SGD 30 of long-term debt to buy fixed assets.

C. issuing SGD 30 in short-term debt to purchase marketable securities.

21. Redline's consolidated gross profit margin for 2007 would be *highest* if Acceletron accounted for inventory using:

A. FIFO, and its functional currency were the U.S. dollar.

B. LIFO, and its functional currency were the U.S. dollar.

C. FIFO, and its functional currency were the Singapore dollar.

22. If the current rate method is used to translate Acceletron's financial statements into U.S. dollars, Redline's consolidated financial statements will *most likely* include Acceletron's:

A. $3,178 in revenues.

B. $118 in long-term debt.

C. negative translation adjustment to shareholder equity.

23. If Acceletron's financial statements are translated into U.S. dollars using the temporal method, Redline's consolidated financial statements will *most likely* include Acceletron's:

A. $336 in inventory.

B. $956 in fixed assets.

C. $152 in accounts receivable.

24. When translating Acceletron's financial statements into U.S. dollars, Redline is *least likely* to use an exchange rate of USD per SGD:

A. 0.671.

B. 0.588.

C. 0.654.

SOLUTIONS FOR READING 25

1. B is correct. IAS 21 requires that the financial statements of the foreign entity first be restated for local inflation using the procedures outlined in IAS 29, "Financial Reporting in Hyperinflationary Economies." Then, the inflation-restated foreign currency financial statements are translated into the parent's presentation currency using the current exchange rate. Under U.S. GAAP, the temporal method would be used with no restatement.
2. C is correct. Ruiz expects the EUR to appreciate against the UAH and expects some inflation in the Ukraine. In an inflationary environment, FIFO will generate a higher gross profit than weighted average cost. For either inventory choice, the current rate method will give higher gross profit to the parent company if the subsidiary's currency is depreciating. Thus, using FIFO and translating using the current rate method will generate a higher gross profit for the parent company, Eurexim SA, than any other combination of choices.
3. B is correct. If the parent's currency is chosen as the functional currency, the temporal method must be used. Under the temporal method, fixed assets are translated using the rate in effect at the time they were acquired.
4. C is correct. Monetary assets and liabilities such as accounts receivable are translated at current (end-of-period) rates regardless of whether the temporal or current rate method is being used.
5. B is correct. When the foreign currency is chosen as the functional currency, the current rate method is used. All assets and liabilities are translated at the current (end-of-period) rate.
6. B is correct. When the foreign currency is chosen as the functional currency, the current rate method must be used and all gains or losses from translation are reported as a cumulative translation adjustment to shareholder equity. When the foreign currency decreases in value (weakens), the current rate method results in a negative translation adjustment in stockholders' equity.
7. B is correct. When the parent's currency is used as the functional currency, the temporal method must be used to translate the subsidiary's accounts. Under the temporal method, monetary assets and liabilities (e.g., debt) are translated at the current (year-end) rate, nonmonetary assets and liabilities measured at historical cost (e.g., inventory) are translated at historical exchange rates, and nonmonetary assets and liabilities measured at current value are translated at the exchange rate at the date when the current value was determined. Because beginning inventory was sold first and sales and purchases were evenly acquired, the average rate is most appropriate for translating inventory and $77 × 0.92 = $71. Long-term debt is translated at the year-end rate of $0.95. $175 × 0.95 = $166.
8. B is correct. Translating the 2007 balance sheet using the temporal method, as is required here, results in assets of $370 million. The translated liabilities and common stock amount to $326 million, meaning that the value for 2007 retained earnings is: $370 million − $326 million = $44 million.

Temporal Method (2007)

Account	C$	Rate	US$
Cash	135	0.95	128
Accounts receivable	98	0.95	93
Inventory	77	0.92	71
Fixed assets	100	0.86	86
Accumulated depreciation	(10)	0.86	(9)
Total assets	400		370
Accounts payable	77	0.95	73
Long-term debt	175	0.95	166
Common stock	100	0.86	86
Retained earnings	48	to balance	44
Total liabilities and shareholders' equity	400		370

9. C is correct. The Canadian dollar would be the appropriate reporting currency when substantially all operating, financing, and investing decisions are based on the local currency. The parent country's inflation rate is never relevant. Earnings manipulation is not justified, and at any rate changing the functional currency would take the gains off of the income statement.

10. C is correct. If the functional currency was changed from the parent currency (U.S. dollar) to the local currency (Canadian dollar), the current rate method would replace the temporal method. The temporal method ignores unrealized gains and losses on nonmonetary assets and liabilities, but the current rate method does not.

11. B is correct. If the Canadian currency is chosen as the functional currency, the current rate method will be used and the current exchange rate will be the rate used to translate all assets and liabilities. Currently, only monetary assets and liabilities are translated at the current rate. Sales are translated at the average rate during the year under either method. Fixed assets are translated using the historical rate under the temporal method but would switch to current rates under the current rate method. Therefore, there will most likely be an effect on sales/fixed assets. Because the cash ratio involves only monetary assets and liabilities it is unaffected by the translation method. Receivables turnover pairs a monetary asset with sales and is thus also unaffected.

12. B is correct. If the functional currency were changed, then Consol-Can would use the current rate method and the balance sheet exposure would be equal to net assets (total assets – total liabilities). In this case, 400 − 77 − 175 = 148.

13. B is correct. Julius is using the current rate method, which is most appropriate when it is operating with a high degree of autonomy.

14. A is correct. If the current rate method is being used (as it is for Julius), the local currency (euro) is the functional currency. When the temporal method is being used (as it is for Augustus), the parent currency (U.S. dollar) is the functional currency.

15. C is correct. When the current rate method is being used, all currency gains and losses are recorded as a cumulative translation adjustment to shareholder equity.

16. C is correct. Under the current rate method, all assets are translated using the year-end 2008 (current) rate of $1.61/€1.00. €2,300 × 1.61 = $3,703.

17. A is correct. Under the current rate method, both sales and cost of goods sold would be translated at the 2008 average exchange rate. The ratio would be the same as reported under the euro. €2,300 − €1,400 = €900, €900/€2300 = 39.1 percent. Or, $3,542 − $2,156 = $1,386, $1,386/$3,542 = 39.1 percent.

18. C is correct. Augustus is using the temporal method in conjunction with FIFO inventory accounting. If FIFO is used, ending inventory is assumed to be composed of the most recently acquired items and thus inventory will be translated at relatively recent exchange rates. To the extent that the average weight used to translate sales differs from the historical rate used to translate inventories, the gross margin will be distorted when translated into U.S. dollars.

19. C is correct. If the U.S. dollar is the functional currency, the temporal method must be used. Revenues and receivables (monetary asset) would be the same under either accounting method. Inventory and fixed assets were purchased when the U.S. dollar was stronger, so at historical rates (temporal method), translated they would be lower. Identical revenues/lower fixed assets would result in higher fixed asset turnover.

20. A is correct. If the U.S. dollar is the functional currency, the temporal method must be used, and the balance sheet exposure will be the net *monetary* assets of 125 + 230 − 185 − 200 = −30 or a net monetary liability of $30. This net monetary liability would be eliminated if fixed assets (non-monetary) were sold to increase cash. Issuing debt, either short-term or long-term, would increase the net monetary liability.

21. A is correct. Because the U.S. dollar has been consistently weakening against the Singapore dollar, cost of sales will be lower and gross profit higher when an earlier exchange rate is used to translate inventory, compared to using current exchange rates. If the Singapore dollar is the functional currency, current rates would be used. Therefore, the combination of the U.S. dollar (temporal method) and FIFO will result in the highest gross profit margin.

22. A is correct. Under the current rate method, revenue is translated at the average rate for the year, SGD 4,800 × 0.662 = $3,178. Debt should be translated at the current rate, SGD 200 × 0.671 = $134. Under the current rate method, Acceletron would have a net asset balance sheet exposure. Since the SGD has been strengthening against the USD, the translation adjustment would be positive rather than negative.

23. B is correct. Under the temporal method, inventory and fixed assets would be translated using historic rates. Accounts receivable is a monetary asset and would be translated at year-end (current) rates. Fixed assets are found as (1,000 × 0.568) + (640 × 0.606) = $956.

24. B is correct. \$0.671/SGD is the current exchange rate. That rate would be used regardless of whether Acceletron uses the current rate or temporal method. \$0.654 was the weighted average rate when inventory was acquired. That rate would be used if the company translated its statements under the temporal method, but not the current rate method. \$0.588/SGD was the exchange rate in effect when long-term debt was issued. As a monetary liability, long-term debt is always translated using current exchange rates. Consequently, that rate is not applicable regardless of how Acceletron translates its financial statements.

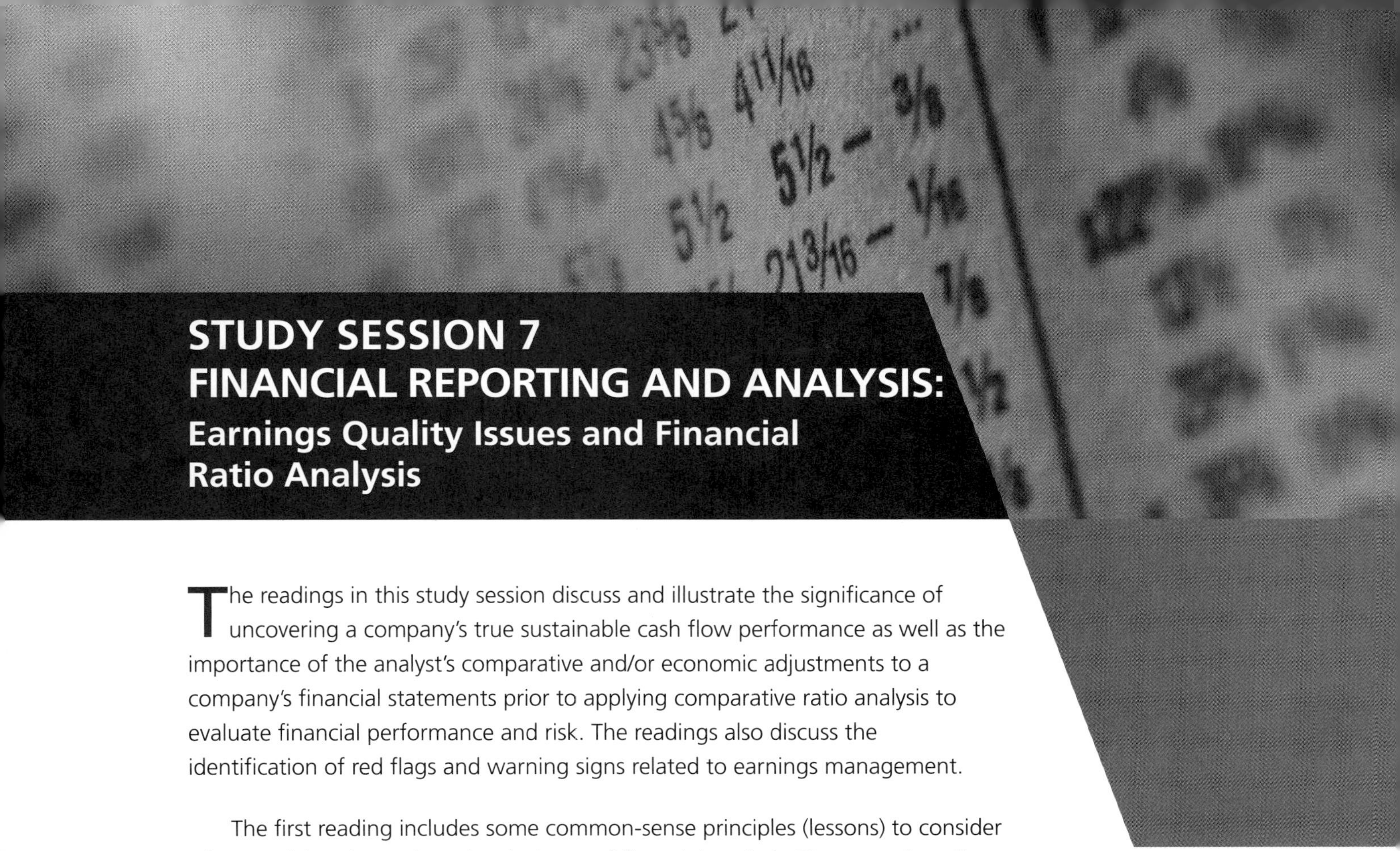

STUDY SESSION 7
FINANCIAL REPORTING AND ANALYSIS:
Earnings Quality Issues and Financial Ratio Analysis

The readings in this study session discuss and illustrate the significance of uncovering a company's true sustainable cash flow performance as well as the importance of the analyst's comparative and/or economic adjustments to a company's financial statements prior to applying comparative ratio analysis to evaluate financial performance and risk. The readings also discuss the identification of red flags and warning signs related to earnings management.

The first reading includes some common-sense principles (lessons) to consider when applying the tools and techniques of financial analysis. The second reading illustrates how an analysis of a company's financial statements can reveal problems. Analysts should be able to critique accruals and other problem areas in the financial statements and footnotes that would suggest that the financial reporting quality of a company has been compromised.

Financial ratios may be used to compare a company's risk and return with that of other companies of various sizes. A financial analyst uses ratio analysis to evaluate a company's profitability, asset utilization, liquidity, and solvency. A significant hurdle in applying ratio analysis is the difficulty of comparing companies that use alternative accounting policies. To achieve comparability, the analyst must identify the accounting differences and adjust the financial statements accordingly.

Note:
New rulings and/or pronouncements issued after the publication of the readings in financial reporting and analysis may cause some of the information in these readings to become dated. Candidates are expected to be familiar with the overall analytical framework contained in the study session readings, as well as the implications of alternative accounting methods for financial analysis and valuation, as provided in the assigned readings. Candidates are not responsible for changes that occur after the material was written.

READING ASSIGNMENTS

Reading 26 The Lessons We Learn
Analysis of Financial Statements, Second Edition, by Pamela P. Peterson, CFA and Frank J. Fabozzi, CFA

Reading 27	Evaluating Financial Reporting Quality *International Financial Statement Analysis,* by Thomas R. Robinson, CFA, Jan Hendrik van Greuning, CFA, Elaine Henry, CFA, and Michael A. Broihahn, CFA
Reading 28	Integration of Financial Statement Analysis Techniques by Jack T. Ciesielski, Jr., CFA

THE LESSONS WE LEARN

by Pamela P. Peterson, CFA and Frank J. Fabozzi, CFA

READING **26**

LEARNING OUTCOMES

The candidate should be able to:	Mastery
a. distinguish among the various definitions of earnings (e.g., EBITDA, operating earnings, net income, etc.);	☐
b. illustrate how trends in cash flow from operations can be more reliable than trends in earnings;	☐
c. provide a simplified description of the accounting treatment for derivatives being used to hedge: ► exposure to changes in the value of assets and liabilities, ► exposure to variable cash flow, and ► a foreign currency exposure of an instrument in a foreign corporation.	☐

INTRODUCTION 1

Financial analysis involves gathering the information about a company, its industry, and the economy, and developing an evaluation of the company's future financial condition and operating performance. The financial scandals of recent years have increased the awareness of the need for more transparency in financial disclosures and more analysis of the available information.

Former Chairman of the Securities and Exchange Commission, Harvey Pitt, summed up this era in his March 20, 2002 testimony before the Committee on Financial Services, U.S. House of Representatives:

> In recent years, corporate leaders have been under increasing pressure from the investment community, including individual investors, to meet elevated expectations.

> They also have been operating under a system that can misalign the incentives of investors and those of management. Our culture over the past decade has fostered a short-term perspective of corporate performance. Corporate leaders and directors have been rewarded for short-term performance, sometimes at the expense of long-term fundamental value. Investors have purchased stock not because they believed in the business or its strategy as an investment over the long-term, but simply under the assumption that stock prices would only go up.

As a result of these problems, we have seen many new laws and regulations, including the Sarbanes–Oxley Act of 2002.

Key to a company's fundamental value is its future financial condition and operating performance. In our analysis of a company, however, we rely upon information supplied by others; in particular, the company's own financial disclosures.

One of the buzzwords of recent years is transparency. *Transparency* in financial reporting means that companies provide information to owners and other stakeholders in an understandable manner. This requires that financial disclosures be clear, reliable, and comparable. Transparency is important in financial disclosures to ensure the ability of stakeholders to evaluate the financial condition and performance of companies. Transparency is viewed as important for the efficient functioning of financial markets.[1]

We have focused on the interpretation of required financial disclosures that companies make, as prescribed by regulatory requirements. But in addition to the wealth of information available through these disclosures, many companies choose to disclose information above and beyond these required disclosures. In its Business Reporting Research Project, the Financial Accounting Standard Board (FASB) analyzed voluntary disclosures of companies. The FASB classified these disclosures into six categories:

1. business data about the company's sales, products, and financial performance
2. management analysis of business data, including goals, trends, impact of strikes, and benchmarking against competitors
3. forward-looking information about products and operations, including patent expirations, growth targets for products or regions, expected growth
4. information about management and shareholders

[1] For a discussion of the issues of transparency in the telecommunications industry, see the testimony of John M. Morrissey before the Subcommittee on Oversight and Investigations Committee on Financial Services, March 21, 2002.

5. background about the company, including discussions of key legislation, industry trends, facilities, and strategies
6. information about intangible assets, such as information about research and development, customer relations, and innovations

These voluntary disclosures should be used to supplement the required disclosures because they provide management's perspective of what drives the company's financial results.

In a perfect world, the system of financial disclosure would provide information that is:

- *Relevant* to the determination of fundamental value
- *Reflective* of the true economics of the transactions
- *Verifiable,* such that estimates and assumptions are reasonable and understood
- *Neutral* with respect to any predetermined result, such as analysts' forecasts
- *Comparable,* enabling the analyst to compare information among companies and over time
- *Complete,* providing sufficient information to understand a company's past, current, and future performance
- *Understandable* to all stakeholders

Of course, we do not live in a perfect world. The improvements in financial disclosures and the audit function, as well as enhanced penalties for misdeeds, will result in better quality financial disclosures. The financial analyst must, however, still be diligent in looking at this information critically.

One of the signs of an increasing awareness and importance of the accuracy of financial statements has been the increased number of companies restating their financial disclosures for "accounting irregularities." Restatements occur when companies correct errors in previously reported financial statement information, with revenue recognition being the most frequent basis for restatements.

In a study of restatements, the General Accounting Office (GAO) reported the frequency of restatements. Using the data from this study, we show the trend of restatements in Exhibit 1.[2] As you can see, though the proportion of companies restating results is small, the number of restatements has increased, coinciding with the revelation of corporate scandals. In terms of who is initiating the

---

[2] *Financial Statement Restatements: Trends, Market Impacts, Regulatory Responses, and Remaining Challenges,* General Accounting Office, Report to Chairman, Committee on Banking, Housing, and Urban Affairs, U.S. Senate, (October 2002).

EXHIBIT 1 **Number of Restatements of NYSE, AMSE, and NASDAQ-Listed Companies, 1997–2002**

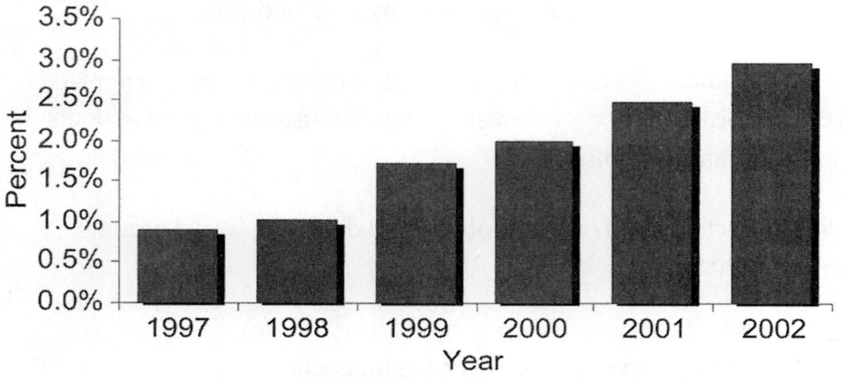

Source: Financial Statement Restatements: Trends, Market Impacts, Regulatory Responses, and Remaining Challenges, General Accounting Office, Report to Chairman, Committee on Banking, Housing, and Urban Affairs, U.S. Senate (October 2002).

restatements, the company itself is the most frequent initiator, initiating 49% of these restatements. What this tells us is that companies are aware of the increased scrutiny of financial disclosures and they are taking measures to ensure that their disclosures are accurate.[3]

2 THE LESSONS

Throughout the curriculum, we have offered tools and techniques that the analyst may apply in performing a financial analysis. We have also pointed out some of the things that analysts missed along the way, which were eventually brought to light in the financial scandals of recent years. From all of this, you should take along with you a number of lessons regarding financial analysis.

Lesson 1: Understand What You Are Looking At

The financial analyst must be aware of the type of disclosure that he or she is looking at.

- Is this a disclosure that is prepared according to generally accepted accounting principles, or is this pro forma information?
- If the disclosure is earnings, specifically what earnings are these? Before or after the effects of an accounting change? Before or after the effects of discontinued items? Before or after extraordinary items? Before or after special items?

The analyst must have a thorough understanding of accounting principles, as well as understand the source of the information.

[3] This also tells us that a financial analyst should try to understand the reasons that companies restate their financial numbers. It is often the case that there are accounting irregularities.

Consider the issue of a company's earnings. Within generally accepted accounting principles, the company's management has some discretion with regard to how it classifies some income and expenses on the income statement. Researchers have observed that investors give less weight to transitory items on the income statement than to permanent items.[4] With that in mind, we can see why companies have wanted to separate transitory from permanent items. But this introduces an element of confusion because there are now many earnings figures to sort through, for example:

- earnings before interest, taxes, depreciation, and amortization (EBITDA)
- operating income
- income before income taxes
- income from continuing operations
- income before extraordinary items
- income before effect of changes in accounting principles
- net income

In addition, companies may develop their own measures that they present alongside the GAAP figures. Consider TXU, which is an energy holding company. For 2004, it reported income that

> Operational earnings, which exclude special items, for the fourth quarter of 2004 were $183 million, $0.67 per share of common stock, compared to $34 million, $0.11 per share for 2003, a 509 percent increase in per share earnings.

This statement by the company's management suggests that the company did well on a continuing basis, producing an increase in earnings. We get a slightly different picture of company performance when we look at GAAP earnings over time, as we see in Exhibit 2, Panel A. The net income declined from $582 million in the 2003 fiscal year to $485 million, whereas net income to common shareholders declined from $560 million to a loss of $386 million.

Why the different financial pictures? It is the terminology: the company's introduction of the term "operational earnings" muddies the waters. The definition provided in the footnote to the company's press release indicates that this is income adjusted for special items, discontinued operations, and the cumulative effect of accounting change. The special items, detailed in its 10-K filings for 2004, include employee severance costs, asset impairments, software write-offs, changes on leased equipment, and consulting and professional fees. Many companies do not consider these items "special," so for comparability purposes, we would want to take a close look at the company's adjustments to arrive at "operational earnings."

So what earnings should the financial analyst use in the analysis of TXU? Probably a number somewhere between the loss of $386 million and income of $887 million. The analyst must delve into the footnotes and explanations of the extraordinary gains and losses, the special items, and discontinued items to determine how much, if any, of these items are likely to recur in the future. For example, in the case of TXU, there is an $849 million charge to arrive at net income for common stockholders for the buyback of exchangeable preferred

[4] See, for example, Mark T. Bradshaw, Matthew Moberg, and Richard G. Sloan, "GAAP Versus the Street: An Empirical Assessment of Two Alternative Definitions of Earnings," *Journal of Accounting Research* 40 (2002), pp. 41–65; or David Burgstahler, James Jiambalvo, and Terry Shevlin, "Do Stock Prices Fully Reflect the Implications of Special Items for Future Earnings?" *Journal of Accounting Research* 40 (2002), pp. 585–612.

EXHIBIT 2 **TXU Corporation's 2004 Earnings**

Panel A. Trends in GAAP Earnings, 1994–2004

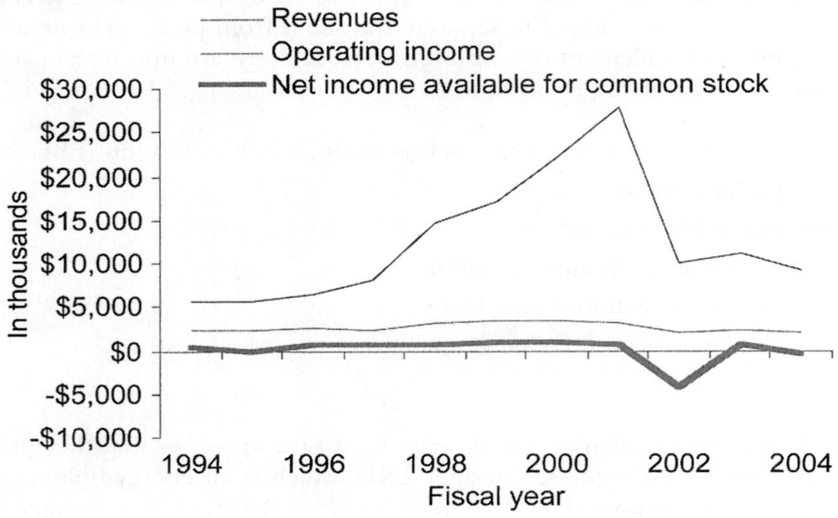

Panel B. TXU and Its Operational Earnings

Net loss to common	−$386
Less: Income from discontinued operations	378
Less: Extraordinary gain	16
Less: Cumulative effect of changes in accounting principles	10
Add: Premium on exchange preferred membership interests	849
Income from continuing operations	$59
Add: Special items	828
Operational earnings	$887

Source: 10-K filings, various years, and TXU News Release, February 2, 2005.

membership interests. From a review of footnote 9 of TXU's 2004 10-K filing, we see that this is a repurchase of preferred stock that reduces paid-in capital, similar to a repurchase of common stock. We would not expect to see this in the future and therefore it is reasonable to back out this charge in using the income for 2004 to help forecast future income to common shareholders.

Lesson 2: Read the Fine Print

The information that companies provide in their balance sheet, income statement, and statement of cash flows is informative; but there is so much more that we can learn from footnotes, the management discussion and analysis, and other disclosures.

The trend in regulation and accounting pertaining to financial reporting is requiring companies to disclose more information in the management discussion and analysis and footnotes. In fact, these items should be the starting place in the examination of financial statements—understanding what is behind the numbers that appear in the balance sheet, income statement, and statement of cash flows. The challenge is that footnotes may be neither concise nor clear. Companies are required to provide these footnotes, but there is no standard for the format or readability. For example, the convoluted nature of the "special purposes entities" of Enron Corporation was evident in the company's own footnotes and the publicly available filings of the special purpose entities. Though it may not have been possible to unravel all the financial threads in this case, there was enough to raise questions.

Many of the companies involved in financial scandals in the past provided information that should have been a red flag (or at least a caution flag) regarding the management of earnings. Consider the case of Waste Management. Waste Management used many different devices, including extending depreciable lives and altering salvage values on depreciable assets, to meet analysts' earnings expectations. Hints of this were offered in its footnotes. For example, in a footnote in its 1995 10-K filing (p. 27), Waste Management disclosed the following:[5]

> In 1995, depreciation and amortization decreased due to the change in the estimated useful life of excess cost over net assets of acquired businesses related to certain acquisitions from 25 to 40 years, effective January 1, 1995, which resulted in decreased amortization expense of approximately $1,488,000 for the year. This change in accounting policy substantially offset the normal increase in depreciation and amortization of property and equipment used to generate increased operating revenues.

In other words, operating earnings were enhanced from the change in the estimated lives of depreciable assets. In 1998, Waste Management restated its earnings for this and other irregularities, becoming at the time the largest restatement of earnings in corporate history.

Lesson 3: If It's Too Good to Be True, It May Be

There are many corporate success stories, such as Microsoft and Wal-Mart Stores, and we enjoy watching these successes. But each of these successes can be explained by the company's comparative or competitive advantage. Value is not created from the proverbial thin air, but rather must come from some advantage the company is able to exploit.

In a study of a large number of U.S. companies, Chan, Karceski, and Lakonishok examine the level and persistence of earnings growth rates.[6] They find that in the period from 1951–1998:

- The median growth rate of earnings is 10% per year.
- After removing dividends, the growth rate of earnings mirrors that of the gross domestic product, between 3% and 3.5%.
- Only 5% of companies have growth rates that exceed 29% per year over 10 years, with most of these highest-growth companies being smaller companies.
- Persistence in sales growth does not always translate to persistence in earnings growth.
- On average, only 3% of companies have growth consistently above the median for five years running.

[5] Formerly USA Waste.

[6] Louis K. C. Chan, Jason Karceski, and Josef Lakonishok, "The Level of Persistence of Growth Rates," *Journal of Finance* 58, no. 2 (2003), pp. 634–684.

If we look at the growth in revenues of Enron Corporation from 1986 through 2000, we see that revenues grew at an average annual rate of 20.29% and earnings grew at a rate of 22.43% per year. You can see the growth in revenues in Exhibit 3, Panel A. In fact, Enron's revenues more than doubled from fiscal year 1999 to 2000.

EXHIBIT 3 **Enron Corporation, Revenues and Capital Structure, 1986 through 2000**

Panel A. Enron Corporation Revenues, 1986–2000

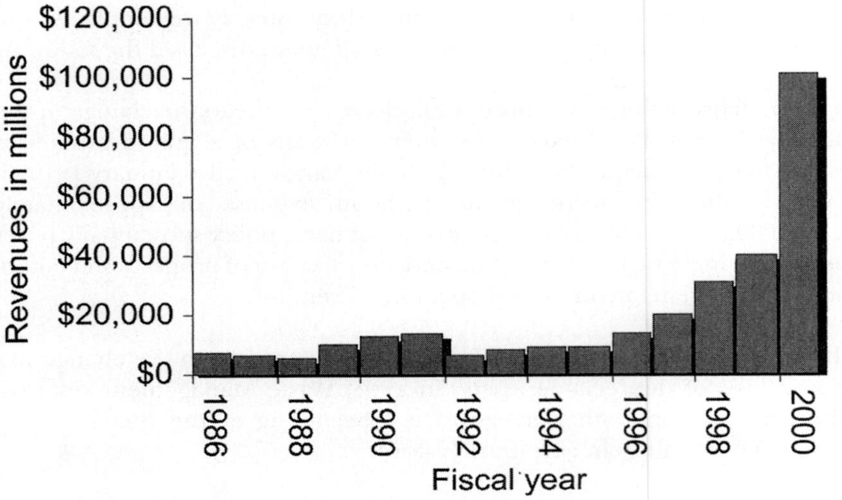

Panel B. Enron Corporation Liabilities and Equity, 1986–2000

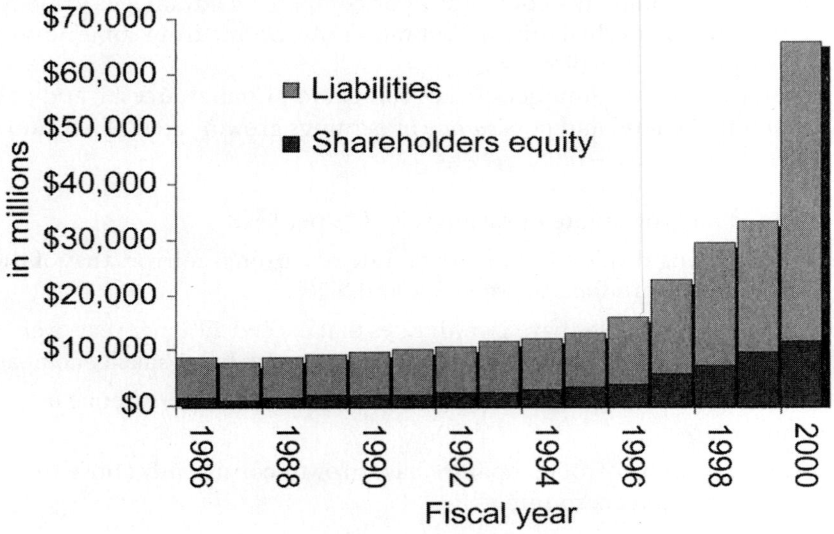

Source: Enron Corporation's 10-K filings, various years, and www.enron.com.

But this growth was not without its problems, as we saw with the eventual scandal and bankruptcy that followed fiscal year 2000. Enron relied heavily on accounting gimmicks and debt financing to fuel its revenue growth. By 2000, Enron reported that over 82% of its assets were financed with debt—and this does not consider the debt that was shifted off the balance sheet through the special purpose entities. We have graphed the reported liabilities and equity of Enron Corporation from 1986 through 2000 in Panel B of this figure. The growth in Enron was based largely on debt financing, which is difficult to sustain over time.

Lesson 4: Follow the Money

An analysis of a company must include an analysis of its cash flows. Alongside the typical financial ratios, a financial analyst should also be looking closely at cash flows—the trends in these flows, as well as how cash flows compare to income. Cash flow information is generally more reliable than earnings information because earnings may include noncash income and expenses items that are arbitrary.

We can see some of the problems of Enron by looking beyond the annual figures to see the patterns emerging on a quarterly basis. Many companies experience seasonal fluctuations in their business, which affects revenues and net income. We often see a difference between a company's cash flow from operations and its operating income, which is resolved over time; in other words, the differences between operating income and cash flow from operations are generally zero, when considered over time.

In the case of the Enron Corporation, whose cash flows we depict in Exhibit 4, Panels A and B, the relation between cash flows and earnings was not as expected. On a quarterly basis, as shown in Panel A, cash flows from operations were largely negative in many quarters in which operating income was positive. In Panel B, we can see how the growth in operating income far exceeded that of cash flows from operations, suggesting that there may have been some management of earnings.

The question arises as to why financial analysts did not see these problems as they occurred. First, hindsight is 50–50 and it is not easy to detect fraudulent acts that distort publicly available financial information. Second, some analysts did point out some problems with Enron Corporation prior to the scandal, but it is difficult for nay-sayers to get attention with a stock that was rising and a company that has investment grade ratings.[7]

Lesson 5: Understand the Risks

There are many risks that a company faces, and the types and extent of these risks vary from company to company, even within the same industry. For example, if you consider airlines and their problem with a high degree of business risk, you can see differences in how these airlines manage these risks, as we show in Exhibit 5. The ratio of debt to equity is wide ranging in this industry, suggesting different willingness to add financial risk to the already substantial business risk.

[7] And still a third issue is that there is a tendency for analysts to be overly optimistic in the near-term in the case of companies issuing debt. See Mark T. Bradshaw, "Playing Favorites: Financing Options Sway Analysts' Thinking," *Investor Relations Quarterly* (June 2004). There is harsh criticism of analysts who missed the problems with Enron. See, for example, "The Watchdogs Didn't Bark: Enron and the Wall Street Analysts," Hearing Before the Senate Governmental Affairs Committee, 107th Cong., Senate Hearing 107–385 (February 27, 2002).

EXHIBIT 4 **Enron Corporation's Operating Income versus Cash Flow from Operations**

Panel A. Quarterly Operating Income and Cash Flow from Operations, 1997–2001

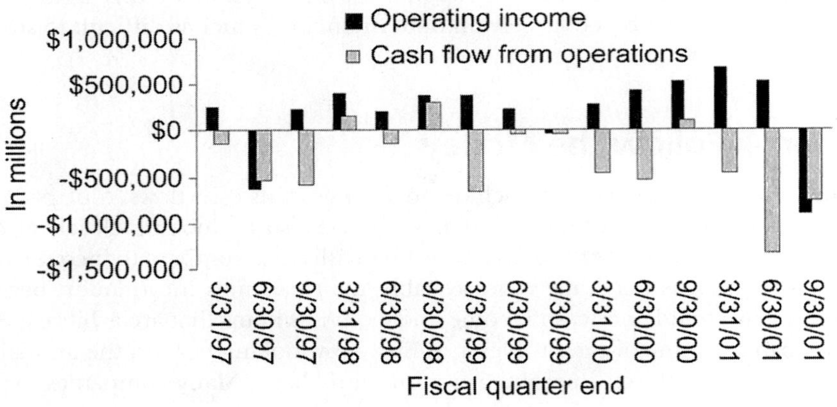

Panel B. Annual Operating Income and Cash Flow from Operations, 1986–2001

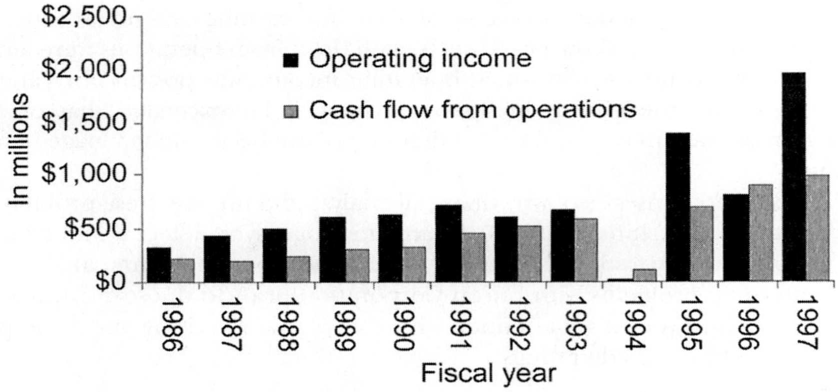

Source: Enron Corporation's 10-K filings, various years, and www.enron.com.

Therefore, there are two dimensions to understand risks: 1) understanding what they are, and 2) understanding how companies deal with these risks.

Types of Risk

The types of risks that a company faces are varied. We can use financial analysis to get an idea of the company's sales, operating, and financial risk. However, there are more specific risks that companies face. We can get an idea of these risks by looking at the company's market risk disclosure (Item 7A in the company's 10-K filing).

EXHIBIT 5 **Long-Term Debt to Equity Ratios of Companies in the Airline Industry**

Airline	Ratio of Long-Term Debt to Equity
AMR Corporation	nmf
Delta Air Lines	nmf
Jet Blue Airways	1.846
Midwest Air Group	0.794
Southwest Airlines	0.308

Note: nmf is undefined because shareholders' equity is negative.
Source: 10-K filings for fiscal year 2004.

Consider the risks disclosed in IBM's *2004 Annual Report* (pp. 33–34):

- interest rate risk
- foreign currency exchange rate risk with respect to debt and non-U.S. dollar-denominated assets and liabilities
- collectibility of accounts receivable
- recoverability of residual values on leased assets

These risks are different, say, from a company that relies on raw materials, such as a manufacturer of food products. For example, Kellogg lists three risks in its *2004 Annual Report* (pp. 28–29):

- foreign exchange risk
- interest rate risk
- price risk with respect to commodities and energy

An analyst may derive information about a company's other risks from the company's disclosure about contingencies (e.g., lawsuits) and segment disclosures.

Management of Risks

Though most companies are exposed to interest rate risk, foreign currency exchange risk, credit risk, and other risks, the analyst must examine how companies manage these risks. For example, many companies use derivatives to affect the magnitude or the direction of such risks.[8] Analysts need to understand the actions and transactions that companies take to manage risks. For example, who are the counterparties in a swap transaction? Is the company hedging their interest rate risk? If so, what means are they using to do so?

Many companies, for example, hedge some of their risk using derivatives, such as forward, futures, and swaps. A company's use of derivatives will be disclosed according to Statement of Financial Accounting Standards No. 133,

[8] Warren Buffett, in the 2004 Annual Report of Berkshire Hathaway, remarks on companies' use of derivatives (p. 11), "Like Hell, derivative trading is easy to enter but difficult to leave."

Accounting for Derivative Instruments and Hedging Activities[9] When a company uses derivatives, it must determine at the outset how this derivative is being used.

- If the derivative is being used to hedge exposure to changes in the value of an asset or liability, the extent to which the hedge is not effective is recognized in the income statement.
- If the derivative is being used to hedge exposure to variable cash flows (such as future cash flows from a forecasted transaction), the effective portion of the derivative's gain or loss goes into comprehensive income (and hence directly to shareholders' equity, bypassing the income statement), and then is recognized as a part of a gain or loss when the forecasted transaction affects earnings.
- If the derivative is being used to hedge a foreign currency exposure of an investment in a foreign corporation, any gain or loss is a part of comprehensive income (and shareholders' equity, bypassing the income statement).

Actually, the accounting for derivatives is much more complicated than this simple description and results in a rather obtuse disclosure. Warren Buffett, in the 2003 Berkshire Hathaway Annual Report (p. 15) sums up this reporting:

> If our derivatives experience—and the Freddie Mac shenanigans of mind-blowing size and audacity that were revealed last year—makes you suspicious of accounting in this arena, consider yourself wised up. No matter how financially sophisticated you are, you can't possibly learn from reading the disclosure documents of a derivatives-intensive company what risks lurk in its positions. Indeed, the more you know about derivatives, the less you will feel you can learn from the disclosures normally proffered you. In Darwin's words, "Ignorance more frequently begets confidence than does knowledge."

And the true test of a company's use of derivatives, according to Warren Buffett, is what it does over a period of time in which there is no growth, because everyone does well in a bull market. As he cleverly points out, "You only learn who has been swimming naked when the tide goes out."[10]

3 THE FUTURE OF FINANCIAL ANALYSIS IN THE POST-SOX ERA

There is no doubt that the financial scandals of the past few years and the resulting legislation, regulation, and rule-making have changed financial analysis. The Sarbanes–Oxley Act of 2002 (SOX) is the single most important legislation affecting financial reporting since the Securities Act of 1933 and the Securities Exchange Act of 1934. SOX provides for more oversight of the auditing function, increased corporate financial disclosures, and improved corporate governance.

[9] This SFAS is amended by SFAS No. 149, Amendment of Statement 133 on *Derivative Instruments and Hedging Activities,* which clarifies some of the more confusing aspects of No. 133.

[10] *Berkshire Hathaway 2004 Annual Report.*

There are many implications of SOX to financial analysis. Examples include the following:

1. The management discussion and analysis section of the 10-K filing is more informative. In particular, this section will provide information about off-balance sheet arrangements.
2. A larger number of events trigger an 8-K filing. The financial analyst therefore has more information about more events related to a company. The additional triggering events include the entry or termination of a material definitive agreement, the completion or asset acquisition or disposition, creation of a financial obligation (direct or off-balance sheet), and changes in the certifying accountant.
3. An adverse opinion with respect to a weakness in internal controls should at least get the attention of the analyst. When SOX's internal control requirement (section 404) is first implemented, we expect a number of companies to have some type of ineffective internal control or weakness. However, beyond the law's initial implementation, a weakness or ineffective control should be a red flag to the financial analyst.

Additionally, there are many provisions in SOX, such as those to seek to reduce conflicts of interest, which provide more confidence in the data reported by companies.

One of the themes of SOX is the responsibility of the "gatekeepers" to our financial markets. Along with auditors, boards of directors, and lawyers, financial analysts are important gatekeepers, with a responsibility to the capital markets. As gatekeepers, financial analysts have a responsibility to interpret financial disclosures, along with other available information, to provide useful information to stakeholders with regard to the company's financial condition and operating performance in the future.

PRACTICE PROBLEMS FOR READING 26

The following information relates to Questions 1–6

Paul Lee, CFA, is an equity analyst with HHK Securities, an investment management firm based in New York. Lee is conducting a financial analysis of Food-for-All, Inc., a U.S. manufacturer of food products with no international operations or procurements. Food-for-All prepares its financial statements in accordance with U.S. GAAP, and its shares are listed on the New York Stock Exchange. Lee prepares trend analysis (Exhibit 1) using information he gathers from the company's financial statements and other disclosures.

EXHIBIT 1 Food-for-All Trend Analysis

	(In million $)				
Fiscal Year Ended 31-December	**2010**	**2009**	**2008**	**2007**	**2006**
Revenues	2,628	2,103	1,682	1,368	1,121
Year over year change	*25%*	*25%*	*23%*	*22%*	
Operating income	1,386	1,016	785	612	477
Net income	964	695	529	407	312
Cash flow from operations	263	329	387	430	453
Year over year change	*–20%*	*–15%*	*–10%*	*–5%*	
Non-GAAP Results					
Operational earnings*	1,400	1,031	805	632	492
Year over year change	*36%*	*28%*	*27%*	*29%*	

*Management defines operational earnings as GAAP operating income excluding special and transitory items.

In reviewing Food-for-All's 2010 annual report, Lee highlights four statements from the Management Discussion and Analysis section and the Footnotes to the financial statements.

Statement 1: "In 2010 both our operating income and our operational earnings increased by 36% compared with a 29% and 28% increase, respectively, in 2009. This increase in earnings reflects the effects of our new business strategy."

Statement 2: "In 2006 we conducted an extensive review of our property, plant and equipment. Since then, we have been increasing the estimated useful life of many of our fixed assets and reducing our depreciation and amortization expense. As a result, in 2010 depreciation expense was reduced by $83 million."

Statement 3: "Food-for-All finances its operations using floating-rate bank debt and equity capital. In 2010 as part of our new business strategy, we sold a significant portion of our receivables. This generated a gain of $12 million."

Statement 4: "The company hedges its exposure to the risk of higher raw material and energy prices by purchasing commodity and energy futures contracts in the open market. It accounts for these derivatives as hedging instruments. For the fiscal year ended 31 December 2010, 94% of the hedges were effective in offsetting gains and losses in raw materials and energy price changes."

1. Which of the statements highlighted by Lee is *least likely* to be an indication of potential earnings management at Food-for-All?

A. Statement 1.

B. Statement 2.

C. Statement 4.

2. Based on Exhibit 1 and the statements highlighted by Lee, the primary reason for the 36% increase in Food-for-All's operating income in 2010 was:

A. the growth of revenues.

B. the sales of receivables.

C. the increase in the estimated useful life of its fixed assets.

3. Based on Lee's trend analysis in Exhibit 1, what is *least likely* to be an indication of potential management of earnings at Food-for-All?

A. The persistent double-digit growth in revenues and earnings.

B. The diverging trends in cash flow from operations and operating income.

C. The consistency between the growth rates of operating income and operational earnings.

4. Based on the trend analysis in Exhibit 1 and the statements highlighted by Lee, what is the *most likely* explanation for the diverging trend in cash flow from operations and operating income?

A. The sale of receivables.

B. The use of floating rate bank debt.

C. The increase in the estimated useful lives of its fixed assets.

5. Which of the following risks is *least likely* to affect Food-for-All's earnings and cash flows?

A. Interest rate risk.

B. Energy price risk.

C. Foreign exchange risk.

6. What impact did the derivatives (futures contracts) have on Food-for-All's 2010 financial statements?

A. The gains or losses on the hedges were recognized in net income.

B. The ineffective portions of the hedges were recognized in net income.

C. The effective portions of the hedges were recognized in comprehensive income.

SOLUTIONS FOR READING 26

1. C is correct. While derivatives are complex, the use of derivatives to hedge risks and accounting for these as hedging instruments is not necessarily an indication of management of earnings. As Lesson 5 explains, analysts need to understand the risks. The use of derivatives to hedge risks is often a prudent business strategy. In this case, management's utilization of derivatives to manage the risk of increased prices of raw materials and energy seems appropriate.
2. C is correct. In 2010, depreciation expense was reduced by 30% or \$83 million. Without this reduction, operating income would have only increased by 28% because operating income would have been \$1,303.
3. C is correct. The fact that there is consistency between the growth rates of operating income and operational earnings does not necessarily imply any earnings management. On the contrary, the consistency in growth between these two measures implies a consistency in the significant special and transitory items that are removed from operating earnings when deriving operational earnings over this timeframe.
4. C is correct. Operating income is increasing while cash flow from operations is decreasing. Changing the useful lives of fixed assets has no impact on cash flow from operations because depreciation is a non-cash item. Such a change does, however, increase operating income as depreciation expense is reduced. Since 2006, the company has been increasing the estimated useful lives of its fixed assets. This is a partial explanation for the increasing difference between operating income and cash flow from operations.
5. C is correct. Since Food-for-All has no international operations or procurements, foreign exchange risk is the least likely risk to affect its earnings and cash flows.
6. C is correct. Food-for-All is using the future contracts to hedge exposures to variable cash flows (future cash flows from a forecasted transaction), i.e., the cost of higher future raw material and energy prices. Therefore, the effective portion of the derivatives gains or losses goes into comprehensive income and then is recognized as a part of gain or loss when the forecasted transactions affect earnings.

EVALUATING FINANCIAL REPORTING QUALITY

by Scott Richardson and İrem Tuna

READING

27

LEARNING OUTCOMES

The candidate should be able to:	Mastery
a. contrast cash-basis and accrual-basis accounting and explain why accounting discretion exists in an accrual accounting system;	☐
b. describe the relation between the level of accruals and the persistence of earnings and the relative multiples that the cash and accrual components of earnings should rationally receive in valuation;	☐
c. discuss the opportunities and motivations for management to intervene in the external financial reporting process and the mechanisms that discipline such intervention;	☐
d. discuss earnings quality and the measures of earnings quality, and compare and contrast the earnings quality of peer companies;	☐
e. explain mean reversion in earnings and how the accruals component of earnings affects the speed of mean reversion;	☐
f. discuss problems with the quality of financial reporting, including revenue recognition, expense recognition, balance sheet issues, and cash flow statement issues, and interpret warning signs of these potential problems.	☐

Note:
New rulings and/or pronouncements issued after the publication of the readings in financial reporting and analysis may cause some of the information in these readings to become dated. Candidates are expected to be familiar with the overall analytical framework contained in the study session readings, as well as the implications of alternative accounting methods for financial analysis and valuation, as provided in the assigned readings. Candidates are not responsible for changes that occur after the material was written.

1 INTRODUCTION

Financial statement analysis involves taking a systematic approach to using information contained in the financial statements to assist in decision making. The set of decision makers using financial statements is varied. However, one thing they have in common is an interest in assessing a company's future cash flow generating capability. Equity investors and analysts, credit investors and analysts, rating agencies, customers, employees, tax authorities, and others all have a need to estimate a company's future cash flows. Although there are many sources of information relevant to such forecasting, one of the principal sources, and our focus in this reading, is the company's financial statements (inclusive of supplemental information to the main financial statements).

Financial reporting quality relates to the accuracy with which a company's reported financials reflect its operating performance and to their usefulness for forecasting future cash flows. Our focus in introducing this topic is on the income statement and the discretion (exercise of choice) embedded in the recording of various revenues and expenses—this affects net income, which is simply net revenue less total expense. Simple measures that capture the aggregate discretion reflected in reported net income are a very effective way to measure financial reporting quality. Companies exercising more (less) discretion can usually be classified as having weaker (stronger) financial reporting quality. This separation is especially useful in identifying companies who will have weaker (stronger) future cash flow generating capability.

The discussion in this reading extends the material introduced in the reading on financial statement analysis techniques. We begin with some fundamentals to highlight the extent of discretion that is embedded in financial statements. This discretion is a necessary part of financial reporting, but it brings with it unintended consequences. Discretion necessitates preparers of financial statements to make numerous "estimates" which suffer from neutral errors as well as strategic manipulation. We will walk through many examples of how discretion in the financial reporting system manifests itself in the form of systematic biases, which analysts would be foolhardy to ignore given the ever-increasing role that accounting numbers play in contracts and asset pricing. Our discussion will be broad, and will be generally from the perspective of an equity or credit analyst. However, much of the material covered is also relevant to the corporate financial analyst for evaluating acquisitions, restructurings, and other investments, and for calculating the value generated by strategic scenarios.

The remainder of this reading is organized as follows: Section 2 introduces discretion in accounting systems, comparing accrual and cash bases of accounting. Understanding this basic, yet often subtle, difference is crucial to all of the material in the reading, as it defines the scope for discretion that resides in the financial statements. Section 3 lays out the general context for financial reporting quality and introduces simple measures of financial reporting quality. Section 4 provides a structure for computing, analyzing, and interpreting various indicators and measures of financial reporting and earnings quality. Section 5 briefly discusses the implications for financial reporting quality of the trend towards fair value accounting. A summary of the key points and practice problems in the CFA Institute multiple-choice format conclude the reading.

DISCRETION IN ACCOUNTING SYSTEMS

2

To understand the issues in evaluating the quality of financial reporting, the analyst should be familiar with the context in which managerial discretion in accounting is exercised and with the principles and objectives of accrual accounting. The following sections provide that background.

2.1 Distinguishing Cash Basis from Accrual Basis Accounting

Our focus on external financial statements centers on the three primary financial statements: the balance sheet, income statement, and statement of cash flows. The balance sheet is a snapshot of the various asset, liability, and equity accounts. It reflects the financial status of the entity at a point in time. The income statement reports revenues less expenses, and the statement of cash flows which, when reported using the indirect method (which starts with net income), articulates how the change in cash observed on the balance sheet can reconcile to reported income.

To help put these statements in context and clarify the importance of accrual accounting, consider a bicycle repair shop, Cadence Cycling. At the start of the current year the owner contributes $100 cash into the business. The opening balance sheet would look as follows:

Cadence Cycling Balance Sheet (Cash-Basis Accounting) as of 1 January 2007

Assets		**Liabilities**	
Cash	100		0
		Equity	
		Common stock	100

During 2007, Cadence Cycling attracted two customers who brought their bikes to the store for service. The first customer pays $20 up front for the bike service and repairs. The second customer does not pay for the service up front; the estimated price for the service is $25. By the end of 2007, Cadence has completed work for the second customer but has not started the work for the first customer (we are ignoring the associated inventory parts to keep the example simple).

Under pure **cash basis** accounting, the only relevant transactions for the financial statements are those that involve cash. Thus, the balance sheet needed for this example includes only cash and cash equivalents, and the income statement (and statement of cash flows) is simply the change in cash and cash equivalents not attributable to external capital providers. The income statement and balance sheet under the cash basis would be as follows:

Cadence Cycling Income Statement (Cash-Basis Accounting) for the Year Ended 31 December 2007

Revenues	
Cash collected from Customer #1	20
Expenses	0
Net income	20

Cadence Cycling Balance Sheet (Cash-Basis Accounting) as of 31 December 2007

Assets		**Liabilities**	
Cash	120		0
		Equity	
		Common stock	100
		Retained earnings	20

Note: We ignored the associated inventory costs to focus the discussion on revenue.

Obviously, we do not see such financial statements in practice for publicly traded companies (although we will see how financial statements can be recast to compute a pure cash basis of earnings, which can be used to benchmark accrued earnings). Instead, we see an accrual accounting system. In contrast to cash basis accounting, under **accrual basis** of accounting it is *not* the cash flow that defines when revenues and expenses are recorded in the financial statements; rather, there is an earnings process that triggers the recognition of revenues and expenses. **Revenues** are increases in net assets that result from the principal income-generating activity of the company, and **expenses** are reductions in net assets associated with the creation of those revenues. Thus, for example, accrual accounting records revenue not when cash is collected, but when a good or service has been provided to the customer. The income statement and balance sheet under the accrual basis for Cadence Cycling would be as follows:

Cadence Cycling Income Statement (Accrual-Basis Accounting) for the Year Ended 31 December 2007

Revenues	
Bike services for Customer #2	25
Expenses	0
Net income	25

Cadence Cycling Balance Sheet (Accrual-Basis Accounting) as of 31 December 2007

Assets		**Liabilities**	
Cash	120	Unearned revenue	20
Receivable	25		
		Equity	
		Common stock	100
		Retained earnings	25

Note: We ignored the associated inventory costs to focus the discussion on revenue.

There is a striking difference in the summary performance measure across the two sets of financial statements. Under the cash basis, Cadence Cycling reports return on average total assets (ROA) of $20/[($100 + $120)/2] = 18.2%, whereas under the accrual basis the ROA is $25/[($100 + $145)/2] = 20.4%. There is good reason to focus on the accrual-based earnings measure of performance, as it gives a better indication of the "true" value-creating activities during the year. The differences between ROA on a cash basis and on an accrual basis of accounting are even greater if we consider investment activities in noncurrent assets (assets that have long useful lives). Under cash basis accounting, if these noncurrent investments, such as the purchase of property, plant, and equipment (PP&E), are paid for with cash, the cash outflow would constitute a reduction to income in the year of the investment, whereas under the accrual basis of accounting that amount initially gets capitalized as an asset and is then periodically depreciated over the useful life of the asset. In the year of the investment, an ROA measure from the cash basis will be substantially lower than under the accrual basis. Conversely, in later periods, if the company makes fewer such investments in PP&E, then ROA will be higher under the cash basis in those future periods as the depreciation charge will continue to flow through the income statement under the accrual basis of accounting. This example naturally leads to the question: What are the relative merits of cash basis and accrual earnings?

One of the main objectives of external financial statements is to provide information that is useful to investors. Accrual accounting has emerged as the accepted method of achieving this objective. Accrual accounting centers on the identification and measurement of assets and liabilities, with accruals representing changes in noncash assets and liabilities. The financial analyst should be able to analyze whether a company's use of discretion in implementing accruals facilitates or hampers investor decision making. The potential usefulness of the accrual system can be seen with the accruals and deferrals related to revenue recognition. For a company that sells a lot of its goods and services on credit terms, waiting until cash is received will not result in timely indication of the future cash flow generating ability of that enterprise. Instead, the company accrues revenues as the good is delivered or the service is provided. This is a desirable property of the accrual accounting system: It provides more timely and relevant information for decision making purposes. For example, if Cadence Cycling sold a bike during 2007 to a customer on credit, then under the cash basis of accounting that sale will not appear in the calculation of income for 2007. Instead, it will be recorded as revenue when the cash is collected in a future period. Under the accrual basis that sale will be recorded as revenue during 2007, with an adjustment for doubtful accounts (i.e., the full amount of the credit sale will be reduced based on an expectation of amounts that are not likely to be collected). The accrual basis of accounting therefore produces a net income figure that is more timely in communicating profit-generating activity to users of financial statements.

It is important to note that these same accruals bring with them discretion in estimating the amount of revenues that get allocated between fiscal periods. A number of questions must be answered before a number for revenue can be assigned to a given time period. For example, were the goods actually delivered? Were the services provided? Do the customers have recourse to return the merchandise? Do the customers have the ability, or credit-worthiness, to pay the receivable when it falls due? The answers to these questions are often subjective and create opportunities for strategic use of accrual accounting. By "strategic use" we mean that accounting numbers such as net income are important in a variety of contractual settings such as executive compensation. The economic incentives created by such contracts create an opportunity for management to be "strategic" or "opportunistic" when making determinations such as when a good has been provided, or how large a provision for doubtful accounts should be. We describe some of these incentives in more detail in Section 2.3.

Considerable research has examined whether cash basis or accrual basis performance measures are superior indicators of future cash flows and stock returns. The broad takeaway from the relevant literature is that accrual accounting earnings are superior to cash accounting earnings at summarizing company performance.[1] However, accrual accounting aggregates numerous estimations with respect to the deferral and accrual of various revenue and expenses. For example, choices on useful life and residual value for the purposes of estimating periodic depreciation, choices on provisioning for doubtful accounts, choices on assumptions for computing post-retirement obligations, etc., are all relevant in determining periodic net income. A simple way to isolate these aggregate accruals is to decompose accrued earnings into a cash flow and accrual component (we cover measurement of the components in Section 3.2). Extensive research has examined the benefits from this decomposition.[2] There is clear evidence that the accrual component of earnings is less persistent (i.e., more transitory) than the cash component of earnings. (To explain *persistence* further, a completely persistent earnings stream is one for which a euro of earnings today implies a euro of earnings for all future periods.) The implication is that while accrual accounting is superior to cash accounting, the accrual component of earnings should receive a lower weighting than the cash component of earnings

[1] See, for example, Dechow (1994).

[2] See, for example, Sloan (1996).

in evaluating company performance. This lower persistence is at least partly attributable to the greater subjectivity involved in the estimation of accruals.

The lower persistence of earnings resulting from high levels of accruals does not have to be a direct result of **earnings management activity** (i.e., deliberate activity aimed at influencing reporting earnings numbers, often with a goal of placing management in a favorable light). The nature of accrual accounting is to accrue and defer past, current, and anticipated future cash receipts and disbursements. The accrual process involves a significant amount of estimation of future cash receipts and payments, and a subjective allocation of past cash receipts and payments. In doing so, the accrual process creates accounts of varying reliability. For example, recording the net realizable value of receivables involves estimation of default risk across a portfolio of debtors. Other examples include estimating recoverable amounts of inventories, depreciating and amortizing long-lived assets, and estimating post-retirement benefit obligations. Estimation errors (either intentional or unintentional) for the various asset, liability, and associated revenue and expense accounts will all lead to lower persistence in earnings. Collectively, these estimations manifest themselves in the magnitude of reported accruals. We will examine detailed examples related to these accounting distortions later in the reading. Specifically, we will introduce some broad measures of accruals that are useful from an investment perspective. To the extent that investors do not assign a lower weighting to accruals (because they are unable to fully comprehend the greater subjectivity involved in the estimation of accruals), securities become mispriced with respect to that information. A good analyst should not make this error: The accrual component of earnings should rationally receive a lower multiple in valuation than the cash component.

2.2 Placing Accounting Discretion in Context

In this section we outline some of the key areas of discretion embedded in the financial statements and identify why this discretion could be used strategically by management. Financial statements prepared under generally accepted accounting principles are riddled with estimates. These estimates lower the reliability of reported earnings as a result of both neutral estimation errors and the opportunistic use of discretion. For example, when estimating the allowance for doubtful accounts on credit sales and the related provision for bad debts, an estimate of 3 percent of sales may be made; but the actual rate of default could turn out to be 5 percent. The 2 percent understatement of expense in the year the provision was created may simply be an error in estimation or it could be the result of management intervention to report a lower expense. Disentangling whether the estimation error is neutral or strategic can be difficult, but the net result is the same for the financial analyst. If you see choices made that tend to over-(under-) state current income, then on average *future* cash flows will be lower (higher) respectively.

Examples of sources of accounting discretion include the following:

- *Revenue recognition*: Provisions for doubtful accounts, warranty provisions, returns and allowances, channel stuffing (forcing more products through a sales distribution channel than the channel can sell), timing of service or provision of goods, etc.
- *Depreciation choices*: Estimation of useful lives, residual value, method choice
- *Inventory choices*: Cost flow assumptions, obsolescence estimation, etc.
- *Choices related to goodwill and other noncurrent assets*: Periodic impairment tests

- *Choices related to taxes*: Valuation allowances
- *Pension choices*: Estimated return on plan assets, discount rates, wage growth, employee turnover, etc.
- *Financial asset/liability valuation*: Recent accounting pronouncements (e.g., SFAS 157 on Fair Value Measurement in the United States)[3] focus on fair value as the basis for recording financial assets and liabilities. For certain types of financial assets and liabilities that rarely trade, there is considerable discretion in specifying the model inputs that would be used to assign a fair value.
- *Stock option expense estimates*: Volatility estimates, discount rates, etc.

The above is only a partial list. Everything other than cash (excluding fraudulently reported cash) is the result of choice. We want to understand this choice and learn how to utilize disclosures in financial statements to quantify the extent that these choices are driving reported earnings.

It is important to keep in mind that the accounting discretion we discuss in this reading is part of a broader set of management decisions and interactions with financial markets that affect investor expectations. For example, the strategic use of accounting discretion can be combined with real business decisions such as the cutting of research and development activity or timing inventory purchases under LIFO accounting (permitted under U.S. GAAP but not IFRS), which also have a direct impact on financial statements. Management also can communicate directly with capital markets via their investor relations departments, conference calls, and conference presentations. There is a large industry set up to facilitate these communications, which are used by companies to explain company performance and help set expectations for future performance.

2.3 Manipulation Incentives

Financial statement information is used in a variety of settings that can create the incentive for the preparers of those statements to be opportunistic when reporting results. In particular, preparers may hope to influence capital markets and/or measured performance under various contracts. We examine these incentives in more detail in the following sections.

2.3.1 Capital Markets

When financial information is reported to capital markets, security prices move. This creates a clear incentive for management to report financial performance that meets or exceeds current expectations and to manage expectations going forward.

Research has focused on the propensity for companies to report earnings that meet various thresholds (e.g., beat historical earnings and beat consensus analyst forecasts). The exhibits below neatly summarize this phenomenon. Exhibit 1 reports the relative frequency of return on the market value equity (defined as net income divided by the market value of equity). The sample included is all U.S. Security and Exchange Commission (SEC) registrants from 1988–2003 (this is effectively all companies with securities that were publicly traded in the United States in that period). The horizontal axis groups companies into "NI (net income) class" buckets. These buckets are formed by cross-sectional ranking all companies into groups based on the magnitude of net income scaled by market capitalization. Each bar corresponds to a 50 basis point

[3] The content of SFAS 157 is included in FASB ASC Topic 820 [Fair Value Measurements and Disclosures].

interval. For example, the bolded vertical bars correspond to firm-years where net income scaled by market capitalization is between 0 and 0.005 for the first bar, and between 0.005 and 0.01 for the second bolded bar. There is a clear "kink" in this distribution where more companies than expected report small profits (the bolded bars) compared to small losses. Some have claimed this kink is at least partly attributable to financial reporting manipulation.

EXHIBIT 1 **Distribution of Net Income Deflated by Market Value of Equity**

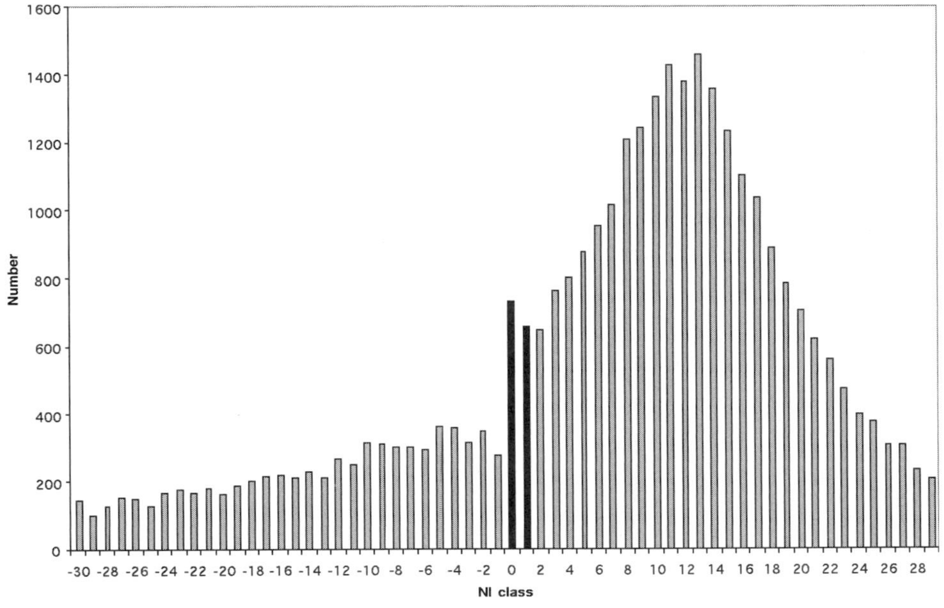

Source: Dechow, Richardson, and Tuna (2003).

Exhibit 2 reports the distribution of forecast errors for the same sample of companies. A forecast error is defined as the difference between reported earnings and the most recent consensus analyst earnings forecast prior to the earnings announcement. There is a clear incidence of an asymmetry around the "zero" forecast error (i.e., where more companies report earnings that slightly exceed sell-side analyst forecasts than companies that report earnings that just miss these forecasts). (*Sell-side analysts* work at firms that sell trading and related services.) This pattern appears to illustrate a combination of earnings management (i.e., opportunistic use of accruals) and **earnings expectations management** (i.e., encouraging analysts to forecast a slightly lower number than they would otherwise).

The target that the company is trying to achieve is a moving benchmark: the consensus sell-side forecast. Using strategic communications with the investment community, management is able to move this benchmark. Likewise, the reported earnings number is a moving target attributable to the discretion afforded to management. The focus on reporting earnings that meet consensus estimates has often been referred to as the **earnings game**. Indeed, there is evidence that this "game" is related to capital market pressures facing a company. If one looks at the pattern of forecast errors throughout the fiscal year, initial forecasts tend to be optimistic relative to reported earnings (i.e., analysts are

EXHIBIT 2 Distribution of Analyst Forecast Errors

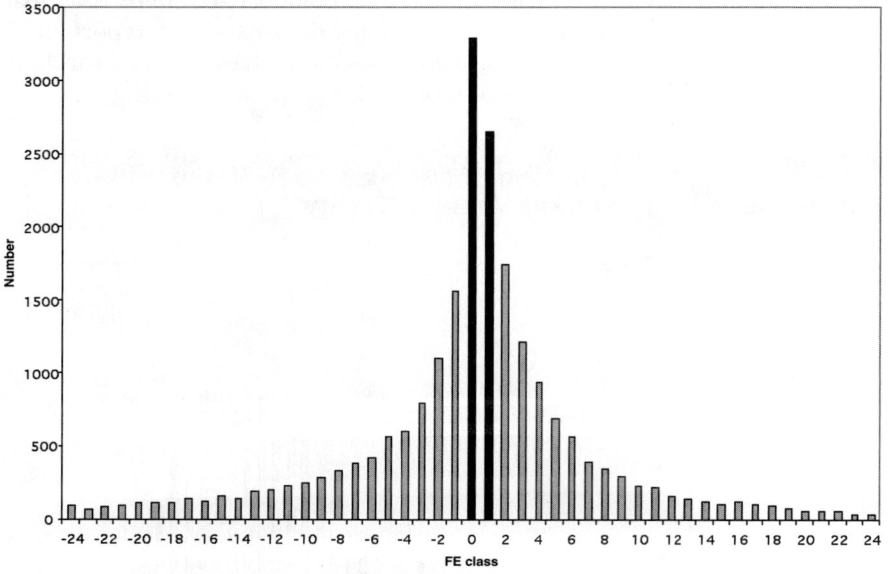

Source: Dechow, Richardson, and Tuna (2001).

forecasting a number early in the year that is greater than what the company ends up reporting), and the later forecasts tend to be pessimistic (i.e., analysts are forecasting a number later in the year that is less than what the company ends up reporting). This switch from early optimism to late pessimism leads to a positive earnings surprise when earnings are finally announced. Exhibit 3 summarizes this pattern for the same sample of companies, and it is clear that this pattern has become increasingly common in more recent years. Furthermore, this pattern is stronger for companies that are subsequently issuing equity, or where insiders are, on average, selling their equity stake.

Besides capital markets, a variety of contracts can provide manipulation incentives, as discussed in the next section.

2.3.2 Contracts

Accounting information is used in a variety of contracts, including managerial contracts and contracts related to financial securities. Both types of contracts can provide the incentive for management to use accounting discretion opportunistically.

For example, managerial compensation is typically set as a function of reported earnings numbers (either in absolute terms or relative to a benchmark) as well as linked to stock price information, which in turn is a function of reported earnings. As an example, Textron Inc. reports in its 2006 proxy statement that the performance criteria used for its short-term and long-term incentive plans includes various financial statement based measures including return on assets, and various profit margin and turnover measures. Financial statement information is regularly used as a basis for the determination of executive compensation. These contracts provide a very direct incentive for management to be opportunistic in their use of accounting discretion.

EXHIBIT 3 Forecast Errors across the Fiscal Year

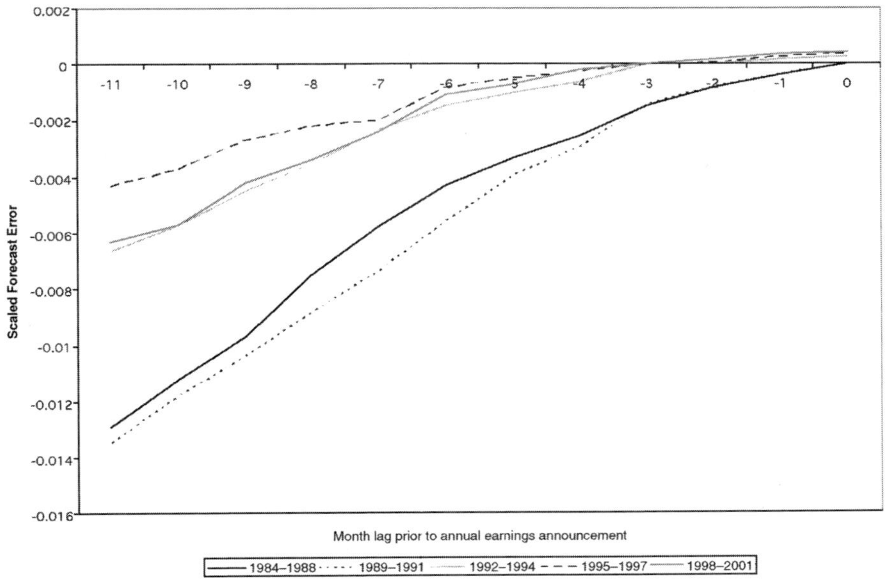

Source: Richardson, Teoh, and Wysocki (2004).

There are other contracts where accounting information also is used, such as debt contracts. Companies with outstanding debt are parties to one or more **debt covenants** (agreements between the company as borrower and its creditors) that typically have a variety of restrictions (e.g., the company must maintain a minimum interest coverage ratio to avoid technical default and potentially costly debt renegotiation) and possibly performance pricing grids where interest costs are explicitly tied to financial performance. Collectively, these contracts provide very clear incentives for management to strategically use the accounting discretion afforded to them.

2.4 Mechanisms Disciplining Management

The discussion thus far points to many opportunities for management to manipulate reported financial results. Should we therefore place very little value on the output of this system? No. Financial statements provide very useful information in part due to the standard set of rules according to which they are prepared despite the discretion allowed by the standards. There are many mechanisms curtailing abuse of that discretion. Some examples of the mechanisms ensuring truthful reporting include:

- *External auditors.* Every public company is required to have their financial statements audited by a registered auditor. This process provides independent verification of the statements. Specifically, the external auditor's responsibility is to express an opinion on the truthfulness of consolidated financial statements, an opinion on management's assessment of internal controls, and an opinion on the effectiveness of internal financial reporting controls. Auditors' opinions that are other than "unqualified" reflect a disagreement about the treatment or disclosure of information in the financial statements.

- *Internal auditors, audit committee, and the board.* The board of directors, through its committees and oversight of internal auditors, has the capacity to act as a check on management.
- *Management certification.* For companies subject to the U.S. Sarbanes–Oxley Act of 2002, the CEO and CFO must now certify the financial statements increasing their litigation risk, so they have more personal risk than formerly in manipulating reported financial results.
- *Lawyers.* Class action lawsuits are a potentially effective way to mitigate incentives to game the financial reporting system.
- *Regulators.* Regulatory actions, up to criminal prosecution for certain misdeeds, can make managers think twice about their actions.
- *General market scrutiny.* Financial journalists, short sellers, activist institutions, employee unions, analysts, etc. are constantly studying financial statements in an effort to identify financial shenanigans.

3 FINANCIAL REPORTING QUALITY: DEFINITIONS, ISSUES, AND AGGREGATE MEASURES

In this section we lay out a broad framework for financial reporting quality, focusing on earnings quality. Earnings quality is typically defined in terms of persistence and sustainability. For example, analysts often claim that earnings are considered to be of high quality when they are sustainable or when they "expect the reported level of earnings to be sustained or continued." These approaches have at their core a view on forecasting future cash flows or earnings which is central to valuation. A summary performance measure that better forecasts future cash flows or earnings is arguably of higher quality than one which is a less effective forecaster, as it better serves that valuation purpose. Other discussions of earnings quality look at the extent of aggressive or conservative choices that have been made in the financial statements of the companies under examination. For example, companies that have used an accelerated depreciation method, have high allowances for inventory obsolescence and doubtful accounts, or have large unearned revenue balances could be considered to have employed conservative accounting choices. This is because earnings have been depressed in the current period. However, given the range of potential earnings outcomes, simply equating choices that lower reported earnings with high earnings quality provides at best a marginal indicator of financial reporting quality as defined in the introduction of this reading. Reporting earnings that are too high or too low results in an inferior earnings measure for the purpose of forecasting future company performance. Accruals are not independent over time. Rather, accruals have a natural self-correcting property. For example, an aggressive accounting choice in the past that capitalized an excess amount of cost into a noncurrent asset will lead to larger write-downs of that asset in future periods. Thus, the earlier aggressive choice (avoiding expensing at the time of capitalization) is associated with a later conservative action (expensing). Focusing on changes in balance sheet accounts, or equivalently the multitude of accruals and deferrals embedded in net income, is an efficient and effective way to capture cross-sectional variation in earnings quality. These accrual-based measures capture both aggressive and conservative accounting choices that impair the ability of accrued earnings to forecast future company performance.

3.1 Mean Reversion in Earnings

Our focus on accruals and deferrals for earnings quality has valuation at its core. Our aim is to identify companies that have earnings which are more persistent or sustainable than their peers. In that context, the analyst should be aware of the empirically observed tendency of earnings at extreme levels to revert back to normal levels (mean reversion in earnings). The phenomenon has an economic explanation. Competitive markets (including the market for corporate control) tend to lead to correction of strategic or managerial problems causing poor performance; poorly performing businesses and segments tend to be abandoned. Subject to barriers to entry, capital migrates toward more profitable businesses and segments, increasing competition and reducing returns. The net effect of these competitive forces is to move earnings back to a "normal" level. Data analyzed by Nissim and Penman (2001) show that this pattern of mean reversion in earnings is very pervasive. Exhibit 4 below summarizes the mean reverting behavior in return on net operating assets (RNOA) for a large sample of SEC registrants. Every year companies are sorted into ten equal groups and the average RNOA for these ten portfolios are tracked over the next six years. There is a clear reversion back to a range between 8–20 percent by the end of six years.

EXHIBIT 4 Mean Reversion in Accounting Rates of Return (Return on Net Operating Assets)

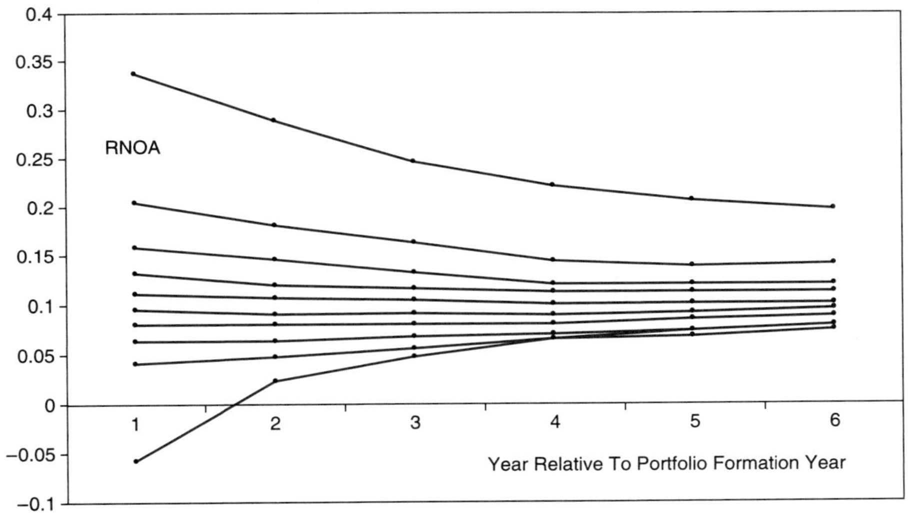

Source: Reprinted from *Review of Accounting Studies 6*, no. 1, by Doron Nissim and Stephen Penman (March 2001), with kind permission of Springer Science and Business Media.

Understanding this reverting property of earnings is of fundamental importance for financial statement analysis. To build a meaningful forecast of future cash flows one should recognize that very low and very high earnings are not expected to continue into the future. Using information in accruals we can improve these forecasts of future cash flow further. As mentioned earlier, earnings have a cash flow and an accrual component. Algebraically, earnings are equal to cash flows plus accruals. When earnings are largely comprised of accruals, the evidence referenced in Section 2.1 suggests that future accounting rates of return and future cash flows would be lower. This is equivalent to saying that earnings will revert back to a normal level even quicker when earnings are largely comprised of accruals as opposed to cash flows. This is not surprising: The accrual component of earnings is where the accounting distortions are greatest and for which we expect there to be lower persistence.

In summary, earnings that are more persistent are viewed as higher quality. This decomposition of earnings into its accrual and cash flow components creates a superior forecast for future earnings and cash flows; furthermore, as already mentioned, earnings components that are less persistent should rationally receive a lower multiple in valuation. In a later section, we will walk through many examples of transactions that give rise to low quality earnings streams. One thing that is common to all of the examples of low earnings quality is the fact that current earnings are temporarily distorted relative to "true" earnings, due to various accounting choices, but cash flows are unaffected.

3.2 Measures of the Accrual Component of Earnings and Earnings Quality

In this section we lay out the framework for measuring the cash and accrual components of earnings using standardized financial statements. We explain various measures of the accrual component of earnings (the cash component being the remainder after subtracting the accrual component from reported earnings). Finally, we present scaled measures of accrual components as simple measures of earnings quality that working analysts can readily compute and use.

Exhibit 5 presents the three primary financial statements in standardized formats. The format selected is based on the one used by Compustat in processing the reported financials of companies trading in the United States, with simplifications.[4] Using a standardized format has advantages in facilitating cross-sectional comparisons across companies.[5] Note that "income before extraordinary items" is possible under U.S. Generally Accepted Accounting Principles (U.S. GAAP) but not under International Financial Reporting Standards (IFRS), and "minority interest" must appear in the equity section under IFRS but can be placed in liabilities, in the equity section, or in between according to U.S. GAAP (Compustat places it in liabilities).[6] Making adjustments for such differences where required is part and parcel of analysts' work.

---

[4] The simplifications include using one line for items that are usually broken down into multiple lines. As examples, "cash and short-term investments" in actual financial statements is often presented in two lines as "cash and cash equivalents" and "short-term investments," and "Common equity—Total" is analyzed into multiple components (Compustat gives seven lines) including "common stock," "capital surplus," "retained earnings," "accumulated other comprehensive income," etc.

[5] A good example of the usefulness of a standardized format relates to the disclosure of depreciation and amortization. Most companies include this charge as part of selling, general, and administrative (SG&A) expenses or cost of goods sold in their regulatory filings. But analysts are able to identify these data from supplemental footnote disclosures, which the data providers capture and then treat systematically.

[6] Effective after 15 December 2008, U.S. GAAP require noncontrolling (minority) interest to be reported separately from the parent's equity but within total equity. This is an example of U.S. GAAP and IFRS converging.

EXHIBIT 5 Financial Statements (in a Standardized Format)

Panel A: Balance Sheet

Cash and short-term investments	a	Debt in current liabilities	i
Receivables (net)	b	Accounts payable	j
Inventories (net)	c	Income taxes payable	k
Other current assets	d	Other current liabilities	l
Total current assets (TCA):	**a+b+c+d**	**Total current liabilities (TCL):**	**i+j+k+l**
Property, plant, and equipment (net)	e	Long-term debt	m
Investments and advances	f	Deferred taxes	n
Intangibles (net)	g	Other noncurrent liabilities	o
Other noncurrent assets	h	**Total noncurrent liabilities (TNL):**	**m+n+o**
Total noncurrent assets (TNA):	**e+f+g+h**	**Minority interest**	**MI**
Total assets	**TCA+TNA**	**Total liabilities (TL):**	**TCL+TNL+MI**
		Preferred stock (book value)	p
		Common equity − Total	q
		Total shareholders' equity (OE)	**p+q**
		Total liabilities and shareholders' equity	**TL + OE**

Panel B: Income Statement

Net revenue	a
Less: Cost of goods sold	b
Less: Selling, general & admin.	c
Operating income before depreciation (OIBD)	**a−b−c**
Less: Depreciation and amortization expense	d
Operating income after depreciation (OIAD)	**OIBD−d**
Less: Interest expense (net)	e
Less: Special items and other nonoperating items	f
Less: Tax expense	g
Income before extraordinary items (IBXI)	**OIAD−e−f−g**
Less: Extraordinary items	h
Net Income (NI)	**IBXI−h**

Panel C: Cash Flow Statement

Income before extraordinary items	**IBXI**
+ Depreciation and amortization expense	a
+ Deferred taxes	b
+ Equity in net loss (earnings)	c
+ (−) Loss (gain) on sale of noncurrent assets	d
+ Other funds from operations	e
+ (−) Decrease (increase) in net working capital	f

(Exhibit continued on next page . . .)

EXHIBIT 5 (continued)

Operating cash flows	**CFO = IBXI + a + b + c + d + e + f**
− Increase in investments	g
+ Sale of investments	h
− Capital expenditures	i
+ Sale of property, plant, and equipment	j
− Acquisitions	k
Investing cash flows	**CFI = − g + h − i + j − k**
+ Sale of common and preferred stock	l
− Stock repurchases and dividends	m
+ Issuance of debt	n
− Reduction of debt	o
Financing cash flows	**CFF = l − m + n − o**
Change in cash and cash equivalents	**CFO + CFI + CFF**

Notes:

1. Debt in current liabilities includes the current portion of long-term debt and notes payable.
2. Equity in net loss (earnings) is sometimes called "equity income or loss, net of dividends."
3. Other funds from operations can include items such as stock-based compensation expense and foreign currency adjustments.
4. In the cash flow statement, "net working capital" is (Accounts receivable + Inventory) − (Accounts payable + Accrued liabilities); the term is not used by Compustat, but is introduced here to summarize four Compustat line items.

The financial statements presented above are based on an accrual accounting system. Other than cash, every line item in the balance sheet is the result of subjective choices surrounding recognition and valuation rules. For example: 1) Receivables are reported on a net basis after making a determination that a sale was made and those credit sales are to customers with sufficient capacity to make good on the amounts they owe; 2) Inventories are also reported on a net basis assuming that there is sufficient future sales demand to be able to sell these items at an amount greater than their historical cost. Similar explanations can be made for every other line item in the balance sheet. Considerable discretion resides throughout the accrual-based financial statements.

In contrast, financial statements based on a pure cash basis are devoid of this discretion: "cash is cash." Absent fraud, there is no disputing ownership and the valuation of cash. Contrasting financial statements prepared on a cash basis with those prepared on an accrual basis is therefore a natural way to identify the extent of discretion embedded in the reported financial statements. Effectively, this amounts to comparing a pure change in cash measure of earnings with the reported earnings under the relevant set of accrual accounting principles (e.g., U.S. GAAP or IFRS). The difference is aggregate accruals or the accrual component of earnings:

$$\text{Aggregate accruals} = \text{Accrual-basis earnings} - \text{Cash earnings} \quad (1)$$

There are several ways that we can decompose reported accrual earnings into a cash flow and accrual component. We can focus on information in the balance sheet, or we can focus on information in the statement of cash flows. We prefer the latter approach because it generates a cleaner measure that is free from the effects of noncash acquisitions and foreign currency translation adjustment effects. We now outline the two approaches to this decomposition of accruals and the definition of a quantity ("accrual ratio") for comparing accruals across companies or for one company over time.

First, using balance sheet data, we can measure the net change across all noncash accounts to compute the aggregate accruals for that fiscal period. With the sample balance sheet reported above, aggregate accruals are simply the change in net assets (net of the cash and debt-related accounts) from the start to the end of the period. We first define **net operating assets** (NOA) as the difference between operating assets (total assets less cash) and operating liabilities (total liabilities less total debt):

$$\text{NOA}_t = [(\text{Total assets}_t - \text{Cash}_t) - (\text{Total liabilities}_t - \text{Total debt}_t)] \quad \textbf{(2)}$$

We exclude cash (shorthand here for "cash and short-term investments") and debt from our measure as these accounts are essentially discretion free. (This is not entirely true as there are some accounting accruals/deferrals embedded in debt, e.g., amortization of discounts/premium, but these can be ignored for our purposes here.)

From a balance sheet perspective, we measure aggregate accruals for period t as the change in NOA over the period:

$$\text{Aggregate accruals}_t^{B/S} = \text{NOA}_t - \text{NOA}_{t-1} \quad \textbf{(3)}$$

We can call the measure presented in Equation 3 **balance-sheet-based aggregate accruals**. To adapt the measure as an indicator of earnings quality, it must be made comparable across companies by adjusting for differences in company size. An easy way to do the adjustment is to deflate (i.e., scale) the aggregate accrual measure by the *average* value of NOA. If one just used the opening or ending value of NOA as the scaling quantity, the ratio would be distorted by companies that have experienced significant growth or contractions during the fiscal period. The scaled measure (which we can call the **balance-sheet-based accruals ratio**) is our first measure of financial reporting quality and given by

$$\text{Accruals ratio}_t^{B/S} = \frac{(\text{NOA}_t - \text{NOA}_{t-1})}{(\text{NOA}_t + \text{NOA}_{t-1})/2} \quad \textbf{(4)}$$

The accruals measures defined in Equations 3 and 4 involve the summation of all of the line items of the balance sheet. If you are interested in subcomponents of accrual activity, then simply focus on the relevant line item from the balance sheet. For example, looking at the change in net receivables over a fiscal period deflated by average NOA will give you a sense of the magnitude of accrued revenue attributable to net credit sales.

We can also look at the statement of cash flows. For this approach we are looking at the difference between reported accrual earnings and the cash flows attributable to operating and investing activities. From a cash flow statement perspective, a measure of aggregate accruals can be defined as follows:[7]

$$\text{Aggregate accruals}_t^{CF} = NI_t - (CFO_t + CFI_t) \quad (5)$$

We can call this **cash-flow-statement-based aggregate accruals**. The corresponding scaled measure (**cash-flow-statement-based accruals ratio**) is our second simple measure of financial reporting quality:

$$\text{Accruals ratio}_t^{CF} = \frac{[NI_t - (CFO_t + CFI_t)]}{(NOA_t + NOA_{t-1})/2} \quad (6)$$

The measures in Equations 5 and 6 aggregate all of the operating and investing activities and their impact on cash flows relative to accrued earnings. The result is a cash-flow-statement-based measure of aggregate accruals. The inclusion of the cash flow from investing activities (CFI_t) in Equations 5 and 6 may require explanation. From a valuation perspective, there are essentially only two sides to the company: the operating side (broadly conceived) and the financing side. However, the cash flow statement splits the operating side into "operating" and "investing" pieces (roughly, current and noncurrent operating pieces). When calculating a broad accruals ratio, the appropriate treatment is to include both cash flow pieces (CFO and CFI). In applying Equations 5 and 6, the analyst should make any needed adjustments for differences in the cash flow statement treatment of interest and dividends across companies being examined.[8] These adjustments ensure consistency in the treatment of operating and financing activities. For example, if Company A treats interest paid as an operating cash outflow (under U.S. GAAP) and Company B treats interest paid as a financing cash flow (under IFRS), the systematic differences in leverage across the two companies could create significant differences in a computed aggregate accrual measure. Treating interest paid consistently across the companies (e.g., as a financing cash outflow) will mitigate this problem.

Example 1 illustrates the calculation of the ratios for an actual company.

[7] In applying Equations 5 and 6 for companies reporting under U.S. GAAP, where comparison with non-U.S. GAAP reporting companies is not an issue, analysts may prefer to use $IBXI_t$ rather than NI_t.

[8] In particular, IFRS allows operating or financing cash flow treatment of interest paid and dividends paid, whereas U.S. GAAP currently specifies operating cash flow treatment of interest paid and financing cash flow treatment of dividends paid.

EXAMPLE 1

The Coca-Cola Company: An Illustration of Accrual Analysis

Below, recent financial statements for the Coca-Cola Company (NYSE: KO) have been put in the format of Exhibit 5.[9]

The Coca-Cola Company Financial Statements in Standardized Format Year Ended 31 December (Amounts in $Millions)

Panel A: Balance Sheet	**2006**	**2005**
Cash and short-term investments	2,590	4,767
Receivables (net)	2,587	2,281
Inventories (net)	1,641	1,424
Other current assets	1,623	1,778
Total current assets	8,441	10,250
Property, plant, and equipment (net)	6,903	5,786
Investments and advances	6,783	6,922
Intangibles (net)	5,135	3,821
Other noncurrent assets	2,701	2,648
Total noncurrent assets	21,522	19,177
Total assets	29,963	29,427
Debt in current liabilities	3,268	4,546
Accounts payable	929	2,315
Income taxes payable	567	797
Other current liabilities	4,126	2,178
Total current liabilities	8,890	9,836
Long-term debt	1,314	1,154
Deferred taxes	608	352
Other noncurrent liabilities	2,231	1,730
Total noncurrent liabilities	4,153	3,236
Minority interest	0	0
Total liabilities	13,043	13,072
Preferred stock (book value)	0	0
Common equity − Total	16,920	16,355
Total shareholders' equity	16,920	16,355
Total liabilities and shareholders' equity	29,963	29,427

(continued on next page. . .)

[9] In Panel A, the balance sheet, "deferred taxes" refers to *accumulated* deferred taxes. In Panel B, the statement of cash flows, "deferred taxes" refers to deferred tax expense related to the single period being reported, 2006. Note also that the concise balance sheet pools cash and cash equivalents and short-term investments into one line so the change in cash and cash equivalents of −2,261 shown in the statement of cash flows cannot be confirmed directly. However, the more detailed balance sheet in the Form 10-K disclosure for Coca-Cola shows that cash and cash equivalents in 2005 to 2006 were \$4,701 and \$2,440, respectively; as \$2,440 − 4,701 = −\$2,261, this confirms the value shown in the statement of cash flows.

(continued)

Panel B: Income Statement	**2006**
Net revenue	24,088
Less: Cost of goods sold	7,358
Less: Selling, general & admin. expenses	9,195
Operating income before depreciation	**7,535**
Less: Depreciation and amortization expense	938
Operating income after depreciation	**6,597**
Less: Interest expense (net)	220
Plus: Special items and other nonoperating items	201
Less: Tax expense	1,498
Income before extraordinary items	**5,080**
Less: Extraordinary items	0
Net income	**5,080**

Panel C: Statement of Cash Flows	**2006**
Income before extraordinary items	5,080
+ Depreciation and amortization expense	938
+ Deferred taxes	−35
+ Equity in net loss (earnings)	124
+ (−) Loss (gain) on sale of noncurrent assets	−303
+ Other funds from operations	768
+ (−) Decrease (increase) in net working capital	−615
Operating cash flows	**5,957**
− Increase in investments	1,045
+ Sale of investments	640
− Capital expenditures	1,407
+ Sale of property, plant, and equipment	112
− Acquisitions	0
Investing cash flows	**−1,700**
+ Sale of common stock	148
− Stock repurchases and dividends	5,327
+ Issuance of debt	617
− Reduction of debt	2,021
Financing cash flows	**−6,583**
Less: Exchange rate effects	65
Change in cash and cash equivalents	**−2,261**

Based on the information given, address the following problems:

1. Calculate net operating assets for Coca-Cola for 2006 and 2005.
2. Calculate balance-sheet-based aggregate accruals for Coca-Cola for 2006.
3. Calculate the balance-sheet-based accruals ratio for Coca-Cola for 2006.
4. Calculate cash-flow-statement-based aggregate accruals for Coca-Cola for 2006.
5. Calculate the cash-flow-statement-based accruals ratio for Coca-Cola for 2006.
6. State and explain which of the measures calculated in Problems 1 through 5 would be appropriate to use in evaluating relative financial reporting quality of a group of companies.

Solutions to 1, 2, and 3: These are given in the worksheet below.

Balance Sheet Computation of Aggregate Accruals

	2006	2005	
Operating Assets			
Total assets	29,963	29,427	
Less: Cash and short-term investments	2,590	4,767	
Operating assets **(A)**	27,373	24,660	
Operating Liabilities			
Total liabilities	13,043	13,072	
Less: Long-term debt	1,314	1,154	
Less: Debt in current liabilities	3,268	4,546	
Operating liabilities **(B)**	8,461	7,372	
Net Operating Assets = (A) − (B)	**18,912**	**17,288**	Solution to 1
Balance-Sheet-Based Aggregate Accruals			
BSA = $\text{NOA}_{2006} - \text{NOA}_{2005}$	**1,624**		Solution to 2
Average Net Operating Assets (AvgNOA)	18,100		
Balance-Sheet-Based Accruals Ratio = BSA/AvgNOA	**8.97%**		Solution to 3

Problem 1: The amount of net operating assets is found as the difference between operating assets (total assets minus cash and short-term investments) and operating liabilities (total liabilities minus total debt). For 2005 and 2006, net operating assets amount to $17,288 million and $18,912 million, respectively.

Problem 2: The amount of balance-sheet-based aggregate accruals for 2006 is found as the change in net operating assets from 2005 to 2006. This amount is $1,624 million.

Problem 3: The balance-sheet-based accruals ratio for 2006 is found by dividing balance-sheet-based aggregate accruals for 2006, $1,624 million, by average net operating assets, (18,912 + 17,288)/2 = $18,100 million. This ratio is equal to 1,624/18,100 = 8.97 percent.

Solutions to 4 and 5: These are given in the worksheet below.

Cash Flow Statement Computation of Aggregate Accruals

	2006	
Income Before Extraordinary Items	5,080	
Less: Operating Cash Flows	5,957	
Less: Investing Cash Flows	−1,700	
Cash-Flow-Statement-Based Aggregate Accruals (A)	**823**	Solution to 4
Cash-Flow-Statement-Based Accruals Ratio = (A)/AvgNOA	**4.55%**	Solution to 5

Note: AvgNOA is 18,100 (see previous worksheet).

Solution to 6: Among the measures presented in Problems 2 through 5, only the size-scaled measures calculated in Problems 3 and 5 are appropriate for cross-company comparisons. The unscaled measures in Problems 2 and 4 would be affected by differences in company size.

Consistent with the discussion above on the balance sheet approach to measuring accruals, we also could focus on current versus noncurrent accruals by looking only at the difference between reported income and operating cash flows for current accruals. It is important to note that while the two approaches (balance sheet and statement of cash flows) are conceptually equivalent, they will not generate the exact same numbers due to a combination of noncash acquisitions, currency translation, and inconsistent classification across the balance sheet and statement of cash flows. These differences, however, are typically small and can be ignored for our purpose. The typical correlation between a broad accrual measure based on balance sheet data with one based on statement of cash flow data is in excess of 0.80. The important thing to remember is to compare companies using the same method. If you prefer to use a balance sheet approach or a statement of cash flow approach, be sure to keep that method constant across companies. If you use different methods across companies, this will distort your comparison. But using one approach systematically will give a very similar rank ordering of companies as using the other approach systematically.

3.3 Applying the Simple Measures of Earnings Quality

The simple measures of earnings quality defined by Equations 4 and 6 are an effective way to partition companies into low and high earnings quality groups. Given the broad discretion afforded to management, it can be difficult to identify specifically which accrual or deferral was manipulated in a given fiscal period. Rather than attempt to measure discretion embedded within each accrual, an effective alternative is to focus on the aggregate. This aggregate measure will reflect the portfolio of discretion and its impact on income for a given fiscal period. In this section we give further examples to illustrate the measures. Example 2 compares two companies. In contrast to Example 1, the original account labels have been retained in the example.

EXAMPLE 2

A Quality-of-Earnings Comparison of Two Companies

Siemens, AG is a global electronics and electrical engineering company headquartered in Munich, Germany. Selected data (in € millions) from Siemens' financial statements for the years ended 30 September 2006, 2005, and 2004 are presented below.

Siemens, AG Fiscal Years Ended 30 September (in Millions of €)

Selected Income Statement Data	2006	2005	2004
Net sales	87,325	75,445	70,237
Income from continuing operations, before tax	4,371	4,185	4,369
Income (loss) from discontinued operations	(54)	(810)	(45)
Net income	3,033	2,248	3,405

Selected Balance Sheet Data	2006	2005	2004
Cash and equivalents	10,214	8,121	12,190
Marketable securities	596	1,789	1,386
Total current assets	51,611	46,803	45,946
Total assets	90,973	86,117	79,518
Short-term debt	2,175	3,999	1,434
Total current liabilities	38,957	39,631	33,372
Long-term debt	13,399	8,436	9,785
Total liabilities	61,667	59,095	52,663

Selected Statement of Cash Flows Data	2006	2005	2004
Net cash provided by (used in) operating activities	4,981	3,121	5,080
Net cash provided by (used in) operating activities – continuing operations	5,174	4,217	4,704

(continued on next page. . .)

(continued)

Selected Statement of Cash Flows Data	2006	2005	2004
Net cash provided by (used in) investing activities	(4,614)	(5,824)	(1,818)
Net cash provided by (used in) investing activities − continuing operations	(4,435)	(5,706)	(1,689)
Net cash provided by (used in) financing activities	1,802	(1,403)	(3,108)

General Electric is a diversified global industrial corporation headquartered in Fairfield, Connecticut, USA. Selected data (in $ millions) from GE's financial statements for the years ended 31 December 2006, 2005, and 2004 are presented below.

General Electric Company and Consolidated Affiliates Years Ended 31 December (in Millions of $)

Selected Income Statement Data	2006	2005	2004
Net sales	163,391	147,956	134,291
Income from continuing operations, before tax	24,620	22,696	20,297
Income (loss) from discontinued operations	163	(1,950)	559
Net income	20,829	16,711	17,160

Selected Balance Sheet Data as of 31 December	2006	2005	2004
Cash and equivalents	14,275	8,825	12,152
Marketable securities	47,826	42,148	56,923
Total current assets	87,456	76,298	93,086
Total assets	697,239	673,321	750,507
Short-term debt	172,153	158,156	157,195
Total current liabilities	220,514	204,970	200,047
Long-term debt	260,804	212,281	207,871
Total liabilities	577,347	555,916	627,083

(continued on next page. . .)

(continued)

Selected Statement of Cash Flows Data	2006	2005	2004
Net cash provided by (used in) operating activities	30,646	37,691	36,493
Net cash provided by (used in) operating activities – continuing operations	33,019	32,664	30,872
Net cash provided by (used in) investing activities	(51,402)	(35,099)	(38,423)
Net cash provided by (used in) investing activities – continuing operations	(51,019)	(29,366)	(30,772)
Net cash provided by (used in) financing activities	23,230	(6,119)	4,594

Based on the information given, address the following:

1. Calculate net operating assets for Siemens and GE for each year presented.
2. Calculate aggregate accruals using both the balance sheet and cash flow statement methods for Siemens and GE for each year presented.
3. Calculate the balance-sheet-based and cash-flow-statement-based accruals ratios for Siemens and GE for each year presented.
4. **A.** State and explain which company had higher earnings quality in 2005 and 2006.

   B. Identify any trends in earnings quality for each company.
5. Would the results of question 4 be different if the accruals ratios were calculated based only on continuing operations?
6. General Electric recorded net financing receivables of $334,232 in 2006 and $292,639 in 2005. It describes these receivables in the notes to its financial statements as largely relating to direct financing leases. Evaluate this disclosure with respect to GE's earnings quality.

Solution to 1: Net operating assets is defined as (total assets − cash and marketable securities) − (total liabilities − total debt). For example, in 2006 Siemens reported total assets of 90,973 and cash and marketable securities of 10,214 + 596 = 10,810. Total liabilities were 61,667 and total debt was 2,175 + 13,399 = 15,574. (90,973 − 10,810) − (61,667 − 15,574) = 80,163 − 46,093 = 34,070. The values for each firm are summarized on the following page.

Net Operating Assets	2006	2005	2004
Siemens	34,070	29,547	24,498
General Electric	490,748	436,869	419,415

Solution to 2: Balance sheet aggregate accruals are defined as the change in net operating assets. As such, only two years' worth of accruals can be calculated from the data given. For example, for Siemens, using the answers to Problem 1, balance sheet aggregate accruals for 2006 equal €34,070 − €29,547 = €4,523.

Balance Sheet Aggregate Accruals	2006	2005
Siemens	4,523	5,049
General Electric	53,879	17,454

Cash flow statement aggregate accruals are defined as net income − (cash flows from operating activity + cash flows from investing activity). For example, for Siemens in 2006, cash flow statement aggregate accruals are found as NI of €3,033 minus [CFO of €4,981 + (CFI of −€4,614)] = €3,033 minus €367 = €2,666.

Cash Flow Statement Aggregate Accruals	2006	2005	2004
Siemens	2,666	4,951	143
General Electric	41,585	14,119	19,090

Solution to 3: The accrual ratio is defined as aggregate accruals divided by average net operating assets. Because the denominator requires an average of two years' data, only two years of accrual ratios can be calculated. For example, for Siemens, average net operating assets for 2006 were (€34,070 + €29,547)/2 = €31,808.5. With aggregate accruals for 2006 of €4,523 and €2,666 by the balance sheet and cash flow statement methods, respectively, the corresponding accrual ratios were €4,523/€31,808.5 = 14.2 percent and €2,666/€31,808.5 = 8.4 percent.

Balance-Sheet-Based Accrual Ratio	2006 (%)	2005 (%)
Siemens	14.2	18.7
General Electric	11.6	4.1

Cash-Flow-Statement-Based Accrual Ratio	2006 (%)	2005 (%)
Siemens	8.4	18.3
General Electric	9.0	3.3

Solution to 4:

A. Using the balance-sheet-based accrual ratio, General Electric has higher earnings quality (i.e., lower accruals ratio) in both years. Using the cash-flow-statement-based measure, GE actually shows lower earnings quality than Siemens only in 2006.

B. Using either earnings quality measure, Siemens shows improving earnings quality from 2005 to 2006, while GE shows deteriorating earnings quality.

Solution to 5: Subtracting the results of discontinued operations from net income and using the cash flow data from continuing operations, the results of the calculations are:

Cash Flow Statement Accruals—Continuing Operations	2006	2005	2004
Siemens	2,348	4,547	435
General Electric	38,666	15,363	16,501
Accrual Ratio—Continuing Operations			
Siemens	7.4%	16.8%	
General Electric	8.3	3.6	

Using continuing operations does not significantly alter either the level or trends in accruals for these companies.

Solution to 6: The $41,593 million change in financing receivables accounts for a large portion of GE's $53,879 million change in net operating assets. Compared to treating the leases as operating leases (see the reading on long-term liabilities), accounting for leases as direct financing leases increases net income in the early years of a lease but the same total net income is recognized over the lease life. Under direct financing lease accounting, operating cash flow is lower, but investing cash flows are higher. When considering the cash versus accrual portions of earnings, this disclosure allows us to conclude that GE's 2006 earnings are likely less persistent (of lower quality) than its 2005 earnings.

Broad measures of aggregate accruals are quite effective in identifying companies with financial reporting quality issues. Using a broad sample of earnings restatements from 1979 through 2002, Richardson, Tuna, and Wu (2002) found strong evidence that these restatements are concentrated in companies reporting the highest level of total accruals. Exhibit 6 summarizes these findings. Every year, SEC registrants are sorted into ten equal-sized groups based on the magnitude of total accruals, using the statement of cash flow definition above (Equation 6). Exhibit 6 reports the relative frequency of earnings restatements across these ten equal-sized groups. The upward sloping line is quite telling: Of the 440 earnings restatements examined, there is a concentration in the highest accrual group (low earnings quality). Specifically, for the lowest accrual group (high earnings quality) only 7.5 percent of the 440 restatements are to be found, but in the highest accrual group we see 18 percent of the 440 restatement companies.

EXHIBIT 6 Relative Frequency of Earnings Restatements as a Function of Aggregate Accruals

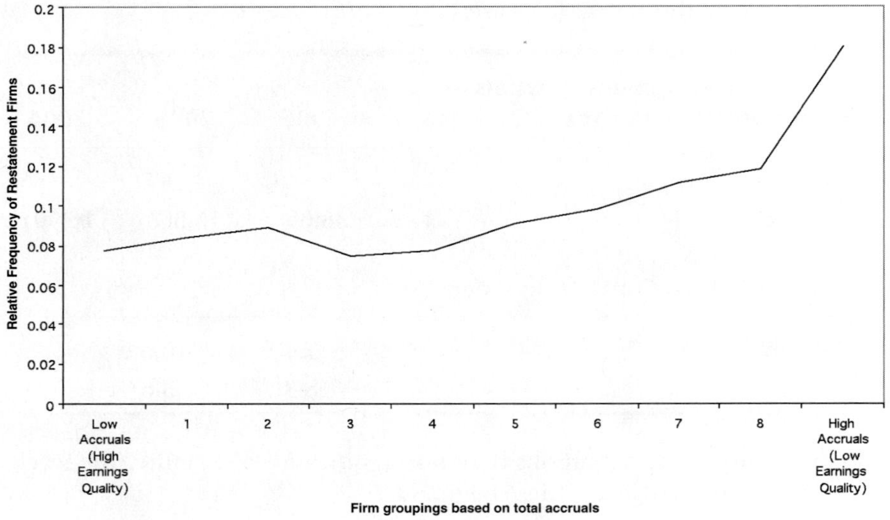

Source: Richardson, Tuna, and Wu (2002).

This ability to discriminate restatement companies from non-restatement companies is beneficial to analysts looking to avoid significant "torpedoes" in their portfolios. This clearly can be seen in Exhibit 7 below. In this exhibit we plot the cumulative equity returns for the 440 earnings restatement companies examined above. We cumulate stock returns for 120 trading days either side of the first press release describing the earnings announcement (i.e., the "0" point on the horizontal axis corresponds to the announcement date). There is a marked decrease in market value around this announcement. For the average company in that group, the loss of market value in the few days surrounding the announcement of the restatement is around 10 percent. Having information ahead of time as to the likelihood of a restatement is clearly of value to the equity investor. The analysis above demonstrates just that: Broad accrual measures are effective in identifying egregious accounting irregularities of the type that precipitate earnings restatements. Importantly, these measures identify such companies well ahead of the restatement announcement. For the 440 restatement companies examined, the announcement date is (on average) more than one year after the fiscal year during which the alleged manipulation occurred.

EXHIBIT 7 **Cumulative Abnormal Returns around Earnings Restatements**

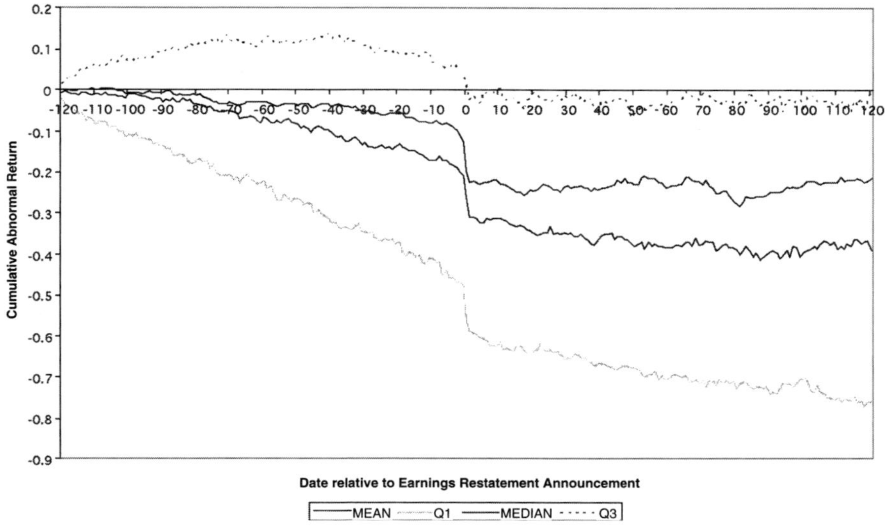

Source: Richardson, Tuna, and Wu (2002).

To make this point even more clear, research also has shown that broad measures of accruals are also leading indicators of SEC enforcement actions. Exhibit 8 reports aggregate accruals for companies subject to SEC enforcement actions. (The measure used [ACC] is the same as what we have called the balance-sheet-based accruals ratio in this reading.) Aggregate accruals are tracked for five years on either side of the period of alleged manipulation giving rise to the enforcement action. The bold (hatched) line reports the average (median) aggregate accruals for the SEC enforcement action sample. For comparison purposes the horizontal line shows the aggregate accruals for the average listed company (a little over 15 percent). Note the clear pattern for companies subject to enforcement actions from the SEC: The accrual measure peaks at between 30−35 percent in the two years prior to the SEC enforcement action.

It is important to note that while this broad approach does not tell us which accruals were used as part of that manipulation, it is effective at summarizing all sources of accruals that were used to achieve an earnings target. More detailed analysis focusing on components of total accruals that are particularly germane to a given sector is likely to generate even more effective discriminatory power to identify earnings restatements. Some examples include focusing on the unearned revenue accounts in the software industry, claim loss development reserves in the insurance industry, loan loss provisions for financial institutions,

EXHIBIT 8 Aggregate Accruals (ACC) around SEC Enforcement Action

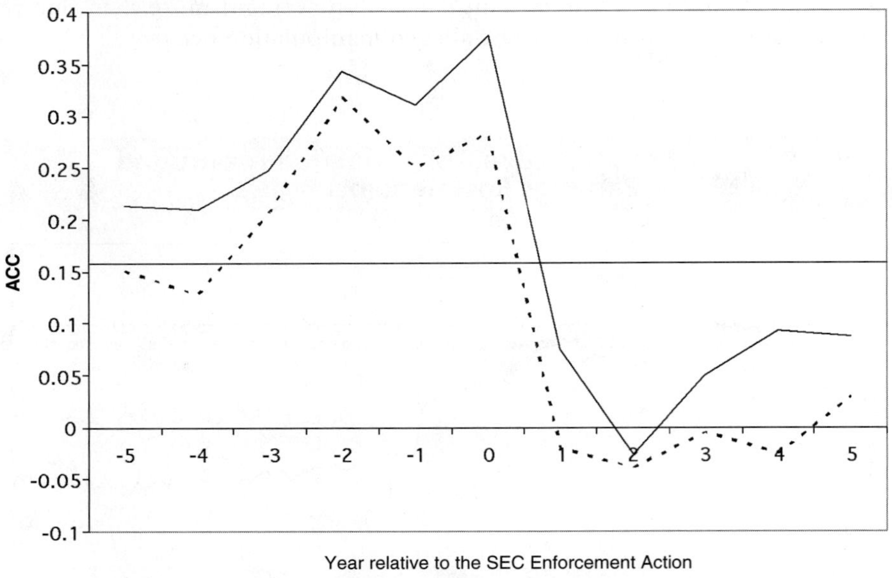

Source: Richardson, Sloan, Soliman, and Tuna (2006).

fair value adjustments for complicated derivative instruments held by financial institutions, inventory adjustments for manufacturing companies, etc.

In the next section we focus on the various component accruals (e.g., provision for doubtful accounts, depreciation choices, unearned revenue, inventory obsolescence, etc.) that drive the aggregate accrual measures we have discussed so far.

4 A FRAMEWORK FOR IDENTIFYING LOW-QUALITY FINANCIAL REPORTING

This section focuses on specific approaches and measures used to quantify financial reporting quality. This framework builds on a sound understanding of the key risk and success factors facing the company. As with any quantitative analysis, the quality of the output depends on the quality of inputs and on a structured analysis of those inputs. Furthermore, the relevance of the reporting quality measures we will discuss 1) varies across companies and 2) can vary through time for a given company. As examples of Point 1, measures related to inventory are particularly relevant for retail and manufacturing companies, measures relating to depreciation choices are particularly relevant for capital intensive companies, and measures relating to off-balance sheet financing vehicles are especially relevant for financial institutions or entities with linked financial subsidiaries. As an example of Point 2, it is often easier for management of a company to "hide" their use of discretion in periods of growth. Consequently, the most effective way to utilize the quantitative measures discussed below is through a combination of peer group comparison and year over year changes.

Sector neutralizing measures of financial reporting quality—by subtracting the mean or median ratio for a given sector group from a given company's ratio—are particularly useful in identifying companies with extreme good or poor quality. However, the degree of homogeneity within a sector or industry group may vary, so supplementing this kind of analysis with information on how the company itself has changed through time can help mitigate any heterogeneity. The company may change through time via divestitures, acquisitions, and changes in strategy. Such changes need to be kept in mind so you have a comparison that is as close to "apples to apples" as possible. Finally, as with any ratio analysis, the analyst should work with standardized financial statements so companies of different sizes are comparable. This is easily achieved by dividing a flow measure from the income statement or statement of cash flows by a measure from the balance sheet such as average total assets.

As we work through the various line items of the financial statements below, it is important to keep in mind the link between the primary financial statements. If there is an issue to be measured in the context of revenues or expenses, there will be an associated implication on the net assets reported in the balance sheet. To keep the sections manageable, we have focused on revenue and expense quality issues. We could easily have included a complete asset and liability section as well, but this would be the flip side of a combination of the revenue and expense items. For example, discussion on the *unearned revenue* account, which typically appears as part of *other current liabilities* on the balance sheet, is subsumed by the discussion of revenue recognition below. Therefore, instead of repeating our discussion, we highlight the relevant asset and liability accounts associated with the respective revenue and expense accounts.

4.1 Revenue Recognition Issues

Mis-stating current revenue, recognizing revenue early, or classifying nonoperating income or gains as resulting from operating activities can make current operating performance appear better than it actually is—generally impairing the persistence or sustainability of reported earnings. The following sections highlight the major types of revenue recognition issues.

4.1.1 Revenue Mis-statement

This section focuses on the discretion available when reporting revenue. Revenue can be over- or understated for a given period. Examples of overstatement include recording smaller provisions for doubtful accounts and warranty provisions. Examples of understatement include recording opportunistic use of unearned revenue. We will discuss these in turn.

4.1.1.1 The Range of Problems Revenue accounting is one of the simplest, yet most challenging aspects of interpreting financial statements. As described in Section 2, accrual accounting records revenue not when cash is collected, but when a good or service has been provided to the customer. Total revenue reported in a given fiscal period is equal to the cash collected from customers plus the increase in net accounts receivable less the increase in unearned revenue (**unearned revenue** or **deferred revenue** is payment received in advance of providing a good or service). Receivables capture credit sales made in the past that as yet have not been collected. While companies have to report these receivables on a net basis by making a best guess as to what will become uncollectible, there is considerable discretion in determining the amount that is expected to be uncollectible. Likewise, unearned revenue contains discretion. The existence of this account typically lowers the reported revenue relative to cash received in the current period. But note that unearned revenues from prior fiscal periods can be used to create revenue in the current fiscal period. For example, if a company collected cash in 2006 for services to be provided over several periods the appropriate treatment is to record that cash collection as a liability in 2006. During future periods a determination has to be made as to whether the services have in fact been provided. Oftentimes there is discretion in deciding when a service has been provided, especially for software companies where the service and licensing agreements are typically bundled together. Related to estimates about credit sales and unearned revenue, companies also must estimate warranty provisions, and sales returns and allowances. The net effect of all of these estimates is the single line item, total revenue, reported at the top of the income statement. Collectively, the discretion embedded in the revenue line item is the culprit for the majority of earnings restatements, fraud cases, and related SEC enforcement actions (Huron Consulting reports that the main driver of earnings restatements in recent years is revenue recognition issues).

4.1.1.2 Warning Signs To detect quality issues with reported revenues, it is best to focus on the balance sheet accounts associated with revenue (accounts receivable and unearned revenue). Large changes in these accounts should be viewed as "red flag" indicators of revenue quality issues. Specifically, large increases in accounts receivable or large decreases in unearned revenue are indicators of low-quality revenue. Companies reporting earnings where a large portion of the revenue is attributable to growth in receivables or a contraction in unearned revenue, on average report lower accounting rates of return and cash flows in the future, and these earnings reversals are not anticipated in a timely fashion by the stock market.[10]

We can use the example of Microsoft to illustrate various revenue recognition issues. In Exhibit 9 we see the balance sheet for the 30 June 2007 fiscal year for Microsoft.

EXHIBIT 9 **Microsoft Corporation Balance Sheets Fiscal Year Ended 30 June 2007 and 30 June 2006 (in $ Millions)**

30 June	2007	2006
Assets		
Current assets:		
Cash and equivalents	**$6,111**	$6,714
Short-term investments (including securities pledged as collateral of $2,356 and $3,065)	**17,300**	27,447
Total cash and short-term investments	**23,411**	34,161
Accounts receivable, net of allowance for doubtful accounts of $117 and $142	***11,338***	*9,316*
Inventories	**1,127**	1,478
Deferred income taxes	**1,899**	1,940
Other	**2,393**	2,115
Total current assets	**40,168**	49,010

(Exhibit continued on next page . . .)

[10] See, for example, Sloan (1996).

EXHIBIT 9 (continued)

30 June	2007	2006
Property and equipment, net	**4,350**	3,044
Equity and other investments	**10,117**	9,232
Goodwill	**4,760**	3,866
Intangible assets, net	**878**	539
Deferred income taxes	**1,389**	2,611
Other long-term assets	**1,509**	1,295
Total assets	**$63,171**	$69,597
Liabilities and stockholders' equity		
Current liabilities:		
Accounts payable	**$3,247**	$2,909
Accrued compensation	**2,325**	1,938
Income taxes	**1,040**	1,557
Short-term unearned revenue	***10,779***	*9,138*
Securities lending payable	**2,741**	3,117
Other	**3,622**	3,783
Total current liabilities	**23,754**	22,442
Long-term unearned revenue	***1,867***	*1,764*
Other long-term liabilities	**6,453**	5,287
Commitments and contingencies		
Stockholders' equity:		
Common stock and paid-in capital − shares authorized 24,000; outstanding 9,380 and 10,062	**60,557**	59,005
Retained deficit, including accumulated other comprehensive income of $1,654 and $1,229	**(29,460)**	(18,901)
Total stockholders' equity	**31,097**	40,104
Total liabilities and stockholders' equity	**$63,171**	$69,597

Note: Italics added by authors.

There is a roughly $1.6 billion increase in the short-term unearned revenue account (the opening balance is $9.138 billion and the closing balance is $10.779 billion, creating a positive change of $1.641 billion), and a roughly $0.1 billion increase in the long-term unearned revenue account (the opening balance is $1.764 billion and the closing balance is $1.867 billion, creating a positive change of $0.103 billion). There is also a roughly $2 billion increase in gross accounts receivable[11] (the opening balance is $9.458 billion and the closing balance is $11.455 billion, creating a positive change of $1.997 billion). Write-offs will reduce the gross accounts receivable balance but do not reflect cash collection. In the absence of footnote information, we can infer a $0.025 billion write-off from the decrease in the allowance for doubtful accounts. To place these

[11] Using the indirect method to arrive at cash flow from operating activities, it is appropriate to use net accounts receivable. This implicitly includes the necessary adjustments for bad debt expense and write-offs. Using the direct method, where cash collected from customers is shown as a separate item, gross accounts receivable and actual write-offs are used to adjust revenue to a cash basis.

magnitudes in context, Microsoft reported revenue of $51.122 billion and net income of $14.065 billion for the fiscal period. The difference between revenue and cash collected from customers can be computed by aggregating the changes in accounts receivable and unearned revenue accounts as follows:

$$\begin{aligned}\text{Revenue} - \text{Cash collected from customers} &= \text{Increase in gross A/R} + \text{Write-offs} - \text{Increase in unearned revenue}\\ &= \$1.997\text{ billion} + 0.025\text{ billion} - (1.641\text{ billion} + 0.103\text{ billion})\\ &= \$0.278\text{ billion.}\end{aligned}$$

The net effect of the increase in receivables, write-offs, and increase in unearned revenue is to report revenue greater by $0.278 billion relative to cash collected from customers. The magnitude of the absolute changes in these accounts is over $3.5 billion, suggesting that Microsoft has considerable flexibility in reporting revenue in a given fiscal period. For example, the unearned revenue account could be built up in periods of strong growth as customers prepay for services, and tapped into when times are tough. In effect, with the unearned revenue account, Microsoft has flexibility to be strategic as to when it chooses to recognize revenue. Note that few companies disclose unearned revenue separately in the financial statements; however, this information can often be found in supplemental footnote disclosures to the financial statements.

To place the accrual items described above (change in accounts receivable and change in unearned revenue) in context, we can express these changes as a fraction of average net operating assets. For the year ended 30 June 2007, Microsoft reports in millions of dollars: opening (closing) total assets of $69,597 ($63,171), opening (closing) cash and short-term investments of $34,161 ($23,411), opening (closing) total liabilities of $29,493 ($32,074), and opening (closing) total debt of $0 ($0). Using the balance-sheet-based accruals ratio described in Equation 4, we can compute aggregate accruals as follows:

	2007	2006
Operating Assets		
Total assets	63,171	69,597
Less: Cash and short-term investments	23,411	34,161
Operating assets (OA)	39,760	35,436
Operating Liabilities		
Total liabilities	32,074	29,493
Less: Long-term debt	0	0
Less: Debt in current liabilities	0	0
Operating liabilities (OL)	32,074	29,493
Net Operating Assets NOA = OA−OL	7,686	5,943
Balance-sheet-based aggregate accruals (= NOA[2007] − NOA[2006])	1,743	
Average Net Operating Assets	6,814.5	
Balance-Sheet-Based Accruals Ratio (= 1,743/6,814.5)	*25.58%*	

The revenue-related accruals in accounts receivable and unearned revenue, calculated as the increase in gross accounts receivable plus write-offs minus the increase in unearned revenue, total $278 million, which accounts for about 16 percent of the total accruals ($278 million/$1,743 million) for the 2007 fiscal year. There are other ways to use this information to make statements about earnings quality. For example, measures of days' sales outstanding (DSO) are useful to inform about revenue quality. DSO is simply the ratio of net accounts receivable divided by total revenue multiplied by 365. This ratio gives a sense for how quickly the company is able to convert its credit sales into cash. Increases in this ratio are a red flag for questionable credit sales that take longer to convert into cash. Of course, in assessing this ratio, one should be careful to see if the company's credit policy or product mix has changed substantially, or whether the company has securitized or factored its receivables (this leads to a dramatic lowering of DSO, which is not sustainable). If you notice that a company has securitized a large portion of its receivables, then do not treat the accompanying improvement in DSO as a signal of improving earnings quality because it is a one-off occurrence. For example, Federated Stores sold its credit card business in 2005, effectively lowering its DSO ratio to zero.

4.1.2 Accelerating Revenue

In addition to the issues described above relating to credit sales and unearned revenue, there is also considerable discretion as to when a sale has been made. The issue here is deciding in which fiscal period revenue should be recognized.

4.1.2.1 The Range of Problems Related to the discussion in Section 4.1.1, revenue is recognized when a good is "delivered" to the customer or a service has been performed. There is considerable discretion as to when the transaction is deemed to have taken place. It is easy to understand the incentives of salespeople who are struggling to meet internal targets toward the end of the fiscal period: To sell as much as possible as the period ends, e.g., by lowering credit standards or by moving sales from the next period to the current fiscal period. This latter option is acceptable as long as the sale has been made, i.e., the good has been delivered and/or the service has been provided. For companies that provide goods or services where it is sometimes difficult to assess the completion of the revenue-generating process (i.e., the delivery of the good or the provision of service), there is the potential for these companies to accelerate the recognition of revenue by reporting revenue in the current period that should be reported in a future period. Companies that provide goods and services as bundled products are a classic example where there may be opportunity for the acceleration of revenues. Consider a company selling computer software licenses with a multiperiod service agreement. The revenue associated with the provision of that service component of the software license should not be recognized at point of sale but at the time the service is provided to the customer. For example, consider a software provider that sells desktop applications in bulk to large corporations on 1 November 2007. This contract comes with built-in options to upgrade and extensive product support for the next two years. A determination needs to be made to allocate the revenue associated with this software sale over the 2007, 2008, and 2009 fiscal periods.

4.1.2.2 Warning Signs The analyst needs to be particularly skeptical about revenue reporting practices when

- top management has a significant portion of vested options in the money;
- the company is trying to maintain its track record of successively meeting analyst forecasts; or
- the company is looking to raise additional financing.

The above are risk factors in the sense of describing circumstances that can provide incentives for accelerating the recognition of revenue.

The warning signs for accelerated revenue are similar to what was described for over-stated revenue: Look for large positive changes in net accounts receivable and large decreases in unearned revenue accounts (to the extent these are separately disclosed). A large increase in accounts receivable could indicate credit sales made late in the fiscal period with associated deteriorations in credit quality. Large decreases in unearned revenue could be indicative of management's aggressive determination that prior goods and services have been delivered/provided in the current fiscal period. Combining an analysis of the accrual activity in revenue-related accounts with the current market environment (e.g., pressing need to meet analyst forecasts or extensive outstanding vested options for top executives) can be an effective way to identify companies who have the incentive to be aggressive in the timing of revenue recognition and who have utilized accrual accounting choices to deliver revenue growth.

A good example is Microstrategy. Exhibit 10 outlines the evolution of Microstrategy's stock price for the 1999–2000 period. Microstrategy announced that it would be restating its earnings in March 2000. They had accelerated the recognition of revenue by booking legitimate future sales orders in the current fiscal period. At first glance this does not seem particularly egregious: after all, these would have been legitimate sales. But placed in the context of significant capital market pressures, where analysts and investors generally were looking for exponential sales growth to support very lofty stock prices, the front-loading of revenues allowed Microstrategy to report very large revenue increases over the 1998–1999 period, fueling the stock price appreciation during 1999. When investors learned that this revenue growth was the result of front-loading future sales, there was a very quick correction in the market. There are numerous other cases of companies accelerating revenue recognition. A skeptical view on receivable growth and changes in unearned revenue, combined with an assessment of incentives to manipulate earnings, can help identify these companies before the stock price collapses.

One way to detect acceleration of revenue recognition is to analyze the ratio of revenue to cash collected from customers. Cash collected from customers can be computed as revenue + decrease (minus increase) in accounts receivable + increase (minus decrease) in deferred income (or "deferred revenue"). In normal circumstances, the relation between revenue and cash collected from customers should be relatively stable. Large swings in revenue as a percent of cash collected from customers could occur for several reasons including the acceleration of revenue. Reported revenue as a percent of cash collected from customers would be expected to initially increase as the aggressive revenue recognition is adopted. Example 3 illustrates one technique of revenue acceleration: bill-and-hold sales.

EXHIBIT 10 Daily Stock Prices for Microstrategy 1 September 1999–29 September 2000

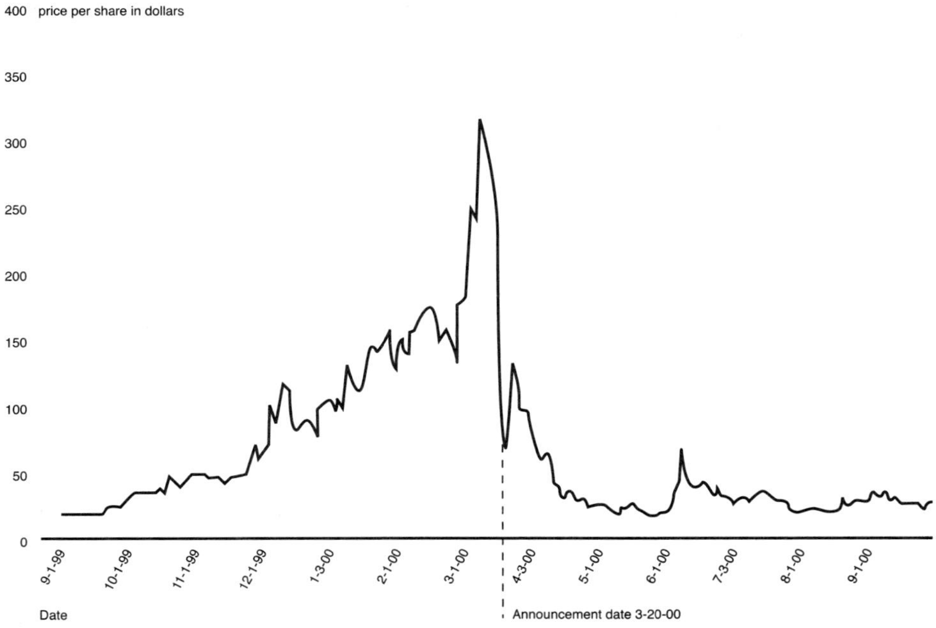

Note: Stock prices have been adjusted to account for the 26 January 2000 2:1 stock split.
Source: GAO (2002), Figure 18, based on the GAO's analysis of NYSE TAQ data.

EXAMPLE 3

Revenue Recognition Practices

Diebold, Inc. (NYSE: DBD) is a leading manufacturer of Automated Teller Machines (ATMs) used in banks, as well as electronic voting machines. Certain of Diebold's financial results for the years ended 31 December 2006, 2005 and 2004 are summarized as follows:

	2006	2005	2004
Revenues	$2,906,232	$2,587,049	$2,357,108
Net income	86,547	96,746	183,797
Cash flow from operating activities	250,424	102,741	221,610
Accounts receivable, net	610,893	676,361	583,658
Deferred income	170,921	136,135	92,862
Other current liabilities	258,103	228,699	202,713

In its 2006 Annual Report, Diebold described its revenue recognition practice as follows:

1. The company considers revenue to be realized or realizable and earned when the following revenue recognition requirements are met: persuasive evidence of an arrangement exists, which is a customer contract; the products or services have been provided to the customer; the sales price is fixed or determinable within the contract; and collectibility is probable. (From the Notes to the Financial Statements)
2. Revenue is recognized only after the earnings process is complete. For product sales, the company determines that the earnings process is complete when the customer has assumed risk of loss of the goods sold and all performance requirements are substantially complete. (From the Management Discussion and Analysis)

On 25 July 2007, Diebold announced it would be delaying the release of its earnings for the second quarter due to regulatory questions about the way it reports revenue. The stock had closed on 24 July at $53.71 per share.

On 2 October 2007, Diebold Inc. issued a press release titled "Diebold Provides Update on Revenue Recognition Practice."

> Diebold, Incorporated has been engaged in an ongoing discussion with the Office of the Chief Accountant (OCA) of the Securities and Exchange Commission (SEC) regarding the company's practice of recognizing certain revenue on a "bill and hold" basis within its North America business segment. As a result of these discussions, Diebold will discontinue the use of bill and hold as a method of revenue recognition in both its North America and international businesses. . . .
>
> The change in the company's revenue recognition practice, and the potential amendment of prior financial statements, would only affect the timing of recognition of certain revenue. While the percentage of the company's global bill and hold revenue varied from period to period, it represented 11 percent of Diebold's total consolidated revenue in 2006. The company does not anticipate that the change in the timing of revenue recognition would impact previously reported cash provided by operating activities or the company's net cash position. . . .
>
> While the company cannot predict with certainty the length of time it will take to complete this analysis and review, it anticipates the process will take at least 30 days. Upon completing this process, Diebold will be in a position to provide updated revenue and earnings guidance for the full-year 2007.

That day, shares continued a slide that had begun with the announced delay, reaching $44.50. As of late 2007, the stock had fallen more than 20 percent since the initial announcement.

In a document titled "Report Pursuant to Section 704 of the Sarbanes–Oxley Act of 2002," the U.S. Securities and Exchange Commission noted that:

Improper accounting for bill-and-hold transactions usually involves the recording of revenue from a sale, even though the customer has not taken title of the product and assumed the risks and rewards of ownership of the products specified in the customer's purchase order or sales agreement. In a typical bill-and-hold transaction, the seller does not ship the product or ships it to a delivery site other than the customer's site. These transactions may be recognized legitimately under GAAP when special criteria are met, including being done pursuant to the buyer's request.

Based on the information given, address the following problems:

1. State whether bill-and-hold sales are consistent with the revenue recognition practices described in Diebold's Annual Report. Explain your response.
2. Describe the incentives for recording revenue on a bill and hold basis.
3. The SEC report notes that bill and hold sales may be appropriate when done at the customer's request. Explain a circumstance in which a customer may choose to be billed for a product that has not been delivered.
4. Critique the argument in the press release of 2 October 2007 that "the change in the company's revenue recognition practice, and the potential amendment of prior financial statements, would only affect the timing of recognition of certain revenue."
5. Describe a warning sign that might alert investors to the presence of improper bill and hold accounting. Illustrate the warning sign for the case of Diebold.

Solution to 1: No, they are not consistent. Diebold says it recognizes revenue only after "the products or services have been provided to a customer." In a bill and hold transaction, "the seller does not ship the product or ships it to a delivery site other than the customer's site."

Solution to 2: Incentives include meeting revenue growth expectations or prior company guidance on revenue growth. Investors may reward positive "surprises" in revenues (revenue in excess of expected revenue) with a higher stock price. Conversely, disappointing news with respect to revenue targets may result in stock price declines. Thus, meeting or exceeding revenue growth expectations can help support the stock price. Furthermore, individual employees may have bonuses that depend in part upon their ability to meet certain sales targets in a given period, creating another incentive to recognize revenue on a bill and hold basis.

In Diebold's case, it is possible that nearly all of the 12.3 percent growth in revenues was provided by the 11 percent of revenue recorded on a bill-and-hold basis. The accounting for the bill-and-hold transaction was not adequately disclosed in the financial statements, and thus it is no surprise that the practice drew negative attention from regulators.

Solution to 3: Customers may also have incentives to "time" their expenditures. For example, they might have provided their own investors with an indication of how much they planned to invest in new capital and may request that some equipment be provided on a bill-and-hold basis in order to meet that guidance. Alternatively, department heads may want to spend any remaining money in their budget at fiscal year-end to avoid budget cuts the following year, and not be particularly concerned about taking possession at the time of purchase. Another reason could be that the seller offers discounts if the buyer "requests" bill and hold.

Solution to 4: The statement is correct in that the bill and hold revenue recognition involves the timing of revenue recognition. However, the statement is incomplete in not pointing out that the effect of bill and hold sales is to speed up the recognition of revenue and often to distort the revenue growth rate in a manner that is temporarily favorable to the company.

Solution to 5: The first sign could come from comparing revenue to cash collections from customers. For Diebold, the calculations for 2005 and 2006 are as follows:

	2006	2005
Revenue	$2,906,232	$2,587,049
Plus decrease (increase) in accounts receivable	65,468	(92,703)
Plus increase in deferred income	34,786	43,273
Equals cash collected from customers	$3,006,486	$2,537,619
Revenue/Cash collected from customers	96.7%	101.9%

In normal circumstances, the relationship between revenue and cash collected from customers would be expected to remain relatively stable. In Diebold's case, there was a 6.1 percent decrease from 2005 to 2006. In particular, the large increase in accounts receivable in 2005 provided a warning sign more than one year in advance of the restatement. As noted earlier, increases in accounts receivable capture aggressive accruals related to revenue recognition.

The net profit margin declined from 7.8 percent in 2004 to 3.7 percent in 2005 and 3.0 percent in 2006. The declining profitability could have been a signal that the company was pricing aggressively for customers willing to accept early billing. At the same time, the deferred income rose by 84 percent between 2004 and 2006 while sales grew just 23 percent.

Taking a more holistic approach to analysis, investors should also have been skeptical of the company's accounting practices on the basis of past infractions. The SEC lawsuit that led to the change was disclosed in the 10-Q filed in August 2006.

4.1.3 Classification of Nonrecurring or Nonoperating Revenue as Operating Revenue

Investors view operating income numbers as being most informative about the ongoing earnings power of a business. For example, many investors base forward price–earnings ratio estimates on forecasts of operating earnings which exclude nonrecurring items. Broadly, management may have an incentive to include nonrecurring revenues in operating income that might not belong there.

4.1.3.1 The Range of Problems Capital markets tend to focus on operating income numbers. This is important, because items that are outside the core operating activity of the company are not as relevant for assessing the long-term cash flow generating capability of the company. For example, a company operating in the retail sector may have a portfolio of financial assets which is required to be periodically revalued. These revaluations, to the extent the securities are held for trading purposes, will be included in net income. But these earnings are not reflective of the core operating activity of the company. Likewise, gains or losses associated with the divestiture of noncurrent assets typically fall outside the core operating activities of most companies; yet these transactions will affect net income. The challenge for the analyst is in separating operating from nonoperating activities. Companies do this as evidenced by the operating, investing, and financing sections of the statement of cash flows and the pro forma earnings numbers that are the focal point of earnings announcements and conference calls. However, there is discretion in making this distinction. Consequently, there is room in defining what is core or operating earnings. One of the advantages of this earnings game for management is the absence of an *ex post* settling up mechanism: For this type of earnings management, there is no accrual or deferral reversal in future periods.

Note that the opportunistic classification of items into operating income as opposed to a nonrecurring item is not about *net income* reported under generally accepted accounting principles. Rather, the issue relates to the earnings number generally provided to the capital markets. This has been described cynically by some as "earnings before bad stuff." Pro forma earnings numbers fall outside of the domain of U.S. GAAP and as such no uniform methodology exists for calculating them.[12]

4.1.3.2 Warning Signs One red flag for the opportunistic classification of nonrecurring items into operating income is to look at the temporal inconsistency with respect to the included revenues and expenses in a company's definition of operating income. For example, if a company excludes different items from its computation of pro forma earnings across quarters, this is a good indication that the company is opportunistically using its discretion to classify items as recurring or nonrecurring. This information can be gleaned from the press releases associated with earnings announcements, and the greater disclosure required currently makes this easier to do.

[12] Note that the SEC cracked down on abuses of reporting pro forma results back in 2001 with Release Nos. 33-8039, 34-45124, FR-59.

4.2 Expense Recognition Issues

Having discussed revenue recognition as it relates to financial reporting quality issues, we will now focus on expense recognition, the other chief area of earnings discretion. Expense issues include

- understating expenses;
- deferring expenses; and
- classifying ordinary expenses as nonrecurring or nonoperating.

We address these in order.

4.2.1 Understating Expenses

Income can be increased by both overstating revenue and understating expenses. In this section, we focus on the improper capitalization of costs.

4.2.1.1 The Range of Problems Our focus in discussing expense recognition will be selling, general, and administrative (SG&A) expenses and the cost of goods sold (COGS).

The classic expense account with considerable discretion is depreciation and amortization, which is typically reported as part of SG&A or COGS on the income statement. Companies are required to determine the capital costs associated with noncurrent assets and then depreciate the depreciable amount (the difference between the capitalized costs and an estimate of the salvage value) over an estimated useful life. Reported depreciation expense is the result of many choices—which costs to capitalize, residual value assumptions, useful life assumptions—as well as an allocation method (e.g., straight line, accelerated or some other method).

Another primary expense account that contains considerable discretion is cost of goods sold (COGS). Accrual accounting only expenses costs associated with inventory when that inventory is sold. For companies with large inventory balances, there is considerable discretion as to the costs that are capitalized into inventory as well as how to value that inventory at the end of the fiscal period. Obsolescence must be accounted for and inventory, as with other assets, cannot be reported on the balance sheet at greater than fair value. Identification of obsolete inventory and valuation at the end of the fiscal period is subjective. As with receivables, care should be taken to monitor significant changes in inventory balances.

4.2.1.2 Warning Signs Financial statements contain ample disclosures related to depreciation and amortization. Companies must disclose their method (straight line or otherwise) along with broad summaries of useful lives. Ratios of depreciation rates relative to the gross value of property, plant and equipment or ratios of changes in depreciation rates relative to contemporaneous sales, can easily be computed and compared to other companies to assess conservative or aggressive depreciation rates.

Financial statement information also can be combined with additional disclosure that companies make at earnings announcements or via conference calls. Companies typically give more detailed information than what you see in the 10-Q or 10-K filing, especially for segment information. A good example of the information contained in conference calls is Ford Motor Company. For the quarter ended 30 September 2004, Ford reported net income of $266 million compared to a net loss of $25 million for the quarter ended 30 September 2003. A key driver of this improved profitability is the financial services arm of Ford. That unit reported an increase of net income from $1.031 billion for Q3, 2003 to $1.425 billion for Q3, 2004. Revenues fell marginally from $6.499 billion for the financial services arm to $6.198 billion, but this was coupled with a significant reduction in depreciation from $2.072 billion to $1.570 billion. Conference call participants were quick to pick this up, and noticed that the bulk of the improvement in the financial services profitability was attributable to growth in Ford Motor Credit, with over half of the improvement coming from lease residual value improvements (i.e., the company reassessed the residual value of its fleet based on recent auctions, increasing residual values and consequently lowering periodic depreciation charges). This choice as to residual value affected the depreciation accrual. The net effect allowed Ford to report a profit for Q3, 2004 as opposed to a loss. This example also illustrates that the information used to identify financial reporting quality issues need not be limited to the financial statements themselves. Conference calls and other company communications provide additional information for the interpretation of reported financial statements. In the case of Ford, it was detailed segment disclosure in the conference call that alerted conference call participants to the reasons Ford moved to a profit in Q3, 2004.

NetFlix is a good example of low-quality financial reporting attributable to depreciation-related choices. NetFlix has a simple business model: It maintains an extensive DVD warehouse with an online distribution channel. This business model was very effective, primarily due to a first mover advantage in implementing the strategy. Part of the financial performance of NetFlix is attributable to the amortization method for its rental library. NetFlix uses an accelerated amortization method known as "sum of the months."[13] Prior to 2004, NetFlix used this accelerated method with a one year useful life assumption. Post 2004, NetFlix switched to a three year useful life assumption for back catalogue DVDs. This had the effect of slowing the expensing of back catalogue DVDs. Going into 2005, the back catalogue DVDs that would have been expensed from the acquisitions during 2004 would be spread out over the next three years. The change in amortization method at NetFlix had the consequence of increasing reported earnings in the year following the change by slowing the expense rate of back catalogue DVDs. Blockbuster is an interesting counter-example. They employ a similar accelerated depreciation method over one year for all DVDs, and have kept this method constant.

Reporting quality issues with inventory can be tracked by monitoring large changes in the inventory balance. Inventory buildup will be explained by companies as necessary to support future product demand. On average, however, an inventory buildup is a good indication that the company has problems with managing its inventory levels and/or has not been sufficiently aggressive in writing down the value of that inventory as the turnover slows. As with the days' sales outstanding ratio discussed for revenue issues, a similar days' inventory outstanding ratio can be looked at to identify inventory quality issues. This ratio is equal to net inventory divided by cost of goods sold multiplied by 365. This ratio gives a sense for how quickly the company is able to convert inventory into revenue. Increases in this ratio may indicate potential problems related to earnings quality. But be careful in treating all increases and decreases equally.

---

[13] Using one year as the useful life and a "sum of the months" digit method, the sum of the months over one year totals 78 ($1 + 2 + 3 + \ldots + 12 = 78$). 12/78 of the amortizable amount would be charged to the first month, 11/78 to the second month, 10/78 to the third month, and so forth.

Companies can shift their inventory management systems leading to significant periodic changes in this ratio. For example, companies expecting some instability in inventory supply chains from overseas locations may rationally build up additional inventory to act as a buffer from potential disruptions. But companies will always try to explain away unfavorable movements in key ratios. The right question to ask of management in this scenario is "Why were supply chains set up with such political risk in the first place?" Finally, for companies utilizing the LIFO cost flow assumption to value their inventories, check the footnotes carefully to see the extent to which LIFO liquidations have contributed to profit in a given fiscal period. If you see a LIFO liquidation has contributed to an improvement in profitability as COGS are lower by "dipping" into the older inventory cost layers, this one time advantage should be removed from current earnings to give a better indication of long-term profitability.

4.2.2 Deferring Expenses

In addition to simply understating expenses, companies are able to shift the recording of expenses across fiscal periods under the accrual accounting system. In this section we look at some of these deferral choices in detail.

4.2.2.1 The Range of Problems One of the largest areas of accounting abuse is the practice of capitalizing costs that should have been expensed. Given the significant discretion in capitalizing costs for various noncurrent assets such as property, plant, and equipment and intangibles, some companies abuse this discretion and include costs in the noncurrent portion of the balance sheet that should have been expensed.

4.2.2.2 Warning Signs The simplest way to get a sense for inappropriate capitalization is to track growth in net noncurrent assets: capitalization activity is what we are interested in. The broad measures of accruals described in Section 2 will flag companies that have experienced significant growth in their net operating assets. On average, this growth in net operating assets is associated with lower future company performance. This is due to a combination of over-investment tendencies from these companies and diminishing marginal returns to investment activity. However, not all companies that grow will perform poorly. Identifying, ex ante, which companies are growing at a rate that is not likely to lead to lower future performance is a challenging task. The approach is to place the asset growth in context relative to sales growth, expected future sales growth both for the company itself and sector group which it belongs to. If a company is growing its asset base in an environment where capacity utilization is very tight and margins are quite attractive, this asset growth is less likely to be indicative of poor future performance as compared to a company which is growing its asset base and has excess capacity and deteriorating margins. But note that this is a challenging task: It is very difficult to separate good asset growth from bad asset growth. Your presumption should be to treat all asset growth as bad and impose a tough standard to reject that hypothesis.

The example below touches on the issue of capitalization of software development costs. It also illustrates the care that must be taken in selecting valuation metrics when costs that might be included in operating expenses are capitalized.

EXAMPLE 4

Expense Recognition for an Information Service Provider

Thomson Corporation, based in Canada, is one of the world's leading information services providers. The software industry is an interesting sector to examine because it allows considerable discretion with respect to capitalization decisions. Software providers are allowed to capitalize costs associated with software development and then amortize these costs over a period in which the product is expected to be sold. Thomson's income statement for the year ended 31 December 2006, along with selected notes related to its treatment of software development costs, is presented below.

The Thomson Corporation Consolidated Statement of Earnings (Millions of U.S. Dollars, except per Common Share Amounts)

	Year Ended 31 December	
	2006	**2005**
Revenues	6,641	6,173
Cost of sales, selling, marketing, general and administrative expenses	(4,702)	(4,351)
Depreciation (notes 11 and 12)	(439)	(414)
Amortization (note 13)	(242)	(236)
Operating profit	1,258	1,172
Net other income (expense) (note 4)	1	(28)
Net interest expense and other financing costs (note 5)	(221)	(221)
Income taxes (note 6)	(119)	(261)
Earnings from continuing operations	919	662
Earnings from discontinued operations, net of tax (note 7)	201	272
Net earnings	1,120	934
Dividends declared on preference shares (note 16)	(5)	(4)
Earnings attributable to common shares	1,115	930
Earnings per common share (note 8):		
Basic and diluted earnings per common share:		
From continuing operations	$1.41	$1.00
From discontinued operations	0.32	0.42
Basic and diluted earnings per common share	$1.73	$1.42

Note 1: Summary of Significant Accounting Policies
Computer software
Capitalized Software for internal use
Certain costs incurred in connection with the development of software to be used internally are capitalized once a project has progressed beyond a conceptual, preliminary stage to that of application development. Costs which qualify for capitalization include both internal and external costs, but are limited to those that are directly related to the specific project. The capitalized amounts, net of accumulated amortization, are included in "Computer software, net" in the consolidated balance sheet. These costs are amortized over their expected useful lives, which range from three to ten years. The amortization expense is included in "Depreciation" in the consolidated statement of earnings.

Capitalized Software to be marketed
In connection with the development of software that is intended to be marketed to customers, certain costs are capitalized once technological feasibility of the product is established and a market for the product has been identified. The capitalized amounts, net of accumulated amortization, are also included in "Computer software, net" in the consolidated balance sheet. The capitalized amounts are amortized over the expected period of benefit, not to exceed three years, and this amortization expense is included in "Cost of sales, selling, marketing, general and administrative expenses" in the consolidated statement of earnings.

Note 12: Computer Software
Computer software consists of the following:

As at 31 December 2006	Cost	Accumulated Amortization	Net Computer Software
Capitalized software for internal use	**1,791**	**(1,228)**	**563**
Capitalized software to be marketed	**212**	**(128)**	**84**
	2,003	**(1,356)**	**647**

As at 31 December 2005	Cost	Accumulated Amortization	Net Computer Software
Capitalized software for internal use	1,608	(1,085)	523
Capitalized software to be marketed	143	(98)	45
	1,751	(1,183)	568

The amortization charge for internal use computer software in 2006 was $241 million (2005 — $224 million) and is included in "Depreciation" in the consolidated statement of earnings. The amortization charge for software intended to be marketed was $25 million (2005 — $21 million) and is included in "Cost of sales, selling, marketing, general and administrative expenses" in the consolidated statement of earnings.

Based on the information given, address the following problems:

1. Contrast Thomson's recognition of software related costs in 2006 with the actual cash spent acquiring and developing the software.
2. Estimate Thomson's 2006 operating profit and earnings from continuing operations assuming Thomson expensed all software related costs when the related cash flows occurred.

3. Contrast the implications for the cash flow statement from expensing software development costs rather than capitalizing and amortizing them.
4. Many analysts use EV/EBITDA (enterprise value divided by earnings before interest, taxes, depreciation and amortization) as a valuation measure for software companies. Enterprise value is simply the sum of the market capitalization and the book value of outstanding debt. Critique the use of this measure when software related costs are being capitalized.

Solution to 1: The total balance for capitalized computer software increased from \$568 in 2005 to \$647 in 2006, a total of \$79. This is the amount by which computer software costs exceeded the amount recognized as an expense on the income statement.

Solution to 2: Operating profit would have been \$1,258 − 79 = \$1,179. The effective tax rate for 2006 is 11.5% [= 119/(1,258 + 1 − 221)]. Net income would be reduced by \$79 adjusted for tax, or \$79(1 − 0.115) = \$70, so the adjusted earnings from continuing operations is \$919 − 70 = \$849. Earnings from continuing operations were effectively overstated by 8.2 percent (= 70/849) relative to cash costs.

Solution to 3: Software development costs would typically be expensed as part of research and development, or in Thomson's case as part of cost of sales. With such treatment, software development costs affect (reduce) cash flow from operating activities. By contrast, capitalized software costs are amortized to expense over time. The initial expenditure is recorded as a cash flow from investing activities. Amortization of the capitalized amount is added back to net income when calculating cash flow from operating activities. In effect, capitalizing software costs reclassifies them from an operating cash flow to an investing cash flow, and then allocates that amount to amortization expense over time.

Solution to 4: EBITDA ignores the costs related to software development by adding amortization back to operating income. Unless either the initial capitalized amount or the subsequent amortization is deducted, investors are effectively ignoring a software company's software development costs altogether in evaluating the company. Because software companies must develop software in order to stay in business, valuing the companies on the basis of EBITDA potentially ignores a critical component of expense, akin to ignoring a retailer's inventory costs. In the case of Thomson, the amortization of software to be marketed is included in SG&A expenses, so it is captured in the computation of EBITDA. However, most of Thomson's software costs are related to software for internal use and were not included in SG&A. Thus using EBITDA in this case would result in ignoring most software costs.

4.2.3 Classification of Ordinary Expenses as Nonrecurring or Nonoperating

The final set of expense issues that we will touch on relate to a possible way to mask a decline in operating performance by reclassifying operating expenses.

4.2.3.1 The Range of Problems There is an incentive for management at companies with deteriorating core income to reclassify some recurring or operating expenses as nonoperating. The issue here is the inappropriate classification of a recurring item that would normally be recorded as part of SG&A or COGS. These costs are then classified as a nonrecurring or special charge and are reported as a separate line item on the income statement. This is easiest for companies that have experienced a genuine special item such as a restructuring. Recurring costs can then be "piggy-backed" onto these nonrecurring items.

4.2.3.2 Warning Signs McVay (2006) examines this issue in detail and identifies one way to track this behavior based on the core operating margin, defined as (Sales − COGS − SGA)/Sales. This ratio represents the pretax return on a money unit (e.g., euro) of sales resulting from the company's operating activities. To use it, analysts should compute year-over-year changes in the core operating margin and look for spikes in the incidence of negative special items for companies that have experienced an increase in this margin. Observing an increase in core operating margins coincident with a negative special item is consistent with opportunistic classification of a recurring expense as a nonrecurring expense. More sophisticated approaches would include building models of expected core operating margin in year t rather than focusing on a simple change in core operating margin. Examples of these sophisticated approaches include building regression-based models that forecast next period's core operating margin using the prior period's core operating margin in addition to other variables such as expected growth rates, macroeconomic conditions, sector affiliation, etc. The goal is the same: To build an expected core operating margin to compare against the realized core operating margin. If you see a large positive unexpected increase in core operating margin and the company contemporaneously reports a negative special item or nonrecurring charge, this may indicate a reclassification of a recurring item as a nonrecurring item. Absent this opportunistic reclassification, the company would not have reported an increase in its core operating margin. Furthermore, this reclassification tendency is stronger for companies that do not regularly report special items, and the expense classification shifting is more pervasive when incentives are greatest (e.g., the desire to meet/beat analyst forecasts). McVay (2006) notes Borden, Inc. as a good example of this type of behavior. The SEC determined that Borden had inappropriately classified $192 million of marketing expenses, which should have been included in standard selling, general, and administrative expenses, as part of a 1992 restructuring charge.

EXAMPLE 5

Core Operating Margin Warning Sign

Based in Canada, NOVA Chemicals Corporation, together with its subsidiaries, engages in the production and marketing of plastics and chemicals. The company operates in three business units: Olefins/Polyolefins, Performance Styrenics, and STYRENIX. NOVA's income statements and an associated note are presented below.

Consolidated Statements of Income (Loss) and Reinvested Earnings (Deficit) (Millions of U.S. Dollars, except Number of Shares and per Share Amounts)

	Year Ended 31 December		
	2006	2005	2004
Revenue	$6,519	$5,616	$5,270
Feedstock and operating costs	5,663	4,906	4,378
Depreciation and amortization	299	290	297
Selling, general and administrative	201	199	274
Research and development	51	50	48
Restructuring charges (Note 14)	985	168	8
	7,199	5,613	5,005
Operating income (loss)	(680)	3	265

14. Restructuring Charges

During the past three years, NOVA Chemicals has undertaken several restructuring steps to reduce costs. As a result of these actions, the Company estimates it will reduce costs by about $100 million per year beginning in 2007. In addition to this, depreciation will be reduced by about $80 million per year in the three reportable segments within the STYRENIX business unit.

In 2006, NOVA Chemicals recorded a restructuring charge of $985 million before-tax ($861 million after-tax) related to the following:

The Company recorded an impairment charge of $860 million related to the STYRENIX business unit assets. The STYRENIX business unit includes the Styrene Monomer, North American Solid Polystyrene and NOVA Innovene European joint venture segments. The STYRENIX business unit has not been profitable due to poor market conditions, and in recent years both NOVA Chemicals and the NOVA Innovene joint venture have reduced production capacity through plant closures. In July 2006, NOVA Chemicals announced it would investigate various alternatives for the STYRENIX business unit, including sale, formation of a joint venture with other producers, or spin out. NOVA Chemicals has assessed the recoverability of the STYRENIX assets and determined that the carrying value exceeded the estimated future cash flows from these assets. Based on this analysis, the fair market value of these STYRENIX facilities was determined to be $242 million.

NOVA Innovene permanently closed its Carrington, UK solid polystyrene facility in October 2006. The Company recorded a restructuring charge of $57 million related primarily to non-cash asset write-downs of the plant including $8 million related to total expected severance and other departure costs. As of December 31, 2006, $5 million of the severance costs was paid to employees.

During 2006, NOVA Chemicals restructured its North American operations to better align resources and reduce costs. As a result, the Company recorded a $53 million restructuring charge related to severance, pension and other employee-related costs. Of this amount, $10 million related to one-time pension curtailment and special termination benefits. Of the remaining $43 million, $22 million has been paid to employees by the end of 2006 with the majority of the remainder to be paid in 2007.

A $15 million charge was recorded related to the accrual of total expected severance costs for the Chesapeake, Virginia polystyrene plant, which was closed in 2006. To date, $3 million has been paid to employees.

NOVA's property, plant, and equipment balance declined from $3,626 in 2005 to $2,719 in 2006. Net operating assets were $3,088 in 2005 and $2,349 in 2006.

Based on the information given, address the following problems:

1. What was NOVA's core operating margin in each of the three years ended 31 December 2006, 2005 and 2004?
2. What was NOVA's balance-sheet-based accruals ratio in 2006?
3. Are there any warning signs related to NOVA's earnings quality based on the information presented?

Solution to 1: Core operating margins, when calculated as (Sales−Cost of sales−SGA)/Sales, for NOVA were 10.0 percent, 9.1 percent, and 11.7 percent in 2006, 2005, and 2004, respectively (feedstock and operating costs being used as the most representative of cost of sales). When calculated using all operating items other than the restructuring charge, core operating margins were 4.7 percent, 3.0 percent, and 5.2 percent, which is directionally similar.

	2006	2005	2004
Revenue	$6,519	$5,616	$5,270
Feedstock and operating costs	5,663	4,906	4,378
Depreciation and amortization	299	290	297
Selling, general and administrative	201	199	274
Research and development	51	50	48
Core operating income	$305	$171	$273
Core operating margin	4.7%	3.0%	5.2%

Solution to 2: The balance-sheet-based accruals ratio is equal to the Change in NOA/Average NOA. In NOVA's case, $(2{,}349 - 3{,}088)/[0.5 \times (2{,}349 + 3{,}088)] = -739/2{,}718.5 = -27.2\%$.

Solution to 3: Yes. The large accrual ratio suggests that a significant portion of NOVA's net income was due to discretionary items. The increase in core operating margin from 2005 to 2006, combined with a large special item in 2006, fits McVay's warning sign that the company may be classifying ordinary operating expenses as nonoperating or nonrecurring. This is an indication of opportunistic use of expense classification. The reported numbers for NOVA should be viewed skeptically.

EXAMPLE 6

The Classification of Expenses

Matsushita Electric Industrial Co., Ltd., best known for its Panasonic brand name, is one of the world's leading manufacturers of electronic and electric products for a wide range of consumer, business, and industrial uses, as well as a wide variety of components. Excerpted below are Matsushita's income statements for the years ended 31 March.

	Yen (Millions)		
Years Ended 31 March	**2007**	**2006**	**2005**
Revenues, costs and expenses:			
Net sales:			
Related companies (Note 4)	250,863	204,740	192,489
Other	8,857,307	8,689,589	8,521,147
Total net sales	9,108,170	8,894,329	8,713,636
Cost of sales (Notes 4 and 16)	(6,394,418)	(6,155,297)	(6,176,046)
Selling, general and administrative expenses (Note 16)	(2,254,211)	(2,324,759)	(2,229,096)
Interest income	30,553	28,216	19,490
Dividends received	7,597	6,567	5,383
Gain from the transfer of the substitutional portion of Japanese Welfare Pension Insurance (Note 10)	—	—	31,509
Other income (Notes 5, 6, 16 and 17)	114,545	147,399	82,819
Interest expense	(20,906)	(21,686)	(22,827)
Goodwill impairment (Note 8)	(30,496)	(50,050)	(3,559)
Other deductions (Notes 4, 5, 7, 8, 15, 16 and 17)	(121,690)	(153,407)	(174,396)
Income before income taxes	439,144	371,312	246,913
Provision for income taxes (Note 11):			
Current	119,465	96,341	96,529
Deferred	72,398	70,748	56,805
	191,863	167,089	153,334
Income before minority interests and equity in earnings (losses) of associated companies	247,281	204,223	93,579
Minority interests	31,131	(987)	27,719
Equity in earnings (losses) of associated companies (Note 4)	1,035	(50,800)	(7,379)
Net income	217,185	154,410	58,481

As shown, Matsushita includes a line "other deductions," which would be understood to be nonoperating items because it appears below such items as "other income" and "interest expense." Without further examination, analysts may be inclined to treat this item as nonoperating or nonrecurring. However, the deductions amount to a high percentage of pre-tax income (as high as 70 percent in 2005) and revenue (2 percent in 2005.) Clearly the distinction is worth further analysis. Consider the associated notes, which are excerpted below.

(4) Investments in and Advances to, and Transactions with Associated Companies
During the years ended March 31, 2006 and 2005, the Company incurred a writedown of 30,681 million yen and 2,833 million yen, respectively, for other-than-temporary impairment of investments and advances in associated companies.

(5) Investments in Securities
During the years ended March 31, 2007, 2006 and 2005, the Company incurred a write down of 939 million yen, 458 million yen and 2,661 million yen, respectively, for other-than-temporary impairment of available-for-sale securities, mainly reflecting the aggravated market condition of certain industries in Japan.

(7) Long-Lived Assets
The Company periodically reviews the recorded value of its long-lived assets to determine if the future cash flows to be derived from these assets will be sufficient to recover the remaining recorded asset values. . . .

(8) Goodwill and Other Intangible Assets
The Company recognized an impairment loss of 27,299 million yen during fiscal 2007 related to goodwill of a mobile communication subsidiary. This impairment is due to a decrease in the estimated fair value of the reporting unit caused by decreased profit expectation and the intensification of competition in a domestic market which was unforeseeable in the prior year.

The Company recognized an impairment loss of 3,197 million yen during fiscal 2007 related to goodwill of JVC due primarily to profit performance in JVC's consumer electronics business being lower than the Company's expectation.

The Company recognized an impairment loss of 50,050 million yen during fiscal 2006 related to goodwill of a mobile communication subsidiary. This impairment is due to a decrease in the estimated fair value of the reporting unit caused by decreased profit expectation and the closure of certain businesses in Europe and Asia.

(15) Restructuring Charges
The Company has provided early retirement programs to those employees voluntarily leaving the Company. The accrued early retirement programs are recognized when the employees accept the offer and the amount can be reasonably estimated. Expenses associated with the closure and integration of locations include amounts such as moving expense of facilities and costs to terminate leasing contracts incurred at domestic and overseas manufacturing plants and sales offices. An analysis of the accrued restructuring charges for the years ended March 31, 2007, 2006 and 2005 is as follows:

	Yen (Millions)		
	2007	**2006**	**2005**
Balance at beginning of the year	1,335	3,407	—
New charges	19,574	48,975	110,568
Cash payments	(10,889)	(51,047)	(107,161)
Balance at end of the year	10,020	1,335	3,407

(16) Supplementary Information to the Statements of Income and Cash Flows
Foreign exchange gains and losses included in other deductions for the years ended March 31, 2007, 2006 and 2005 are losses of 18,950 million yen, 13,475 million yen and 7,542 million yen, respectively.

Included in other deductions for the year ended March 31, 2006 are claim expenses of 34,340 million yen.

Based on the information given, address the following problems:

1. Based on the description in the notes for each item, comment on whether it is appropriate to treat the following charges as nonoperating or nonrecurring:
   - A. Investments in and Advances to, and Transactions with Associated Companies
   - B. Investments in Securities
   - C. Long-Lived Assets
   - D. Goodwill and Other Intangible Assets
   - E. Restructuring Charges
   - F. Supplementary Information to the Statements of Income and Cash Flows
2. How would analyzing balance-sheet-based or cash-flow-statement-based accruals ratios help in assessing the impact of movements in the accounts above? (No calculations are needed.)

Solutions to 1: Discretion is required in analyzing many items. When in doubt, analysts may wish to prepare separate sets of financial statements to understand the effect of treating individual items in different manners.

- **A.** Classifying changes in the value of the investments as nonoperating is appropriate for a nonfinancial company such as Matsushita.
- **B.** Securities held available for sale are typically used as alternatives to investing in low-yielding cash. Treating losses on such securities as nonoperating is appropriate. Again, however, persistent losses raise the question of whether management is capable of selecting worthwhile alternative investments.
- **C.** The value of long-lived assets is typically charged to expense over time as depreciation, which is considered to be an operating item. The impairment charges shift future depreciation expense into the current year, which reduces the future depreciation and also suggests that past depreciation charges were too low. Analysts should reclassify the impairment expense to treat it on par with normal depreciation.
- **D.** Accounting principles call for periodic testing of goodwill for impairment. No amortization expense is otherwise charged. Because the impairment does not offset a normal operating expense, it can be appropriate to classify it as nonoperating, as Matsushita does. However, analysts should pay attention to goodwill impairment. Large impairments can appear conservative at the time they are announced, but the need for them can result from previous aggressive accounting (aggressive at least from an after-the-fact perspective). In the case of Matsushita, it appears that management overpaid for its past investments.
- **E.** Early retirement programs and expenses associated with the closure and integration of locations include amounts such as moving expense of facilities and costs to terminate leasing contracts. Given

that these expenses would be incurred from time to time as part of normal business operations, they should be reclassified as operating expenses.

F. Matsushita is an international operation and should thus be expected to incur foreign currency gains and losses as part of normal operations, although they are typically considered outside management's control. Foreign exchange gains are typically treated as adjustments to net financing costs and are treated as nonoperating.

Solution to 2: Marketable securities (if treated as short-term investments) and equity investments would not be included in either net operating assets or cash flow from operating activities, so the accruals ratios would provide the correct interpretation of these items. Foreign currency and goodwill may appear in a balance-sheet-driven accruals ratio, but not in the ratio based on the cash flow statement. These were also items of questionable operating significance, so the mixed treatment in an accruals ratio reflects the ambiguity. The charges to long-lived assets and for restructuring would deservedly be reflected in the accruals ratios.

4.3 Balance Sheet Issues

The focus of our discussion has been quality of earnings issues as contained in various revenue and expense accounts. There are additional sources of information related to the balance sheet that pertain to our discussion of earnings quality. We will introduce this topic with brief discussion of two balance sheet issues, off-balance sheet debt and goodwill.

4.3.1 Off-Balance Sheet Liabilities

Off-balance sheet debt includes items not reported in the body of the balance sheet but that might be associated with an obligation for future payments. Information contained here is related to our discussion of earnings quality, as the net assets that are acquired from this off-balance sheet financing are a form of growth that an on-balance sheet measure of accruals would fail to capture.

4.3.1.1 The Range of Problems Current accounting standards allow for a significant portion of assets and liabilities to avoid recognition in the primary financial statements. A consequence of this is that companies will appear to have less leverage than they actually do when leverage is measured using only on-balance sheet information. The classic example is leases. U.S. GAAP recognizes two types of leases (operating and capital) and provides different accounting rules for each. The distinction between the two types of leases rests primarily on a consideration of the present value of minimum lease payments relative to the fair value of the asset leased (greater than 90 percent constitutes a capital lease under U.S. GAAP), and a consideration of whether the life of the lease is greater than 75 percent of the useful life of the leased asset (greater than 75 percent constitutes a capital lease under U.S. GAAP). There are other issues to consider such as the existence of a bargain purchase option, but they typically are less relevant for the determination of whether a lease is operating or not. The treatment of operating leases relative to capital leases is dramatically different. An operating lease treats the cash outflow associated with the lease as a rental expense which will flow through the income statement over the life of the lease. With a capital lease, the fair value of the asset is recognized as both an asset and liability at inception of the lease, and subsequently amortized over the life of the lease. Companies have a strong preference for operating lease classification, as this keeps the lease obligation off the balance sheet. With the current rules under U.S. GAAP, there is significant discretion in structuring the terms of the lease contract so as not to trigger one of the thresholds described above.

Currently there are few companies reporting capital leases: Operating leases have become the norm, largely attributable to their preferred accounting treatment. Estimates range to over $1 trillion dollars for the amount of undiscounted future cash flow obligations associated with operating leases for SEC registrants. This is clearly a nontrivial issue. The use of operating leases is pervasive in the retail sector with companies such as Walgreen, Wal-Mart, CVS, and others having very large off-balance sheet operating lease obligations. The consequence of bringing these leases onto the balance sheet will be to increase leverage ratios; and depending on how these companies amortize the value of the leased asset, there could also be significant impacts on reported income directly.

4.3.1.2 Warning Signs While the FASB has governed the determination of operating and capital leases and the appropriate accounting treatment, SEC disclosures have improved in recent years with the addition of tabular presentation of future cash flow obligations associated with debt, operating leases, and other commitments in the 10-K. From these disclosures it is now possible to identify future cash flow obligations from many contractual obligations including current operating leases. These numbers can be discounted to their present value to get a rough estimate of the off-balance sheet obligations, which in turn can be brought on to the balance sheet and amortized using the companies' reported depreciation schedule for other noncurrent assets. Furthermore, tracking year-over-year changes in these off-balance sheet leases can highlight less transparent financing activities for these companies, which are arguably as important as on-balance sheet financing activities for forecasting future company performance.

The following example explores the use of off-balance sheet debt of a major U.S. retailer.

EXAMPLE 7

Off-Balance Sheet Debt

In its 10-K for the year ended 31 January 2007, Wal-Mart's (NYSE: WMT) balance sheet included total obligations under capital leases of $3,798 million, of which $285 million was due within one year and the remainder was long-term. The notes to the financial statements also broke out the following information regarding long-term contractual obligations:

> **Contractual Obligations and Other Commercial Commitments**
> The following table sets forth certain information concerning our obligations and commitments to make contractual future payments, such as debt and lease agreements, and contingent commitments:

	Payments Due during Fiscal Years Ending 31 January				
(in Millions)	**Total**	**2008**	**2009–2010**	**2011–2012**	**Thereafter**
Recorded Contractual Obligations:					
Long-term debt	$32,650	$ 5,428	$ 9,120	$ 5,398	$12,704
Commercial paper	2,570	2,570	—	—	—
Capital lease obligations	5,715	538	1,060	985	3,132
Unrecorded Contractual Obligations:					
Noncancelable operating leases	*10,446*	*842*	*1,594*	*1,332*	*6,678*
Interest on long-term debt	17,626	1,479	2,482	1,705	11,960
Undrawn lines of credit	6,890	3,390	—	3,500	—
Trade letters of credit	2,986	2,986	—	—	—
Standby letters of credit	2,247	2,247	—	—	—
Purchase obligations	15,168	11,252	3,567	126	223
Total commercial commitments	$96,298	$30,732	$17,823	$13,046	$34,697

Based on the information given, address the following problems:

1. Contrast the relative importance of on- and off-balance sheet treatment of contractual obligations for Wal-Mart.
2. Determine the relative importance of Wal-Mart's off-balance sheet obligations, given that Wal-Mart's 2007 cost of sales was $264 billion.
3. Estimate the impact on Wal-Mart's financial statements if operating leases were treated as though they were capital leases.

Solution to 1: Wal-Mart lists $40.9 billion of recorded contractual obligations ($32.650 + $2.570 + 5.715), and $55.4 ($10.446 + $17.626 + $6.890 + $2.986 + $2.247 + $15.168) billion of future obligations that are not recorded on the balance sheet.

Solution to 2: Noncancellable operating leases are similar in nature to capital leases, or assets financed with debt. They should be treated as though they were capital leases. The interest on long-term debt is the total future sum, and represents a financing cost rather than an actual liability. Analysis of interest coverage ratios should be adequate, with no adjustments to financial statements required. Undrawn lines of credit represent credit available, not currently in use. It is a potential obligation rather than an actual one. Letters of credit and purchase obligations are normal parts of business, and the related amounts ($20.4 billion) are small relative to Wal-Mart's operations. Wal-Mart's 2007 cost of sales was $264 billion—so the $15 billion in purchase obligations (which will eventually flow through cost of sales) amounts to less than three weeks' worth of the actual purchases by Wal-Mart.

Solution to 3: The present value of Wal-Mart's operating leases can be estimated by comparing them to its capital leases. Ideally, an analyst would discount the future capital lease payments, $5,715, to their carrying value of $3,798 to determine the implicit interest rate (an internal rate of return), then discount the operating lease obligations at the same rate. However, the disclosures give only broad ranges of when the payments are due, so analysts must estimate the timing. A shortcut approach is to simply apply the same overall discount to each type of lease. So, if the present value of capital leases is $3,798/$5,715 = 66.5% of the future payments, the present value of operating leases would be estimated at $10,446 × 0.665 = $6,942. To capitalize the operating leases, the analyst would add $6,942 to property, plant, and equipment and also to long-term liabilities. Leverage ratios, asset turnover, and other ratios involving assets and liabilities would be affected. In addition, the existing lease payments would ideally be allocated to depreciation and interest components rather than the current classification as rent. This would also impact interest coverage ratios and operating margins. The precise impact would depend on the amortization assumptions made. Note: Operating lease obligations of $10.4 billion are 1.83 times larger than the $5.7 billion in capital leases. The operating leases are slightly longer duration, as evidenced by the fact that 64 percent ($6,678/$10,446) of the payments are due in more than five years, compared with 55 percent ($3,132/$5,715) of the capital lease payments. Because the payments are due over a longer time horizon, their discounted value is lower, and the $6.9 billion estimated value is somewhat high (though considerably more accurate than the current balance sheet valuation of zero).

4.3.2 Goodwill

Goodwill is an intangible asset, subject to an annual impairment test, that is typically paid for in a business combination when the consideration paid to acquire the target exceeds the fair value of the target's net assets. For a company with many past acquisitions, the impairment of goodwill can have a major effect on reported financials.

4.3.2.1 The Range of Problems When a company acquires another company and records part of the acquisition price as goodwill, the goodwill is capitalized as an asset and no periodic amortization charges are taken against it. Instead, companies evaluate goodwill and other acquired intangible assets for impairment annually or whenever events or changes in circumstances indicate that the value of such an asset is impaired. This assessment requires estimates of the future cash flows associated with continued use of the asset, growth rates, and general market conditions. There is considerable discretion in conducting this impairment test, and this is one of the key risks associated with the external audit function: Auditors typically hire external appraisers to help with their assessment of fair value of goodwill and other intangibles.

4.3.2.2 Warning Signs Disclosures for goodwill can be found in the supplemental information to the primary financial statements. Typically, a company will provide tabular disclosure for year-over-year changes in reported goodwill. Given the inherent subjectivity in how this account is valued, analysts should look carefully at changes (or the absence of an impairment given overall economic conditions) in reported goodwill. Companies that continue to report goodwill on their balance sheets, but that have market capitalization less than the book value of equity, are certainly worthy of detailed examination to understand why an impairment was not taken. Karthik and Watts (2007) provide an interesting illustration of this situation for Orthodontic Centers of America (OCA). For the fiscal year ended 31 December 2003, OCA had reported book value of equity in excess of the market value of equity, yet continued to report a sizeable goodwill on its balance sheet ($87 million out of its $660 million total assets were attributable to goodwill). OCA was subsequently delisted from the stock exchange and in 2006 filed for bankruptcy.

4.4 Cash Flow Statement Issues

The material discussed in the preceding sections has highlighted many problems with earnings measures as predictors of a company's ability to generate future free cash flows. In this section, we outline a few caveats related to blindly following cash-flow-based measures. We will discuss three key items: 1) classification issues in the cash flow statement, 2) omitted investing and financing activities, and 3) real earnings management activity.

4.4.1 Classification Issues

Accounting standards define cash and cash equivalents to include only very short-term highly liquid investments. This narrow definition leads to the possibility that companies' investment of cash in liquid assets may appear in the investing as well as the operating section of the statement of cash flows.[14]

Many firms carry large cash balances which are invested in a portfolio of reasonable liquid investments. These cash balances are kept for various reasons. For example, Microsoft Corporation holds very large cash balances in part to help finance new investment opportunities when they arise, eliminating the need to obtain costly external financing. The cash that companies like Microsoft hold is not always invested in highly liquid short-term investments such as Treasury bills because companies can often obtain higher expected rates of return by investing elsewhere. To the extent that cash is invested in marketable securities such as equity and other fixed-income products, these investments are not strictly "cash equivalents" under most accounting standards. This allows companies to classify them as longer term investments. The result is that some liquid investments end up appearing in the investing section of the statement of cash flows. If the analyst focuses solely on an operating cash flow number, these "investing" cash flows will be missed. An easy solution to this problem is to take a holistic view to cash flows, and include operating and investing cash flows when assessing financial reporting quality. The aggregate accrual measures described in this reading do this for you by capturing the net cash flow generated from both operating and investing activities.

4.4.2 Omitted Investing and Financing Activities

The aggregate accrual measures outlined in this reading are based solely on investing and financing activity that is reported in the primary financial statements. There are certain types of investing and financing activity that are 1) not

[14] Note that the IASB in its 2007 revision to IAS 1 Presentation of Financial Statements has decided to make "cash" rather than "cash and cash equivalents" the basis for presenting the statement of cash flows. See the document FSP-0710b08a-obs at *www.iasb.org* for more information.

reported in *either* the balance sheet or statement of cash flows, or 2) not reported in the financial statements at all. An example of the first category is common-stock-based acquisition activity. Such activity will be picked up via the balance sheet measure of aggregate accruals, and the net assets acquired through the acquisition will be reported in the balance sheet post-acquisition for the new entity. It is important for the analyst to utilize both a balance-sheet-based and cash-flow-statement-based measure of aggregate accruals so as not to miss capturing the effects of such activity. An example of the second category is operating leases. This was described in detail back in section 4.3.1. The recommended approach is to capitalize the operating lease and adjust the balance sheet to reflect this off-balance sheet source of asset growth. What the analyst should pay attention to is not the existence of operating leases per se, but growth in operating lease activity. A good example is JetBlue Airways Corporation (NASDAQ: JBLU). Like most airline operators JetBlue makes extensive use of operating leases in its business model. From the perspective of 2007, over the last three years JetBlue has expanded extensively in part by increasing the use of operating leases related to terminal usage and flight equipment. The following three panels are extracted from the annual reports filed by JetBlue for the fiscal years ended 31 December 2004 through 31 December 2006.

EXHIBIT 11

Panel A. Contractual Obligations for Year Ended December 31, 2004 (in Millions)

	Payments Due in						
	Total	**2005**	**2006**	**2007**	**2008**	**2009**	**Thereafter**
Long-term debt(1)	$ 2,011	$ 173	$ 166	$ 163	$ 179	$ 129	$1,201
Operating leases	*1,035*	*110*	*114*	*98*	*92*	*88*	*533*
Flight equipment obligations	7,280	820	1,120	1,170	1,210	1,240	1,720
Short-term borrowings	44	44	—	—	—	—	—
Facilities and other(2)	271	143	28	28	30	27	15
Total	$10,641	$1,290	$1,428	$1,459	$1,511	$1,484	$3,469

Panel B. Contractual Obligations for Year Ended December 31, 2005 (in Millions)

	Payments Due in						
	Total	**2006**	**2007**	**2008**	**2009**	**2010**	**Thereafter**
Long-term debt	$ 3,400	$ 284	$ 282	$ 304	$ 207	$ 200	$2,123
Lease commitments	*1,707*	*157*	*155*	*145*	*129*	*119*	*1,002*
Flight equipment obligations	6,440	1,115	1,170	1,200	1,230	1,180	545
Short-term borrowings	65	65	—	—	—	—	—
Financing obligations and other	2,439	188	83	115	147	158	1,748
Total	$14,051	$1,809	$1,690	$1,764	$1,713	$1,657	$5,418

(Exhibit continued on next page . . .)

EXHIBIT 11 (continued)

Panel C. Contractual Obligations for Year Ended December 31, 2006 (in Millions)

	Payments Due in						
	Total	**2007**	**2008**	**2009**	**2010**	**2011**	**Thereafter**
Long-term debt and capital lease obligations (1)	$ 4,312	$ 350	$ 387	$ 282	$ 275	$ 271	$2,747
Lease commitments	*2,177*	*217*	*216*	*190*	*170*	*159*	*1,225*
Flight equipment obligations	5,705	775	835	965	1,030	1,000	1,100
Short-term borrowings	39	39	—	—	—	—	—
Financing obligations and other (2)	2,333	147	119	138	147	168	1,614
Total	$14,566	$1,528	$1,557	$1,575	$1,622	$1,598	$6,686

Note: Italics within added by the authors.

There is a clear increase in the extent of operating lease activity for JetBlue over the three years from 2004 through 2006. To the extent that the growth in operating lease activity is not associated with asset growth that is recorded on the balance sheet, this lease activity represents an investing activity that is missing from the primary financial statements—limiting the potential usefulness of the statement-of-cash-flow- or balance-sheet-based measures of aggregate accruals. A recommended approach is to capitalize the future cash flow obligations reported in the contractual obligation tables that companies are required to disclose (at least in the United States). As described in section 4.3.1, simple assumptions with respect to discount rates and treatment of the cash flows that extend beyond five years are sufficient for our purposes. This capitalized amount then gets added to the asset and liability side of the balance sheet. Given that our measures focus on net operating asset growth, this growth in operating lease activity will lead to a direct change in our aggregate accrual measures as the liability side of this transaction is a financing activity.

4.4.3 Real Earnings Management Activity

Our focus on financial reporting quality has concentrated on the embedded discretion in the accrual-based accounting system. We have ignored real operating decisions that management may take to meet the same capital market and contracting pressures described in section 2.3. For example, management may cut the budget for research and development activity toward the end of the fiscal period when it becomes clear they are struggling to meet earnings-based targets. Note that under U.S. GAAP research and development expenditures are expensed in the year that they are incurred and not capitalized for expensing over future periods. Such myopic behavior is not uncommon for management. The longer-term implications from these real operating decisions are to sacrifice future free cash flows at the expense of meeting short-term earnings targets.

4.5 A Summary of Financial Reporting Quality Warning Signs

In the course of this reading we have presented some key indicators of possibly low-quality financial reporting. In Exhibit 12 we indicate some key red flags to look for across the various revenue, expense, and balance sheet issues. We include the main warning signs discussed in the text as well as a selection of other warning signs that the reader may find helpful for further study. The expanded list is only a selection, of course.

EXHIBIT 12 Accounting Warning Signs (Selection)

Category	Observation	Potential Interpretation
Revenues and gains	Large increases in accounts receivable or large decreases in unearned revenue	Financial statement indicator of potential for revenue quality issues
	Large swings in the ratio of revenue to cash collected from customers	Financial statement indicator of potential revenue acceleration issues
	Recognizing revenue early; for example: ▶ Bill-and-hold sales ▶ Lessor use of capital lease classification ▶ Recording sales of equipment or software prior to installation and acceptance by customer	Acceleration in the recognition of revenue boosts reported income masking a decline in operating performance
	Classification of nonoperating income or gains as part of operations	Income or gains may be nonrecurring and may not relate to true operating performance. May mask a decline in operating performance
	Recognizing revenue from barter transactions	Value of transaction may be overstated. Both parties may be striving to report revenues where no cash flow occurs. Revenues and expenses may be overstated
	Growth in revenues out of line with industry, peers, inventory growth, receivables growth, or cash flow from operations	May indicate aggressive reporting of sales. If receivables are growing more rapidly than sales, may indicate that credit standards have been lowered or that shipments have been accelerated. If inventories are growing more rapidly than sales, may indicate a slowdown in demand for the company's products
	Large proportion of revenue occurs in the last quarter of the year for a nonseasonal business	May indicate aggressive reporting of sales or acceleration of shipments at year end

(Exhibit continued on next page . . .)

EXHIBIT 12 (continued)

Category	Observation	Potential Interpretation
Expenses and losses	Inconsistency over time in the items included in operating revenues and operating expenses	May indicate opportunistic use of discretion to boost reported operating income
	Classification of ordinary expenses as nonrecurring or nonoperating	May reflect an attempt to mask a decline in operating performance
	Increases in the core operating margin (Sales − COGS − SGA)/Sales accompanied by spikes in negative special items	May indicate opportunistic classification of recurring expenses as nonrecurring
	Use of non-conservative depreciation and amortization estimates, assumptions, or methods; for example, long depreciable lives	May indicate actions taken to boost current reported income. Changes in assumptions may indicate an attempt to mask problems with underlying performance in the current period
	Buildup of high inventory levels relative to sales or decrease in inventory turnover ratios	May indicate obsolete inventory or failure to take needed inventory write-downs
	Deferral of expenses by capitalizing expenditures as an asset; for example: ► Customer acquisition costs ► Product development costs	May boost current income at the expense of future income. May mask problems with underlying business performance
	Lessee use of operating leases	May result in higher net income in early years under an operating lease, not reflecting depreciation expense and interest expense. Leased asset and associated liability not reflected on balance sheet
	Use of reserves, such as ► *Restructuring or impairment charges reversed in a subsequent period* ► *Use of high or low level of bad debt reserves relative to peers*	May allow company to "save" profits in one period to be used when needed in a later period. May be used to smooth earnings and mask underlying earnings variability
Balance sheet issues (may also impact earnings)	Lessee preference for operating lease classification	Tends to reduce leverage ratios based only on on-balance sheet items
	Market value less than book value for companies with substantial reported goodwill	May indicate that appropriate goodwill impairments have not been taken

(Exhibit continued on next page . . .)

EXHIBIT 12 (continued)

Category	Observation	Potential Interpretation
	Use of aggressive acquisition accounting, such as write-off of purchased in-process research and development costs[15]	May indicate that assets and liabilities are not recorded at economic cost to the entity and that earnings may be overstated in future years relative to peers
	Use of special purpose vehicles (SPVs)[16]	Assets and/or liabilities may not be properly reflected on the balance sheet. Income may also be overstated by sales to the special purpose entity or a decline in the value of assets transferred to the SPE
	Large changes in deferred tax assets and liabilities	May have near term cash flow consequences. Particularly investigate the reason for the existence of deferred tax asset valuation allowances
	Sales of receivables with recourse	The use of debt may not be fully reflected on the balance sheet and the risks of non-collection may not be reflected for receivables
	Use of unconsolidated joint ventures or equity method investees when substantial ownership (near 50 percent) exists	May reflect off-balance sheet liabilities. Profitability ratios may be overstated due to share on income reported in income statement but related sales or assets are not reflected in parent financial statements

Note: Points not discussed in the text have been italicized in the table.

Source: Adapted from Stowe, Robinson, Pinto, McLeavey (2002), Chapter 1, Table 1-1, with additions and deletions.

THE IMPLICATIONS OF FAIR VALUE REPORTING FOR FINANCIAL REPORTING QUALITY: A BRIEF DISCUSSION

5

As a final point of discussion before concluding, it is worth noting how the recent push from the FASB and the IASB to bring greater relevance to the financial statements has the ironic side effect of increasing accounting discretion. The IASB and FASB recently have made serious efforts to embrace fair value accounting as a basis for financial reporting. The general theme is that the balance sheet should reflect fair values of assets and liabilities. While for some assets, such as equity investments in companies listed on the New York Stock Exchange, the fair value is readily determinable and easily audited (just pick up a copy of the *Wall Street Journal* on the last day of the fiscal period and multiply the number of

[15] **Purchased in-process research and development costs** are the costs of research and development in progress at an acquired company; often part of an acquired company's purchase price is allocated to such costs.

[16] A **special purpose vehicle** is a nonoperating entity created to carry out a specified purpose, such as leasing assets or securitizing receivables. The use of SPVs is frequently related to off-balance sheet financing (financing that does not currently appear on the balance sheet).

shares held by the quoted market price), it is not as clear for some other assets. For example, how should one value a large block of equity or bonds in another public entity? Should a discount from the current market value be recorded from the market impact cost associated with selling such a large position? What about investments in private entities where there is no observable market (even for over-the-counter corporate bond trading in the United States, it is difficult to get an accurate price). This is not to mention the more common problem of valuing assets whose economic lives are quite long and may be quite specific to the entity—for example, specialized manufacturing equipment. The turmoil in credit markets over the summer of 2007, stemming from concerns about the collateral quality for many securitized asset-backed securities, illustrates the difficulty in identifying reliable estimates of fair value for many assets (even financial assets) that reside on company balance sheets. Of course, the FASB and IASB have very detailed guidelines defining approaches one can take to place a fair value on such items. But ultimately, fair value accounting opens the door for considerable discretion to be placed on balance sheet valuations.

What is an analyst to do when faced with this increasing uncertainty about balance sheet valuations? First, remember that financial statements should be used as an anchor for your valuation. Keep in mind that there is considerable discretion in the financial statements; appreciate where it is and be skeptical of the numbers presented to you. Second, search for disclosures relating to how the values of assets and liabilities reported in the balance sheet are determined. Financial statements should not be read in isolation from the detailed footnotes accompanying them. There is often useful detail in those footnotes that greatly assists in understanding the choices made by a company in a given fiscal period. With sufficient disclosure about the choices a company has made, it is possible to reverse engineer and place companies back on an equal footing with respect to that choice set.

SUMMARY

We have touched on major themes in financial reporting quality. This is a broad area with considerable academic and practitioner research. Indeed, many of the techniques described here are used by analysts to make security recommendations and by asset managers in making portfolio allocation decisions. The interested reader would be well served by exploring this topic in greater detail. Among the points the reading has made are the following:

- Financial reporting quality relates to the accuracy with which a company's reported financial statements reflect its operating performance and to their usefulness for forecasting future cash flows. Understanding the properties of accruals is critical for understanding and evaluating financial reporting quality.
- The application of accrual accounting makes necessary use of judgment and discretion. On average, accrual accounting provides a superior picture to a cash basis accounting for forecasting future cash flows.
- Earnings can be decomposed into cash and accrual components. The accrual component has been found to have less persistence than the cash component and therefore 1) earnings with higher accrual components are less persistent than earnings with smaller accrual components, all else equal, and 2) the cash component of earnings should receive a higher weighting in evaluating company performance.
- Aggregate accruals = Accrual earnings − Cash earnings
- Defining net operating assets as $NOA_t = [(\text{Total assets}_t - \text{Cash}_t) - (\text{Total liabilities}_t - \text{Total debt}_t)]$ one can derive the following balance-sheet-based and cash-flow-statement-based measures of aggregate accruals/the accruals component of earnings:
  - $\text{Aggregate accruals}_t^{B/S} = NOA_t - NOA_{t-1}$
  - $\text{Aggregate accruals}_t^{CF} = NI_t - (CFO_t + CFI_t)$

  With corresponding scaled measures that can be used as simple measures of financial reporting quality:
  - $\text{Accruals ratio}_t^{B/S} = \dfrac{(NOA_t - NOA_{t-1})}{(NOA_t + NOA_{t-1})/2}$
  - $\text{Accruals ratio}_t^{CF} = \dfrac{[NI_t - (CFO_t + CFI_t)]}{(NOA_t + NOA_{t-1})/2}$
- Aggregate accruals ratios are useful to rank companies for the purpose of evaluating earnings quality. Companies with high (low) accruals ratios are companies with low (high) earnings quality. Companies with low (high) earnings quality tend to experience lower (higher) accounting rates of return and relatively lower excess stock returns in future periods.
- Sources of accounting discretion include choices related to revenue recognition, depreciation choices, inventory choices, choices related to goodwill and other noncurrent assets, choices related to taxes, pension choices, financial asset/liability valuation, and stock option expense estimates.
- A framework for detecting financial reporting problems includes examining reported financials for revenue recognition issues and expense recognition issues.

- Revenue recognition issues include overstatement of revenue, acceleration of revenue, and classification of nonrecurring or nonoperating items as operating revenue.
- Expense recognition issues include understating expenses, deferring expenses, and the classification of ordinary expenses as nonrecurring or nonoperating expenses.
- Discretion related to off-balance sheet liabilities (e.g., in the accounting for leases) and the impairment of goodwill also can affect financial reporting quality.

PRACTICE PROBLEMS FOR READING 27

1. Which of the following mechanisms is *least likely* to discourage management manipulation of earnings?

A. Debt covenants.

B. Securities regulators.

C. Class action lawsuits.

2. High earnings quality is *most likely* to:

A. result in steady earnings growth.

B. improve the ability to predict future earnings.

C. be based on conservative accounting choices.

3. The *best* justification for using accrual-based accounting is that it:

A. reflects the company's underlying cash flows.

B. reflects the economic nature of a company's transactions.

C. limits management's discretion in reporting financial results.

4. The *best* justification for using cash-based accounting is that it:

A. is more conservative.

B. limits management's discretion in reporting financial results.

C. matches the timing of revenue recognition with that of associated expenses.

5. Which of the following is *not* a measure of aggregate accruals?

A. The change in net operating assets.

B. The difference between operating income and net operating assets.

C. The difference between net income and operating and investing cash flows.

6. Consider the following balance sheet information for Profile, Inc.:

Year Ended 31 December	2007	2006
Cash and short-term investments	14,000	13,200
Total current assets	21,000	20,500
Total assets	97,250	88,000
Current liabilities	31,000	29,000
Total debt	50,000	45,000
Total liabilities	87,000	79,000

Profile's balance-sheet-based accruals ratio in 2007 was *closest* to:

A. 12.5%.

B. 13.0%.

C. 16.2%.

7. Rodrigue SA reported the following financial statement data for the year ended 2007:

Average net operating assets	39,000
Net income	14,000
Cash flow from operating activity	17,300
Cash flow from investing activity	(12,400)

Rodrigue's cash-flow-based accruals ratio in 2007 was *closest* to:

A. −8.5%.

B. −19.1%.

C. 23.3%.

8. Cash collected from customers is *least likely* to differ from sales due to changes in:

A. inventory.

B. deferred revenue.

C. accounts receivable.

9. Reported revenue is *most likely* to have been reduced by management's discretionary estimate of:

A. warranty provisions.

B. inventory damage and theft.

C. interest to be earned on credit sales.

10. Zimt AG reports 2007 revenue of €14.3 billion. During 2007, its accounts receivable rose by €0.7 billion, accounts payable increased by €1.1 billion, and unearned revenue increased by €0.5 billion. Its cash collections from customers in 2007 were *closest* to:

A. €14.1 billion.

B. €14.5 billion.

C. €15.2 billion.

11. Cinnamon Corp. began the year with $12 million in accounts receivable and $31 million in deferred revenue. It ended the year with $15 million in accounts receivable and $27 million in deferred revenue. Based on this information, the accrual-basis earnings included in total revenue were *closest* to:

A. $1 million.

B. $7 million.

C. $12 million.

12. Which of the following is *least likely* to be a warning sign of low-quality revenue?

A. A large decrease in deferred revenue.

B. A large increase in accounts receivable.

C. A large increase in the allowance for doubtful accounts.

13. An unexpectedly large reduction in the unearned revenue account is *most likely* a sign that the company:

A. accelerated revenue recognition.

B. overstated revenue in prior periods.

C. adopted more conservative revenue recognition practices.

14. Canelle SA reported 2007 revenue of €137 million. Its accounts receivable balance began the year at €11 million and ended the year at €16 million. At year-end, €2 million of receivables had been securitized. Canelle's cash collections from customers (in € millions) in 2007 were *closest* to:

A. €130.

B. €132.

C. €134.

15. In order to identify possible understatement of expenses with regard to noncurrent assets, an analyst would *most likely* beware management's discretion to:

A. accelerate depreciation.

B. increase the residual value.

C. reduce the expected useful life.

16. A sudden rise in inventory balances is *least likely* to be a warning sign of:

A. understated expenses.

B. accelerated revenue recognition.

C. inefficient working capital management.

17. A warning sign that a company may be deferring expenses is sales revenue growing at a slower rate than:

A. unearned revenue.

B. noncurrent liabilities.

C. property, plant, and equipment.

18. An asset write-down is *least likely* to indicate understatement of expenses in:

A. prior years.

B. future years.

C. the current year.

19. Ranieri Corp. reported the following 2007 income statement:

Sales	93,000
Cost of sales	24,500
SG&A	32,400
Interest expense	800
Other income	1,400
Income taxes	14,680
Net income	22,020

Ranieri's core operating margin in 2007 was *closest* to:

A. 23.7%.

B. 38.8%.

C. 73.7%.

20. Sebastiani AG reported the following financial results for the years ended 31 December:

	2007	2006
Sales	46,574	42,340
Cost of sales	14,000	13,000
SGA	13,720	12,200
Operating income	18,854	17,140
Income taxes	6,410	5,656
Net income	12,444	11,484

Compared to core operating margin in 2006, Sebastiani's core operating margin in 2007 was:

A. lower.

B. higher.

C. unchanged.

21. A warning sign that ordinary expenses are now being classified as nonrecurring or nonoperating expenses is:

A. falling core operating margin followed by a spike in positive special items.

B. a spike in positive special items followed by falling core operating margin.

C. falling core operating margin followed by a spike in negative special items.

22. Which of the following obligations must be reported on a company's balance sheet?

A. Capital leases.

B. Operating leases.

C. Purchase commitments.

23. The *most accurate* estimate for off-balance sheet financing related to operating leases consists of the sum of:

A. future payments.

B. future payments less a discount to reflect the related interest component.

C. future payments plus a premium to reflect the related interest component.

24. The intangible asset goodwill represents the value of an acquired company that cannot be attached to other tangible assets. This noncurrent asset account is charged to an expense:

A. as amortization.

B. when it becomes impaired.

C. at the time of the acquisition.

25. Total accruals measured using the balance sheet is *most likely* to differ from total accruals measured using the statement of cash flows when the company has made acquisitions:

A. financed by debt.

B. in exchange for cash.

C. in exchange for stock.

SOLUTIONS FOR READING 27

1. A is correct. Because debt covenants typically mandate a certain level of financial performance, they can serve to *encourage* rather than discourage earnings manipulation.
2. B is correct. Earnings quality is typically defined in terms of persistence and sustainability. By contrast, earnings may be manipulated to deliver steady growth. Conservatism in accounting choices may reduce the persistence of earnings as the accounting often reverts to the mean over time.
3. B is correct. Accrual accounting is based on the "matching principle" under which revenues and the associated expenses are recognized concurrently even when the cash flow timing may differ.
4. B is correct. Cash accounting does not rely on discretionary estimates but rather on actual cash flows. This may be either more or less conservative than accrual-based accounting.
5. B is correct. A is the balance sheet aggregate accrual measure, while C is the cash flow aggregate accrual measure.
6. A is correct. Net operating assets = (Assets − Cash and short-term investments) − (Liabilities − Total debt), or in Profile's case, (97,250 − 14,000) − (87,000 − 50,000) = 46,250 in 2007 and 40,800 in 2006. The accrual ratio in 2007 is the change in NOA divided by average NOA, or (46,250 − 40,800)/[(46,250 + 40,800)/2] = 5,450/43,525 = 12.5%.
7. C is correct. The accrual ratio is [NI − (CFO + CFI)]/NOA or [14,000 − (17,300 − 12,400)]/39,000 = 9,100/39,000 = 23.3%.
8. A is correct. Sales = Cash collected from customers + Increase in accounts receivable − Increase in deferred revenue.
9. A is correct. Reported sales results are affected by management's estimates of, among other things, uncollectible receivables, warranty costs, and returns.
10. A is correct. Cash collected from customers = Sales − Net increase in accounts receivable + Net increase in deferred revenue. Cash collected from customers = 14.3 billion sales − 0.7 billion increase in receivables + 0.5 billion increase in unearned revenue = €14.1 billion.
11. B is correct. Revenue was increased by a $3 million accrual for the change in receivables and also by the $4 million reduction in deferred revenue. Accrual-basis earnings were therefore $7 million.
12. C is correct. The allowance for doubtful accounts *excludes* items from reported revenue and accounts receivable. An increase in this account *reduces* the discretionary accrual related to the change in accounts receivable.
13. A is correct. Deferred/unearned revenue represents cash collected from customers that will be recognized as revenue in the future. A decrease in this account means the revenue has been recognized. An unexpected decrease could signal accelerated revenue recognition.
14. A is correct. Ending receivables should be adjusted to add the €2 million of securitized receivables. Then cash collections can be calculated as €137 − (5 + 2) = €130.

15. B is correct. By increasing the residual value estimate, management would lower the total depreciation expense to be recognized over time.
16. B is correct. A rise in inventory balances could suggest poor inventory management efficiency, or also that costs that should be recognized in cost of goods sold are being capitalized as inventory. It would not affect the revenue line.
17. C is correct. PP&E growing at a faster rate than sales may indicate that expenses are being inappropriately capitalized.
18. C is correct. An asset write-down *increases* expense in the current year, but reduces depreciation in future periods (and possibly indicates that depreciation was too low in prior periods).
19. B is correct. Core operating margin is (Sales − COGS − SGA)/Sales, or (93,000 − 24,500 − 32,400)/93,000 = 36,100/93,000 = 38.8%.
20. C is correct. Although COGS/Sales improved and SGA/Sales deteriorated, the total effect was no change. 17,140/42,340 = 40.5% and 18,854/46,574 = 40.5%.
21. C is correct. One way to spot misclassification of ordinary expenses is to look for spikes in the incidence of special items for companies that previously experienced decreasing core operating margin.
22. A is correct. Capital leases are treated as though the related asset were purchased and financed using debt.
23. B is correct. The future payments should be discounted to the present value at a rate approximating the company's cost to finance debt of a similar nature.
24. B is correct. Goodwill is charged to expense only if it becomes impaired.
25. C is correct. Stock-based acquisitions do not flow through the cash flow statement.

INTEGRATION OF FINANCIAL STATEMENT ANALYSIS TECHNIQUES

by Jack T. Ciesielski, Jr., CFA

READING

28

LEARNING OUTCOMES

The candidate should be able to:	Mastery
a. demonstrate the use of a framework for the analysis of financial statements, given a particular problem, question, or purpose (e.g., valuing equity based on comparables, critiquing a credit rating, obtaining a comprehensive picture of financial leverage, evaluating the perspectives given in management's discussion of financial results);	☐
b. identify financial reporting choices and biases that affect the quality and comparability of companies' financial statements and illustrate how such biases affect financial decisions;	☐
c. evaluate the quality of a company's financial data and recommend appropriate adjustments to improve quality and comparability with similar companies, including adjustments for differences in accounting rules, methods, and assumptions;	☐
d. predict the impact on financial statements and ratios, given a change in accounting rules, methods, or assumptions;	☐
e. analyze and interpret the effects of balance sheet modifications, earnings normalization, and cash-flow-statement-related modifications on a company's financial statements, financial ratios, and overall financial condition.	☐

Note:
New rulings and/or pronouncements issued after the publication of the readings in financial reporting and analysis may cause some of the information in these readings to become dated. Candidates are expected to be familiar with the overall analytical framework contained in the study session readings, as well as the implications of alternative accounting methods for financial analysis and valuation, as provided in the assigned readings. Candidates are not responsible for changes that occur after the material was written.

INTRODUCTION 1

It is important to keep in mind that financial analysis is the means to the end, and not the end itself. Rather than try to apply every possible technique and tool to every situation, it is more important for the investor to understand the proper type of analysis to apply in a given situation.

The primary reason for performing financial analysis is to facilitate an economic decision. Before making such decisions as whether to lend to a particular long-term borrower or to invest a large sum in a common stock, venture capital vehicle, or private equity candidate, an investor wants to put the odds of a successful outcome on his or her side. Rather than leaving outcomes to chance, financial analysis should identify potential losses and make the potential favorable outcomes more visible.

The purpose of this reading is to provide examples of the effective use of financial analysis in decision making. The framework for the analysis is shown in Exhibit 1. Each of the three case studies is set in a different type of company and has a different focus/purpose and context for the analysis. However, each case study follows the basic framework.

EXHIBIT 1 A Financial Statement Analysis Framework

Phase	Sources of Information	Examples of Output
1. Define the purpose and context of the analysis.	▶ The nature of the analyst's function, such as evaluating an equity or debt investment or issuing a credit rating ▶ Communication with client or supervisor on needs and concerns ▶ Institutional guidelines related to developing specific work product	▶ Statement of the purpose or objective of analysis ▶ A list (written or unwritten) of specific questions to be answered by the analysis ▶ Nature and content of report to be provided ▶ Timetable and budgeted resources for completion
2. Collect input data.	▶ Financial statements, other financial data, questionnaires, and industry/economic data ▶ Discussions with management, suppliers, customers, and competitors ▶ Company site visits (e.g., to production facilities or retail stores)	▶ Organized financial statements ▶ Financial data tables ▶ Completed questionnaires, if applicable
3. Process input data, as required, into analytically useful data.	▶ Data from the previous phase	▶ Adjusted financial statements ▶ Common-size statements ▶ Ratios and graphs ▶ Forecasts
4. Analyze/interpret the data.	▶ Input data and processed data	▶ Analytical results

(Exhibit continued on next page . . .)

EXHIBIT 1 (continued)

Phase	Sources of Information	Examples of Output
5. Develop and communicate conclusions and recommendations (e.g., with an analysis report).	▶ Analytical results and previous reports ▶ Institutional guidelines for published reports	▶ Analytical report answering questions posed in Phase 1 ▶ Recommendation regarding the purpose of the analysis, such as whether to make an investment or grant credit
6. Follow-up.	▶ Information gathered by periodically repeating above steps as necessary to determine whether changes to holdings or recommendations are necessary	▶ Updated reports and recommendations

CASE STUDY 1: LONG-TERM EQUITY INVESTMENT

2

The portfolio manager for the food sector of a large public employee pension fund wants to take a long-term equity stake in a publicly traded food company, and has become interested in Nestlé S.A. (SWX Swiss Exchange: NESN and OTC [NY ADR]: NSRGY), a truly global company. In its 2007 management report, Nestlé's management outlined its long-term objectives for organic growth, continuous margin improvement, and improvement in return on invested capital. The management report indicated the following general strategic direction: "We continue to believe that our greatest opportunity to create value for our shareholders is through further transforming our Food and Beverages business into a Nutrition, Health, and Wellness offering and by improving its performance further." Those stated objectives captured the portfolio manager's attention, and the manager has become intrigued with Nestlé as an investment possibility. He commissions an analyst to evaluate Nestlé for consideration as a core holding. Before investing in the company, the portfolio manager has several concerns that he has conveyed to the analyst:

- What are Nestlé's sources of earnings growth? How sustainable is Nestlé's performance? In other words, do the company's reported earnings represent economic reality? And if their performance is indeed robustly reported, will it be repeatable for, say, five to ten years while the pension fund treats the common stock as a core holding?
- In determining the quality of earnings over a long-term time frame, the portfolio manager wants to understand the relationship of earnings to cash flow.
- Having started out in the investment business as a lending officer, the portfolio manager wants to know how well Nestlé's balance sheet takes into account the company's full rights and obligations. Can the capital structure of the company support future operations and strategic plans? Even if the investor is primarily concerned with the earnings power of a possible investee, the balance sheet matters. For example, if asset write-downs or new legal liabilities cripple a company's financial standing, it is difficult for

a company to sustain profitability if it has to repair its balance sheet. Worse still for an investor: If "repairing the balance sheet" means the issuance of dilutive stock, it can be even more costly to existing investors.

The analyst develops a plan of analysis to address the portfolio manager's concerns by following the framework in Exhibit 1. Phases 3 and 4 will be the focus of most of the work.

Phase 1: Define a Purpose for the Analysis

The analyst articulates the purpose and context of the analysis as isolating the factors that have driven the company's financial success and assessing their sustainability, while delineating and understanding the risks that may upset the sustainability of returns.

Phase 2: Collect Input Data

The analyst finds that Nestlé has an extensive library of financial statements on its website. After gathering several years of annual reports, he is ready to begin processing the data.

Phase 3: Process Data/Phase 4: Analyze/Interpret the Processed Data

The analyst intends to accomplish his purpose stated in Phase 1 through a series of financial analyses, including:

- A DuPont analysis;[1]
- An analysis of the composition of Nestlé's asset base;
- An analysis of Nestlé's capital structure;
- A study of the company's segments and the allocation of capital among them;
- An examination of the company's accruals in reporting as they affect earnings quality;
- A study of the company's cash flows and their adequacy for the company's continued operations and strategies; and
- Decomposition and analysis of the company's valuation.

While processing the input data consistent with the needs of the analyses above, the analyst plans to simultaneously interpret and analyze the resulting data. In his view, Phases 3 and 4 of the framework are best considered jointly.

[1] A reminder to the reader: This case study is an example, and starting financial statement analysis with a DuPont analysis is not a mandate. Alternatively, another analyst might have preferred starting with a time-series common-size income statement. This analyst might be more interested in the trends of various income and expense categories as a financial statement analysis starting point than in the sources of returns on shareholder equity. It depends on the perspective of the individual analyst.

DuPont Analysis

For several reasons, the analyst decides that the best way to first investigate Nestlé is through the lens of a DuPont analysis. The investment is expected to be in the company's common stock, and ultimately, the DuPont analysis isolates the components affecting the return on common equity. Furthermore, the disaggregation of ROE components leads to more threads to follow in assessing the drivers of Nestlé's performance. The analyst also intends to investigate the quality of the earnings and the underlying cash flows, as well as investigating the common shareholders' standing in the Nestlé capital structure.

One basic premise underlying all research and analysis is to constantly look beneath the level of information presented—to constantly strive for disaggregation within information presented, whether it is a single line on a financial statement or within segments of an entire entity. This search for granularity can reveal the sources of a company's earnings drivers; it can also highlight weaker operations being masked by stronger ones in the aggregate. That premise of "seeking granularity" underlies DuPont analysis: By isolating the different components of return on equity, it helps the analyst find potential operational flaws and provides a springboard for dialogue with management about possible problems.

The analyst begins to process the data gathered in Phase 2 to assemble the information required for the DuPont analysis. Exhibit 2 shows the last three years of income statements for Nestlé; Exhibit 3 shows the last four years of Nestlé balance sheets. From his study of the income statement, the analyst notes that Nestlé has a significant amount of income from associates. In 2007, this amounted to CHF 1,280 million, or 11.2 percent, of Nestlé's net income (referred to by Nestlé as "profit for the period"). The income from associates[2] is a pure net income figure, after taxes and with no related revenue in the income statement. Much of the income relates to Nestlé's 30 percent stock ownership of L'Oreal, a cosmetics company.

The analyst's interest is to evaluate the company on a decomposed basis as much as possible in order to isolate any problem operations or to find misunderstood or unidentified opportunities. Including the net investments and returns of associates with full reported value of Nestlé's own assets and income would introduce noise into the analytical signals produced by the DuPont analysis. The returns earned by affiliates are not under the direct control of Nestlé's management as are the "pure Nestlé" operations and resources. To avoid making incorrect inferences about the profitability of Nestlé's operations, the analyst wants to remove the effects of the investments in associates from the balance sheet and income statement. Otherwise, DuPont analysis components such as net profit margin and total asset turnover will combine the impact of pure Nestlé operations with operations of associated companies. Conclusions drawn about Nestlé-only business would be based on flawed information.

The analyst restated the 2004 balance sheet from the published version to take into account several accounting changes Nestlé made as of 1 January 2005. Those adjustments would have affected 31 December 2004 balances if the financial statements had been restated for that year. In order to keep the DuPont analysis as logically consistent as possible throughout all the periods of study, he restated the 2004 balance sheet for those adjustments by isolating the 1 January 2005 adjustments from the 2005 financial statements, and restating the 31 December 2004 year end balances for them. They included changes for

[2] Associates are companies in which Nestlé has the power to exercise a significant influence but does not exercise control. They are accounted for by the equity method.

EXHIBIT 2 Nestlé S.A. Income Statements 2007–2005 (in Millions of CHF)

	2007	2006	2005
Sales	107,552	98,458	91,115
Cost of goods sold	(45,037)	(40,713)	(37,917)
Distribution expenses	(9,104)	(8,244)	(7,402)
Marketing and administration expenses	(36,512)	(34,465)	(32,421)
Research and development costs	(1,875)	(1,734)	(1,499)
EBIT before restructuring and impairments[3]	**15,024**	**13,302**	**11,876**
Net other income/(expenses)[4]	(590)	(516)	(920)
Profit before interest and taxes	14,434	12,786	10,956
Net financing cost			
Financial income	576	537	605
Financial expense	(1,492)	(1,218)	(1,192)
Profit before taxes and associates (EBT)	**13,518**	**12,105**	**10,369**
Taxes	(3,416)	(3,293)	(2,647)
Share of results of associates	1,280	963	896
Profit from continuing operations	**11,382**	**9,775**	**8,618**
Net profit/(loss) on discontinued operations	0	74	(14)
Profit for the period	**11,382**	**9,849**	**8,604**
of which attributable to minority interests	733	652	523
of which attributable to shareholders of the parent (Net profit)	10,649	9,197	8,081
Earnings per share from continuing operations			
Basic earnings per share	CHF 27.81	CHF 23.71	CHF 20.82
Diluted earnings per share	CHF 27.61	CHF 23.56	CHF 20.63

employee benefits plan accounting (IAS 19 adoption), lease classification (IFRIC 4 adoption), a reclassification of a warrants premium, and the cumulative effect on their investment of L'Oreal's first-time adoption of International Financial Reporting Standards. The revisions made by the analyst to the as-reported 2004 balance sheet are shown in Exhibit 4.

[3] Expenses include depreciation and amortization of 3,211; 3,061; and 2,728 for 2007, 2006, and 2005, respectively.

[4] Includes impairments of 482, 134, and 608 for 2007, 2006, and 2005, respectively.

EXHIBIT 3 Nestlé S.A. Balance Sheets 2007–2004 (in Millions of CHF)

	2007	2006	2005	2004 (Revised)
Assets				
Liquid assets				
Cash and cash equivalents	6,594	5,278	4,658	4,902
Short term investments	2,902	6,197	12,735	10,380
	9,496	11,475	17,393	15,282
Trade and other receivables	15,421	14,577	14,291	11,809
Assets held for sale	22	74	633	0
Inventories	9,272	8,029	8,162	7,025
Derivative assets	754	556	645	585
Prepayments and accrued income	805	594	641	584
Total current assets	35,770	35,305	41,765	35,285
Non-current assets				
Net property, plant and equipment	22,065	20,230	18,990	17,208
Investments in associates	8,936	8,430	7,073	5,197
Deferred tax assets	2,224	2,433	2,466	2,173
Financial assets	4,213	2,778	2,513	2,410
Employee benefits assets	811	343	69	32
Goodwill	33,423	28,513	26,990	23,854
Intangible assets	7,217	3,773	2,852	2,028
Total non-current assets	78,889	66,500	60,953	52,902
Total assets	114,659	101,805	102,718	88,187
Liabilities and equity				
Current liabilities				
Trade and other payables	14,179	12,572	11,117	9,074
Liabilities directly associated with assets held for sale	7	0	38	0
Financial liabilities	24,541	15,494	18,841	14,722
Tax liabilities	856	884	705	584
Derivative liabilities	477	470	922	856
Accruals and deferred income	3,266	3,059	4,231	3,892
Total current liabilities	43,326	32,479	35,854	29,128
Non-current liabilities				
Financial liabilities	6,129	6,952	8,277	10,891
Employee benefits liabilities	5,165	5,415	5,747	5,704
Deferred tax liabilities	1,398	706	240	16
Other payables	1,091	366	185	327
Provisions	3,316	3,039	3,347	3,004
Total non-current liabilities	17,099	16,478	17,796	19,942
Total liabilities	60,425	48,957	53,650	49,070
Total equity attributable to shareholders of the parent	52,085	50,991	47,498	38,068
Minority interests	2,149	1,857	1,570	1,049
Total equity	54,234	52,848	49,068	39,117
Total liabilities and equity	114,659	101,805	102,718	88,187

EXHIBIT 4 Modifications to 2004 Balance Sheets (in Millions of CHF)

	As Reported	IAS 19 Effect (1)	IFRIC 4 Effect (2)	IAS 39 Warrant Premium Classification (3)	L'Oreal IFRS Adoption (4)	Revised
Assets						
Cash and cash equivalents	4,902					4,902
Short term investments	10,380					10,380
Liquid assets	15,282					15,282
Trade and other receivables	11,809					11,809
Inventories	7,025					7,025
Derivative assets	585					585
Prepayments and accrued income	584					584
Total current assets	35,285					35,285
Non-current assets						
Net property, plant and equipment	17,052		156			17,208
Investments in associates	4,091				1,106	5,197
Deferred tax assets	1,469	702	2			2,173
Financial assets	2,410					2,410
Employee benefits assets	928	(896)				32
Goodwill	23,854					23,854
Intangible assets	2,028					2,028
Total non-current assets	51,832	(194)	158		1,106	52,902
Total assets	87,117	(194)	158		1,106	88,187
Liabilities and equity						
Current liabilities						
Trade and other payables	9,074					9,074
Financial liabilities	14,722					14,722
Tax liabilities	584					584
Derivative liabilities	856					856
Accruals and deferred income	3,839			53		3,892
Total current liabilities	29,075					29,128
Non-current liabilities						
Financial liabilities	10,731		160			10,891
Employee benefits liabilities	3,234	2,470				5,704
Deferred tax liabilities	447	(431)				16
Other payables	327					327
Provisions	3,004					3,004
Total non-current liabilities	17,743					19,942
Total liabilities	46,818	2,039	160	53		49,070

(Exhibit continued on next page . . .)

EXHIBIT 4 (continued)

	As Reported	IAS 19 Effect (1)	IFRIC 4 Effect (2)	IAS 39 Warrant Premium Classification (3)	L'Oreal IFRS Adoption (4)	Revised
Equity						
Total equity attributable to parent shareholders	39,236	(2,219)	(2)	(53)	1,106	38,068
Minority interests	1,063	(14)				1,049
Total equity	40,299	(2,233)				39,117
Total liabilities and equity	87,117	(194)	158	0	1,106	88,187

(1) IAS 19 was implemented in 2006, with comparative restatement made to January 1, 2005. The 1/1/05 adjustments were imposed on the 12/31/04 balance sheet by the analyst, taken from the Accounting Policies footnote of 2006 Annual Report, p. 21.

(2) IFRIC 4 required the company to recognize additional finance lease assets and obligations that were not previously considered to be lease arrangements. The 2005 adjustments were carried back to the end of 2004. The amounts were found in the Accounting Policies footnote of 2006 Annual Report, p. 21.

(3) IAS 39 changed the classification of premiums associated with Nestlé warrants included in a bond issue. The 1/1/05 adjustments were imposed on the 12/31/04 balance sheet by the analyst, taken from the Accounting Policies footnote of 2005 Annual Report, p. 23.

(4) L'Oreal adopted International Financial Reporting Standards as of 1/1/05. The cumulative effect was carried back to 12/31/04, as found in footnote d) to the 2005 Consolidated Statement of Changes in Equity, page 11.

The analyst draws the data shown in Exhibit 5 from Exhibits 2, 3 and 4 for the preparation of DuPont analysis:

EXHIBIT 5 Data Needed for DuPont Analysis (in Millions of CHF)

	2007	2006	2005	2004
Income Statement Data:				
Revenue	107,552	98,458	91,115	—
EBIT	14,434	12,786	10,956	—
EBT	13,518	12,105	10,369	—
Profit from continuing operations	11,382	9,775	8,618	—
Share of results of associates	1,280	963	896	—
Profit ex-associates	10,102	8,812	7,722	—
Balance Sheet Data:				
Total assets	114,659	101,805	102,718	88,187
Investments in associates	8,936	8,430	7,073	5,197
Total assets, ex-associates	105,723	93,375	95,645	82,990
Shareholders' equity	54,234	52,848	49,068	39,117

The five-way decomposition of ROE needs to be expanded to account for the presence of the investment in associates and the share of income they provide to Nestlé. Subtracting the investment from total assets results in a figure that more closely represents Nestlé's own asset base; subtracting the share of results of associates from the net income allows for the analysis of exclusively Nestlé profitability resulting from that exclusively Nestlé asset base. Exhibit 6 shows the results of expanding the DuPont analysis.

The net profit margin component and the asset turnover component require adjustments to remove the impact of the associates on the return on assets. To adjust the net profit margin component, the analyst subtracts the associates' income from the net income, and divides it by earnings before taxes. Recall that the number referred to as EBT is profit before taxes and associates (Exhibit 2). In 2007 terms, this was represented by (CHF 11,382 net income − 1,280 income from associates)/CHF 13,518 earnings before taxes = 74.73 percent. Interest burden and EBIT or operating profit margin are calculated as usual. Interest burden is calculated by dividing the profit before taxes and associates by the profit before interest and taxes: CHF 13,518/14,434 = 93.65 percent for 2007. The EBIT margin is simply the earnings before interest and taxes (operating profit or income) divided by sales: CHF 14,434/107,552 = 13.42 percent.

Multiplying the three components together produces the net profit margin of Nestlé—9.39 percent in 2007—excluding the associates' earnings. Calculating the net profit margin in the usual fashion—*with* the net income figure including the associates' earnings—yields 10.58 percent (CHF 11,382/107,552). That profit margin is not representative of the Nestlé-only operations. Dividing the net profit margin by the net profit margin *without* associates income (10.58%/9.39% = 112.67%) quantifies the magnifying effect of the associates'

EXHIBIT 6 Expanded DuPont Analysis

	2007	2006	2005
Tax burden (ex-associates)	74.73%	72.80%	74.47%
× Interest burden	93.65%	94.67%	94.64%
× EBIT margin	13.42%	12.99%	12.02%
= Net profit margin (ex-associates)	9.39%	8.95%	8.47%
× Associates' effect on net profit margin	112.67%	111.78%	111.43%
= Net Profit Margin	**10.58%**	**10.00%**	**9.44%**
Total asset turnover (ex-associates)	1.080	1.042	1.020
Effect of associates investments on turnover	(0.086)	(0.079)	(0.065)
× Total Asset Turnover	**0.994**	**0.963**	**0.955**
= Return on assets	10.52%	9.63%	9.02%
× Leverage	**2.02**	**2.01**	**2.16**
= Return on Equity	**21.25%**	**19.36%**	**19.48%**
Traditional ROE Calculation:			
Net income /	11,382	9,849	8,604
Average stockholders' equity	53,541	50,958	44,093
= Return on Equity	**21.26%**	**19.33%**	**19.51%**
(Differences in ROE calculations due to rounding)			

income on Nestlé's own margins. Where the "Nestlé-only" entity really earned 9.39 percent on every sales dollar, inclusion of the associates' income in net profit inflates the net profit margins by 12.67 percent (112.67% × 9.39% = 10.58%); a level that is not representative of what the Nestlé-only entity is capable of producing.

A similar picture of the net profit margin over time emerges from the DuPont analysis after neutralizing the effect of the associates' earnings. The margin would be greater in each year if the associates' earnings were included in net profit, as compared to looking at Nestlé alone. While Nestlé showed a consistent upward trend in the three years, the analysis excluding associates' earnings shows that the company's profit margins are not necessarily as large without the boost from associates' earnings.

To calculate a "Nestlé-only" total asset turnover, the asset base also needs to be neutralized for the amount of the investment in associates. In 2007, the adjusted total assets were CHF 105,723 (CHF 114,659 − 8,936 = 105,723); for 2006, the adjusted total assets were CHF 93,375 (CHF 101,805 − 8,430 = 93,375). Dividing the average of the two figures into 2007's sales yields a "Nestlé-only" total asset turnover rate of 1.080 (CHF 107,552/[(CHF 105,723 + 93,375)/ 2] = 1.080). Calculating the total asset turnover from the consolidated financial statements with amounts unadjusted for investments in associates yields a measure of 0.994 (CHF 107,552/ [(CHF 114,659 + 101,805)/ 2] = 0.994). The difference between the asset turnover based on unadjusted financial statement amounts and the "Nestlé-only" asset turnover reveals the effect on total asset turnover of the investment in associates: a decrease of 0.087 in 2007.

The adjustments thus far have isolated the operational aspects of Nestlé performance and the assets that produced them from non-Nestlé operations. The resulting return on asset signal from the DuPont analysis is free from bias introduced by the affiliates' results, and the contribution to the overall return on assets from the non-Nestlé components is clearly identified.

The financial leverage ratio has not been adjusted by the analyst in similar fashion to profit margins and asset turnover. The DuPont components, profit margins and asset turnover, function fairly discretely: Nestlé assets produce a certain pretax return, as do the non-Nestlé assets. In the DuPont analysis, the assets are isolated from each other and it is possible to see the contributions of each to the aggregate performance. It might be tempting to likewise adjust the financial leverage ratio by subtracting the investment in associates from total assets and equity, but it would not improve the DuPont analysis. Without knowledge of how the investment in associates was financed—all debt, all from internally generated cash flow, or a blend—it would be arbitrary to erase the investment amount from the asset base and equity base to arrive at an adjusted financial leverage figure. If such information was available, the analyst might calculate separate financial leverage components as well. In Nestlé's case, such information is unavailable, and the analyst simply considers the investment to be part of the total assets supported by common equity. The inherent assumption is that a similar capital structure finances the associates' assets and the Nestlé-only assets.

From Exhibit 6, multiplying the three conventionally-calculated (including the effect of the associates) ROE components yields the return on equity shown in the top row of Exhibit 7. The return on equity exhibits a smooth, steadily increasing trend when examined without adjusting for investment in associates; however, the analyst wants to see the ROE for Nestlé alone and compare it to the aggregate ROE. Calculating the ROE on a "Nestlé-only" basis is done by multiplying the net profit margin ex-associates' investment by the total asset turnover ex-associates' investment by the financial leverage. For 2007, the Nestlé-only ROE was 20.48 percent (9.39% × 1.080 × 2.02 = 20.48%). Exhibit 7 shows the ROE prepared on the two bases and the contribution of the associates'

EXHIBIT 7 **ROE Performance Due to Investment in Associates**

	2007 (%)	2006 (%)	2005 (%)
Return on equity	21.25	19.36	19.48
Nestlé-only ROE	20.48	18.75	18.66
Associates' contribution to ROE	0.77	0.61	0.82

investment to ROE. The trend is similar for the two ROE calculations, but the magnitudes of the ROE based on Nestlé only are lower.

Although the analyst is satisfied with the trend and magnitude of the Nestlé return on equity, he is now aware that a significant amount of Nestlé's profitability is attributable to the investments in associates. He is convinced that in order to completely understand Nestlé's earnings drivers, he needs to understand these investments as well. He is somewhat concerned that the spread between "Nestlé-only" profit margins and the aggregate profit margins has widened over the past three years: Referring to Exhibit 6, the spread was 1.19 percent in 2007, higher than the 1.05 percent in 2006, which was higher than the 0.97 percent spread in 2005. In fact, the associate income for the past two years has made all the difference between double-digit net profit margins and single-digit profit margins. The analyst makes note to investigate the valuation aspects of the investment holdings later. For now, he is interested in learning more about the drivers of Nestlé's growth and revenues.

Asset Base Composition

The analyst examines the composition of the balance sheet over time, as shown in Exhibit 8.

EXHIBIT 8 **Asset Composition as a Percentage of Total Assets**

	2007	2006	2005	2004
Cash and equivalents	5.8	5.2	4.5	5.6
Short-term investments	2.5	6.1	12.4	11.8
Trade and other receivables	13.4	14.3	13.9	13.4
Inventory	8.1	7.9	7.9	8.0
Other current	1.4	1.2	1.9	1.3
Total Current	**31.2**	**34.7**	**40.6**	**40.1**
PP&E, net	19.2	19.9	18.5	19.5
Intangibles	35.4	31.7	29.1	29.3
Other noncurrent	14.1	13.7	11.8	11.1
Total	**99.9***	**100.0**	**100.0**	**100.0**

* Does not add to 100 percent due to rounding.

While he expected significant investments in current assets, inventory, and physical plant assets—given that Nestlé is a food manufacturer and marketer—he is surprised to see so much investment in intangible assets, indicating that Nestlé's success may be due in part to successful acquisitions. The increasing proportion of the asset mix in intangibles and the reduction in short-term investments are consistent with growth through acquisition. The investing section of the statement of cash flows, Exhibit 9, supports this fact:

EXHIBIT 9 Nestlé Investing Activity, 2004–2007 (in Millions of CHF)

Investing Activities	Total	2007	2006	2005	2004
Capital expenditure	(15,841)	(4,971)	(4,200)	(3,375)	(3,295)
Expenditure on intangible assets	(2,802)	(619)	(689)	(758)	(736)
Sale of property, plant and equipment	887	323	98	220	246
Acquisition of businesses	(19,329)	(11,232)	(6,469)	(995)	(633)
Disposal of businesses	1,362	456	447	193	266
Cash flows with associates	1,047	264	323	259	201
Other investing cash flows	(229)	26	(30)	(202)	(23)
Total investing cash flow	(34,905)	(15,753)	(10,520)	(4,658)	(3,974)
Acquisitions % of total investing activities	55.4%	71.3%	61.5%	21.4%	15.9%

For the four-year period, the acquisition of businesses was a significant part of the total resources dedicated to investment activities—over half for the entire time frame. In the largest acquisition year, 2007, Nestlé acquired Gerber and Novartis Medical Nutrition; the two purchases accounted for 85 percent (CHF 9,535/11,232) of the total cash invested in 2007 for business acquisitions.

Capital Structure Analysis

The analyst then examined Nestlé's long-term capital structure by constructing a chart on a common-size basis, displayed in Exhibit 10 below.

Although the DuPont analysis indicated that the company had de-leveraged somewhat over the last three years—financial leverage decreased from 2.16 in 2005 to 2.02 in 2007—the leverage ratio alone does not show much about the

EXHIBIT 10 Percent of Long-Term Capital Structure

	2007	2006	2005	2004
Long-term financial liabilities	8.6	10.0	12.4	18.4
Other long-term liabilities	15.4	13.7	14.2	15.3
Total equity	76.0	76.2	73.4	66.2
Total long-term capital	**100.0**	**99.9***	**100.0**	**99.9***

* Does not add to 100 percent due to rounding.

nature of the leverage. For example, the financial burden imposed by bond debt is more onerous and bears more consequences in the event of default than does restructuring provisions or employee benefit plan obligations. A look at Exhibit 10 reveals that Nestlé has been making its capital structure substantially less financially risky over the last five years. Not only is the proportion of the less risky equity financing rising—from 66.2 percent in 2004 to 76.0 percent in 2007—the more risky long-term financial liabilities have become a significantly smaller part of the capital mix, dropping to 8.6 percent in 2007 from 18.4 percent in 2004. Meanwhile, the "other long-term liabilities" (primarily employee benefit plan obligations and provisions) have remained at nearly the same proportion of the financing mix over the period.

Given the de-leveraging occurring in the long-term capital structure, the analyst wonders if there has been any offsetting change in the company's working capital accounts. He decides to examine Nestlé's liquidity situation; and from the financial statements in Exhibits 2 and 3, he constructs the table shown in Exhibit 11.

EXHIBIT 11 Nestlé Working Capital Accounts and Ratios, 2004–2007

	2007	2006	2005	2004
Current ratio	0.83	1.09	1.16	1.21
Quick ratio	0.58	0.80	0.88	0.93
Defensive interval ratio[5]	100.7	114.4	149.4	
Days' sales outstanding (DSO)	50.9	53.5	52.3	
Days on hand of inventory (DOH)	70.1	72.6	73.1	
Number of days payables	−105.5	−106.5	−94.4	
Cash conversion cycle	15.5	19.6	31.0	

A significant increase in the current portion of the financial liabilities is responsible for the current ratio's deterioration between 2006 and 2007. He notes that the company's quick ratio and defensive interval ratio have also deteriorated in the last few years. The company seems to be responding by more aggressively managing its receivables and inventories; both receivables DSOs and inventory DOHs have improved in 2007 over 2006. While the decline in the actual working capital ratios is a concern, it is mitigated by the improvement in the management of receivables, inventory, and payables. Those improvements provide evidence that the company's managers are moving in the right direction on the management of working capital.

Segment Analysis/Capital Allocation

To understand any geopolitical investment risks, as well as the economies in which Nestlé operates, the analyst wants to know which geographic areas are of the greatest importance to the company. One issue the analyst confronts is the fact that Nestlé reports segment information by management responsibility and

[5] For 2007, the daily cash expenditure = [45,037 + 9,104 + 36,512 + 1,875 − 3,211 + (590 − 482) + (1492 − 576)]/365 = 247.5. The defensive interval ratio is 24,917/247.5 = 100.7.

geographical area (hereafter referred to as "segment"), not by segments based exclusively on geographic areas. From the segment information in Exhibit 12, he notes that the European business, while still growing, is a lesser part of the revenue stream than two years ago; Nestlé Americas and Asia, Oceania, and Africa sectors show a similar decline as a percentage of revenues. All of the geographic sectors are growing in terms of absolute amount of revenues and EBIT, but they appear proportionally smaller each year because of the way Nestlé displays its Waters, Nutrition, and Other Food and Beverage segments: Their operations are not segmented geographically, but are shown on a global basis. Not only are they not included in the geographic information, they have also grown significantly in the last several years through acquisition: As pointed out earlier, the company acquired Gerber and Novartis Medical Nutrition in 2007. Those acquisitions, included into the non-geographic categories, make the three geographic categories look less material in the aggregate, from year to year. Nevertheless, the Americas sector appears to be the single most significant segment in terms of size and growth of both sales and EBIT.

Because of a realignment of segments in 2006 and the lack of complete restated data, the analyst cannot make meaningful comparisons to years before 2005.

The analyst is curious about the company's capital allocation decisions based on the geographic segments. Exhibit 13 shows the segment information regarding Nestlé's capital expenditures and assets.

EXHIBIT 12 **Sales and EBIT by Segment (in Millions of CHF)**

							Year-to-Year % Change	
Sales	**2007**	**% total**	**2006**	**% total**	**2005**	**% total**	**2007**	**2006**
Europe	28,464	26.5	26,652	27.1	25,599	28.1	6.8	4.1
Americas	32,917	30.6	31,287	31.8	28,956	31.8	5.2	8.1
Asia, Oceania, and Africa	16,556	15.4	15,504	15.7	14,296	15.7	6.8	8.4
Nestlé Waters	10,404	9.7	9,636	9.8	8,787	9.6	8.0	9.7
Nestlé Nutrition	8,434	7.8	5,964	6.1	5,270	5.8	41.4	13.2
Other Food and Beverage	3,458	3.2	2,728	2.8	2,245	2.5	26.8	21.5
Pharma	7,319	6.8	6,687	6.7	5,962	6.5	9.5	12.2
	107,552		98,458		91,115			
EBIT								
Europe	3,412	22.7	3,109	23.4	3,082	26.0	9.7	0.9
Americas	5,359	35.7	4,946	37.2	4,364	36.7	8.4	13.3
Asia, Oceania, and Africa	2,697	18.0	2,571	19.3	2,334	19.7	4.9	10.2
Nestlé Waters	851	5.7	834	6.3	709	6.0	2.0	17.6
Nestlé Nutrition	1,447	9.6	1,009	7.6	932	7.8	43.4	8.3
Other Food and Beverage	548	3.6	371	2.8	273	2.3	47.4	35.9
Pharma	2,435	16.2	2,136	16.0	1,833	15.4	14.0	16.5
Unallocated Items	(1,725)	−11.5	(1,674)	−12.6	(1,651)	−13.9		
	15,024		13,302		11,876			

Using the information from Exhibit 12 to calculate EBIT margins, and using the information about the asset and capital expenditure distribution from Exhibit 13, the analyst constructs the table in Exhibit 14, ranked by descending order of EBIT profitability.

Although the segmentation is not purely geographical, the analyst can still make some judgments about the allocation of capital. On the premise that the largest investments in assets will require a similar proportion of capital expenditures, he calculates a ratio of capital expenditures proportion to total asset proportion for the last three years, and compares them to the current EBIT profitability ranking. The resulting table is shown in Exhibit 15.

EXHIBIT 13 Asset and Capital Expenditure Segment Information (in Millions of CHF)

	Assets*			Capital Expenditures		
	2007	2006	2005	2007	2006	2005
Europe	15,794	15,566	14,387	932	812	797
Americas	19,503	19,191	19,228	1,371	1,125	908
Asia, Oceania, and Africa	9,153	8,741	8,153	675	588	546
Nestlé Waters	9,298	8,884	8,468	1,043	923	601
Nestlé Nutrition	13,990	3,774	2,577	271	194	134
Other Food and Beverage	1,792	1,473	1,011	269	141	86
Pharma	7,120	6,028	4,978	276	286	209
	76,650	63,657	58,802	4,837	4,069	3,281

* Assets do not equal total assets on the balance sheet due to unallocated and non-segment assets.

EXHIBIT 14 EBIT Margins, Asset, and Capital Expenditure Proportions by Segment

	EBIT Margins			% of Total Assets			% of Total Cap Ex		
	2007	2006	2005	2007	2006	2005	2007	2006	2005
Pharma	33.27	31.94	30.74	9.3	9.5	8.5	5.7	7.0	6.4
Nestlé Nutrition	17.16	16.92	17.69	18.3	5.9	4.4	5.6	4.8	4.1
Asia, Oceania, and Africa	16.29	16.58	16.33	11.9	13.7	13.9	14.0	14.5	16.6
Americas	16.28	15.81	15.07	25.4	30.1	32.7	28.3	27.6	27.7
Other Food and Beverage	15.85	13.60	12.16	2.3	2.3	1.7	5.6	3.5	2.6
Europe	11.99	11.67	12.04	20.6	24.5	24.5	19.3	20.0	24.3
Nestlé Waters	8.18	8.66	8.07	12.1	14.0	14.4	21.6	22.7	18.3
				100.0	100.0	100.0	100.0	100.0	100.0

EXHIBIT 15 Ratio of Capital Expenditures Percent to Total Asset Percent Ranked by EBIT Margin

	2007 EBIT	2007	2006	2005
Pharma	33.27	0.61	0.74	0.75
Nestlé Nutrition	17.16	0.31	0.81	0.93
Asia, Oceania, and Africa	16.29	1.18	1.06	1.19
Americas	16.28	1.11	0.92	0.85
Other Food and Beverage	15.85	2.43	1.52	1.53
Europe	11.99	0.94	0.82	0.99
Nestlé Waters	8.18	1.79	1.62	1.27

A ratio of 1 indicates that the segment's proportion of capital expenditures is the same as its proportion of total assets. A ratio *below* 1 indicates that the segment is being allocated a lesser proportion of capital expenditures than its proportion of total assets; if a trend develops, the segment will become less significant over time. A ratio *above* 1 indicates the company is growing the segment. Comparing the ratio to the EBIT margin percentage gives the analyst an idea of whether the company is investing its capital in the most profitable segments.

Pharma, by the nature of the business, has significant research and development expenses and yet has the highest margins. It requires little in the way of invested assets and maintenance capital expenditures. Nutrition has similar characteristics, but to a lesser degree. The two are the highest EBIT margin segments, yet Nestlé has invested in both of them at a less aggressive rate, judging by the ratio of capital expenditures proportions to total assets proportions. The Nutrition segment, however, received significant investment in 2007 through the acquisition of Novartis Medical Nutrition and Gerber. The Pharma segment, consisting largely of U.S. eye care company Alcon, is extremely profitable but is an outlier in terms of Nestlé's current portfolio. Given the differences in the food and pharmaceutical businesses, it would seem unlikely that the world's largest food company would elect to seriously grow the pharmaceutical segment. However, investment in Pharma is consistent with the objective stated in the management report to be recognized as a leader in Nutrition, Health, and Wellness. It was the strategy of transformation that initially appealed to the portfolio manager.

Investments in the Asia, Oceania, and Africa and the Americas segments have typically been in "growth" mode over the last three years; the proportion of capital expenditures to the proportion of total assets in each of these two segments is typically slightly above 1 annually. Given that these are large and well-margined segments, the capital allocation decisions appear reasonable.

The Other Food and Beverage segment appears problematic: While its EBIT margin is on almost the same level as the Asia, Oceania, and Africa and Americas segments, it is still the third lowest segment in terms of profitability. Yet the capital expenditures devoted to it over the last three years are in a rapid growth mode. It may be that the segment is a catch-all, or it may be the development of another line of business that will become more visible in the future; for now, the analyst notes that while it could be a problem or a promise, it is a small part of Nestlé's asset base, revenues, and EBIT and thus not of great concern at this time.

The Nestlé Waters segment is a much greater concern to the analyst. Its EBIT margin is about two-thirds of the next highest-ranked segment; and at

8.18 percent, it is well below the 13.42 percent company-wide EBIT margin (see Exhibit 6). Even after allowing for the fact that the Waters segment was charged with a CHF 210 million goodwill write-down in 2007, the segment's EBIT margin was only 10.20 percent—still well below the other segments. The fact that the Waters segment was the source of a goodwill write-down is also a sign that operating weaknesses might be present; otherwise, the cash flow assumptions used in the goodwill testing might have been high enough to prevent the write-down. Nestlé Waters is a significant part of the asset base at 12.1 percent in 2007, and it appears to be a high-maintenance operation. In each of the last three years, the ratio of capital expenditures proportion to total assets proportion shows the segment to be in a growth mode, with a ratio of 1.79, 1.62, and 1.27 in 2007, 2006, and 2005, respectively. In 2007 and 2006, the only segment to have greater absolute dollar capital expenditures was the more highly profitable Americas segment; in 2005, Nestlé Waters was outranked in terms of capital expenditures only by the Americas and Europe segments. In a worst-case scenario, if the company were to continue to allocate capital towards the lowest-margined businesses, the overall Nestlé-only returns might be impacted negatively. As a result, Nestlé might become more dependent on its investment in associates to sustain performance.

The analyst decides to look at Nestlé from a product group standpoint as well. The sales and EBIT information are shown in Exhibit 16.

To further examine capital allocation decisions, the analyst garners the asset and capital expenditure information by product group from the financial statements, as shown in Exhibit 17. The total assets and capital expenditures differ between the presentations by segment and product group. Nestlé presents its assets for the product groups on an *average* basis rather than on a year-end basis as it does for the segment reporting. Further, a significant amount of assets is unallocated to segments, but there is no unallocated amount by product groups. Capital expenditures by segment and product group represent additional investments in PP&E during the year, but the unallocated amount of capital expenditures is far greater by product group.

EXHIBIT 16 **Sales and EBIT Segment Information by Product Group (in Millions of CHF)**

							Year to Year % Change	
Sales	**2007**	**% of Total**	**2006**	**% of Total**	**2005**	**% of Total**	**2007**	**2006**
Beverages	28,245	26.3	25,882	26.3	23,842	26.2	9.1	8.6
Milk Products, Nutrition, and Ice cream	29,106	27.1	25,435	25.8	23,275	25.5	14.4	9.3
Prepared Dishes and Cooking Aids	18,504	17.2	17,635	17.9	16,673	18.3	4.9	5.8
Confectionery	12,248	11.4	11,399	11.6	10,794	11.8	7.4	5.6
Pet Care	12,130	11.3	11,420	11.6	10,569	11.6	6.2	8.1
Pharmaceutical Products	7,319	6.8	6,687	6.8	5,962	6.5	9.5	12.2
	107,552	100.0	98,458	100.0	91,115	100.0	9.2	8.1

(Exhibit continued on next page . . .)

EXHIBIT 16 (continued)

Sales	2007	% of Total	2006	% of Total	2005	% of Total	Year to Year % Change 2007	Year to Year % Change 2006
EBIT								
Beverages	4,854	32.3	4,475	33.6	4,131	34.8	8.5	8.3
Milk Products, Nutrition, and Ice cream	3,744	24.9	3,003	22.6	2,598	21.9	24.7	15.6
Prepared Dishes and Cooking Aids	2,414	16.1	2,323	17.5	2,176	18.3	3.9	6.8
Confectionery	1,426	9.5	1,309	9.8	1,257	10.6	8.9	4.1
Pet Care	1,876	12.5	1,730	13.0	1,532	12.9	8.4	12.9
Pharmaceutical Products	2,435	16.2	2,136	16.1	1,833	15.4	14.0	16.5
	16,749	111.5	14,976	112.6	13,527	113.9	11.8	10.7
Unallocated Items	(1,725)	−11.5	(1,674)	−12.6	(1,651)	−13.9		
	15,024	100.0	13,302	100.0	11,876	100.0		

EXHIBIT 17 Asset and Capital Expenditure Segment Information by Product Group (in Millions of CHF)

	Assets			Capital Expenditures		
	2007	2006	2005	2007	2006	2005
Beverages	17,937	16,640	15,105	1,409	1,105	752
Milk Products, Nutrition, and Ice cream	23,047	17,970	15,516	933	702	689
Prepared Dishes and Cooking Aids	10,959	10,553	9,386	305	272	261
Confectionery	6,663	6,319	5,745	316	258	194
Pet Care	15,652	15,763	15,030	402	345	274
Pharmaceutical Products	6,704	5,492	4,538	155	122	97
	80,962	72,737	65,320	3,520	2,804	2,267

Using the information from Exhibit 16 to calculate EBIT margins and the information about the asset and capital expenditure distribution from Exhibit 17, the analyst constructs the table in Exhibit 18, ranked by descending order of EBIT profitability in 2007.

EXHIBIT 18 **EBIT Margins, Assets, and Capital Expenditures Proportions by Product Group**

	EBIT Margins			% of Total Assets			% of Cap Ex		
	2007	2006	2005	2007	2006	2005	2007	2006	2005
Pharmaceutical Products	33.27	31.94	30.74	8.3	7.6	6.9	4.4	4.4	4.3
Beverages	17.19	17.29	17.33	22.2	22.9	23.1	40.0	39.4	33.2
Pet Care	15.47	15.15	14.50	19.3	21.7	23.0	11.4	12.3	12.1
Prepared Dishes and Cooking Aids	13.05	13.17	13.05	13.5	14.5	14.4	8.7	9.7	11.5
Milk Products, Nutrition, and Ice cream	12.86	11.81	11.16	28.5	24.7	23.8	26.5	25.0	30.4
Confectionery	11.64	11.48	11.65	8.2	8.7	8.8	9.0	9.2	8.6
				100.0	100.0	100.0	100.0	100.0	100.0

He again prepares a schedule of the proportions of capital expenditures and the proportion of total assets for each of the product groups, and calculates the ratio of capital expenditure proportions to total asset proportions, ranked by the 2007 EBIT margin. The resulting table is shown in Exhibit 19.

EXHIBIT 19 **Ratio of Capital Expenditures Percent to Total Asset Percent Ranked by EBIT Margin**

	2007 EBIT Margin	2007	2006	2005
Pharmaceutical Products	33.27	0.53	0.58	0.62
Beverages	17.19	1.80	1.72	1.44
Pet Care	15.47	0.59	0.57	0.53
Prepared Dishes and Cooking Aids	13.05	0.64	0.67	0.80
Milk Products, Nutrition, and Ice cream	12.86	0.93	1.01	1.28
Confectionery	11.64	1.10	1.06	0.98

The analyst uses this information to make some important observations:

- The Beverages product group has a significantly higher EBIT margin than Nestlé Waters EBIT margin of 8.18 percent. Because Nestlé Waters is contained within the Beverages product group, the EBIT margins of the other products within the product group category—primarily soluble coffee, according to Nestlé's 2007 Management Report—must be much

EXHIBIT 20 **EBIT Margin of Beverages with and without Waters (Millions of CHF)**

	Beverages	Waters	Beverages ex-Waters
Total Beverage Sales	28,245	10,404	17,841
EBIT	4,854	851	4,003
EBIT %	17.19%	8.18%	22.44%

EXHIBIT 21 **Ratio of Capital Expenditures Percent to Total Asset Percent Ex-Nestlé Waters, Ranked by EBIT Margin**

	2007 EBIT Margin	2007	2006	2005
Pharmaceutical Products	33.27	0.67	0.76	0.73
Beverages	22.44	1.22	0.81	0.78
Pet Care	15.47	0.74	0.74	0.62
Prepared Dishes and Cooking Aids	13.05	0.80	0.88	0.95
Milk Products, Nutrition, and Ice cream	12.86	1.17	1.33	1.52
Confectionery	11.64	1.38	1.38	1.15

greater. The analyst removes the Waters sales and EBIT from the total product group (Exhibit 20) and finds that the remaining business is by far the most profitable segment after pharmaceuticals.

- The analyst reworks the ratios presented in Exhibit 19 excluding the assets and capital expenditures for the Nestlé Waters segment. The result in Exhibit 21 shows that management is allocating its capital expenditures to the Beverages business on a growth basis the last year but at a lower rate than for Beverages with Waters. Given the margins of the product group without Waters, this is a favorable discovery, but the amount allocated to Waters is problematic.
- Less favorable to note under either the original or revised exhibits: The two lowest-ranked product groups—Milk Products, Nutrition, and Ice cream and Confectionery—have been allocated capital expenditures at a "growth mode" rate for each of the last three years. If the trend continues and margins in these segments do not grow, Nestlé's company-wide margins could suffer. Further, the allocation to Pharmaceutical Products, the most profitable segment, is cause for concern.

Accruals and Earnings Quality

The consistent profitability exhibited by Nestlé is a desirable attribute, as hoped for and expected of a company operating primarily in the food industry where the demand for the product is typically not cyclical. However, the analyst wants to understand how important a role accruals may play in the company's performance; he is concerned in case the consistency is a result of earnings management. He decides to examine the balance-sheet-based accruals and cash-flow-based accruals over the last few years. From the Nestlé financial statements, he assembles the information and intermediate calculations shown in Exhibit 22.

EXHIBIT 22 Selected Balance Sheet and Statement of Cash Flows Information (in Millions of CHF)

	2007	2006	2005	2004	2003
Balance Sheet Accrual Info:					
Total assets	114,659	101,805	102,718	88,187	89,561
Cash and short-term investments	9,496	11,475	17,393	15,282	15,128
Operating assets (A)	105,163	90,330	85,325	72,905	74,433
Total liabilities	60,425	48,957	53,650	49,070	51,738
Long-term debt	6,129	6,952	8,277	10,891	15,419
Debt in current liabilities	24,541	15,494	18,841	14,722	14,064
Operating liabilities (B)	29,755	26,511	26,532	23,457	22,255
Net Operating Assets (A) − (B)	75,408	63,819	58,793	49,448	52,178
Balance-sheet-based aggregate accruals (YTY Δ in NOA)	11,589	5,026	9,345	(2,730)	1,587
Average net operating assets	69,614	61,306	54,121	50,813	51,385
Statement of Cash Flows Accrual Info:					
Profit from continuing operations	11,382	9,775	8,618	7,031	6,593
Operating cash flow	(13,439)	(11,676)	(10,205)	(10,412)	(10,125)
Investing cash flow	15,753	10,520	4,658	3,974	4,728
Cash-flow-based aggregate accruals	13,696	8,619	3,071	593	1,196

The accruals ratios for the last five years are shown in Exhibit 23.

EXHIBIT 23 Accruals Ratios (in Millions of CHF)

	2007	2006	2005	2004	2003
B/S aggregate accruals (YTY Δ in NOA)	11,589	5,026	9,345	(2,730)	1,587
Divided by: Average net operating assets	69,614	61,306	54,121	50,813	51,385
Balance-sheet-based accruals ratio	**16.6%**	**8.20%**	**17.3%**	**−5.4%**	**3.1%**
Cash-flow-based aggregate accruals	13,696	8,619	3,071	593	1,196
Divided by: Average net operating assets	69,614	61,306	54,632	51,324	51,385
CF accruals ratio	**19.7%**	**14.1%**	**5.6%**	**1.2%**	**2.3%**

The analyst notes that the absolute level of accruals present in the balance sheet is not extremely high, but it is much higher in the most recent year than in the earlier years. Furthermore, the balance-sheet-based accruals ratio has fluctuated significantly. The analyst's concern with the accruals ratio fluctuations is that they could indicate the use of accruals to "time" earnings.

A slightly different, but no less concerning, trend exists for the cash-flow-based accrual ratio. The accruals ratio is low in the early years of the analysis and increases steadily over time. In 2007 and 2006, they are significantly higher than in the earlier years, indicating a higher degree of accruals present in the company's earnings.

Cash Flow Relationships

Given his concerns about the possible use of accruals to manage earnings, the analyst decides to study the company's cash flow and its relationship to net income. He begins his analysis with the compilation of Nestlé's statements of cash flows shown in Exhibit 24.

EXHIBIT 24 Nestlé Statements of Cash Flows, 2003–2007 (in Millions of CHF)

	2007	2006	2005	2004	2003
Operating activities:					
Profit from continuing operations	11,382	9,775	8,618	7,031	6,593
Less share of results of associates	(1,280)	(963)	(896)	(1,588)	(593)
Depreciation of property, plant, and equipment	2,620	2,581	2,382	2,506	2,408
Impairment of property, plant, and equipment	225	96	360	130	148
Amortisation of goodwill	NA	NA	NA	1,599	1,571
Impairment of goodwill	251	38	218	0	0
Depreciation of intangible assets	591	480	346	278	255
Impairment of intangible assets	6	0	30	0	74
Increase/(decrease) in provisions and deferred taxes	162	(338)	(526)	55	312
Decrease/(increase) in working capital	82	348	(315)	227	(688)
Other operating cash flows	(600)	(341)	(12)	174	45
Operating cash flow	13,439	11,676	10,205	10,412	10,125
Investing activities:					
Capital expenditure	(4,971)	(4,200)	(3,375)	(3,295)	(3,337)
Expenditure on intangible assets	(619)	(689)	(758)	(736)	(682)
Sale of property, plant and equipment	323	98	220	246	244
Acquisition of businesses	(11,232)	(6,469)	(995)	(633)	(1,950)
Disposal of businesses	456	447	193	266	725
Cash flows with associates	264	323	259	201	208
Other investing cash flows	26	(30)	(202)	(23)	64
Investing cash flow	(15,753)	(10,520)	(4,658)	(3,974)	(4,728)

(Exhibit continues on next page . . .)

EXHIBIT 24 (continued)

	2007	2006	2005	2004	2003
Financing activities:					
Dividend paid to shareholders of the parent	(4,004)	(3,471)	(3,114)	(2,800)	(2,705)
Purchase of treasury shares	(5,455)	(2,788)	(1,553)	(715)	(318)
Sale of treasury shares	980	906	1,295	573	660
Cash flows with minority interests	(205)	(191)	5	(189)	(197)
Bonds issued	2,023	1,625	1,617	558	2,305
Bonds repaid	(2,780)	(2,331)	(2,443)	(903)	(693)
Increase in other non-current financial liabilities	348	134	279	162	0
Decrease in other non-current financial liabilities	(99)	(289)	(207)	(845)	(134)
Increase/(decrease) in current financial liabilities	9,851	(14)	(492)	(1,204)	(2,930)
Decrease/(increase) in short-term investments	3,238	6,393	(1,910)	(2,564)	(2)
Other financing cash flows	0	(4)	2	0	0
Financing cash flow	3,897	(30)	(6,521)	(7,927)	(4,014)
Translation differences on flows	(64)	(360)	336	(494)	(457)
Increase/(decrease) in cash and cash equivalents	1,519	766	(638)	(1,983)	926
Cash and cash equivalents at beginning of year	5,278	4,658	4,902	7,074	6,338
Effects of exchange rate changes on opening balance	(203)	(146)	394	(189)	(190)
Cash and cash equivalents retranslated at beginning of year	5,075	4,512	5,296	6,885	6,148
Cash and cash equivalents at end of period	6,594	5,278	4,658	4,902	7,074
Cash interest paid	788	599	437	578	532
Cash taxes paid	3,072	2,811	2,540	2,523	2,267

The analyst's most pressing concern: Are Nestlé's operating earnings backed by cash flow, or does the pattern presented by the accrual measures above indicate that the operating earnings may be more of an accounting result? To convince himself of the genuineness of the Nestlé earnings, he first compares the operating cash flow before interest and taxes to the operating income, adjusted for accounting changes as shown in Exhibit 25.

EXHIBIT 25 Operating Cash Flow to Operating Income, 2003–2007 (in Millions of CHF)

	2007	2006	2005	2004	2003
Operating cash flow	13,439	11,676	10,205	10,412	10,125
Cash interest paid	788	599	437	578	532
Cash taxes paid	3,072	2,811	2,540	2,523	2,267
Operating cash flow before interest and taxes	17,299	15,086	13,182	13,513	12,924
Operating income, equalized:					
Profit before interest and taxes	14,434	12,786	10,956	8,487	8,901
Amortisation of goodwill	—	—	—	1,599	1,571
Operating income, adjusted for accounting changes	14,434	12,786	10,956	10,086	10,472
Operating cash flow before interest and taxes/Operating income	**1.20**	**1.18**	**1.20**	**1.34**	**1.23**

To keep the comparisons between cash flow and earnings symmetrical, the analyst added the cash paid for interest and taxes to the operating cash flow. The resulting operating cash flow before interest and taxes is the relevant operating cash flow for comparison to the operating income. This revision makes the cash from operations more directly comparable to accrual basis operating income; it is effectively the operating income (profit before earnings and taxes or EBIT) on a cash basis. In another adjustment to make all comparisons analogous, the analyst added goodwill amortisation to the 2003 and 2004 operating income amounts. International Financial Reporting Standard 3, "Business Combinations," suspended the amortisation of goodwill after 31 March 2004; to subtract the amortisation in just two years of operating earnings would result in a misleading trend in the ratio of the relevant operating cash flow to operating earnings.

The analyst is encouraged by the fact that the operating cash flow before interest and taxes substantially exceeded the operating earnings in 2007, and in fact, for each of the last five years. With the exception of 2004, the ratio of the relevant operating cash flow to operating earnings has consistently been around 1.20.

Knowing that Nestlé has made a number of acquisitions, the analyst decides to examine the relationship between operating cash flow and total assets. The total assets reflect the sum total of management's resource allocations. The relationship is shown in Exhibit 26.

EXHIBIT 26 Operating Cash Flow to Total Assets, 2003–2007 (in Millions of CHF)

	2007	2006	2005	2004	2003
Operating cash flow	13,439	11,676	10,205	10,412	10,125
Average total assets	108,232	102,262	95,453	88,874	88,457
Cash return on total assets	12.4%	11.4%	10.7%	11.7%	11.4%

The 2007 cash return on total assets is the highest in the five-year span and fairly consistent during the entire period. A similar pattern of returns, albeit of a higher magnitude, results if operating cash flow before interest and taxes is used. Nevertheless, the analyst is encouraged to do more cash flow analysis due to the results of the accruals analysis, coupled with the slight volatility in the relationship between operating cash flow and operating income. He decides to compare cash flow to reinvestment, debt, and debt-servicing capacity, as shown in Exhibit 27.

The current cash flow measures for each metric are strong: Reinvestment needs have been covered by cash flow by a factor of 2.40 in 2007 and 2.39 in 2006, indicating ample resources for the company's reinvestment program. Those two measures are only slightly lower than the cash flow reinvestment coverage of the prior three years. The decrease is the result of higher amounts of capital expenditures in the recent years compared to the earlier years.

The 2007 cash flow to total debt ratio of 55.5 percent indicates that the company is not highly leveraged. The ratio is high enough to indicate additional borrowing could be arranged should an investment opportunity arise. Further, the analyst notes that Nestlé has the capacity to pay off its debt in approximately four

EXHIBIT 27 **Operating Cash Flow to Reinvestment, Debt, and Debt-Servicing Capacity, 2003–2007 (in Millions of CHF)**

	2007	2006	2005	2004	2003
Cash flow to reinvestment:					
Operating cash flow	13,439	11,676	10,205	10,412	10,125
Capital expenditures	4,971	4,200	3,375	3,295	3,337
Expenditures on intangible assets	619	689	758	736	682
	5,590	4,889	4,133	4,031	4,019
Cash flow to reinvestment	**2.40**	**2.39**	**2.47**	**2.58**	**2.52**
Cash flow to total debt:					
Operating cash flow before interest and taxes	17,299	15,086	13,182	13,513	12,924
Current debt (Short-term financial liabilities)	24,541	15,494	18,841	14,722	15,419
Current derivative liabilities	477	470	922	856	846
Long-term debt (Long-term financial liabilities)	6,129	6,952	8,277	10,891	14,064
	31,147	22,916	28,040	26,469	30,329
Cash flow to total debt	**55.5%**	**65.8%**	**47.0%**	**51.1%**	**42.6%**
Cash flow interest coverage:					
Operating cash flow before interest and taxes	17,299	15,086	13,182	13,513	12,924
Interest paid	788	599	437	578	532
Cash flow interest coverage	**22.0**	**25.2**	**30.2**	**23.4**	**24.3**

years even while maintaining its current reinvestment policy [31,147/(13,439 − 5,590)].

Finally, the cash flow interest coverage ratio indicates more than satisfactory financial strength in the current year, with cash flow 22.0 times the interest paid. Like the cash flow to total debt ratio, it indicates that the company actually has plenty of financial capacity to add more debt if there is an investment reason. However, the current cash flow to interest is much lower than it was only two years ago at 30.2 times. The analyst is not overly concerned given the recent acquisitions by Nestlé.

Decomposition and Analysis of the Company's Valuation

At this point, the analyst believes he has obtained sufficient information about the company's sources of earnings and returns on shareholder equity, its capital structure, the results of its capital allocation decisions, and its earnings quality. Before he makes his report to the portfolio manager, he wants to study the company's market valuation. During his reading of the annual report, he noted that Nestlé owns significant equity stakes in Alcon (NYSE:ACL), a U.S. ophthalmic products company (77.4 percent), and L'Oreal (Paris exchange: OR), a French cosmetics company (30.0 percent). By virtue of majority ownership in Alcon, Nestlé consolidates the company in its own financial statements, while L'Oreal is handled in the financial statements as an investment, because Nestlé's ownership stake does not give it control. While these companies contribute to the earnings of Nestlé as a whole, they also are valued in the public markets separately and their discrete valuations may be very different from a pure Nestlé valuation. To determine the value that the market is placing solely on Nestlé operations, the analyst first removes the value of the Alcon and L'Oreal holdings from the Nestlé market value, as shown in Exhibit 28.

EXHIBIT 28 **Nestlé Market Value without Alcon and L'Oreal as of 31 December 2007 (Currency in Millions, except Share Prices)**

L'Oreal Value:	
12/31/2007 share price	€97.98
Shares held by Nestlé (millions)	178.381
L'Oreal holding value	€17,478
12/31 euro/CHF rate	1.657
L'Oreal holding value in Swiss francs	CHF 28,961
Alcon Value:	
12/31/2007 share price	$140.78
Shares held by Nestlé (millions)	230.250
Alcon holding value	$32,415
12/31 USD/CHF rate	1.126
Alcon holding value in Swiss francs	CHF 36,499
Nestlé Market Value, with and without holdings	
Nestlé 12/31/2007 share price	CHF 497.77
Shares outstanding (millions)	393.073

(Exhibit continued on next page . . .)

EXHIBIT 28 (continued)

Nestlé market capitalization	CHF 195,661
Value of L'Oreal holding	(28,961)
Value of Alcon holding	(36,499)
Implied value of Nestlé operations	CHF 130,201
Pro rata market value:	
L'Oreal	14.8%
Alcon	18.7%
Nestlé	66.5%
	100.0%

The value of the L'Oreal and Alcon holdings is approximately one-third of the value of Nestlé's market capitalization. The analyst now wants to remove their earnings from the earnings of the combined entity (Exhibit 29) so as to make price/earnings comparison for Nestlé earnings alone. For L'Oreal, this is simple: L'Oreal and Nestlé both report on an IFRS basis and Nestlé discloses in its annual report that L'Oreal has contributed CHF 1,302 to the current year earnings.

It is a more complicated, and less precise, exercise to remove the Alcon earnings from the consolidated whole. Alcon's financial statements are filed in the United States and are prepared on a U.S. GAAP basis. Although Alcon is responsible for providing Nestlé with information on an IFRS basis, there is no publicly available reconciliation showing differences in reported earnings. The analyst can only estimate the amount of Alcon net earnings embedded in Nestlé's earnings on an IFRS basis. In reading the 2007 Management Review of Nestlé, he noted a mention of Alcon's sales and EBIT for 2007: CHF 6,700 and 2,300, respectively. Referencing the 2007 consolidated statement of earnings found in the U.S. 20-F filing, he retrieves the other post-EBIT items and converts them into Swiss franc amounts using the average rate for 2007, found in the Nestlé 2007 financial statements. Those amounts are then combined with the EBIT; the resulting pretax figure is taxed at the Nestlé effective rate.

The estimate is crude, because it implicitly assumes the four non-EBIT item amounts, pulled from the U.S. financial statements, would be the same under IFRS. The analyst does note, however, that the revenues on an IFRS basis were nearly the same amount as on a U.S. basis, when converted into Swiss francs at the average 2007 exchange rate. The Management Review mentioned that Alcon had 2007 revenues of CHF 6,700 million; converted into U.S. dollars at an average rate of 1.196, the dollar equivalent revenues are $5,602 million compared to the $5,599 million presented in the Alcon 20-F. Apparently, no significant difference exists between the revenues on an IFRS basis or U.S. GAAP basis. Applying the same exercise to the IFRS-based EBIT of CHF 2,300 million mentioned in the Management Review, the U.S. dollar equivalent is $1,923 million, compared to the 20-F amount of $1,892 million. The analyst excludes the U.S. GAAP charge for in-process R&D from the 20-F EBIT amount; in-process R&D is capitalized under IFRS. The difference in the EBIT figures is minor, only about 2 percent, giving the analyst some comfort that the two bases of accounting produce much the same results for a large part of the reported Alcon earnings.

After isolating the different earnings sources, the analyst prepares the table shown in Exhibit 30, which compares the different market values and price/earnings ratios.

EXHIBIT 29 Calculation of Nestlé Earnings without Alcon and L'Oreal as of 12/31/2007 (All Currency in Millions)

From Alcon 20-F, Restated into CHF at Average 2007 CHF/USD Exchange Rate of 1.196

	In US $	In CHF
Calculation of Alcon estimated IFRS earnings:		
EBIT		2,300.0
Gain from foreign currency, net	$11.2	13.4
Interest income	69.3	82.9
Interest expense	(50.0)	(59.8)
Other, net	15.4	18.4
Total after-EBIT items		54.9
Earnings before income taxes		2,354.9
Income taxes at 25.3% (Nestlé's effective tax rate)		595.8
Estimated Alcon contribution to net income		1,759.1
Minority interest percentage: (1–77.4%)		22.6%
Portion allocable to minority interest		397.6
Portion allocable to Nestlé group shareholders		1,361.5
Calculation of non-Alcon minority interest:		
Reported profit attributable to minority interests		733.0
Less: Alcon-related portion		(397.6)
Non-Alcon minority interest		335.4
Calculation of Nestlé stand-alone earnings:		
Nestlé consolidated earnings		11,382.0
Less: L'Oreal earnings		(1,302.0)
Less: Estimated Alcon contribution to net income		(1,759.1)
Nestlé stand-alone earnings		8,320.9
Non-Alcon minority interest		(335.4)
Nestlé stand-alone earnings to shareholders		7,985.5

At the time of the analysis (early 2008), Nestlé's common stock traded at a price/earnings multiple of 18.4 based on its year-end stock price and trailing earnings: a discount of 17 percent to the price/earnings multiple of 22.2 for the S&P 500 at year end 2007. Yet once earnings and available market value of the non-Nestlé holdings are taken out of the price/earnings valuation, the shares of the "Nestlé-only" company are selling on an even more discounted basis: at 16.3 times earnings, the discount to the overall market's price/earnings multiple was a steeper 27 percent. The analyst believes the discount is inappropriate for a company with the demonstrated cash flow and low financial leverage of Nestlé; it also seems severe in terms of the company's returns on equity. The analyst concludes that Nestlé shares may be undervalued relative to the market.

At this time, the analyst believes that he has processed and analyzed the data sufficiently to pull together his findings and make his report to the portfolio manager.

EXHIBIT 30 Comparison of Decomposed Nestlé Earnings and Price/Earnings Ratios (CHF in Millions)

	Market Values	Earnings (Group Shareholder Level)	Respective P/Es:
Alcon	36,499	1,361.5	26.8
L'Oreal	28,961	1,302.0	22.2
Implied Nestlé-only	130,201	7,985.5	16.3
Actual	195,661	10,649.0	18.4

Recap in %:	Market Value (%)	Earnings (%)
L'Oreal	14.8	12.8
Alcon	18.7	12.2
Nestlé	66.5	75.0
	100.0	100.0

Phase 5: Develop and Communicate Conclusions and Recommendations (e.g., with an Analysis Report)

As a result of the analyses performed, the analyst has gathered sufficient evidence regarding many of the operational and financial characteristics of Nestlé and believes he is able to address the concerns initially expressed by the portfolio manager. Summary points he will cover in his report are divided into two classes: support for an investment in Nestlé shares and causes for concern.

Support for an Investment in Nestlé Shares

- Nestlé's earnings growth and returns have come from its own operations, acquisitions, and investments in associates. Nestlé has the financial stability to fund growth in its existing operations and carry out its growth-by-acquisition strategy. The company's current liquidity and cash flows are more than adequate for future operating and investment purposes. The company has low leverage, and the capital structure is capable of supporting future operations and strategic plans.
- The company's margins and ROE have been consistently positive and generally have exhibited an upward trend. The disaggregation of the effects of income from associates on margins and ROE indicates that the investment in associates has improved ROE and margins but has not been the primary driver of ROE or margins. Nestlé's performance appears sustainable.
- The operating cash flows have consistently exceeded the operating earnings. The ratio of operating cash to operating income has been fairly consistent, approximately 1.20, and gives confidence in the quality of the

earnings. Measures comparing cash flows to reinvestment, debt, and debt-servicing capacity indicate strength in financial capacity.

- Nestlé has been increasing its size by acquisitions, evidenced by the growth of goodwill in its asset mix, and its cash return on assets has been increasing over the last three years. The current cash return on total assets is the highest in the five-year span. The acquisitions appear to be generating the required cash to justify the acquisitions.
- Decomposing the earnings into Nestlé-only, L'Oreal, and Alcon and considering the respective P/Es, it appears that the implied Nestlé-only portion is undervalued. The implied Nestlé-only portion has a far lower P/E than Alcon, L'Oreal, or the market. This should be considered an opportunity, given Nestlé's demonstrated cash flows and low financial leverage.

Causes for Concern

- The increases in balance-sheet-based and cash flow accrual ratios raised the possible issue of earnings management. However, this concern was alleviated by the comparison of operating cash flows with various measures as noted above.
- The company has some unusual priorities in the allocation of capital expenditures. The low-margined Waters business seems to be taking in an inordinate amount of the company's capital expenditures. This will be an area of constant monitoring if the company makes an investment in Nestlé common stock.
- The research department's monitoring cost, in terms of time and effort, for an investment in Nestlé common stock may require an analyst to follow two additional companies. While Nestlé is viewed by the market as just one company, the presence of Alcon and L'Oreal are important separable components that reflect considerably on the aggregate Nestlé performance. If an investment in Nestlé stock requires an analyst to follow two additional companies, there is less analytical capacity available for other investments to be evaluated or to be monitored on a continuing basis.

The analyst concludes that Nestlé represents a good investment opportunity and recommends it as such.

Phase 6: Follow-up

Because of the discounted value of Nestlé shares and the financial strength and stability of the company, the portfolio manager decides to commit the pension fund to a core investment holding of Nestlé common stock. The portfolio manager is somewhat troubled with the resource allocation within the company, and wants to continually re-evaluate the holding. Unproductive capital spending may be a trigger for eliminating the holding. The analyst is charged with updating his findings in the initial research report at each reporting period, with a particular emphasis on the company's progress and continued investment in the Waters segment; the quality measures expressed by the accruals tests; and the cash flow support of earnings, with particular regard to returns on assets.

3

CASE STUDY 2: OFF-BALANCE SHEET LEVERAGE FROM OPERATING LEASES

The quantitative analyst for a large equity mutual fund has become concerned that the fund's research analysts may not be looking for off-balance sheet financing as much as they should. While the fund's investment philosophy has always been rooted in understanding the fundamentals of an investee company, the accounting scandals of the early 2000s and the more recent credit crisis in the United States has convinced the quantitative analyst the fund should be focusing more efforts on determining the unseen financial leverage that companies may be employing. Due to the nature of the fund's investments in service industries, there has been little concern with unseen financial leverage.

The fund's investment philosophy has always led them to invest in service industries, with little operating leverage or inventory risk, and to avoid industries with high financial and operating leverage, such as the airline and retail industries. The companies in the latter industries are capital-intensive and typically have highly leveraged balance sheets, and also employ off-balance sheet leverage in the form of operating leases. Investors in those industries, as a result, are inclined to look for off-balance sheet financing. However, because the fund invests in service industries, off-balance sheet financing is assumed to be a non-issue. The quantitative analyst wonders if this is in fact true.

Phase 1: Define a Purpose for the Analysis

As a result of this concern, the quantitative analyst decides to look for companies in the fund's holdings where off-balance sheet financing may be an issue. He decides to focus on identifying companies with potentially unrecorded capital leases. The objective is not to come up with a point estimate of unrecorded leases or other sources of off-balance sheet financing, but rather to discover any companies in the fund's portfolio that might have hidden leverage and, if in fact such leverage exists, to analyze the impact of the leverage.

Phase 2: Collect Input Data

To identify companies with potentially unrecorded leases, the quantitative analyst filters the fund's holdings using a financial database. He compares the ratio of 7.4 times the current rent (operating lease) expense to total assets with a threshold percentage of 5 percent. 7.4 is the present value factor on a ten-year constant payment discounted at 6 percent; multiplying 7.4 times the rental expense generates an estimate of the incremental assets and debt under a ten-year capital lease discounted at 6 percent. While there is no way of knowing the actual terms of all the leases held by companies in the fund's holdings, the analyst assumes a ten-year lease is representative of current-lease terms.

The ratio of the estimated incremental assets and liabilities to total assets is compared to 5 percent. The quantitative analyst is only concerned with major understatements of assets and liabilities due to off-balance sheet treatment of operating leases and selects a 5 percent understatement threshold for further investigation of portfolio companies. If the ratio of "hidden" assets to total assets exceeds 5 percent for any of the companies in the fund's holdings, that company's information will be subjected to further analysis to see if in fact there are significant assets and liabilities that could be justifiably capitalized on the balance sheet.

Phase 3: Process Data/Phase 4: Analyze/Interpret the Processed Data

The screening process, shown in Exhibit 31, identifies a company that surprises the quantitative analyst: French advertising company Publicis Groupe (Euronext Paris: PUB).

EXHIBIT 31 Publicis Groupe: Operating Lease Expense Capitalized at 7.4 Times

2007 lease expense	€189.0
Lease multiplier	7.40
Estimated incremental assets and debt	€ 1,398.6
2007 total assets	€12,244.0
Estimated incremental assets to total reported assets	11%

The quantitative analyst is puzzled: Not only does the company lack heavy machinery or retail outlets to finance invisibly through operating leases, but even for a service company it is highly people-intensive. According to the Publicis Groupe annual report, there were 43,808 employees at the end of 2007; it has large office space needs to accommodate those employees. Publicis Groupe does business in virtually every country in the world and owns few offices, primarily leasing.

At 11 percent of total reported assets, the situation demands closer investigation by the analyst responsible for covering Publicis Groupe (the PG analyst). The PG analyst consults the 2007 annual report and finds that Publicis Groupe has significant long-term lease obligations through 2012, with another €455 million beyond that. He assumes that the post-2012 lease payments will be the same amount as in 2012, extinguishing the entire amount of the €455 million by 2016. From a scan of the company's debt schedule, he sees that the company has issued a Eurobond due in 2012 with an effective interest rate of 4.3 percent. He then assumes that the lease borrowing rate that Publicis Groupe would bear on the operating leases if they were capitalized might approximate 4.5 percent. From the payment schedule, he constructs the estimated present value of discounted lease payments shown in Exhibit 32.

EXHIBIT 32 Publicis Groupe: Operating Lease Payments and Present Value (in Millions)

Operating Lease Payments	At 12/31/2007	PMT PV
2008	€215	€206
2009	186	170
2010	160	140
2011	141	118
2012	136	109
2013	136	104

(Exhibit continued on next page . . .)

EXHIBIT 32 (continued)

Operating Lease Payments	At 12/31/2007	PMT PV
2014	136	100
2015	136	96
2016	47	32
	€1,293	€1,075

With the refined estimate of incremental asset basis and debt, the PG analyst revises balance sheet amounts and ratios with the new information on a pro forma basis, as shown in Exhibit 33.

Regardless of the leverage measure under scrutiny, Publicis Groupe becomes significantly more leveraged in the capitalization of the operating lease pro forma scenario than under the present operating lease reporting. In Exhibit 34, the analyst examines the impact on interest coverage if the operating leases are capitalized.

While Publicis Groupe still has ample interest coverage, the ratio presents a far different picture of financial strength than the as-reported figures. The PG analyst consults with the mutual fund's internal strategist, who is forecasting an economic slowdown. The PG analyst concludes that this will reduce advertising spending, which will adversely affect Publicis Groupe.

EXHIBIT 33 Publicis Groupe: 2007 Leverage Ratios after Capitalizing Operating Leases

	As Reported	Pro Forma
Financial leverage:		
Total assets	€12,244	
Total assets including estimated incremental assets based on capitalizing operating leases		€13,319
Total equity	€2,225	€2,225
Financial leverage	**5.50**	**5.99**
Debt to equity:		
Estimated incremental liability based on capitalizing operating leases	—	€1,075
Long-term financial debt	1,293	1,293
Total long-term financial debt	€1,293	€ 2,368
Long-term financial debt to equity:	**58.1%**	**106.4%**
Debt to long-term capital:		
Long-term financial debt	€1,293	€2,368
Total equity	2,225	2,225
Long-term capital (L-T financial debt + equity)	€3,518	€4,593
Long-term financial debt to long-term capital	**36.8%**	**51.6%**

EXHIBIT 34 Publicis Groupe: 2007 Interest Coverage Ratio without and with Capitalizing Operating Leases

	As Reported	Pro Forma
Earnings before interest and taxes	€746	€746
Average rent expense (2007 and 2006)		191
Estimated depreciation expense on newly recognized assets (€1,075.3M/9 years, the estimated lease term)		(119)
Revised EBIT		**€818**
Average interest rate on debt		4.5%
Interest expense as reported	€73.0	€73.0
Assumed interest expense on leases (4.5% × 1075.3)		48.4
Adjusted interest expense		**€121.4**
Interest coverage	**10.2**	**6.7**

Phase 5: Develop and Communicate Conclusions and Recommendations (e.g., with an Analysis Report)

The financial strength of the company, as evidenced by the debt and interest coverage ratios, does not appear as great when the operating leases are capitalized. Further, the PG analyst is concerned with the possible market response to a change in accounting for operating leases. In the most recent update of their Memorandum of Understanding for achieving accounting standard convergence, completed 11 September 2008, the FASB and the IASB agreed to develop a new lease standard by 2011. One likely reform is that all leases, including those currently defined as operating leases, might be required to be capitalized.

If Publicis Groupe was required to capitalize its lease obligations, then the balance sheet of Publicis Groupe would show far less available capacity for adding debt than currently. The ratios would deteriorate as shown by the pro forma information. While it is possible that bankers, bond investors, and shareholders make such adjustments in their lending decisions and in valuing the equity, the PG analyst is not convinced of the market's efficiency and is concerned with a decline in value when the hidden leverage is shown on the balance sheet. Given the significant hidden leverage within Publicis Groupe and a negative macroeconomic outlook, the PG analyst recommends that the fund decrease its holding in Publicis Groupe.

Phase 6: Follow-up

The quantitative analyst and PG analyst will continue to observe the value of Publicis Groupe to get feedback on the decision. Accounting pronouncements and changes will be monitored for potential impact on financial statements. They are both watching for and ready to assess the impact of a change in the accounting treatment of operating leases, should it occur, on the value of companies with significant hidden leverage.

4 CASE STUDY 3: ANTICIPATING EFFECTS OF CHANGES IN ACCOUNTING STANDARDS

The quantitative analyst of the large equity mutual fund, consistent with his mandate to monitor accounting pronouncements and changes, decides to look further at the technical plans on the websites of the International Accounting Standards Board and the Financial Accounting Standards Board.[6] In looking at the websites, he becomes aware of some very near-term efforts at the FASB in the United States to change the accounting for securitizations.

Currently under Statement 140, a company can remove financial assets from its balance sheet by placing them into a qualified special purpose entity, which then issues securities representing interests in those assets. If carried out in accordance with Statement 140 accounting, this transaction results in the recognition of a sale of the assets and their elimination from the balance sheet. The qualified special purpose entity, and the securities issued by it, does not appear on the seller's balance sheet. The combination of asset removal and nonrecognition of liabilities may have a powerfully beneficial effect on financial leverage presented in the balance sheet.

The FASB has considered eliminating the concept of a "qualified" special purpose entity from the securitization accounting contained in Statement 140, and requiring consideration of such vehicles under the accounting requirements of FASB Interpretation 46, Revised (FIN 46(R)). The revised accounting standards would make a sale treatment of financial instruments—such as mortgage loans, accounts receivable, or credit card receivables—through a securitization much less likely. Companies could still securitize financial assets, but they would not be as easily removed from the balance sheet as under Statement 140. Liabilities issued in connection with the securitizations would also be likely to be shown on the company's balance sheet.

If the FASB's plans come to pass, then the United States accounting for securitizations would be closer to the accounting contained in International Accounting Standard 39, Financial Instruments: Recognition and Measurement. If the proposed accounting changes are to be applied to *existing* securitization transactions, it will probably cause companies to reconsolidate assets onto their balance sheets, along with associated liabilities, that had previously been accounted for as being sold. That could cause drastic changes in the leverage of companies that had been securitizing financial assets.

Knowing that the mutual fund has holdings in several financial institutions that frequently securitize assets, the quantitative analyst contacted the financial analyst responsible for the financial institutions and advised him to look into the potential changes.

Phase 1: Define a Purpose for the Analysis

The financial analyst's objective is to identify financial institutions with securitizations that might be susceptible to the potential new accounting treatment, to analyze the effect this would have on reported leverage, and to consider the consequences of the reported leverage.

The financial analyst realized that the mutual fund's large holding in Discover Financial Services (NYSE: DFS) could be at risk from the possible account-

[6] www.iasb.org/Current+Projects/IASB+Projects/IASB+Work+Plan.htm and www.fasb.org/project/, respectively.

ing changes. She knows that the SEC requires companies to disclose the anticipated effects of new accounting pronouncements in the Management's Discussion and Analysis (MD&A) section of the 10-K filing. However, this disclosure does not occur until after a standard had been issued, and occurs with varying degrees of diligence by companies affected by a particular accounting pronouncement. Rather than waiting for the FASB to issue the pronouncement, and perhaps finding adequate disclosure of the effects of it in the 2008 10-K issued in early 2009, she decides to use existing disclosures to estimate the impact of the FASB's intended changes in securitization accounting. She considers it far more important to estimate the direction of changes in balance sheet leverage now, rather than wait for an exact amount.

Phase 2: Collect Input Data

She obtains the current 2008 10-Q filings and the 2007 10-K filing for Discover Financial Services (Discover Financial), and notices that the MD&A section and the segment information footnote presents certain financial data on a "managed basis." On this basis, the information is presented as if Discover Financial's sale treatment of credit card receivables had never occurred; instead the financial data is shown as if the securitization had been treated as a secured borrowing, with the assets remaining on the balance sheet and also including the securitization liabilities on the balance sheet.

Phase 3: Process Data/Phase 4: Analyze/Interpret the Processed Data

Using the balance sheets and the "managed basis" data related to securitization adjustments, she revises the reported balance sheet as of year end 30 November 2007 to a managed basis as shown in Exhibit 35.

EXHIBIT 35 **Discover Financial Services: Removing Effects of "Sale" Treatment Securitizations ($ in Thousands)**

Assets	Reported	Securitization Adjustments	Managed Basis
Cash and cash equivalents	$8,787,095		$8,787,095
Available-for-sale securities	420,837		420,837
Held-to-maturity securities	104,602		104,602
Loans receivable:			
Loan portfolio:			
Credit card	23,468,965	$28,599,309	52,068,274
Commercial loans	234,136		234,136
Other consumer loans	251,194		251,194
Total loan portfolio	23,954,295		52,553,604
Total loan receivables	23,954,295	$28,599,309	52,553,604
Allowance for loan losses	(916,844)		(916,844)
Net loan receivables	23,037,451		51,636,760

(Exhibit continued on next page . . .)

EXHIBIT 35 (continued)

Assets	Reported	Securitization Adjustments	Managed Basis
Accrued interest receivable	139,414		139,414
Amounts due from asset securitization	3,093,472		3,093,472
Premises and equipment, net	658,492		658,492
Goodwill	255,421		255,421
Intangible assets, net	98,043		98,043
Other assets	781,278		781,278
Assets of discontinued operations	0		0
Total assets	$37,376,105	$28,599,309	$65,975,414
Liabilities and Stockholders' Equity			
Total liabilities	$31,776,683	$28,599,309	$60,375,992
Total stockholders' equity	5,599,422		5,599,422
Total liabilities and equity	$37,376,105	$28,599,309	$65,975,414

The managed basis information indicates that loan receivables and total assets have increased by $28.6 billion; the analyst assumes that the increase relates solely to the credit card loan portfolio. No additional information is provided that describes how the short-term and long-term liabilities would be affected by the inclusion of the securities resulting from the application of the managed basis. Therefore, the analyst adjusts for the impact under the heading of "total liabilities," implicitly assuming that the liabilities recognized would be the same as the assets recognized.

The adjustments have a significant impact on the balance sheet. Total assets increase 77 percent; total liabilities increase 90 percent. She then applies the same adjustment to the balance sheets as of 29 February 2008 and 31 May 2008 using information from the respective MD&A sections of the filings, and produces the schedule shown in Exhibit 36. The presentation shows 30 November 2007 on the left and 31 May 2008 on the right.

On an as-reported basis, the company appears to have become less leveraged over the last six months. Financial leverage (total assets divided by total equity) was 6.67 at 30 November 2007 and decreased to 5.85 by 31 May 2008. Discover Financial's application of Statement 140 treated its securitizations of receivables as if they were asset sales instead of secured borrowings. This has the effect of decreasing overall leverage. When calculating the financial leverage ratio on a pro forma managed basis—as if the securitized receivables were still the assets of the company—Discover Financial shows higher leverage but similar improvement over the same period. On a managed basis, the financial leverage was 11.78 at 30 November 2007 and decreased to 10.53 by 31 May 2008. The Statement 140 sale treatment understated leverage by 43 percent (11/30/07), 43 percent (2/29/08), and 44 percent (5/31/08) in the three respective periods.

Another measure of financial leverage, liabilities as a percentage of total assets, shows the as-reported liabilities would be 82.9 percent of total capital at 31 May 2008. That proportion is 90.5 percent in a calculation based on managed basis figures. While financial leverage on either basis (as-reported or managed) shows a lessening of leverage over the six-month period, that decline is less on a

EXHIBIT 36 Discover Financial Services: Revised Balance Sheets and Leverage Ratios ($ in Thousands)

	30 Nov 2007		29 Feb 2008		31 May 2008	
Discover Financial Assets	**Reported**	**Managed Basis**	**Reported**	**Managed Basis**	**Reported**	**Managed Basis**
Cash and cash equivalents	$8,787,095	$8,787,095	$8,286,290	$8,286,290	$8,765,384	$8,765,384
Available-for-sale securities	420,837	420,837	792,979	792,979	958,784	958,784
Held-to-maturity securities	104,602	104,602	99,527	99,527	96,371	96,371
Loans receivable:						
Loans held for sale	0	0	349,072	349,072	714,632	714,632
Loan portfolio:						
Credit card	23,468,965	52,068,274	19,895,527	46,353,256	18,683,242	46,022,670
Commercial loans	234,136	234,136	312,211	312,211	387,540	387,540
Other consumer loans	251,194	251,194	485,871	485,871	716,649	716,649
Total loan portfolio	23,954,295	52,553,604	20,693,609	47,151,338	19,787,431	47,126,859
Total loan receivables	23,954,295	52,553,604	21,042,681	47,500,410	20,502,063	47,841,491
Allowance for loan losses	(916,844)	(916,844)	(860,378)	(860,378)	(846,775)	(846,775)
Net loan receivables	23,037,451	51,636,760	20,182,303	46,640,032	19,655,288	46,994,716
Accrued interest receivable	139,414	139,414	122,765	122,765	131,388	131,388
Amounts due from asset securitization	3,093,472	3,093,472	2,935,494	4,192,534	2,705,638	2,705,638
Premises and equipment, net	658,492	658,492	567,475	567,475	556,030	556,030
Goodwill	255,421	255,421	255,421	255,421	255,421	255,421
Intangible assets, net	98,043	98,043	57,900	57,900	56,030	56,030
Other assets	781,278	781,278	922,578	922,578	839,911	839,911
Assets of discontinued operations	0	0	3,105,327	3,105,327	213,297	213,297
Total Assets	$37,376,105	$65,975,414	$37,328,059	$65,042,828	$34,233,542	$61,572,970
Liabilities and stockholders' equity						
Total liabilities	$31,776,683	$60,375,992	$31,673,718	$59,388,487	$28,383,851	$55,723,279
Total stockholders' equity	5,599,422	5,599,422	5,654,341	5,654,341	5,849,691	5,849,691
Total liabilities and equity	$37,376,105	$65,975,414	$37,328,059	$65,042,828	$34,233,542	$61,572,970
Financial leverage	6.67	11.78	6.60	11.50	5.85	10.53
Incremental leverage	5.11		4.90		4.67	
Understatement of leverage	–43%		–43%		–44%	
Liabilities as percent of capital	85.0%	91.5%	84.9%	91.3%	82.9%	90.5%

managed basis. Further, the absolute level of leverage would be significantly increased in a standard change like the one contemplated by the FASB.

The financial analyst then looks to the MD&A for information on the effects the managed basis would have on the income statement. While net interest income, provision for loan losses, and other income would change, the net income would be unaffected. It appears that the balance sheet impacts are those of concern.

Phase 5: Develop and Communicate Conclusions and Recommendations (e.g., with an Analysis Report)

The balance sheet effects concern the financial analyst on several levels. First, she is concerned that the current accounting treatment for securitizations masks the company's true leverage. Second, she is concerned that expected changes by standard setters will force Discover Financial to present a balance sheet that is more highly leveraged than investors have come to expect. That may raise concerns among other market participants about the company's financial standing, possibly weakening the company's valuation. Third, she is concerned that the company may try to offset the effects of the anticipated accounting change by raising equity, which would dilute the company's ownership and also possibly weaken the company's valuation.

She believes it is highly probable that the FASB will act on the project to change Statement 140 accounting and that it can only portend negative effects for the company's holding in Discover Financial Services. She recommends that the company reduce its holdings in Discover Financial Services.

Phase 6: Follow-up

Specifically, the quantitative analyst and financial analyst will continue to observe the value of Discover Financial Services to get feedback on the decision. Generally, accounting pronouncements and changes will be monitored for potential impact on financial statements and on company valuation.

SUMMARY

The three case studies demonstrate the use of financial analysis in decision making. Each case is set in a different type of industry: manufacturing, service, and financial service. The different focus, purpose, and context for each analysis result in different techniques and tools being applied to the analysis. However, each case demonstrates the use of a common financial statement analysis framework. In each case, an economic decision is arrived at; this is consistent with the primary reason for performing financial analysis: to facilitate an economic decision.

PRACTICE PROBLEMS FOR READING 28

The following information relates to Questions 1–8

Sergei Leenid, CFA, is a long-only fixed income portfolio manager for the Parliament Funds. He has developed a quantitative model, based on financial statement data, to predict changes in the credit ratings assigned to corporate bond issues. Before applying the model, Leenid first performs a screening process to exclude bonds that fail to meet certain criteria relative to their credit rating. Existing holdings that fail to pass the initial screen are individually reviewed for potential disposition. Bonds that pass the screening process are evaluated using the quantitative model to identify potential rating changes.

Leenid is concerned that a pending change in accounting rules could affect the results of the initial screening process. One current screen excludes bonds when the financial leverage ratio (equity multiplier) exceeds a given level and/or the interest coverage ratio falls below a given level for a given bond rating. For example, any "A" rated bond of a company with a financial leverage ratio exceeding 2.0 or an interest coverage ratio below 6.0 would fail the initial screening. The failing bonds are eliminated from further analysis using the quantitative model.

The new accounting rule would require substantially all leases to be capitalized on a company's balance sheets. To test whether the change in accounting rules will affect the output of the screening process, Leenid collects a random sample of "A" rated bonds issued by companies in the retail industry, which he believes will be among the industries most affected by the change.

Two of the companies, Silk Road Stores and Colorful Concepts, recently issued bonds with similar terms and interest rates. Leenid decides to thoroughly analyze the potential effects of the change on these two companies and begins by gathering information from their most recent annual financial statements (Exhibit 1).

After examining lease disclosures, Leenid estimates the average lease term for each company at 8 years with a fairly consistent lease expense over that time. He believes the leases should be capitalized using 6.5 percent, the rate at which both companies recently issued bonds.

EXHIBIT 1 Selected Financial Data for Silk Road Stores and Colorful Concepts

	Silk Road	Colorful Concepts
Revenue	3,945	7,049
EBIT	318	865
Interest expense	21	35
Income taxes	121	302
Net income	176	528
Average total assets	2,075	3,844
Average total equity	1,156	2,562
Lease expense	213	406

While examining the balance sheet for Colorful Concepts, Leenid also discovers that the company has a 204 ending asset balance (188 beginning) for investments in associates, primarily due to its 20 percent interest in the equity of Exotic Imports. Exotic Imports is a specialty retail chain and in the most recent year reported 1,230 in sales, 105 in net income, and had average total assets of 620.

1. If the accounting rules were to change, Silk Road's assets would increase by approximately:

A. 1,297.

B. 1,576.

C. 1,704.

2. If the accounting rules were to change, Silk Road's interest coverage ratio would be *closest* to:

A. 3.03.

B. 3.50.

C. 5.04.

3. If the accounting rules were to change, Silk Road's financial leverage ratio would be *closest* to:

A. 1.37.

B. 1.79.

C. 2.92.

4. Will the change in accounting rules impact the result of the initial screening process for Colorful Concepts?

A. It passes the screens now, but will not pass if the accounting rules change.

B. It passes the screens now and will continue to pass if the accounting rules change.

C. It fails the screens now and will continue to fail if the accounting rules change.

5. Based on Leenid's analysis of the results of the initial screening, relative to Colorful Concepts the bond rating of Silk Road should be:

A. lower.

B. higher.

C. the same.

6. Ignoring the potential impact of any accounting change and excluding the investment in associates, the net profit margin for Colorful Concepts would be *closest* to:

A. 6.0%.

B. 7.2%.

C. 7.5%.

7. Ignoring the impact of any accounting change, the asset turnover ratio for Colorful Concepts excluding the investments in associates would:

A. stay the same.

B. increase by 0.10.

C. decrease by 0.10.

8. Excluding the investments in associates would result in the interest coverage ratio for Colorful Concepts being:

A. lower.

B. higher.

C. the same.

The following information relates to Questions 9–15

Quentin Abay, CFA, is an analyst for a private equity firm interested in purchasing Bickchip Enterprises, a conglomerate. His first task is to determine the trends in ROE and the main drivers of the trends using DuPont analysis. To do so he gathers the data in Exhibit 1.

EXHIBIT 1 Selected Financial Data for Bickchip Enterprises (€ Thousands)

	2009	2008	2007
Revenue	72,448	66,487	55,781
Earnings before interest and tax	6,270	4,710	3,609
Earnings before tax	5,101	4,114	3,168
Net income	4,038	3,345	2,576
Asset turnover	0.79	0.76	0.68
Assets/Equity	3.09	3.38	3.43

After conducting the DuPont analysis, Abay believes that his firm could increase the ROE without operational changes. Further, Abay thinks that ROE could improve if the company divested segments that were generating the lowest returns on capital employed (total assets less non-interest-bearing liabilities). Segment EBIT margins in 2009 were 11 percent for Automation Equipment, 5 percent for Power and Industrial, and 8 percent for Medical Equipment. Other relevant segment information is presented in Exhibit 2.

EXHIBIT 2 Segment Data for Bickchip Enterprises (€ Thousands)

	Capital Employed			Capital Expenditures (Excluding Acquisitions)		
Operating Segments	**2009**	**2008**	**2007**	**2009**	**2008**	**2007**
Automation Equipment	10,705	6,384	5,647	700	743	616
Power and Industrial	15,805	13,195	12,100	900	849	634
Medical Equipment	22,870	22,985	22,587	908	824	749
	49,380	42,564	40,334	2,508	2,416	1,999

Abay is also concerned with earnings quality, so he intends to calculate Bickchip's cash-flow-based accruals ratio and the ratio of operating cash flow before interest and taxes to operating income. To do so, he prepares the information in Exhibit 3.

EXHIBIT 3 Earnings Quality Data for Bickchip Enterprises (€ Thousands)

	2009	2008	2007
Net income	4,038	3,345	2,576
Net cash flow provided by (used in) operating activity[a]	9,822	5,003	3,198
Net cash flow provided by (used in) investing activity	(10,068)	(4,315)	(5,052)
Net cash flow provided by (used in) financing activity[b]	(5,792)	1,540	(2,241)
Average net operating assets	43,192	45,373	40,421
[a] includes cash paid for taxes of:	(1,930)	(1,191)	(1,093)
[b] includes cash paid for interest of:	(1,169)	(596)	(441)

9. Over the three-year period presented in Exhibit 1, Bickchip's return on equity is *best* described as:

A. stable.

B. trending lower.

C. trending higher.

10. Based on the DuPont analysis, Abay's belief regarding ROE is *most likely* based on:

A. leverage.

B. profit margins.

C. asset turnover.

11. Based on Abay's criteria, the business segment *best* suited for divestiture is:

A. medical equipment.

B. power and industrial.

C. automation equipment.

12. Bickchip's cash-flow-based accruals ratio in 2009 is *closest* to:

A. 9.9%.

B. 13.4%.

C. 23.3%.

13. The cash-flow-based accruals ratios from 2007 to 2009 indicate:

A. improving earnings quality.

B. deteriorating earnings quality.

C. no change in earnings quality.

14. The ratio of operating cash flow before interest and taxes to operating income for Bickchip for 2009 is *closest* to:

A. 1.6.

B. 1.9.

C. 2.1.

15. Based on the ratios for operating cash flow before interest and taxes to operating income, Abay should conclude that:

A. Bickchip's earnings are backed by cash flow.

B. Bickchip's earnings are not backed by cash flow.

C. Abay can draw no conclusion due to the changes in the ratios over time.

The following information relates to Questions 16–21

Michael Wetstone is an equity analyst covering the software industry for a public pension fund. Prior to comparing the financial results of Software Services Inc. and PDQ GmbH, Wetstone discovers the need to make adjustments to their respective financial statements. The issues preventing comparability, using the financial statements as reported, are the sale of receivables and the impact of minority interests.

Software Services sold $267.5 million of finance receivables to a special purpose entity. PDQ does not securitize finance receivables. An abbreviated balance sheet for Software Services is presented in Exhibit 1.

EXHIBIT 1 Abbreviated Balance Sheet for Software Services ($ 000)

Year Ending:	31 December 2009
Total current assets	1,412,900
Total assets	3,610,600
Total current liabilities	1,276,300
Total liabilities	2,634,100
Total equity	976,500

A significant portion of PDQ's net income is explained by its 20 percent minority interest in Astana Systems. Wetstone collects certain data (Exhibit 2) related to both PDQ and Astana in order to estimate the financials of PDQ on a stand-alone basis.

EXHIBIT 2 Selected Financial Data Related to PDQ and Astana Systems

	PDQ (€ in 000)	Astana ($ in 000)
Earnings before tax (2009)	41,730	15,300
Income taxes (2009)	13,562	5,355
Net income (2009)	28,168	9,945
Market capitalization (recent)	563,355	298,350
Average $/€ exchange rate in 2009	1.55	
Current $/€ exchange rate	1.62	

16. Compared to holding securitized finance receivables on the balance sheet, treating them as sold had the effect of reducing Software Services' reported financial leverage by:

A. 6.8%.
B. 7.4%.
C. 9.2%.

17. Had the securitized finance receivables been held on the balance sheet, Software Services' ratio of liabilities to total capital would have been *closest* to:

A. 73.0%.
B. 74.8%.
C. 80.4%.

18. How much of PDQ's value can be explained by its equity stake in Astana?

A. 6.5%.
B. 10.6%.
C. 20.0%.

19. On a "solo" basis, PDQ's P/E ratio is *closest* to:

A. 19.6.
B. 21.0.
C. 24.5.

20. The adjusted financial statements were created during which phase of the financial analysis process?

A. Data collection.
B. Data processing.
C. Data interpretation.

21. The estimate of PDQ's solo value is crude because of:

A. the potential differences in accounting standards used by PDQ and Astana.
B. the differing risk characteristics of PDQ and Astana.
C. differences in liquidity and market efficiency where PDQ and Astana trade.

SOLUTIONS FOR READING 28

1. A is correct. The capitalized value of Silk Road's leases, the amount by which assets would increase, is estimated as the present value of the operating lease expense (payments). The present value of 8 payments of 213 at 6.5 percent is 1,297.
2. B is correct. Adjusted EBIT = EBIT + Lease expense − Adjustment to depreciation = 318 + 213 − (1,297/8) = 369. Adjusted interest expense = Interest expense + Assumed interest expense on leases = 21 + (0.065 × 1,297) = 105.3. Adjusted interest coverage ratio = 369/105.3 = 3.50.
3. C is correct. The capitalized value of the leases is added to assets and liabilities but does not impact equity. On an adjusted basis, Silk Road's financial leverage ratio = (2,075 + 1,297)/1,156 = 2.92.
4. A is correct. Without the accounting change, Colorful Concepts has a financial leverage ratio = 3,844/2,562 = 1.50 and an interest coverage ratio = 865/35 = 24.71. These are both passing ratios. With the accounting change, the capitalized value of Colorful Concept's leases is 2,472. The financial leverage ratio = (3,844 + 2,472)/2,562 = 2.46 and the interest coverage ratio = [865 + 406 − (2,472/8)]/[35 + (2,472 × 0.065)] = 4.91. These are both failing ratios. The change in interest rate coverage is particularly dramatic.
5. A is correct. Silk Road has higher unadjusted and adjusted financial leverage ratios and lower unadjusted and adjusted interest coverage ratios than Colorful Concepts. Silk Road is riskier based on the financial leverage and interest coverage ratios, so it should have a lower bond rating.
6. B is correct. The investment in Exotic Imports is accounted for using the equity method and 20 percent of Exotic Import's net income is included in the net income of Colorful Concepts. The net profit margin excluding the investment in Exotic Imports is (528 – 21)/7,049 = 7.2 percent. (If the investment in Exotic Imports is included, net profit margin is 7.5 percent.)
7. B is correct. The asset turnover ratio (sales/average total assets) without adjustment is 7,049/3,844 = 1.83. To compute the asset turnover ratio excluding investments in associates, the average investment in associates [(204 + 188)/2 = 196] is deducted from average total assets. The adjusted asset turnover ratio is 7,049/(3,844 − 196) = 1.93. The asset turnover ratio increased by 0.10.
8. C is correct. The calculation for interest coverage is EBIT/interest expense, neither of which is affected by the investment in associates.
9. C is correct. The ROE has been trending higher. ROE can be calculated by multiplying (net profit margin) × (asset turnover) × (financial leverage). Net profit margin is net income/sales. In 2007 the net profit margin was 2,576/55,781 = 4.6% and the ROE = 4.6% × 0.68 × 3.43 = 10.8%. Using the same method, ROE was 12.9 percent in 2008 and 13.6 percent in 2009.
10. A is correct. The DuPont analysis shows that profit margins and asset turnover have both increased over the last three years, but leverage has declined. The reduction in leverage offsets a portion of the improvement in profitability and turnover. Thus, ROE would have been higher if leverage had not decreased.

11. B is correct. The Power and Industrial segment has the lowest EBIT margins but uses about 31 percent of the capital employed. Further, Power and Industrial's proportion of the capital expenditures has increased from 32 percent to 36 percent over the three years. Its capital intensity only looked to get worse, as the segment's percentage of total capital expenditures was higher than its percentage of total capital in each of the three years. If Abay is considering divesting segments that do not earn sufficient returns on capital employed, this segment is most suitable.

12. A is correct. The cash-flow-based accruals ratio = [NI − (CFO + CFI)]/(Average NOA) = [4,038 − (9,822 − 10,068)]/43,192 = 9.9%.

13. A is correct. The cash-flow-based accruals ratio falls from 11.0 percent in 2007 to 5.9 percent in 2008, and then rises to 9.9 percent in 2009. However, the change over the three-year period is a net modest decline, indicating a slight improvement in earnings quality.

14. B is correct. Net cash flow provided by (used in) operating activity has to be adjusted for interest and taxes, as necessary, in order to be comparable to operating income (EBIT). Bickchip, reporting under IFRS, chose to classify interest expense as a financing cash flow so the only necessary adjustment is for taxes. The operating cash flow before interest and taxes = 9,822 + 1,930 = 11,752. Dividing this by EBIT of 6,270 yields 1.9.

15. A is correct. Operating cash flow before interest and taxes to operating income rises steadily (not erratically) from 1.2 to 1.3 to 1.9. The ratios over 1.0 and the trend indicate that earnings are supported by cash flow.

16. A is correct. The leverage ratio is measured as total assets/total equity. As reported, this was $3,610,600/$976,500 = 3.70. Had the securitized receivables been held on the balance sheet, assets would have been $267,500 higher, or $3,878,100, and equity would have been unchanged. The ratio would then have been 3.97. The ratio of 3.70 as reported is 6.8 percent less than 3.97: 1 − 3.7/3.97 = 0.068.

17. B is correct. If the receivables had been held on the balance sheet, both assets and liabilities would have been $267,500 higher: $2,901,600/ $3,878,100 = 74.8%.

18. A is correct. PDQ owns 20 percent of Astana (0.2 × 298,350 = $59,670). Translated at the current exchange rate of $1.62 per euro that is €36,833. 36,833/563,355 = 0.0654 or 6.5%.

19. A is correct. PDQ's solo market capitalization is 563,355 − 36,833 = 526,522. To calculate its solo net income, because Astana is accounted for using the equity method, 20 percent of Astana's net income of $9,945 is translated at the average exchange rate of $1.55/€ and deducted from PDQ's net income to produce €26,884 in adjusted net income for PDQ. P/E = 526,522/26,884 = 19.6.

20. B is correct. Adjusted financial statements are created during the data processing phase of the financial analysis process.

21. A is correct. Estimates of Astana's impact on PDQ's financial statements are crude due to the potential differences in accounting standards used by the two firms. Based on the currencies each reports in, Astana is likely using U.S. GAAP and PDQ is likely using IFRS. Pricing (market capitalization) should reflect the other potential differences.

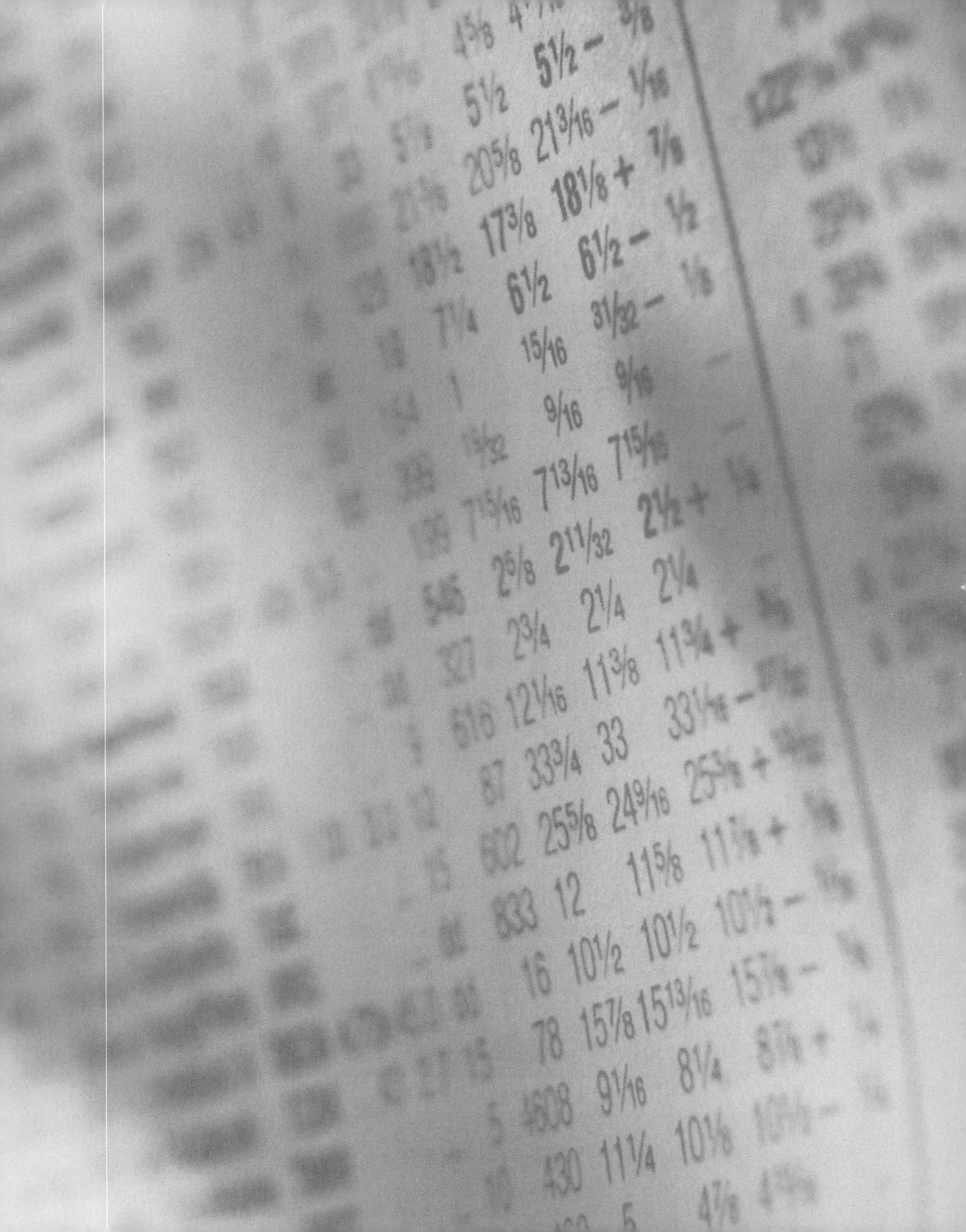

GLOSSARY

A priori probability A probability based on logical analysis rather than on observation or personal judgment.

Abandonment option The ability to terminate a project at some future time if the financial results are disappointing.

Abnormal earnings See *Residual income.*

Absolute dispersion The amount of variability present without comparison to any reference point or benchmark.

Absolute frequency The number of observations in a given interval (for grouped data).

Absolute valuation model A model that specifies an asset's intrinsic value.

Accelerated methods of depreciation Depreciation methods that allocate a relatively large proportion of the cost of an asset to the early years of the asset's useful life.

Account With the accounting systems, a formal record of increases and decreases in a specific asset, liability, component of owners' equity, revenue, or expense.

Account format A method of presentation of accounting transactions in which effects on assets appear at the left and effects on liabilities and equity appear at the right of a central dividing line; also known as T-account format.

Accounting estimates Estimates of items such as the useful lives of assets, warranty costs, and the amount of uncollectible receivables.

Accounting profit (income before taxes or **pretax income)** Income as reported on the income statement, in accordance with prevailing accounting standards, before the provisions for income tax expense.

Accounting risk The risk associated with accounting standards that vary from country to country or with any uncertainty about how certain transactions should be recorded.

Accounts payable Amounts that a business owes to its vendors for goods and services that were purchased from them but which have not yet been paid.

Accounts receivable turnover Ratio of sales on credit to the average balance in accounts receivable.

Accrual basis Method of accounting in which the effect of transactions on financial condition and income are recorded when they occur, not when they are settled in cash.

Accrued expenses (accrued liabilities) Liabilities related to expenses that have been incurred but not yet paid as of the end of an accounting period—an example of an accrued expense is rent that has been incurred but not yet paid, resulting in a liability "rent payable."

Accrued interest Interest earned but not yet paid.

Accumulated benefit obligation Under U.S. GAAP, a measure used in estimating a defined-benefit pension plan's liabilities, defined as "the actuarial present value of benefits (whether vested or non-vested) attributed by the pension benefit formula to employee service rendered before a specified date and based on employee service and compensation (if applicable) prior to that date."

Accumulated depreciation An offset to property, plant, and equipment (PPE) reflecting the amount of the cost of PPE that has been allocated to current and previous accounting periods.

Acquiring company, or **acquirer** The company in a merger or acquisition that is acquiring the target.

Acquisition The purchase of some portion of one company by another; the purchase may be for assets, a definable segment of another entity, or the purchase of an entire company.

Acquisition method A method of accounting for a business combination where the acquirer is required to measure each identifiable asset and liability at fair value. This method was the result of a joint project of the IASB and FASB aiming at convergence in standards for the accounting of business combinations.

Active factor risk The contribution to active risk squared resulting from the portfolio's different-than-benchmark exposures relative to factors specified in the risk model.

Active investment managers Managers who hold portfolios that differ from their benchmark portfolio in an attempt to produce positive risk-adjusted returns.

Active portfolio In the context of the Treynor-Black model, the portfolio formed by mixing analyzed stocks of perceived nonzero alpha values. This portfolio is ultimately mixed with the passive market index portfolio.

Active return The return on a portfolio minus the return on the portfolio's benchmark.

Active risk The standard deviation of active returns.

Active risk squared The variance of active returns; active risk raised to the second power.

Active specific risk or **asset selection risk** The contribution to active risk squared resulting from the portfolio's active weights on individual assets as those weights interact with assets' residual risk.

Active strategy In reference to short-term cash management, an investment strategy characterized by monitoring and attempting to capitalize on market conditions to optimize the risk and return relationship of short-term investments.

Activity ratios (asset utilization or **operating efficiency ratios)** Ratios that measure how efficiently a company performs day-to-day tasks, such as the collection of receivables and management of inventory.

Addition rule for probabilities A principle stating that the probability that *A* or *B* occurs (both occur) equals the probability that *A* occurs, plus the probability that *B* occurs, minus the probability that both *A* and *B* occur.

Add-on interest A procedure for determining the interest on a bond or loan in which the interest is added onto the face value of a contract.

Adjusted beta Historical beta adjusted to reflect the tendency of beta to be mean reverting.

Adjusted present value (APV) As an approach to valuing a company, the sum of the value of the company, assuming no use of debt, and the net present value of any effects of debt on company value.

Adjusted R^2 A measure of goodness-of-fit of a regression that is adjusted for degrees of freedom and hence does not automatically increase when another independent variable is added to a regression.

After-tax cash flow (ATCF) Net operating income less debt service and less taxes payable on income from operations.

After-tax equity reversion (ATER) Sales price less disposition costs, amortized mortgage loan balance, and capital gains taxes.

Agency costs Costs associated with the conflict of interest present when a company is managed by non-owners. Agency costs result from the inherent conflicts of interest between managers and equity owners.

Agency costs of equity The smaller the stake that managers have in the company, the less is their share in bearing the cost of excessive perquisite consumption or not giving their best efforts in running the company.

Agency problem, or **principal-agent problem** A conflict of interest that arises when the agent in an agency relationship has goals and incentives that differ from the principal to whom the agent owes a fiduciary duty.

Agency relationships An arrangement whereby someone, an agent, acts on behalf of another person, the principal.

Aging schedule A breakdown of accounts into categories of days outstanding.

Allowance for bad debts An offset to accounts receivable for the amount of accounts receivable that are estimated to be uncollectible.

Alpha (or **abnormal return**) The return on an asset in excess of the asset's required rate of return; the risk-adjusted return.

Alternative hypothesis The hypothesis accepted when the null hypothesis is rejected.

American Depositary Receipt A negotiable certificate issued by a depositary bank that represents ownership in a non-U.S. company's deposited equity (i.e., equity held in custody by the depositary bank in the company's home market).

American option An option contract that can be exercised at any time until its expiration date.

Amortization The process of allocating the cost of intangible long-term assets having a finite useful life to accounting periods; the allocation of the amount of a bond premium or discount to the periods remaining until bond maturity.

Amortizing and accreting swaps A swap in which the notional principal changes according to a formula related to changes in the underlying.

Analysis of variance (ANOVA) The analysis of the total variability of a dataset (such as observations on the dependent variable in a regression) into components representing different sources of variation; with reference to regression, ANOVA provides the inputs for an *F*-test of the significance of the regression as a whole.

Annual percentage rate The cost of borrowing expressed as a yearly rate.

Annuity A finite set of level sequential cash flows.

Annuity due An annuity having a first cash flow that is paid immediately.

Anticipation stock Excess inventory that is held in anticipation of increased demand, often because of seasonal patterns of demand.

Antidilutive With reference to a transaction or a security, one that would increase earnings per share (EPS) or result in EPS higher than the company's basic EPS—antidilutive securities are not included in the calculation of diluted EPS.

Arbitrage 1) The simultaneous purchase of an undervalued asset or portfolio and sale of an overvalued but equivalent asset or portfolio, in order to obtain a riskless profit on the price differential. Taking advantage of a market inefficiency in a risk-free manner. 2) A trading strategy designed to generate a guaranteed profit from a transaction that requires no capital commitment or risk bearing on the part of the trader. A simple example of an arbitrage trade would be the simultaneous purchase and sale of the same security in different markets at different prices. 3) The condition in a financial market in which equivalent assets or combinations of assets sell for two different prices, creating an opportunity to profit at no risk with no commitment of money. In a well-functioning financial market, few arbitrage opportunities are possible. 4) A risk-free operation that earns an expected positive net profit but requires no net investment of money.

Arbitrage opportunity An opportunity to conduct an arbitrage; an opportunity to earn an expected positive net profit without risk and with no net investment of money.

Arbitrage portfolio The portfolio that exploits an arbitrage opportunity.

Arithmetic mean The sum of the observations divided by the number of observations.

Arrears swap A type of interest rate swap in which the floating payment is set at the end of the period and the interest is paid at that same time.

Asian call option A European-style option with a value at maturity equal to the difference between the stock price at maturity and the average stock price during the life of the option, or $0, whichever is greater.

Asset beta The unlevered beta; reflects the business risk of the assets; the asset's systematic risk.

Asset purchase An acquisition in which the acquirer purchases the target company's assets and payment is made directly to the target company.

Asset retirement obligations (AROs) The fair value of the estimated costs to be incurred at the end of a tangible asset's service life. The fair value of the liability is determined on the basis of discounted cash flows.

Assets Resources controlled by an enterprise as a result of past events and from which future economic benefits to the enterprise are expected to flow.

Asset-based approach Approach that values a private company based on the values of the underlying assets of the entity less the value of any related liabilities.

Asset-based loan A loan that is secured with company assets.

Asset-based valuation An approach to valuing natural resource companies that estimates company value on the basis of the market value of the natural resources the company controls.

Assignment of accounts receivable The use of accounts receivable as collateral for a loan.

Asymmetric information The differential of information between corporate insiders and outsiders regarding the company's performance and prospects. Managers typically have more information about the company's performance and prospects than owners and creditors.

At the money An option in which the underlying value equals the exercise price.

Autocorrelation The correlation of a time series with its own past values.

Automated Clearing House An electronic payment network available to businesses, individuals, and financial institutions in the United States, U.S. Territories, and Canada.

Autoregressive (AR) model A time series regressed on its own past values, in which the independent variable is a lagged value of the dependent variable.

Available-for-sale investments Debt and equity securities not classified as either held-to-maturity or held-for-trading securities. The investor is willing to sell but not actively planning to sell. In general, available-for-sale securities are reported at fair value on the balance sheet.

Backtesting With reference to portfolio strategies, the application of a strategy's portfolio selection rules to historical data to assess what would have been the strategy's historical performance.

Backward integration A merger involving the purchase of a target ahead of the acquirer in the value or production chain; for example, to acquire a supplier.

Backwardation A condition in the futures markets in which the benefits of holding an asset exceed the costs, leaving the futures price less than the spot price.

Balance of payments accounts A country's record of international trading, borrowing, and lending.

Balance sheet (statement of financial position or **statement of financial condition)** The financial statement that presents an entity's current financial position by disclosing resources the entity controls (its assets) and the claims on those resources (its liabilities and equity claims), as of a particular point in time (the date of the balance sheet).

Balance sheet ratios Financial ratios involving balance sheet items only.

Balance-sheet-based accruals ratio The difference between net operating assets at the end and the beginning of the period compared to the average net operating assets over the period.

Balance-sheet-based aggregate accruals The difference between net operating assets at the end and the beginning of the period.

Band-of-investment method A widely used approach to estimate an overall capitalization rate. It is based on the premise that debt and equity financing is typically involved in a real estate transaction.

Bank discount basis A quoting convention that annualizes, on a 360-day year, the discount as a percentage of face value.

Bargain purchase When a company is acquired and the purchase price is less than the fair value of the net assets. The current treatment of the excess of fair value over the purchase price is different under IFRS and U.S. GAAP. The excess is never accounted for as negative goodwill.

Basic earnings per share (EPS) Net earnings available to common shareholders (i.e., net income minus preferred dividends) divided by the weighted average number of common shares outstanding during the period.

Basis point value (BPV) Also called *present value of a basis point* or *price value of a basis point* (PVBP), the change in the bond price for a 1 basis point change in yield.

Basis swap 1) An interest rate swap involving two floating rates. 2) A swap in which both parties pay a floating rate.

Bayes' formula A method for updating probabilities based on new information.

Bear hug A tactic used by acquirers to circumvent target management's objections to a proposed merger by submitting the proposal directly to the target company's board of directors.

Bear spread An option strategy that involves selling a put with a lower exercise price and buying a put with a higher exercise price. It can also be executed with calls.

Before-tax cash flow A measure of the expected annual cash flow from the operation of a real estate investment after all expenses but before taxes.

Benchmark A comparison portfolio; a point of reference or comparison.

Benchmark value of the multiple In using the method of comparables, the value of a price multiple for the comparison asset; when we have comparison assets (a group), the mean or median value of the multiple for the group of assets.

Bernoulli random variable A random variable having the outcomes 0 and 1.

Bernoulli trial An experiment that can produce one of two outcomes.

Beta A standardized measure of systematic risk based upon an asset's covariance with the market portfolio.

Bill-and-hold basis Sales on a bill-and-hold basis involve selling products but not delivering those products until a later date.

Binomial model A model for pricing options in which the underlying price can move to only one of two possible new prices.

Binomial random variable The number of successes in n Bernoulli trials for which the probability of success is constant for all trials and the trials are independent.

Binomial tree The graphical representation of a model of asset price dynamics in which, at each period, the asset moves up with probability p or down with probability $(1 - p)$.

Block Orders to buy or sell that are too large for the liquidity ordinarily available in dealer networks or stock exchanges.

Blockage factor An illiquidity discount that occurs when an investor sells a large amount of stock relative to its trading volume (assuming it is not large enough to constitute a controlling ownership).

Bond equivalent yield A calculation of yield that is annualized using the ratio of 365 to the number of days to maturity. Bond equivalent yield allows for the restatement and comparison of securities with different compounding periods.

Bond indenture A legal contract specifying the terms of a bond issue.

Bond option An option in which the underlying is a bond; primarily traded in over-the-counter markets.

Bond yield plus risk premium approach An estimate of the cost of common equity that is produced by summing the before-tax cost of debt and a risk premium that captures the additional yield on a company's stock relative to its bonds. The additional yield is often estimated using historical spreads between bond yields and stock yields.

Bond-equivalent basis A basis for stating an annual yield that annualizes a semiannual yield by doubling it.

Bond-equivalent yield The yield to maturity on a basis that ignores compounding.

Bonding costs Costs borne by management to assure owners that they are working in the owners' best interest (e.g., implicit cost of non-compete agreements).

Book value equity per share The amount of book value (also called carrying value) of common equity per share of common stock, calculated by dividing the book value of shareholders' equity by the number of shares of common stock outstanding.

Book value of equity (or **book value)** Shareholders' equity (total assets minus total liabilities) minus the value of preferred stock; common shareholders' equity.

Bootstrapping earnings An increase in a company's earnings that results as a consequence of the idiosyncrasies of a merger transaction itself rather than because of resulting economic benefits of the combination.

Bottom-up analysis With reference to investment selection processes, an approach that involves selection from all securities within a specified investment universe, i.e., without prior narrowing of the universe on the basis of macroeconomic or overall market considerations.

Bottom-up forecasting approach A forecasting approach that involves aggregating the individual company forecasts of analysts into industry forecasts, and finally into macroeconomic forecasts.

Bottom-up investing An approach to investing that focuses on the individual characteristics of securities rather than on macroeconomic or overall market forecasts.

Box spread An option strategy that combines a bull spread and a bear spread having two different exercise prices, which produces a risk-free payoff of the difference in the exercise prices.

Break point In the context of the weighted average cost of capital (WACC), a break point is the amount of capital at which the cost of one or more of the sources of capital changes, leading to a change in the WACC.

Breakeven point The number of units produced and sold at which the company's net income is zero (revenues = total costs).

Breakup value or **private market value** The value derived using a sum-of-the-parts valuation.

Breusch–Pagan test A test for conditional heteroskedasticity in the error term of a regression.

Broker 1) An agent who executes orders to buy or sell securities on behalf of a client in exchange for a commission. 2) *See* Futures commission merchants.

Brokerage The business of acting as agents for buyers or sellers, usually in return for commissions.

Build-up method A method for determining the required rate of return on equity as the sum of risk premiums, in which one or more of the risk premiums is typically subjective rather than grounded in a formal equilibrium model.

Built-up method A method of identifying the basic elements of the overall capitalization rate.

Bull spread An option strategy that involves buying a call with a lower exercise price and selling a call with a higher exercise price. It can also be executed with puts.

Bundling Offering two or more products for sale as a set.

Business risk The risk associated with operating earnings. Operating earnings are uncertain because total revenues and many of the expenditures contributed to produce those revenues are uncertain.

Butterfly spread An option strategy that combines two bull or bear spreads and has three exercise prices.

Buy-side analysts Analysts who work for investment management firms, trusts, and bank trust departments, and similar institutions.

Call An option that gives the holder the right to buy an underlying asset from another party at a fixed price over a specific period of time.

Cannibalization Cannibalization occurs when an investment takes customers and sales away from another part of the company.

Cap 1) A contract on an interest rate, whereby at periodic payment dates, the writer of the cap pays the difference between the market interest rate and a specified cap rate if, and only if, this difference is positive. This is equivalent to a stream of call options on the interest rate. 2) A combination of interest rate call options designed to hedge a borrower against rate increases on a floating-rate loan.

Capital account A record of foreign investment in a country minus its investment abroad.

Capital allocation line (CAL) A graph line that describes the combinations of expected return and standard deviation of return available to an investor from combining the optimal portfolio of risky assets with the risk-free asset.

Capital asset pricing model (CAPM) An equation describing the expected return on any asset (or portfolio) as a linear function of its beta relative to the market portfolio.

Capital budgeting The allocation of funds to relatively long-range projects or investments.

Capital charge The company's total cost of capital in money terms.

Capital market line (CML) The line with an intercept point equal to the risk-free rate that is tangent to the efficient frontier of risky assets; represents the efficient frontier when a risk-free asset is available for investment.

Capital rationing A capital rationing environment assumes that the company has a fixed amount of funds to invest.

Capital structure The mix of debt and equity that a company uses to finance its business; a company's specific mixture of long-term financing.

Capitalization rate The divisor in the expression for the value of a perpetuity.

Capitalized cash flow model (method) In the context of private company valuation, valuation model based on an assumption of a constant growth rate of free cash flow to the firm or a constant growth rate of free cash flow to equity.

Capitalized inventory costs Costs of inventories including costs of purchase, costs of conversion, other costs to bring the inventories to their present location and condition, and the allocated portion of fixed production overhead costs.

Caplet Each component call option in a cap.

Capped swap A swap in which the floating payments have an upper limit.

Captive finance subsidiary A wholly-owned subsidiary of a company that is established to provide financing of the sales of the parent company.

Capture hypothesis A theory of regulatory behavior that predicts that regulators will eventually be captured by special interests of the industry being regulated.

Carried interest A share of any profits that is paid to the general partner (manager) of an investment partnership, such as a private equity or hedge fund, as a form of compensation designed to be an incentive to the manager to maximize performance of the investment fund.

Carrying amount (book value) The amount at which an asset or liability is valued according to accounting principles.

Cash In accounting contexts, cash on hand (e.g., petty cash and cash not yet deposited to the bank) and demand deposits held in banks and similar accounts that can be used in payment of obligations.

Cash basis Accounting method in which the only relevant transactions for the financial statements are those that involve cash.

Cash conversion cycle (net operating cycle) A financial metric that measures the length of time required for a company to convert cash invested in its operations to cash received as a result of its operations; equal to days of inventory on hand + days of sales outstanding − number of days of payables.

Cash equivalents Very liquid short-term investments, usually maturing in 90 days or less.

Cash flow additivity principle The principle that dollar amounts indexed at the same point in time are additive.

Cash flow at risk (CFAR) A variation of VAR that reflects the risk of a company's cash flow instead of its market value.

Cash flow from operations (cash flow from operating activities or **operating cash flow)** The net amount of cash provided from operating activities.

Cash flow statement (statement of cash flows) A financial statement that reconciles beginning-of-period and end-of-period balance sheet values of cash; consists of three parts: cash flows from operating activities, cash flows from investing activities, and cash flows from financing activities.

Cash offering A merger or acquisition that is to be paid for with cash; the cash for the merger might come from the acquiring company's existing assets or from a debt issue.

Cash price or **spot price** The price for immediate purchase of the underlying asset.

Cash ratio A liquidity ratio calculated as (cash + short-term marketable investments) divided by current liabilities; measures a company's ability to meet its current obligations with just the cash and cash equivalents on hand.

Cash settlement A procedure used in certain derivative transactions that specifies that the long and short parties engage in the equivalent cash value of a delivery transaction.

Cash-flow-statement-based accruals ratio The difference between reported net income on an accrual basis and the cash flows from operating and investing activities compared to the average net operating assets over the period.

Cash-flow-statement-based aggregate accruals The difference between reported net income on an accrual basis and the cash flows from operating and investing activities.

Cash-generating unit The smallest identifiable group of assets that generates cash inflows that are largely independent of the cash inflows of other assets or groups of assets.

Catalyst An event or piece of information that causes the marketplace to re-evaluate the prospects of a company.

Central limit theorem A result in statistics that states that the sample mean computed from large samples of size n from a population with finite variance will follow an approximate normal distribution with a mean equal to the population mean and a variance equal to the population variance divided by n.

Centralized risk management or **companywide risk management** When a company has a single risk management group that monitors and controls all of the risk-taking activities of the organization. Centralization permits economies of scale and allows a company to use some of its risks to offset other risks. (See also *enterprise risk management*.)

Chain rule of forecasting A forecasting process in which the next period's value as predicted by the forecasting equation is substituted into the right-hand side of the equation to give a predicted value two periods ahead.

Chart of accounts A list of accounts used in an entity's accounting system.

Cheapest to deliver A bond in which the amount received for delivering the bond is largest compared with the amount paid in the market for the bond.

Cherry-picking When a bankrupt company is allowed to enforce contracts that are favorable to it while walking away from contracts that are unfavorable to it.

Classical growth theory A theory of economic growth based on the view that the growth of real GDP per person is temporary and that when it rises above subsistence level, a population explosion eventually brings it back to subsistence level.

Classified balance sheet A balance sheet organized so as to group together the various assets and liabilities into subcategories (e.g., current and noncurrent).

Clean surplus accounting Accounting that satisfies the condition that all changes in the book value of equity other than transactions with owners are reflected in income. The bottom-line income reflects all changes in shareholders' equity arising from other than owner transactions. In the absence of owner transactions, the change in shareholders' equity should equal net income. No adjustments such as translation adjustments bypass the income statement and go directly to shareholders equity.

Clean surplus relation The relationship between earnings, dividends, and book value in which ending book value is equal to the beginning book value plus earnings less dividends, apart from ownership transactions.

Clearinghouse An entity associated with a futures market that acts as middleman between the contracting parties and guarantees to each party the performance of the other.

Clientele effect The preference some investors have for shares that exhibit certain characteristics.

Closeout netting Netting the market values of *all* derivative contracts between two parties to determine one overall value owed by one party to another in the event of bankruptcy.

Coefficient of variation (CV) The ratio of a set of observations' standard deviation to the observations' mean value.

Cointegrated Describes two time series that have a long-term financial or economic relationship such that they do not diverge from each other without bound in the long run.

Collar An option strategy involving the purchase of a put and sale of a call in which the holder of an asset gains protection below a certain level, the exercise price of the put, and pays for it by giving up gains above a certain level, the exercise price of the call. Collars also can be used to provide protection against rising interest rates on a floating-rate loan by giving up gains from lower interest rates.

Combination A listing in which the order of the listed items does not matter.

Commercial paper Unsecured short-term corporate debt that is characterized by a single payment at maturity.

Committed lines of credit A bank commitment to extend credit up to a pre-specified amount; the commitment is considered a short-term liability and is usually in effect for 364 days (one day short of a full year).

Commodity forward A contract in which the underlying asset is oil, a precious metal, or some other commodity.

Commodity futures Futures contracts in which the underlying is a traditional agricultural, metal, or petroleum product.

Commodity option An option in which the asset underlying the futures is a commodity, such as oil, gold, wheat, or soybeans.

Commodity swap A swap in which the underlying is a commodity such as oil, gold, or an agricultural product.

Common size statements Financial statements in which all elements (accounts) are stated as a percentage of a key figure such as revenue for an income statement or total assets for a balance sheet.

Common-size analysis The restatement of financial statement items using a common denominator or reference item that allows one to identify trends and major differences; an example is an income statement in which all items are expressed as a percent of revenue.

Company fundamental factors Factors related to the company's internal performance, such as factors relating to earnings growth, earnings variability, earnings momentum, and financial leverage.

Company share-related factors Valuation measures and other factors related to share price or the trading characteristics of the shares, such as earnings yield, dividend yield, and book-to-market value.

Comparable company A company that has similar business risk; usually in the same industry and preferably with a single line of business.

Comparables (comps, guideline assets, guideline companies) Assets used as benchmarks when applying the method of comparables to value an asset.

Comparative advantage A person or country has a comparative advantage in an activity if that person or country can perform the activity at a lower opportunity cost than anyone else or any other country.

Compiled financial statements Financial statements that are not accompanied by an auditor's opinion letter.

Complement In probability, with reference to an event S, the event that S does not occur; in economics, a good that is used in conjunction with another good.

Completed contract A method of revenue recognition in which the company does not recognize any revenue until the contract is completed; used particularly in long-term construction contracts.

Component cost of capital The rate of return required by suppliers of capital for an individual source of a company's funding, such as debt or equity.

Compounding The process of accumulating interest on interest.

Comprehensive income All changes in equity other than contributions by, and distributions to, owners; income under clean surplus accounting; includes all changes in equity during a period except those resulting from investments by owners and distributions to owners; comprehensive income equals net income plus other comprehensive income.

Conditional expected value The expected value of a stated event given that another event has occurred.

Conditional heteroskedasticity Heteroskedasticity in the error variance that is correlated with the values of the independent variable(s) in the regression.

Conditional probability The probability of an event given (conditioned on) another event.

Conditional variances The variance of one variable, given the outcome of another.

Confidence interval A range that has a given probability that it will contain the population parameter it is intended to estimate.

Conglomerate discount The discount possibly applied by the market to the stock of a company operating in multiple, unrelated businesses.

Conglomerate merger A merger involving companies that are in unrelated businesses.

Consistent With reference to estimators, describes an estimator for which the probability of estimates close to the value of the population parameter increases as sample size increases.

Consolidation The combining of the results of operations of subsidiaries with the parent company to present financial statements as if they were a single economic unit. The assets, liabilities, revenues and expenses of the subsidiaries are combined with those of the parent company, eliminating intercompany transactions.

Constant dividend payout ratio policy A policy in which a constant percentage of net income is paid out in dividends.

Constant maturity swap or **CMT swap** A swap in which the floating rate is the rate on a security known as a constant maturity treasury or CMT security.

Constant maturity treasury or **CMT** A hypothetical U.S. Treasury note with a constant maturity. A CMT exists for various years in the range of 2 to 10.

Contango A situation in a futures market where the current futures price is greater than the current spot price for the underlying asset.

Contingent claims Derivatives in which the payoffs occur if a specific event occurs; generally referred to as options.

Contingent consideration Potential future payments to the seller that are contingent on the achievement of certain agreed on occurrences.

Continuing residual income Residual income after the forecast horizon.

Continuous random variable A random variable for which the range of possible outcomes is the real line (all real numbers between ($-\infty$ and $+\infty$) or some subset of the real line.

Continuous time Time thought of as advancing in extremely small increments.

Continuously compounded return The natural logarithm of 1 plus the holding period return, or equivalently, the natural logarithm of the ending price over the beginning price.

Contra account An account that offsets another account.

Contribution margin The amount available for fixed costs and profit after paying variable costs; revenue minus variable costs.

Control premium An increment or premium to value associated with a controlling ownership interest in a company.

Controlling interest An investment where the investor exerts control over the investee, typically by having a greater than 50 percent ownership in the investee.

Convenience yield The nonmonetary return offered by an asset when the asset is in short supply, often associated with assets with seasonal production processes.

Conventional cash flow A conventional cash flow pattern is one with an initial outflow followed by a series of inflows.

Conversion factor An adjustment used to facilitate delivery on bond futures contracts in which any of a number of bonds with different characteristics are eligible for delivery.

Convertible debt Debt with the added feature that the bondholder has the option to exchange the debt for equity at prespecified terms.

Corporate governance The system of principles, policies, procedures, and clearly defined responsibilities and accountabilities used by stakeholders to overcome the conflicts of interest inherent in the corporate form.

Corporate raider A person or organization seeking to profit by acquiring a company and reselling it, or seeking to profit from the takeover attempt itself (e.g., greenmail).

Corporation A legal entity with rights similar to those of a person. The chief officers, executives, or top managers act as agents for the firm and are legally entitled to authorize corporate activities and to enter into contracts on behalf of the business.

Correlation A number between -1 and $+1$ that measures the comovement (linear association) between two random variables.

Correlation analysis The analysis of the strength of the linear relationship between two data series.

Cost approach to value A method of valuing property based on site value plus current construction costs less accrued depreciation.

Cost averaging The periodic investment of a fixed amount of money.

Cost leadership The competitive strategy of being the lowest cost producer while offering products comparable to those of other firms, so that products can be priced at or near the industry average.

Cost of capital The rate of return that suppliers of capital require as compensation for their contribution of capital.

Cost of carry The cost associated with holding some asset, including financing, storage, and insurance costs. Any yield received on the asset is treated as a negative carrying cost.

Cost of carry model A model for pricing futures contracts in which the futures price is determined by adding the cost of carry to the spot price.

Cost of debt The cost of debt financing to a company, such as when it issues a bond or takes out a bank loan.

Cost of equity The required rate of return on common stock.

Cost of goods sold For a given period, equal to beginning inventory minus ending inventory plus the cost of goods acquired or produced during the period.

Cost of preferred stock The cost to a company of issuing preferred stock; the dividend yield that a company must commit to pay preferred stockholders.

Cost recovery method A method of revenue recognition in which the seller does not report any profit until the cash amounts paid by the buyer—including principal and interest on any financing from the seller—are greater than all the seller's costs for the merchandise sold.

Cost structure The mix of a company's variable costs and fixed costs.

Cost-of-service regulation Regulation that allows prices to reflect only the actual average cost of production and no monopoly profits.

Covariance A measure of the co-movement (linear association) between two random variables.

Covariance matrix A matrix or square array whose entries are covariances; also known as a variance–covariance matrix.

Covariance stationary Describes a time series when its expected value and variance are constant and finite in all periods and when its covariance with itself for a fixed number of periods in the past or future is constant and finite in all periods.

Covered call An option strategy involving the holding of an asset and sale of a call on the asset.

Covered interest arbitrage A transaction executed in the foreign exchange market in which a currency is purchased (sold) and a forward contract is sold (purchased) to lock in the exchange rate for future delivery of the currency. This transaction should earn the risk-free rate of the investor's home country.

Crawling peg A policy regime is one that selects a target path for the exchange rate with intervention in the foreign exchange market to achieve that path.

Creative response Behavior on the part of a firm that allows it to comply with the letter of the law but violate the spirit, significantly lessening the law's effects.

Credit With respect to double-entry accounting, a credit records increases in liability, owners' equity, and revenue accounts or decreases in asset accounts; with respect to borrowing, the willingness and ability of the borrower to make promised payments on the borrowing.

Credit analysis The evaluation of credit risk; the evaluation of the creditworthiness of a borrower or counterparty.

Credit derivatives A contract in which one party has the right to claim a payment from another party in the event that a specific credit event occurs over the life of the contract.

Credit risk or **default risk** The risk of loss caused by a counterparty's or debtor's failure to make a promised payment.

Credit scoring model A statistical model used to classify borrowers according to creditworthiness.

Credit spread option An option on the yield spread on a bond.

Credit swap A type of swap transaction used as a credit derivative in which one party makes periodic payments to the other and receives the promise of a payoff if a third party defaults.

Credit VAR, **default VAR**, or **credit at risk** A variation of VAR that reflects credit risk.

Credit-linked notes Fixed-income securities in which the holder of the security has the right to withhold payment of the full amount due at maturity if a credit event occurs.

Creditor nation A country that during its entire history has invested more in the rest of the world than other countries have invested in it.

Creditworthiness The perceived ability of the borrower to pay what is owed on the borrowing in a timely manner; it represents the ability of a company to withstand adverse impacts on its cash flows.

Cross-product netting Netting the market values of all contracts, not just derivatives, between parties.

Cross-sectional analysis Analysis that involves comparisons across individuals in a group over a given time period or at a given point in time.

Cross-sectional data Observations over individual units at a point in time, as opposed to time-series data.

Cumulative distribution function A function giving the probability that a random variable is less than or equal to a specified value.

Cumulative relative frequency For data grouped into intervals, the fraction of total observations that are less than the value of the upper limit of a stated interval.

Currency forward A forward contract in which the underlying is a foreign currency.

Currency option An option that allows the holder to buy (if a call) or sell (if a put) an underlying currency at a fixed exercise rate, expressed as an exchange rate.

Currency swap A swap in which each party makes interest payments to the other in different currencies.

Current account A record of receipts from exports of goods and services, payments for imports of goods and services, net income and net transfers received from the rest of the world.

Current assets, or **liquid assets** Assets that are expected to be consumed or converted into cash in the near future, typically one year or less.

Current cost With reference to assets, the amount of cash or cash equivalents that would have to be paid to buy the same or an equivalent asset today; with reference to liabilities, the undiscounted amount of cash or cash equivalents that would be required to settle the obligation today.

Current credit risk The risk associated with the possibility that a payment currently due will not be made.

Current exchange rate For accounting purposes, the spot exchange rate on the balance sheet date.

Current liabilities Short-term obligations, such as accounts payable, wages payable, or accrued liabilities, that are expected to be settled in the near future, typically one year or less.

Current rate method Approach to translating foreign currency financial statements for consolidation in which all assets and liabilities are translated at the current exchange rate. The current rate method is the prevalent method of translation.

Current ratio A liquidity ratio calculated as current assets divided by current liabilities.

Current taxes payable Tax expenses that have been recognized and recorded on a company's income statement but which have not yet been paid.

Cyclical businesses Businesses with high sensitivity to business- or industry-cycle influences.

Daily settlement See *Marking to market.*

Data mining The practice of determining a model by extensive searching through a dataset for statistically significant patterns.

Day trader A trader holding a position open somewhat longer than a scalper but closing all positions at the end of the day.

Days of inventory on hand (DOH) An activity ratio equal to the number of days in the period divided by inventory turnover over the period.

Days of sales outstanding (DSO) An activity ratio equal to the number of days in period divided by receivables turnover.

Dead-hand provision A poison pill provision that allows for the redemption or cancellation of a poison pill provision only by a vote of continuing directors (generally directors who were on the target company's board prior to the takeover attempt).

Dealing securities Securities held by banks or other financial intermediaries for trading purposes.

Debit With respect to double-entry accounting, a debit records increases of asset and expense accounts or decreases in liability and owners' equity accounts.

Debt covenants Agreements between the company as borrower and its creditors.

Debt incurrence test A financial covenant made in conjunction with existing debt that restricts a company's ability to incur additional debt at the same seniority based on one or more financial tests or conditions.

Debt rating approach A method for estimating a company's before-tax cost of debt based upon the yield on comparably rated bonds for maturities that closely match that of the company's existing debt.

Debt ratings An objective measure of the quality and safety of a company's debt based upon an analysis of the company's ability to pay the promised cash flows, as well as an analysis of any indentures.

Debt with warrants Debt issued with warrants that give the bondholder the right to purchase equity at prespecified terms.

Debtor nation A country that during its entire history has borrowed more in the rest of the world than other countries have lent in it.

Debt-to-assets ratio A solvency ratio calculated as total debt divided by total assets.

Debt-to-capital ratio A solvency ratio calculated as total debt divided by total debt plus total shareholders' equity.

Debt-to-equity ratio A solvency ratio calculated as total debt divided by total shareholders' equity.

Decentralized risk management A system that allows individual units within an organization to manage risk. Decentralization results in duplication of effort but has the advantage of having people closer to the risk be more directly involved in its management.

Deciles Quantiles that divide a distribution into 10 equal parts.

Decision rule With respect to hypothesis testing, the rule according to which the null hypothesis will be rejected or not rejected; involves the comparison of the test statistic to rejection point(s).

Declaration date The day that the corporation issues a statement declaring a specific dividend.

Deductible temporary differences Temporary differences that result in a reduction of or deduction from taxable income in a future period when the balance sheet item is recovered or settled.

Deep in the money Options that are far in-the-money.

Deep out of the money Options that are far out-of-the-money.

Default risk premium An extra return that compensates investors for the possibility that the borrower will fail to make a promised payment at the contracted time and in the contracted amount.

Defensive interval ratio A liquidity ratio that estimates the number of days that an entity could meet cash needs from liquid assets; calculated as (cash + short-term marketable investments + receivables) divided by daily cash expenditures.

Deferred tax assets A balance sheet asset that arises when an excess amount is paid for income taxes relative to accounting profit. The taxable income is higher than accounting profit and income tax payable exceeds tax expense. The company expects to recover the difference during the course of future operations when tax expense exceeds income tax payable.

Deferred tax liabilities A balance sheet liability that arises when a deficit amount is paid for income taxes relative to accounting profit. The taxable income is less than the accounting profit and income tax payable is less than tax expense. The company expects to eliminate the liability over the course of future operations when income tax payable exceeds tax expense.

Defined benefit obligation Under IFRS, the liability of a defined benefit pension.

Defined-benefit pension plans Plan in which the company promises to pay a certain annual amount (defined benefit) to the employee after retirement. The company bears the investment risk of the plan assets.

Defined-contribution pension plans Individual accounts to which an employee and typically the employer makes contributions, generally on a tax-advantaged basis. The amounts of contributions are defined at the outset, but the future value of the benefit is unknown. The employee bears the investment risk of the plan assets.

Definition of value (or **standard of value**) A specification of how "value" is to be understood in the context of a specific valuation.

Definitive merger agreement A contract signed by both parties to a merger that clarifies the details of the transaction, including the terms, warranties, conditions, termination details, and the rights of all parties.

Degree of confidence The probability that a confidence interval includes the unknown population parameter.

Degree of financial leverage (DFL) The ratio of the percentage change in net income to the percentage change in operating income; the sensitivity of the cash flows available to owners when operating income changes.

Degree of operating leverage (DOL) The ratio of the percentage change in operating income to the percentage change in units sold; the sensitivity of operating income to changes in units sold.

Degree of total leverage The ratio of the percentage change in net income to the percentage change in units sold; the sensitivity of the cash flows to owners to changes in the number of units produced and sold.

Degrees of freedom (df) The number of independent observations used.

Delivery A process used in a deliverable forward contract in which the long pays the agreed-upon price to the short, which in turn delivers the underlying asset to the long.

Delivery option The feature of a futures contract giving the short the right to make decisions about what, when, and where to deliver.

Delta The relationship between the option price and the underlying price, which reflects the sensitivity of the price of the option to changes in the price of the underlying.

Delta hedge An option strategy in which a position in an asset is converted to a risk-free position with a position in a specific number of options. The number of options per unit of the underlying changes through time, and the position must be revised to maintain the hedge.

Delta-normal method A measure of VAR equivalent to the analytical method but that refers to the use of delta to estimate the option's price sensitivity.

Dependent With reference to events, the property that the probability of one event occurring depends on (is related to) the occurrence of another event.

Dependent variable The variable whose variation about its mean is to be explained by the regression; the left-hand-side variable in a regression equation.

Depreciation The process of systematically allocating the cost of long-lived (tangible) assets to the periods during which the assets are expected to provide economic benefits.

Deregulation The elimination or phasing out of regulations on economic activity.

Derivative A financial instrument whose value depends on the value of some underlying asset or factor (e.g., a stock price, an interest rate, or exchange rate).

Derivatives dealers Commercial and investment banks that make markets in derivatives.

Descriptive statistics The study of how data can be summarized effectively.

Designated fair value instruments Financial instruments that an entity chooses to measure at fair value per IAS 39 or SFAS 159. Generally, the election to use the fair value option is irrevocable.

Diff swaps A swap in which the payments are based on the difference between interest rates in two countries but payments are made in only a single currency.

Differential expectations Expectations that differ from consensus expectations.

Differentiation The competitive strategy of offering unique products or services along some dimensions that are widely valued by buyers so that the firm can command premium prices.

Diffuse prior The assumption of equal prior probabilities.

Diluted earnings per share (diluted EPS) Net income, minus preferred dividends, divided by the number of common shares outstanding considering all dilutive securities (e.g., convertible debt and options); the EPS that would result if all dilutive securities were converted into common shares.

Diluted shares The number of shares that would be outstanding if all potentially dilutive claims on common shares (e.g., convertible debt, convertible preferred stock, and employee stock options) were exercised.

Dilution A reduction in proportional ownership interest as a result of the issuance of new shares.

Diminishing balance method An accelerated depreciation method, i.e., one that allocates a relatively large proportion of the cost of an asset to the early years of the asset's useful life.

Direct debit program An arrangement whereby a customer authorizes a debit to a demand account; typically used by companies to collect routine payments for services.

Direct financing lease A type of finance lease, from a lessor perspective, where the present value of the lease payments (lease receivable) equals the carrying value of the leased asset. The revenues earned by the lessor are financing in nature.

Direct format (direct method) With reference to the cash flow statement, a format for the presentation of the statement in which cash flow from operating activities is shown as operating cash receipts less operating cash disbursements.

Direct income capitalization approach Division of net operating income by an overall capitalization rate to arrive at market value.

Direct sales-comparison approach Method of valuing property based on recent sales prices of similar properties.

Direct write-off method An approach to recognizing credit losses on customer receivables in which the company waits until such time as a customer has defaulted and only then recognizes the loss.

Dirty surplus accounting Accounting in which some income items are reported as part of stockholders' equity rather than as gains and losses on the income statement; certain items of comprehensive income bypass the income statement and appear as direct adjustments to shareholders' equity.

Dirty surplus items Items that affect comprehensive income but which bypass the income statement.

Disbursement float The amount of time between check issuance and a check's clearing back against the company's account.

Discount To reduce the value of a future payment in allowance for how far away it is in time; to calculate the present value of some future amount. Also, the amount by which an instrument is priced below its face value.

Discount for lack of control An amount or percentage deducted from the pro rata share of 100 percent of the value of an equity interest in a business to reflect the absence of some or all of the powers of control.

Discount for lack of marketability An amount or percentage deducted from the value of an ownership interest to reflect the relative absence of marketability.

Discount interest A procedure for determining the interest on a loan or bond in which the interest is deducted from the face value in advance.

Discount rate Any rate used in finding the present value of a future cash flow.

Discounted cash flow analysis In the context of merger analysis, it is an estimate of a target company's value found by discounting the company's expected future free cash flows to the present.

Discrete random variable A random variable that can take on at most a countable number of possible values.

Discrete time Time thought of as advancing in distinct finite increments.

Discriminant analysis A multivariate classification technique used to discriminate between groups, such as companies that either will or will not become bankrupt during some time frame.

Dispersion The variability around the central tendency.

Divestiture The sale, liquidation, or spin-off of a division or subsidiary.

Dividend coverage ratio The ratio of net income to dividends.

Dividend discount model (DDM) A present value model of stock value that views the intrinsic value of a stock as present value of the stock's expected future dividends.

Dividend discount model based approach An approach for estimating a country's equity risk premium. The market rate of return is estimated as the sum of the dividend yield and the growth rate in dividends for a market index. Subtracting the risk-free rate of return from the estimated market return produces an estimate for the equity risk premium.

Dividend displacement of earnings The concept that dividends paid now displace earnings in all future periods.

Dividend imputation tax system A taxation system which effectively assures that corporate profits distributed as dividends are taxed just once, at the shareholder's tax rate.

Dividend policy The strategy a company follows with regard to the amount and timing of dividend payments.

Dividend payout ratio The ratio of cash dividends paid to earnings for a period.

Dividend rate The most recent quarterly dividend multiplied by four.

Dividends per share The dollar amount of cash dividends paid during a period per share of common stock.

Double declining balance depreciation An accelerated depreciation method that involves depreciating the asset at double the straight-line rate. This rate is multiplied by the book value of the asset at the beginning of the period (a declining balance) to calculate depreciation expense.

Double taxation system Corporate earnings are taxed twice when paid out as dividends. First, corporate earnings are taxed regardless of whether they will be distributed as dividends or retained at the G-13 corporate level, and second, dividends are taxed again at the individual shareholder level.

Double-entry accounting The accounting system of recording transactions in which every recorded transaction affects at least two accounts so as to keep the basic accounting equation (assets = liabilities + owners' equity) in balance.

Down transition probability The probability that an asset's value moves down in a model of asset price dynamics.

Downstream A transaction between two affiliates, an investor company and an associate company such that the investor company records a profit on its income statement. An example is a sale of inventory by the investor company to the associate.

Drag on liquidity When receipts lag, creating pressure from the decreased available funds.

Due diligence Investigation and analysis in support of a recommendation; the failure to exercise due diligence may sometimes result in liability according to various securities laws.

Dummy variable A type of qualitative variable that takes on a value of 1 if a particular condition is true and 0 if that condition is false.

Dumping The sale by a foreign firm of exports at a lower price than the cost of production.

DuPont analysis An approach to decomposing return on investment, e.g., return on equity, as the product of other financial ratios.

Duration A measure of an option-free bond's average maturity. Specifically, the weighted average maturity of all future cash flows paid by a security, in which the weights are the present value of these cash flows as a fraction of the bond's price. A measure of a bond's price sensitivity to interest rate movements.

Dutch Book theorem A result in probability theory stating that inconsistent probabilities create profit opportunities.

Dynamic hedging A strategy in which a position is hedged by making frequent adjustments to the quantity of the instrument used for hedging in relation to the instrument being hedged.

Earnings at risk (EAR) A variation of VAR that reflects the risk of a company's earnings instead of its market value.

Earnings expectation management Attempts by management to encourage analysts to forecast a slightly lower number for expected earnings than the analysts would otherwise forecast.

Earnings game Management's focus on reporting earnings that meet consensus estimates.

Earnings management activity Deliberate activity aimed at influencing reporting earnings numbers, often with the goal of placing management in a favorable light; the opportunistic use of accruals to manage earnings.

Earnings per share The amount of income earned during a period per share of common stock.

Earnings yield Earnings per share divided by price; the reciprocal of the P/E ratio.

Economic exposure The risk associated with changes in the relative attractiveness of products and services offered for sale, arising out of the competitive effects of changes in exchange rates.

Economic growth The expansion of production possibilities that results from capital accumulation and technological change.

Economic growth rate The annual percentage change in real GDP.

Economic order quantity–reorder point An approach to managing inventory based on expected demand and the predictability of demand; the ordering point for new inventory is determined based on the costs of ordering and carrying inventory, such that the total cost associated with inventory is minimized.

Economic profit See *Residual income.*

Economic sectors Large industry groupings.

Economic value added (EVA®) A commercial implementation of the residual income concept; the computation of EVA® is the net operating profit after taxes minus the cost of capital, where these inputs are adjusted for a number of items.

Economies of scale In reference to mergers, it is the savings achieved through the consolidation of operations and elimination of duplicate resources.

Effective annual rate The amount by which a unit of currency will grow in a year with interest on interest included.

Effective annual yield (EAY) An annualized return that accounts for the effect of interest on interest; EAY is computed by compounding 1 plus the holding period yield forward to one year, then subtracting 1.

Efficiency In statistics, a desirable property of estimators; an efficient estimator is the unbiased estimator with the smallest variance among unbiased estimators of the same parameter.

Efficient frontier The portion of the minimum-variance frontier beginning with the global minimum-variance portfolio and continuing above it; the graph of the set of portfolios offering the maximum expected return for their level of variance of return.

Efficient portfolio A portfolio offering the highest expected return for a given level of risk as measured by variance or standard deviation of return.

Elasticity A measure of sensitivity; the incremental change in one variable with respect to an incremental change in another variable.

Electronic funds transfer The use of computer networks to conduct financial transactions electronically.

Empirical probability The probability of an event estimated as a relative frequency of occurrence.

Enhanced derivatives products companies (EDPC) A type of subsidiary engaged in derivatives transactions that is separated from the parent company in order to have a higher credit rating than the parent company.

Enterprise risk management A form of *centralized risk management* that typically encompasses the management of a broad variety of risks, including insurance risk.

Enterprise value (EV) Total company value (the market value of debt, common equity, and preferred equity) minus the value of cash and investments.

Enterprise value multiple A valuation multiple that relates the total market value of all sources of a company's capital (net of cash) to a measure of fundamental value for the entire company (such as a pre-interest earnings measure).

Entry price The price paid to buy an asset.

Equilibrium The condition in which supply equals demand.

Equitizing cash A strategy used to replicate an index. It is also used to take a given amount of cash and turn it into an equity position while maintaining the liquidity provided by the cash.

Equity Assets less liabilities; the residual interest in the assets after subtracting the liabilities.

Equity carve-out A form of restructuring that involves the creation of a new legal entity and the sale of equity in it to outsiders.

Equity charge The estimated cost of equity capital in money terms.

Equity dividend rate Income rate that reflects the relationship between equity income and equity capital.

Equity forward A contract calling for the purchase of an individual stock, a stock portfolio, or a stock index at a later date at an agreed-upon price.

Equity method A basis for reporting investment income in which the investing entity recognizes a share of income as earned rather than as dividends when received. These transactions are typically reflected in Investments in Associates or Equity Method Investments.

Equity options Options on individual stocks; also known as stock options.

Equity risk premium The expected return on equities minus the risk-free rate; the premium that investors demand for investing in equities.

Equity swap A swap transaction in which at least one cash flow is tied to the return to an equity portfolio position, often an equity index.

Error autocorrelation The autocorrelation of the error term.

Error term The portion of the dependent variable that is not explained by the independent variable(s) in the regression.

Estimate The particular value calculated from sample observations using an estimator.

Estimated (or **fitted) parameters** With reference to regression analysis, the estimated values of the population intercept and population slope coefficient(s) in a regression.

Estimation With reference to statistical inference, the subdivision dealing with estimating the value of a population parameter.

Estimator An estimation formula; the formula used to compute the sample mean and other sample statistics are examples of estimators.

Eurodollar A dollar deposited outside the United States.

European-style option or **European option** An option contract that can only be exercised on its expiration date.

Event Any outcome or specified set of outcomes of a random variable.

Excess kurtosis Degree of peakedness (fatness of tails) in excess of the peakedness of the normal distribution.

Exchange for physicals (EFP) A permissible delivery procedure used by futures market participants, in which the long and short arrange a delivery procedure other than the normal procedures stipulated by the futures exchange.

Exchange rate The value of the U.S. dollar in terms of other currencies in the foreign exchange market.

Exchange ratio The number of shares that target stockholders are to receive in exchange for each of their shares in the target company.

Ex-dividend Trading ex-dividend refers to shares that no longer carry the right to the next dividend payment.

Ex-dividend date The first date that a share trades without (i.e., "ex") the dividend.

Ex-dividend price The price at which a share first trades without (i.e., "ex") the right to receive an upcoming dividend.

Exercise or **exercising the option** The process of using an option to buy or sell the underlying.

Exercise date The day that employees actually exercise the options and convert them to stock.

Exercise price (strike price, striking price, or **strike)** The fixed price at which an option holder can buy or sell the underlying.

Exercise rate or **strike rate** The fixed rate at which the holder of an interest rate option can buy or sell the underlying.

Exhaustive Covering or containing all possible outcomes.

Exit price The price received to sell an asset or transfer a liability.

Expanded CAPM An adaptation of the CAPM that adds to the CAPM a premium for small size and company-specific risk.

Expectational arbitrage Investing on the basis of differential expectations.

Expected holding-period return The expected total return on an asset over a stated holding period; for stocks, the sum of the expected dividend yield and the expected price appreciation over the holding period.

Expected value The probability-weighted average of the possible outcomes of a random variable.

Expensed Taken as a deduction in arriving at net income.

Expenses Outflows of economic resources or increases in liabilities that result in decreases in equity (other than decreases because of distributions to owners); reductions in net assets associated with the creation of revenues.

Expiration date The date on which a derivative contract expires.

Exports The goods and services that we sell to people in other countries.

Exposure to foreign exchange risk The risk of a change in value of an asset or liability denominated in a foreign currency due to a change in exchange rates.

External growth Company growth in output or sales that is achieved by buying the necessary resources externally (i.e., achieved through mergers and acquisitions).

Externality The effect of an investment on other things besides the investment itself.

Face value (also **principal, par value, stated value,** or **maturity value)** The amount of cash payable by a company to the bondholders when the bonds mature; the promised payment at maturity separate from any coupon payment.

Factor A common or underlying element with which several variables are correlated.

Factor risk premium (or **factor price)** The expected return in excess of the risk-free rate for a portfolio with a sensitivity of 1 to one factor and a sensitivity of 0 to all other factors.

Factor sensitivity (also **factor betas** or **factor loadings)** An asset's sensitivity to a particular factor; a measure of the response of return to each unit of increase in a factor, holding all other factors constant.

Fair market value The market price of an asset or liability that trades regularly.

Fair value The amount at which an asset (or liability) could be bought (or incurred) or sold (or settled) in a current transaction between willing parties, that is, other than in a forced or liquidation sale; the price that would be received to sell an asset or paid to transfer a liability in an orderly transaction between market participants at the measurement date.

Fiduciary call A combination of a European call and a risk-free bond that matures on the option expiration day and has a face value equal to the exercise price of the call.

Finance lease (capital lease) Essentially, the purchase of some asset by the buyer (lessee) that is directly financed by the seller (lessor).

Financial analysis The process of selecting, evaluating, and interpreting financial data in order to formulate an assessment of a company's present and future financial condition and performance.

Financial distress Heightened uncertainty regarding a company's ability to meet its various obligations because of lower or negative earnings.

Financial flexibility The ability to react and adapt to financial adversities and opportunities.

Financial futures Futures contracts in which the underlying is a stock, bond, or currency.

Financial leverage The extent to which a company can effect, through the use of debt, a proportional change in the return on common equity that is greater than a given proportional change in operating income; also, short for the financial leverage ratio.

Financial leverage ratio A measure of financial leverage calculated as average total assets divided by average total equity.

Financial reporting quality The accuracy with which a company's reported financials reflect its operating performance and their usefulness for forecasting future cash flows.

Financial risk The risk that environmental, social, or governance risk factors will result in significant costs or other losses to a company and its shareholders; the risk arising from a company's obligation to meet required payments under its financing agreements.

Financial transaction A purchase involving a buyer having essentially no material synergies with the target (e.g., the purchase of a private company by a company in an unrelated industry or by a private equity firm would typically be a financial transaction).

Financing activities Activities related to obtaining or repaying capital to be used in the business (e.g., equity and long-term debt).

First-differencing A transformation that subtracts the value of the time series in period $t - 1$ from its value in period t.

First-in, first-out (FIFO) The first in, first out, method of accounting for inventory, which matches sales against the costs of items of inventory in the order in which they were placed in inventory.

First-order serial correlation Correlation between adjacent observations in a time series.

Fixed asset turnover An activity ratio calculated as total revenue divided by average net fixed assets.

Fixed charge coverage A solvency ratio measuring the number of times interest and lease payments are covered by operating income, calculated as (EBIT + lease payments) divided by (interest payments + lease payments).

Fixed costs Costs that remain at the same level regardless of a company's level of production and sales.

Fixed exchange rate An exchange rate pegged at a value decided by the government or central bank and that blocks the unregulated forces of demand and supply by direct intervention in the foreign exchange market.

Fixed-income forward A forward contract in which the underlying is a bond.

Fixed-rate perpetual preferred stock Nonconvertible, noncallable preferred stock with a specified dividend rate that has a claim on earnings senior to the claim of common stock, and no maturity date.

Flexible exchange rate An exchange rate is determined by demand and supply with no direct intervention in the foreign exchange market by the central bank.

Flip-in pill A poison pill takeover defense that dilutes an acquirer's ownership in a target by giving other existing target company shareholders the right to buy additional target company shares at a discount.

Flip-over pill A poison pill takeover defense that gives target company shareholders the right to purchase shares of the acquirer at a significant discount to the market price, which has the effect of causing dilution to all existing acquiring company shareholders.

Float In the context of customer receipts, the amount of money that is in transit between payments made by customers and the funds that are usable by the company.

Float factor An estimate of the average number of days it takes deposited checks to clear; average daily float divided by average daily deposit.

Floating-rate loan A loan in which the interest rate is reset at least once after the starting date.

Floor A combination of interest rate put options designed to hedge a lender against lower rates on a floating-rate loan.

Floor traders or **locals** Market makers that buy and sell by quoting a bid and an ask price. They are the primary providers of liquidity to the market.

Floored swap A swap in which the floating payments have a lower limit.

Floorlet Each component put option in a floor.

Flotation cost Fees charged to companies by investment bankers and other costs associated with raising new capital.

Focus The competitive strategy of seeking a competitive advantage within a target segment or segments of the industry, either on the basis of cost leadership (**cost focus**) or differentiation (**differentiation focus**).

Foreign currency The money of other countries regardless of whether that money is in the form of notes, coins, or bank deposits.

Foreign currency transactions Transactions that are denominated in a currency other than a company's functional currency.

Foreign exchange market The market in which the currency of one country is exchanged for the currency of another.

Forward contract An agreement between two parties in which one party, the buyer, agrees to buy from the other party, the seller, an underlying asset at a later date for a price established at the start of the contract.

Forward dividend yield A dividend yield based on the anticipated dividend during the next 12 months.

Forward integration A merger involving the purchase of a target that is farther along the value or production chain; for example, to acquire a distributor.

Forward P/E (also **leading P/E** or **prospective P/E**) A P/E calculated on the basis of a forecast of EPS; a stock's current price divided by next year's expected earnings.

Forward price or **forward rate** The fixed price or rate at which the transaction scheduled to occur at the expiration of a forward contract will take place. This price is agreed on at the initiation date of the contract.

Forward rate agreement (FRA) A forward contract calling for one party to make a fixed interest payment and the other to make an interest payment at a rate to be determined at the contract expiration.

Forward swap A forward contract to enter into a swap.

Franking credit A tax credit received by shareholders for the taxes that a corporation paid on its distributed earnings.

Free cash flow The actual cash that would be available to the company's investors after making all investments necessary to maintain the company as an ongoing enterprise (also referred to as free cash flow to the firm); the internally generated funds that can be distributed to the company's investors (e.g., shareholders and bondholders) without impairing the value of the company.

Free cash flow hypothesis The hypothesis that higher debt levels discipline managers by forcing them to make fixed debt service payments and by reducing the company's free cash flow.

Free cash flow method Income approach that values an asset based on estimates of future cash flows discounted to present value by using a discount rate reflective of the risks associated with the cash flows.

Free cash flow to equity The cash flow available to a company's common shareholders after all operating expenses, interest, and principal payments have been made, and necessary investments in working and fixed capital have been made.

Free cash flow to equity model A model of stock valuation that views a stock's intrinsic value as the present value of expected future free cash flows to equity.

Free cash flow to the firm The cash flow available to the company's suppliers of capital after all operating expenses (including taxes) have been paid and necessary investments in working and fixed capital have been made.

Free cash flow to the firm model A model of stock valuation that views the value of a firm as the present value of expected future free cash flows to the firm.

Frequency distribution A tabular display of data summarized into a relatively small number of intervals.

Frequency polygon A graph of a frequency distribution obtained by drawing straight lines joining successive points representing the class frequencies.

Friendly transaction A potential business combination that is endorsed by the managers of both companies.

Full price The price of a security with accrued interest.

Functional currency The currency of the primary economic environment in which an entity operates.

Fundamental beta A beta that is based at least in part on fundamental data for a company.

Fundamental factor models A multifactor model in which the factors are attributes of stocks or companies that are important in explaining cross-sectional differences in stock prices.

Fundamentals Economic characteristics of a business such as profitability, financial strength, and risk.

Future value (FV) The amount to which a payment or series of payments will grow by a stated future date.

Futures commission merchants (FCMs) Individuals or companies that execute futures transactions for other parties off the exchange.

Futures contract A variation of a forward contract that has essentially the same basic definition but with some additional features, such as a clearinghouse guarantee against credit losses, a daily settlement of gains and losses, and an organized electronic or floor trading facility.

Futures exchange A legal corporate entity whose shareholders are its members. The members of the exchange have the privilege of executing transactions directly on the exchange.

Gains Asset inflows not directly related to the ordinary activities of the business.

Gamma A numerical measure of how sensitive an option's delta is to a change in the underlying.

General Agreement on Tariffs and Trade An international agreement signed in 1947 to reduce tariffs on international trade.

Generalized least squares A regression estimation technique that addresses heteroskedasticity of the error term.

Geometric mean A measure of central tendency computed by taking the nth root of the product of n non-negative values.

Giro system An electronic payment system used widely in Europe and Japan.

Going-concern assumption The assumption that the business will maintain its business activities into the foreseeable future.

Going-concern value A business's value under a going-concern assumption.

Goodwill An intangible asset that represents the excess of the purchase price of an acquired company over the value of the net assets acquired.

Government sector surplus or **deficit** An amount equal to net taxes minus government expenditure on goods and services.

Grant date The day that options are granted to employees; usually the date that compensation expense is measured if both the number of shares and option price are known.

Greenmail The purchase of the accumulated shares of a hostile investor by a company that is targeted for takeover by that investor, usually at a substantial premium over market price.

Gross domestic product A money measure of the goods and services produced within a country's borders over a stated time period.

Gross income multiplier (GIM) A ratio derived from the market; sales price divided by annual gross income equals GIM.

Gross profit (gross margin) Sales minus the cost of sales (i.e., the cost of goods sold for a manufacturing company).

Gross profit margin The ratio of gross profit to revenues.

Grouping by function With reference to the presentation of expenses in an income statement, the grouping together of expenses serving the same function, e.g., all items that are costs of good sold.

Grouping by nature With reference to the presentation of expenses in an income statement, the grouping together of expenses by similar nature, e.g., all depreciation expenses.

Growth accounting A tool that calculates the contribution to real GDP growth of each of its sources.

Growth investors With reference to equity investors, investors who seek to invest in high-earnings-growth companies.

Growth option or **expansion option** The ability to make additional investments in a project at some future time if the financial results are strong.

Growth phase A stage of growth in which a company typically enjoys rapidly expanding markets, high profit margins, and an abnormally high growth rate in earnings per share.

Guideline public companies Public-company comparables for the company being valued.

Guideline public company method A variation of the market approach; establishes a value estimate based on the observed multiples from trading activity in the shares of public companies viewed as reasonably comparable to the subject private company.

Guideline transactions method A variation of the market approach; establishes a value estimate based on pricing multiples derived from the acquisition of control of entire public or private companies that were acquired.

Harmonic mean A type of weighted mean computed by averaging the reciprocals of the observations, then taking the reciprocal of that average.

Hedge ratio The relationship of the quantity of an asset being hedged to the quantity of the derivative used for hedging.

Hedging A general strategy usually thought of as reducing, if not eliminating, risk.

Held-for-trading securities (trading securities) Debt or equity financial assets bought with the intention to sell them in the near term, usually less than three months; securities that a company intends to trade.

Held-to-maturity investments Debt (fixed-income) securities that a company intends to hold to maturity; these are presented at their original cost, updated for any amortization of discounts or premiums.

Herfindahl–Hirschman Index A measure of market concentration that is calculated by summing the squared market shares for competing companies in an industry; high HHI readings or mergers that would result in large HHI increases are more likely to result in regulatory challenges.

Heteroskedastic With reference to the error term of a regression, having a variance that differs across observations.

Heteroskedasticity The property of having a nonconstant variance; refers to an error term with the property that its variance differs across observations.

Heteroskedasticity-consistent standard errors Standard errors of the estimated parameters of a regression that correct for the presence of heteroskedasticity in the regression's error term.

Histogram A bar chart of data that have been grouped into a frequency distribution.

Historical cost In reference to assets, the amount paid to purchase an asset, including any costs of acquisition and/or preparation; with reference to liabilities, the amount of proceeds received in exchange in issuing the liability.

Historical equity risk premium approach An estimate of a country's equity risk premium that is based upon the historical averages of the risk-free rate and the rate of return on the market portfolio.

Historical exchange rates For accounting purposes, the exchange rates that existed when the assets and liabilities were initially recorded.

Historical method A method of estimating VAR that uses data from the returns of the portfolio over a recent past period and compiles this data in the form of a histogram.

Historical simulation (or **back simulation)** Another term for the historical method of estimating VAR. This term is somewhat misleading in that the method involves not a *simulation* of the past but rather what *actually happened* in the past, sometimes adjusted to reflect the fact that a different portfolio may have existed in the past than is planned for the future.

Holder-of-record date The date that a shareholder listed on the corporation's books will be deemed to have ownership of the shares for purposes of receiving an upcoming dividend; two business days after the ex-dividend date.

Holding period return The return that an investor earns during a specified holding period; a synonym for total return.

Holding period yield (HPY) The return that an investor earns during a specified holding period; holding period return with reference to a fixed-income instrument.

Homogenization Creating a contract with standard and generally accepted terms, which makes it more acceptable to a broader group of participants.

Homoskedasticity The property of having a constant variance; refers to an error term that is constant across observations.

Horizontal analysis Common-size analysis that involves comparing a specific financial statement with that statement in prior or future time periods; also, cross-sectional analysis of one company with another.

Horizontal common-size analysis A form of common-size analysis in which the accounts in a given period are used as the benchmark or base period, and every account is restated in subsequent periods as a percentage of the base period's same account.

Horizontal merger A merger involving companies in the same line of business, usually as competitors.

Hostile transaction An attempt to acquire a company against the wishes of the target's managers.

Human capital The value of skills and knowledge possessed by the workforce.

Hurdle rate The rate of return that must be met for a project to be accepted.

Hypothesis With reference to statistical inference, a statement about one or more populations.

Hypothesis testing With reference to statistical inference, the subdivision dealing with the testing of hypotheses about one or more populations.

Identifiable intangible An intangible that can be acquired singly and is typically linked to specific rights or privileges having finite benefit periods (e.g., a patent or trademark).

If-converted method A method for accounting for the effect of convertible securities on earnings per share (EPS) that specifies what EPS would have been if the convertible securities had been converted at the beginning of the period, taking account of the effects of conversion on net income and the weighted average number of shares outstanding.

Illiquidity discount See *Liquidity discount.*

Impairment Diminishment in value as a result of carrying (book) value exceeding fair value and/or recoverable value.

Impairment of capital rule A legal restriction that dividends cannot exceed retained earnings.

Implied repo rate The rate of return from a cash-and-carry transaction implied by the futures price relative to the spot price.

Implied volatility The volatility that option traders use to price an option, implied by the price of the option and a particular option-pricing model.

Implied yield A measure of the yield on the underlying bond of a futures contract implied by pricing it as though the underlying will be delivered at the futures expiration.

Imports The goods and services that we buy from people in other countries.

Imputation In reference to corporate taxes, a system that imputes, or attributes, taxes at only one level of taxation. For countries using an imputation tax system, taxes on dividends are effectively levied only at the shareholder rate. Taxes are paid at the corporate level but they are *attributed* to the shareholder. Shareholders deduct from their tax bill their portion of taxes paid by the company.

Income Increases in economic benefits in the form of inflows or enhancements of assets, or decreases of liabilities that result in an increase in equity (other than increases resulting from contributions by owners).

Income approach Valuation approach that values an asset as the present discounted value of the income expected from it.

Income statement (statement of operations or **profit and loss statement)** A financial statement that provides information about a company's profitability over a stated period of time.

Income tax paid The actual amount paid for income taxes in the period; not a provision, but the actual cash outflow.

Income tax payable The income tax owed by the company on the basis of taxable income.

Income tax recoverable The income tax expected to be recovered, from the taxing authority, on the basis of taxable income. It is a recovery of previously remitted taxes or future taxes owed by the company.

Incremental cash flow The cash flow that is realized because of a decision; the changes or increments to cash flows resulting from a decision or action.

Indenture A written contract between a lender and borrower that specifies the terms of the loan, such as interest rate, interest payment schedule, maturity, etc.

Independent With reference to events, the property that the occurrence of one event does not affect the probability of another event occurring.

Independent and identically distributed (IID) With respect to random variables, the property of random variables that are independent of each other but follow the identical probability distribution.

Independent projects Independent projects are projects whose cash flows are independent of each other.

Independent variable A variable used to explain the dependent variable in a regression; a right-hand-side variable in a regression equation.

Index amortizing swap An interest rate swap in which the notional principal is indexed to the level of interest rates and declines with the level of interest rates according to a predefined schedule. This type of swap is frequently used to hedge securities that are prepaid as interest rates decline, such as mortgage-backed securities.

Index option An option in which the underlying is a stock index.

Indexing An investment strategy in which an investor constructs a portfolio to mirror the performance of a specified index.

Indirect format (indirect method) With reference to cash flow statements, a format for the presentation of the statement which, in the operating cash flow section, begins with net income then shows additions and subtractions to arrive at operating cash flow.

Industry structure An industry's underlying economic and technical characteristics.

Infant-industry argument The argument that it is necessary to protect a new industry to enable it to grow into a mature industry that can compete in world markets.

Inflation premium An extra return that compensates investors for expected inflation.

Information ratio (IR) Mean active return divided by active risk; or alpha divided by the standard deviation of diversifiable risk.

Initial margin requirement The margin requirement on the first day of a transaction as well as on any day in which additional margin funds must be deposited.

Initial public offering (IPO) The initial issuance of common stock registered for public trading by a formerly private corporation.

In-process research and development Research and development costs relating to projects that are not yet completed, such as have been incurred by a company that is being acquired.

In-sample forecast errors The residuals from a fitted time-series model within the sample period used to fit the model.

Instability in the minimum-variance frontier The characteristic of minimum-variance frontiers that they are sensitive to small changes in inputs.

Installment Said of a sale in which proceeds are to be paid in installments over an extended period of time.

Installment method (installment-sales method) With respect to revenue recognition, a method that specifies that the portion of the total profit of the sale that is recognized in each period is determined by the percentage of the total sales price for which the seller has received cash.

Intangible assets Assets lacking physical substance, such as patents and trademarks.

Interest coverage A solvency ratio calculated as EBIT divided by interest payments.

Interest rate A rate of return that reflects the relationship between differently dated cash flows; a discount rate.

Interest rate call An option in which the holder has the right to make a known interest payment and receive an unknown interest payment.

Interest rate cap or **cap** A series of call options on an interest rate, with each option expiring at the date on which the floating loan rate will be reset, and with each option having the same exercise rate. A cap in general can have an underlying other than an interest rate.

Interest rate collar A combination of a long cap and a short floor, or a short cap and a long floor. A collar in general can have an underlying other than an interest rate.

Interest rate floor or **floor** A series of put options on an interest rate, with each option expiring at the date on which the floating loan rate will be reset, and with each option having the same exercise rate. A floor in general can have an underlying other than the interest rate.

Interest rate forward See *Forward rate agreement.*

Interest rate option An option in which the underlying is an interest rate.

Interest rate parity A formula that expresses the equivalence or parity of spot and forward rates, after adjusting for differences in the interest rates.

Interest rate put An option in which the holder has the right to make an unknown interest payment and receive a known interest payment.

Interest rate swap A swap in which the underlying is an interest rate. Can be viewed as a currency swap in which both currencies are the same and can be created as a combination of currency swaps.

Intergenerational data mining A form of data mining that applies information developed by previous researchers using a dataset to guide current research using the same or a related dataset.

Internal rate of return (IRR) Rate of return that discounts future cash flows from an investment to the exact amount of the investment; the discount rate that makes the present value of an investment's costs (outflows) equal to the present value of the investment's benefits (inflows).

Interquartile range The difference between the third and first quartiles of a dataset.

Interval With reference to grouped data, a set of values within which an observation falls.

Interval scale A measurement scale that not only ranks data but also gives assurance that the differences between scale values are equal.

In-the-money Options that, if exercised, would result in the value received being worth more than the payment required to exercise.

Intrinsic value or **exercise value** The value of an asset given a hypothetically complete understanding of the asset's investment characteristics; the value obtained if an option is exercised based on current conditions.

Inventory The unsold units of product on hand.

Inventory blanket lien The use of inventory as collateral for a loan. Though the lender has claim to some or all of the company's inventory, the company may still sell or use the inventory in the ordinary course of business.

Inventory turnover An activity ratio calculated as cost of goods sold divided by average inventory.

Inverse floater A floating-rate note or bond in which the coupon is adjusted to move opposite to a benchmark interest rate.

Inverse price ratio The reciprocal of a price multiple, e.g., in the case of a P/E ratio, the "earnings yield" E/P (where P is share price and E is earnings per share).

Investing activities Activities which are associated with the acquisition and disposal of property, plant, and equipment; intangible assets; other long-term assets; and both long-term and short-term investments in the equity and debt (bonds and loans) issued by other companies.

Investment constraints Internal or external limitations on investments.

Investment objectives Desired investment outcomes; includes risk objectives and return objectives.

Investment opportunity schedule A graphical depiction of a company's investment opportunities ordered from highest to lowest expected return. A company's optimal capital budget is found where the investment opportunity schedule intersects with the company's marginal cost of capital.

Investment strategy An approach to investment analysis and security selection.

Investment value The value to a specific buyer, taking account of potential synergies based on the investor's requirements and expectations.

IRR rule An investment decision rule that accepts projects or investments for which the IRR is greater than the opportunity cost of capital.

Joint probability The probability of the joint occurrence of stated events.

Joint probability function A function giving the probability of joint occurrences of values of stated random variables.

Joint venture An entity (partnership, corporation, or other legal form) where control is shared by two or more entities called venturers.

Justified (fundamental) P/E The price-to-earnings ratio that is fair, warranted, or justified on the basis of forecasted fundamentals.

Justified price multiple (or **warranted price multiple** or **intrinsic price multiple)** The estimated fair value of the price multiple, usually based on forecasted fundamentals or comparables.

Just-in-time method Method of managing inventory that minimizes in-process inventory stocks.

***k*th order autocorrelation** The correlation between observations in a time series separated by *k* periods.

Kurtosis The statistical measure that indicates the peakedness of a distribution.

Labor productivity The quantity of real GDP produced by an hour of labor.

Lack of marketability discount An extra return to investors to compensate for lack of a public market or lack of marketability.

Laddering strategy A form of active strategy which entails scheduling maturities on a systematic basis within the investment portfolio such that investments are spread out equally over the term of the ladder.

Last-in, first-out (LIFO) The last in, first out, method of accounting for inventory, which matches sales against the costs of items of inventory in the reverse order the items were placed in inventory (i.e., inventory produced or acquired last are assumed to be sold first).

Law of one price The condition in a financial market in which two equivalent financial instruments or combinations of financial instruments can sell for only one price. Equivalent to the principle that no arbitrage opportunities are possible.

Leading dividend yield Forecasted dividends per share over the next year divided by current stock price.

Leading P/E (or **forward P/E** or **prospective P/E)** A stock's current price divided by the next year's expected earnings.

Legal risk The risk that failures by company managers to effectively manage a company's environmental, social, and governance risk exposures will lead to lawsuits and other judicial remedies, resulting in potentially catastrophic losses for the company; the risk that the legal system will not enforce a contract in case of dispute or fraud.

Legislative and regulatory risk The risk that governmental laws and regulations directly or indirectly affecting a company's operations will change with potentially severe adverse effects on the company's continued profitability and even its long-term sustainability.

Lemons problem The potential for asymmetric information to bring about a general decline in product quality in an industry.

Leptokurtic Describes a distribution that is more peaked than a normal distribution.

Lessee The party obtaining the use of an asset through a lease.

Lessor The owner of an asset that grants the right to use the asset to another party.

Level of significance The probability of a Type I error in testing a hypothesis.

Leverage In the context of corporate finance, leverage refers to the use of fixed costs within a company's cost structure. Fixed costs that are operating costs (such as depreciation or rent) create operating leverage. Fixed costs that are financial costs (such as interest expense) create financial leverage.

Leveraged buyout (LBO) A transaction whereby the target company management team converts the target to a privately held company by using heavy borrowing to finance the purchase of the target company's outstanding shares.

Leveraged floating-rate note or **leveraged floater** A floating-rate note or bond in which the coupon is adjusted at a multiple of a benchmark interest rate.

Leveraged recapitalization A post-offer takeover defense mechanism that involves the assumption of a large amount of debt that is then used to finance share repurchases; the effect is to dramatically change the company's capital structure while attempting to deliver a value to target shareholders in excess of a hostile bid.

Liabilities Present obligations of an enterprise arising from past events, the settlement of which is expected to result in an outflow of resources embodying economic benefits; creditors' claims on the resources of a company.

LIFO layer liquidation (LIFO liquidation) With respect to the application of the LIFO inventory method, the liquidation of old, relatively low-priced inventory; happens when the volume of sales rises above the volume of recent purchases so that some sales are made from relatively old, low-priced inventory.

LIFO reserve The difference between inventory reported as FIFO and inventory reported as LIFO (FIFO inventory value less LIFO inventory value).

Likelihood The probability of an observation, given a particular set of conditions.

Limit down A limit move in the futures market in which the price at which a transaction would be made is at or below the lower limit.

Limit move A condition in the futures markets in which the price at which a transaction would be made is at or beyond the price limits.

Limit up A limit move in the futures market in which the price at which a transaction would be made is at or above the upper limit.

Linear association A straight-line relationship, as opposed to a relationship that cannot be graphed as a straight line.

Linear interpolation The estimation of an unknown value on the basis of two known values that bracket it, using a straight line between the two known values.

Linear regression Regression that models the straight-line relationship between the dependent and independent variable(s).

Linear trend A trend in which the dependent variable changes at a constant rate with time.

Liquidation To sell the assets of a company, division, or subsidiary piecemeal, typically because of bankruptcy; the form of bankruptcy that allows for the orderly satisfaction of creditors' claims after which the company ceases to exist.

Liquidation value The value of a company if the company were dissolved and its assets sold individually.

Liquidity A company's ability to satisfy its short-term obligations using assets that are most readily converted into cash; the ability to trade a futures contract, either selling a previously purchased contract or purchasing a previously sold contract.

Liquidity discount A reduction or discount to value that reflects the lack of depth of trading or liquidity in that asset's market.

Liquidity premium An extra return that compensates investors for the risk of loss relative to an investment's fair value if the investment needs to be converted to cash quickly.

Liquidity ratios Financial ratios measuring the company's ability to meet its short-term obligations.

Liquidity risk The risk that a financial instrument cannot be purchased or sold without a significant concession in price due to the size of the market.

Local currency The currency of the country where a company is located.

Lockbox system A payment system in which customer payments are mailed to a post office box and the banking institution retrieves and deposits these payments several times a day, enabling the company to have use of the fund sooner than in a centralized system in which customer payments are sent to the company.

Locked limit A condition in the futures markets in which a transaction cannot take place because the price would be beyond the limits.

Logit model A qualitative-dependent-variable multiple regression model based on the logistic probability distribution.

Log-linear model With reference to time-series models, a model in which the growth rate of the time series as a function of time is constant.

Log-log regression model A regression that expresses the dependent and independent variables as natural logarithms.

London Interbank Offer Rate (LIBOR) The Eurodollar rate at which London banks lend dollars to other London banks; considered to be the best representative rate on a dollar borrowed by a private, high-quality borrower.

Long The buyer of a derivative contract. Also refers to the position of owning a derivative.

Longitudinal data Observations on characteristic(s) of the same observational unit through time.

Long-lived assets (or **long-term assets**) Assets that are expected to provide economic benefits over a future period of time, typically greater than one year.

Long-term contract A contract that spans a number of accounting periods.

Long-term debt-to-assets ratio The proportion of a company's assets that is financed with long-term debt.

Long-term equity anticipatory securities (LEAPS) Options originally created with expirations of several years.

Long-term liability An obligation that is expected to be settled, with the outflow of resources embodying economic benefits, over a future period generally greater than one year.

Look-ahead bias A bias caused by using information that was not available on the test date.

Losses Asset outflows not directly related to the ordinary activities of the business.

Lower bound The lowest possible value of an option.

Macaulay duration The duration without dividing by 1 plus the bond's yield to maturity. The term, named for one of the economists who first derived it, is used to distinguish the calculation from modified duration. (See also *modified duration.*)

Macroeconomic factor A factor related to the economy, such as the inflation rate, industrial production, or economic sector membership.

Macroeconomic factor model A multifactor model in which the factors are surprises in macroeconomic variables that significantly explain equity returns.

Maintenance margin requirement The margin requirement on any day other than the first day of a transaction.

Management buyout (MBO) A corporate transaction in which management repurchases all outstanding common stock, usually using the proceeds of debt issuance.

Managerialism theories Theories that posit that corporate executives are motivated to engage in mergers to maximize the size of their company rather than shareholder value.

Manufacturing resource planning (MRP) The incorporation of production planning into inventory management. A MRP analysis provides both a materials acquisition schedule and a production schedule.

Margin The amount of money that a trader deposits in a margin account. The term is derived from the stock market practice in which an investor borrows a portion of the money required to purchase a certain amount of stock. In futures markets, there is no borrowing so the margin is more of a down payment or performance bond.

Marginal investor An investor in a given share who is very likely to be part of the next trade in the share and who is therefore important in setting price.

Market approach Valuation approach that values an asset based on pricing multiples from sales of assets viewed as similar to the subject asset.

Market efficiency A finance perspective on capital markets that deals with the relationship of price to intrinsic value. The **traditional efficient markets formulation** asserts that an asset's price is the best available estimate of its intrinsic value. The **rational efficient markets formulation** asserts that investors should expect to be rewarded for the costs of information gathering and analysis by higher gross returns.

Market-extraction method Method used to estimate the overall capitalization rate by dividing the sale price of a comparable income property into the net operating income.

Market price of risk The slope of the capital market line, indicating the market risk premium for each unit of market risk.

Market rate The rate demanded by purchasers of bonds, given the risks associated with future cash payment obligations of the particular bond issue.

Market risk The risk associated with interest rates, exchange rates, and equity prices.

Market risk premium The expected excess return on the market over the risk-free rate.

Market share test The percentage of a market that a particular firm supplies; used as the primary measure of monopoly power.

Market timing Asset allocation in which the investment in the market is increased if one forecasts that the market will outperform T-bills.

Market value of invested capital The market value of debt and equity.

Marketability discount A reduction or discount to value for shares that are not publicly traded.

Market-oriented investors With reference to equity investors, investors whose investment disciplines cannot be clearly categorized as value or growth.

Marking to market A procedure used primarily in futures markets in which the parties to a contract settle the amount owed daily. Also known as the *daily settlement.*

Markowitz decision rule A decision rule for choosing between two investments based on their means and variances.

Mark-to-market The revaluation of a financial asset or liability to its current market value or fair value.

Matching principle The accounting principle that expenses should be recognized when the associated revenue is recognized.

Matching strategy An active investment strategy that includes intentional matching of the timing of cash outflows with investment maturities.

Materiality The condition of being of sufficient importance so that omission or misstatement of the item in a financial report could make a difference to users' decisions.

Matrix pricing In the fixed income markets, to price a security on the basis of valuation-relevant characteristics (e.g., debt-rating approach).

Mature growth rate The earnings growth rate in a company's mature phase; an earnings growth rate that can be sustained long term.

Mature phase A stage of growth in which the company reaches an equilibrium in which investment opportunities on average just earn their opportunity cost of capital.

Maturity premium An extra return that compensates investors for the increased sensitivity of the market value of debt to a change in market interest rates as maturity is extended.

Mean The sum of all values in a distribution or dataset, divided by the number of values summed; a synonym of arithmetic mean.

Mean absolute deviation With reference to a sample, the mean of the absolute values of deviations from the sample mean.

Mean excess return The average rate of return in excess of the risk-free rate.

Mean reversion The tendency of a time series to fall when its level is above its mean and rise when its level is below its mean; a mean-reverting time series tends to return to its long-term mean.

Mean–variance analysis An approach to portfolio analysis using expected means, variances, and covariances of asset returns.

Measure of central tendency A quantitative measure that specifies where data are centered.

Measure of location A quantitative measure that describes the location or distribution of data; includes not only measures of central tendency but also other measures such as percentiles.

Measurement scales A scheme of measuring differences. The four types of measurement scales are nominal, ordinal, interval, and ratio.

Median The value of the middle item of a set of items that has been sorted into ascending or descending order; the 50th percentile.

Merger The absorption of one company by another; two companies become one entity and one or both of the pre-merger companies ceases to exist as a separate entity.

Mesokurtic Describes a distribution with kurtosis identical to that of the normal distribution.

Method based on forecasted fundamentals An approach to using price multiples that relates a price multiple to forecasts of fundamentals through a discounted cash flow model.

Method of comparables An approach to valuation that involves using a price multiple to evaluate whether an asset is relatively fairly valued, relatively undervalued, or relatively overvalued when compared to a benchmark value of the multiple.

Minimum-variance frontier The graph of the set of portfolios that have minimum variance for their level of expected return.

Minimum-variance portfolio The portfolio with the minimum variance for each given level of expected return.

Minority active investments Investments in which investors exert significant influence, but not control, over the investee. Typically, the investor has 20 to 50% ownership in the investee.

Minority interest (noncontrolling interest) The proportion of the ownership of a subsidiary not held by the parent (controlling) company.

Minority passive investments (passive investments) Investments in which the investor has no significant influence or control over the operations of the investee.

Mismatching strategy An active investment strategy whereby the timing of cash outflows is not matched with investment maturities.

Mispricing Any departure of the market price of an asset from the asset's estimated intrinsic value.

Mixed factor models Factor models that combine features of more than one type of factor model.

Mixed offering A merger or acquisition that is to be paid for with cash, securities, or some combination of the two.

Modal interval With reference to grouped data, the most frequently occurring interval.

Mode The most frequently occurring value in a set of observations.

Model risk The use of an inaccurate pricing model for a particular investment, or the improper use of the right model.

Model specification With reference to regression, the set of variables included in the regression and the regression equation's functional form.

Modified duration A measure of a bond's price sensitivity to interest rate movements. Equal to the Macaulay duration of a bond divided by one plus its yield to maturity.

Molodovsky effect The observation that P/Es tend to be high on depressed EPS at the bottom of a business cycle, and tend to be low on unusually high EPS at the top of a business cycle.

Momentum indicators Valuation indicators that relate either price or a fundamental (such as earnings) to the time series of their own past values (or in some cases to their expected value).

Monetary assets and liabilities Assets and liabilities with value equal to the amount of currency contracted for, a fixed amount of currency. Examples are cash, accounts receivable, mortgages receivable, accounts payable, bonds payable, and mortgages payable. Inventory is not a monetary asset. Most liabilities are monetary.

Monetary/nonmonetary method Approach to translating foreign currency financial statements for consolidation in which monetary assets and liabilities are translated at the current exchange rate. Nonmonetary assets and liabilities are translated at historical exchange rates (the exchange rates that existed when the assets and liabilities were acquired).

Money market The market for short-term debt instruments (one-year maturity or less).

Money market yield (or **CD equivalent yield**) A yield on a basis comparable to the quoted yield on an interest-bearing money market instrument that pays interest on a 360-day basis; the annualized holding period yield, assuming a 360-day year.

Moneyness The relationship between the price of the underlying and an option's exercise price.

Money-weighted rate of return The internal rate of return on a portfolio, taking account of all cash flows.

Monitoring costs Costs borne by owners to monitor the management of the company (e.g., board of director expenses).

Monopolization The possession of monopoly power in the relevant market and the willful acquisition or maintenance of that power, as distinguished from growth or development as a consequence of a superior product, business acumen, or historical accident.

Monte Carlo simulation method An approach to estimating a probability distribution of outcomes to examine what might happen if particular risks are faced. This method is widely used in the sciences as well as in business to study a variety of problems.

Multicollinearity A regression assumption violation that occurs when two or more independent variables (or combinations of independent variables) are highly but not perfectly correlated with each other.

Multiple linear regression Linear regression involving two or more independent variables.

Multiple linear regression model A linear regression model with two or more independent variables.

Multiple *R* The correlation between the actual and forecasted values of the dependent variable in a regression.

Multiplication rule for probabilities The rule that the joint probability of events A and B equals the probability of A given B times the probability of B.

Multi-step format With respect to the format of the income statement, a format that presents a subtotal for gross profit (revenue minus cost of goods sold).

Multivariate distribution A probability distribution that specifies the probabilities for a group of related random variables.

Multivariate normal distribution A probability distribution for a group of random variables that is completely defined by the means and variances of the variables plus all the correlations between pairs of the variables.

Mutually exclusive events Events such that only one can occur at a time.

Mutually exclusive projects Mutually exclusive projects compete directly with each other. For example, if Projects A and B are mutually exclusive, you can choose A or B, but you cannot choose both.

***n* Factorial** For a positive integer n, the product of the first n positive integers; 0 factorial equals 1 by definition. n factorial is written as $n!$.

Negative serial correlation Serial correlation in which a positive error for one observation increases the chance of a negative error for another observation, and vice versa.

Neoclassical growth theory A theory of economic growth that proposes that real GDP per person grows because technological change induces a level of saving and investment that makes capital per hour of labor grow.

Net asset balance sheet exposure When assets translated at the current exchange rate are greater in amount than liabilities translated at the current exchange rate. Assets exposed to translation gains or losses exceed the exposed liabilities.

Net book value The remaining (undepreciated) balance of an asset's purchase cost. For liabilities, the face value of a bond minus any unamortized discount, or plus any unamortized premium.

Net borrower A country that is borrowing more from the rest of the world than it is lending to it.

Net exports The value of exports of goods and services minus the value of imports of goods and services.

Net income (loss) The difference between revenue and expenses; what remains after subtracting all expenses (including depreciation, interest, and taxes) from revenue.

Net lender A country that is lending more to the rest of the world than it is borrowing from it.

Net liability balance sheet exposure When liabilities translated at the current exchange rate are greater than assets translated at the current exchange rate. Liabilities exposed to translation gains or losses exceed the exposed assets.

Net operating assets The difference between operating assets (total assets less cash) and operating liabilities (total liabilities less total debt).

Net operating cycle An estimate of the average time that elapses between paying suppliers for materials and collecting cash from the subsequent sale of goods produced.

Net operating profit less adjusted taxes, or **NOPLAT** A company's operating profit with adjustments to normalize the effects of capital structure.

Net present value (NPV) The present value of an investment's cash inflows (benefits) minus the present value of its cash outflows (costs).

Net profit margin (profit margin or **return on sales)** An indicator of profitability, calculated as net income divided by revenue; indicates how much of each dollar of revenues is left after all costs and expenses.

Net realisable value Estimated selling price in the ordinary course of business less the estimated costs necessary to make the sale.

Net revenue Revenue after adjustments (e.g., for estimated returns or for amounts unlikely to be collected).

Netting When parties agree to exchange only the net amount owed from one party to the other.

New growth theory A theory of economic growth based on the idea that real GDP per person grows because of the choices that people make in the pursuit of profit and that growth can persist indefinitely.

Node Each value on a binomial tree from which successive moves or outcomes branch.

No-growth company A company without positive expected net present value projects.

No-growth value per share The value per share of a no-growth company, equal to the expected level amount of earnings divided by the stock's required rate of return.

Nominal exchange rate The value of the U.S. dollar expressed in units of foreign currency per U.S. dollar.

Nominal rate A rate of interest based on the security's face value.

Nominal risk-free interest rate The sum of the real risk-free interest rate and the inflation premium.

Nominal scale A measurement scale that categorizes data but does not rank them.

Nonconventional cash flow In a nonconventional cash flow pattern, the initial outflow is not followed by inflows only, but the cash flows can flip from positive (inflows) to negative (outflows) again (or even change signs several times).

Noncurrent Not due to be consumed, converted into cash, or settled within one year after the balance sheet date.

Noncurrent assets Assets that are expected to benefit the company over an extended period of time (usually more than one year).

Nondeliverable forwards (NDFs) Cash-settled forward contracts, used predominately with respect to foreign exchange forwards.

Nonearning assets Cash and investments (specifically cash, cash equivalents, and short-term investments).

Nonlinear relation An association or relationship between variables that cannot be graphed as a straight line.

Nonmonetary assets and liabilities Assets and liabilities that are not monetary assets and liabilities. Nonmonetary assets include inventory, fixed assets, and intangibles, and nonmonetary liabilities include deferred revenue.

Nonparametric test A test that is not concerned with a parameter, or that makes minimal assumptions about the population from which a sample comes.

Nonstationarity With reference to a random variable, the property of having characteristics such as mean and variance that are not constant through time.

Nontariff barrier Any action other than a tariff that restricts international trade.

Normal backwardation The condition in futures markets in which futures prices are lower than expected spot prices.

Normal contango The condition in futures markets in which futures prices are higher than expected spot prices.

Normal distribution A continuous, symmetric probability distribution that is completely described by its mean and its variance.

Normalized earnings Earnings adjusted for nonrecurring, noneconomic, or other unusual items to eliminate anomalies and/or facilitate comparisons.

Normalized earnings per share (or **normal earnings per share)** The earnings per share that a business could achieve currently under mid-cyclical conditions.

Normalized P/E P/Es based on normalized EPS data.

North American Free Trade Agreement An agreement, which became effective on January 1, 1994, to eliminate all barriers to international trade between the United States, Canada, and Mexico after a 15-year phasing-in period.

Notes payable Amounts owed by a business to creditors as a result of borrowings that are evidenced by (short-term) loan agreements.

***n*-Period moving average** The average of the current and immediately prior $n - 1$ values of a time series.

NPV rule An investment decision rule that states that an investment should be undertaken if its NPV is positive but not undertaken if its NPV is negative.

NTM P/E Next twelve months P/E: current market price divided by an estimated next twelve months EPS.

Null hypothesis The hypothesis to be tested.

Number of days of inventory An activity ratio equal to the number of days in a period divided by the inventory ratio for the period; an indication of the number of days a company ties up funds in inventory.

Number of days of payables An activity ratio equal to the number of days in a period divided by the payables turnover ratio for the period; an estimate of the average number of days it takes a company to pay its suppliers.

Number of days of receivables Estimate of the average number of days it takes to collect on credit accounts.

Objective probabilities Probabilities that generally do not vary from person to person; includes a priori and objective probabilities.

Off-balance sheet financing Arrangements that do not result in additional liabilities on the balance sheet but nonetheless create economic obligations.

Official settlements account A record of the change in official reserves, which are the government's holdings of foreign currency.

Off-market FRA A contract in which the initial value is intentionally set at a value other than zero and therefore requires a cash payment at the start from one party to the other.

Offsetting A transaction in exchange-listed derivative markets in which a party re-enters the market to close out a position.

One third rule The rule that, on the average, with no change in technology, a 1 percent increase in capital per hour of labor brings a 1/3 percent increase in labor productivity.

One-sided hypothesis test (or **one-tailed hypothesis test**) A test in which the null hypothesis is rejected only if the evidence indicates that the population parameter is greater than (smaller than) θ_0. The alternative hypothesis also has one side.

Operating activities Activities that are part of the day-to-day business functioning of an entity, such as selling inventory and providing services.

Operating breakeven The number of units produced and sold at which the company's operating profit is zero (revenues = operating costs).

Operating cycle A measure of the time needed to convert raw materials into cash from a sale; it consists of the number of days of inventory and the number of days of receivables.

Operating lease An agreement allowing the lessee to use some asset for a period of time; essentially a rental.

Operating leverage The use of fixed costs in operations.

Operating profit (operating income) A company's profits on its usual business activities before deducting taxes.

Operating profit margin (operating margin) A profitability ratio calculated as operating income (i.e., income before interest and taxes) divided by revenue.

Operating return on assets (operating ROA) A profitability ratio calculated as operating income divided by average total assets.

Operating risk The risk attributed to the operating cost structure, in particular the use of fixed costs in operations; the risk arising from the mix of fixed and variable costs; the risk that a company's operations may be severely affected by environmental, social, and governance risk factors.

Operations risk or **operational risk** The risk of loss from failures in a company's systems and procedures (for example, due to computer failures or human failures) or events completely outside of the control of organizations (which would include "acts of God" and terrorist actions).

Opportunity cost The value that investors forgo by choosing a particular course of action; the value of something in its best alternative use.

Opportunity set The set of assets available for investment.

Optimal capital structure The capital structure at which the value of the company is maximized.

Optimizer A specialized computer program or a spreadsheet that solves for the portfolio weights that will result in the lowest risk for a specified level of expected return.

Option A financial instrument that gives one party the right, but not the obligation, to buy or sell an underlying asset from or to another party at a fixed price over a specific period of time. Also referred to as contingent claims.

Option price, option premium, or **premium** The amount of money a buyer pays and seller receives to engage in an option transaction.

Orderly liquidation value The estimated gross amount of money that could be realized from the liquidation sale of an asset or assets, given a reasonable amount of time to find a purchaser or purchasers.

Ordinal scale A measurement scale that sorts data into categories that are ordered (ranked) with respect to some characteristic.

Ordinary annuity An annuity with a first cash flow that is paid one period from the present.

Ordinary least squares (OLS) An estimation method based on the criterion of minimizing the sum of the squared residuals of a regression.

Ordinary shares (common stock or **common shares)** Equity shares that are subordinate to all other types of equity (e.g., preferred equity).

Organic growth Company growth in output or sales that is achieved by making investments internally (i.e., excludes growth achieved through mergers and acquisitions).

Orthogonal Uncorrelated; at a right angle.

Other comprehensive income Changes to equity that bypass (are not reported in) the income statement; the difference between comprehensive income and net income.

Other post-employment benefits Promises by the company to pay benefits in the future, other than pension benefits, such as life insurance premiums and all or part of health care insurance for its retirees.

Other receivables Amounts owed to the company from parties other than customers.

Outcome A possible value of a random variable.

Outliers Small numbers of observations at either extreme (small or large) of a sample.

Out-of-sample forecast errors The differences between actual and predicted value of time series outside the sample period used to fit the model.

Out-of-sample test A test of a strategy or model using a sample outside the time period on which the strategy or model was developed.

Out-of-the-money Options that, if exercised, would require the payment of more money than the value received and therefore would not be currently exercised.

Overall capitalization rate A ratio in property valuation; net operating income divided by sale price. Also known as the going-in rate.

Overnight index swap (OIS) A swap in which the floating rate is the cumulative value of a single unit of currency invested at an overnight rate during the settlement period.

Owners' equity The excess of assets over liabilities; the residual interest of shareholders in the assets of an entity after deducting the entity's liabilities.

Paired comparisons test A statistical test for differences based on paired observations drawn from samples that are dependent on each other.

Paired observations Observations that are dependent on each other.

Pairs arbitrage A trade in two closely related stocks that involves buying the relatively undervalued stock and selling short the relatively overvalued stock.

Pairs arbitrage trade A trade in two closely related stocks involving the short sale of one and the purchase of the other.

Pairs trading An approach to trading that uses pairs of closely related stocks, buying the relatively undervalued stock and selling short the relatively overvalued stock.

Panel data Observations through time on a single characteristic of multiple observational units.

Parameter A descriptive measure computed from or used to describe a population of data, conventionally represented by Greek letters.

Parameter instability The problem or issue of population regression parameters that have changed over time.

Parametric test Any test (or procedure) concerned with parameters or whose validity depends on assumptions concerning the population generating the sample.

Partial regression coefficients or **partial slope coefficients** The slope coefficients in a multiple regression.

Partnership A business owned and operated by more than one individual.

Passive portfolio A market index portfolio.

Passive strategy In reference to short-term cash management, it is an investment strategy characterized by simple decision rules for making daily investments.

Payables turnover An activity ratio calculated as purchases divided by average trade payables.

Payer swaption A swaption that allows the holder to enter into a swap as the fixed-rate payer and floating-rate receiver.

Payment date The day that the company actually mails out (or electronically transfers) a dividend payment.

Payment netting A means of settling payments in which the amount owed by the first party to the second is netted with the amount owed by the second party to the first; only the net difference is paid.

Payoff The value of an option at expiration.

Payout policy The principles by which a company distributes cash to common shareholders by means of cash dividends and/or share repurchases.

Payout ratio The percentage of total earnings paid out in dividends in any given year (in per-share terms, DPS/EPS).

Pecking order theory The theory that managers take into account how their actions might be interpreted by outsiders and thus order their preferences for various forms of corporate financing. Forms of financing that are least visible to outsiders (e.g., internally generated funds) are most preferable to managers and those that are most visible (e.g., equity) are least preferable.

PEG The P/E-to-growth ratio, calculated as the stock's P/E divided by the expected earnings growth rate.

PEG ratio The ratio of P/E-to-growth, calculated as the stock's P/E divided by the expected earnings growth rate in percent.

Per unit contribution margin The amount that each unit sold contributes to covering fixed costs—that is, the difference between the price per unit and the variable cost per unit.

Percentage-of-completion A method of revenue recognition in which, in each accounting period, the company estimates what percentage of the contract is complete and then reports that percentage of the total contract revenue in its income statement.

Percentiles Quantiles that divide a distribution into 100 equal parts.

Perfect capital markets Markets in which, by assumption, there are no taxes, transactions costs, or bankruptcy costs, and in which all investors have equal ("symmetric") information.

Perfect collinearity The existence of an exact linear relation between two or more independent variables or combinations of independent variables.

Performance appraisal The evaluation of risk-adjusted performance; the evaluation of investment skill.

Performance guarantee A guarantee from the clearinghouse that if one party makes money on a transaction, the clearinghouse ensures it will be paid.

Performance measurement The calculation of returns in a logical and consistent manner.

Period costs Costs (e.g., executives' salaries) that cannot be directly matched with the timing of revenues and which are thus expensed immediately.

Periodic inventory system An inventory accounting system in which inventory values and costs of sales are determined at the end of the accounting period.

Periodic rate The quoted interest rate per period; the stated annual interest rate divided by the number of compounding periods per year.

Permanent differences Differences between tax and financial reporting of revenue (expenses) that will not be reversed at some future date. These result in a difference between the company's effective tax rate and statutory tax rate and do not result in a deferred tax item.

Permutation An ordered listing.

Perpetual inventory system An inventory accounting system in which inventory values and costs of sales are continuously updated to reflect purchases and sales.

Perpetuity A perpetual annuity, or a set of never-ending level sequential cash flows, with the first cash flow occurring one period from now.

Pet projects Projects in which influential managers want the corporation to invest. Often, unfortunately, pet projects are selected without undergoing normal capital budgeting analysis.

Plain vanilla swap An interest rate swap in which one party pays a fixed rate and the other pays a floating rate, with both sets of payments in the same currency.

Platykurtic Describes a distribution that is less peaked than the normal distribution.

Point estimate A single numerical estimate of an unknown quantity, such as a population parameter.

Point of sale Systems that capture transaction data at the physical location in which the sale is made.

Poison pill A pre-offer takeover defense mechanism that makes it prohibitively costly for an acquirer to take control of a target without the prior approval of the target's board of directors.

Poison puts A pre-offer takeover defense mechanism that gives target company bondholders the right to sell their bonds back to the target at a pre-specified redemption price, typically at or above par value; this defense increases the need for cash and raises the cost of the acquisition.

Pooled estimate An estimate of a parameter that involves combining (pooling) observations from two or more samples.

Pooling of interests accounting method A method of accounting in which combined companies were portrayed as if they had always operated as a single economic entity. Called pooling of interests under U.S. GAAP and uniting of interests under IFRS. (No longer allowed under U.S. GAAP or IFRS.)

Population All members of a specified group.

Population mean The arithmetic mean value of a population; the arithmetic mean of all the observations or values in the population.

Population standard deviation A measure of dispersion relating to a population in the same unit of measurement as the observations, calculated as the positive square root of the population variance.

Population variance A measure of dispersion relating to a population, calculated as the mean of the squared deviations around the population mean.

Portfolio implementation problem The part of the execution step of the portfolio management process that involves the implementation of portfolio decisions by trading desks.

Portfolio performance attribution The analysis of portfolio performance in terms of the contributions from various sources of risk.

Portfolio possibilities curve A graphical representation of the expected return and risk of all portfolios that can be formed using two assets.

Portfolio selection/composition problem The part of the execution step of the portfolio management process in which investment strategies are integrated with expectations to select a portfolio of assets.

Position trader A trader who typically holds positions open overnight.

Positive serial correlation Serial correlation in which a positive error for one observation increases the chance of a positive error for another observation, and a negative error for one observation increases the chance of a negative error for another observation.

Posterior probability An updated probability that reflects or comes after new information.

Potential credit risk The risk associated with the possibility that a payment due at a later date will not be made.

Power of a test The probability of correctly rejecting the null—that is, rejecting the null hypothesis when it is false.

Precautionary stocks A level of inventory beyond anticipated needs that provides a cushion in the event that it takes longer to replenish inventory than expected or in the case of greater than expected demand.

Pre-investing The strategy of using futures contracts to enter the market without an immediate outlay of cash.

Premise of value The status of a company in the sense of whether it is assumed to be a going concern or not.

Prepaid expense A normal operating expense that has been paid in advance of when it is due.

Present value (PV) The present discounted value of future cash flows: For assets, the present discounted value of the future net cash inflows that the asset is expected to generate; for liabilities, the present discounted value of the future net cash outflows that are expected to be required to settle the liabilities.

Present (price) value of a basis point (PVBP) The change in the bond price for a 1 basis point change in yield. Also called *basis point value* (BPV).

Present value of growth opportunities (or **value of growth**) The difference between the actual value per share and the no-growth value per share.

Present value model or **discounted cash flow model** A model of intrinsic value that views the value of an asset as the present value of the asset's expected future cash flows.

Presentation currency The currency in which financial statement amounts are presented.

Pretax margin A profitability ratio calculated as earnings before taxes divided by revenue.

Price discovery A feature of futures markets in which futures prices provide valuable information about the price of the underlying asset.

Price limits Limits imposed by a futures exchange on the price change that can occur from one day to the next.

Price momentum A valuation indicator based on past price movement.

Price multiple The ratio of a stock's market price to some measure of value per share.

Price relative A ratio of an ending price over a beginning price; it is equal to 1 plus the holding period return on the asset.

Price to book value A valuation ratio calculated as price per share divided by book value per share.

Price to cash flow A valuation ratio calculated as price per share divided by cash flow per share.

Price to sales A valuation ratio calculated as price per share divided by sales per share.

Priced risk Risk for which investors demand compensation for bearing (e.g., equity risk, company-specific factors, macroeconomic factors).

Price-setting option The operational flexibility to adjust prices when demand varies from forecast. For example, when demand exceeds capacity, the company could benefit from the excess demand by increasing prices.

Principal The amount of funds originally invested in a project or instrument; the face value to be paid at maturity.

Prior probabilities Probabilities reflecting beliefs prior to the arrival of new information.

Prior transaction method A variation of the market approach; considers actual transactions in the stock of the subject private company.

Private sector surplus or **deficit** An amount equal to saving minus investment.

Probability A number between 0 and 1 describing the chance that a stated event will occur.

Probability density function A function with non-negative values such that probability can be described by areas under the curve graphing the function.

Probability distribution A distribution that specifies the probabilities of a random variable's possible outcomes.

Probability function A function that specifies the probability that the random variable takes on a specific value.

Probit model A qualitative-dependent-variable multiple regression model based on the normal distribution.

Production-flexibility The operational flexibility to alter production when demand varies from forecast. For example, if demand is strong, a company may profit from employees working overtime or from adding additional shifts.

Profitability ratios Ratios that measure a company's ability to generate profitable sales from its resources (assets).

Project sequencing To defer the decision to invest in a future project until the outcome of some or all of a current project is known. Projects are sequenced through time, so that investing in a project creates the option to invest in future projects.

Projected benefit obligation Under U.S. GAAP, a measure used in estimating a defined-benefit pension plan's liabilities, defined as "the actuarial present value as of a date of all benefits attributed by the pension benefit formula to employee service rendered prior to that date. The projected benefit obligation is measured using assumptions as to future compensation if the pension benefit formula is based on those future compensation levels."

Projected unit credit method Method used under IFRS to estimate the defined benefit obligation; for each period in which employees provide services, they earn a portion of the post-employment benefits that the company has promised to pay.

Proportionate consolidation A method of accounting for joint ventures where the venturer's share of the assets, liabilities, income and expenses of the joint venture are combined on a line-by-line basis with similar items on the venturer's financial statements.

Protective put An option strategy in which a long position in an asset is combined with a long position in a put.

Provision In accounting, a liability of uncertain timing or amount.

Proxy fight An attempt to take control of a company through a shareholder vote.

Proxy statement A public document that provides the material facts concerning matters on which shareholders will vote.

Pseudo-random numbers Numbers produced by random number generators.

Pull on liquidity When disbursements are paid too quickly or trade credit availability is limited, requiring companies to expend funds before they receive funds from sales that could cover the liability.

Purchase method A method of accounting for a business combination where the acquiring company allocates the purchase price to each asset acquired and liability assumed at fair value. If the purchase price exceeds the allocation, the excess is recorded as goodwill.

Purchased in-process research and development costs Costs of research and development in progress at an acquired company; often, part of the purchase price of an acquired company is allocated to such costs.

Purchasing power gain A gain in value caused by changes in price levels. Monetary liabilities experience purchasing power gains during periods of inflation.

Purchasing power loss A loss in value caused by changes in price levels. Monetary assets experience purchasing power losses during periods of inflation.

Purchasing power parity The equal value of different monies.

Pure discount instruments Instruments that pay interest as the difference between the amount borrowed and the amount paid back.

Pure factor portfolio A portfolio with sensitivity of 1 to the factor in question and a sensitivity of 0 to all other factors.

Pure-play method A method for estimating the beta for a company or project; it requires using a comparable company's beta and adjusting it for financial leverage differences.

Put An option that gives the holder the right to sell an underlying asset to another party at a fixed price over a specific period of time.

Put–call parity An equation expressing the equivalence (parity) of a portfolio of a call and a bond with a portfolio of a put and the underlying, which leads to the relationship between put and call prices.

Put–call–forward parity The relationship among puts, calls, and forward contracts.

***p*-Value** The smallest level of significance at which the null hypothesis can be rejected; also called the marginal significance level.

Pyramiding Controlling additional property through reinvestment, refinancing, and exchanging.

Qualifying special purpose entities Under U.S. GAAP, a special purpose entity structured to avoid consolidation that must meet qualification criteria.

Qualitative dependent variables Dummy variables used as dependent variables rather than as independent variables.

Quality of earnings analysis The investigation of issues relating to the accuracy of reported accounting results as reflections of economic performance; quality of earnings analysis is broadly understood to include not only earnings management, but also balance sheet management.

Quantile (or **fractile**) A value at or below which a stated fraction of the data lies.

Quartiles Quantiles that divide a distribution into four equal parts.

Quick assets Assets that can be most readily converted to cash (e.g., cash, short-term marketable investments, receivables).

Quick ratio, or **acid test ratio** A stringent measure of liquidity that indicates a company's ability to satisfy current liabilities with its most liquid assets, calculated as (cash + short-term marketable investments + receivables) divided by current liabilities.

Quintiles Quantiles that divide a distribution into five equal parts.

Quota A quantitative restriction on the import of a particular good, which specifies the maximum amount that can be imported in a given time period.

Random number An observation drawn from a uniform distribution.

Random number generator An algorithm that produces uniformly distributed random numbers between 0 and 1.

Random variable A quantity whose future outcomes are uncertain.

Random walk A time series in which the value of the series in one period is the value of the series in the previous period plus an unpredictable random error.

Range The difference between the maximum and minimum values in a dataset.

Rate of return The proportional annual benefit that results from making an investment.

Rate-of-return regulation Regulation that seeks to keep the rate of return in the industry at a competitive level by not allowing excessive prices to be charged.

Ratio scales A measurement scale that has all the characteristics of interval measurement scales as well as a true zero point as the origin.

Ratio spread An option strategy in which a long position in a certain number of options is offset by a short position in a certain number of other options on the same underlying, resulting in a risk-free position.

Rational efficient markets formulation See *Market efficiency*.

Real exchange rate The relative price of foreign-made goods and services to U.S.-made goods and services.

Real GDP per person Real GDP divided by the population.

Real options Options that relate to investment decisions such as the option to time the start of a project, the option to adjust its scale, or the option to abandon a project that has begun.

Real risk-free interest rate The single-period interest rate for a completely risk-free security if no inflation were expected.

Realizable value (settlement value) With reference to assets, the amount of cash or cash equivalents that could currently be obtained by selling the asset in an orderly disposal; with reference to liabilities, the undiscounted amount of cash or cash equivalents expected to be paid to satisfy the liabilities in the normal course of business.

Recapture premium Provision for a return of investment, net of value appreciation.

Receivables turnover An activity ratio equal to revenue divided by average receivables.

Receiver swaption A swaption that allows the holder to enter into a swap as the fixed-rate receiver and floating-rate payer.

Reconciliation Resolving differences in indications of value when estimating market value.

Regime With reference to a time series, the underlying model generating the times series.

Regression coefficients The intercept and slope coefficient(s) of a regression.

Regulatory risk The risk associated with the uncertainty of how derivative transactions will be regulated or with changes in regulations.

Rejection point (or **critical value**) A value against which a computed test statistic is compared to decide whether to reject or not reject the null hypothesis.

Relative dispersion The amount of dispersion relative to a reference value or benchmark.

Relative frequency With reference to an interval of grouped data, the number of observations in the interval divided by the total number of observations in the sample.

Relative strength (RSTR) indicators Valuation indicators that compare a stock's performance during a period either to its own past performance or to the performance of some group of stocks.

Relative valuation models A model that specifies an asset's value relative to the value of another asset.

Rent seeking The pursuit of wealth by capturing economic rent—consumer surplus, producer surplus, or economic profit.

Reorganization Agreements made by a company in bankruptcy under which a company's capital structure is altered and/or alternative arrangements are made for debt repayment; U.S. Chapter 11 bankruptcy. The company emerges from bankruptcy as a going concern.

Replacement value The market value of a swap.

Report format With respect to the format of a balance sheet, a format in which assets, liabilities, and equity are listed in a single column.

Reporting unit An operating segment or one level below an operating segment (referred to as a component).

Reputational risk The risk that a company will suffer an extended diminution in market value relative to other companies in the same industry due to a demonstrated lack of concern for environmental, social, and governance risk factors.

Required rate of return The minimum rate of return required by an investor to invest in an asset, given the asset's riskiness.

Residual autocorrelations The sample autocorrelations of the residuals.

Residual claim The owners' remaining claim on the company's assets after the liabilities are deducted.

Residual dividend approach A dividend payout policy under which earnings in excess of the funds necessary to finance the equity portion of company's capital budget are paid out in dividends.

Residual dividend policy A policy in which dividends are paid from any internally generated funds remaining after such funds are used to finance positive NPV projects.

Residual income (or **economic profit** or **abnormal earnings**) Earnings for a given time period, minus a deduction for common shareholders' opportunity cost in generating the earnings.

Residual income method (or **excess earnings method**) Income approach that estimates the value of all intangible assets of the business by capitalizing future earnings in excess of the estimated return requirements associated with working capital and fixed assets.

Residual income model (RIM) (also **discounted abnormal earnings model** or **Edwards-Bell-Ohlson model**) A model of stock valuation that views intrinsic value of stock as the sum of book value per share plus the present value of the stock's expected future residual income per share.

Residual loss Agency costs that are incurred despite adequate monitoring and bonding of management.

Retail method An inventory accounting method in which the sales value of an item is reduced by the gross margin to calculate the item's cost.

Return on assets (ROA) A profitability ratio calculated as net income divided by average total assets; indicates a company's net profit generated per dollar invested in total assets.

Return on common equity (ROCE) A profitability ratio calculated as (net income − preferred dividends) divided by average common equity; equal to the return on equity ratio when no preferred equity is outstanding.

Return on equity (ROE) A profitability ratio calculated as net income divided by average shareholders' equity.

Return on invested capital (ROIC) The after-tax net operating profits as a percent of total assets or capital.

Return on total capital A profitability ratio calculated as EBIT divided by the sum of short- and long-term debt and equity.

Revaluation The process of valuing long-lived assets at fair value, rather than at cost less accumulated depreciation. Any resulting profit or loss is either reported on the income statement and/or through equity under revaluation surplus.

Revenue The amount charged for the delivery of goods or services in the ordinary activities of a business over a stated period; the inflows of economic resources to a company over a stated period.

Reverse stock split A reduction in the number of shares outstanding with a corresponding increase in share price, but no change to the company's underlying fundamentals.

Reviewed financial statements A type of non-audited financial statements; typically provide an opinion letter with representations and assurances by the reviewing accountant that are less than those in audited financial statements.

Revolving credit agreements The strongest form of short-term bank borrowing facilities; they are in effect for multiple years (e.g., 3–5 years) and may have optional medium-term loan features.

Rho The sensitivity of the option price to the risk-free rate.

Risk budgeting The establishment of objectives for individuals, groups, or divisions of an organization that takes into account the allocation of an acceptable level of risk.

Risk governance The setting of overall policies and standards in risk management.

Risk management The process of identifying the level of risk an entity wants, measuring the level of risk the entity currently has, taking actions that bring the actual level of risk to the desired level of risk, and monitoring the new actual level of risk so that it continues to be aligned with the desired level of risk.

Risk premium The expected return on an investment minus the risk-free rate.

Risk-neutral probabilities Weights that are used to compute a binomial option price. They are the probabilities that would apply if a risk-neutral investor valued an option.

Risk-neutral valuation The process by which options and other derivatives are priced by treating investors as though they were risk neutral.

Robust The quality of being relatively unaffected by a violation of assumptions.

Robust standard errors Standard errors of the estimated parameters of a regression that correct for the presence of heteroskedasticity in the regression's error term.

Root mean squared error (RMSE) The square root of the average squared forecast error; used to compare the out-of-sample forecasting performance of forecasting models.

Roy's safety first criterion A criterion asserting that the optimal portfolio is the one that minimizes the probability that portfolio return falls below a threshold level.

Rule of 70 A rule that states that the number of years it takes for the level of a variable to double is approximately 70 divided by the annual percentage growth rate of the variable.

Rule of 72 The principle that the approximate number of years necessary for an investment to double is 72 divided by the stated interest rate.

Safety stock A level of inventory beyond anticipated needs that provides a cushion in the event that it takes longer to replenish inventory than expected or in the case of greater than expected demand.

Safety-first rules Rules for portfolio selection that focus on the risk that portfolio value will fall below some minimum acceptable level over some time horizon.

Sales Generally, a synonym for revenue; "sales" is generally understood to refer to the sale of goods, whereas "revenue" is understood to include the sale of goods or services.

Sales returns and allowances An offset to revenue reflecting any cash refunds, credits on account, and discounts from sales prices given to customers who purchased defective or unsatisfactory items.

Sales risk Uncertainty with respect to the quantity of goods and services that a company is able to sell and the price it is able to achieve; the risk related to the uncertainty of revenues.

Sales-type lease A type of finance lease, from a lessor perspective, where the present value of the lease payments (lease receivable) exceeds the carrying value of the leased asset. The revenues earned by the lessor are operating (the profit on the sale) and financing (interest) in nature.

Salvage value The amount the company estimates that it can sell the asset for at the end of its useful life.

Sample A subset of a population.

Sample excess kurtosis A sample measure of the degree of a distribution's peakedness in excess of the normal distribution's peakedness.

Sample kurtosis A sample measure of the degree of a distribution's peakedness.

Sample mean The sum of the sample observations, divided by the sample size.

Sample selection bias Bias introduced by systematically excluding some members of the population according to a particular attribute—for example, the bias introduced when data availability leads to certain observations being excluded from the analysis.

Sample skewness A sample measure of degree of asymmetry of a distribution.

Sample standard deviation The positive square root of the sample variance.

Sample statistic or **statistic** A quantity computed from or used to describe a sample.

Sample variance A sample measure of the degree of dispersion of a distribution, calculated by dividing the sum of the squared deviations from the sample mean by the sample size minus 1.

Sampling The process of obtaining a sample.

Sampling distribution The distribution of all distinct possible values that a statistic can assume when computed from samples of the same size randomly drawn from the same population.

Sampling error The difference between the observed value of a statistic and the quantity it is intended to estimate.

Sampling plan The set of rules used to select a sample.

Sandwich spread An option strategy that is equivalent to a short butterfly spread.

Sarbanes–Oxley Act An act passed by the U.S. Congress in 2002 that created the Public Company Accounting Oversight Board (PCAOB) to oversee auditors.

Scaled earnings surprise Unexpected earnings divided by the standard deviation of analysts' earnings forecasts.

Scalper A trader who offers to buy or sell futures contracts, holding the position for only a brief period of time. Scalpers attempt to profit by buying at the bid price and selling at the higher ask price.

Scatter plot A two-dimensional plot of pairs of observations on two data series.

Scenario analysis Analysis that shows the changes in key financial quantities that result from given (economic) events, such as the loss of customers, the loss of a supply source, or a catastrophic event; a risk management technique involving examination of the performance of a portfolio under specified situations. Closely related to stress testing.

Screening The application of a set of criteria to reduce a set of potential investments to a smaller set having certain desired characteristics.

Seats Memberships in a derivatives exchange.

Sector neutral Said of a portfolio for which economic sectors are represented in the same proportions as in the benchmark, using market-value weights.

Sector neutralizing Measure of financial reporting quality by subtracting the mean or median ratio for a given sector group from a given company's ratio.

Sector rotation strategy A type of top-down investing approach that involves emphasizing different economic sectors based on considerations such as macroeconomic forecasts.

Securities Act of 1933 An act passed by the U.S. Congress in 1933 that specifies the financial and other significant information that investors must receive when securities are sold, prohibits misrepresentations, and requires initial registration of all public issuances of securities.

Securities Exchange Act of 1934 An act passed by the U.S. Congress in 1934 that created the Securities and Exchange Commission (SEC), gave the SEC authority over all aspects of the securities industry, and empowered the SEC to require periodic reporting by companies with publicly traded securities.

Securities offering A merger or acquisition in which target shareholders are to receive shares of the acquirer's common stock as compensation.

Security market line (SML) The graph of the capital asset pricing model.

Segment debt ratio Segment liabilities divided by segment assets.

Segment margin Segment profit (loss) divided by segment revenue.

Segment ROA Segment profit (loss) divided by segment assets.

Segment turnover Segment revenue divided by segment assets.

Sell-side analysts Analysts who work at brokerages.

Semideviation The positive square root of semivariance (sometimes called semistandard deviation).

Semilogarithmic Describes a scale constructed so that equal intervals on the vertical scale represent equal rates of change, and equal intervals on the horizontal scale represent equal amounts of change.

Semivariance The average squared deviation below the mean.

Sensitivity analysis Analysis that shows the range of possible outcomes as specific assumptions are changed.

Serially correlated With reference to regression errors, errors that are correlated across observations.

Service period The period benefited by the employee's service, usually the period between the grant date and the vesting date.

Settlement date or **payment date** The date on which the parties to a swap make payments.

Settlement period The time between settlement dates.

Settlement price The official price, designated by the clearinghouse, from which daily gains and losses will be determined and marked to market.

Settlement risk When settling a contract, the risk that one party could be in the process of paying the counterparty while the counterparty is declaring bankruptcy.

Share repurchase A transaction in which a company buys back its own shares. Unlike stock dividends and stock splits, share repurchases use corporate cash.

Shareholders' equity Total assets minus total liabilities.

Share-the-gains, share-the-pains theory A theory of regulatory behavior that holds that regulators must take account of the demands of three groups: legislators, who established and oversee the regulatory agency; firms in the regulated industry; and consumers of the regulated industry's products.

Shark repellents A pre-offer takeover defense mechanism involving the corporate charter (e.g., staggered boards of directors and supermajority provisions).

Sharpe ratio The average return in excess of the risk-free rate divided by the standard deviation of return; a measure of the average excess return earned per unit of standard deviation of return.

Sharpe's measure Reward-to-volatility ratio; ratio of portfolio excess return to standard deviation.

Short The seller of a derivative contract. Also refers to the position of being short a derivative.

Shortfall risk The risk that portfolio value will fall below some minimum acceptable level over some time horizon.

Simple interest The interest earned each period on the original investment; interest calculated on the principal only.

Simple random sample A subset of a larger population created in such a way that each element of the population has an equal probability of being selected to the subset.

Simple random sampling The procedure of drawing a sample to satisfy the definition of a simple random sample.

Simulation Computer-generated sensitivity or scenario analysis that is based on probability models for the factors that drive outcomes.

Simulation trial A complete pass through the steps of a simulation.

Single-payment loan A loan in which the borrower receives a sum of money at the start and pays back the entire amount with interest in a single payment at maturity.

Single-step format With respect to the format of the income statement, a format that does not subtotal for gross profit (revenue minus cost of goods sold).

Sinking fund factor Amount that must be set aside each period to have $1 at some future point in time.

Skewed Not symmetrical.

Skewness A quantitative measure of skew (lack of symmetry); a synonym of skew.

Sole proprietorship A business owned and operated by a single person.

Solvency With respect to financial statement analysis, the ability of a company to fulfill its long-term obligations.

Solvency ratios Ratios that measure a company's ability to meet its long-term obligations.

Sovereign yield spread An estimate of the country spread (country equity premium) for a developing nation that is based on a comparison of bonds yields in country being analyzed and a developed country. The sovereign yield spread is the difference between a government bond yield in the country being analyzed, denominated in the currency of the developed country, and the Treasury bond yield on a similar maturity bond in the developed country.

Spearman rank correlation coefficient A measure of correlation applied to ranked data.

Special purpose entity (special purpose vehicle or **variable interest entity)** A non-operating entity created to carry out a specified purpose, such as leasing assets or securitizing receivables; can be a corporation, partnership, trust, limited liability, or partnership formed to facilitate a specific type of business activity.

Specific identification method An inventory accounting method that identifies which specific inventory items were sold and which remained in inventory to be carried over to later periods.

Spin-off A form of restructuring in which shareholders of a parent company receive a proportional number of shares in a new, separate entity; shareholders end up owning stock in two different companies where there used to be one.

Split-off A form of restructuring in which shareholders of the parent company are given shares in a newly created entity in exchange for their shares of the parent company.

Split-rate tax system In reference to corporate taxes, a split-rate system taxes earnings to be distributed as dividends at a different rate than earnings to be retained. Corporate profits distributed as dividends are taxed at a lower rate than those retained in the business.

Spread An option strategy involving the purchase of one option and sale of another option that is identical to the first in all respects except either exercise price or expiration.

Spreadsheet modeling As used in this book, the use of a spreadsheet in executing a dividend discount model valuation, or other present value model valuation.

Spurious correlation A correlation that misleadingly points towards associations between variables.

Stable dividend policy A policy in which regular dividends are paid that reflect long-run expected earnings. In contrast to a constant dividend payout ratio policy, a stable dividend policy does not reflect short-term volatility in earnings.

Standard cost With respect to inventory accounting, the planned or target unit cost of inventory items or services.

Standard deviation The positive square root of the variance; a measure of dispersion in the same units as the original data.

Standard normal distribution (or **unit normal distribution)** The normal density with mean equal to 0 and standard deviation (σ) equal to 1.

Standardized beta With reference to fundamental factor models, the value of the attribute for an asset minus the average value of the attribute across all stocks, divided by the standard deviation of the attribute across all stocks.

Standardized unexpected earnings (SUE) Unexpected earnings per share divided by the standard deviation of unexpected earnings per share over a specified prior time period.

Standardizing A transformation that involves subtracting the mean and dividing the result by the standard deviation.

Stated annual interest rate or **quoted interest rate** A quoted interest rate that does not account for compounding within the year.

Stated rate (nominal rate or **coupon rate)** The rate at which periodic interest payments are calculated.

Statement of cash flows (cash flow statement) A financial statement that reconciles beginning-of-period and end-of-period balance sheet values of cash; provides information about an entity's cash inflows and cash outflows as they pertain to operating, investing, and financing activities.

Statement of changes in shareholders' equity (statement of owners' equity) A financial statement that reconciles the beginning-of-period and end-of-period balance sheet values of shareholders' equity; provides information about all factors affecting shareholders' equity.

Statement of retained earnings A financial statement that reconciles beginning-of-period and end-of-period balance sheet values of retained income; shows the linkage between the balance sheet and income statement.

Static trade-off theory of capital structure A theory pertaining to a company's optimal capital structure; the optimal level of debt is found at the point where additional debt would cause the costs of financial distress to increase by a greater amount than the benefit of the additional tax shield.

Statistic A quantity computed from or used to describe a sample of data.

Statistical factor models A multifactor model in which statistical methods are applied to a set of historical returns to determine portfolios that best explain either historical return covariances or variances.

Statistical inference Making forecasts, estimates, or judgments about a larger group from a smaller group actually observed; using a sample statistic to infer the value of an unknown population parameter.

Statistically significant A result indicating that the null hypothesis can be rejected; with reference to an estimated regression coefficient, frequently understood to mean a result indicating that the corresponding population regression coefficient is different from 0.

Statistics The science of describing, analyzing, and drawing conclusions from data; also, a collection of numerical data.

Statutory merger A merger in which one company ceases to exist as an identifiable entity and all its assets and liabilities become part of a purchasing company.

Stock grants The granting of stock to employees as a form of compensation.

Stock options (stock option grants) The granting of stock options to employees as a form of compensation.

Stock purchase An acquisition in which the acquirer gives the target company's shareholders some combination of cash and securities in exchange for shares of the target company's stock.

Stock-out losses Profits lost from not having sufficient inventory on hand to satisfy demand.

Storage costs or **carrying costs** The costs of holding an asset, generally a function of the physical characteristics of the underlying asset.

Straddle An option strategy involving the purchase of a put and a call with the same exercise price. A straddle is based on the expectation of high volatility of the underlying.

Straight-line method A depreciation method that allocates evenly the cost of a long-lived asset less its estimated residual value over the estimated useful life of the asset.

Strangle A variation of a straddle in which the put and call have different exercise prices.

Strap An option strategy involving the purchase of two calls and one put.

Strategic transaction A purchase involving a buyer that would benefit from certain synergies associated with owning the target firm.

Stratified random sampling A procedure by which a population is divided into subpopulations (strata) based on one or more classification criteria. Simple random samples are then drawn from each stratum in sizes proportional to the relative size of each stratum in the population. These samples are then pooled.

Stress testing A set of techniques for estimating losses in extremely unfavorable combinations of events or scenarios.

Strip An option strategy involving the purchase of two puts and one call.

Structured note A variation of a floating-rate note that has some type of unusual characteristic such as a leverage factor or in which the rate moves opposite to interest rates.

Subjective probability A probability drawing on personal or subjective judgment.

Subsidiary merger A merger in which the company being purchased becomes a subsidiary of the purchaser.

Subsistence real wage rate The minimum real wage rate needed to maintain life.

Sum-of-the-parts valuation A valuation that sums the estimated values of each of a company's businesses as if each business were an independent going concern.

Sunk cost A cost that has already been incurred.

Supernormal growth Above average or abnormally high growth rate in earnings per share.

Surprise The actual value of a variable minus its predicted (or expected) value.

Survey approach An estimate of the equity risk premium that is based upon estimates provided by a panel of finance experts.

Survivorship bias Bias that may result when failed or defunct companies are excluded from membership in a group.

Sustainable growth rate The rate of dividend (and earnings) growth that can be sustained over time for a given level of return on equity, keeping the capital structure constant and without issuing additional common stock.

Swap An agreement between two parties to exchange a series of future cash flows.

Swap spread The difference between the fixed rate on an interest rate swap and the rate on a Treasury note with equivalent maturity; it reflects the general level of credit risk in the market.

Swaption An option to enter into a swap.

Synthetic call The combination of puts, the underlying, and risk-free bonds that replicates a call option.

Synthetic forward contract The combination of the underlying, puts, calls, and risk-free bonds that replicates a forward contract.

Synthetic index fund An index fund position created by combining risk-free bonds and futures on the desired index.

Synthetic lease A lease that is structured to provide a company with the tax benefits of ownership while not requiring the asset to be reflected on the company's financial statements.

Synthetic put The combination of calls, the underlying, and risk-free bonds that replicates a put option.

Systematic factors Factors that affect the average returns of a large number of different assets.

Systematic sampling A procedure of selecting every kth member until reaching a sample of the desired size. The sample that results from this procedure should be approximately random.

Takeover A merger; the term may be applied to any transaction, but is often used in reference to hostile transactions.

Takeover premium The amount by which the takeover price for each share of stock must exceed the current stock price in order to entice shareholders to relinquish control of the company to an acquirer.

Tangible assets Long-term assets with physical substance that are used in company operations, such as land (property), plant, and equipment.

Tangible book value per share Common shareholders' equity minus intangible assets from the balance sheet, divided by the number of shares outstanding.

Target balance A minimum level of cash to be held available—estimated in advance and adjusted for known funds transfers, seasonality, or other factors.

Target capital structure A company's chosen proportions of debt and equity.

Target company, or **target** The company in a merger or acquisition that is being acquired.

Target payout ratio A strategic corporate goal representing the long-term proportion of earnings that the company intends to distribute to shareholders as dividends.

Target semideviation The positive square root of target semivariance.

Target semivariance The average squared deviation below a target value.

Tariff A tax that is imposed by the importing country when an imported good crosses its international boundary.

Tax base (tax basis) The amount at which an asset or liability is valued for tax purposes.

Tax expense An aggregate of an entity's income tax payable (or recoverable in the case of a tax benefit) and any changes in deferred tax assets and liabilities. It is essentially the income tax payable or recoverable if these had been determined based on accounting profit rather than taxable income.

Tax loss carry forward A taxable loss in the current period that may be used to reduce future taxable income.

Tax risk The uncertainty associated with tax laws.

Taxable income The portion of an entity's income that is subject to income taxes under the tax laws of its jurisdiction.

Taxable temporary differences Temporary differences that result in a taxable amount in a future period when determining the taxable profit as the balance sheet item is recovered or settled.

***t*-Distribution** A symmetrical distribution defined by a single parameter, degrees of freedom, that is largely used to make inferences concerning the mean of a normal distribution whose variance is unknown.

Technical indicators Momentum indicators based on price.

Temporal method A variation of the monetary/nonmonetary translation method that requires not only monetary assets and liabilities, but also nonmonetary assets and liabilities that are measured at their current value on the balance sheet date to be translated at the current exchange rate. Assets and liabilities are translated at rates consistent with the timing of their measurement value. This method is typically used when the functional currency is other than the local currency.

Tender offer A public offer whereby the acquirer invites target shareholders to submit ("tender") their shares in return for the proposed payment.

Tenor The original time to maturity on a swap.

Terminal price multiple The price multiple for a stock assumed to hold at a stated future time.

Terminal share price The share price at a particular point in the future.

Terminal value of the stock (or **continuing value of the stock**) The analyst's estimate of a stock's value at a particular point in the future.

Termination date The date of the final payment on a swap; also, the swap's expiration date.

Terms of trade The quantity of goods and services that a country exports to pay for its imports of goods and services.

Test statistic A quantity, calculated based on a sample, whose value is the basis for deciding whether or not to reject the null hypothesis.

Theory of contestable markets A hypothesis concerning pricing behavior that holds that even though there are only a few firms in an industry, they are forced to price their products more or less competitively because of the ease of entry by outsiders. The key aspect of a contestable market is relatively costless entry into and exit from the industry.

Theta The rate at which an option's time value decays.

Tie-in sales Purchases of one product that are permitted by the seller only if the consumer buys another good or service from the same firm.

Time series A set of observations on a variable's outcomes in different time periods.

Time to expiration The time remaining in the life of a derivative, typically expressed in years.

Time value decay The loss in the value of an option resulting from movement of the option price toward its payoff value as the expiration day approaches.

Time value of money The principles governing equivalence relationships between cash flows with different dates.

Time value or **speculative value** The difference between the market price of the option and its intrinsic value, determined by the uncertainty of the underlying over the remaining life of the option.

Time-period bias The possibility that when we use a time-series sample, our statistical conclusion may be sensitive to the starting and ending dates of the sample.

Time-series data Observations of a variable over time.

Time-weighted rate of return The compound rate of growth of one unit of currency invested in a portfolio during a stated measurement period; a measure of investment performance that is not sensitive to the timing and amount of withdrawals or additions to the portfolio.

Tobin's *q* The ratio of the market value of debt and equity to the replacement cost of total assets.

Top-down analysis With reference to investment selection processes, an approach that starts with macro selection (i.e., identifying attractive geographic segments and/or industry segments) and then addresses selection of the most attractive investments within those segments.

Top-down forecasting approach A forecasting approach that involves moving from international and national macroeconomic forecasts to industry forecasts and then to individual company and asset forecasts.

Top-down investing An approach to investing that typically begins with macroeconomic forecasts.

Total asset turnover An activity ratio calculated as revenue divided by average total assets.

Total invested capital The sum of market value of common equity, book value of preferred equity, and face value of debt.

Total probability rule A rule explaining the unconditional probability of an event in terms of probabilities of the event conditional on mutually exclusive and exhaustive scenarios.

Total probability rule for expected value A rule explaining the expected value of a random variable in terms of expected values of the random variable conditional on mutually exclusive and exhaustive scenarios.

Total return swap A swap in which one party agrees to pay the total return on a security. Often used as a credit derivative, in which the underlying is a bond.

Tracking error The standard deviation of the difference in returns between an active investment portfolio and its benchmark portfolio; also called tracking error volatility, tracking risk, and active risk.

Tracking portfolio A portfolio having factor sensitivities that are matched to those of a benchmark or other portfolio.

Tracking risk The standard deviation of the differences between a portfolio's returns and its benchmark's returns; a synonym of active risk.

Trade credit A spontaneous form of credit in which a purchaser of the goods or service is financing its purchase by delaying the date on which payment is made.

Trade receivables (commercial receivables or **accounts receivable)** Amounts customers owe the company for products that have been sold as well as amounts that may be due from suppliers (such as for returns of merchandise).

Trade-weighted index The average exchange rate, with individual currencies weighted by their importance in U.S. international trade.

Trading securities (held-for-trading securities) Securities held by a company with the intent to trade them.

Traditional efficient markets formulation See *Market efficiency*.

Trailing dividend yield Current market price divided by the most recent quarterly per-share dividend multiplied by four.

Trailing P/E (or **current P/E)** A stock's current market price divided by the most recent four quarters of earnings per share.

Transaction exposure The risk of a change in value between the transaction date and the settlement date of an asset or liability denominated in a foreign currency.

Transactions motive In the context of inventory management, the need for inventory as part of the routine production–sales cycle.

Transition phase The stage of growth between the growth phase and the mature phase of a company in which earnings growth typically slows.

Translation exposure The risk associated with the conversion of foreign financial statements into domestic currency.

Treasury shares Shares that were issued and subsequently repurchased by the company.

Treasury stock method A method for accounting for the effect of options (and warrants) on earnings per share (EPS) that specifies what EPS would have been if the options and warrants had been exercised and the company had used the proceeds to repurchase common stock.

Tree diagram A diagram with branches emanating from nodes representing either mutually exclusive chance events or mutually exclusive decisions.

Trend A long-term pattern of movement in a particular direction.

Trimmed mean A mean computed after excluding a stated small percentage of the lowest and highest observations.

Trust receipt arrangement The use of inventory as collateral for a loan. The inventory is segregated and held in trust, and the proceeds of any sale must be remitted to the lender immediately.

***t*-Test** A hypothesis test using a statistic (*t*-statistic) that follows a *t*-distribution.

Two-sided hypothesis test (or **two-tailed hypothesis test)** A test in which the null hypothesis is rejected in favor of the alternative hypothesis if the evidence indicates that the population parameter is either smaller or larger than a hypothesized value.

Type I error The error of rejecting a true null hypothesis.

Type II error The error of not rejecting a false null hypothesis.

U.S. interest rate differential The U.S. interest rate minus the foreign interest rate.

U.S. official reserves The government's holding of foreign currency.

Unbiasedness Lack of bias. A desirable property of estimators, an unbiased estimator is one whose expected value (the mean of its sampling distribution) equals the parameter it is intended to estimate.

Unbilled revenue (accrued revenue) Revenue that has been earned but not yet billed to customers as of the end of an accounting period.

Unclassified balance sheet A balance sheet that does not show subtotals for current assets and current liabilities.

Unconditional heteroskedasticity Heteroskedasticity of the error term that is not correlated with the values of the independent variable(s) in the regression.

Unconditional probability (or **marginal probability)** The probability of an event *not* conditioned on another event.

Underlying An asset that trades in a market in which buyers and sellers meet, decide on a price, and the seller then delivers the asset to the buyer and receives payment. The underlying is the asset or other derivative on which a particular derivative is based. The market for the underlying is also referred to as the spot market.

Underlying earnings (or **persistent earnings, continuing earnings,** or **core earnings)** Earnings excluding nonrecurring components.

Unearned fees Unearned fees are recognized when a company receives cash payment for fees prior to earning them.

Unearned revenue (deferred revenue) A liability account for money that has been collected for goods or services that have not yet been delivered; payment received in advance of providing a good or service.

Unexpected earnings (also **earnings surprise)** The difference between reported earnings per share and expected earnings per share.

Unidentifiable intangible An intangible that cannot be acquired singly and that typically possesses an indefinite benefit period; an example is accounting goodwill.

Unit root A time series that is not covariance stationary is said to have a unit root.

Uniting of interests method A method of accounting in which combined companies were portrayed as if they had always operated as a single economic entity. Called pooling of interests under U.S. GAAP and uniting of interests under IFRS. (No longer allowed under U.S. GAAP or IFRS.)

Units-of-production method A depreciation method that allocates the cost of a long-lived asset based on actual usage during the period.

Univariate distribution A distribution that specifies the probabilities for a single random variable.

Unlimited funds An unlimited funds environment assumes that the company can raise the funds it wants for all profitable projects simply by paying the required rate of return.

Up transition probability The probability that an asset's value moves up.

Upstream A transaction between two affiliates, an investor company and an associate company such that the associate company records a profit on its income statement. An example is a sale of inventory by the associate to the investor company.

Valuation The process of determining the value of an asset or service on the basis of variables perceived to be related to future investment returns, or on the basis of comparisons with closely similar assets.

Valuation allowance A reserve created against deferred tax assets, based on the likelihood of realizing the deferred tax assets in future accounting periods.

Valuation ratios Ratios that measure the quantity of an asset or flow (e.g., earnings) in relation to the price associated with a specified claim (e.g., a share or ownership of the enterprise).

Value The amount for which one can sell something, or the amount one must pay to acquire something.

Value at risk (VAR) A money measure of the minimum value of losses expected during a specified time period at a given level of probability.

Value investors With reference to equity investors, investors who are focused on paying a relatively low share price in relation to earnings or assets per share.

Variable costs Costs that fluctuate with the level of production and sales.

Variance The expected value (the probability-weighted average) of squared deviations from a random variable's expected value.

Variation margin Additional margin that must be deposited in an amount sufficient to bring the balance up to the initial margin requirement.

Vega The relationship between option price and volatility.

Venture capital investors Private equity investors in development-stage companies.

Venturers The owners of a joint venture. Each is active in the management and shares control of the joint venture.

Vertical analysis Common-size analysis using only one reporting period or one base financial statement; for example, an income statement in which all items are stated as percentages of sales.

Vertical common-size analysis The most common type of common-size analysis, in which the accounts in a given period are compared to a benchmark item in that same year.

Vertical merger A merger involving companies at different positions of the same production chain; for example, a supplier or a distributor.

Versioning Selling a product in slightly altered forms to different groups of consumers.

Vested benefit obligation Under U.S. GAAP, a measure used in estimating a defined-benefit pension plan's liabilities, defined as the "actuarial present value of vested benefits."

Vested benefits Future benefits promised to the employee regardless of continuing service. Benefits typically vest after a specified period of service or a specified period of service combined with age.

Vesting date The date that employees can first exercise stock options; vesting can be immediate or over a future period.

Visibility The extent to which a company's operations are predictable with substantial confidence.

Volatility As used in option pricing, the standard deviation of the continuously compounded returns on the underlying asset.

Voluntary export restraint An agreement between two governments in which the government of the exporting country agrees to restrain the volume of its own exports.

Warehouse receipt arrangement The use of inventory as collateral for a loan; similar to a trust receipt arrangement except there is a third party (i.e., a warehouse company) that supervises the inventory.

Weighted average cost An inventory accounting method that averages the total cost of available inventory items over the total units available for sale.

Weighted harmonic mean See *Harmonic mean.*

Weighted mean An average in which each observation is weighted by an index of its relative importance.

Weighted-average cost of capital (WACC) A weighted average of the after-tax required rates of return on a company's common stock, preferred stock, and long-term debt, where the weights are the fraction of each source of financing in the company's target capital structure.

White knight A third party that is sought out by the target company's board to purchase the target in lieu of a hostile bidder.

White squire A third party that is sought out by the target company's board to purchase a substantial minority stake in the target—enough to block a hostile takeover without selling the entire company.

White-corrected standard errors A synonym for robust standard errors.

Winner's curse The tendency for the winner in certain competitive bidding situations to overpay, whether because of overestimation of intrinsic value, emotion, or information asymmetries.

Winsorized mean A mean computed after assigning a stated percent of the lowest values equal to one specified low value, and a stated percent of the highest values equal to one specified high value.

Working capital The difference between current assets and current liabilities.

Working capital management The management of a company's short-term assets (such as inventory) and short-term liabilities (such as money owed to suppliers).

Working capital turnover A comparison of revenues with working capital to produce a measure that shows how efficiently working capital is employed.

World Trade Organization An international organization that places greater obligations on its member countries to observe the GATT rules.

Write-down A reduction in the value of an asset as stated in the balance sheet.

Yield The actual return on a debt security if it is held to maturity.

Yield beta A measure of the sensitivity of a bond's yield to a general measure of bond yields in the market that is used to refine the hedge ratio.

Yield spread The difference between the yield on a bond and the yield on a default-free security, usually a government note, of the same maturity. The yield spread is primarily determined by the market's perception of the credit risk on the bond.

Yield to maturity The annual return that an investor earns on a bond if the investor purchases the bond today and holds it until maturity.

Zero-cost collar A transaction in which a position in the underlying is protected by buying a put and selling a call with the premium from the sale of the call offsetting the premium from the purchase of the put. It can also be used to protect a floating-rate borrower against interest rate increases with the premium on a long cap offsetting the premium on a short floor.

INDEX

J